Isolationism

ADVANCE PRAISE FOR *ISOLATIONISM*

"At a time when many are urging America to retreat internationally, Kupchan's illuminating history of US foreign policy reminds us of isolationism's pitfalls as well as its continuing allure. Scholars and policy makers alike will benefit from this book's trenchant analysis of America's past and wise counsel about how to forge a more balanced, realistic, and enduring foreign policy going forward."

> —**Peter Trubowitz**, Professor of International
> Relations, London School of Economics

"Charles Kupchan reminds us that a globally assertive foreign policy is more the exception than the norm in American history. Even those who do not fully agree with his arguments will find this book sharply argued, provocative, and engaging."

> —**Hal Brands**, Henry A. Kissinger Distinguished Professor
> of Global Affairs, Johns Hopkins School of
> Advanced International Studies (SAIS)

"Astute political history."

> —*Kirkus*

Isolationism

A History of America's Efforts to Shield Itself from the World

CHARLES A. KUPCHAN

A Council on Foreign Relations Book

OXFORD
UNIVERSITY PRESS

OXFORD
UNIVERSITY PRESS

Oxford University Press is a department of the University of Oxford. It furthers
the University's objective of excellence in research, scholarship, and education
by publishing worldwide. Oxford is a registered trade mark of Oxford University
Press in the UK and certain other countries.

Published in the United States of America by Oxford University Press
198 Madison Avenue, New York, NY 10016, United States of America.

Library of Congress Cataloging-in-Publication Data
Names: Kupchan, Charles, author.
Title: Isolationism : a history of America's efforts to shield itself from the world / Charles A. Kupchan.
Other titles: History of America's efforts to shield itself from the world
Description: New York, NY : Oxford University Press, [2020] | Includes index. |
Identifiers: LCCN 2020019840 (print) | LCCN 2020019841 (ebook) |
ISBN 9780199393022 (hardback) | ISBN 9780199393251 (epub) |
Subjects: LCSH: United States—Foreign relations—History. | Isolationism—United States—History.
Classification: LCC E183.7 .K86 2020 (print) | LCC E183.7 (ebook) | DDC 327.73—dc23
LC record available at https://lccn.loc.gov/2020019840
LC ebook record available at https://lccn.loc.gov/2020019841

1 3 5 7 9 8 6 4 2

Printed by Sheridan Books, Inc., United States of America

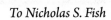

To Nicholas S. Fish

The Council on Foreign Relations (CFR) is an independent, nonpartisan membership organization, think tank, and publisher dedicated to being a resource for its members, government officials, business executives, journalists, educators and students, civic and religious leaders, and other interested citizens in order to help them better understand the world and the foreign policy choices facing the United States and other countries. Founded in 1921, CFR carries out its mission by maintaining a diverse membership, with special programs to promote interest and develop expertise in the next generation of foreign policy leaders; convening meetings at its headquarters in New York and in Washington, DC, and other cities where senior government officials, members of Congress, global leaders, and prominent thinkers come together with CFR members to discuss and debate major international issues; supporting a Studies Program that fosters independent research, enabling CFR scholars to produce articles, reports, and books and hold roundtables that analyze foreign policy issues and make concrete policy recommendations; publishing *Foreign Affairs*, the preeminent journal on international affairs and U.S. foreign policy; sponsoring Independent Task Forces that produce reports with both findings and policy prescriptions on the most important foreign policy topics; and providing up-to-date information and analysis about world events and American foreign policy on its website, www.cfr.org.

The Council on Foreign Relations takes no institutional positions on policy issues and has no affiliation with the U.S. government. All views expressed in its publications and on its website are the sole responsibility of the author or authors.

TABLE OF CONTENTS

PREFACE

The United States is in the midst of a bruising debate about its role in the world. Not since the interwar era have Americans been so divided over the scope and nature of their engagement abroad. President Donald Trump's America First approach to foreign policy certainly amplified the controversy. His isolationist, unilateralist, protectionist, and anti-immigrant proclivities marked a sharp break with the brand of internationalism that the country had embraced since World War II. But Trump's election was a symptom as much as a cause of the nation's rethink of its approach to the world. Decades of war in the Middle East with little to show for it, rising inequality and the hollowing out of the nation's manufacturing sector, political paralysis over how to fix a dysfunctional immigration policy—these and other trends have been causing Americans to ask legitimate questions about whether U.S. grand strategy has been working to their benefit. The COVID-19 pandemic then caused a severe economic downturn the likes of which the nation had not experienced since the 1930s—the last time the United States made the mistake of beating a strategic retreat in the face of mounting trouble abroad. Adding to the urgent and heated nature of this rethink of American foreign policy is China's rise and the threat it poses to the liberal international order that took shape during the era of the West's material and ideological dominance.

Isolationism speaks directly to this unfolding debate over the future of the nation's engagement with the world. It does so primarily by looking back, by probing America's isolationist past. Although most Americans know little about it, the United States in fact has an impressive isolationist pedigree. In his Farewell Address of 1796, President George Washington set the young nation on a clear course: "It is our true policy to steer clear of permanent alliances with any portion of the foreign world." The isolationist impulse embraced by Washington and the other Founders guided the nation for much of its history prior to the Japanese attack on Pearl Harbor in 1941.

My starting premise is not that the United States should or will return to the grand strategy of nonentanglement urged on the nation by its first president. But America's isolationist past does have much to teach us about the nation's current geopolitical predicament. Many readers may find this assertion puzzling. After all, the United States has spent much of the last eighty years strenuously trying to run the world through a global network of international institutions, alliances, and military bases. Beginning during World War II and continuing well into the twenty-first century, successive administrations have sought to open up and knit together international markets while maintaining strategic commitments in virtually all quarters of the globe.

America's sustained enthusiasm for international engagement is, however, the exception, not the rule, across the nation's history. Prior to the country's entry into World War II, Americans were generally averse to foreign entanglement, shunned alliances and other binding pacts, backed tariffs to protect the domestic economy, and embraced successive waves of anti-immigrant sentiment. In short, Trump's America First grand strategy was in many respects a throwback to an earlier era. He explicitly linked his approach to the world to the America First Committee, the group of diehard isolationists that formed in 1940 to block the nation's entry into World War II. Trump's foreign policy was not some bolt from the blue. On the contrary, the notion of America First has deep roots in the nation's history and identity—precisely why mining the nation's past can shed considerable light on the present and future.

Trump's embrace of America First was hardly the only reason I felt compelled to study the nation's isolationist past. Indeed, I started this book in 2012, well before Trump came into office. A number of considerations led me to embark on a project aimed at telling the story of isolationism across the full arc of American history. Multiple warning signs suggested that the fall of the Berlin Wall and the end of the Cold War made fragile the activist brand of internationalism that Americans had embraced during the second half of the twentieth century. After Iraq invaded Kuwait in 1990, the Senate in 1991 approved by only a close margin—52 to 47—President George H. W. Bush's war to expel Iraqi forces. President Bill Clinton then dragged his feet when it came to using the U.S. military to put a stop to the bloodshed that afflicted the Balkans during the 1990s. Especially after the Republican takeover of Congress in 1994, the bipartisan compact of centrist Democrats and Republicans that had long supported a robust and steady brand of U.S. engagement abroad began to unravel. Politics no longer stopped at the water's edge. All the while, coverage of foreign affairs in the print and broadcast media fell off precipitously. Americans were losing interest in the rest of the world.

The terror attacks of September 11, 2001, abruptly halted the nation's inward turn. The wars in Afghanistan and Iraq initially galvanized the nation and helped

restore a bipartisan consensus on the conduct of statecraft. But political polarization only intensified as those wars dragged on, prompting many Americans
to ask why their tax dollars were going toward the construction of schools in
Afghanistan rather than in Alabama. Conversations with family, friends, and
fellow Americans I would meet in the course of travels around the country revealed growing discontent with the nation's embroilment in the Middle East. It
was no surprise that President Barack Obama was keen to get the United States
out of its ongoing wars in Afghanistan and Iraq. As he campaigned for reelection,
one of his common refrains was "now is the time to focus on nation-building
here at home." Obama clearly sensed that the public was tiring of foreign entanglement. In the end, the post–September 11 wars ended up reinforcing, not
arresting, the nation's inward turn.

Prompted by these developments, I began to explore U.S. grand strategy
prior to World War II, putting particular focus on tracing the evolution of isolationism from the founding era through Pearl Harbor. The history was fasci-
nating and illuminating. From the debates among the Founders to President
Franklin Roosevelt's battle with the America First Committee, the history
spoke directly to the nation's ongoing dialogue about the scope and nature
of its role in a changing world. After I had canvassed the existing literature
on the subject and realized that no one had yet told the full story of isolationism and its connection to the American experience, I set out to fill this
important gap.

Once I had embarked on this project, I became only more convinced of the
importance of probing and unpacking American isolationism. I set the research
aside from 2014 to 2017, while working for President Obama on the National
Security Council. During this time, I had a firsthand look at the struggle that
took place between a president who was determined to end the post–September
11 wars and a tumultuous Middle East that made it hard for the United States
to get out. Beneath the surface of the administration's handling of the tough issues of the day in Afghanistan, Iraq, Syria, Ukraine, Russia, and elsewhere was
a broader debate over whether the United States should step away from its
days as global guardian and scale back at least some of its onerous international
commitments. Trump brought that debate to the surface, questioning the need
for America's core alliances in Europe and Asia and pledging to bring U.S. troops
home from the Middle East. Like Obama, he too ran into obstacles as he sought
to make good on his promises to shed foreign entanglements. But his willingness
to embrace isolationist, unilateralist, and protectionist language and objectives
set the stage for the full-throated debate over foreign policy that unfolded during
his presidency. The COVID-19 pandemic, which coupled economic wreckage
with the closing of the nation's borders, only bolstered an inward turn among
elites and the public alike.

Completing the task that I began in 2012 has further strengthened my conviction that understanding the current trajectory of U.S. grand strategy requires
looking back. The Federalist Papers, Washington's Farewell Address, the debates
over overseas expansion that followed the Spanish-American War in 1898, the
Senate's consideration of U.S. participation in the League of Nations in 1919–
1920—examining these and other seminal episodes from the nation's past
provides crucial insight into its present and future engagement with the world.
The allure of natural security that comes with geographic separation from other
great powers, the yearning for autonomy in the conduct of statecraft, the costs
and benefits of the nation's messianic impulse to spread abroad the virtues of
political and economic liberty—these and other indelible elements of the
American experience continue to shape U.S. grand strategy. As Americans debate the future of their role in the world, they need to consider the full span of
the nation's history—its isolationist as well as its internationalist past.

My main objective in writing this book is to provide readers a go-to volume
for understanding American isolationism. I aim, in accessible fashion, to tell the
story of America's efforts to shield itself from the world—from the founding era
through the Trump presidency. At the same time, I do take a stand on where
U.S. grand strategy should be headed going forward. I put myself in the "selective engagement" school. I believe that the United States has dramatically
overreached since the end of the Cold War—especially in the aftermath of the
terror attacks of September 11. Accordingly, a major strategic retrenchment is in
order; the United States needs to off-load at least some of its surfeit of foreign
entanglements.

I disagree, however, with the growing chorus of voices calling for the United
States to pull out of its major strategic positions around the world, including
those in Europe and East Asia. Rather, the United States should focus on retrenchment from the strategic periphery—in particular, from the Middle East.
Countering the threats posed by Russia and China gives the United States
good reason to stay put in Europe and East Asia until both regions enjoy a self-
sustaining stability. In contrast, U.S. interventions in Afghanistan, Iraq, Syria,
and Libya have produced little good. It is past time for the nation to cut its losses.

Calling for selective engagement and judicious retrenchment is hardly to endorse an isolationist grand strategy. On the contrary, a deliberate and thoughtful
pullback from strategic overreach is the best insurance against a rash and dangerous retreat. Nonetheless, in the service of fostering a full and wide-ranging
debate over the options Americans have before them, I do seek in this book to
refurbish isolationism and rehabilitate its reputation. Isolationism deservedly
became a political pejorative following America's strategic abdication during the
interwar era. Ever since, the political mainstream has marginalized those calling
for strategic retrenchment and attacked them as irresponsible isolationists. But

the dark history of the nation's run for cover as fascism and militarism were sweeping Europe and Asia should not be allowed to tarnish the notion of strategic restraint. For much of America's history, isolationism served the nation well. Under the right circumstances and in the right places, geopolitical detachment will effectively advance the national interest. In this book, I seek to evaluate soberly the costs and benefits of the nation's isolationist traditions—as well as the internationalist alternatives. In doing so, I aim to help Americans find the middle ground between doing too much and doing too little.

I have been fortunate to have had two wonderful intellectual homes while writing this book: Georgetown University's School of Foreign Service and the Council on Foreign Relations. Both institutions are one hundred years old, having been born after the close of World War I to help lay a foundation for U.S. internationalism and shape America's new role in global affairs. It is perhaps ironic that a scholar based at these two institutions has written a book on isolationism and calls for the United States to pull back from an excess of foreign commitments. It is, no doubt, a sign of the times, a changing America, and a changing world.

My colleagues and students at Georgetown and the Council on Foreign Relations have made invaluable contributions to this book. Dean Joel Hellman has helped make the School of Foreign Service an ideal place to marry teaching and research and to produce policy-relevant scholarship. Richard Haass, the president of the Council on Foreign Relations, and James Lindsay, its director of studies, supported this project from the outset and both read the manuscript and provided astute feedback.

The Council also convened two study groups at which a gathering of diverse scholars critiqued the draft manuscript. I am deeply indebted to the following members of these study groups for their oral and/or written input: Michael Barnett, John Milton Cooper, James Goldgeier, William Hitchcock, Brian Katulis, Melvyn Leffler, Michael Mandelbaum, Christopher Preble, William Ruger, Paul Stares, Stephen Wertheim, and Thomas Wright. Special thanks go to James Lindsay for chairing these review groups and for painstakingly poring over the manuscript. Peter Trubowitz and Mary Elise Sarotte also read the book in draft form and provided detailed and perceptive comments. I would also like to thank two anonymous reviewers who provided excellent comments. It was my great fortune to be able to draw on the expertise of such learned colleagues as I finalized the book.

I benefited enormously from a team of research assistants based at both the Council on Foreign Relations and Georgetown. Oliver Bloom first began working on the book as my research associate at the Council in 2012, and then continued to lend a hand from afar right up until I completed the manuscript. His contributions were invaluable, as were those of David Gevarter, who provided research and feedback as I was finalizing the book. Heartfelt thanks go to my other research associates at the Council, all of whom provided important input: Isabella Bennett, Alyssa Dougherty, Kyle Evanoff, Madison Freeman, Theresa Lou, Connor Mills, and Zachary Shapiro. I benefited from the excellent research support provided by three Georgetown students: Adam Kline, Arjun Mehrotra, and Emma Rhodes. I am also grateful to the other students and interns who lent a hand, including John Askona, Mark Bailey, Rachel Berkowitz, Jeremy Carp, Leticia Chacon, Simon Engler, Nicholas Fletcher, Keagan Ingersoll, Ludwig Jung, Ryan Musto, Lauren Overton, Venesa Rugova, Gabriela Saenz, Dayana Sarova, and Ian van Son.

My literary agent, Andrew Wylie, has enthusiastically supported this project since he saw the first draft of the book proposal. I appreciate his wise counsel. David McBride and the rest of the team at Oxford University Press toiled over the manuscript. They have been a pleasure to work with.

I am indebted to Simma, my wife, and Maia, Nina, and Samuel, my children, for their love, support, and patience—all welcome gifts for an author at work. I wrote most of this book in my kitchen. It probably was not an ideal venue from the perspective of concentration. But hot cups of espresso were only a step away. And I found no preferable alternative when it came to drafting a book in the midst of three young children. Escaping to the third floor or heading to an office would have meant missing out on too much joy. My mother, Nancy Kupchan Sonis, and my brother and his family, Clifford, Sandy, and Nicholas Kupchan, were also constant sources of love and support.

I dedicate this book to Nicholas S. Fish, who passed away on January 2, 2020. I met Nick during my first day of college; we lived across the hall from each other. Soon, we were roommates and the very best of friends. Nick spent the last decade serving on the City Council of Portland, Oregon, where he devoted himself to all the right causes. He was a person of uncommon decency, committed to serving the public good. Public service ran in his bloodstream. Nick's father, Hamilton Fish IV, served in the U.S. House of Representatives. His grandfather, Hamilton Fish III, was also a member of Congress and a staunch opponent of the nation's entry into World War II. His great-great-grandfather, Hamilton Fish, served as secretary of state to President Ulysses Grant. His great-great-great-grandfather, Nicholas Fish, served in the Revolutionary War. It is a fitting tribute to Nick that both his great-great-grandfather and his grandfather figure in the pages that follow. The world is a better place for Nick's having graced it.

Chevy Chase, MD
June 2020

NOTE ON QUOTATIONS

The author has modernized spelling and capitalization in quotations in order to enhance readability. In addition, quotations that start in the middle of a sentence begin with a lower-case letter even when they are capitalized in the original.

1

American Isolationism:
Past as Prelude?

In his inaugural address on January 20, 2017, President Donald Trump promised to remake America's engagement with the world. "From this day forward," he proclaimed, "a new vision will govern our land. From this day forward, it's going to be only America first. America first. Every decision on trade, on taxes, on immigration, on foreign affairs will be made to benefit American workers and American families. We must protect our borders from the ravages of other countries making our products, stealing our companies and destroying our jobs. . . . America will start winning again, winning like never before."[1]

The "America First" refrain—the same terminology embraced by Americans seeking to block the nation's entry into World War II—harkened back to the isolationism, xenophobia, and protectionism of the interwar era. Minutes after taking office, President Trump effectively pledged to dismantle the liberal brand of U.S. internationalism that had prevailed since World War II. He would soon go on to question the value of the nation's core alliances and strive to off-load what he saw as an excess of foreign commitments; he would cut back on immigration and invest in a wall on the border with Mexico; he would step away from open trade, canceling trade pacts and imposing tariffs.

Trump was not the first U.S. president to demonstrate discontent with the nation's role as global guardian and seek to lighten the burdens of international leadership. Indeed, President Barack Obama struggled over the course of his two terms in office to pull back from lengthy conflicts in the broader Middle East. He wanted U.S. forces out of Iraq and Afghanistan, and was leery of new entanglements in the region. One particular turn of events starkly illustrated Obama's more reluctant attitude toward projecting American power—his refusal to enforce his own red line against the use of chemical weapons in Syria's civil war.

On August 20, 2012, after reports of alleged chemical attacks by Syria's government against its own citizens, Obama warned against the further use of chemical weapons: "that's a red line for us . . . there would be enormous consequences if we start seeing movement on the chemical weapons front or the use of chemical weapons."[2] A year later, a chemical attack took place in Ghouta, a densely populated suburb of Damascus, killing some 1,400 civilians, including hundreds of children. Stomach-turning photographs of gassed toddlers provoked international outrage. After concluding that forces under the command of Syrian president Bashar al-Assad had carried out the lethal attack, Obama was ready to retaliate with military strikes against the regime, determined to enforce the red line he had drawn a year earlier. However, he faced uncertain support at home and abroad for military action. As a consequence, Obama announced on August 31 that he would seek congressional approval before launching strikes.

The hard sell began. In an address to the nation on September 10, Obama affirmed that "I determined that it is in the national security interests of the United States to respond to the Assad regime's use of chemical weapons through a targeted military strike."[3] Secretary of State John Kerry helped build the case for the use of force, testifying before Congress that a failure to act "would undermine our standing, degrade America's security and our credibility, and erode our strength in the world."[4] Well aware that Americans feared yet another quagmire in the Middle East, Obama and Kerry both went out of their way to stress that military action would be limited. "I will not pursue an open-ended action like Iraq or Afghanistan," Obama insisted. Kerry added that the strikes would be "unbelievably small."[5]

Despite such forceful assurances of only limited American involvement, many members of Congress appeared unconvinced; Democrats and Republicans alike expressed deep reservations. Support from the Republican-controlled House appeared out of reach. Even the Democratic-controlled Senate was wavering. Opinion polls revealed similar reluctance among the American public, with only twenty-nine percent favoring military strikes.[6] Having sought, and failed, to obtain a popular mandate, Obama decided to back off. When Russia conveniently offered an alternative course of action—a diplomatic effort to rid Syria of its chemical arsenal—the White House readily signed up.

The reversal was stunning. The Syrian government had violated a red line set down by the American president. The U.S. Navy had vessels on station in the eastern Mediterranean, at the ready to launch cruise missiles. France had also prepared its strike aircraft to participate in the operation. Nonetheless, Obama's determination that the nation's security required military action had collided with a reluctant Congress—and with his own misgivings about the prospect of U.S. involvement in yet another war in the Middle East. Obama felt strongly that the nation had already overreached in the region and needed to retrench: "Any president who was thoughtful, I believe, would recognize that after over a decade of war, with obligations that are still to this day requiring great amounts of resources and attention in Afghanistan, with the experience of Iraq, with the strains that it's placed on our military—any thoughtful president would hesitate about making a renewed commitment in the exact same region of the world with some of the exact same dynamics and the same probability of an unsatisfactory outcome."[7]

It is against the backdrop of Obama's more discriminating and reluctant brand of statecraft that his failure to honor his own red line marked a historical turning point. Ever since World War II, American foreign policy had rested on a solid bipartisan consensus in favor of liberal internationalism—a brand of statecraft that sought to anchor global stability through a combination of U.S. power and international partnership. But over Obama's eight years in office, signs of a steady inward turn were readily apparent. He labored to shrink the defense budget and America's strategic footprint abroad. He twisted the arms of America's allies to get them to shoulder a larger share of international burdens. He raised the bar when it came to military intervention and wanted to end the nation's days as the global policeman of first and last resort. Although he fell short, he tried his best to withdraw from both Afghanistan and Iraq. With the exception of a temporary surge of forces into Afghanistan, he studiously avoided the large-scale involvement of U.S. ground forces, instead turning to air power, drone strikes, special operations, and the manpower of local forces with which the U.S. military could partner.

Downsizing America's footprint abroad was a direct reflection of Obama's elevation of domestic priorities and his sense that the nation had become geopolitically overstretched. Amid both an economic downturn and long and costly wars in Iraq and Afghanistan, Obama was anything but apologetic about his desire to rein in the scope of the nation's foreign entanglements. On the contrary, he was forthright in touting retrenchment as a political asset, running a televised campaign ad on the subject during his reelection campaign and mentioning the need to focus on "nation-building here at home" multiple times during his third presidential debate with Mitt Romney.[8] Obama saw lightening America's load abroad as not just a geopolitical necessity but also a winning electoral strategy. His political judgment proved correct.

True to form, Obama cautiously and through methodical deliberation arrived at a new and more discriminating brand of U.S. statecraft that he deemed in synch with public sentiment. He was still committed to a grand strategy that looked to a mix of American power and multilateral partnership to promote international order, but he wanted to deploy less of both—a "liberal internationalism lite" that would enable the United States to pull back from an excess of foreign entanglements. Obama sought to uphold *Pax Americana*, but to do so more cheaply.

In contrast, Donald Trump sought to dismantle *Pax Americana*. Catering to a political base that felt it was on the losing end of the open and globalized world fashioned under America's watch, Trump did not want to preserve the current system at lower cost; he wanted to take it down. He unfurled an America First foreign policy that explicitly challenged the primary tenets of American state-craft since World War II. He questioned the durability of America's strategic commitments to its principal allies in both Europe and Asia, going so far as to deem NATO "obsolete" and expressing his desire to withdraw from the alliance. He abruptly extracted U.S. troops from northern Syria in October 2019, even though the move sold out the Kurdish allies who had played a central role in fighting ISIL. He withdrew from multiple international pacts, including the Paris Agreement on climate change and the Iran nuclear deal. He canceled emerging free-trade deals with both Pacific and Atlantic partners in favor of tariffs and trade wars. He responded to the COVID-19 crisis by going it alone, shunning international teamwork, and turning his back on the World Health Organization. Trump generally delivered on an America First approach to foreign policy that was decidedly isolationist, unilateralist, and protectionist in tone and substance.

Many in the Republican Party followed Trump's lead. Republicans had long backed a muscular foreign policy—and scored points with American voters for doing so. But Trump's pledges to end endless wars resonated with a Republican base weary of economic duress and almost two decades of inconclusive conflicts in the Middle East. So, too, have many Republicans joined Trump in backing away from the multilateralism of the post–World War II era, preferring the autonomy that comes with going it alone. The liberal internationalist compact between power and partnership is falling prey to this combination of isolationism and unilateralism.

America has been backing away from the world, raising the prospect that the nation's isolationist past could be a prelude to its future. This prospect is made all the more likely by the economic disruption caused by the COVID-19 pandemic; after all, the Great Depression helped produce the isolationist retreat of the 1930s. At this inflection point in American history, the United States is not about to again embrace geopolitical detachment and crouch behind protective barriers. America still maintains a vast network of overseas bases, posts thousands of troops abroad, sustains a defense budget that dwarfs that of all other countries, and remains a powerhouse of global trade and investment. Nonetheless, the isolationist instincts that throughout much of American history prevailed over the temptations of geopolitical ambition are making a comeback. The United States is headed toward a new and as yet uncharted brand of international engagement—with profound implications for the nation and the rest of the world. Forged amid World War II and solid into the twenty-first century, the political foundations of *Pax Americana* are finally cracking.

Isolationist Beginnings

Although America's current yearning to pull away from foreign entanglement constitutes a stark departure from its recent track record of determined global engagement, the impulse is hardly new. Indeed, this inward turn resonates strongly with America's further past; in the broad swath of American history, the last eighty years of "deep engagement" with the rest of the world are the exception, not the rule.[9] From the founding era until the Spanish-American War of 1898, the United States generally shunned geopolitical entanglement with foreign nations. Yes, the nation's birth did require a war to break away from Great Britain, which in turn prompted Americans to turn to the French for help. In 1778, the Thirteen Colonies concluded an alliance with France, which enabled them to prevail against the British in their struggle for independence. But the pact was the ultimate marriage of convenience, reluctantly embraced by the Founders only because it was necessary to break free from Britain. The United States promptly reneged on the alliance in 1793 when the French were in need of American help for their own war with Britain. Americans did embark on another war against the British in 1812. But the Royal Navy was obstructing the nation's vital seaborne commerce, an infringement on sovereignty that many Americans deemed to warrant the use of force.

Apart from these geopolitical engagements with Britain and France, the Founders were adamant that the United States should avoid foreign entanglement. In his Farewell Address of 1796, President George Washington was explicit: "The great rule of conduct for us in regard to foreign nations is in extending our commercial relations, to have with them as little political connection as possible. . . . It is our true policy to steer clear of permanent alliances with any portion of the foreign world."[10] This dictum would guide U.S. statecraft for generations to come. Indeed, after Washington reneged on the nation's alliance with France in 1793, it would not be until after World War II—a gap of roughly 150 years—that the United States was again prepared to countenance formal alliance with a foreign power.[11]

Neither Washington nor any of his compatriots thought of the "great rule" as "isolationist"—a term that would not come into popular usage until the twentieth century. After all, the United States during its founding era was anything but isolated; the colonial presence of Europe's great powers and Native American tribes both stood in the way of the union's well-being and territorial expansion. Americans during the country's early years were understandably obsessed with its vulnerability to predation and to the threats that would be posed to its republican institutions should the nation be constantly embroiled in wars. Indeed, it was precisely because of this vulnerability that Washington articulated a grand strategy that envisioned and aspired to geopolitical isolation. Nonentanglement would keep foreign powers at bay, enable the United States to concentrate on territorial consolidation and expansion, and inoculate the country against the risk of domestic tyranny by obviating the need for large standing armies and overweening federal institutions.

Building on Washington's "great rule," this book defines isolationism as a grand strategy aimed at disengagement with foreign powers and the avoidance of enduring strategic commitments beyond the North American homeland. In doctrinal terms, implementing the "great rule" meant avoiding alliances as well as other forms of entanglement with foreign nations, shunning territorial possessions outside North America, and assuming strategic obligations beyond the homeland only on a temporary and exigent basis.[12] Given the presence of Europe's imperial powers in America's neighborhood, it took time for the United States to disentangle itself from great-power rivalry. But from the nation's earliest days, the Founders sought to ease Europe out of the Western Hemisphere so as to enable the United States to enjoy strategic isolation and the natural geographic advantages of flanking oceans and territorial girth.

Geopolitical isolation did not mean economic autarky. Washington made amply clear that his admonition was against only strategic, not commercial, engagement with foreign nations. Americans were avid traders, keen to enlarge foreign trade, if necessary by defending their economic pursuits through military means. During the nineteenth century, the United States sent armed forces abroad dozens of times, primarily to defend its citizens and their commercial interests.[13]

Even as Washington's "great rule" cautioned against foreign entanglement, it by no means precluded territorial expansion. Following their successful separation from Great Britain, Americans were ardent expansionists when it came to the westward settlement and annexation of a large swath of North America. Indeed, they saw westward expansion as a strategic imperative and were determined to construct a formidable North American redoubt that would then enjoy the security of natural boundaries, geographic isolation, and strategic nonentanglement.[14] Over the course of the nineteenth century, Americans made good use of their increasing wealth and might to enlarge their union, relying on a combination of diplomacy and force to expand to the Pacific coast. Native Americans in their way were ruthlessly eliminated or shunted aside. In the service of expanding the union, the United States seized a sizable piece of Mexico in the Mexican-American War (1846–1848), bought Alaska from Russia in 1867, and tried several times—unsuccessfully—to grab hold of Canadian territory. Americans from early on also aspired to hemispheric ascendancy. The Monroe Doctrine of 1823, although the United States did not assertively back it up until the end of the nineteenth century, warned European powers away from any new imperial adventures in the Western Hemisphere, indicating a growing U.S. desire to hold sway over its own neighborhood.

The United States harbored ideological as well as material aspirations. Guided by the concept of Manifest Destiny, many Americans saw westward expansion as part of a messianic obligation to spread the virtues of republican government. And even if they restricted their geopolitical ambition to North America, their ideological ambition extended much further; the United States was to serve as a beacon of freedom and expand liberty around the world through the example of American democracy. The nation's exceptional experiment in political and economic liberty would be a global model, spreading by virtue of its own success.

This record of commercial activism overseas, territorial expansion across North America, and republican messianism abroad may seem at odds with the claim that the United States long adhered to a grand strategy of isolationism. But amid these expansive impulses, Americans remained dead set against taking on enduring geopolitical commitments outside North America, preferring to bank on the natural security afforded by the Atlantic and Pacific Oceans to keep them safe from the dangers of involvement in great-power rivalry. To be sure, from the founding era forward, isolationism and internationalism were in constant tension. The United States had no choice but to engage with European powers that had substantial strategic footholds in the Western Hemisphere. Foreign trade also pulled the country into global affairs, prompting the United States to regularly dispatch forces abroad to defend commercial interests. Nonetheless, time and again, Congress shot down proposals to expand into the Caribbean, Latin America, and the Pacific. Time and again, the United States passed on opportunities to use military force to support the spread of republican ideals in other quarters. A grand strategy of geopolitical isolation enjoyed a virtual lock on American politics.

The United States did start to break away from its isolationist roots at the end of the nineteenth century. It began to build battleships in the 1890s and then made good use of them in the Spanish-American War, which produced a bout of U.S. expansion into the Caribbean and the Pacific. The nation's entry into World War I in 1917 also represented a stark departure from the decades of isolation that had come before. Indeed, the United States directly contravened the Founders by voluntarily inserting itself into a new round of great-power bloodletting on the other side of the Atlantic. But these detours, by provoking a backlash against military intervention abroad, in the end did more to consolidate isolationism than to weaken it. The allure of internationalism prevailed, but only temporarily.

The U.S. colonization of the Philippines in 1898 triggered a bloody insurgency, quickly impressing upon Americans their distaste for ruling over foreign peoples. Entry into World War I, despite having tipped the scales in favor of

Europe's democracies, soured Americans on involvement in great-power conflict, precipitating a pronounced strategic pullback during the interwar years.
The United States continued its heavy-handed engagement in the Americas, but
it effectively retreated to a grand strategy of hemispheric isolation. Even as Nazi
Germany conquered much of Europe and Imperial Japan progressively carved up
China, the United States insisted on maintaining a distant neutrality. As danger
mounted, America was nowhere to be found. Americans belatedly agreed early
in 1941 to begin providing substantial military support to nations fighting fascism. But it would not be until the Japanese attack on Pearl Harbor at the end
of that year that the United States finally entered the war, clearing the way for a
durable brand of internationalism to take hold. It is America's pronounced passivity during the dark history of the interwar era that gave isolationism the bad
name that it has today.

How and why was isolationism able to maintain its hold on U.S. statecraft
from its founding days until the 1940s? Did isolationism serve well America's
interests by keeping adversaries at bay? Or does it deserve its tarnished reputation as a strategy of dangerous delusion that abdicates international responsibility and invites aggression? Why is isolationist sentiment making a comeback
and what are the implications for America and the world? These are some of the
guiding questions explored in the chapters that follow.

The Agenda

The Story of Isolationism

This book has three broad objectives. First, it tells the story of American isolationism. This work is the first to provide a comprehensive political and intellectual history of the subject. It therefore addresses a knowledge gap among
not just the foreign policy cognoscenti, but also the broader public. For many
Americans as well as publics around the world, America's recent past is relatively familiar ground—the United States' triumph in World War II, its patient
successes against the Soviet Union during the Cold War, and the determined,
even if vexing, fight against terrorism that followed the attacks of September 11.
About what came before, however, most people tend to be largely unaware; they
know much less about the dogged isolationism that for much of America's history guided its role in the world. As historian Walter Russell Mead has observed,
America's foreign policy elites and its public have exhibited a "deep lack of interest in the history of American foreign policy" prior to 1941.[15]

Despite isolationism's long hold on the practice of U.S. statecraft, the subject
has yet to be examined from the perspective of the *longue durée*. Distinguished
volumes have addressed specific episodes, including the founding era, the

Senate's rejection of the League of Nations after World War I, and the strategic retreat of the interwar era.[16] But no author has traced isolationism's intellectual and political evolution across American history. This book will do just that, offering a synthetic treatment of a subject that, despite its centrality to the nation's development and its contemporary relevance, remains notably understudied. Even if it has been in abeyance since World War II, isolationism continues to be part of America's creed and needs to be better understood by policy makers and the public alike. The contemporary comeback of isolationist sentiment makes this inquiry all the more important.

The Rehabilitation of Isolationism

The second main objective of this book is to refurbish isolationism's reputation and rediscover the strategic advantages it afforded America during its impressive ascent. This study does *not* call for the United States to return to isolationism. On the contrary, it maintains that the country should continue to uphold its core strategic commitments in Europe and Asia. But this book does argue that the United States needs to retrench from an excess of foreign commitments in the strategic periphery. In making the case for doing so, it draws lessons from the nation's isolationist past—exposing its dangers, but also rediscovering its considerable benefits. Rehabilitating isolationism will help ensure that grand strategies of restraint again enter the mainstream of American debate. Contrary to conventional wisdom, limiting foreign entanglement long served America well—and, if pursued in measured fashion, can do so again. In today's world of economic interdependence, cybernetworks, and aircraft and ballistic missiles, no nation can enjoy strategic immunity. Nonetheless, it is time to reclaim the enduring truth that standing apart from trouble abroad often constitutes wise statecraft.

Rehabilitating isolationism is a tall order given the heavy beating it has taken since the nation's dangerous and irresponsible bout of passivity during the interwar era. Beginning soon after the country's entry into World War II in 1941, American officials and opinion makers regularly unleashed unflinching condemnations of isolationism, setting the tone for the generations that followed. President Franklin Roosevelt warned that, "there could be no safety in passivity; no sanctuary in isolation." His successor, Harry Truman, was more strident, referring to isolationism as "a confession of mental and moral bankruptcy," a "counsel of despair," and a "futile and vulnerable shield."[17] Truman's secretary of state, Dean Acheson, quipped that isolationists wanted to "pull down the blinds and sit in the parlor with a loaded gun, waiting."[18] As the scholar Robert Tucker wrote in 1972, "in the American political vocabulary there are few terms carrying greater opprobrium than isolationism."[19]

Through the end of the Cold War and into the twenty-first century, isolationism and its few adherents have continued to be vilified in the harshest of
terms. As Secretary of State Kerry was making the case for air strikes against
the Syrian regime to retaliate for its use of chemical weapons, he admonished
reluctant senators that "this is not the time for armchair isolationism."[20] Bret
Stephens, then a columnist for the *Wall Street Journal*, wrote that Republican resistance to U.S. strikes was "exposing the isolationist worm eating its way through
the GOP apple," and Senator John McCain (R-Arizona) labeled Senator Rand
Paul (R-Kentucky) and other isolationists "wacko birds."[21] Many members of
the Republican foreign policy establishment signed "Never Trump" letters
during the 2016 campaign—due in part to Trump's isolationist and unilateralist
leanings.[22] As the scholar Andrew Bacevich has noted, the isolationist label has
been a powerful political pejorative since the 1940s—and remains so:

> The term isolationism is not likely to disappear from American polit-
> ical discourse anytime soon. It's too useful. Indeed, employ this verbal
> cudgel to castigate your opponents and your chances of gaining entrée
> to the nation's most prestigious publications improve appreciably.
> Warn about the revival of isolationism and your prospects of making
> the grade as a pundit or candidate for high office suddenly brighten.[23]

While opprobrium toward America's interwar strategy is fully warranted,
the broader indictment of isolationism is not. Indeed, aversion to foreign ambition enabled the United States to rise in virtually unmolested fashion over the
course of the nineteenth century. As the chapters that follow make clear, isolationism was born of sound strategic logic, not delusion; steering clear of foreign
entanglement allowed the United States to advance democracy and prosperity
at home and to avoid war abroad. This strategy rested on self-evident geographic
realities; assuming the United States could succeed in getting Europe's imperial powers to quit its neighborhood, the nation would indeed enjoy relative
isolation. As Thomas Jefferson put it, "America has a hemisphere to itself. . . .
The insulated state in which nature has placed the American continent, should
so far avail it that no spark of war kindled in the other quarters of the globe
should be wafted across the wide oceans which separate us from them."[24] The
Founders, and the generations of statesmen that followed, recognized that the
United States was blessed with a natural—even if imperfect—security afforded
by flanking oceans and weaker and relatively pacific neighbors to its north and
south. The lawyer and State Department official Bernard Fensterwald observed
as much in 1958: "'Isolationism' was a marked success during the nineteenth
and early twentieth centuries; by adhering to this policy, we expanded across the
continent and became the strongest single power in the world."[25]

America's interwar retreat admittedly constituted a naïve denial of the dangers posed by Nazi Germany and Imperial Japan. American policy makers took isolationism way too far; their search for strategic immunity ended in strategic delusion. But the isolationist excesses of the interwar era do not justify the blanket indictment of isolationist thinking that has prevailed since World War II. A strategy of detachment has been too thoroughly rejected, preventing Americans from considering and benefiting from its potential merits.[26] Americans counseling pullback should not be dismissed as unpatriotic; they need to be heard and their arguments carefully considered. Most candidates for high office still feel the need to promise a new American century and the indefinite extension of *Pax Americana*. Instead, they should feel free to speak forthrightly about how the United States can best navigate a changing global landscape. As historian Christopher Nichols notes, isolationism continues to be denigrated, but its "inherent caution serves as a bulwark against hasty interventions and their likely unintended consequences."[27]

So, too, would it be a mistake to dismiss the merits of isolationism on the grounds that globalization and interdependence make geopolitical detachment obsolete and infeasible. To be sure, Washington's "great rule" of nonentanglement emerged when flanking oceans provided a significant measure of strategic immunity and before the United States had emerged as a major power. Times and conditions have indeed changed. In an era of intercontinental missiles and transnational terrorism, adjoining oceans are less protective than they used to be. The United States is currently far more powerful in economic and military terms than it was in the nineteenth century, meaning that many quarters of the globe have become dependent upon an American presence as a source of stability. Globalization has dramatically advanced commercial and financial interdependence, giving the United States a vested interest in defending an open trading order and damping down potential geopolitical disruptions to the flow of goods and finance.

But there are more similarities between the distant past and the emerging present than meet the eye. The Founders banked on the natural security afforded by the nation's enviable location. Today, Americans in increasing numbers are coming to the conclusion that staying out of distant fights may do more to protect the nation than extending its reach to far-off lands. The Founders believed that the United States could most effectively promote prosperity by embracing protective tariffs while expanding international trade. Today, Americans are again looking to tariffs to protect jobs at home and open markets abroad. The Founders feared that ambition abroad would lead to the excessive centralization of power in the hands of the U.S. government, impairing freedom at home. Today, Americans are again concerned that the federal government's response to foreign threats is impairing the privacy and liberty of the American people. So, too, are they legitimately concerned that the "imperial presidency" has compromised Congress's constitutional authority over matters of war and peace.[28] The logic of shielding America from a dangerous world again has intrinsic appeal; the arguments that sustained isolationism in the past resonate with many of the arguments that are today politically ascendant in the United States.

These political and ideological linkages between America's past, present, and future provide this book's conceptual anchor. They ensure that a work that is principally a history of isolationism also speaks directly to where the United States' relationship with the world may be headed. This book's reclamation of the virtues of isolationism does not constitute an endorsement of an American retreat from the global stage. But rediscovery of isolationism's merits—along with sober acknowledgment of its drawbacks—will help the country reclaim its most valuable tenets. Those tenets should figure prominently in the informed and searching debate that Americans need to have about the country's future role in the world.

Engaging in that debate is an urgent priority; the United States has been living with a dangerous gap between its commitments abroad and the economic and political resources needed to sustain them. As Walter Lippmann, one of the most influential journalists of his generation, wrote in 1943, "in foreign relations, as in all other relations, a policy has been formed only when commitments and power have been brought into balance. . . . The nation must maintain its objectives and its power in equilibrium, its purposes within its means and its means equal to its purposes, its commitments related to its resources and its resources adequate to its commitments."[29] The United States' purposes and its means have been out of kilter, which is why many Americans have been calling for efforts to scale back foreign commitments and restore a balance between the nation's objectives and its economic and political resources.

Donald Trump's isolationist pronouncements may have shocked the establishment, but they certainly resonated with an electoral base that has been struggling to make ends meet. Even before he came on the scene, opinion surveys were picking up a discernible inward turn among the public—precisely why Obama tried to rein in foreign entanglements and why Trump ran on a neo-isolationist platform. According to a 2013 Pew Research Center survey, titled "American International Engagement on the Rocks," the U.S. electorate has been turning its back on foreign affairs. "The depth and duration of the public's disengagement," the report notes, "goes well beyond the periodic spikes in isolationist sentiment that have been observed over the past 50 years."[30] A separate poll revealed that over fifty percent of Americans believed the United States should "mind its own business internationally," by historical standards a very high level of isolationist sentiment.[31]

The United States needs to pull back from an excess of foreign commitments if it is to bring ends and means back into alignment—and the nation's isolationist past provides valuable guidance for doing so. The country can and must draw lessons from the isolationist playbook to advance its interests as it seeks to restore an equilibrium between its objectives and its power. An informed, cautious, and selective pullback is far preferable to a precipitous retreat—precisely what may lie in store should internationalist overreach prompt Americans to again embrace isolationist excess.[32] Finding the middle ground between internationalist and isolationist extremes is one of America's paramount challenges in the years ahead. The grand strategy of judicious retrenchment offered in this book's concluding chapter seeks to arrive at that middle ground. It seeks to extract the wisdom of America's isolationist as well as its internationalist traditions to bring purposes and means back into balance. Excavating the tension between isolationism and internationalism can help restore prudence to U.S. statecraft.

The Reinterpretation of Isolationism and Internationalism

The third objective of this book is to offer a fresh account of the sources of isolationism and internationalism, casting a new light on the historical trajectory of American statecraft. This reinterpretation entails investigating the ideological roots of isolationism, exploring why it dominated U.S. strategy for so long, and explaining how and why it eventually gave way to an ambitious brand of internationalism.

American Exceptionalism and Isolationism. This historical reinterpretation begins with a reevaluation of the impact of American exceptionalism on U.S. grand strategy. The doctrine of American exceptionalism holds that the United States represents a unique experiment in political and economic liberty that it is destined to share with the rest of the world. Today, belief in the exceptional character of the American experiment serves as the ideological foundation of the nation's ambitious global role; for reasons of both self-interest and altruism, the United States has a responsibility to expend blood and treasure to share with others its unique prowess in producing prosperity and liberty. To be sure, U.S. behavior at home and abroad has not always lined up with the nation's virtuous sense of self. And material interests, threats, and opportunities have played at least as important a role as ideology in shaping U.S. foreign policy. Nonetheless, American statesmen regularly deploy the exceptionalist narrative to justify the sacrifices needed to sustain *Pax Americana*. Indeed, paeans to American exceptionalism have long been a litmus test for patriotism.

Barack Obama and Donald Trump were only the most recent presidents to join the chorus. During the 2012 election campaign, Obama made clear where he stood on the issue: "The United States has been, and will always be, the one indispensable nation in world affairs. This is one of the many examples of why America is exceptional."[33] In his State of the Union Address on February 4, 2020, Trump followed suit: "Our ancestors built the most exceptional republic ever to exist in all of human history, and we are making it greater than ever before. . . . The American Age, the American Epic, the American adventure has only just begun."[34]

It may be obligatory for contemporary American politicians to tout the nation's exceptional character and its indispensability as a global guardian. But for much of the country's history, belief in American exceptionalism fueled isolationism rather than ambitious efforts to re-create the world in America's image. Indeed, from the founding era through the end of the nineteenth century, the notion of American exceptionalism served as isolationism's ideological anchor.[35] Precisely because the American experiment was unique and exceptional, the United States needed to protect it by remaining aloof from the perils and corrupting influences that lay beyond its borders. The chief objective of U.S. grand strategy was to shield the nation from a dangerous world.

Early Americans indeed believed passionately in the exceptional nature of the American experiment. Grounded in Protestant notions of redemption, they saw their young country as the New Israel, a chosen nation whose mission it was to elevate mankind spiritually, politically, and economically. Herman Melville succinctly captured the spirit of American exceptionalism in his 1850 book *White-Jacket*:

> We Americans are the peculiar, chosen people—the Israel of our time; we bear the ark of the liberties of the world. . . . God has predestinated, mankind expects, great things from our race; and great things we feel in our souls. The rest of the nations must soon be in our rear. We are the pioneers of the world; the advance guard, sent on through the wilderness of untried things, to break a new path in the New World that is ours.[36]

But despite the scope of this ambition, fulfilling America's role as "the pioneers of the world" mandated keeping the rest of the world at bay, not dominating it. Only by shielding the nation from the monarchism, imperialism, corruption, and inequality of the Old World would Americans be able to perfect their union. The alternative would be contamination by the ills the settlers were so determined to leave behind. "Why quit our own to stand upon foreign ground?" George Washington asked in his Farewell Address. "Why . . . entangle our peace and prosperity in the toils of European ambition, rivalship, interest, humor or caprice?"[37]

Americans accepted that they had an urgent calling beyond their shores; as the activist and author Thomas Paine put it in his widely read pamphlet *Common Sense*, "we have it in our power, to begin the world all over again."[38] The United States, however, was destined to save the world by example, not by dominion. To do otherwise would risk jeopardizing America's redemptive mission. In the words of John Quincy Adams, who served as both secretary of state (1817–1825) and president (1825–1829), the nation "goes not abroad, in search of monsters to destroy. She is the well-wisher to the freedom and independence of all," but only through "the countenance of her voice, and the benignant sympathy of her example. She well knows that by once enlisting under other banners than her own, were they even the banners of foreign independence, she would involve herself beyond the power of extrication, in all the wars of interest and intrigue."[39] Adams, according to historian Albert Weinberg, believed that "America could save the world only if it remained free to save itself."[40]

Multiple versions of isolationist logic congealed as America matured— including geographic, unilateralist, libertarian, racist, and pacifist variants. Indeed, isolationism's political strength emerged from the support it enjoyed from diverse constituencies, with strident nationalists on the right often teaming up with progressives on the left to block foreign expansion. Nonetheless, isolationism's ideological variants were all informed and anchored by an enduring belief that realizing the exceptional nature of the American experiment required sheltering the nation from the dangers of foreign entanglement. Throughout much of the nation's history, the doctrine of American exceptionalism mandated isolationism; the United States was to change the world—but only by example, not foreign ambition. The country's aggressive expansion across North America, which included the elimination or subjugation of Native Americans and the seizure of land from Mexico, was in obvious tension with this exceptionalist narrative. But in political discourse and the public imagination, westward expansion under the guise of Manifest Destiny was to fulfill, not depart from, the nation's messianic mission. In Melville's words, "we are the pioneers of the world; the advance guard, sent on through the wilderness of untried things, to break a new path in the New World that is ours."

The Enemy Within. A second important reinterpretation of the sources of isolationism follows naturally. Isolationism holds that the best way to safeguard the nation is to steer clear of external adversaries. It is a doctrine commonly understood to call for detachment from *foreign* enemies. Isolationism's ideological origins, however, actually stem not just from fear of enemies abroad but also of enemies at home. Yes, early Americans, with good reason, worried about the threats posed by the imperial ambitions of Britain, France, and Spain. But they were at least as worried about the enemy within—*domestic* threats to American democracy. The vulnerability of the American experiment to internal hazards teamed up with the dangers posed by foreign powers to convince the Founders to embrace isolationism.

The identity of the enemy within was anything but constant. During their first decades of independence, Americans were fearful that European powers, aided by their transplanted agents in the New World, were determined to restore monarchic rule—hence the need to keep Britain and France at a distance. As the United States grew in wealth and territory during the first half of the nineteenth century, its citizens worried that expansion abroad would prompt the federal government to amass overweening power; the prevention of foreign ambition was necessary to avoid tyranny at home. After the Civil War, domestic reconstruction and social cohesion topped the agenda; should the United States seek conquest abroad, it would only divert resources from the home front and bring into the national community unwanted ethnic diversity. It was Anglo-Saxons who made the American people exceptional, and preserving social homogeneity took precedence over geopolitical ambition. Beginning in the late nineteenth century, the rapid advance of industrialization fueled fear of excessive corporate power and the exploitation of American workers. An expensive foreign policy would only further magnify the self-interested sway of industrialists and financiers. The nation's entry into World War I intensified these concerns. During the interwar era, keeping arms merchants and other war-profiteering capitalists in check required strict neutrality—even in the face of the increasing international menace posed by Germany and Japan.

The restoration of monarchy, the overreach of the federal government, the diversion of resources from domestic investment, ethnic and racial dilution, the unchecked power of banks and corporations—Americans saw these and other domestic challenges to the American experiment as at least as dangerous as the threats posed by foreign enemies. It was in the service of confronting both external and internal perils that Americans of all political stripes rallied behind isolationism. Warding off foreign threats while defending freedom and prosperity from the enemy within meant the avoidance of entanglement with the enemy abroad. Only by holding themselves aloof from the outside world could Americans, in the famous words of John Winthrop, an English immigrant who arrived in 1630, serve as a "city upon a hill."[41]

For much of the nation's history, Americans thus understood the fulfillment of their exceptional experiment in political and economic liberty as mandating isolation, not foreign ambition. The injunction against entanglement abroad was motivated by fear of the enemy within as much as of foreign adversaries. Only if Americans jealously protected their own republican practices and institutions would they be able to fulfill their messianic mission by serving as a democratic exemplar for the rest of the world. These essential reinterpretations of isolationism provide a new understanding of both its sources and its durability.

<u>*Isolationism as National Creed.*</u> Other scholars have offered valuable explanations of isolationism's ideological origins and longevity. Some view American isolationism as the product of geographic determinism. The United States steered clear of foreign entanglement because it could; flanking oceans afforded it natural security.[42] Some see it as a product of the geopolitical weakness that came with America's youth; the United States simply did not have the military might to maintain strategic commitments beyond its immediate neighborhood.[43] Others view partisanship, regionalism, and competing allegiances to countries of origin as the main sources of isolationism. The incompatible political and economic interests of the nation's north, south, interior, and west, along with the conflicting attachments of English, Irish, French, German, and other immigrants to their motherlands, produced stalemate, effectively blocking America from expanding abroad.[44] For these scholars, understanding the sources of the nation's aversion to foreign entanglement means unpacking the narrow economic and electoral interests of America's competing regions, parties, and immigrant communities.

Geographic separation and the nation's relative weakness certainly figured prominently in the appeal of isolationism. So, too, did sectional and partisan politics have a long and consequential impact on U.S. statecraft. During the nation's early years, the North preferred a geopolitical tilt toward Britain while the South leaned toward alignment with France. A combination of pacifism, commercial interest, and partisanship prompted northerners to oppose the War of 1812, which most southerners supported. During the late 1800s, the South tended to oppose the naval building program backed by many northerners, but then became more internationalist, supporting the nation's entry into World War I and its participation in the League of Nations. The Midwest supported overseas expansion during the late 1890s, but opposed entry into World War I, and during the 1930s eclipsed the coastal regions as the main bastion of isolationist sentiment. Sectional preferences were the product of the economic interests, ideological proclivities, ethnic makeup, and partisan affiliations of the nation's different regions.[45]

As the following chapters will make clear, however, isolationism dominated American grand strategy even as technological change diminished the strategic advantages of flanking oceans and the growth of U.S. power made possible increased foreign ambition. Moreover, isolationism lasted as long as it did not because of sectional and partisan disagreement, but because it enjoyed substantial support across region, party, and ethnic group.[46] Isolationist sentiment ebbed and flowed among sections and parties, and the regional and partisan alignments that regularly blocked overseas expansion changed over time. Nonetheless, isolationism persisted across time, party, and region because it was embedded in the nation's identity and infused its politics. Even if they were motivated by different ideological and material concerns, Americans remained convinced that enhancing their security and advancing their country's calling as an exceptional nation required steering clear of foreign entanglement. As historian Selig Adler concludes in his own examination of why isolationism long dominated American statecraft, "the answer to this strange paradox lies in the fact that the isolationist impulse has been woven into the warp and woof of the American epic."[47] Manfred Jonas, also a historian of the subject, agrees that the nation's attachment to isolationism was due "not to geography, nor politics, nor class structure, nor ethnic background," but to deeply and widely held views about the nation and its role in the world.[48]

Geography, the nation's relative power, and partisan, regional, and ethnic preferences certainly contributed to isolationism's longevity. But what mattered most was a conception of American exceptionalism that equated the success of the American experiment with geopolitical isolation. Only by pursuing "honest friendship with all nations, entangling alliances with none," as Thomas Jefferson put it in his first inaugural address, could the nation keep at bay the enemy afar while subduing the enemy within.[49] In this respect, isolationism is best understood not as a matter of policy but as a matter of national identity and creed. As Christopher Nichols observes, "the inner logic of isolationist arguments turned on the inner life of the nation and on visions of national self-definition."[50] Fueled by overriding concern about protecting and advancing America's exceptional character and its redemptive mission, political separation from the outside world came to define the country's sense of self. For successive generations, the equation of American purpose with geopolitical isolation effectively banished from political discourse the option of strategic commitment abroad.

From the founding era until Japan's attack on Pearl Harbor—with notable detours during the Spanish-American War and World War I—isolationism was to America's national identity and sense of purpose what internationalism has been since World War II. Today, to call someone an isolationist is to tar them as a heretic. America's sense of self is inseparable from its role as the world's "indispensable nation." But for much of America's history prior to the 1940s, isolationism was the only game in town and its adherents ruled the roost; the few arguing for foreign entanglements were the heretics. Shielding the American experiment from the outside world became part and parcel of the nation's political creed, not just a foreign policy strategy. That isolationism was creed more than policy is precisely why it persisted over time in the face of technological change that reduced America's geographic advantage, the nation's pronounced rise in economic and military power, and shifting partisan and regional alignments.

From Isolationism to Internationalism. This book's reinterpretation of the sources of isolationism provides a compelling account of not only why it dominated U.S. statecraft for so long, but also why the transition from isolationism to a durable internationalism proved so difficult and politically fraught. The Spanish-American War of 1898 was a watershed. After more than a century of shunning territorial acquisitions beyond North America, President William McKinley (1897–1901) presided over an unprecedented bout of overseas expansion. The United States not only expelled Spain from Cuba, but also embarked on the military occupation of the island and wrested control of Puerto Rico, Hawaii, the Philippines, Guam, Samoa, and the Wake Islands. Just as the nation's exceptionalist narrative had anchored isolationism, it also justified this new outward push. By the 1890s, many Americans had come to fear that the closing of the continental frontier and the end of westward expansion would compromise the nation's exceptional experiment in liberty and prosperity. Having completed Manifest Destiny at home, Americans needed to direct their expansive energies abroad if they were to sustain their messianic mission.

This ideological justification for overseas expansion succeeded in overturning the nation's attachment to isolationism—but it also ran head-on into the reality that the United States in 1898 became an imperial power. Even if most Americans, at least initially, embraced the nation's newly acquired geopolitical heft, they soon found that they had little appetite for ruling over other peoples. The United States had launched a successful war to end Spain's ruthless oppression of Cubans, but in doing so had itself become an imperial and cruel overlord. A break with isolationism intended to further the nation's exceptionalist calling ended up jeopardizing the nation's messianic mission. An isolationist backlash and strategic retreat followed—even though the United States did not give up the territories it had seized. The brand of internationalism that emerged in 1898 was simply too realist and bellicose for an American polity convinced of its idealist cause and exceptional character. The United States was to have ended European imperialism, not replicated it. The nation's first run at internationalism failed to endure.

President Woodrow Wilson (1913–1921) learned from McKinley's mistakes—but he ended up overcorrecting by putting on offer an idealist brand of internationalism intended to overturn the dictates of realism. Rather than casting the internationalist cause in terms of power and interests, he framed it in terms of ideals and principles. He initially steered clear of World War I, a conflict that he saw as another Old World struggle rooted in pointless geopolitical rivalry—one not worthy of American intervention. Prompted by German attacks on U.S. shipping, Wilson then entered the war in 1917, justifying his change of heart exclusively on idealist grounds—to make the world safe for democracy and build a peaceful postwar order fashioned on republican government and the rule of law. Finally, the United States would deliver on its obligation to remake the world. But Wilson dramatically overreached by embracing idealist aspirations that bore little resemblance to a world at war and that committed the

United States to postwar obligations abroad for which many Americans had little enthusiasm. The Senate ended up rejecting U.S. participation in the League of Nations—Wilson's brainchild for building a new postwar order. His idealist excess cleared the way for another isolationist backlash and strategic retreat.

It would not be until World War II that Franklin Roosevelt and his successors fashioned liberal internationalism—a brand of U.S. engagement in the world that would prove politically sustainable because it rested on both realist and idealist foundations. Liberal internationalism married interests and ideals, power and partnership. The United States would project its strength abroad to further its strategic and economic interests in a manner consistent with geopolitical realities. At the same time, it would seek to further the nation's exceptionalist mission by pursuing a rules-based international order that would advance international partnership and spread American values. Idealist in ambition, realist in implementation, liberal internationalism proved sufficiently compelling to bring to an end isolationism's long run.

The consolidation of liberal internationalism led not just to isolationism's demise but to the global ambition of *Pax Americana*. In short order, the United States transitioned from hemispheric isolation and geopolitical detachment to worldwide strategic engagement. The country began the 1940s with no alliances and little interest in foreign entanglement beyond its hemisphere. It ended the decade with strategic commitments in most quarters of the globe. It had also overseen the construction of a network of international institutions, including the United Nations, intended to ensure both geopolitical and economic stability. The United States had successfully transformed itself from a detached exemplar into an activist crusader bent on deploying American power and purpose to spread republican ideals.[51]

It is no accident that the United States swung from dogged isolationism to unstinting internationalism; both were born of American exceptionalism. The sense of unique national character and mission that initially inspired Americans to shun foreign entanglement also prompted them, after Pearl Harbor, to abandon it in favor of global engagement. Self-separation was to have protected the American experiment, neutralized the enemy within, and enabled the United States to make the world anew. But geopolitical detachment failed to achieve its objective. The Japanese attack on Pearl Harbor burst the myth of strategic immunity, and Nazism and fascism were taking the world down a dark path inimical to the values that America was destined to share globally.

If the world could not be saved by American example, it would have to be saved by American action. If the United States could not preserve the American experiment by standing aloof, it would have to do so by exporting that experiment to the rest of the world. Its mission as a chosen nation confronted the United States with an either/or proposition. To redeem the world it either had to retreat from it to preserve the American experiment as a pristine exemplar, or it had to venture out as a crusader and transform the world in America's image; there was no middle road. The new goal was to make the world safe for an America that was no longer seeking to shun it, but instead seeking to run it. A national narrative that revolved around keeping the world at bay while changing it through example gave way to one committed to U.S. activism in the service of remaking the world in its image. Faced with this duality, the United States set out in World War II not just to deny Germany and Japan their expansionist goals, but also to defeat them, occupy them, and transform them into like-minded states. After the close of the war, the United States led the effort to erect the panoply of alliances and institutions that would keep the peace while spreading republican ideals and open markets.

The shift from isolationism to hegemonic ambition, from exemplar to crusader state, was driven not just by the logic of American exceptionalism and the new means required for the country to fulfill its self-appointed role as redeemer nation. In addition, politicians needed to refashion the national creed in order to dismantle isolationism's grip on U.S. grand strategy. Richard Olney, who was secretary of state from 1895 to 1897 and a frustrated supporter of a more ambitious foreign policy, described isolationism's hold as follows: "A rule of policy originating with Washington, preeminently wise for his epoch, ever since taught in schools, lauded on the platform, preached in the pulpit, and displayed in capitals and italics in innumerable political manuals and popular histories, almost becomes part of the mental constitution of the generations to which it descends. They accept it without knowing why and they act upon it without the least regard to their wholly new environment."[52] Walter Mead makes a similar observation about the political environment a half-century later: "So powerful were these older historical traditions that their hold on the American public imagination posed the greatest single obstacle to the generation of statesmen charged with the development of American foreign policy for the 1940s." Mead contends that this "myth of virtuous isolation ... presented itself as the eternal and unchanging creed of the American people through the generations. It was the foreign policy equivalent of the Bill of Rights: the one true faith, handed down from on high."[53]

Breaking this mold and overturning "the foreign policy equivalent of the Bill of Rights" required not just a minor adjustment to the playbook. It required a bold stroke—one capable of shifting deeply entrenched public attitudes. Hence the redefinition of how America would go about fulfilling its mission as redeemer nation and the stark switch in the American narrative from exemplar to crusader state. Hence the dramatic swing, as Louis Hartz notes, from isolationism to a grand strategy of global activism that was its "polar counterpart."[54]

The End of the Cold War, the Onset of Strategic Excess, and the Isolationist Backlash. World War II thus marked a historic turning point for U.S. grand strategy. The United States began to practice a brand of global engagement aimed at both vanquishing adversaries and transforming them into liberal democracies and market economies, thereby seeking to spread worldwide the American experiment. The U.S. strategy of containment during the Cold War similarly aimed at not only blocking Soviet expansionism, but also eliminating communism as an ideological rival to democratic capitalism. This transformational ambition became a hallmark of U.S. foreign policy after Pearl Harbor, continuing from World War II, through the Cold War, and beyond.

An activist version of exceptionalism had considerable potential to lead to strategic overreach. Remaking the world through exertion required far greater effort than doing so through example. Nonetheless, until the fall of the Berlin Wall the presence of a peer competitor kept in check the scope of American ambition. The United States did engage in bouts of strategic excess during the Cold War—the Vietnam War arguably the most notable instance. But geopolitical realities generally imposed restraint and moderation on America's Cold War grand strategy. The United States and its democratic allies ultimately prevailed because of strategic patience and foresight, not rash ambition.

The collapse of the Soviet Union did, however, then clear the way for an era of strategic excess. With the defeat of Soviet communism, the realization of America's messianic mission was at hand. As famously framed by the scholar Frank Fukuyama, democracy would finally triumph and bring about "the end of history."[55] Amid the unipolar moment, the United States could use its monopoly on material power to universalize republican values and institutions.[56] President George W. Bush stated as much in his 2002 National Security Strategy:

> Freedom is the non-negotiable demand of human dignity; the birthright of every person—in every civilization. Throughout history, freedom has been threatened by war and terror; it has been challenged by the clashing wills of powerful states and the evil designs of tyrants; and it has been tested by widespread poverty and disease. Today, humanity holds in its hands the opportunity to further freedom's triumph over all these foes. The United States welcomes our responsibility to lead in this great mission.[57]

Since the founding era, Americans had been determined, in the words of Thomas Paine, "to begin the world all over again." At last, the United States could fulfill its exceptionalist calling.

American power may have been unchecked, but the result was overreach, not the completion of the nation's messianic mission. NATO's eastward expansion was to consolidate democracy and peace in Europe. Instead, it ended up contributing to the return of geopolitical confrontation with Russia. The United

States helped guide China into the World Trade Organization, a move that was intended to expand its middle class, liberalize its politics, and tame its geopolitical ambition. Instead, it quickened China's rise as America's new peer competitor. The interventions in Afghanistan, Iraq, and Libya were to bring about political transformations and establish democratic beachheads in a region long plagued by autocracy. They have done nothing of the sort. Policy makers in Washington aided and abetted the Arab Spring, seeing it as a sign that the Middle East was finally breaking America's way. But the political upheaval has instead unleashed generations of instability.

These strategic errors were the product of ideological excess and over-confidence in the ability of American power to shape global affairs; since the 1990s, the idealist ambitions of *Pax Americana* have gone unchecked by realist constraints, producing successive bouts of strategic overreach. Americans are today reacting against this overreach. Remaking the world in America's image has proved a costly and futile proposition. As a consequence, the pendulum is swinging back from internationalism toward isolationism—a trend only reinforced by the economic stagnation that has afflicted many American workers, the dire economic impact of the COVID-19 pandemic, and the domestic unrest that broke out across the nation following the police killing of George Floyd in Minneapolis. The United States went out to save the world. But America's exertions seem to have gone awry. The international order erected by the United States and its allies after World War II is faltering; illiberalism is on the march in many quarters of the globle. In the meantime, American's own exceptional experiment is falling prey to economic discontent, social division, and political dysfunction. The nation's efforts to make the world anew appear not only to have been in vain, but also to have come at the expense of prosperity and liberty for Americans themselves.

The United States seems to be coming full circle, moving from isolationism, to liberal internationalism, and now back to isolationism. How far back in the direction of isolationism the pendulum swings remains to be seen. As Hartz approvingly paraphrases the views of diplomat and historian George Kennan, "Americans seem to oscillate between fleeing from the rest of the world and embracing it with too ardent a passion. An absolute morality is inspired either to withdraw from 'alien' things or to transform them: it cannot live in comfort constantly by their side."[58] It is conceivable that the United States will again recoil from alien things and that isolationist excess will prevail. It is also possible that the United States will finally succeed in finding the middle ground between running the world and running away from it. Instead of withdrawing from or seeking to transform alien things, can Americans instead live in comfort by their side? The outcome of this building debate on America's role in the world will have a major impact on the global politics of the twenty-first century.

The Plan

This volume examines the trajectory of isolationist thinking and practice by focusing on critical strategic debates, seminal moments when Americans were forced to confront the nature and scope of their relationship with the rest of the world. The episodes explored are selective rather than exhaustive, but taken together they illuminate the ideological and political landscape that gave rise to isolationism and sustained it for so much of American history. The story unfolds through the debates among and decisions of the main protagonists—executive branch officials, members of Congress, opinion makers, corporate leaders, and public activists who shaped both public discourse and policy. The book narrates isolationism's ideological origins, the sources of its political pull, and its impact on statecraft, exposing how its multiple variants enabled it to appeal to diverse constituencies across time. It then goes on to explore the struggle between isolationism and alternative forms of internationalism between 1898 and 1941, explaining how and why isolationism maintained its tight grip on U.S. statecraft during the interwar era. The bulk of the book covers the story of isolationism from the founding era until America's entry into World War II in 1941. The final section of the volume then goes on to chart the rise and fall of liberal internationalism after World War II, examines isolationism's current comeback, and concludes with an assessment of what form of U.S. statecraft may lie ahead.

Even as it reveals the distinctive nature of the alternative logics of isolationism at play during different periods, the book also weaves isolationism's intellectual and political trajectory into a broader whole. It demonstrates that isolationism's multiple variants drew on the notion of American exceptionalism and the accompanying fear that entanglement abroad, both in spirit and in deed, would jeopardize the nation's natural security, expose it to the enemy within, and compromise the American experiment. This conviction became deeply embedded in the nation's identity, making challenges to it both rare and politically perilous. The story of isolationism also serves to refurbish its blemished reputation, making clear that restraint amid ascent advanced the nation's interests, enabling the United States to sidestep the great-power rivalry that usually accompanies the rise of a newcomer. Indeed, isolationism's success helps explain its longevity. It was not until after the delusionary isolationism of the interwar era that American leaders durably overcame nonentanglement's powerful allure by merging realist and idealist versions of internationalism in the 1940s.

The next chapter maps out isolationism's ideological and political origins. It presents an anatomy of isolationism, revealing the diverse—and, at times, contradictory—logics that compelled a steadily rising America to generally steer clear of foreign commitments. Thereafter, the book proceeds chronologically, conceptually packaging U.S. statecraft into three main eras. Part I, The

Era of Isolationism, covers U.S. statecraft from the founding era until the embrace of imperial ambition in 1898. Part II, The Defeat of Realist and Idealist Internationalism, focuses on the period from the Spanish-American War until U.S. entry into World War II in 1941. Part III, The Rise and Fall of Liberal Internationalism, covers the onset of *Pax Americana* and its ongoing demise, running from the early 1940s through the presidency of Donald Trump.

Part I begins with Chapter Three, which explores the Revolutionary War—America's initial bid to disentangle itself from Europe—and the early formation of a consensus among the Founders in favor of an isolationist grand strategy. Chapter Four chronicles U.S. efforts to distance itself from the French Revolutionary Wars and Napoleonic Wars, as well as the U.S. decision to embark on a second conflict with Britain in 1812. It was during this era that isolationism became doctrine.

The Napoleonic Wars as well as the War of 1812 came to a close in 1815, enabling the United States to enjoy an unprecedented period of peace, prosperity, and political comity—what one Boston newspaper called "an Era of Good Feelings."[59] As Chapter Five chronicles, under the guise of the Monroe Doctrine and Manifest Destiny, Americans aggressively expanded westward and sought to limit Europe's imperial presence in the Western Hemisphere. Nonetheless, they resolutely guarded against commitments outside North America and repeatedly resisted the temptation to advance the democratic cause by materially supporting the stirrings of republican government in Latin America and Europe. Chapter Six focuses on the Civil War and its aftermath, when America again had a head of expansionist steam. The United States consolidated its extension to the Pacific coast and purchased Alaska. Buoyed by the growing economic and military strength of the country, the nation's leaders were tempted to go further, eyeing the potential annexation of territories in Latin America, the Caribbean, and the Pacific. But the isolationist consensus again prevailed, ultimately defeating the urge to expand beyond North America.

Part II covers the tug-of-war that took place between isolationism and internationalism between 1898 and 1941. It examines the onset—and ultimate defeat—of the realist and idealist brands of internationalism on offer during this era. Chapter Seven focuses on the sources of America's imperial turn in 1898—a sharp historical breakpoint. It explores the social, ideological, and geopolitical developments that prompted Americans, for the first time in the nation's history, to countenance overseas expansion and rule over colonial territories. Chapter Eight examines in greater detail the outbreak and strategic impact of the Spanish-American War, chronicling the nation's unprecedented decision to extend its territorial reach into the Caribbean and Pacific. It recounts the nation's enthusiastic abandonment of isolationism, but then explores why, especially in the face of the bloody U.S. occupation of the Philippines, many Americans soon soured on "republican imperialism" and returned to their traditional aversion to foreign entanglement. Reconciling the nation's exceptional character with its sudden embrace of imperial ambition proved a bridge too far.

Chapter Nine interprets the rise of Wilsonian idealism as a political compromise between isolationism and imperialism. President Woodrow Wilson sought to craft a principled brand of American internationalism that would allow the nation to remain true to its exceptional character while projecting its power abroad. He guided the United States into World War I to, in his own words, "vindicate the principles of peace and justice," and then worked hard to ensure that idealist values would shape the postwar order.[60] But just as the imperial adventurism of 1898 prompted a swift retreat, so too did U.S. involvement in World War I produce a sharp backlash. The Senate ended up rejecting U.S. participation in the League of Nations, setting the stage for the strategic pullback of the interwar era. Wilson's idealist vision proved too much for a nation whose skepticism of foreign entanglement had just been reinforced by participation in World War I.

Chapter Ten explores the 1920s—a decade of "isolationist internationalism" during which the United States sought to exercise global sway through its economic strength while retracting its strategic commitments beyond the Western Hemisphere.[61] By tapping into Wall Street's diplomatic leverage and turning to multilateral pacts to limit armament and geopolitical rivalry, the United States searched for a way to wield international influence while minimizing strategic liabilities.

Chapter Eleven focuses on the years between the Great Depression and the Japanese attack on Pearl Harbor—an era of stubborn and delusionary isolationism. Americans turned sharply inward amid the economic duress of the 1930s. As the menace posed by the Axis powers progressively mounted, the main response of the United States was to cordon itself off from the trouble brewing in both Europe and East Asia. After the outbreak of World War II, President Roosevelt finally began to provide military support to those fighting fascism, but he had to battle the isolationists each step of the way. And despite the string of strategic successes enjoyed by Nazi Germany and Imperial Japan in 1940 and 1941, the United States still refused to join the fight. America's terribly late entry into the war came only at the end of 1941, when the nation was forced to fight by Japan's surprise attack on Pearl Harbor.

Part III covers the rise of liberal internationalism during the 1940s and its demise after the end of the Cold War. The isolationists went silent after the attack on Pearl Harbor, clearing the way for the liberal brand of internationalism that took root during World War II. Since this book focuses primarily on the impact of the isolationist impulse on U.S. history, it moves quickly through World War II and the Cold War era. Isolationism was largely in remission from the end of 1941 through the fall of the Berlin Wall, enabling the pace of the historical narrative to quicken and to focus principally on the few episodes during which voices favoring nonentanglement tried, even if unsuccessfully, to pull the United States back from global engagement. American statecraft has remained predominantly internationalist since the Cold War's end. But isolationist sentiment has been making a comeback amid economic duress, partisan polarization, and strategic overreach, warranting a more detailed look at U.S. statecraft over the past two decades.

Chapter Twelve examines the ideological and political roots of liberal internationalism and the sources of its durability during the balance of the twentieth century. The paramount threats posed by Nazi Germany, Imperial Japan, and then the Soviet Union, coupled with the merging of realist and idealist brands of internationalism, solidified broad bipartisan support for the combination of power and partnership needed to defeat adversaries and sustain *Pax Americana*. Isolationists challenged the internationalist consensus during the early Cold War, but were effectively marginalized by the mid-1950s. Voices counseling nonentanglement again pushed back in response to the Vietnam War. But the Iranian revolution and the Soviet invasion of Afghanistan helped revive the bipartisan compact behind liberal internationalism, which would then last through the end of the Cold War.

Chapter Thirteen chronicles the demise of liberal internationalism over the course of the Clinton, Bush, Obama, and Trump administrations. Following the end of the Cold War, bipartisan support for a brand of statecraft that relied on equal parts of power and partnership came to an end. The Republicans generally became the party of power while the Democrats strongly favored partnership, ending the centrist compact that sustained liberal internationalism and setting the stage for wide oscillations in policy as power changed hands in Washington. The polarization and incoherence, coupled with ideological triumphalism, produced the strategic overreach of the post–Cold War era.

President Clinton embraced a brand of statecraft that relied heavily on partnership and multilateral institutions, using force only gingerly. The Republicans then veered in the opposite direction. In the aftermath of the September 11 attacks, President George W. Bush opted for unilateralism and the assertive use of force in the Middle East, resulting in quagmires in Afghanistan and Iraq that reawakened the nation's isolationist instincts. President Obama responded by turning to a scaled-back version of liberal internationalism aimed at orchestrating a strategic retrenchment and lightening the nation's footprint abroad. But he was hampered by turmoil abroad and intractable polarization at home.

President Trump then followed with his America First approach to statecraft, which was an explicit return to the isolationist, unilateralist, and protectionist grand strategy that preceded the onset of liberal internationalism. The chapter probes the political and ideological origins of Trump's foreign policy, and chronicles the battle between Trump's more isolationist preferences and a foreign policy establishment still committed to a robust global role for the United States. The result was an erratic and inconstant foreign policy; one day, Trump appeared ready to retreat from an unruly world, the next to run rough-shod over it.

This book's conclusion, Chapter Fourteen, looks both back and ahead, extracting lessons from America's isolationist and internationalist past to inform its statecraft moving forward. The strategic, political, and socio-economic forces that long sustained a grand strategy of nonentanglement are making a come-back, producing a growing gap between the nation's role in the world and the political will needed to sustain that role. The search is on for a foreign policy that brings America's means and its purposes back into alignment. A world that is in the midst of geopolitical flux and a surge in illiberalism still needs American leadership. At the same time, this more unruly world, coupled with polarization and economic dislocation at home, tempts Americans to step away from it. The challenge ahead is finding a brand of statecraft that continues to promote global stability and order while enjoying the support of the American electorate.

It remains to be seen whether Americans are up to the task. They have tired of the exertions required to sustain an expansive notion of *Pax Americana* and become skeptical of the benefits of doing so. Amid economic uncertainty, increasing social diversity, and intense political division, they are understand-ably calling for a realignment of priorities and a greater focus of attention and resources on the home front. A strategic retrenchment is coming; the key ques-tion is whether it occurs by design or default. As America's isolationist instincts reawaken, much rides on the nation's ability to find the elusive middle ground between doing too much and doing too little—between remaking the world in its image and disentangling itself from that world.

2

An Anatomy of Isolationism

The term "isolationism" came into common usage in the United States in the 1930s—and it already had distinctly negative connotations. Admiral Alfred Thayer Mahan, who in the late nineteenth century was one of the nation's most passionate advocates of a "blue-water" navy, in 1890 warned against "our self-imposed isolation" and predicted that "when the opportunities for gain abroad are understood, the course of American enterprise will cleave a channel by which to reach them."[1] At the close of World War I, supporters of the League of Nations explicitly deployed the isolationist label against those who opposed U.S. participation in the global body. Following the Senate's rejection of U.S. participation in the League in 1919 and 1920, organizations such as the Council on Foreign Relations and the Carnegie Endowment for International Peace dedicated themselves to studying and promoting internationalism and exposing the dangers of isolationism.

Such efforts to tarnish isolationism fell short. During the interwar era, the United States embraced strategic passivity outside the Western Hemisphere—even after Nazi Germany and Imperial Japan had made amply clear their aggressive ambitions. Interwar critics did lay the groundwork for the more vigorous and successful discrediting of isolationism that occurred during the 1940s, but it took the Japanese attack on Pearl Harbor to push isolationism to the fringes of American politics. As Senator Arthur Vandenberg (R-Michigan), formerly a resolute supporter of isolationism, wrote in his diary, "in my own mind, my convictions regarding international cooperation and collective security for peace took firm form on the afternoon of the Pearl Harbor attack. That day ended isolationism for any realist."[2]

That it took from the nation's birth until 1941 for Americans to abandon their isolationist roots speaks to its long dominance of American politics and statecraft. President George Washington's 1796 dictum that the United States should have with foreign nations "as little political connection as possible" set the tone for the decades that followed; until the imperial turn of 1898 the country shunned strategic commitments beyond North America.[3] Prior to the end of the nineteenth century, nonentanglement was the only game in town. Even so, Americans did not consider themselves isolated, one of the reasons that they did not conceive of their nation's statecraft as "isolationist." Europe's imperial powers had sizable holdings in the Western Hemisphere and kept on station the fleets and soldiers needed to protect their territories. Potential enemies were nearby, not on the other side of the Atlantic. Moreover, Americans were hardly passive when it came to territorial and commercial expansion. From early on, they aimed to become, in the words of Alexander Hamilton, "an ascendant in the system of American affairs" by eventually driving Europe's imperial powers from the Western Hemisphere.[4] They were ruthlessly acquisitive in North America, by 1848 expanding their maturing union all the way to the Pacific coast. They were determined to trade in all quarters of the globe—and to use military force to defend American merchants as needed.

Such ardor for territorial expansion across North America and commercial activism beyond the nation's shores has prompted some scholars of U.S. foreign policy to dismiss the notion that the United States ever was isolationist. Historian Robert Kagan argues that the United States was a "dangerous nation" from the start and that Americans have always pursued "aggressive expansionism" and "acquisitive materialism."[5] Political scientist Bear Braumoeller calls U.S. isolationism a "myth," maintaining that even during the 1920s, after the United States had refused to enter the League of Nations and pulled away from strategic engagement in Europe and East Asia, the nation was deeply engaged abroad, adroitly using its commercial and financial strength—"banks rather than tanks"—to pursue its objectives.[6] Historians Warren Cohen and Melvyn Leffler offer a similar perspective, contending that the United States wielded considerable influence over global affairs after World War I by relying on its financial, rather than its military, strength.[7]

These considered objections to the isolationist moniker are, simply put, off the mark. From 1789 until 1941, with notable departures in 1898 and during World War I, the United States *was* strikingly isolationist. Yes, Americans were avid and restless merchants, constantly looking for new markets abroad. Yes, Americans were bent on expanding westward across North America, in the process repeatedly attempting (but failing) to wrest control of Canadian territory, grabbing a sizable chunk of Mexico, and purchasing Alaska. Yes, African Americans and Native Americans suffered grievously as the union matured and enlarged. Yes, the United States was from early on intent on driving Europe's imperial powers from the Western Hemisphere, clearing the way for the union to enjoy uncontested sway in its neighborhood. And yes, beginning in 1898 the United States became far more interventionist in the Caribbean and Latin America after it drove Spain from the region and took a major step toward finally fulfilling Hamilton's aspiration that the nation become "an ascendant in the system of American affairs."

But when it came to pursuing geopolitical ambition farther afield, Americans were decidedly opposed. Indeed, their primary geopolitical focus until World War II was on countering adjacent challengers. As Alexander Hamilton articulated in *Federalist No. 24*, Americans faced two proximate threats—from the European powers whose imperial possessions surrounded the United States and from Native Americans:

> Though a wide ocean separates the United States from Europe, yet there are various considerations that warn us against an excess of confidence or security. On one side of us, and stretching far into our rear, are growing settlements subject to the dominion of Britain. On the other side, and extending to meet the British settlements, are colonies and establishments subject to the dominion of Spain. This situation and the vicinity of the West India Islands, belonging to these two powers, create between them, in respect to their American possessions and in relation to us, a common interest. The savage tribes on our Western frontier ought to be regarded as our natural enemies, their natural allies, because they have most to fear from us, and most to hope from them.[8]

Westward expansion, determined efforts to ease European powers out of America's neighborhood, and neutralization of the threat from "savage tribes" were generally deemed to be strategic imperatives, not matters of choice. Moreover, Americans pursued such expansion in the service of isolation; the dismantling of Europe's imperial holdings in the Western Hemisphere and the clearing out of Native Americans would permit the United States to enjoy the natural security afforded by its geographic location. Westward expansion would not only eliminate threats to the nation's security, but also provide the arable land needed for America's growing population to thrive. The nation's other prerequisite for prosperity was foreign trade. The United States was from the outset a trading nation; the seaborne trade of cotton, tobacco, cod, and other commodities helped fuel the American economy. The expansion of overseas trade—and, if necessary, the defense of such trade by force—followed logically.

But what the United States did not do—and what qualifies it as an isolationist nation par excellence—was take on enduring strategic commitments beyond its immediate neighborhood. Until 1898, Americans repeatedly turned their backs on opportunities to expand beyond North America. They regularly debated, but consistently rejected, proposals to wrest control of noncontiguous territories, including Cuba, the Danish West Indies, Haiti, Hawaii, and Santo Domingo. Between 1898 and 1941, they began to enforce their claim to hemispheric hegemony, made a run at imperial expansion in the Pacific, and intervened in Europe amid World War I. But these forays produced a sharp political backlash and a strategic retreat. Throughout, with the exception of the nation's entry into World War I, the United States sought to avoid entanglement in great-power rivalry and resisted the temptation, which was so enthusiastically embraced by other states of similar rank, to extend its reach into and to exert its influence over distant strategic theaters. The test of America's isolationist credentials was not its mounting ambition in the Western Hemisphere or its insatiable commercial appetite. These were foreordained. What was optional was following in the footsteps of Europe's imperial powers and seeking to shape the balance of power in theaters far afield. On this front, the United States passed the isolationist test with flying colors.

From its founding until 1898, the United States refused to take on strategic commitments outside North America. Between 1898 and 1941, it defended hemispheric hegemony, but strayed beyond the Western Hemisphere only on a limited and exceptional basis. It is this abstinence that marks the nation as isolationist and makes its rise historically distinctive. While Europe's great powers were building and defending far-flung empires, the United States for the most part held back. While its peers were seeking to maximize their influence and strength by projecting their power abroad, the United States was building its power only at and close to home. Even after the United States became a country of the top rank by the turn of the twentieth century, it generally shunned rather than strived for geopolitical sway commensurate with its material strength.

Such restraint amid ascent made America's rise truly exceptional. Moreover, in a country distinguished by its intractable partisan divisions and deep ideological divides, isolationism's bipartisan support was a rarity. As historian Selig Adler has noted, "few policies in American history were so fixed and so stable as non-intervention."[9] The remainder of this chapter examines the roots and staying power of American isolationism, exploring its political and intellectual origins and evolution.

Isolationism's Origins

Americans cannot claim full authorship of isolationism; the idea of geopolitical detachment from great-power rivalry had already gained traction in the motherland—Great Britain. Although England had earlier pursued continental ambitions, it eventually came to practice a grand strategy of isolation when it came to Europe's great powers. Banking on the strategic immunity afforded by the English Channel, the British kept their distance from continental rivalries in order to focus on seaborne commerce with their imperial periphery. In the early 1500s, Henry VIII's advisers were quite clear about the broad outlines of English strategy: "Let us in God's name leave off our attempts against the *terra firma*. The natural situation of islands seems not to consort with conquests of that kind. . . . When we would enlarge ourselves, let it be that way we can, and to which it seems the eternal Providence hath destined us, which is by the sea."[10] To be sure, there were significant differences of opinion about how best to distance Britain from great-power rivalry. Tories generally argued for complete isolation from the Continent, while Whigs maintained that Britain should intervene in Europe as needed to sustain a stable balance of power.[11] But both approaches entailed shunning foreign alliances that would only diminish Britain's room for maneuver. As a foreign policy pamphlet published in London in 1744 put it, "A prince or state ought to avoid all treaties, except such as tend towards promoting commerce or manufactures, or reducing an exorbitant power that is becoming terrible to all its neighbors. All other alliances may be looked upon as so many encumbrances."[12]

America's Founders read widely and were well-schooled in British strategy. The idea and practice of strategic isolation were thus not entirely homegrown.[13] Nonetheless, America's version of isolationism was quite different from Britain's. Whereas Britain was about twenty miles from the Continent at the English Channel's narrowest point, America was 3,000 miles away from Europe. For the United States, the direct threat from Europe was more remote and the prospect of intervening in European affairs less tempting. Moreover, whereas Britain isolated itself from the Continent in order to focus on constructing and defending an overseas empire, the United States until the end of the nineteenth century had no interest whatsoever in taking on far-flung strategic commitments, nor did it have the capability to do so. To be sure, the United States became a trading nation with an economy buoyed by foreign commerce and tariffs on imports.[14] But in America's case, the flag did not follow trade. Whereas Britain built a globe-spanning network of colonies, defended by the world's premier fleet, the United States sought only commerce, not enduring commitments. It did not build heavy warships capable of projecting power across long distances until the late 1800s, instead investing in the vessels needed for coastal defense and the protection of merchant ships against Barbary corsairs and other commerce raiders. Britain steered clear of the Continent in order to pursue overseas empire. In contrast, the United States steered clear of Europe's great powers to trade with all, but extend strategic commitments to none.

America's marriage of commercial ambition with strategic detachment also distinguishes its brand of isolationism from other versions. Japan during the Tokugawa shogunate (1603–1867) embraced an isolationist grand strategy (*sakoku*), but it practiced a much more stringent variety. Edicts adopted during the 1630s barred Japanese from leaving the country and severely restricted the entry of foreigners to Japan. Foreign commerce was tightly controlled. In effect, Japan sought to seal itself off from the outside world. In contrast, throughout its decades of isolationism, the United States remained an immigrant nation and its citizens zealously pursued foreign commerce. The nation's Founders were worldly and well-traveled; many of its early leaders were experienced diplomats and had served abroad. The United States may have been stubbornly isolationist when it came to strategic entanglement abroad, but was very much engaged in global affairs when it came to commerce and diplomacy.

American isolationism was unique in one final—and crucial—respect: it was an end as well as a means, a fundamental maxim of U.S. statecraft and not just an instrumental practice. Britain pursued strategic isolation from the Continent in the service of overseas expansion. The Tokugawa shogunate secluded Japan in order to eliminate the cultural and religious influence of Europeans and other outsiders as well as to undercut the growing power of local warlords who were benefiting from foreign trade. American isolationism, as outlined below, was similarly a means for achieving specific ends, both at home and abroad.

Yet American isolationism was also an end in itself. The United States was destined to break the mold of great-power rivalry and play by a more enlightened and humane rule book. Its responsibility to chart this new course became part of the narrative of American exceptionalism—a defining element in the new nation's evolving identity. When the nation's first president in 1796 outlined his vision of U.S. statecraft, steering clear of foreign entanglement was far more than a policy recommendation; it was, in Washington's own words, "the great rule of conduct for us."[15] Admittedly, Americans of different regions and political persuasions embraced differing versions of the exceptionalist narrative. But isolationism was common to all of them, precisely why it enjoyed such widespread political support and became central to the American creed. Isolationism lasted as long as it did because it was rooted in who Americans were and what they stood for. What follows is an anatomy of American isolationism that investigates its ideological sources and explores how its multiple variants were both defined by and came to define American exceptionalism.

The Logics of Isolationism

American isolationism rested on six distinct, but interlocking, logics: 1) *capitalizing on natural security*; 2) *serving as redeemer nation*; 3) *advancing liberty and prosperity at home*; 4) *preserving freedom of action abroad*; 5) *protecting social homogeneity*; and 6) *promoting pacifism*. These six logics of isolationism were present from early on, and they all figured as elements in the evolving narrative of American exceptionalism. Nonetheless, their salience changed over time depending on domestic as well as international developments. So, too, were there regional differences in the ideological strength of these variants; for example, libertarian strains of isolationism ran stronger in the South, while pacifist strains held more sway in the North. The regional and ideological diversity of isolationist doctrine was a considerable source of its political durability, enabling it to long dominate American statecraft—despite the nation's growing power, technological change, generational turnover, shifting control of the executive and legislative branches, and variation in the political and economic interests of America's different sections.

Capitalizing on Natural Security

Exceptional geography made possible America's embrace of isolationism by providing natural security. Vast expanses of water flanked North America's eastern and western coasts. To the north and south of the developing nation were relatively weak neighbors. To its west was an ample allotment of fertile land beckoning settlers, much of it unpopulated or thinly populated. During America's early decades, the British, Spanish, French, and Russian presence in the Western Hemisphere as well as conflicts with Native Americans did compromise this natural security. But a number of developments would eventually allow the maturing nation to reap the full benefits of its fortunate location: the high rate of population growth in the United States; the disease, violence, and forced removal that weakened Native Americans; U.S. efforts to end European colonialism in its neighborhood; and independence movements in the Caribbean and Latin America that expedited Europe's retreat. In the meantime, distance itself would help keep at bay the predatory intentions of Europe's imperial powers. As Hamilton explained in *Federalist No. 8*, "Europe is at a great distance from us. Her colonies in our vicinity will be likely to continue too much disproportioned in strength to be able to give us any dangerous annoyance."[16]

America's exceptional and providential location was first and foremost a function of the nation's watery distance from Europe's great powers, which made it not only difficult for Europeans to remain dominant in the Western Hemisphere, but also unnatural. As Thomas Paine argued in his widely read pamphlet *Common Sense*, "even the distance at which the Almighty hath placed England and America, is a strong and natural proof, that the authority of the one, over the other, was never the design of Heaven."[17] The task at hand for Americans was to fashion a union strong and coherent enough to ward off Europe's imperial predations. In Hamilton's words, "if we are wise enough to preserve the Union we may for ages enjoy an advantage similar to that of an insulated situation."[18] The United States should do nothing to compromise that insulation and should instead, as President Washington put it in his Farewell Address, "steer clear of permanent alliances with any portion of the foreign world."[19]

America's distance from Europe not only provided it ready protection, but also meant that it resided in a separate geopolitical system. Strategic theaters were naturally defined by proximity. Nations located close to each other were destined to be geopolitical rivals. Felix Gilbert summarizes Hamilton's views on this subject as follows: "States situated in the same geographic area were tied together in a continuous power struggle arising from clashing interests. They were members of the same political system which extended as far as its natural geographical limits."[20] In contrast, countries distant from each other enjoyed strategic separation; for them geopolitical competition was a choice, not foreordained by geography. According to Paine, "it is evident they [England and America] belong to different systems; England to Europe, America to itself."[21]

Accordingly, the United States had to avoid adventurous behavior far afield that would unnecessarily invite molestation by distant nations. By staying out of other strategic theaters, America would encourage foreign powers to stay out of its strategic theater. According to Paine, "any submission to, or dependence on Great Britain, tends directly to involve this continent in European wars and quarrels; and sets us at variance with nations, who would otherwise seek our friendship, and against whom, we have neither anger nor complaint."[22] Washington laid out a similar perspective in the Farewell Address: "Europe has a set of primary interests, which to us have none, or a very remote relation. . . . Hence therefore it must be unwise in us to implicate ourselves, by artificial ties, in the ordinary vicissitudes of her politics."[23] The practice of isolationism was thus meant to reinforce America's natural invulnerability; distance would keep other powers at bay as long as the United States kept its strategic distance from them.

Americans' sense of natural security also stemmed from its ample allotment of land, not just from protective oceans to the east and west. Europe was crowded with nations, setting them against each other in constant competition for land and power. In Paine's words, "Europe is too thickly planted with kingdoms to be long at peace."[24] In contrast, North America had few residents and fewer nations—Native Americans were not accorded standing—offering a much more benign political and strategic environment. Indeed, that more benign environment was one of America's main sources of appeal; many immigrants to the New World had risked the trip across the Atlantic in search of open land, greater liberty, and less warfare.

The girth of North America—in particular, its vast interior—made it very difficult to conquer. Britain's naval superiority enabled it to threaten America's coastal areas. But molesting the hinterland was another matter altogether. Indeed, Paine pointed to the sheer size of North America as one of the reasons that the colonies should be free from British rule: "There is something very absurd, in supposing a continent to be perpetually governed by an island. In no instance hath nature made the satellite larger than its primary planet."[25] The strategic consequence of the nation's deep interior was reinforced by the rapid population growth sustained by a seemingly unlimited allotment of arable land. America's demographic advantage, coupled with its strategic depth, promised to indemnify it against both proximate and European challengers.[26] Abraham Lincoln, although perhaps overstating the case, spelled out this aspect of natural security in an address in 1838:

> We find ourselves in the peaceful possession, of the fairest portion of the earth, as regards extent of territory, fertility of soil, and salubrity of climate.... At what point shall we expect the approach of danger? By what means shall we fortify against it?—Shall we expect some transatlantic military giant, to step the Ocean, and crush us at a blow? Never!—All the armies of Europe, Asia and Africa combined, with all the treasure of the earth (our own excepted) in their military chest; with a Buonaparte for a commander, could not by force, take a drink from the Ohio, or make a track on the Blue Ridge, in a trial of a thousand years.[27]

The notion of natural security had an economic component as well. As mentioned above, the United States was from the start a trading nation. The Founders may have differed as to whether the country should remain primarily agrarian or instead pursue industrialization, but they were in agreement that it should maximize foreign trade. Geopolitical isolation would further this objective by enabling the United States to trade with all countries. Embroilment in geopolitical rivalries would, in contrast, impair free commerce and give belligerent nations cause to interrupt trade with the United States. In Paine's words, "as Europe is our market for trade, we ought to form no partial connection with any part of it. It is the true interest of America to steer clear of European contentions." Jefferson was in complete agreement: "Commerce with all nations, alliance with none, should be our motto." John Quincy Adams offered a similar formulation, urging the United States to "look to *commerce* and *navigation*, and not to empire as her means of communication with the rest of the human family."[28]

Many of the Founders believed not only that an isolationist foreign policy would boost foreign trade, but also that maximizing foreign commerce would enhance the nation's security. The allure of doing business with the United States, they held, would ultimately convince other powers to pursue pacific relations with America. Paine maintained that "our plan is commerce, and that, well attended to, will secure us peace and friendship of all Europe; because it is the interest of all Europe to have America a free port."[29] Jefferson, too, viewed open trade as an investment in international stability.[30] As he put it in 1785, "I think all the world would gain by setting commerce at perfect liberty."[31] Not all the Founders agreed. Hamilton, for one, expressed skepticism about trade's pacifying effects: "Has commerce hitherto done any thing more than change the objects of war," he asked. "Have there not been as many wars founded upon commercial motives since that has become the prevailing system of nations, as were before occasioned by the cupidity of territory or dominion?"[32] Nonetheless, Hamilton, like his colleagues, staunchly supported an isolationist statecraft that would advance the prospects for open commerce. In this respect, protecting and expanding America's commercial links abroad helped fashion a consensus among America's early leaders that the nation should bank on its natural security.

As President Washington prepared his Farewell Address, he consulted Hamilton on its content. One of the issues they debated was whether to present the injunction against alliance with foreign powers as a temporary function of the strategic weakness of a young nation or a more enduring feature of U.S. strategy—a function of America's permanent geographic good fortune. They decided on the latter, precisely why the address had a timeless quality and referred to the admonition against foreign entanglement as "our true policy" and "the great rule of conduct for us."[33] Washington's appreciation of the nation's natural security, as well as his definitive statement of its implications for U.S. statecraft, would guide U.S. grand strategy for decades to come.

Serving as Redeemer Nation

The narrative of American exceptionalism posited not only the nation's geographic good fortune but also its unique political character. Whereas America's geographic bounty was unto itself, its exceptional experiment in political and economic liberty was to be shared with others. Indeed, the United States was the redeemer, the chosen nation, the repository of human progress that would serve as a global beacon. Americans—elites and the public alike—believed that destiny had endowed them with an obligation to impart their political wisdom to the rest of the world. Since many immigrants to the United States had come in search of economic opportunity and political and religious freedom, their character and convictions made them well-suited to be the foot soldiers of this messianic mission.

America's self-appointed role as redeemer nation emerged in part from religious faith. New England, in particular, was home to a fervent strain of Protestantism holding that divine redemption was possible in this world, not only in the next. These committed Protestants saw the United States as the New Israel—a nation tasked with a divinely inspired redemptive mission. American messianism also came in a secular variant, one holding that it was the nation's duty to advance a brand of political, religious, and economic freedom that would become a standard-bearer for the world. Especially in less religious communities and during periods of diminished religious fervor, belief in the unique and exemplary nature of the American experiment helped anchor the country's commitment to serve as the world's redeemer nation. As historian Lawrence Kaplan notes, "Calvinist expectations of a New Jerusalem in turn received reinforcement from the secular thought of the Enlightenment."[34] The result was a distinctive strain of American exceptionalism rooted in both religious conviction and rationalist conceptions of human progress.

Logically, this sense of national mission should have prompted zealous entanglement abroad; at least in theory, the global promotion of the American experiment required nothing less. Paradoxically, however, American messianism had the opposite effect. Fearful of compromising their experiment by venturing into an outside realm that was politically blemished and war-prone, Americans were determined to protect the exceptional character of their nation by keeping the outside world at bay. They would stand behind their obligation to spread American values and institutions, but they would fulfill this mission by example, not by action. To pursue a more forceful and ambitious foreign policy, they believed, would jeopardize, not advance, that mission. Entanglement in great-power politics would necessitate a centralized government and a large military establishment, both of which were inimical to domestic liberty. Geopolitical ambition would also force the United States to play by the bellicose and selfish rules of the Old World, ruining its hope of constructing an international realm governed by reason and law rather than power politics. As historian Walter McDougall has observed, the American embrace of isolationism was driven as much by the nation's obsession with its providential calling as by its geographic separation.[35]

Religious Messianism. As for the religious foundations of the nation's messianic calling, Calvinism—the main Protestant denomination in the United States—embraced two contrasting conceptions of redemption. A conservative and pessimistic variant held humans to be irremediably flawed and took redemption to be possible only in the world to come. In contrast, a progressive and optimistic variant held that humans could improve themselves through individual worship, moral behavior, and good works, opening up the possibility of redemption in this world. This progressive variant, which came to dominate New England, also saw religious freedom and political liberty as inseparable and defining features of American society. For believers, this intermingling of religious and political conceptions of redemption set the nation on a course to build God's kingdom on earth.[36]

Historians continue to debate the ebb and flow of religiosity among New Englanders.[37] The spread of commercialism in the North did produce a secularizing trend, exposing religious idealism to the tempering effects of material ambition.[38] Nonetheless, two waves of religious revivalism, known as Great Awakenings, stoked religious fervor. The first ran from the 1720s to the 1740s. The surge in religious zeal strengthened dissent against established churches, bolstering the progressive variants of Protestantism that held out the prospect of divine redemption in this world. The second Great Awakening ran from the 1790s into the 1840s. Against the backdrop of American independence and the young nation's growing population, territory, and prosperity, it deepened the linkage between religious and secular conceptions of America's role as redeemer nation. Some historians draw a direct line between this wave of religious revivalism and westward expansion under the guise of Manifest Destiny. In the minds of Protestant evangelists, territorial expansion and the maturation of republican institutions were welcome and reassuring markers of an unfolding religious redemption.[39] Principles of religious freedom and individual worship aligned with principles of political liberty, leading, in the words of Andrew Preston, to a "Christian republicanism."[40]

Throughout the eighteenth and nineteenth centuries, sermons, literature, and political discourse ensured that America's sense of national mission was infused with both religious and political purpose. Missionaries had a hand in advocating and facilitating westward expansion and, by the late 1800s, many had become passionate advocates of expansion abroad. An excerpt from a poem, published in 1780 by Timothy Dwight, an author and Congregationalist minister who in 1795 became the president of Yale University, exemplifies this intermingling of the sacred and the secular in shaping American messianism:

> Hail Land of light and joy! thy power shall grow
> Far as the seas, which round thy regions flow;
> Through earth's wide realms thy glory shall extend,
> And savage nations at thy scepter bend. . . .
> No more shall War her fearful horrors found,
> Nor strew her thousands on th' embattled ground;
> No more on earth shall Rage and Discord dwell,
> But sink with Envy to their native hell.
> Then, then an heavenly kingdom shall descend,
> And Light and Glory through the world extend.[41]

It was not only religious leaders who drew on such imagery. In *Common Sense*, Paine asserted that "the cause of America is in a great measure the cause of all mankind." He went on to claim that "we have it in our power to begin the world over again. A situation, similar to the present, hath not happened since the days of Noah until now. The birthday of a new world is at hand."[42] Independence only strengthened the conviction that the United States was indeed destined to fulfill a providential mission. According to political scientist Susan Materese, "America's victory [against Britain] was conventionally interpreted as the work of Providence and as proof of God's blessing, while America's democratic institutions were perceived to reflect the ideals of the kingdom of God on Earth."[43] In *Federalist No. 2*, John Jay wrote, "this country and this people seem to have been made for each other, and it appears as if it were the design of Providence."[44] Jefferson proposed that the young nation adopt as a national seal an image of the children of Israel led by a heavenly pillar of light. He was, according to historian Walter LaFeber, "confident that Americans were the new chosen people of God."[45] In his farewell address, President Andrew Jackson told Americans that "Providence . . . has chosen you as the guardians of freedom, to preserve it for the benefit of the human race."[46] This view even had adherents in England. Richard Price, an English preacher and moral philosopher, affirmed in 1784 that "it is a conviction I cannot resist that the independence of the English colonies in America is one of the steps ordained by Providence to introduce these times. . . . Perhaps there never existed a people on whose wisdom and virtue more depended or to whom a station of more importance in the plan of Providence has been assigned."[47]

The second Great Awakening, coupled with territorial expansion and rapid growth in population and prosperity, strengthened the discourse portraying the United States as a chosen nation in both sacred and material terms. Horace Bushnell, a Congregational minister, said in 1837, "there are too many prophetic signs admonishing us, that Almighty Providence is pre-engaged to make this a truly great nation."[48] In 1846, author J. Sullivan Cox compared the nation's expansion under the guise of Manifest Destiny to the biblical experience of the Jewish people in the Sinai desert: "Call it what you will, *destiny*, or what not; it is leading us as a cloud by day and a pillar of fire by night."[49] In his 1850 novel, *White-Jacket*, Melville referred to the United States as "the political Messiah," alerting his readers that "he has come in us."[50] In 1890, Washington Gladden, a Congregational pastor, cast America's westward expansion in messianic terms: "Here, upon these plains, the problems of history are to be solved; here, if anywhere, is to rise that city of God, the New Jerusalem, whose glories are to fill the earth."[51]

Such biblical imagery was commonplace through the end of the nineteenth century—and was applied to the land itself, not just those who were settling it. Designation of the United States as the promised land went hand in hand with the labeling of its citizens as the chosen nation. Although Americans were determined to subdue, settle, and make productive their vast and untamed wilderness, they also saw the nation's expanse as affording spiritual retreat—in the words of historian Roderick Nash, "the medium through which God spoke most clearly."[52] The nation's interior offered not just arable land but the ideal venue for Americans to realize their providential calling. As Henry David Thoreau put it in 1851, "I believe that Adam in paradise was not so favorably situated on the whole as is the backwoodsman in America."[53]

Secular Messianism. A religiously inspired conception of the United States as the redeemer nation dominated during America's early decades. Manifest Destiny drew in part on this religious narrative, casting westward expansion as the fulfillment of the nation's providential calling. But over the course of the nineteenth century—and particularly after the second Great Awakening—this religious narrative gave way to a more secular version, due to both a decline in the public's religiosity and the nation's growing territorial girth and economic bounty. America's self-evident success gave rise to a complementary strain of messianism that was grounded in the secular rather than the sacred. According to Matarese, many Americans still understood their nation as the New Jerusalem, but in a way that became "modified and secularized" over the course of the 1800s.[54]

This secular narrative understood America's uniqueness as resting on three main elements: the advanced stage of the nation's political and social liberty; the superiority of its Anglo-Saxon population; and the quality and size of its territory. This triple endowment would enable the United States to advance, if not complete, the quest for political and social finality—the secular counterpart to God's kingdom on earth.

Even in devoted Puritan communities in New England, political redemption—and not just religious salvation—was central to the nation's evolving identity. The Enlightenment was born in Europe, but its ideals would be perfected in the United States, leading to, in Matarese's words, "a kind of secular utopia."[55] Europeans may have begun the historic process of liberating mankind from monarchic oppression, but it was up to Americans to finish the task; political liberty, via republican government, would be the nation's bequest to the rest of the world. In the words of Kentucky politician Henry Clay, "we should become the center of a system which would constitute the rallying point of human freedom against all the despotism of the Old World."[56] Even among the more religiously inclined, such as Timothy Dwight, the Congregational pastor turned Yale president, this secular narrative had considerable appeal: "It is a very common and just remark that the progress of Liberty, of Science, and of Empire has been with that of the sun, from east to west, since the beginning of time. . . . It is evident that the Empire of North-America will be the last on earth; from the second, that it will be the most glorious. Here the progress of temporal things towards perfection will undoubtedly be finished."[57]

The embrace of Enlightenment principles had implications not just for the character of the nation's governing institutions but also for the conduct of its statecraft. America's foreign policy was to be as unique as its domestic liberty. Drawing on the work of European thinkers such as Voltaire, David Hume, and Jean-Jacques Rousseau, many of America's Founders favored a foreign policy based on reason and law, not on coercion and balance-of-power logic. Indeed, the pursuit of a pacified, rules-based brand of statecraft informed the preference for geopolitical isolation. Strategic engagement with Europe would inevitably draw the United States into a world of rivalry and conflict. Instead, the United States should seek to banish from the Western Hemisphere Europe's great powers and their imperial designs. As President James Monroe (1817–1825) declared in his Annual Message to Congress in 1823, "in the wars of European powers, in matters relating to themselves, we have never taken any part, nor does it comport with our policy to do so. . . . We should consider any attempt on their part to extend their system to any portion of this hemisphere, as dangerous to our peace and security."[58]

The secular narrative of America's role as redeemer rested on the nation's commitment not just to liberty and law, but also to social equity. The Old World was beset by aristocratic privilege, social hierarchy, class conflict, and economic inequality. The United States, in contrast, would be free of class hierarchy and social impediments to economic opportunity. Americans were "born equal," in the words of Alexis de Tocqueville, the astute French observer of early America.[59] For many Americans, social equality and economic mobility were some of the nation's most alluring assets. In Europe, according to Jefferson, "the dignity of man is lost in arbitrary distinctions, where the human species is classed into several stages of degradation, where the many are crouched under the weight of the few." In America, he countered, "the poorest laborer stood on equal ground with the wealthiest Millionary," and "no other distinction between man and man had ever been known, but that of persons in office exercising powers by authority of the laws, and private individuals."[60]

Louis Hartz describes "the historic ethos of American life" as "its bourgeois hungers, its classlessness, the spirit of equality that pervaded it." This ethos, Hartz explains, "saturated the American sense of mission, not with a Christian universalism, but with a curiously Hebraic kind of separatism."[61] Americans were determined to keep their distance from Europe's social ills and to build a more open and mobile society. In the words of Kaplan, a religious sense of national mission "received reinforcement from the secular thought of the Enlightenment, which contrasted the simple, egalitarian, free society of eighteenth-century America with the complex, class-ridden, war-plagued societies of Europe."[62]

Race also figured prominently in the secular version of the redeemer narrative—often intermingled with its religious variant. For Horace Bushnell, the Congregational minister, providence not only ensured that the United States would become a "truly great nation," but also endowed it with a special population capable of fulfilling that destiny: "Out of all the inhabitants of the world, too, a select stock, the Saxon, and out of this the British family, the noblest of stock was chosen to people our country."[63] Washington Gladden agreed that it seemed by divine ordination that "the great mass of these inhabitants of the New World belong to the Aryan race, whose teeming millions have been hurrying westward ever since the dawn of time."[64] Josiah Strong, a Protestant clergyman and social activist, contended that Anglo-Saxons were completing the mission begun by Hebrews, Greeks, and Romans. "Anglo-Saxon civilization," he insisted, "is more favorable than any other to the spread of those principles whose universal triumph is necessary to that perfection of the race to which it is destined."[65]

The final dimension of this secular narrative connected the exceptional character of the American population to the exceptional size and quality of the nation's territory—what Hartz calls "the magnificent material setting" of the New World.[66] North America's abundant and fertile soil afforded its settlers not just economic opportunity but also political and social freedom. Yeoman farmers, shopkeepers in small towns, settlers heading west to subdue new lands—they represented the vanguard of the American experiment. They owned their land and enjoyed the fruits of their own labor, exemplifying the political and economic liberty unique to the United States.[67] And just as the wilderness offered spiritual restoration, so did it offer refuge from the social impurities of city life. Even as Americans congregated in cities and turned forests into productive farms, they were determined to preserve the sanctity of the backcountry.[68] By the second half of the 1800s, political momentum was building for the federal protection of wilderness areas. President Ulysses Grant was the first to establish national parkland, in 1872 designating over two million acres of Wyoming as Yellowstone National Park.

Exemplar or Crusader State? These religious and secular narratives of America's messianic mission took strong hold among elites and the public alike. In theory, belief in the nation's exceptional character and the widespread commitment to sharing America's extraordinary religious, ideological, and material progress with the rest of the world should have produced an unstinting enthusiasm for foreign engagement. After all, if the United States was to fulfill its mission of changing the world, it would have to be very much *in* the world.

Paradoxically, however, American exceptionalism encouraged an isolationist, not an internationalist, impulse. Americans indeed believed that they were destined to change the world, but they were intent on doing so through example, not through a crusading messianism.[69] Admittedly, this issue frequently provoked considerable controversy; the nation's elected representatives regularly engaged in pitched debates over the costs and benefits of leading only by example, with influential voices at times calling for a more activist and interventionist stance. The independence movements in Latin America that started in the late 1700s tempted the United States to deepen its involvement in the region, with Secretary of State James Monroe noting in 1811 that "as inhabitants of the same Hemisphere, as neighbors, the United States cannot be unfeeling spectators of so important a moment."[70] Similar sentiments in favor of intervention emerged during the liberal revolutions that swept Europe in 1848. Prominent Americans saw both occasions as opportunities to be seized by the United States, warranting direct involvement in order to advance the spread of the American experiment.

Until 1898, such advocacy for a more activist approach to fulfilling the nation's redemptive mission in the end proved futile; supporters of foreign intervention were repeatedly overruled by those insistent that the United States should encourage the export of democracy only by example. To be sure, the United States regularly dispatched forces overseas during the course of the nineteenth century. But it did so to protect its traders, citizens, and investments, not in the service of fostering progressive change in foreign lands. It was not until the Spanish-American War that elites and the public alike were ready to countenance the spread of America's ideals through the projection of U.S. power abroad.

Four key suppositions, elaborated upon in the remainder of this chapter, ensured that the nation's exceptionalist calling favored exemplarism rather than more activist engagement. First, Americans feared that the exertions entailed in pursuing a more ambitious foreign policy would, by imperiling domestic liberty, do more to compromise than to advance the American experiment. Early Americans were far from confident in the durability of their experiment in political liberty; Europe's track record on this front gave them plenty of cause for concern. They worried that projecting American power abroad, which would require a more centralized federal government, higher taxation, and a standing military establishment, would directly threaten republican freedoms. As such, foreign intervention in the service of replicating the American experiment elsewhere risked jeopardizing that experiment at home. Instead, the country should focus on protecting and advancing its own exceptional political character, thereby making republican government more attractive to others and increasing the likelihood that it spread by example.[71]

Second, as mentioned above, Americans believed that the fulfillment of their country's destiny as an exceptional nation depended in part on its ability to eschew power politics in favor of a brand of statecraft guided by law and reason. Particularly in the North, where idealism and pacifism had strong religious and ideological appeal, Americans saw themselves as escaping not just the tyranny and social hierarchy of the Old World, but also its recurring cycles of coercion, predation, and war.[72] The United States was destined to chart a new path— one that would demonstrate the appeal of geopolitical restraint and peaceful diplomacy rather than imperial expansion. To intervene abroad, even with the most noble of intentions, would therefore be to compromise the nation's calling and promise. If America tried to spread its ideals through coercion rather than example, it would end up being no different from its rapacious and predatory predecessors. As Secretary of State Adams put it before the House of Representatives during a Fourth of July oration in 1821, "she knows well that by once enlisting under other banners than her own, were they even banners of foreign independence, she would involve herself beyond the power of extrication, in all the wars of interest and intrigue, of individual avarice, envy, and ambition, which assume the colors and usurp the standard of freedom. The fundamental maxims of her policy would insensibly change from liberty to force."[73]

Third, early Americans were quite sober about the prospects for successfully fostering republican government beyond their own shores. They believed that their nation was endowed with an exceptional location, people, and land. Other countries lacked such good fortune and were therefore not in a position to be able to replicate the American experiment. Americans therefore had to be appropriately guarded about the likely efficacy of efforts to foster progressive change abroad. Skepticism that countries in Latin America would successfully embrace republican government, for example, helped convince the nation's leaders to refrain from more activist support for independence movements in the region. Catholicism, social hierarchy, and ethnic heterogeneity made it likely that independence would be accompanied by monarchy and despotism, not democracy. As Adams wrote in his diary in 1821 following a conversation with Henry Clay, who favored more activist U.S. support for republican movements in Latin America, "so far as they are contending for independence, I wish well to their cause; but I have not yet seen and do not now see any prospect that [Latin Americans] will establish free and liberal institutions of government."[74]

Early Americans were not only mindful of the difficulties entailed in promoting democracy and freedom, but also unconvinced of the geopolitical benefits that would accrue should they in fact succeed. To be sure, Americans were committed in principle to sharing their political and economic advancements with the rest of the world, and some believed that doing so would have beneficial geopolitical effects.[75] But the compulsion was primarily moral in nature, not one motivated by the belief, so prevalent today, that the spread of democracy and capitalism would ensure peace among nations. Indeed, Alexander Hamilton in *Federalist No. 6* made short shrift of the notion that a democratic and commercialized world would make for a more peaceful world:

> Have republics in practice been less addicted to war than monarchies? Are not the former administered by *men* as well as the latter? Are there not aversions, predilections, rivalships, and desires of unjust

acquisitions, that affect nations as well as kings? Are not popular assemblies frequently subject to the impulses of rage, resentment, jealousy, avarice, and of other irregular and violent propensities? . . . Has commerce hitherto done anything more than change the objects of war? . . . Have there not been as many wars founded upon commercial motives since that has become the prevailing system of nations, as were before occasioned by the cupidity of territory or dominion? Has not the spirit of commerce, in many instances, administered new incentives to the appetite, both for the one and for the other? Let experience, the least fallible guide of human opinions, be appealed to for an answer to these inquiries.[76]

Such skepticism about the prospects for replicating the American experiment and the concrete benefits of doing so tempered enthusiasm for a more activist brand of messianism. In light of the poor prospects for the durable spread of republican government and the limited geopolitical benefits in sight, the nation should share its exceptional experiment with other nations only through example rather than more risky and costly means. The United States should serve as a guiding beacon, but not more.

Fourth, the racial variant of the redeemer narrative served as a further check on the potential emergence of a crusading messianism. The nation's Anglo-Saxon populace was a source of its exceptional character; the homogeneity of that populace needed to be vigilantly protected. Fear of the citizenry's dilution on repeated occasions prompted the United States to back away from foreign adventures that had the potential to increase the diversity of its population. During the second half of the nineteenth century, several administrations embarked on efforts to annex new territories in the Caribbean and Latin America—but were regularly blocked by voices warning against the inclusion of "inferior peoples" in the nation's body politic. Restrictions on immigration similarly aimed at protecting the country's white population from further dilution. To be sure, the "cult of Anglo-Saxonism" would by the turn of the twentieth century become a potent source of a new crusaderism, fueling calls for Britain and the United States to team up in the service of spreading their shared culture and language.[77] But prior to the end of the nineteenth century, America's sense of racial superiority reinforced the impulse to cordon the nation off from the outside world rather than venture forth.

The political complexions of the North and South magnified the degree to which these ideological considerations produced a strong preference for exemplarism over a more activist messianism.[78] The North more enthusiastically embraced the idealist notion that the United States, as the New Israel, had an obligation to change the world. So, too, were northerners more comfortable

with the stronger institutions of government needed to oversee an activist foreign policy. At the same time, however, the North was also home to a religiously
inspired pacifism and was supportive of an international order governed by the
rule of law, not coercion. Accordingly, despite its readiness and willingness to
export American ideals, that task would have to be pursued through example,
not through more coercive methods that would conflict with American ideals.

The South was less wedded to the notion that the nation's foreign policy
should aim at building an international order guided by law and reason. However,
southerners were also less convinced of the nation's idealist obligations to replicate the American experiment abroad. Furthermore, southerners were animated
by libertarian fears of political centralization, and therefore wary of foreign
engagements that would encourage greater federalization and potentially give
rise to a large standing army and navy. Accordingly, they were no more ready
than northerners to resort to coercive means to spread the American experiment
abroad. Northerners and southerners certainly had their political differences,
but they nonetheless arrived, even if for contrasting reasons, at a notion of the
nation's redemptive mission that decidedly favored an isolationist exemplarism
over an internationalist messianism.

Advancing Liberty and Prosperity at Home

America's advanced forms of political and economic freedom figured prominently in the nation's exceptionalist narrative. Fear that ambition abroad would
come at the expense of such freedom at home was another important source of
America's tenacious embrace of isolationism. The Founders did differ on important issues of statecraft, including whether to tilt toward Britain or France during
the union's early years. But they generally agreed that over the longer term the
nation needed to shun foreign entanglement if it was to preserve its experiment
in political and economic liberty. Multiple considerations led to this conclusion.

During the confederation period (1781–1789) and into its early years as a
federation, the nation's leaders saw disunion as a chief domestic threat. They
feared that the individual states might form their own alliances with foreign
powers, thereby pulling the confederation apart and setting its members against
one another. The strategic implications of geography again came into play. As
John Jay wrote in *Federalist No. 5*, "considering our distance from Europe, it
would be more natural for these confederacies to apprehend danger from one
another than from distant nations, and therefore that each of them should be
more desirous to guard against the others by the aid of foreign alliances, than to
guard against foreign dangers by alliances between themselves."[79] Indeed, many
representatives at the Continental Congress argued that America's separate
states should be free to form their own alliances with other countries.[80]

The potential for foreign manipulation and subversion exacerbated the threat of disunion. Republican government, by virtue of its accessibility, was vulnerable to the corrupting influence of foreign powers. As Hamilton noted in *Federalist No. 22*, "one of the weak sides of republics, among their numerous advantages, is that they afford too easy an inlet to foreign corruption."[81] In *Federalist No. 7*, he worried that the union, "by the destructive contentions of the parts into which she was divided, would be likely to become a prey to the artifices and machinations of powers equally the enemies of them all."[82] Washington agreed, noting in his Farewell Address that "history and experience prove that foreign influence is one of the most baneful foes of republican government."[83] Intense partisan and regional disagreements over policy made the country especially ripe for external manipulation, inviting Britain or France in particular to seek to insert themselves into American politics.

The Founders pursued two antidotes to the threat posed by foreign manipulation and the prospect of each state going its own way on matters of foreign policy. The first was to enhance the power of the central government, endowing it, in Hamilton's words, with the authority to oversee "the superintendence of our intercourse, political and commercial, with foreign countries."[84] The second was to steer clear of foreign commitments, avoiding the alliances that might pull the separate states apart and leave them, as Hamilton put it, "entangled in all the pernicious labyrinths of European politics and wars."[85]

Isolation would thus prevent disunion by removing a source of discord among the separate states and denying foreign powers the opportunity to manipulate and set them against each other. So, too, was geopolitical detachment a useful instrument for avoiding political infighting in a country deeply divided along sectional lines over foreign alignment. If northerners and southerners could not agree on whether to tilt toward Britain or France, steering clear of both powers was an attractive political compromise. Indeed, Washington's admonition against entangling alliances in his Farewell Address was in part meant to inoculate American politics against the intractable political divisions that would accompany alignment with a foreign power.[86]

Some of the Founders feared too much union as well as too little. Jefferson thought it virtually inevitable that the demands associated with projecting American power abroad would lead to excessive centralization, if not domestic tyranny. James Madison was concerned primarily about preserving the separation of powers and feared that foreign ambition would jeopardize political equilibrium among the executive, judicial, and legislative branches. Accordingly, both Jefferson and Madison saw the avoidance of foreign entanglement as necessary for the stable operation of republican government. Hamilton also supported a grand strategy of geopolitical detachment, but unlike Jefferson and Madison, believed that implementing that strategy required *strong* institutions of governance. A weak union would be perceived by other nations as a strategic vulnerability, inviting predation that would compromise America's independence and its domestic liberties. Centralized and capable governance, on the other hand, would ward off foreign powers contemplating aggression, and thereby protect American liberty. Strong institutions of governance were required not to project the nation's power abroad, but to keep other nations at bay. Jefferson, Madison, and Hamilton had differing views of how best to structure the nation's governing institutions, but they all arrived at the conclusion that domestic liberty required strategic isolation.

Fear of a turn to tyranny was an obsession during America's early decades—and with good reason. Efforts elsewhere to establish democratic institutions had not fared well. In England, the Stuarts eventually turned to the army to put down a recalcitrant Parliament, plunging the country into civil war. The Glorious Revolution of 1688 strengthened Parliament's powers, but England remained a monarchy with limited suffrage and was an expanding imperial power that imposed its will on other peoples. In France, popular revolution was giving way to despotism and military adventurism just as the American experiment was getting under way. Against this backdrop, Jeffersonians tended to see foreign ambition and domestic tyranny as inseparable twins. Geopolitical ambition required a strong central government and a large military establishment, both of which were inimical to liberty. As Jefferson wrote from Paris in 1789, "there are instruments so dangerous to the rights of the nation, and which place them so totally at the mercy of their governors, that those governors, whether legislative or executive, should be restrained from keeping such instruments on foot, but in well-defined cases. Such an instrument is a standing army."[87] Washington agreed, warning in his Farewell Address against "those overgrown military establishments which, under any form of government, are inauspicious to liberty, and which are to be regarded as particularly hostile to republican liberty."[88]

Jefferson and Washington were not unsympathetic to the concerns of Jay and Hamilton, noted above, that the American union needed to be cohesive enough to avoid foreign predation and internal strife. If each state pursued its own foreign policy, each would be too weak to resist foreign interference, and competing allegiances could pit the individual states against one another. In Washington's words, "they must derive from union an exemption from those broils and wars between themselves, which so frequently afflict neighboring countries not tied together by the same governments." Accordingly, banding together was a necessary antidote to both foreign and homegrown conflict. But Jefferson preferred keeping that cohesion to the bare minimum—and restricting it to the realm of foreign policy. In his own words: "I wish to see our states made one as to all foreign, and several as to all domestic matters."[89]

Madison shared Jefferson's preoccupation with the preservation of domestic freedom, but he came at the issue from a somewhat different perspective. For Madison, the main challenge was preserving the separation of powers—the system of checks and balances that the Founders embraced to provide Americans capable governance across an expansive territory without compromising their liberty.[90] On matters of national security, the Founders implemented the separation of powers by designating the president the commander-in-chief, granting Congress the authority to declare war, appointing the House of Representatives as the keeper of the purse, and making the Senate the overseer of treaties and appointments. Even with such built-in checks, Jefferson wanted to restrict the authorities of the federal government primarily to those needed to forestall foreign predation. In contrast, Madison favored a more capable federal government on matters of domestic as well as foreign policy as long as that government was constrained by the separation of powers—what he called the "compound republic."[91]

The compound republic was, however, a finely tuned political system that required exemption from the demands of foreign ambition if the internal checks and balances that protect domestic freedom were to be maintained. In Madison's own words, "the fetters imposed on liberty at home have ever been forged out of the weapons provided for defence against real, pretended, or imaginary dangers from abroad."[92] The political equilibrium on which the compound republic rested thus depended on the nation's strategic isolation. The exertions of great-power competition would inevitably tilt the government toward excessive centralization, compromising the liberty derived from a delicate system of checks and balances. If the United States was to countenance the more capable institutions needed to provide effective government and keep other powers at bay, it needed to protect those institutions against dangerous imbalances by avoiding foreign entanglement.[93]

Hamilton was far more concerned about the potential for tyranny to be imposed on the nation by foreign powers than he was about the risks of home-grown despotism. Accordingly, he worried that the nation's system of governance would be too weak, not too strong. Weak governance would be on show to the world and therefore invite foreign meddling. As Hamilton asserted at the Constitutional Convention in 1787, "no government could give us tranquility and happiness at home, which did not possess sufficient stability and strength to make us respectable abroad." He stipulated that "unless your government is respectable, foreigners will invade your rights; and to maintain tranquility you must be respectable—even to maintain neutrality you must maintain a strong government."[94] Hamilton's comfort with centralized federal institutions, including a central bank, followed naturally.

Some historians view Hamilton as the one Founder who bucked isolationist thinking and instead advocated for a strong nation that would follow in the footsteps of Great Britain and rise as a great power.[95] But, for Hamilton, the goal of centralized governance was not to enable the United States to project its power abroad. On the contrary, a stronger federal government, coupled with the protection afforded by flanking oceans, would grant the nation immunity from foreign interference. Liberty was to be preserved by keeping other powers at bay; isolation, not foreign ambition, was the pathway to freedom. Indeed, as Washington composed his Farewell Address in 1796, Hamilton successfully pressed the president to present his admonition against foreign entanglement as an enduring rule, not just a temporary strategy suited to a young and fledgling nation.[96]

In sum, for Jefferson and Madison, geopolitical isolation would advance domestic freedom by obviating the need for a strong, centralized government and preserving a finely tuned separation of powers. In contrast, Hamilton thought that more centralized governance was necessary to ward off foreign predation, thereby ensuring the nation's isolation from great-power rivalry and its immunity from tyrannical rule imposed by others. In the end, all three equated the preservation of liberty at home with the avoidance of entanglement abroad.

The Founders saw geopolitical detachment as the best guarantor of not only liberty, but also prosperity. Foreign ambition had the potential to compromise the nation's economic well-being on multiple fronts. For starters, given its size, its natural abundance, and its ready access to rivers and seas, the United States was destined to look to foreign trade to help build prosperity. Taking advantage of its location and natural resources to maximize international commerce meant avoiding armed conflicts that had the potential to hamper trade. Geopolitical rivalries brought with them severed economic ties, embargoes, attacks on merchant shipping, and other disruptions to commercial activity—as Americans had learned during both the colonial and revolutionary eras. Simply put, enemies were bad for business.

As Washington admonished in his Farewell Address, the United States should deepen its commercial relations with foreign nations but "have with them as little political connection as possible."[97] In similar fashion, Jefferson affirmed that he supported "free commerce with all nations, political connection with none."[98] John Adams agreed that "the business of America with Europe was commerce, not politics or war."[99] This consensus was reflected in the Model Treaty adopted by Congress in 1776, which was to serve as a template for formalizing the country's relations with other nations. It focused almost exclusively on commercial ties, made no mention of alliances or other kinds of strategic commitments, and only touched on geopolitics by, for example, providing for arms transfers and other indirect forms of security assistance.

Foreign ambition also had the potential to stunt economic growth by distorting commerce at home and siphoning resources away from productive investment. Other than ensuring the free flow of commerce among America's individual states, the Founders believed that the federal government should intervene as little as possible in the domestic economy. Foreign entanglement made that outcome unlikely; the large and centralized government needed to conduct expensive wars would as a matter of course be compelled to interfere in the country's economy. In addition, the costs of a standing army and navy would require high levels of taxation that would weigh on growth and prosperity. Indeed, as discussed in the following chapter, the British sought to extract additional revenue from the colonies to help defray the costs of the French and Indian War (1754–1763), so Americans were well aware of the economic downside of armed conflict. Instead, the nation should avoid geopolitical rivalry and thereby obviate the need for an extractive and expensive federal government.

This libertarian critique of the potential impact of big government on commerce also came in a progressive variant—one more focused on the potential for inequality than interference. Should the United States engage in foreign ambition, the costs incurred would weigh on the prosperity of ordinary Americans and inevitably exacerbate inequities within American society. Jefferson and his fellow travelers, for example, were concerned that the instruments needed to fund wars—in particular, a central bank and public debt—would eventually create a wealthy and excessively influential creditor class, replicating one of Europe's primary political and social ills.[100] According to Jefferson, establishing a central bank would run the following risks:

> This institution is one of the most deadly hostility existing, against the principles & form of our constitution. . . . An institution like this, penetrating by its branches every part of the Union, acting by command & in phalanx may in a critical moment, upset the government. I deem no government safe which is under the vassalage of any self-constituted authorities, or any other authority than that of the nation, or its regular functionaries. What an obstruction could not this bank of the U.S., with all its branch banks, be in time of war? It might dictate to us the peace we should accept, or withdraw its aids. Ought we then to give further growth to an institution so powerful, so hostile?[101]

Especially as industrialization advanced over the course of the nineteenth century, this progressive critique of foreign ambition targeted the corporate elite more broadly, not just financiers. In the early 1900s, progressives were concerned about growing inequality, urban poverty, social stratification, and excessive corporate influence over commerce—as well as about the potential

emergence of an industrial and financial elite with a vested interest in foreign expansion. As discussed in Chapter Eleven, this sentiment arguably peaked during
the 1930s, when many Americans blamed the armaments industry and corporate self-interest for pushing the nation into World War I. The ensuing suspicion
of the connection between corporate pressure and foreign ambition contributed
significantly to the political durability of isolationist sentiment during the
interwar years.

Preserving Freedom of Action Abroad

Early Americans sought not just liberty at home but also freedom of action beyond their shores. Indeed, the libertarian impulse ran particularly strong when
it came to the conduct of the nation's statecraft. Historian Andrew Preston
traces this unilateralist streak to the yearning for political liberty that defined
the American experience as well as the premium placed on religious freedom
by Protestantism. "Produced by an intense combination of republicanism and
Protestantism," Preston writes, "a strong libertarian ethos pervaded U.S. foreign policy."[102] Americans were willing to tolerate obligations to their own
government—as long as they were kept to a minimum—but they were dead set
against obligations to foreign governments, especially when it came to matters
of geopolitics. If and when the United States were to act beyond its borders, it
wanted to have a free hand and to act as it saw fit. This insistence on unilateral
action served to reinforce the nation's isolationist leanings. Leery of the alliances
and political compacts that usually accompany engagement abroad, the United
States regularly chose to forgo foreign commitments that might come to con-
strain its autonomy.

Three fundamental convictions animated the nation's early embrace of unilateralism. The first was principled; the United States needed to avoid alliances or
other types of political commitments that could impair the ability of the president or Congress to exercise its constitutional authorities. Independence from
Britain meant just that—the nation's freedom to make its own decisions about
the conduct of foreign relations. As President Washington wrote to Hamilton in
1796, "if we are to be told by a foreign Power . . . what we shall do, and what we
shall not do, we have Independence yet to seek."[103]

The second was ideological; as it charted its own course as the redeemer nation, the United States needed to make a clean break with the dangerous geopolitical traditions of the Old World. Realizing the nation's exceptionalist
calling meant conducting a statecraft based on Enlightenment principles, not on
alliances and manipulation of the balance of power. Jay in *Federalist No. 4* laid out
a common American view of Europe's proclivity to engage in senseless conflict,
a proclivity the Founders were determined to leave behind:

It is too true, however disgraceful it may be to human nature, that nations in general will make war whenever they have a prospect of getting
anything by it; nay, absolute monarchs will often make war when their
nations are to get nothing by it, but for the purposes and objects merely
personal, such as thirst for military glory, revenge for personal affronts,
ambition, or private compacts to aggrandize or support their particular
families or partisans. These and a variety of other motives, which affect
only the mind of the sovereign, often lead him to engage in wars not
sanctified by justice or the voice and interests of his people.[104]

The third consideration was pragmatic; alliance with other countries risked
dragging the United States into conflicts that might contravene its interests,
while unilateralism protected the nation's ability to more carefully choose its
fights. Preserving freedom of action abroad would enable the United States to
fully exploit the advantages of its natural security, while "political connection" to
other countries would entangle the United States in their disputes. As Jefferson
wrote in 1799, "I am not for linking ourselves by new treaties with the quarrels
of Europe, entering that field of slaughter to preserve their balance, or joining in
the confederacy of Kings to war against the principles of liberty."[105]

This yearning for autonomy was so strong that it compelled the United States
to commit an act of bald perfidy during its early years. Faced with the prospect
of defeat at the hands of Britain amid its bid for independence, the United States
concluded a military alliance with France in 1778. Thereafter, direct French
assistance in the fight against Britain played a vital role in enabling the United
States to prevail. Nonetheless, after war broke out between France and Britain
in 1793, the United States refused to honor its military obligations to France.
Instead, President Washington declared neutrality, angering not just the French
but also Jefferson and other Founders who favored a pro-French diplomatic
tilt. This awkward turn of events prompted Washington in his Farewell Address
to warn his countrymen to rely only on "*temporary* alliances for *extraordinary*
emergencies."[106]

Although the treaty with France effectively lapsed with Washington's proclamation of neutrality in 1793, Congress went on to unilaterally annul the treaty
in 1798. However, it was not until 1800 that the United States and France of-
ficially agreed to dissolve their alliance. Thereafter, the United States jealously
guarded its freedom of action abroad, not concluding another formal alliance
until after World War II. In the early nineteenth century, it declined an offer
from Britain to work together to support newly independent countries in Latin
America, instead preferring a unilateral declaration of its own vision for the
Western Hemisphere—the Monroe Doctrine of 1823. As the United States
expanded into the Pacific at the end of the century, it similarly steered clear of

great-power pacts in favor of the freedom of action spelled out in the Open Door Policy of 1899, which called for trade with China to be equal for all countries. In a bold statement of the nation's aversion to geopolitical commitments beyond its neighborhood, the Senate after the close of World War I rejected U.S. partic-ipation in the League of Nations—a body designed and ardently supported by America's own president, Woodrow Wilson.

It should not be surprising that the main exception to this norm of unilater-alism was America's willingness to join pacts that limited or constrained, rather than mandated, international action. The United States, for example, played a leading role in negotiating the Kellogg-Briand Pact of 1928, which committed signatories to renounce war in favor of the peaceful resolution of disputes. This unusual foray into the realm of multilateral diplomacy was aimed at avoiding, not deepening, foreign entanglement; it would be easier for the United States to practice isolationism if other nations did so as well.

Protecting Social Homogeneity

Isolationism was also born of the nation's effort to preserve social homogeneity and the dominance of its white population. Americans may have anointed their country the redeemer nation, but not all of the land's inhabitants were capable of delivering redemption. Protestants, not Catholics, were to build the New Israel and perfect religious and political liberty. Indeed, many Americans had come to the New World to escape the hierarchy and strictures of the Catholic Church. Race mattered even more than religion. Native Americans were deemed unfit to contribute to advancing the American experiment and needed to be pushed out of the way. Blacks were enslaved even though the practice was at odds both with the founding principle that "all men are created equal" and with the nation's commitment to advancing political liberty. This contradiction would prove po-litically unsolvable; divergence between the North and South over slavery's ac-ceptability would eventually split the union asunder.

The goal of protecting America's social homogeneity shaped isolationism from early on. Concern about social dilution slowed America's westward expan-sion. The Founders were committed to westward enlargement, but they gener-ally preferred to hold off on integrating new territories into the union until they were populated predominantly by English-speaking whites. After purchasing the Louisiana Territory from France in 1803, Jefferson wanted statehood to await the arrival of many more Anglo-Saxons to offset the large numbers of Native Americans, French, Spaniards, and Creoles who populated the area.[107] He supported territorial expansion, but was keen to ensure that such expan-sion not jeopardize the homogeneity of the union's population. According to

Jefferson, the United States should eventually "cover the whole northern, if not the southern continent, with a people speaking the same language, governed in similar forms, & by similar laws: nor can we contemplate, with satisfaction, either blot or mixture on that surface."[108] As the union's enlargement eventually tilted the political balance of power in favor of states opposed to slavery, the South's aversion to such "mixture" prompted its secession and the Civil War. The economic self-interest of slaveholders was a strong motivation, but so too was the South's commitment to preserving racial hierarchy.

If fear of social dilution slowed the union's expansion in North America, farther afield it helped block it altogether. On repeated occasions during the course of the nineteenth century, the U.S. government and public debated the merits of territorial expansion into the Caribbean, Latin America, and the Pacific. But until the outbreak of the Spanish-American War in 1898, the country repeatedly backed away from the temptation—in no small part because of an aversion to ruling over "inferior peoples" or incorporating them into the nation's population.[109] Even after the Civil War and the abolition of slavery, the United States kept its distance from Haiti, Santo Domingo, Cuba, and other nearby territories that risked adding to America's black population. Many Americans were also skeptical that nonwhites would make good democratic citizens; they were incapable of responsible self-government. So, too, did the predominance of Catholicism in Latin America make the region's population unfit for potential inclusion in a republic.[110] In contrast, American society was mainly white, Protestant, and English-speaking, making it uniquely suited to advance the frontier of political liberty.

The priority placed on preserving social homogeneity also prompted efforts to restrict immigration, which at times played a role in reinforcing isolationist sentiment. During the second half of the nineteenth century, the United States put restrictions on Chinese immigrants, both to prevent social dilution and to protect jobs. Limits on immigration from "Asiatic" zones increased after the turn of the century. In the 1920s, the United States imposed immigration quotas based on country of origin, leading to a dramatic decrease in arrivals of Catholics and Jews from southeastern Europe in favor of Protestants from the north. The isolationism of the interwar era went hand in hand with anti-immigrant sentiment, reinforcing the aversion to foreign entanglement. In periods during which the United States was implicated in international conflicts, it also put restraints— including surveillance and forced incarceration—on immigrant populations it deemed to be potentially disloyal—French in the 1790s, Germans during World War I, and Japanese during World War II. Engagement in foreign conflicts fueled anti-immigrant sentiment aimed at disarming the enemy within and protecting social homogeneity by keeping foreigners out.[111]

Promoting Pacifism

Pursuit of a brand of U.S. statecraft that would be guided by Enlightenment principles rather than realpolitik was another central element of America's exceptionalist narrative. Especially in New England, this strain of exceptionalism took the form of a principled commitment to pacifism, which in turn served as an ideological source of isolationism. During the nation's early decades, pacifism took hold primarily among religious communities in the North—the Mennonites and Quakers in particular. Congregants of the peace churches regularly refused to join the fight during the Revolutionary War. In these communities, aversion to war was a by-product of faith; taking up arms was a violation of religious conviction. As one Quaker testimonial explained, "we are, therefore incited by a sincere concern for the peace and welfare of our country, publicly to declare against every usurpation of power and authority, in opposition to the laws and government, and against all combinations, insurrections, conspiracies, and illegal assemblies: and as we are restrained from them by the conscientious discharge of our duty to almighty God."[112] Although George Washington complained that such individuals seemed "notoriously disaffected to the cause of American liberty," he nonetheless instructed the authorities responsible for conscription to exempt from military service those persons "conscientiously scrupulous against it in every case."[113]

American pacifists were also staunch opponents of going to war with Britain in 1812, teaming up with the many other northerners who were against the war for strategic and economic reasons. In the words of Jonathan Whipple, a Quaker from Massachusetts, "my brother and I had had such thorough training against all of this man-destroying business, that their operations seemed inhumane, savage, and barbarous enough to us. No Christianity about, or in, such business ... And we were summoned to go and 'kill the Britons.' ... But we could have nothing to do with such business."[114] In the end, northern opposition to the war did little to change the course of the conflict, and ultimately provoked a backlash that weakened the North's political voice. Nonetheless, popular reaction against the War of 1812 helped spawn the institutionalization of the pacifist movement. The New York Peace Society, the nation's first pacifist organization, formed in 1815—largely in response to the war. Other local peace societies soon opened, followed by a nationwide body, the American Peace Society.

Despite the emergence of a national network, pacifists had a muted impact on public debate in the aftermath of the War of 1812. The peace movement became more active and influential during the Mexican-American War. Pacifists argued that the conflict was both immoral and unjustified, helping build significant public opposition to the war. Henry David Thoreau argued that the U.S. government was "liable to be abused and perverted before the people can act through it. Witness the present Mexican war, the work of comparatively a few individuals using the standing government as their tool; for, in the outset, the people would not have consented to this measure." Thoreau was famously jailed in the summer of 1846 for refusing to pay Massachusetts tax on the grounds that he did not want to enable the state "to commit violence and shed innocent blood."[115]

The pacifist movement became better organized, more vocal, and more politically consequential after the Spanish-American War and the bloody U.S. occupation of the Philippines that followed. In the Philippines, some 4,000 American soldiers and hundreds of thousands of Filipino insurgents and civilians died between 1899 and 1902. The pacifists not only gained political momentum as a result of the conflict, but also broadened their antiwar agenda to include support for mediation and peacemaking, disarmament, and anti-imperialism. In the 1900 presidential election, the Democratic candidate, William Jennings Bryan, ran on an anti-imperialist platform, giving the pacifist movement greater legitimacy and political leverage.

The pacifists broadened their message as the new century progressed. The United States had enjoyed a long run of economic growth, embarked on an ambitious naval building program, and acquired an inventory of imperial possessions. Bryan's anti-imperialist message had a significant measure of public appeal, but he fell well short of winning the presidency; many Americans welcomed the nation's new geopolitical heft. Accordingly, prominent pacifists such as William James, Jane Addams, and Randolph Bourne had to adapt their critique of U.S. foreign policy to a nation that had acquired the material and political wherewithal to leave behind its isolationist past. Rather than exploiting industrialization, economic growth, and a growing navy to pursue imperial conquest, they argued, the United States should focus on addressing social ills at home. Instead of expanding abroad through coercive means, the nation should turn its energies to fixing domestic ills—poverty, inequality, excessive corporate influence—and return to spreading its ideals only through example. As debate over America's entry into World War I heated up, the pacifists argued vociferously that the nation should play the role of mediator, not combatant. And after the war drew to a close, many pacifists opposed the postwar settlement for being too punitive and realist, helping to block Woodrow Wilson's bid to ratify the Versailles Treaty and secure the nation's membership in the League of Nations. Thereafter, pacifists became one of many political camps contributing to America's inward turn during the two interwar decades.

On balance, pacifism played a less prominent role than other ideological sources of isolationism in shaping American grand strategy. The peace movement and its principled aversion to armed conflict consistently struggled to enter the political mainstream. Pacifism on its own was not a sufficiently strong force to produce a foreign policy of isolation. Nonetheless, pacifists on occasion did line up with isolationists driven by other concerns to thwart those supporting foreign entanglement. Even though left-leaning pacifists and right-wing unilateralists were hardly ideological kin, they at times confronted internationalists with a blocking coalition. Democratic pacificists opposed U.S. entry into the League of Nations because the body was insufficiently progressive, but ended up in the same camp as Republican conservatives, who opposed the League because they deemed it far too idealist. Pacifism thus worked alongside isolationism's other ideological variants to ensure its dominating influence over U.S. grand strategy from the nation's founding until World War II.

* * *

Capitalizing on natural security; serving as redeemer nation; advancing liberty and prosperity at home; preserving freedom of action abroad; protecting social homogeneity; promoting pacifism—these six interlocking logics shape the story of American isolationism that unfolds in the following chapters.

THE ERA OF ISOLATIONISM, 1789–1898

Part I of this book's historical narrative covers the emergence of a grand strategy of isolationism during the French and Indian War (1754–1763) and the Revolutionary era, its articulation and formalization during the 1790s—in particular, by President George Washington in his Farewell Address of 1796—and its implementation and evolution over the course of the nineteenth century. Isolationism was in its heyday from the founding era through the end of the 1800s; it was central to the nation's exceptionalist narrative and embedded in its creed. The United States proved quite adept at turning strategic ideology into strategic reality—although geopolitical detachment did not come easily. Americans engaged in a dogged effort to realize the natural security afforded by the nation's geographic dispensation and growing strength. Implementing a grand strategy of isolationism took two wars against Britain, followed by deft diplomacy and bouts of coercion with Britain, France, Russia, and Spain to shepherd them out of North America and, eventually, the Western Hemisphere. While pushing Europe's great powers from their neighborhood, Americans vigorously expanded westward, shunting aside Native Americans as they incorporated new lands and sources of wealth and constructed a union that would stretch from coast to coast. By the turn of the century, the United States had become the formidable North American redoubt that the Founders had envisaged.

Despite their sustained continental expansion and the growing confidence and power that came with it, Americans held back from taking on enduring commitments outside North America. To be sure, the nation during its earliest decades did not have the economic or military strength to range far afield. At least at the outset, strategic restraint emerged from necessity as much as choice. But even after the Civil War, when the United States experienced a dramatic increase in its wealth and power, it held back from territorial expansion beyond the continental home-land. More adventurous U.S. leaders on occasion made determined runs at annexing islands in the Caribbean and Pacific or building an isthmian canal. However, they all fell short, foiled by a legislative branch that was unwilling to depart from Washington's "great rule." An enduring political commitment to nonentanglement guided the conduct of statecraft.

The ideological variant of isolationism that most influenced strategic debate varied over time. Capitalizing on the natural security afforded by flanking oceans was a consistent priority. So, too, was the United States' obligation to serve as a redeemer nation by pursuing a path that would showcase the advantages of republicanism at home and restraint abroad. Demonstrating the benefits of geopolitical detachment would help counter the appeal of the balance-of-power logic that dominated rela-tions among European states. Even after the end of the Napoleonic Wars and the formation of the Concert of Europe—a great-power forum es-tablished in 1815 aimed at preventing major war—Americans tended to regard Europe as still beholden to power politics and inescapably prone to war. Moreover, they saw the Concert as a conservative instrument for repressing liberal threats to monarchic rule and feared joint European in-tervention to suppress or reverse independence movements challenging Spanish rule in the Americas—all the more reason for the United States to ward Europeans away from interference in the Western Hemisphere.

Other isolationist logics complemented and reinforced the imperatives of taking advantage of the nation's geographic bounty and fulfilling its exceptionalist calling. During the founding era, Americans feared that the political centralization and militarization that would accompany great-power entanglement would imperil domestic liberty. Neutralizing this threat from within mandated geopolitical detachment. After the War of 1812 and amid diminishing concern about great-power entan-glement, Americans focused more on preserving their freedom of ac-tion abroad and establishing a norm of noninterference in the affairs of other nations. Between 1820 and 1850, the United States passed on numerous opportunities to support the spread of republicanism in Latin America and Europe. Prior to and after the Civil War, sectional differences over slavery and race relations were a potent source of isolationism. Disagreement over whether new territories would be slave-holding and opposition to the incorporation of more nonwhites into the body politic blocked prospective expansion into the Caribbean and Latin America. By the 1880s, concern about diluting the nation's social homogeneity not only stood in the way of expansion, but also began to produce anti-immigrant legislation. Pacifism was arguably the least influential of isolationism's ideological variants, but it did become politically consequential during times of conflict—especially during the War of 1812 and the Mexican-American War.

Debate about whether the nation should continue to adhere to its self-imposed isolation intensified during the 1880s and 1890s as the U.S. economy expanded and as foreign powers enlarged their fleets and the scope of their imperial holdings. The United States embarked on a significant naval buildup in the 1880s, followed by the construction of a battleship fleet in the 1890s. The ability to project power to overseas theaters fueled greater temptation to use that power, undermining the long-standing political consensus behind isolationism. The emerging struggle between budding internationalists and traditional isolationists began to fall along partisan lines, with Republicans in the more commercialized North backing naval construction and a more ambitious foreign policy, while Democrats in the more agrarian South generally resisted such ambition. Initially, the isolationists continued to prevail even in the face of the naval buildup—but only for so long. The Spanish-American War of 1898 and the major bout of extracontinental expansion that accompanied it marked a clear break with the isolationist consensus that had held since the founding era.

Washington's "great rule" prevailed for over a century—despite the country's political and economic maturation and dramatic change in its geopolitical circumstance and potential. A grand strategy of isolationism lasted so long in part because it unquestionably served the nation's interests, allowing Americans to focus on continental expansion, economic development, and political consolidation of the union. By the end of the nineteenth century, the United States had experienced remarkable growth in population and prosperity—indeed, it had emerged as a world-class power. All the while, strategic restraint enabled it to avoid molestation by Europe's great powers and to evade the imperial adventures that might have distracted the union and embroiled it in distant conflicts. In the meantime, anticolonial sentiment in the Caribbean and Latin America helped push Europe's great powers from the Western Hemisphere, clearing the way for the United States to attain hemispheric dominance at low cost. An isolationist grand strategy succeeded in enabling America's rise while endowing the nation with remarkable security.

3

The Revolutionary Era:
Contemplating Nonentanglement

President George Washington set the United States on an isolationist course when he warned Americans in 1796 "to steer clear of permanent alliances with any portion of the foreign world."[1] Nonetheless, it was well before Washington's Farewell Address that Americans began to covet the prospect of detachment from Europe. Immigrants to the New World sought not only economic opportunity and religious freedom, but also escape from the interstate violence that regularly plagued Europe.[2] During the late 1600s and into the eighteenth century, millions of soldiers and civilians died in a succession of large-scale conflicts, including the War of the Grand Alliance (1688–1697), the Great Northern War (1700–1721), and the wars of succession in Spain (1700–1713), Poland (1733–1738), and Austria (1740–1748).

Colonists in the New World did not initially succeed in leaving behind the violence-prone statecraft of the Old World. Beginning in the late 1600s, the American colonists found themselves in a series of conflicts with the French and Spanish, usually over territory. The Seven Years' War, which ran from 1756 to 1763, then drew the Thirteen Colonies into a conflict among Europe's major powers, impressing upon Americans the dangers that came with political attachment to the Old World.

The Seven Years' War pitted a British-led coalition that included Prussia and Portugal against a French-led coalition that included Spain, Austria, and Russia. The war engulfed both sides of the Atlantic, with the conflict in the North American theater commonly known as the French and Indian War. The American colonists fought alongside their British compatriots to defeat a mixed force of French soldiers, Canadian settlers, and Native Americans. French Canada fell to the British, the British seized Florida from Spain, and France ceded to Britain its territories east of the Mississippi.

These military successes notwithstanding, the war left the American colonies ever more wary of their strategic connection to Europe. The British decided to help cover the costs of the war by imposing additional financial burdens on the American colonies. The aggrieved colonies retaliated by obstructing commerce with Britain. This clash over issues of taxation and trade would fuel America's growing estrangement from Britain, culminating in the colonies' revolt against British rule in 1775.

Further alienating the American colonists was the fact that the British left a sizable contingent of troops west of Appalachia following the close of the French and Indian War—in part to block America's westward expansion and limit its territorial girth and geopolitical potential. In 1763, London issued a proclamation formally prohibiting colonial expansion beyond the Appalachians. Britain's overt efforts to put limits on the territory and prosperity of its North American brethren only encouraged the colonists to become more resentful of British rule.

France's territorial losses in North America and the terms of the Treaty of Paris (1763) that brought the Seven Years' War to a close also meant the effective end of a credible French threat to British North America. The balance of power had decisively shifted in favor of Britain. With Spain having neither the intent nor the ability to pose a significant military threat to the colonies, Americans no longer needed Britain to help them resist the imperial designs of other Europeans.

Americans thus emerged from the French and Indian War contemplating more seriously than ever before the prospect of separation from Britain. Many of the Founders came of age during the war, and its consequences helped shape their conviction in favor of independence.[3] The conflict may have brought the colonists short-term gains, but it also left them wary of again getting dragged into European conflicts—against their will. As John Adams stated in 1775, "we ought to lay it down, as a first principle and maxim never to be forgotten, to maintain an entire neutrality in all future European wars."[4] In *Common Sense*, Thomas Paine explicitly blamed the colonies' tensions with France and Spain on their connection to Britain: "Let Britain waive her pretentions to the continent, or the continent throw off the dependence, and we should be at peace with France and Spain, were they at war with Britain.... France and Spain never were, nor perhaps ever will be our enemies as *Americans*, but as our being the *subjects of Great Britain*."[5]

Support for breaking away from Britain mounted in step with the growing tensions over taxation and trade that emerged from the French and Indian War. In 1774 the colonies agreed to form the Continental Congress, the representative body that would provide governance during their struggle for independence. Combat between British troops and the Massachusetts militia broke out in April 1775, marking the beginning of the Revolutionary War and setting the stage for Congress's declaration of independence in July 1776.

In the years during and immediately after the struggle for independence, two defining elements of U.S. grand strategy clearly emerged. First, the colonies sought not only independence from Britain but also strategic dominance in their own neighborhood. Alexander Hamilton envisaged the United States holding sway over the Western Hemisphere and becoming "the arbiter of Europe in America."[6] Thomas Jefferson wanted the country to "cover the whole northern, if not the southern continent."[7] Such ambitions were more than idle rhetoric. The Continental Army in the winter of 1775–1776 made several expeditions into Canada to seize Montreal and Quebec, expecting Canadians to join them in seeking to end British rule and potentially become the "fourteenth colony."[8] However, Canadians were of a different mind and sided with the British to rebuff the American force. According to military historians Robert Coakley and Stetson Conn, "nowhere did the Canadians show much inclination to rally to the American cause; the French habitants remained indifferent, and the small British population gave its loyalty to the [British] governor general."[9] After repeated American forays had all failed by the summer of 1776, American forces fell back to New York, with one of their commanders, Brigadier General John Sullivan, lamenting that "I am sufficiently mortified and sincerely wish I had never seen this fatal country."[10]

During the negotiations with Britain to end the Revolutionary War, a chief U.S. aim was getting the British to hand over Canada. But Americans ultimately abandoned this demand in the service of securing independence and peace. As the Continental Congress instructed John Adams after appointing him as the lead negotiator in 1779, "it is of the utmost importance to the peace and commerce of the United States that Canada and Nova Scotia should be ceded . . . yet a desire to terminating the war hath induced us not to make the acquisition of these objects an ultimatum on the present occasion."[11] At other moments, Congress changed its mind, encouraging its negotiators to insist that Britain cede Canada as part of a peace agreement.[12] Pragmatism eventually won out and limited U.S. war aims, but Americans had made clear even before British recognition of their independence that they aspired to strategic domination over their neighborhood. To that end, they did secure from the British as part of the peace settlement the Northwest Territory, effectively doubling the size of the country.

The second distinguishing feature of U.S. grand strategy to emerge during and after the Revolutionary War seemed to contradict the first. Even as the United States envisaged dominance in its own hemisphere, it contemplated geopolitical isolation from the rest of the world. The United States wanted to be independent and free from molestation by its neighbors, but its geopolitical ambitions stopped there. Several considerations informed this early isolationist turn in American statecraft.

First, the nation's youthful weakness constrained its ambition; the United States did not have the military or economic wherewithal to assume geopolitical commitments beyond its immediate neighborhood. When the Revolutionary War commenced, the British had the world's most powerful navy, while the Continental Navy consisted primarily of converted merchant vessels, which were minimally capable of disrupting British maritime operations. Engaging British forces on land and looking to Britain's European rivals to tie down the Royal Navy in other theaters were America's best bets. Early America could send merchant ships and cruisers capable of trade protection over long distances, but otherwise had to restrict the geographic scope of its ambitions. Indeed, even after the United States had achieved independence from Britain and transitioned from a loose confederation to a more capable federation, President Washington believed that the young nation needed at least two decades of peace to build up the strength necessary to adequately defend the homeland.[13]

A second rationale for the United States to keep its geopolitical distance from Europe was the fact that the American economy was heavily reliant on seaborne commerce, making the new nation keen to trade, not fight, with Europe's great powers.[14] The decision to break away from Britain had been triggered in part by discontent with an international trading order based on imperial preferences and London's control over colonial trade. Instead, the United States wanted both the world's oceans and its own ports to be open to all commerce. In the spring of 1784, the Confederation Congress instructed U.S. envoys to pursue an international trading system free of imperial preferences.[15] To this end, the United States was to avoid political connections with other countries to ensure that geopolitics not get in the way of the flow of trade. In the words of John Adams, "if we give exclusive privileges in trade, or form perpetual alliances offensive and defensive with the powers in one scale, we infallibly make enemies of those in the other."[16]

The goal was first and foremost to maximize U.S. prosperity. Some of the Founders also believed that the free flow of commerce would make for a more peaceful world. Jefferson believed that in pursuing an open trading system the United States was pursuing a goal "so valuable to mankind as the total emancipation of commerce and the bringing together all nations for a free interconnection of happiness."[17] Adams agreed that free trade would serve as a check against conflict among nations.[18] This belief that international commerce would tame geopolitical rivalry was not shared by all the Founders. Hamilton, for example, was a decided skeptic; he foresaw that wars would be fought over commerce, asking, "is not the love of wealth as domineering and enterprising a passion as that of power or glory?"[19]

In keeping with the widespread belief in America's obligation and ability to chart a new and exceptional historical course, America's earliest diplomats were instructed not just to liberalize international trade but also to keep protocol and pomp to a minimum, to dress modestly, and to focus their work narrowly on commercial issues. As John Adams told the French foreign minister, "the dignity of North America does not consist in diplomatic ceremonials or any of the subtleties of etiquette; it consists solely in reason, justice, truth, the rights of mankind, and the interests of the nations of Europe."[20] Although Adams was engaging in a significant amount of hyperbole, his statement makes clear that many Americans did conceive of themselves as leaving behind not only imperial preferences but also what they saw as the anachronistic world of palace intrigue, secret diplomacy, and power politics.

The Continental Congress in September 1776 approved the so-called Model Treaty to provide guidance as efforts to formalize relations with France and Spain proceeded and to serve as a general template for American statecraft moving forward. The Model Treaty made quite clear that expanding commerce with other countries was the nation's top diplomatic priority. While the United States should avoid formal political connections to France and other nations, the document instructed U.S. diplomats to deepen commercial ties through open and reciprocal trade. It also stipulated that neutrals should have the right to trade with belligerents, except for contraband, which included more than two dozen military items such as "great guns," and "bombs with their fuses."[21] Although the United States would soon seek the assistance of France in its war with Britain, the logic informing the Model Treaty was that the allure of access to U.S. trade would be sufficient to secure that objective and convince the French to recognize American independence. The U.S. delegation to Paris was instructed to request from the French eight warships, but also to studiously avoid any mention of mutual defense obligations.[22] Indeed, Article VIII of the Model Treaty maintained that if Great Britain were to attack France after the conclusion of a treaty between France and the United States, America's only obligation to France would be to refrain from providing any military assistance or contraband to Britain.

Although America's leaders saw themselves as seeking to escape the world of geopolitical rivalry and power balancing by breaking away from the Old World, the Model Treaty was at the same time based on a sober calculation of national interest. In light of its long-standing rivalry with Great Britain in North America and Europe, France was the obvious candidate to help America defeat the British. As the Model Treaty was taking shape, some voices advocated offering the French territorial prizes—in particular, the West Indies—to sweeten the pot and secure French support for America's cause. At least at the outset, however, Congress resisted making any prospective commitments to territorial change and saw such pledges as inconsistent with the U.S. commitment to fashioning a new brand of statecraft based on Enlightenment principles.[23] At the same time, American leaders knew well that the European powers were playing by the traditional rules of the Old World, and that the United States had to behave accordingly in dealing with them. As Thomas Jefferson recorded John Adams's statement during the deliberations over confederation in the summer of 1776 (belying his contrary statement to the French foreign minister), "reason, justice, and equity, never had weight enough, on the face of the earth, to govern the councils of men. It is interest alone which does it, and it is interest alone which can be trusted."[24]

Adams's insight proved prescient when it came to securing French support. "Interest alone" was sufficient to induce the French to deepen trade ties with the United States and to help America's war effort by sending, albeit secretly, gunpowder and other military supplies. But the help stopped there. Americans were misguided in believing that the allure of commerce would be enough to induce the French to recognize U.S. independence and enter the war on America's behalf.[25] Indeed, Adams, who had been one of the architects of the Model Treaty, later admitted that "there was not sufficient temptation to France to join us."[26]

As the war took a turn for the worse and further setbacks seemed inevitable in the absence of more assistance from abroad, America's leaders recognized that they had to offer more than commerce if they were to secure the help they needed to prevail against Britain. The surrender of Fort Ticonderoga to the British in July 1777 as well as dwindling financial resources helped convince American leaders that concluding a military alliance with France was necessary to avert defeat. With the nascent nation's back up against the wall, the Founders had little choice but to resort to the geopolitical instruments of the Old World if they were to break free from that world.

The United States and France signed two treaties in Paris in February 1778. The Treaty of Amity and Commerce recognized the effective independence of the United States and laid out the terms of trade between the two countries.[27] The Treaty of Alliance committed both parties to join together "against the enterprises of their common enemy . . . and aid each other mutually with their good offices, their counsels, and their forces."[28] Great Britain declared war against France the following month, with Spain entering the fray against Britain in June 1779. The ensuing engagements in Europe, as expected, succeeded in diverting British assets from the North American theater, helping the Americans turn the tide. In the summer of 1778, the French began to participate in maritime operations alongside their American compatriots, and soon thereafter began contributing soldiers to the battles on land.

Although French involvement in the war proved essential to securing America's eventual victory and its *de jure* independence, its strategic partnership with France did more to strengthen than to undercut America's distaste for alliance. France's military assistance was more than welcome, but the same was not true of the political constraints that accompanied it. Their alliance of 1778 prohibited both the United States and France from negotiating a peace settlement with Britain "without the formal consent of the other first obtained."[29] In keeping with such terms, the commission that Congress had appointed to negotiate peace with Britain had initially been instructed to consult with the French prior to concluding terms with the British. But the Americans soon took matters into their own hands and crafted a peace agreement with London at odds with the strategic objectives of France and Spain.[30] France enticed Spain to enter the war in 1779 by pledging to secure Spanish war aims, including claims to Gibraltar and Florida, that were not coordinated with the United States.[31] American negotiators ended up suspicious that France maintained designs on North America and was seeking to limit U.S. expansion beyond the Appalachians. In the meantime, Spain took positions on Gibraltar, Florida, and other territorial issues that helped convince the United States to go its own way in concluding a peace treaty with Britain.

Alliance with France helped the United States attain its primary objective—independence—but it also enmeshed Americans, in the words of historian Samuel Flagg Bemis, in "the baleful realm of European diplomacy of the eighteenth century."[32] Even after independence was at hand, Americans remained wary of the geopolitical aspirations of Europe's major powers in the Western Hemisphere and feared that Europe's monarchies would ultimately seek to scuttle America's fragile experiment in representative government. As the next chapter details, such concerns about entrapment in the geopolitical and monarchical aspirations of Europe weighed heavily on the new nation's reluctance to honor its alliance with France after the outbreak of war between France and Britain in 1793.

A final debate that sheds considerable light on U.S. grand strategy during the Revolutionary era concerns potential U.S. entry into the League of Armed Neutrality. Russia took the lead in forming the League in 1780 as a means of preserving the right of neutral countries to trade with all parties, including belligerents. As long as their ships were not carrying contraband, neutral countries had the right to defend their fleets against molestation. The United States initially requested inclusion in the League, the terms of which were quite consistent with the Model Treaty, but its belligerent status precluded participation. By 1783, eight countries had joined the pact, including Sweden, Denmark, Prussia, and Portugal.[33]

After the close of the Revolutionary War, the United States was eligible to join the League, and gave serious consideration to doing so in order to advance its commercial interests. In the end, Congress in 1783 decided against U.S. participation on the grounds that the pact risked embroiling the country in European rivalries. Hamilton, joined by James Madison, argued before Congress that the nation would be "unwilling, at this juncture, to become a party to a confederacy which may hereafter too far complicate the interests of the United States with the politics of Europe."[34] In the resolution setting forth the decision against joining the League, Congress concluded that "the true interest of these States requires that they should be as little as possible entangled in the politics and controversies of European nations."[35] America's abiding interest in protecting overseas commerce was trumped by its aversion to the potential constraints associated with joining an international pact. The nation's unilateralist impulses were alive and well even as it was taking its first steps.

* * *

The Revolutionary era was a formative period for U.S. statecraft. Americans began to aspire to hemispheric dominance, but confronted head-on the many obstacles standing in their way. From the outset, the Founders made clear their aversion to alliance and their desire to adhere to a principled brand of statecraft based on nonentanglement, commerce, and Enlightenment values. But they soon realized that achieving their geopolitical aims required compromising their principles and concluding an alliance with France. The alliance played a central role in enabling the United States to break free of Britain. But discord with France and Spain over the terms of the peace settlement with Britain soon reinforced American distrust of entanglement with Europe. Congress's rejection of U.S. participation in the League of Armed Neutrality also revealed early on the nation's distaste for international pacts and its strong preference for unilateral action. Americans were contemplating nonentanglement, but strategic detachment from Europe remained far off.

From the French Revolution to the War of 1812: Isolationism as Doctrine

The Ideological Foundations of Early U.S. Statecraft

While up to twenty percent of American colonists remained loyal to the British crown during the Revolutionary War, the unifying effects of America's struggle for independence paved over many of the other sharp ideological differences within American society.[1] After the close of the war, these cleavages rose to the surface, shaping the nation's politics and the conduct of its foreign policy. Multiple arenas of political and ideological contestation emerged, many of them running along North/South lines. The two-party system that took shape during President Washington's first term (1789–1792) exacerbated sectional rivalry. The Federalists became the dominant party in the North, while the Democratic-Republicans (hereafter referred to as Republicans) dominated in the South.

In broad terms, the North was more commercialized, urbanized, and committed to a religiously inspired progressivism, while the South was more agrarian, rural, and libertarian. Accordingly, the North tilted toward Britain, which it saw as a model for a modern American economy fueled by urbanization and manufacturing, while the South tilted toward France and its more agrarian lifestyle. North/South differences also played out over slavery and over constitutional reform and how much power to vest in the federal government. Indeed, differences over the appropriate reach of the federal government were a primary source of the partisan and personal rancor that mounted after independence. Jefferson, for example, railed against Hamilton's call for a national bank, national debt, and a political economy resembling Britain's, charging that this agenda constituted a veiled attempt to replace republican government with the trappings of monarchical rule.[2] Hamilton harbored reciprocal disdain for Jefferson's preference for an agrarian America with a weak central government.[3] With Hamilton serving as Washington's secretary of the treasury and Jefferson as his secretary of state, the personal and ideological feud between the two mounted, eventually contributing to Jefferson's decision to resign from the cabinet in 1793.[4]

These core ideological differences over the nation's developmental path and its governing institutions continued well into the nineteenth century. Nonetheless, they did not prevent the Founders from reaching general agreement on the need for collective governance over a number of principal policy areas. One such area was interstate commerce and foreign trade. Even Jefferson, one of the most tenacious advocates of states' rights, recognized that the federal government needed control over commerce. Frustrated by the unwillingness of European nations to agree to improved trade arrangements with a newly independent America, he concluded that the nation had to rely on collective governance to effectively wield its economic power.[5]

So, too, was there agreement that the union needed to be sufficiently centralized to resist foreign predation. Hamilton in *Federalist No. 7* spoke for many of the Founders in expressing concern about "the probability of incompatible alliances between the different states or confederacies and different foreign nations, and the effects of this situation upon the peace of the whole." He maintained that "America, if not connected at all, or only by the feeble tie of a simple league, offensive and defensive, would, by the operation of such jarring alliances, be gradually entangled in all the pernicious labyrinths of European politics and wars; and by the destructive contentions of the parts into which she was divided, would be likely to become a prey to the artifices and machinations of powers equally the enemies of them all. Divide et impera must be the motto of every nation that either hates or fears us."[6] The constitution that took effect in 1789 accordingly endowed the nation with a single foreign policy, and granted the federal government the power to tax, as well as to "raise and support Armies" and "to provide and maintain a Navy."[7]

Even as they took these centralizing steps, the Founders put clear limits on the authority of the federal government, fearful of the potential for federal institutions to become too strong and compromise political liberty. Although the Constitution made provision for a standing army, the Founders struggled to find the right balance between a military establishment adequate to defend the nation and one that risked becoming a tool of domestic repression. Accordingly, they made the president the commander-in-chief but offset that authority by charging Congress with the appropriation of funds for the army and restricting the term of such funding to no longer than two years. As James Madison described the logic behind this provision, "the best possible precaution against danger from standing armies is a limitation of the term for which revenue may be appropriated to their support."[8] In practice and in law the militias of the individual states remained the primary repositories of military capability for decades to come. Even Hamilton, who viewed a standing army as essential for defending against foreign predation and knitting together a stable union, felt the need to reassure skeptics. He argued that due to the natural security afforded by geography, the United States would need to maintain only a small army—one that, although capable of suppressing "a small faction, or an occasional mob, or insurrection," would not be strong enough to "enforce encroachments against the united efforts of the great body of the people."[9]

The ongoing debate about how best to structure institutions capable of providing for the nation's defense was not just theoretical. No longer afforded the protection that had come with being an appendage of the British Empire, the United States had to worry about threats from Britain, France, Spain, and American Indians (Native Americans dealt the U.S. Army a decisive defeat at the Battle of Wabash in 1791), as well as pirate attacks against U.S. merchant ships operating in distant waters. Moreover, by the early 1790s Europeans were again at war with each other, giving the new republic added reason to worry about entanglement in Old World rivalries. The French Revolution in 1789 spawned roughly a decade of conflict that engulfed a host of countries, including Austria, Britain, Russia, Portugal, the Netherlands, Prussia, and Spain. That Europe's conservative monarchies were keen to quash the French Revolution and restore Bourbon rule concerned Americans already preoccupied with the fragility of their republican experiment.

Closer to U.S. shores, the slave revolt that broke out in 1791 in the French colony of Saint-Domingue (Haiti) further complicated America's geopolitical environment. France was ultimately unable to put down the rebellion, with Haiti becoming independent in 1804. The French lost a major foothold in the Western Hemisphere, which contributed to Napoleon's decision in 1803 to sell the Louisiana Territory—a major trading post for Haiti—to the United States.[10] A setback for the French was clearly a boon for the United States. At the same time, the independence of Haiti, even if consistent with America's anti-imperialist agenda, was not universally welcomed in the United States. Indeed, President Jefferson (1801–1809), despite pressure to do so from Federalists, refused to recognize Haitian independence largely because it entailed the emancipation of the island's slaves.[11] Recognition of Haiti, many southerners feared, could trigger a slave insurrection in the United States. This would not be the last time that America's internal divisions over slavery and race relations would impact foreign policy.

France's departure from Haiti as well as its sale of the Louisiana Territory to the United States opened up new prospects for the union's enlargement. Americans were intent on proceeding with westward expansion, and were continuing to contemplate the prospect of gaining hold of Canada. Influential Americans were also eyeing Mexico, Cuba, and Puerto Rico as potential acquisitions.[12] Some

historians view this expansive ambition as a refutation of the nation's isolationist pedigree. Robert Kagan, for example, concludes that "the principles that
guided American foreign policy in the era of the early republic were not isolation and nonentanglement. . . . American liberalism was inherently entangling."
According to Kagan, Americans fully embraced the notion that it was their role
in the world to venture forth to defeat tyranny; it was only their "debilitating
weakness" that was holding them back.[13]

Kagan, however, conflates a desire for hemispheric dominance with
more wide-ranging aspirations. Apart from defending commercial shipping
against Barbary pirates and other bandits around the world, the United States
during its early decades did not have geopolitical ambitions beyond its own
region. On the contrary, its leaders were intent on severing the nation's geopolitical connection to Europe. Indeed, the determination of Americans to
establish hemispheric hegemony was about pushing Europeans out of their
neighborhood. Far from being "inherently entangling," U.S. grand strategy
aimed at enabling the country to take advantage of its natural geographic
isolation.

Kagan also conflates America's readiness to lead by example with a more
zealous and activist approach to spreading democracy. Americans self-
consciously shied away from opportunities to spread republican government
through force rather than example. They deemed such intervention to be inconsistent with their own commitment to the principle of self-determination, and
feared that their own political liberty would be threatened by the strong central
government and military establishment needed to project U.S. power abroad.
The preservation and advancement of the American experiment dictated a
policy of isolation, not entanglement. As the following chapters will make clear,
Americans for more than a century after independence steered clear of efforts
to export democracy through force not because of weakness but because they
very deliberately chose not to do so. Indeed, Jefferson's refusal to recognize the
independence of Haiti was a sobering sign of America's cautionary approach to
supporting liberal change—even in areas close to home.

Kagan makes one other error in his effort to argue that an entangling ambition was from the outset "baked into" American exceptionalism. He contends
that the Founders believed that the character of a nation's government was an
important determinant of a nation's foreign policy and that the United States
would be more secure if it was able to further the advance of republican government elsewhere and align itself with more liberal regimes. He argues, for example, that Americans were uneasy fashioning a military alliance with France in
1788 because it was an absolutist monarchy. They then grew much more comfortable with the alliance after the French Revolution in 1789. Kagan also argues
that Hamilton's deep-seated affinity for Britain was based on the character of its

government, believing that its liberal proclivities made it a more natural ally of the United States.[14]

To be sure, most Americans welcomed the French Revolution as a sign that republican government was enlarging its foothold. But there is no compelling historical evidence to back up the claim that America's reluctance to ally with France at the outbreak of the Revolutionary War was a product of France's monarchical ways, or that U.S. attitudes toward the alliance changed for the better after the overthrow of the French monarchy. America's alliance with France emerged from a hard-headed strategic calculus of what it would take for the colonies to break away from Britain; political developments inside France were largely irrelevant. Indeed, some of the Founders were alarmed by the political turmoil that engulfed France after its revolution in 1789 and feared the unrest could jeopardize its alliance with the United States. Hamilton, for example, was disconcerted, not heartened, by the French Revolution, which he saw as a source of bloodshed and mob rule, not deliberative democracy.[15] And although Hamilton may have tilted toward Britain as a model for American development, he hardly saw the country in benign terms, viewing it, like all others, as motivated by the inescapable game of power politics—precisely why the United States needed to keep its distance.

It is also the case that many of the Founders were quite explicit in rejecting the notion that the United States should choose its friends and allies on the basis of the character of their governments. In his Farewell Address, Washington warned that "it is folly in one nation to look for disinterested favors from another. . . . There can be no greater error than to expect or calculate upon real favors from nation to nation."[16] In the words of John Adams, "no attachment between nations arising merely from a similarity of laws and government is ever very strong, or sufficient to bind nations together who have opposite or even different interests."[17] As the United States contemplated alliance with France, Adams warned against assuming that alignment with the French would prove durable, warning that "the time might come when we should be obliged to call upon Britain to defend us against France."[18] Hamilton believed that regimes of all types were out for their own good and dismissed the notion of "perpetual peace between the states," expressing skepticism that republics are "pacific" and "less addicted to war than monarchies."[19] And Jefferson was disappointed about the way revolutionary France treated the United States, dashing his hopes that the two countries might enjoy a special affinity.[20]

The Founders certainly hoped for the spread of the experiment in republican government that they were overseeing. In Jefferson's words, "we are pointing out the way to struggling nations who wish, like us, to emerge from their tyrannies."[21] But they were quite adamant that America's relationships with other countries would be shaped by their interests, not by the character of their governments.

And they were equally adamant that to the degree the United States aided and abetted the spread of democracy, it should do so by example, not through more activist means.

Finalizing the Break from Europe

The Revolutionary War came to a close with Britain's recognition of the United States as "free sovereign and independent" in the Treaty of Paris, signed in September 1783.[22] Nonetheless, the United States was hardly free of a geopolitical connection to Europe. Its military alliance with France continued. Spain reclaimed a major portion of Florida as a result of the Treaty of Paris, and Spanish Florida's border with the United States was in dispute. Britain did cede the Northwest Territory to the United States, but both Britain and Spain were determined to use the sizable territory they still held in North America to keep the United States geopolitically weak and prevent it from expanding beyond the Mississippi. Britain looked to Native Americans to help contain the United States, while the Spanish closed the Mississippi to U.S. commerce a mere nine months after the Treaty of Paris. Neither Britain nor France granted the United States the unrestricted trade that it was hoping for, with the British denying U.S. merchants access to lucrative markets in the British West Indies.

Given America's continuing geopolitical and commercial entanglements with Europe, France's declaration of war against Britain in February 1793 confronted the United States with a host of difficult strategic choices. Not only did the United States have a treaty-based obligation to come to France's aid should it be at war with Britain, but the French, by taking on Britain as well as a host of other European monarchies, were acting in the name of spreading popular government—a mission similar to America's own. Nonetheless, neither fidelity nor common cause prevailed, with President Washington declaring in April 1793 that the United States would remain neutral in the war between Britain and France. Washington was effectively turning the nation's back on the country that had recently come to America's rescue during its own struggle against monarchy.

In keeping with the practice of neutrality, the United States continued to trade with both Britain and France, prompting both belligerents to obstruct U.S. shipping. Such interference with U.S. commerce sharpened political divisions over whether the United States should tilt to Britain or France, miring the conduct of statecraft in partisan polarization. John Jay in 1794 negotiated a treaty with Britain aimed at deescalating tensions with the British by resolving a number of geopolitical and commercial issues. Especially in the aftermath of Washington's refusal to honor the alliance with France, the move outraged those favoring closer alignment with the French. The intensity of domestic quarreling over grand strategy figured prominently in Washington's Farewell Address in 1796, which counseled against both partisan division and foreign entanglement. Washington's plea was to little avail. Relations with France continued to deteriorate, leading in 1798 to the outbreak of the Quasi-War—an undeclared naval conflict between the United States and France. Underscoring the fraught politics of grand strategy, Congress the same year passed the Alien and Sedition Acts, which sought to silence pro-French voices and repress domestic dissent.

The decisive tilt toward Britain did not last long. The Treaty of Mortefontaine, signed in 1800 and ratified the following year, ended the Quasi-War and amicably dissolved the U.S. alliance with France. In 1803, the United States purchased the Louisiana Territory from the French for $15 million, almost doubling the size of the country and removing France as an impediment to westward expansion. In the meantime, the Jay Treaty led to only a temporary reprieve in tensions between the United States and Britain. Ongoing British harassment of U.S. merchant ships eventually encouraged the United States to declare war on Britain in 1812. Although the War of 1812 ended in a military stalemate, it did secure for the United States unobstructed maritime commerce and an end to British efforts to block westward expansion by arming Native Americans. The Treaty of Mortefontaine and the sale of the Louisiana Territory had already largely disentangled the United States from France. The Treaty of Ghent, which in early 1815 brought the War of 1812 to a close and finalized the transfer of the Northwest Territory from British to American control, marked a similar disentanglement of the United States from Britain.[23] Americans had made major progress in attaining the geopolitical detachment from Europe that they had been seeking since the declaration of independence.

This chapter examines five pivotal episodes of strategy-making during the 1793-to-1815 period: the decision to effectively abrogate the treaty with France in 1793; the Jay Treaty of 1794; Washington's Farewell Address in 1796; the passage of the Alien and Sedition Acts in 1798; and the decision to go to war against Britain in 1812.

The Abrogation of the Alliance with France

News of the outbreak of war between France and Britain in February 1793 forced the Founders to stake out their positions on whether to uphold the nation's alliance with France. Hamilton in 1792 had proposed annulling the pact. He saw nullification of the treaty as a means of currying favor with London and reorienting U.S. strategy away from France toward Britain.[24] He also argued that the revolution had brought to power an illegitimate French government, effectively releasing the United States from the obligations it had undertaken to the French monarchy.[25] The execution of King Louis XVI in January 1793 consolidated Hamilton's assessment of the French Revolution as a radical and dangerous development from which the United States should keep its distance.[26] By April, when Washington was making his decision on whether to uphold the alliance, Hamilton's advice had moderated somewhat. Well aware that some of his colleagues—especially Republicans—would firmly resist outright nullification of the alliance, he advised the president to declare an impartial neutrality.

Jefferson and his political allies staunchly opposed not only formal nullification of the alliance but also a declaration of neutrality, interpreting both moves as part of a Federalist plot to spoil U.S. relations with France. Many in Jefferson's camp were troubled by the radical turn in the French Revolution, but generally believed, in Lawrence Kaplan's words, "that France was fighting America's battle abroad."[27] The French helped the Americans defeat monarchy on their side of the Atlantic, and it now behooved Americans to stand by the French as they took on Britain, Austria, Prussia, and other monarchies in Europe.

Their opposition to nullification and neutrality notwithstanding, Jefferson and his political allies exercised their own cautionary restraint when it came to upholding the alliance. They in fact held back from arguing that the United States should enter the war on France's behalf. Fearful that direct intervention would mean another war with Britain for which the country was not prepared, Jefferson argued that the United States should honor the alliance in theory, but not in practice. He wanted to refrain from joining the conflict, but to proceed with economic assistance to France, including by using U.S. vessels to resupply the French with goods from the French West Indies. He also wanted to use U.S. restraint as a bargaining chip with the British, suggesting that they be asked to vacate the forts that they still maintained in America's North and agree to let American merchants trade in the British West Indies in return for U.S. willingness to refrain from entering the war on France's behalf.[28] Jefferson's camp recommended avoiding a formal declaration of neutrality, thereby enabling the United States at least nominally to uphold the alliance.

Amid increasing rancor among his advisers, Washington settled on the middle course to which Hamilton had gravitated. He was unwilling to formally renounce the alliance as Hamilton had initially preferred, but was equally unwilling to honor it. Accordingly, on April 22, 1793, Washington issued a Proclamation of Neutrality, declaring that the country would "adopt and pursue a conduct friendly and impartial toward the belligerent powers." The proclamation also threatened legal action against any American caught "committing, aiding, or abetting hostilities against" the belligerents.[29]

Washington's unambiguous announcement that the United States would not honor the 1778 alliance precipitated a diplomatic crisis with France. The French minister in the United States, Edmond Charles Genêt, refused to adhere to the policy of neutrality and proceeded to use U.S. ports to ready French privateers and dispatch them to attack and seize British shipping. He also wrote directly to Washington, complaining that "the Federal government, far from manifesting any regard for our generous conduct towards this country ... or for the reiterated demonstrations of our real and disinterested friendship, were sacrificing our interests to those of our enemies, by their interpretation of the treaties which exist between us."[30] The U.S. government requested that the French government recall Genêt, which it eventually did, somewhat easing the strain in relations that had emerged.

The Proclamation of Neutrality was equally disruptive of relations between Federalists and Republicans; far from settling their dispute over the merits of alliance with France, their disagreement intensified. Hamilton dug in, publishing under the pseudonym Pacificus seven essays defending neutrality. He maintained that the United States had no obligation to defend France in an offensive war and that the United States could not risk inviting retaliatory attacks on its territory by aligning with the French. He also argued that France had fought on behalf of the United States during its war against Britain only out of self-interest; the French were seeking to derive economic and strategic benefit from a weakened Britain. Since the United States had no self-interested rationale for siding with France in 1793, it had no obligation to reciprocate France's earlier military assistance. Moreover, the American people owed gratitude to Louis XVI, not to the French people. Due to the king's "sole power," Hamilton argued, "if there was any kindness in the decision, demanding a return of kindness from us, it was the kindness of Louis the XVI ... [which cannot] be equitably transferred from him to others, who had no share in the decision."[31]

Madison, writing under the pseudonym Helvidius, presented the Jeffersonian rebuttal. He suggested that it was "ignominious perfidy" for a country to fail to come to the aid of an ally at war—even if its government had changed since the alliance's inception. He also argued that Washington had violated the Constitution since the alliance with France involved a treaty, meaning that only Congress had the right to effectively suspend it and declare neutrality. In addition, Madison accused the Federalists of being closet monarchists "who hate our republican government and the French Revolution."[32] Such dismay among Republicans with the declaration of neutrality, along with Secretary of State Jefferson's poisoned relationship with Hamilton, helped convince the former to step down. Jefferson initially submitted his letter of resignation in July indicating his intent to depart in September. At Washington's request, Jefferson stayed in his post until the end of the year.[33]

The U.S. decision to remain neutral as revolutionary France took on its neighboring monarchies revealed a great deal about the strategic orientation of early America. In effect, the Founders—including Jefferson and his fellow Republicans—wanted nothing to do with the nation's military obligations to France, exposing the deep-seated discomfort with alliance that had become apparent during the era of the Model Treaty. During the Revolutionary War, they overcame that reluctance and concluded an alliance with France out of strategic necessity. In 1793, in contrast, they perceived only strategic downsides in honoring the alliance with France; entering the war would likely pit the United States against Britain as well as Europe's other monarchies. To be sure, the Founders could not bring themselves to annul the 1778 alliance. Hamilton was tempted to do so, but ultimately concluded that he did not have to fight that battle; a declaration of neutrality would effectively produce the same outcome. Even among pro-French Republicans, however, there was scant support for upholding the alliance and coming to the aid of the country that had helped the United States break free of British rule. The main debate was between those who wanted to formalize publicly American neutrality and those who wanted to stand by the alliance in principle, but refrain from honoring it in practice.

The decision to withhold strategic support to France also exposed the striking limits to America's willingness to sustain costs in the service of promoting republican government. The growing power of the Jacobins and the execution of King Louis XVI in January 1793 certainly marked a militant turn in the course of the French Revolution. But France, especially in the context of the wars that began in 1792, was effectively doing America's bidding by taking on Europe's main monarchies. Nonetheless, the United States was unwilling to lend a hand—even in the face of its alliance commitments. Americans were in principle keen on sharing their experiment in republican government with the rest of the world. Their failure to support France in 1793, however, made it amply clear that they were not willing to run strategic risks to do so.

Finally, the debate over whether to honor the alliance with France underscored the intense partisanship that had engulfed debate over the conduct of U.S. statecraft. In the end, the substantive difference between Federalists and Republicans was not that significant; Hamilton wanted a public declaration of neutrality, while Jefferson counseled neutrality only in practice. Their disagreement over whether to tilt toward Britain or France was, however, so embedded in partisan and sectional politics that the question of whether to uphold the 1778 alliance proved uniquely divisive. The intensity of the bitterness stemmed from the personal rivalry that had emerged between Hamilton and Jefferson as well as the broader debate between North and South as to whether the country should follow Britain's trajectory and become more urbanized and centralized or follow France's trajectory and remain more agrarian and localized. Jefferson's resignation was a testament to the consequence of this political divide and helped set the stage for the mounting partisan rivalry over foreign policy that would soon follow.

The Jay Treaty of 1794

Despite Washington's decision in favor of neutrality, relations with Britain remained fraught. Americans continued to insist that they were free to trade with all belligerents. The British responded by interdicting American ships bound for French ports, impressing their sailors and seizing their cargo. Additionally, the United States made no progress in getting the British to give up their remaining military outposts on U.S. territory, to cease arming Native Americans, or to drop restrictions on trade. Unconvinced that neutrality alone was enough to prevent hostilities with Britain, Washington dispatched John Jay to London to try to improve relations.[34]

The so-called Jay Treaty was signed on November 19, 1794. As a result of the pact, Britain eased its restrictions on U.S. trade and granted its former colony preferential trade status; agreed to withdraw by 1796 from the eight northern forts on U.S. territory at which it still maintained a military presence; and resolved to settle through arbitration a number of contentious issues, including wartime debts and the demarcation of the U.S.-Canadian border.[35] In return, the United States granted Britain preferential trade status and acquiesced in British interference in neutral shipping, including by letting the British bring into U.S. ports goods seized from ships that were resupplying the French. Hamilton also assured the British envoy to Philadelphia, George Hammond, that the United States would not join Sweden and Denmark in taking up arms to defend neutral shipping against British harrassment. Hammond sent to London the following description of U.S. policy: "It was the settled policy of the government in every contingency even in that of an open contest with Great Britain, to avoid entangling itself with European connections, which could only tend to involve this country in disputes, wherein it might have no possible interest, and commit it in a common cause with allies, from whom in the moment of danger, it could derive no succor."[36]

In effect, the United States was backing down on President Washington's 1793 commitment to the right of neutrals to trade freely with belligerents—hopeful that the concession would deescalate tensions with Britain and significantly lower the chances of war. In addition, U.S. seaborne commerce—both imports and exports—was expanding significantly during the 1790s, giving the United States a compelling interest in keeping such commerce flowing by tolerating British interference with neutral shipping.[37] The United States was letting pragmatism trump principle—just as Washington had done when he backed away from honoring the alliance with France.

The Jay Treaty succeeded in clearing the way for increased trade and more amicable relations with Britain—but it had the opposite effect on ties between the United States and France. The United States had not only reneged on its alliance with France but also concluded a new treaty with France's enemy. In response to what France saw as a double betrayal, it eventually began to interdict American shipping and seize U.S. merchant vessels. In return, the United States began to disrupt French shipping, leading to what came to be known as the Quasi-War (1798–1800). Relations between the United States and France sank to their poorest since American independence.

The Jay Treaty also had brought relations between Federalists and Republicans to a new low. Coming on the heels of Washington's declaration of neutrality, which was itself a bitter pill for Jefferson and his allies, many Republican leaders were outraged by what they saw as Jay's capitulation to the British. The treaty also elicited public opposition, especially among, but not restricted to, Republican voters. Protests broke out; opponents of the treaty accused Jay of treason and hung him in effigy. With Jacobin extremism in full swing in France, Federalists retorted that Republicans were "a despicable mobocracy" and "Gallic jackals."[38]

The domestic fallout stemming from the Jay Treaty consolidated a political landscape divided between two opposing parties whose bases largely ran along North/South lines.[39] In the lead-up to the 1796 presidential election, angry Republicans rallied behind Jefferson's bid to best John Adams, Washington's vice president and the Federalist candidate. The further institutionalization and regionalization of the nation's party system intensified the already bitter partisan rivalry. The fisticuffs over the Jay Treaty also made clear that differences over foreign policy had the potential to cause deep rifts in the body politic. Indeed, American politicians vilified one another at least as intensely as they did potential foreign adversaries, giving rise to increasing concern about the enemy within. In addition, the French openly backed Jefferson, meaning that anxiety also mounted over the influence of foreign agents and their ability to manipulate the nation's politics.

Washington's Farewell Address

The campaign for the 1796 election was dominated by the bitter partisan controversy arising from the Proclamation of Neutrality, the Jay Treaty, and the broader dispute raging between pro-British Federalists and pro-French Republicans. Pointing to the "reign of terror" in France, the Federalists intensified their effort to affiliate Jeffersonians with chaos and mob rule. The Republicans countered that Federalists favored monarchy and aristocratic rule. Pierre August Adet, who had replaced Genêt as France's envoy to the United States, added to the partisan animosity by openly attacking the Federalists in the lead-up to the election and urging voters to cast their ballots for the Republican candidate, Thomas Jefferson.[40]

Unwilling to run for a third term and with the November election fast approaching, President Washington in the summer of 1796 decided that before leaving office he would share his hopes and fears with the American people. Washington asked Hamilton to take the lead on drafting the document, working from a version that Madison had drafted in 1792 as a potential valedictory speech.[41] Hamilton retained some of Madison's points but also made major revisions, placing much more focus on partisan politics and on foreign policy. He also strengthened the isolationist orientation of the address.[42]

The text that Washington eventually published in the *American Daily Advertiser* on September 19, 1796, reflected his preoccupation with two paramount threats to the nation's well-being: partisan rivalry and foreign entanglement. These two concerns were of course intimately linked. The nation's parties and regions were deeply divided over whether the country should favor Britain or France, and the Proclamation of Neutrality and Jay Treaty had brought the disagreement to a head. The political atmosphere was so heated that Washington felt obligated to start his address with a disclaimer aimed at instilling trust, noting that since he was not running for office, his remarks were "the disinterested warnings of a parting friend, who can possibly have no personal motive to bias his counsel."[43]

Washington followed his disclaimer by encouraging Americans to remain mindful that they have been blessed with union, a free constitution, and liberty. Drawing on the exceptionalist narrative that had already become part of the country's political discourse, he wished "that heaven may continue to you the choicest tokens of its beneficence," and went on to call on the nation to serve as a model for the rest of the world. Washington expressed hope that "the happiness of the people of these states, under the auspices of liberty, may be made complete by so careful a preservation and so prudent a use of this blessing as will acquire to them the glory of recommending it to the applause, the affection, and adoption of every nation which is yet a stranger to it." He ventured that "it will be worthy of a free, enlightened, and at no distant period, a great nation, to give to mankind the magnanimous and too novel example of a people always guided by an exalted justice and benevolence." Washington affirmed that due to its "detached and distant situation" America was exceptional in terms of geography, not just political character. "Why forego the advantages of so peculiar a situation? Why quit our own to stand upon foreign ground?" he asked. The United States was set to share its blessing with the rest of the world, but would do so through example, not through the projection of the power that it was destined to acquire.

A strong and cohesive union was essential if the United States was to fulfill its mission as a "magnanimous and too novel example" for the rest of the world. In Washington's words, "it is of infinite moment that you should properly estimate the immense value of your national union to your collective and individual happiness." Domestic unity would help ensure the physical well-being of Americans by providing "proportionably greater security from external danger, a less frequent interruption of their peace by foreign nations; and, what is of inestimable value, they must derive from union an exemption from those broils and wars between themselves." At stake was not just physical security, but also the preservation of domestic liberty. Should Americans find themselves in conflict—with foreign powers or with themselves—they would confront "the necessity of those overgrown military establishments which, under any form of government, are inauspicious to liberty, and which are to be regarded as particularly hostile to republican liberty."

Washington was by no means counseling against a strong and capable government. Indeed, he affirmed that "a government of as much vigor as is consistent with the perfect security of liberty is indispensable. Liberty itself will find in such a government, with powers properly distributed and adjusted, its surest guardian." A cohesive union would keep other powers at bay and forestall domestic conflict, helping the United States maintain political institutions that were strong enough to provide good governance but restrained enough to safeguard liberty.

Washington may have held the American experiment in high opinion, but one of the main thrusts of his address was that preserving domestic unity while safeguarding liberty would be no easy task. Indeed, Washington devoted the bulk of his attention—his discourse ran thirty-two handwritten pages, over 7,000 words—to this experiment's vulnerability. In his mind, acute threats to the United States came not only from foreign enemies but also from partisan division—the enemy within. In Washington's words, "the unity of government which constitutes you one people is . . . a main pillar in the edifice of your real independence. . . . But as it is easy to foresee that . . . much pains will be taken, many artifices employed to weaken in your minds the conviction of this truth; as this is the point in your political fortress against which the batteries of internal and external enemies will be most constantly and actively (though often covertly and insidiously) directed."

As for "internal" enemies, partisan and regional divisions were the chief threats. Washington warned Americans of "the danger of parties in the state, with particular reference to the founding of them on geographical discriminations. . . . The alternate domination of one faction over another, sharpened by the spirit of revenge, natural to party dissension . . . is itself a frightful despotism." The passion and disorder produced by partisan rivalry will tempt Americans "to seek security and repose in the absolute power of an individual," leading to the "ruins of public liberty." Factional strife also "opens the door to foreign influence and corruption," meaning that "the policy and the will of one country are subjected to the policy and will of another."

Sectional rivalry was equally dangerous. Washington urged Americans to be on guard, "indignantly frowning upon the first dawning of every attempt to alienate any portion of our country from the rest, or to enfeeble the sacred ties which now link together the various parts." Perceived incompatibilities between "Northern and Southern, Atlantic and western," were mere "misrepresentations" propagated by "designing men [who] may endeavor to excite a belief that there is a real difference of local interests and views." Washington exhorted Americans to direct their loyalties to the collective nation, not their region or locality: "The name of American, which belongs to you in your national capacity, must always exalt the just pride of patriotism more than any appellation derived from local discriminations."

The second main thrust of Washington's address was to "warn against the mischiefs of foreign intrigue." Washington began his discussion of U.S. statecraft by linking it to his remarks on the need for domestic unity, cautioning Americans against favoritism or animosity to Britain, France, or any other power: "Nothing is more essential than that permanent, inveterate antipathies against particular nations, and passionate attachments for others, should be excluded." On one hand, Washington explained, "ill-will and resentment" toward a particular country can be a recipe for war, "contrary to the best calculations of policy." On the other hand, he counseled, "there can be no greater error than to expect or calculate upon real favors from nation to nation." He warned that "a passionate attachment of one nation for another" is likely to facilitate "the illusion of an imaginary common interest in cases where no real common interest exists." Furthermore, Washington continued, the "insidious wiles" of foreign powers have the potential to undermine the loyalty of ordinary Americans, giving "ambitious, corrupted, or deluded citizens (who devote themselves to the favorite nation), facility to betray or sacrifice the interests of their own country."

Instead of embracing favoritism or animosity to other nations, Washington argued, "just and amicable feelings towards all should be cultivated." Harkening back to the Model Treaty, he explained that doing so required focusing relations with other powers primarily on commerce: "The great rule of conduct for us in regard to foreign nations is in extending our commercial relations, to have with them as little political connection as possible." Washington concluded that "it is our true policy to steer clear of permanent alliances with any portion of the foreign world."

Not only did Washington articulate with striking clarity his adherence to an isolationist grand strategy, but he also made clear that avoiding foreign entanglement was "the great rule of conduct for us" and "our true policy"—in other words, it was a doctrine, not a strategy to be followed only temporarily during the nation's relative weakness. Washington did acknowledge that the United States was destined to emerge as a major power. But the appropriate aspiration accompanying America's rise should be immunity from predation, not overseas ambition. As he put it, "the period is not far off when we may defy material injury from external annoyance; when we may take such an attitude as will cause the neutrality we may at any time resolve upon to be scrupulously respected; when belligerent nations, under the impossibility of making acquisitions upon us, will not lightly hazard giving us provocation." Washington's strategic vision was time-unlimited in no small part because it was rooted in the immutable realities of geography. America's "detached and distant situation" meant that it operated in its own strategic theater. In contrast, "Europe has a set of primary interests which to us have none; or a very remote relation. . . . Hence, therefore, it must be unwise in us to implicate ourselves by artificial ties in the ordinary vicissitudes of her politics."[44] Based simply on matters of geography, America's entanglement in the politics of Europe would be "artificial."

In light of ongoing disagreement between Federalists and Republicans over the nation's alliance with France, Washington's two main themes were in obvious tension with each other; the call for political unity was at odds with the warning against alliance. Such tension should not be surprising; the Farewell Address was a political as well as a strategic statement. Despite Washington's insistence that his words were "the disinterested warnings of a parting friend," he was burnishing his own record, defending his decisions, and seeking to put opponents on the defensive.

Nonetheless, Washington could hardly ignore the issue of the alliance with France, and instead sought to address it in a nuanced, if not disingenuous, fashion. Effectively, he relied on the same awkward logic that he had deployed in the Proclamation of Neutrality in 1793. On the surface, he stood by the 1778 alliance and indicated that he was warning against further, not existing, commitments. To this end, his call for the United States to minimize its political connections with other nations came with an important caveat: "So far as we have already formed engagements, let them be fulfilled with perfect good faith. Here let us stop." Three paragraphs later, when warning Americans "to steer clear of permanent alliances with any portion of the foreign world," he issued a similar qualification: "so far, I mean, as we are now at liberty to do it; for let me not be understood as capable of patronizing infidelity to existing engagements. I hold the maxim no less applicable to public than to private affairs, that honesty is always the best policy. I repeat it, therefore, let those engagements be observed in their genuine sense. But, in my opinion, it is unnecessary and would be unwise to extend them."

Washington, however, could not leave the issue there; these statements stood in direct contradiction to his 1793 decision in favor of neutrality. "I was well satisfied," he therefore went on to explain, "that our country, under all the circumstances of the case, had a right to take, and was bound in duty and interest to take, a neutral position." Washington asserted that "justice and humanity" compel the nation to preserve "peace and amity," in no small part because the United States needs "to gain time" in order "to progress without interruption." He was effectively admitting that he was letting pragmatism take precedence over principle, warning against "infidelity to existing engagements," but putting such infidelity into practice because it was not in America's interest to go to war with Britain. As if ultimately trying to justify unprincipled behavior in principled terms, Washington concluded his discussion of the French alliance by asserting that "we may safely trust to temporary alliances for extraordinary emergencies," suggesting that the alliance with France was time-limited (which it was not) and operative only when needed. This formulation provided at least some measure of logical justification for warning against "permanent alliances" while calling on the nation, at least nominally, to fulfill "already formed engagements."

As could be expected, many Republicans reacted scornfully to the Farewell Address. With reference to Washington's warning against permanent alliances, William Duane, a prominent journalist supportive of the Republicans, wrote: "This extraordinary advice is fully exemplified in your departure from the spirit and principle of the treaty with France, which was declared to be permanent, and exhibits this very infidelity you reprobate in a most striking and lamentable light."[45] Madison similarly interpreted the address as little more than a thinly veiled effort to further degrade U.S. relations with France and scuttle the alliance between the two nations.[46]

Washington's warning against permanent alliance proved to be quite consequential. The United States and France agreed in 1800 to annul their alliance. Washington's crystalline articulation of isolationism would then serve as a guidepost for U.S. grand strategy for decades to come. Washington's call for domestic unity was far less effective; leading up to the November election, and for long thereafter, partisan and regional cleavages continued to roil the nation's politics. Indeed, the domestic divide eventually grew so intense that the union broke apart in 1861. In 1862, with the Civil War in full swing, the Farewell Address was read aloud in Congress on February 22, Washington's birthday. Since 1896, the Senate has continued this tradition on an annual basis.[47]

The Alien and Sedition Acts of 1798

John Adams, a Federalist, won the 1796 election by only three electoral votes, with Thomas Jefferson, a Republican, coming in second, thereby claiming the vice presidency.[48] The close vote, the divided executive, and the partisan passions left behind by the bitter campaign made for a combustible mix. France's overt intervention in the campaign had heightened the political animosity between Federalists and Republicans, which only intensified as France stepped up its disruption of U.S. trade after Adams's victory. The French government unilaterally renounced elements of its commercial and defense treaties with the United States and ordered its navy to obstruct American shipping.[49]

Beginning after the 1796 election and running until a negotiated Franco-American settlement in 1800, France seized even more U.S. vessels than did Britain.[50] The U.S. Navy had dwindled in size after the Revolutionary War, leaving the nation with little capability to fight back. Congress responded by authorizing in 1798 the acquisition of new warships. It also voted to rescind the existing treaties with France and authorized U.S. vessels to subdue and seize armed French vessels in U.S. waters and to confiscate their cargo.[51] Although Congress did not formally issue a declaration of war, this turn of events commenced the Quasi-War between France and the United States. The French had the upper hand in the maritime conflict, but the United States succeeded in capturing dozens of French ships.

At roughly the same time that an undeclared war with France was taking shape, the U.S. government was also pursuing steps to disarm France's supporters at home. Against the backdrop of mounting tensions with the French and their interference in the election, President Adams and the Federalist-controlled Congress passed a number of bills, known as the Alien and Sedition Acts, aimed at suppressing domestic dissent and disarming France's Republican sympathizers. Fear of the enemy within and its manipulation by a foreign adversary led to hostility toward immigrants as well as infringements on the civil liberties of American citizens. The Alien and Sedition Acts empowered the U.S. government to target, including by arrest, deportation, and incarceration, resident aliens as well as American citizens deemed to be acting as foreign agents or expressing "malicious" criticism of the federal government.[52]

Congress passed four separate pieces of legislation, approving the first bill on June 18, 1798, and passing the other three over the course of the next four weeks. The legislation raised the residency requirement for citizenship from five to fourteen years, thereby restricting suffrage for new immigrants, many of whom were French and tended to back the Republicans. The acts granted the executive the power to imprison or deport both resident aliens deemed to be "dangerous to the peace and safety of the United States" and any citizen of a nation with which the United States was at war.[53] Aliens from enemy nations became ineligible for citizenship. Finally, the legislation authorized fines and imprisonment for individuals who "write, print, utter, or publish . . . any false, scandalous and malicious" material against the federal government.[54] This law led to the arrest of over a dozen pro-Republican newspaper editors as well as the imprisonment of Matthew Lyon, a Republican member of Congress from Vermont, for his heated criticism of President Adams. Lyon was charged with multiple offenses, including publishing an editorial attributing to Adams an "unbounded thirst for ridiculous pomp, foolish adulation, and selfish avarice."[55]

Just as the Founders had feared, a combination of entanglement in European rivalries, foreign interference in U.S. politics, and partisan enmity was leading to the loss of liberty at home. Escalating tensions with France were mixing with intense partisanship to produce overt infringements of civil liberty. Amid the heated atmosphere, political opposition shaded into treason, with Federalists deeming the most strident voices deserving of prosecution and jail. Meanwhile, the loyalties of new immigrants and resident aliens were as a matter of course suspect; granting voting rights to newcomers needed to be delayed, and individuals deemed to be serving as foreign agents needed to be subject to imprisonment or deportation. A letter Adams's nephew wrote to Abigail Adams, the president's wife, made plain the anti-immigrant sentiment of the day: "The grand cause of all our present difficulties, may be traced . . . to so many *hordes of foreigners* immigrating to America. . . . Let us no longer pray, that America may become an asylum to all nations."[56]

Republicans saw the Alien and Sedition Acts as little more than an overt effort to suppress political opposition and limit freedom of speech. Without recourse in a Congress controlled by Federalists, Jefferson and his allies mounted their resistance by turning to state legislatures that they controlled. Working behind the scenes, partly to avoid accusations of sedition, Jefferson helped draft the Kentucky Resolution, the first version of which passed the state assembly in November 1798. Madison did the same for the Virginia Resolution, which the Virginia assembly passed the following month. Both resolutions concluded that the Alien and Sedition Acts violated the Constitution and the principles of republican government.

The Virginia Resolution asserted that the acts enlarged the power of the federal government in a manner that risked transforming "the present republican system of the United States, into an absolute, or at best a mixed monarchy." It also claimed that the legislation "subverts the general principles of free government" and that it "levelled against that right of freely examining public characters and measures, and of free communication among the people thereon, which has ever been justly deemed, the only effectual guardian of every other right."[57] It concluded by declaring the Alien and Sedition Acts to be "unconstitutional" and invited other states to concur. The Kentucky Resolution went further, stipulating that individual states had the right to nullify laws that they deem to be unconstitutional. The states that are party to the Constitution, the resolution affirmed, "being sovereign and independent, have the unquestionable right to judge of its infraction; and that a nullification, by those sovereignties, of all unauthorized acts done under color of that instrument, is the rightful remedy."[58]

Although the responses of Virginia and Kentucky to the Alien and Sedition Acts had the makings of a constitutional crisis, other states did not follow suit, damping down the escalating confrontation between federal authority and states' rights. The stalemate also eased as the Federalists' effort to use the Alien and Sedition Acts to disarm their Republican opponents produced a political backlash. Many Americans saw the acts as overreach—an attempt to use the threat posed by France to inflate the danger of the enemy within and silence political opponents.[59] Moreover, with the French keen to focus their military efforts on their European adversaries and the United States looking to benefit from unfettered trade with France, the two governments negotiated an end to the Quasi-War in 1800. The Treaty of Mortefontaine, signed in September 1800, ended naval hostilities, formally terminated the alliance of 1778, and recognized mutual trading rights.[60] Peace with France only intensified the public's skepticism of the Alien and Sedition Acts. The Republicans successfully capitalized on such perceptions of Federalist overreach during the presidential campaign in 1800, helping Thomas Jefferson defeat Adams's bid for reelection.[61]

Soon after taking office, Jefferson pardoned those serving sentences under the Sedition Act and Congress thereafter repaid their fines. Only the Alien Enemies Act—the provision providing for the imprisonment or deportation of aliens from enemy nations—survived Jefferson's presidency. Indeed, although revised, this act has remained on the books until today, serving as the legal basis for the removal or internment of U.S. residents hailing from enemy nations, including citizens and noncitizens of Japanese, German, and Italian ancestry during World War II. The era of the Quasi-War with France marked the first time, but not the last, that a threat from abroad, combined with partisan politics, led to the persecution of the perceived enemy within.

The War of 1812

The Quasi-War made France an overt geopolitical rival of the United States, eroding the Republicans' traditional preference for alignment with the French. The coup of November 1799 and Napoleon's consequent political ascent distanced America's political establishment even further from the French, snuffing out any remaining expectation that France would bring republican government to Europe. For Madison, this development "left America the only theater on which true liberty can have a fair trial."[62] Although he long stood by the U.S. alliance with France, Jefferson was also chagrined by France's absolutist turn, helping clear the way for the alliance's formal nullification through ratification of the Treaty of Mortefontaine in 1801.[63]

In the meantime, the Federalist enthusiasm for alignment with Britain had also waned. By 1800, peace had broken out with France and reciprocal trade relations restored, while Britain continued to disrupt U.S. shipping and impress sailors, undermining residual sentiment in favor of a tilt toward Britain. The partisan rancor of the 1790s, the excesses of the Alien and Sedition Acts, and the constitutional challenges posed by the Kentucky and Virginia resolutions helped convince leaders on both sides of the aisle that not only security, but also domestic liberty and unity, necessitated disentanglement from Europe. In his inaugural address on March 4, 1801, Jefferson affirmed that "we are all Republicans, we are all Federalists" and called for "peace, commerce, and honest friendship with all nations, entangling alliances with none."[64] In a letter to the American diplomat William Short the following October, he asserted that "we have a perfect horror at everything like connecting ourselves with the politics of Europe" and that "we wish to let every treaty we have drop off, without renewal."[65]

By the time of Jefferson's presidency, Federalists and Republicans had thus ended their feud over whether the nation should tilt toward France or Britain, instead agreeing that the country should avoid political connections with all.[66] Washington's Farewell Address had laid out a strategic vision, but it also had a political objective: to undercut Republicans and their support for alliance with France. By 1801, however, its admonitions had lost their partisan edge and instead been embraced by Republicans and Federalists alike. Both parties had arrived at the conclusion that the nation's security as well as its internal cohesion would be best served by a grand strategy of geopolitical isolation. As Jefferson put it in his inaugural address, the United States was a "chosen country, with room enough for our descendants to the thousandth and thousandth generation," while being "kindly separated by nature and a wide ocean from the exterminating havoc of one quarter of the globe."[67]

America's political leadership had thus returned to the consensus enshrined in the Model Treaty of 1776, which called for deepening the nation's commercial engagement abroad while shunning political and strategic connections. The revival of this earlier orientation was understandable. Over the course of the 1790s, geopolitical tilts toward either Britain or France had produced little good. In contrast, the expansion of foreign trade was unquestionably working to the nation's benefit. Despite the efforts of both Britain and France to disrupt America's seaborne commerce, the value of U.S. trade roughly doubled over the course of the decade.[68] Napoleon's wars against his European adversaries served only to draw the United States even more deeply into transatlantic commerce, with American merchants taking advantage of the nation's status as a neutral trader and the appetite for goods generated by the conflict.

Accordingly, protecting seaborne commerce emerged as one of the earliest foreign policy challenges facing Jefferson. At the top of his agenda was countering raids from North Africa's Barbary pirates against U.S. merchant ships in the Mediterranean and Atlantic. American shipping had been protected by the British fleet prior to independence, and then by the French fleet during the Revolutionary War. Thereafter, the United States dealt with the ongoing threat of Barbary piracy primarily through a combination of monetary tribute to fore-stall attacks and ransom payments to free U.S. sailors taken hostage.

Jefferson took a more forceful approach, in no small part because he had at his disposal the naval assets to do so. During the second half of the 1790s, the United States had built a small naval force to counter Barbary piracy and prosecute the Quasi-War with France. On the eve of Jefferson's presidency, Congress approved the acquisition of additional warships, in large part to con-front the Barbary threat. In 1801, Jefferson ordered U.S. naval attacks against both pirate vessels and Tripoli. By 1804, most of the U.S. Navy was on station in the Mediterranean.[69] The following spring, a band of mercenaries led by U.S. Marines attacked and seized the port city of Derne, threatening a further ad-vance on Tripoli. Thereafter, the Pasha of Tripoli and U.S. negotiators reached a diplomatic agreement that ended hostilities, led to the release of remaining American prisoners (after another ransom payment), and ended, at least tempo-rarily, Barbary attacks on U.S. shipping.

For the first time in its history, the United States had engaged both its naval and ground forces in an overseas theater. The action was, however, in keeping with the nation's determination to use foreign policy primarily as a commercial instrument. Jefferson limited American objectives to protecting the nation's sea-borne commerce and its citizens; he was seeking neither to establish the U.S. Navy as a dominant force in the Mediterranean nor to bring republican govern-ment to distant lands. The United States turned to the use of force to defend its commercial interests, not to extend its geopolitical reach.

As for relations with Britain and France, Jefferson enjoyed a temporary break in their interference with U.S. shipping as a consequence of the Treaty of Mortefontaine as well as the Peace of Amiens in 1802. The Treaty of Amiens brought to a close a decade of war between France and Britain, thereby ending their efforts to disrupt neutral trade. France also posed a diminished threat to U.S. territory after its loss of Haiti and sale of the Louisiana Territory. Jefferson did not immediately pursue statehood in order to buy time for more Anglo-Saxons to settle the area, but the purchase did mark the beginning of a sustained era of westward expansion.

Britain and France returned to war in 1803, prompting both powers to again disrupt American shipping. Britain also stepped up impressment, in no small part to augment the number of sailors it could devote to the fight against Napoleon. After Britain attacked a U.S. Navy vessel off the coast of Norfolk in 1807, Jefferson responded by imposing an embargo on all exports and restricting imports from Britain. Despite regular violations of the embargo, foreign trade fell sharply—by some ninety percent between 1807 and the defeat of Napoleon in 1814.[70] The hardship imposed on U.S. merchants provoked considerable opposition to the ban, particularly in the North.[71] American merchant vessels, many of them ported in northern states, were carrying an increasing share of transatlantic trade, making the embargo particularly costly to shippers and their customers. Indeed, it was in part because of the growing volume of foreign commerce that the U.S. government decided to take a harder line on violation of its neutral trading rights than it did during the 1790s.

The embargo did significantly more harm to the U.S. economy than to that of either Britain or France, by 1809 compelling the United States to abandon it and instead press for recognition of the U.S. right to neutral trade. While commerce with France was nominally reopened in 1810, the British refused any accommodation and continued to disrupt U.S. shipping and impress sailors. Since Britain was the dominant sea power in the Atlantic, its navy was able to take a significant toll on U.S. trade with continental Europe. Such interference with seaborne trade was not the only source of American animosity toward Britain. Whereas the French had effectively abandoned their territories in North America, the British stayed put in Canada and thus posed the main overland threat to the United States. Americans also resented British efforts to aid and abet Native American resistance along the northwest frontier. In addition, with Republicans in control of Congress and the White House—James Madison took over from Jefferson after winning the 1808 election—the party that had long harbored anti-British sentiment was in charge of guiding statecraft.

These sources of hostility toward Britain ultimately fashioned a Republican consensus in favor of resorting to force to break Britain's stranglehold on the nation's seaborne commerce. Congress passed a declaration of war on June 17, 1812, which Madison signed the following day. The primary motivation behind the U.S. decision for war was commercial—to end British interference with U.S. trade. In Madison's words in his fourth Annual Message to Congress, the United States had no choice but to defend "our commercial rights and our maritime independence."[72] But, unlike in the Mediterranean, where the United States resorted to the use of force to pursue purely commercial objectives, in its own hemisphere Americans harbored geopolitical ambition. The goal of driving the British from Canada and advancing the U.S. bid for unchallenged primacy in North America loomed large in the decision for war. Expelling the British from Canada would also deny them the ability to support Native American tribes that were in the way of America's westward expansion. The United States might even be able to wrest control of Florida from Spain, a British ally.[73] To these ends, the United States made several attempts to invade Canada during the war—none of which succeeded.

Republicans buttressed these commercial and geopolitical objectives with a number of potent ideological justifications for war. Returning to the narrative of the Revolutionary era, supporters of hostilities against Britain cast the conflict as a second war of independence. President Madison argued that "the American people were not an independent people, but colonists and vassals" if they had "shrunk . . . from manly resistance."[74] Representative John Calhoun (R-South Carolina) insisted that "if we submit to the pretensions of England . . . the independence of this country is lost. . . . This is the second struggle for our liberty."[75] Republicans also invoked the country's exceptional mission as a redeemer nation. According to Madison, the nation's failure to stand up to Britain "would have been a degradation blasting our best and proudest hopes; it would have struck us from the high rank where the virtuous struggles of our fathers had placed us, and have betrayed the magnificent legacy which we hold in trust for future generations." Supporters of the war, in the words of historian Padraig Riley, "projected the American state as the guardian of universal democracy."[76] So, too, were Madison, Jefferson, and their political compatriots keen to demonstrate that the looser republic they favored was well suited to taking on a formidable foreign adversary while preserving domestic liberties. The conflict, according to a pro-Republican newspaper, demonstrated "the practicability of a republic, such as ours, for the purposes of war."[77]

A further ideological justification for the war was the perceived need to protect the nation's racial hierarchy. Britain was backing Native American adversaries of the United States as well as prohibiting slave trade within the British Empire and encouraging other countries to follow suit. The fight against Britain was regularly touted as a sacrifice needed not just to preserve American democracy against British monarchism, but also to defeat Britain's "savage allies" and to defend slaveholding. Furthermore, Republicans portrayed impressment as a form of white slavery; some 6,000 sailors were illegally apprehended from U.S. ships and forced into service on British vessels. War against Britain was a fight for white emancipation.[78]

Noticeably missing from prowar ideological discourse was consideration of the impact of a U.S. conflict with Britain on the ongoing European effort to defeat Napoleonic France. Britain was leading the struggle against a French nation that had forsaken its republican calling and instead embraced dictatorship and territorial conquest. At least in theory, the United States might have been reluctant to distract from that mission.[79] But the opposite was the case. Republicans capitalized on war in Europe to risk taking on a much stronger adversary, calculating that Britain would have to keep the bulk of its forces on the other side of the Atlantic to fight Napoleon.[80]

To be sure, Republicans did lose their appetite for alliance with France following Napoleon's ascent and they did not seriously consider renewing the alliance with France even amid serious setbacks during the War of 1812.[81] Nonetheless, the fact that Britain was in the midst of seeking to defeat Napoleonic

France—an aggressor state that had trampled on liberal ideals—did not deter the United States from declaring war against Britain. Britain posed a more immediate threat to U.S. commerce and territory than did France; Britain was thus the enemy of choice. In Jefferson's words, "we resist the enterprises of England first, because they first come vitally home to us."[82] Republicans may have justified the War of 1812 on the need to defend democracy at home, but they paid scant attention to the implications of their actions for the welfare of republican ideals further afield. The calculations of U.S. decision makers turned on geopolitical considerations, with little regard for the political character of powers on the other side of the Atlantic.

The justifications for war and the patriotism it engendered succeeded in sustaining sufficient congressional and public support for the conflict. The war declaration passed the House by a vote of 79 to 49, and the Senate by a vote of 19 to 13. But despite Republican claims of a "second struggle for our liberty," their efforts to rally national unity fell short; not a single Federalist voted in favor of war. Federalists opposed the war due to the economic costs it imposed on the northern states and were against an invasion of Canada, in part because it would turn the United States into an aggressor. Harkening back to the 1790s, Federalists also suspected that Republicans would use the war against Britain to revive the prospects for alliance with France; rumors circulated that Napoleon planned to send 10,000 troops across the Atlantic to join the fight.[83] A Federalist senator from New York remarked that the conflict was "a war of party, & not of the country."[84]

Opponents of the war did more than voice their disapproval. New Englanders broached the possibility of secession.[85] Citizens asked to serve in state militias regularly refused; of 5,000 men called up by the New York governor, only 1,500 showed up. When the militia marched north to the Canadian border to mount an attack on Montreal, most of the contingent refused to cross the border and instead headed home. According to historian Harvey Strum, "never again in American history did citizens reveal their refusal to fight more blatantly than in the War of 1812."[86] Smuggling across the border continued throughout the war; many northerners preferred to trade with the enemy rather than to fight it. Opposition to the war was to spawn an organized pacifist movement that extended beyond antiwar activists in religious communities. Peace societies were founded in Massachusetts, New York, and Ohio in 1815. Other state chapters followed, with the American Peace Society opening its doors in New York in 1828.

Against the backdrop of ongoing conflict, Republicans pilloried antiwar Federalists as British sympathizers—the new enemy within. Many Republicans called into question the loyalty of their political opponents—just as the Federalists had done to Republicans during the Quasi-War with France. One

Republican newspaper commented that "we have more to fear" from opponents of the war "than from the most formidable operations of the enemy."[87] Federalists and Republicans in some cases came to blows over the war, with the violence in Baltimore on one occasion leading to a fatality. Influential Republicans contemplated the possibility of taking up arms against Federalist opponents of the war and apprehending them as traitors.[88] Despite the fact that the nation was at war—indeed, because of it—the partisan and sectional divide over foreign policy ran especially deep.

* * *

The War of 1812 ended without a clear victory by either side. The United States was no match for the British at sea. On interior lakes and rivers, the two countries effectively fought to a draw. On land, the United States enjoyed notable successes, but also notable defeats—including Britain's occupation of Washington, D.C., and the burning of the White House and Capitol in August 1814. The agreement that ended the war, the Treaty of Ghent, reflected the outcome on the battlefield, effectively restoring the territorial status quo that existed before the conflict began.

Despite the ambiguous military outcome, most Americans, with considerable coaching from their Republican leaders, understood the War of 1812 to have been a success.[89] A still-young republic had held its own against imperial Britain. The United States won the closing battles, including General Andrew Jackson's famous victory in New Orleans. The British succeeded in holding Canada, but they did agree to cease their support for a Native American buffer state on the northwest frontier, effectively clearing the way for westward expansion. Perhaps most important, the United States achieved its chief war aim—a return to unmolested transatlantic trade and the economic benefits that came with it. The defeat of France, more than U.S. pressure, lay behind this change in British policy. Indeed, the British refused to include in the Treaty of Ghent recognition of America's maritime rights or a ban on impressment. But even if the United States fell short of the principled agreement it sought, it had nonetheless broken free of the restrictions on trade that had originally prompted the declaration of war against Britain.

In going to war in 1812, the United States seemingly contravened the consensus against foreign entanglement that had congealed over the course of the 1790s. The country deliberately chose to take on the world's premier naval power and enmesh itself in Europe's rivalries. In effect, however, the United States was risking entanglement only in the service of isolation; the end of separating itself from Europe justified the means of going to war against Britain. And France, even for Republicans, had hardly demonstrated any goodwill toward the United States, having continued to disrupt U.S. shipping even after the U.S. declaration of war against Britain. Americans were seeking to close out the era of subservience to Europe and eliminate Europe's remaining presence in North America, thereby bringing the United States closer to hemispheric isolation and realization of the natural security afforded by geography. As Kaplan comments, "The name of isolationist belongs not to the opponents of war, but to the war party itself."[90]

Many Americans emerged from the War of 1812 believing that they had indeed rid themselves of British coercion and succeeded in making a definitive geopolitical break with Europe. As Jefferson remarked after the close of the war, "the less we have to do with the amities or enmities of Europe, the better."[91] On the other side of the Atlantic, the Concert of Europe cleared the way for an extended period of great-power peace. No longer did the United States need to navigate conflicts among European powers or the complexities of trade with belligerents. Commercial connections with all, political connections with none, was becoming a reality, not just an aspiration. So, too, was the country drawing closer to President Washington's hope for greater political unity. In much the same way that questions of grand strategy had provoked political discord in the 1790s, the War of 1812 proved to be hugely divisive, again pitting parties and sections against one another over defining matters of statecraft. Americans therefore emerged from the war more convinced than ever that domestic unity depended on geopolitical isolation. The demise of the Federalists after 1815—in part due to their opposition to the war—cleared the way for an era of unprecedented political consensus focused on nation-building and westward expansion while steering clear of strategic entanglement with Europe.

5

Westward Expansion and the Monroe Doctrine: The Limits of Hemispheric Ambition

From the end of the War of 1812 until the outbreak of the Civil War in 1861, the United States focused on two main goals: the union's consolidation and expansion. The first objective required building up both institutions and infrastructure—a strengthened presidency, a central bank, a peacetime navy to protect seaborne trade, and the roads, railroads, canals, steamboats, and ports needed to promote economic growth and integration. The second objective required a mix of diplomacy and force. With Europe's imperial powers the United States negotiated its way to new territories. By 1820, it had already struck a deal with Britain to resolve outstanding border issues with Canada and concluded a treaty with Spain that ceded Florida to the United States. Americans took a more coercive approach when it came to Native Americans and Mexicans, when necessary turning to the use of force to push across North America. By the time the Mexican-American War came to an end in 1848, Americans had made it to the Pacific coast, wresting control of a large swath of land from Mexico and negotiating the transfer of the Oregon territory from Britain.

Americans demonstrated perseverance and determination when it came to westward expansion across North America, but they had very little appetite for venturing further afield. As during the founding era, Americans were keen traders and were always looking to expand their access to foreign markets. Moreover, they actively debated additional territorial expansion into Latin America and the Caribbean. Nonetheless, Americans demurred, going no farther than the Rio Grande. They even passed on repeated opportunities to intervene on behalf of republican aspirations in Latin America and Europe, guided by a cautionary reluctance to interfere in the domestic affairs of other countries. A union that was experiencing phenomenal growth in territory, population, and prosperity nonetheless continued to abide by President Washington's 1796 admonition against political connections beyond the nation's borders. In the aftermath of the War of 1812, disentanglement from foreign nations was hardly a done deal, but it appeared to be at hand.

Nonetheless, Americans had good reason to remain wary of European intentions. Even if the end of the Napoleonic Wars and the formation of the Concert of Europe held out the prospect of a more peaceful Europe and led to the reopening of transatlantic trade, the establishment of the Concert was not entirely good news for the United States. Peace in Europe freed up Britain to focus its attention and resources on other strategic theaters. The great-power members of the Concert divided the territory of weaker neighbors among themselves and suppressed liberal political movements on the Continent. These were not reassuring developments for Americans and raised concerns that Spain might seek to reclaim some of its colonial holdings in America's neighborhood. Such concerns were reflected in the promulgation of the Monroe Doctrine in 1823, which warned Europe against any new colonial outposts in the Western Hemisphere.

The Monroe Doctrine provoked pique on the other side of the Atlantic, but Europeans overreacted; the United States did not back up its words with deeds. The mere prospect of U.S. participation in a diplomatic conference held in Panama in 1826 provoked a firestorm of opposition to the nation's political engagement in Central America. To be sure, the United States did provoke a war with Mexico in 1846 that led to the annexation of roughly half of Mexico's territory. But the United States otherwise tended to tread lightly in the rest of Latin America. Americans generally took a hands-off approach to the fortunes of republican ideals in the region, convinced that Creole aristocracies, mixed races, and Catholicism would stand in the way of successful democracy. Active support for liberal movements in Europe was similarly absent. The United States kept its distance, preferring not to take sides or risk entanglement in Europe's political intrigues.

Although the conduct of foreign policy generated its fair share of political controversy, debate over statecraft—at least until the 1820s—no longer provoked the bitter partisanship that it had before. Federalists suffered from their opposition to the War of 1812 and their own internal divisions, clearing the way for Republican domination. The ascendancy of the Republicans also stemmed from their embrace of central elements of the Federalist platform, including a more capable federal government, a national bank, investment in infrastructure, and tariffs to protect the nation's emerging industrial base. James Monroe, a Republican from Virginia as was Madison, won a landslide victory in the presidential election of 1816. He believed that his role was "not to be head of a party, but of the nation itself."[1] Following one of Monroe's tours aimed at building national unity, a Boston journalist in 1817 pronounced an "Era of Good

Feelings," a phrase that was to catch on.[2] The lopsided congressional election of 1818–1819 further strengthened Republican control, effectively bringing to an end the two-party system that had dominated the union's early years.

The political quiescence did not last long. The Republicans soon experienced plenty of factional infighting despite their political dominance.[3] Indeed, the election of John Quincy Adams in 1824—which was decided in the House since no candidate won a majority in the electoral vote—and of Andrew Jackson in 1828—Jackson was a populist president opposed to the Republican enthusiasm for stronger federal authority—led to the return of a two-party system. Jacksonian Democrats came to dominate the South while the Whigs eventually inherited the Hamiltonian mantle of the North's Federalists. Moreover, the escalating sectional divide over slavery would inflame debate over domestic and foreign policy for decades to come—ultimately splitting the union asunder. Nonetheless, the "Era of Good Feelings" was one of unusual political harmony; the United States had made remarkable progress in extricating itself from the geopolitics of Europe and the union was enjoying further consolidation and expansion. Following the War of 1812, in the words of historian Bradford Perkins, "reality and dream ossified into dogma, as they never had for the Founding Fathers."[4]

Consolidating and Expanding the Union

The population and political reach of the United States moved rapidly westward after the War of 1812. Before the war, roughly one-seventh of the nation's population lived west of the Appalachians. By 1840, one-third did so.[5] At the outbreak of the war, the United States was composed of eighteen states. By the end of the 1840s, there were thirty states in the union. Westward expansion prompted and was furthered by a burst of state-building in the form of both more capable political institutions and the construction of the far more extensive transportation network needed to move goods and people over long distances. Between 1816 and 1840, Americans built over 3,300 miles of canals.[6]

The prospect of material gain was the driving force behind westward expansion. Settlers were seeking arable land and new commercial opportunities. Southerners were particularly keen to extend slavery and cotton plantations to the west; cotton exports boomed after the end of the War of 1812 and the subsequent resuscitation of transatlantic trade. The state-building ambition of the federal government, which aided and abetted the westward flow of Americans, had geopolitical as well as economic intent. Pushing out the frontier would eliminate the threat posed to U.S. territory by Native Americans and European powers, bringing closer to realization the natural geographic security envisaged by the Founders.

The second Great Awakening, which stoked widespread religious fervor that peaked between 1830 and 1850, provided ideological backing for westward expansion. This second wave of revivalism extended well beyond the more religious communities of New England. Indeed, evangelism won many adherents in settlement communities on the frontier, fostered in part by traveling ministers and a growing missionary network that followed settlers westward. This religious revival mixed with westward expansion to generate a variant of the redeemer narrative that emphasized the nation's internal development rather than its messianic calling abroad. The United States still had a responsibility to share its experiment with the rest of the world. But for now, the primary mission was at home. The priority of Americans was to settle and tame the nation's interior—to turn what Abraham Lincoln called "the fairest portion of the earth" into a new Eden through the arrival of Christianity, republican government, and productivity and prosperity.[7] Secular and sacred justifications for westward expansion combined under the rubric of Manifest Destiny—the term popularized during the 1840s to capture the obligatory and ineluctable nature of the nation's march across the continent. In the words of historian Ernest Lee Tuveson, "What happened was that the possibilities for territorial expansion . . . came into a kind of chemical combination with the general Protestant theology of the millennium."[8]

Westward expansion for the most part enjoyed strong political support across the nation's regions; the prospect of arable land, economic opportunity, and continental security had equally strong allure in the North and South. Differences over whether the expansion of slavery should accompany the expansion of territory did, however, provoke a deep sectional rift—one that would slow the pace and scope of westward expansion and eventually help ignite the Civil War. The Missouri Compromise of 1820, at least temporarily, did succeed in reconciling westward expansion with sectional disagreement over the extension of slavery. The legislation preserved a political balance in Congress between the North and South by pairing the admission of Maine as a free state with that of Missouri as a slave state, and then prohibiting slavery in the Louisiana Territory (with the exception of Missouri) north of the 36°30′ parallel. This accommodation cleared the way for the continuation of expansion until the outbreak of the Mexican-American War in 1846, which prompted Representative David Wilmot (D/Free Soil-Pennsylvania) to submit to Congress a proposal to ban slavery in any territories that would be acquired from Mexico as a result of the war.[9] The legislation passed in the House but was defeated in the Senate, intensifying sectional conflict over expansion.

In 1854, the Kansas-Nebraska Act superseded the Missouri Compromise by permitting slavery above the 36°30´ parallel at the discretion of the local population. This maneuver opened the door to the further enlargement of the union. But it also deepened a two-party system that was already running along sectional lines, with the Republicans taking over from the Whigs the abolitionist agenda of the North and the Democrats representing the slaveholding interests of the South. Furthermore, the political balance of power was shifting decidedly in the North's favor. After California joined the union in 1850, free states outnumbered slaveholding states in the Senate, they had a larger population and thus greater weight in the House, and the wealth generated by the more commercialized economies of free states was fast outpacing that of the more agrarian South.[10] This growing political and economic imbalance meant that the stage was set for the South's secession—and the war that followed.

The westward extension of the frontier, whether or not it meant the spread of slavery, was blood-soaked. Native Americans bore the brunt of the suffering, experiencing a massive depopulation due to warfare, massacres, starvation, disease, and forced removal. Policy toward Native Americans evolved over time, with their organized removal to lands west of the Mississippi—primarily Oklahoma—beginning in 1830. In 1850, the United States began to transfer Native Americans to dedicated reservations to free up more arable land and to reduce the level of violence as white settlers continued to move west. State-sponsored warfare, more spontaneous settler violence against Native Americans, and the ills that accompanied repeated dislocation exacted a terrible toll.

As for foreign powers that were in America's way, the United States tended to take a far less coercive approach, opting for diplomacy rather than violence. After the War of 1812 ended, the United States struck a series of territorial bargains with Britain in the service of consolidating the nation's territory and borders. The Rush-Bagot Treaty and the Anglo-American Convention of 1818 set the boundary between the United States and Canada, limited militarization of the border region, and provided for joint Anglo-American control of the Oregon Country. In 1819, the United States and Spain concluded the Adams-Onís Treaty, which ceded Florida to the United States and established the border between Spanish Mexico and U.S.-claimed lands to the north. In 1842, the Webster-Ashburton Treaty settled residual border disputes between the United States and British Canada. Washington and London returned to the negotiating table in 1846, agreeing to divide the Oregon Territory at the 49° parallel, except for Vancouver Island, which remained in British hands. Lasting rapprochement between the United States and the United Kingdom and the demilitarization of the U.S.-Canadian border would await the turn of the century. But these diplomatic breakthroughs succeeded in getting Britain largely out of the way of western expansion and resolving potential conflicts over America's northern border.[11]

From the close of the War of 1812 until the outbreak of the Spanish-American War in 1898, the United States relied exclusively on diplomacy to clear Spain and Britain out of the way of westward expansion. Native Americans, however, were not alone in suffering violence as Americans pursued Manifest Destiny. When it came to Mexico, which attained independence from Spain in 1821, the United States eventually resorted to war to fulfill its territorial aspirations. The stage was set for eventual conflict when Texans revolted against the Mexican government, declaring independence in 1836 after a seven-month war with Mexican forces. By that time, American settlers represented upward of eighty percent of Texas's population, and "most Americans viewed the Texas Revolution . . . as a race war between brown Mexicans and white Texians."[12] Nonetheless, the United States did not yet open its doors to Texas, keen to avoid both a potential war with Mexico and the sectional dispute that would have accompanied the effort to integrate a large slaveholding territory into the union.[13]

James Polk, a Democrat who had represented Tennesee in Congress and then served as its governor, ran in the 1844 election on an expansionist platform, which included an explicit call for the annexation of Texas. Congress approved the annexation a few days before Polk took office in March 1845, and Texas became the twenty-eighth state at the end of that year. Polk then took advantage of a dispute with Mexico over Texas's southern border to orchestrate war with Mexico, which the United States handily won. The deal that accompanied the end of the war extended Texas's border to the Rio Grande and transferred to the United States much of what is today California, New Mexico, Arizona, Nevada, Utah, Wyoming, and Colorado—all for a price of $18.25 million.[14] In 1854, the Gadsden Purchase brought additional Mexican territory into the union. Some influential voices called for the United States to annex all of Mexico. But most Americans were not interested in either ruling over or integrating territory occupied primarily by a "mongrel" mix of Native Americans and blacks; they tended to view Mexico as "an immoral nation and Mexicans themselves as an inferior race practicing a suspect religion."[15]

Such opposition to annexation of lands occupied primarily by nonwhites served as a major obstacle to expansion into Latin America and the Caribbean throughout most of the nineteenth century.[16] Racial objections to territorial acquisitions beyond North America overrode the strong enthusiasm for expansion that emerged in the wake of the Mexican-American War. Along with Oregon, the acquisitions that resulted from the defeat of Mexico increased U.S. territory by roughly fifty percent. According to historian Amy Greenberg, "it was the crowning moment for Manifest Destiny" and would fuel calls for further expansion: "Victory in Mexico spurred expansionists in both sections of the country to push for more land, in Hawaii, Central America, the Yucatán, and particularly Cuba."[17] Nonetheless, as chronicled below, concern about dilution of the nation's racial and religious homogeneity as well as other constraints on expansion blocked this outward push until 1898. As LaFeber observes, "Out of the smoke and excitement of American expansionism in the 1850s, only the Gadsden Purchase actually emerged, although Cuba, Central America, Canada, and Hawaii were heatedly discussed."[18]

The issue of race plagued ongoing debate over territorial acquisitions in North America as well as farther afield. Westward expansion continued to exacerbate sectional tensions, with North and South parting ways over whether lands ceded by Mexico would be slaveholding. Southerners generally supported the war and saw it as a prized opportunity to extend slavery, while northerners for the most part were against the conflict with Mexico, viewed it as a war of aggression, and opposed the spread of slavery. This sectional divide only mounted during the 1850s, especially after the repeal of the Missouri Compromise in 1854. After his election in 1860, President Lincoln halted the further enlargement of the union in order to reduce sectional tensions. The move, however, backfired; the South viewed the further extension of slavery as essential to offsetting the North's growing political and economic dominance.[19] Conflict beckoned.

Projecting American Power: Commercial Ambition, Strategic Restraint

Despite the political difficulties entailed in navigating sectional differences over the westward extension of slavery, the United States eagerly expanded across North America during the decades after the War of 1812. Statecraft beyond North America stood in stark contrast. Successive administrations continued to honor the admonition of the Founders against foreign entanglement—and not just with Europe's imperial powers. Even in its own neighborhood, the United States refrained from extending geopolitical commitments; with the exception of its land grab from Mexico, it generally stayed out of Latin American and Caribbean affairs—save for the occasional short-term intervention aimed at protecting U.S. citizens and their economic interests. The nation's growing strength certainly tempted its leaders to embrace greater external ambition in the Western Hemisphere. President James Monroe in 1823 sternly warned Europeans off imperial ventures in Latin America, and Henry Clay, a Republican/ Whig who represented Kentucky in the House and Senate in addition to serving as secretary of state from 1825 to 1829, called for the United States to serve as the economic and geopolitical center of an "American system" that would encompass the hemisphere. But the bold rhetoric did not translate into action;

U.S. statecraft continued to be constrained by a political establishment that remained staunchly isolationist when it came to strategic commitments beyond North America.[20]

As during the founding era, Americans during the first half of the nineteenth century keenly sought to expand international trade and tap new markets. Exports tripled by the middle of the 1800s while imports quadrupled, with import duties providing the lion's share of federal revenue.[21] The size of the U.S. Navy increased in step with the overseas flow of trade. The U.S. Navy in 1822 established the West Indies Squadron, which patrolled the Caribbean, as well as the Pacific Squadron, which generally covered the waters extending from the coast of South America to Hawaii. The East Indies Squadron followed in 1835, patrolling the Pacific to Hawaii's west as well as the Indian Ocean. The Africa Squadron, which started operating in 1842, patrolled Africa's west coast. The United States made frequent use of its new naval capability, carrying out missions in numerous far-off locales, including Sumatra, Argentina, Peru, Nicaragua, China, Fiji, Uruguay, and Panama. Between 1852 and 1854, Commodore Perry famously mounted expeditions to Japan, leading to the country's economic opening to the West. In 1856, Congress passed the Guano Islands Act, which authorized U.S. citizens to peacefully claim uninhabited islands to collect guano—bird and bat excrement regularly used in making fertilizer and gunpowder. Americans soon laid claim to dozens of islands in far-flung seas.[22]

These missions and acquisitions, however, were all about expanding commerce, not projecting geopolitical influence or taking on new strategic commitments. In justifying to Congress the nation's increasing naval strength and reach, President John Quincy Adams argued in 1825 that "it were, indeed, a vain and dangerous illusion to believe that in the present or probable condition of human society a commerce so extensive and so rich as ours could exist and be pursued in safety without the continual support of a military marine."[23] Countering piracy, protecting American citizens and property, patrolling trade routes—these were the main missions of America's expanding fleet. When military officials sought to do more—Commodore Perry, for example, proposed colonizing the Ryukyu Islands as part of his effort to "open" Japan—they were regularly rebuffed by the civilian leadership.[24]

Resort to the use of force to change regimes abroad was similarly off-limits. In only one instance—in Nicaragua in 1857—did U.S. forces go into action with the primary aim of effecting regime change. Except in this case, the main objective of the U.S. operation was to *reverse* regime change, not enable it. The American military acted to secure the removal of William Walker, a U.S. citizen who had mounted a private effort to take control of Nicaragua and establish it as an English-speaking, slaveholding country that would attract American immigrants. The United States was using its growing power to prevent, not extend, new strategic commitments beyond its shores. Even as America's ability to extend its geopolitical reach grew in step with its naval power, its political readiness to do so remained quite limited.

The Debate over Hemispheric Ambition

During the decade following the end of the War of 1812, Americans heatedly debated whether to annex territories in the Caribbean and Latin America— or at least become more actively engaged in shaping political developments in the region. A number of factors augured for a new level of American ambi- tion. Independence movements were advancing in Latin America, giving the United States the opportunity to support the spread of republican government and expedite the departure of Europe's imperial powers from the hemisphere. Southerners eyed the annexation of new territory—Cuba, in particular—as a means of protecting slavery and strengthening the political weight of slave- holding states, while northerners saw in territorial expansion new commercial opportunities. The "Era of Good Feelings," coupled with the nation's growing population, prosperity, and power tempted Americans to make good on the as- piration of the Founders to establish the United States, in Hamilton's words, as "an ascendant in the system of American affairs . . . erecting one great American system, superior to the control of all transatlantic force or influence."[25]

A more ambitious strategy toward the hemisphere certainly had its advocates. Henry Clay long advocated for an "American system" that foresaw the union's consolidation as the pathway to hemispheric dominance. The nation's commer- cial and political success, Clay argued before Congress in 1820, would make the people of South America "yet more anxious to imitate our institutions, and to secure to themselves and to their posterity the same freedom which we enjoy." He maintained that the United States "should become the center of a system which would constitute the rallying point of human freedom against all the des- potism of the Old World," and went on to proclaim:"Let us become real and true Americans, and place ourselves at the head of the American system."[26] Clay envisioned a U.S.-led pan-American bloc committed to open trade, republican government, and leadership "by the force of example and by moral influence"— a system that would serve as a counterweight to a Europe still wedded to mon- archy and imperial trade preferences.[27]

Although Clay's vision of a hemispheric bloc anchored by the United States had many supporters, it did not come to fruition, stymied by a formidable cadre of opponents counseling a much more cautious and hands-off approach to the nation's southern neighbors. While serving as secretary of state, James Monroe made clear as early as 1811 that the United States, while supportive of the aspirations of its neighbors for independence, would be an interested spectator, not an active participant, in their quest for self-government. In Monroe's words, "the disposition shown by most of the Spanish provinces to separate from Europe and to erect themselves into independent states excites great interest here. As inhabitants of the same Hemisphere, as neighbors, the United States cannot be unfeeling spectators of so important a moment." But, Monroe cautioned, "the destiny of those provinces must depend on themselves."[28]

As Spain's Latin American colonies began to break away, beginning with Venezuela in 1811, the United States kept its distance. It not only refused to lend a hand, but also demurred on recognizing the new republics. Several considerations produced such caution. First, Spain still maintained its foothold in Florida, and the United States was loath to take steps that might alienate the Spanish crown and prolong its stay. Second, Washington feared that its intervention in Spanish Latin America could trigger geopolitical competition between Spain and the United States, prompting the Spanish to seek to reassert control over their colonies. Third, many Americans were skeptical that independent states in Latin America would be able to sustain republican government. They viewed Creole aristocracies, Catholicism, and the region's racial diversity as major impediments to stable democracy. Finally, the Founders' antipathy to interference in the domestic affairs of other nations still maintained a powerful, principled hold on U.S. policy. The United States was acquiring the ability to project its political influence beyond its shores, but doing so was inconsistent with President Washington's admonition against foreign entanglement.[29]

Strategic restraint, coupled with diplomacy, paid off, in 1819 yielding the Adams-Onís Treaty and the transfer of Spanish Florida to the United States. Once in control of Florida, the U.S. government felt less in thrall to Spain, prompting renewed debate about a more assertive U.S. policy toward Latin America, including recognizing the independence of Spain's former colonies. Secretary of State John Quincy Adams consistently made the case for continued restraint to President Monroe, who was inclined to provide active support to the republican cause. In an effort to undercut Clay and his dogged support for greater U.S. engagement, Adams wrote to Monroe in 1820 that "as to an American system, we have it; we constitute the whole of it; there is no community of interests or of principles between North and South America."[30]

The following year, the contest between Clay and Adams intensified. In May 1821, Clay called for the United States to support Latin American independence "by all means short of actual war." Doing so "would give additional tone, and hope, and confidence to the friends of liberty throughout the world."[31] Adams fundamentally disagreed in both private and public. In a speech on July 4, 1821, before the House of Representatives, he offered a rousing rebuttal—an address that has taken its place alongside Washington's Farewell Address as a definitive and eloquent defense of isolationism.

Adams's case against Clay's call for a more activist and assertive U.S. policy rested on three main arguments. First, despite the nation's growing ability to project its power and influence, Adams insisted that its security still depended upon keeping its distance from foreign entanglement. He was confident that the countries of Latin America would succeed in defeating imperial rule, noting in March 1821 that he had never doubted "that the final issue of their present struggle would be their entire independence of Spain." But Adams also insisted "that it was our true policy and duty to take no part in the contest," and he called for honoring "the principle of neutrality to *all* foreign wars."[32] In his July 4 speech, Adams famously declared that the United States "goes not abroad, in search of monsters to destroy." Even if motivated by a noble cause, what might begin as limited involvement risked irretrievably drawing the United States into unwanted and unwise commitments: "She well knows that by once enlisting under other banners than her own, were they even banners of foreign independence, she would involve herself beyond the power of extrication, in all the wars of interest and intrigue, of individual avarice, envy, and ambition, which assume the colors and usurp the standard of freedom."[33]

Second, echoing one of the main concerns of the Founders, Adams warned that ambition abroad could well come at the expense of freedom at home. Staying out of foreign wars was in his view "fundamental to the continuance of our liberties and of our Union."[34] He was concerned not only about the potential centralization of power that preoccupied Washington in his Farewell Address. Adams also worried that entanglement abroad would compromise the nation's exceptional character and its commitment to a brand of statecraft based on principle rather than power. He observed that the United States "has, in the lapse of nearly half a century, without a single exception, respected the independence of other nations while asserting and maintaining her own." To change course and pursue interference in the affairs of others would mean that "the fundamental maxims of her policy would insensibly change from liberty to force. . . . She might become the dictatress of the world. She would be no longer the ruler of her own spirit."[35] Intervention "in foreign wars, even wars for freedom," he reiterated on January 31, 1822, would "change the very foundations of our government from *liberty to power*."[36]

Third, Adams, like many of his colleagues, was skeptical that independence from Spain would bring republican government to America's southern neighbors; social hierarchy, Catholicism, and mixed race were not conducive to democratic government. "So far as they are contending for independence, I wish well their cause;" Adams wrote, "but I had seen and yet see no prospect that [Latins] would establish free and liberal institutions of government."[37] His doubts about the readiness of Latin America for republican government made Adams even more convinced that the United States should remain aloof from the region's struggles for independence. Adams concluded in his July 4 speech that the United States should be "the well-wisher to the freedom and independence of all," but "the champion and vindicator only of her own. She will recommend the general cause by the countenance of her voice, and the benignant sympathy of her example."[38] The United States may have been destined to spread republican government to the rest of the world, but it would do so by serving as a model, not through intervention in the affairs of other countries.

Adams's views initially prevailed over those of the camp calling for greater U.S. activism, forestalling any direct support to Latin America's new republics and helping convince Monroe to withhold recognition. In 1822, however, Monroe changed course and began recognizing Latin America's newly independent countries. With Spain having effectively come to terms with the loss of its colonies—it lacked both the will and the resources to reverse their independence—Monroe, driven in part by public pressure, deemed it advantageous to move ahead with recognition.[39] In 1823, he then laid out what later came to be known as the Monroe Doctrine, ostensibly inserting the United States more fully into hemispheric affairs. The move proved to be primarily rhetorical, however, producing little change to America's aversion to entanglement in the affairs of its southern neighbors.

The Monroe Doctrine

It was a British initiative more than the advance of independence movements in Latin America that spurred President Monroe to embrace a more assertive policy toward the hemisphere. British trade with Latin America had benefited handsomely from Spain's setbacks, prompting London in 1823 to propose to Washington that the two countries team up to support the independence of Spain's former colonies. British foreign secretary George Canning recommended that London and Washington stand together against "the recovery of the colonies" and oppose their transfer "to any other power," effectively warning all Europeans against harboring new imperial designs on Latin America.[40]

The proposal intrigued Monroe, who viewed it as an opportunity to extend U.S. influence in its neighborhood while promoting better relations with Britain. In addition, he saw cooperation with the British as a preventative measure against future European aggression. Monroe worried that if Europe's imperial powers took on new territories in Latin America, "they would, in the next instance, invade us."[41] Moreover, the conservative bent of most of Europe's major powers heightened fears of European intervention in the Americas to suppress independence movements in favor of Spanish rule. At the Congress of Verona in

1822, the members of the Concert, despite British objections, approved France's intervention in Spain to put down a rebellion against the monarchy. The following year, a sizable French force invaded Spain and restored the rule of King Ferdinand VII. Against this backdrop, Monroe was tempted to pursue a pact between the United States and Britain that could make European intervention in the Americas less likely and help distance the British from the continental monarchies. Monroe, however, also saw downsides to accepting the British proposal. A joint initiative with the British would contravene the Founders' admonition against entanglement in rivalries among Europe's great powers.[42] It would also extend to former Spanish territories in Latin America an effective U.S. commitment to defend their independence. Undecided about how to proceed, Monroe sought the advice of two of his predecessors—Thomas Jefferson and James Madison.

Jefferson and Madison both recommended that Monroe accept the British offer. Jefferson saw the proposal as advancing a number of paramount interests. He believed that taking up Canning on his proposal would enable the United States to draw its long-standing adversary into its camp. Cooperation with Great Britain would lure it away from Europe's tyrannical traditions and "detach her from the band of despots, bring her mighty weight into the scale of free government." Since Britain "is the nation which can do us the most harm of any one," Jefferson continued, "with her on our side we need not fear the whole world." Jefferson concluded that "if . . . we can effect a division in the body of the European powers, and draw over to our side its most powerful member, surely we should do it."[43] His analysis made clear that even after the Treaty of Ghent Americans tended to see Britain, due to its unmatched naval strength and ongoing imperial presence in the Western Hemisphere, as the foreign power posing the greatest potential threat to U.S. interests.

Jefferson also contended that teaming up with Britain was entirely consistent with the guiding principles of statecraft embraced during the founding era: "Our first and fundamental maxim should be, never to entangle ourselves in the broils of Europe; our 2d never to suffer Europe to intermeddle in Cis-Atlantic affairs. America, North & South, has a set of interests distinct from those of Europe, and peculiarly her own." In Jefferson's mind, taking up Canning's proposal would enable the United States to honor both principles; the United States could avoid entanglement in European affairs while pushing Europe out of its hemisphere. Even if a pact with Britain drew the United States into a war to defend Latin America against the return of European imperialism, "the war in which the present proposition might engage us . . . is not her war, but ours. Its object is to introduce and to establish the American system, of ousting from our land all foreign nations, of never permitting the powers of Europe to intermeddle with the affairs of our nations. It is to maintain our own principle, not to depart from it."[44]

Madison arrived at a similar conclusion, although he focused more on the importance of fashioning close ties between the United States and the newly independent states of Latin America. He argued that the United States should stand by its southern neighbors due to "our sympathy with their liberty & independence, [and] the deep interests we have in the most friendly relations with them." Madison maintained that "it is particularly fortunate that the policy of G. Britain, though guided by calculations different from ours, has presented a co-operation for an object the same with ours. With that co-operation we have nothing to fear from the rest of Europe; and with it the best reliance on success to our just & laudable views. There ought not to be any backwardness therefore, I think, in meeting her in the way she has proposed."[45]

Such unambiguous advice from his predecessors weighed heavily on Monroe, who was particularly concerned that Europe's continental monarchies could well seek the restoration of Spanish rule in Latin America.[46] Yet again, however, Monroe's more wary secretary of state made the case for exercising due caution. Adams argued that the United States should steer clear of Britain's offer and avoid extending political commitments to either Britain or Latin America's newly independent countries.

Adams was motivated in part by hopes of eventually adding Texas and Cuba to the union, and therefore wanted to avoid a pact with Britain that could preclude the future annexation of these territories—Texas had been under Spanish rule until 1821 and Cuba was still a Spanish colony. In his own summary of a cabinet meeting on the issue on November 7, 1823, Adams expressed his views as follows: "Without entering now into the enquiry of the expediency of our annexing Texas or Cuba to our Union, we should at least keep ourselves free to act as emergencies may arise, and not tie ourselves down to any principle which might immediately afterwards be brought to bear against ourselves." In addition, he was reluctant to tether U.S. diplomacy to that of Great Britain, concerned that doing so would not only constitute entanglement in Europe's rivalries, but also subordinate the United States to Britain's role as an overseer of the Americas. According to his notes from the November 7 cabinet meeting, Adams argued that the nation should not "come in as a cock-boat in the wake of the British man-of-war." Finally, Adams wanted not just Spain and France out of its neighborhood, but all European powers, including Britain and Russia. Adams was particularly keen to warn off Russia, which had in 1821 claimed sovereignty over Alaska and the Pacific Northwest (roughly what is today Washington and Oregon).[47]

Monroe ultimately found Adams's advice persuasive. He backed away from the British proposal in favor of a unilateral declaration of America's opposition to any new imperial forays in the Western Hemisphere. Monroe's initial inclination was to deliver a rhetorical broadside—a speech that would not only issue a strategic warning against future European interference in Latin America but also deliver an ideological blow to European monarchy. Monroe wanted to take sides in Europe's ongoing struggle between absolutism and republicanism by recognizing Greek independence from Turkey and censuring France's intervention in Spain to put down the rebellion against King Ferdinand VII.[48]

Adams successfully pushed back yet again, arguing before the cabinet that U.S. policy should entail "earnest remonstrance against the interference of the European powers by force with South America, but to disclaim all interference on our part with Europe; to make an American cause, and adhere inflexibly to that."[49] Adams also talked Monroe out of giving any formal U.S. assistance to Greece or recognizing Greek independence. In the meantime, he lobbied Congress to back away from a proposed resolution that called on the president to dispatch a diplomatic representative to Greece. The supporters of the resolution made the case that the United States had an obligation to provide at least symbolic and moral support to the Greek cause. But Adams insisted that inserting the United States into European affairs was not worth the risk of provoking European ire. He shared the view of Representative John Randolph (R-Virginia), who spoke for many when he insisted that the duty of Congress was to "guard the interests of the people of the United States, not to guard the rights of other people."[50] The House voted overwhelmingly to table the resolution.[51]

The Annual Message to Congress that Monroe delivered on December 2, 1823, reflected Adams's call "to make an American cause, and adhere inflexibly to that." Monroe admonished Europeans against new imperial adventures in the Western Hemisphere, while also pledging that the United States would refrain from interference in European affairs. The main thrust of what came to be called the Monroe Doctrine was that the United States and Europe should stay out of each other's neighborhoods. Referring to European powers, Monroe warned that "we should consider any attempt on their part to extend their system to any portion of this hemisphere as dangerous to our peace and safety." He reassured governments on the other side of the Atlantic that "with the existing colonies or dependencies of any European power we have not interfered and shall not interfere." But he also made clear that any new "interposition for the purpose of oppressing" the people of the Western Hemisphere would be seen as "the manifestation of an unfriendly disposition toward the United States." Monroe declared that "the American continents, by the free and independent condition which they have assumed and maintain, are henceforth not to be considered as subjects for future colonization by any European powers."

At the same time that he cautioned Europe against future interference in the Western Hemisphere, Monroe pledged that the United States would reciprocate when it came to Europe. He noted that Americans "have always been anxious and interested spectators" of European affairs and that they favored "the liberty and happiness of their fellow-men on that side of the Atlantic." But Monroe also affirmed that the United States would avoid entanglement in Europe's geopolitics: "In the wars of the European powers in matters relating to themselves we have never taken any part, nor does it comport with our policy to do so." While expressing his disappointment about the ongoing repression of liberal movements on the other side of the Atlantic, Monroe acknowledged pragmatic acceptance of Europe's political preferences. It was the policy of the United States, he asserted, "not to interfere in the internal concerns of any of its powers; to consider the government de facto as the legitimate government for us; to cultivate friendly relations with it."[52]

Monroe's 1823 Annual Message thus ended up being quite a conservative statement of the nation's strategic objectives. On the surface, Monroe extended an ambitious American claim to a *droit de regard* over the Western Hemisphere. But in reality, he laid out the modest scope of the nation's geopolitical intent. Monroe warned only against any *new* imperial adventures in the Americas, while accepting "the existing colonies or dependencies of any European power." And when it came to Europe's own affairs, the United States would not only take a hands-off approach, but it would confer legitimacy upon and pursue amicable relations with liberal and illiberal governments alike. The United States may have been the redeemer nation, but it was certainly taking its time in fulfilling its messianic obligation beyond its shores.

Despite Monroe's explicit deference to Europe's own political preferences, European leaders reacted to his speech with disdain. Clemens von Metternich, Austria's foreign minister, wrote that the U.S. president had "astonished Europe by a new act of revolt, more unprovoked, fully as audacious, and no less dangerous than the former." A French newspaper derided Monroe as "a dictator armed with a right of suzerainty over the entire New World."[53] The Russian emperor, Tsar Alexander, wrote that the speech "enunciates views and pretensions so exaggerated, it establishes principles so contrary to the rights of the European powers, that it merits only the most profound contempt."[54]

The harsh reaction notwithstanding, Europeans actually had little to worry about. Monroe did recognize the independence of Spain's former dependencies and he laid claim to greater American influence over the Western Hemisphere. Moreover, the address won broad public support by tapping into the long-standing national aspiration for more hemispheric sway. Monroe's vision of a more ambitious brand of U.S. statecraft also complemented well the nation-building agenda that he laid out in the same speech, which included a call for major investment in domestic infrastructure.

Nonetheless, Monroe's speech led to no significant change in U.S. policy. Latin American governments generally welcomed a principled U.S. stance against new bouts of European imperialism. But the United States continued

to avoid more activist engagement in the region. When a number of newly independent countries in the region requested that the United States make good
on its new policy by providing economic and military assistance, Washington
turned them down.[55] When Britain reasserted control over the Falkland Islands
in 1833 and established British Honduras as a crown colony in 1862—moves
that violated the spirit and letter of the Monroe Doctrine—the United States
did nothing. To be sure, President James Polk launched a war against Mexico in
1846, a conflict that led to the incorporation into the United States of a substantial portion of Mexican territory. But it would not be until the end of the century that the United States would seek to assert dominance over its hemisphere
by pushing Europeans out of the Americas and regularly resorting to coercive
measures to pursue its economic and geopolitical interests in the Caribbean and
Latin America.

The Panama Congress

Monroe may have articulated a new vision of hemispheric ambition, but there
was little prospect of turning rhetorical aspiration into reality given Congress's
tenacious commitment to geopolitical isolation. Despite the country's growing
ability to project its power and influence beyond its borders—and the nationalistic temptation to do so—the Founders' injunction against entangling
commitments continued to guide U.S statecraft. The ideological and political
strength of this isolationist consensus became clear during debate over U.S. participation in the Panama Congress of 1826.

Venezuelan leader Simón Bolívar was the most prominent figure behind
Latin America's push for independence. In 1826, he hosted a diplomatic
conference in Panama City to which the United States was invited. The
objectives were to discuss the prospects for cooperation among American
republics and to map out their relationships with Spain and other European
powers. President John Quincy Adams, who had taken office in 1825,
as well as his secretary of state, Henry Clay, supported U.S. participation. Many members of Congress were staunchly opposed. The question
of whether the United States should send a delegation to the conference
proved remarkably controversial, triggering a heated political debate
that a New York newspaper called of "extraordinary magnitude" and "the
most difficult and delicate that has been presented to the public since the
commencement of our glorious revolution."[56] Historian Charles William
Hackett labeled consideration of the issue "one of the severest parliamentary battles in [Congress's] history."[57] Indeed, many scholars of this era tend
to see the dispute over U.S. participation in the Panama meeting as marking
the end of the "Era of Good Feelings" and the beginning of a new two-party

system divided between progressive Whigs in the North and Jacksonian Democrats in the South.

The mere prospect of attendance at the meeting provoked a political firestorm because it served as a litmus test of the nation's readiness for a more adventurous brand of statecraft. Indeed, when he appealed to Congress to approve and fund the mission to Panama, President Adams explicitly argued that it was time for the nation to move beyond George Washington's admonition against foreign entanglement and instead help consolidate independence and republican institutions in Latin America. Effectively, the greater strategic reach envisaged in the Monroe Doctrine was going up against the doctrinal isolationism set forth in the Farewell Address. The ensuing debate in Congress revealed profound antipathy to a more activist U.S. role in Latin America. The Monroe Doctrine may have been well received when it was delivered in 1823. Nonetheless, after the invitation to the Panama meeting forced Congress to more fully consider the scope of U.S. engagement in Latin America, legislators proved remarkably reluctant to countenance an emboldened U.S. role in the Western Hemisphere— even one that entailed only diplomatic representation at a regional conference.

Consistently cautious about deeper U.S. engagement in Latin America, Adams was initially reluctant to support the dispatch of a U.S. delegation to the Panama Congress, fearful that it risked committing the United States to supporting, and possibly defending, the region's newly independent countries. However, according to historian Jeffrey Malanson, "once he had received assurances . . . that the United States would not be required to take part in any discussions, debates, or negotiations of a belligerent or binding sort, he agreed to attend."[58] Adams publicly broached the issue in the Annual Message to Congress that he delivered on December 6, 1825. He noted that he had already accepted the invitation to the Panama Congress, and that the next step entailed the appointment of the members of the delegation. Well aware that many members of Congress would harbor reservations about participation, he reassured them that U.S. representatives to the meeting would take part only "so far as may be compatible with that neutrality from which it is neither our intention nor the desire of the other American states that we should depart."[59]

Despite the qualification, the announcement of impending U.S. participation in the conference stunned many members of the House and Senate, who were upset that Adams had not consulted the legislature before accepting the invitation. More important, they were concerned that participation would constitute a tacit, if not explicit, U.S. commitment to the independence of Spain's former colonies, a move that risked provoking the Spanish. Sending a U.S. delegation to Panama would therefore contravene the injunction of the Founders against extending political connections to other countries and would risk entangling the United States in a new round of rivalry with a European power.[60]

The stage was set for a major confrontation between the White House and Congress. When Adams at the end of December requested Senate approval of his nominees for the delegation, the Senate Foreign Relations Committee took it upon itself to evaluate whether the United States should participate in the Congress, not just to assess the qualifications of Adams's proposed ministers. The committee proceeded—unanimously—to vote down the dispatch of a delegation on the grounds "that it is not expedient, at this time, for the United States to send any Ministers to the Congress of American nations, assembled at Panama."[61] Opponents of U.S. participation then filibustered for months.

The full Senate eventually approved the mission in March of 1826—more out of loyalty to Adams than enthusiasm for participation in the Congress.[62] After another combative discussion in the House, that chamber begrudgingly authorized funding for the delegation. The Senate concurred, clearing the way for the dispatch of the mission. But one delegate died before he could attend and the other arrived after the meeting had concluded.[63] And even though Congress did in the end agree to the mission, debate in both the Senate and House revealed widespread opposition to Adams's effort to insert the United States into Latin American affairs. Indeed, Congress's profound reluctance to support U.S. participation in what was nothing more than a diplomatic gathering effectively closed off serious debate about implementation of the Monroe Doctrine for the ensuing two decades. According to Malanson, the political row over the Panama Congress "represented the nadir of the Monroe Doctrine."[64]

Multiple strains of isolationist logic informed opposition to U.S. participation in the Panama Congress. For starters, detractors of the mission remained convinced that it would end up saddling the United States with political and strategic commitments beyond its borders—commitments that they deemed inconsistent with U.S. interests and with the foundational principles of U.S. grand strategy. In making his case for U.S. participation, Adams went out of his way to address such concerns. The delegation would not "take part in any deliberations of a belligerent character; that the motive of their attendance is neither to contract alliances, nor to engage in any undertaking or project importing hostility to any other nation." He stressed that participation would reinforce the restriction on colonization set forth in the Monroe Doctrine, but that each country was solely responsible for making good on this commitment. In Adams's words, "an agreement between all the parties represented at the meeting that each will guard *by its own means* against the establishment of any future European colony within its borders, may be found advisable."[65]

Many senators found Adams's arguments unconvincing. Senator Robert Hayne (Jacksonian Democrat [JD]-South Carolina) claimed that U.S. participation in the Panama meeting would "violate the maxim of the Father of his Country [George Washington], which enjoins upon us, as the most sacred of duties, 'to cultivate peace and honest friendship with all nations, entangling alliances with none.'"[66] Senator Hugh White (JD/Whig-Tennessee) similarly declared that "if this mission should be advised, a new era will have commenced in the history of our foreign relations. Have peace with, and good will towards, all nations; entangling alliances with none—has been our cardinal principle in times past." Many senators were worried that the Monroe Doctrine had already effectively extended a strategic commitment by encouraging leaders in Latin America to believe that the United States would, if need be, help defend them against a European effort to reassert colonial rule. For Senator White, attendance at the Panama Congress would only confirm this notion: "If we send Ministers, and an agreement is entered into, then, indeed, will the United States be *pledged*" to the defense of the region.[67] White, Hayne, and a good number of other senators were skeptical of Adams's claim that U.S. participation would not compromise the nation's neutrality, arguing that attendance at the conference would automatically make the United States a co-belligerent of Latin America's republics and poison the country's relationship with Spain.

Despite these objections, the full Senate eventually overturned the negative recommendation of the Foreign Relations Committee and approved the delegation, leaving it to Adams to convince the House to appropriate funds for the mission. Aware of the objections raised in the Senate, he directly confronted the claim that he was breaking with the Founders by departing from the guidance contained in Washington's Farewell Address. Adams argued that Washington's injunction against political connections with other countries was "founded upon the circumstances in which our country and the world around us were situated at the time when it was given." With respect to Europe, he maintained that the United States still enjoyed a "detached and distant situation"—and should continue to steer clear. But times had changed in Latin America, which had been transformed from a colonial outpost of Europe into a region populated by republics. And with these new republics, Adams maintained, "we have an immensely growing commercial, and must have and have already important political, connections; with reference to whom our situation is neither distant nor detached; whose political principles and systems of government, congenial with our own, must and will have an action and counteraction upon us and ours to which we cannot be indifferent if we would."[68]

Adams thus made the admonitions of the Farewell Address temporal and geographically circumscribed rather than timeless and universal. He also argued that the United States should base its relations with other countries on the character of their governments, contravening Washington's counsel that the nation "should hold an equal and impartial hand" with all countries.[69] For Adams, political connections were a "must" with Latin America, whose principles and systems of government were "congenial with our own." In contrast, Europe was still enthralled to monarchy, and hence "has still her set of primary interests with which we have little or a remote relation. Our distant and detached situation with reference to Europe remains the same." Adams concluded that "the acceptance of this invitation, therefore, far from conflicting with the counsel or the policy of Washington, is directly deducible from and conformable with it."[70]

Adams's arguments may have been reasoned and reasonable, but he was way ahead of his times. Many members of Congress recoiled at the prospect of amending Washington's admonitions against foreign entanglement—even if with respect to only Latin America. Like the Senate, the House in the end remained loyal to Adams and approved funding for the Panama Mission. But it had minimal enthusiasm for Adams's reinterpretation of the Farewell Address. Indeed, his efforts to provide a geopolitical and ideological justification for a more activist foreign policy in the Western Hemisphere provoked a sharp backlash.

Representative Louis McLane (F/JD-Delaware) proposed an amendment reaffirming that the United States would continue its original policy of shunning political connections with all countries, including those in Latin America.[71] His stated goal was "to embrace all those principles which had characterized the policy of the United States from our earliest history . . . [and] to preserve that policy unimpaired."[72] James Hamilton (JD-South Carolina) chided Adams for attempting to reinterpret the Farewell Address, noting that it was "founded on the then and ever enduring circumstances of our country."[73] James Buchanan (R/JD-Pennsylvania), who would later become secretary of state (1845–1849) and president (1857–1861), declared, "a crisis has now arrived, in which it is the duty of this House to take a firm stand in favor of the ancient and the approved policy of the country." He argued that Adams was misguided to draw any distinctions between Europe and Latin America when it came to geopolitical engagement; the United States should keep its distance from both. "We have ourselves grown great," Buchanan insisted, "by standing alone, and pursuing an independent policy. This path has conducted us to national happiness and national glory. Let us never abandon it."[74] Edward Livingston (JD-Louisiana) turned Adams's argument on its head, contending that it was the Monroe Doctrine, not the Farewell Address, that was circumstantial and time-limited. Latin America's newly independent nations may have needed U.S. support in 1823, but no longer in 1826. Monroe's address was "related only to the state of things that then existed. . . . The circumstances under which the declaration was made, have passed away."[75]

If McLane's amendment aimed primarily at defending the doctrinal isolationism of the Farewell Address, a second amendment, proposed by William Rives (JD/Whig-Virginia), was about avoiding binding commitments and preserving the nation's right to unilateral action. Rives wanted to prohibit any "compact or engagement" that would constitute a pledge on behalf of the

United States to uphold the independence of the hemisphere's new republics.[76] Many members shared his discomfort with the potential for participation in the Panama Congress to constitute a tacit commitment to uphold the Monroe Doctrine, by force if necessary. The United States should reserve the right to act as it saw fit, and not allow itself to be hemmed in by expectations that it would defend the independence of the hemisphere's new republics.

Many in Congress were also skeptical about the prospects for republican government in Latin America and therefore doubted that U.S. support was worth the effort. Senator John Berrien (JD-Georgia) contended that incompatible cultures would prevent any meaningful connection between the United States and the republics of Latin America, which "differ from us in every particular, in language, religion, laws, manners, customs, habits, as a mass, and as individuals. . . . Are not their interests, in many respects, different from ours?"[77] During the debate in the House, John Forsyth (R/JD-Georgia) agreed, noting that "our will cannot control our neighbors, unless enforced by our power." Expressing doubts about the viability of democratic governance in Latin America, he asked, "do we mean to force our American neighbors to be free, contrary to their wishes?"[78]

The House set aside the proposed amendments—in large part because many members did not believe the chamber had the authority to issue diplomatic instructions to the president—and instead voted forward a clean appropriations bill by a vote of 134 to 60, which the Senate then approved on May 3, 1826, by a vote of 23 to 19.[79] The mission would go forward. But the bruising debate in Congress revealed little appetite for moving beyond the strict interpretation of isolationism that emerged from the founding era. It did not help matters that Congress's tortured consideration of the issue contributed to such a lengthy delay in the arrival of the U.S. delegate that he missed the meeting. Adams's bid to push U.S. statecraft beyond its previous limits thus turned into a political fiasco. His appeals to Congress to make good on the more ambitious brand of statecraft articulated in the Monroe Doctrine won over very few members. According to Malanson, "by 1826 . . . many felt that the doctrine had served its purpose and now belonged to the annals of history."[80]

The Return of the Two-Party System

The prospect of U.S. participation in the Panama Congress produced such heated debate primarily because it was a test of the nation's readiness for foreign entanglement. But a number of other political and ideological forces were also in play. Debate over participation became a proxy for a broadening split that was emerging within the Republican Party. A modernizing wing, led by Adams and Clay, envisaged a stronger federal government that would guide commercial expansion, provide protective tariffs for the North's emerging industries, invest in infrastructure, and open new markets through economic and political engagement beyond the nation's borders. The export of republican institutions and the spread of political and religious pluralism were part of the agenda; the United States would play a more prominent role in shaping the world beyond its borders.

In the meantime, a populist wing of the party was forming in opposition to Adams's agenda; John Calhoun, Andrew Jackson, and Senator Martin Van Buren (D-New York) were among its key figures. This faction was hostile to the further centralization of power in the hands of the federal government and to a more activist brand of U.S. statecraft, focusing instead on the interests of agrarian slaveholders, the protection of states' rights, and the need to keep the nation's foreign relations restricted to commercial engagement. The populists took sharp exception to the more cosmopolitan program of the modernizers. They wanted to keep shielding the nation from the world beyond its borders, not go out and shape it.

Even though debate over participation in the Panama Congress dominated the congressional session that followed Adams's Annual Message in December, populist Republicans objected to other aspects of the vision he laid out in his address. Adams used the speech to describe a bold agenda that included significant investments in canals and roads, an enlarged navy with far-ranging missions, and new educational institutions and scientific explorations. In making the case for public investment, he argued that the United States needed to capitalize on its political and economic success to take its place among the ranks of major powers: "While foreign nations less blessed with that freedom which is power than ourselves are advancing with gigantic strides in the career of public improvement, were we to slumber in indolence or fold up our arms and proclaim to the world that we are palsied by the will of our constituents, would it not be to cast away the bounties of Providence and doom ourselves to perpetual inferiority?"[81]

The populists recoiled at Adams's vision, believing that it constituted, according to historian Robert Remini, little more than "one gigantic grab for power" by the federal government.[82] Adams's opponents resented his overall agenda—but then focused their obstructive ire on blocking participation in the Panama Congress. Referring to Adams's decision to accept the invitation to the Panama meeting without first consulting Congress, Senator Van Buren remarked that "the inroads which the insinuating, not to say insidious, influence of Executive authority has made upon the rights and privileges of this body . . . are great indeed."[83] Opposition to participation in Panama became a rallying cry for the populists and, in the view of many historians, was one of the "political harbingers of the Jacksonian period."[84] Adams's ambitious program for "public improvement" and the perceived threat it posed to states' rights proved to be, in Malanson's words, "the first salvo in a renewed oppositional political system."[85]

The "Era of Good Feelings" was giving way to the return of an antagonistic two-party system, a transformation quickened by Adams's speech and the ensuing debate over the Panama Congress. Indeed, voting in Congress on the issue generally ran along regional and socio-economic lines, with representatives from the more commercialized North and urban centers in the South generally supporting U.S. participation, and those from more remote and agrarian areas in the South generally against sending a U.S. delegation. Opponents of U.S. participation explicitly justified their position by referencing the South's struggle to preserve its political rights, claiming that they were acting in the "spirit of '98"—a reference to the era of the Alien and Sedition Acts of 1798, which many southerners saw as little more than partisan overreach by the North.[86] The political ascent of Jacksonian Democrats in the South and Whigs in the North institutionalized the reemergence of a political system divided along sectional lines. References to the "spirit of '98" made clear that the feud between Jeffersonian and Hamiltonian traditions was alive and well.

Race, Slavery, and U.S. Statecraft

Debate over the Panama Congress laid bare one other issue that helped fuel the return of a two-party system: racism and the sectional divide over slavery. By proposing U.S. participation in the conference, Adams was effectively endorsing a more cosmopolitan and activist brand of statecraft in a nonwhite region. Moreover, the Americans dispatched to Panama would be engaging their Latin American counterparts on an equal footing. Opponents of the mission expressed disdain for the prospect of American diplomats participating in negotiations with mixed-race delegates from Latin America. Many in Congress thought that the United States should remain aloof from what they saw, in the words of historian Matthew Karp, as "a second-rate region defined primarily by aspects of racial difference."[87] Representative John Randolph, for example, was repulsed by the notion of U.S. delegates working "beside the native African, their American descendants, the mixed breeds, the Indians, and the half breeds, without any offense or scandal at so motley a mixture."[88] Religious prejudice reinforced racist opposition to deepening U.S. engagement in Latin America. Protestants uncomfortable with the increasing number of Catholic immigrants wanted the United States to cordon itself off from the predominantly Catholic populations of Latin America. According to historian Paul Naish, "native-born Protestant Americans uneasy about the rapid influx of immigrant Papists shuddered at Cuba and Brazil as models of societies with Catholic majorities. . . . Latin America's casual race relations, unstable governments, and exotic Catholicism kept it at a secure re-move from the United States."[89]

Congress's debate over U.S. participation in the Panama Congress similarly exposed and intensified sectional differences over slavery and the relationship between independence movements and abolition. The North and South may have agreed on Monroe's admonition against European imperialism in America's neighborhood, but they differed on the future of slavery in the hemisphere. Congressional delegations from the North, eyeing markets in Latin America and supporting abolition, generally favored U.S. participation in the conference. In contrast, congressional delegations from the South, for the most part opposed to participation in the conference, worried that direct U.S. support for indepen-dence movements in Latin America would by association endorse abolition—and ultimately threaten slavery at home.

Senator Berrien did not mince his words when it came to the prospect of conducting diplomacy with free blacks: "We receive no mulatto Consuls, or black Ambassadors from her [Haiti]. And why? Because the peace of eleven States in this Union will not permit the fruits of a successful negro insurrection to be exhibited among them. It will not permit black Consuls and Ambassadors to establish themselves in our cities, and to parade through our country, and give their fellow blacks in the United States, proof in hand of the honors which await them, for a like successful effort on their part."[90] Relatedly, one southern senator who ended up supporting participation in the conference did so largely to defend slaveholding; he wanted the U.S. delegation to warn Latin Americans against invading Cuba or fomenting insurrection among its slaves. At the time, rumors were circulating that Mexico and Colombia intended to team up to in-vade and liberate the island.[91]

The North/South differences over slavery that contributed to sectional dis-agreement over U.S. participation in the Panama Congress were to continue to stymie debate about U.S. engagement in the Caribbean and Latin America for the ensuing decades. With the North looking to expand commerce and free labor and the South looking primarily to defend, if not expand, the geographic scope of slavery, this regional divide proved to be an insurmountable obstacle to those advocating for a more expansive policy. Americans were determined to proceed westward across their continent—and therefore came up with innova-tive solutions, such as the Missouri Compromise, to reconcile expansion with the sectional divide over slavery. But when it came to expansion further afield, no such solutions were forthcoming. Sectional differences over slavery played an important role in ensuring that Manifest Destiny stopped at the water's edge.

In 1848, President Polk announced his intent to buy Cuba from Spain and admit it to the union, a proposal that he and other Democrats saw as a way to augment the South's clout in Congress. The prospect of a lucrative increase in trade attracted support among northerners. Nonetheless, Spanish opposition to giving up Cuba and sectional disagreement over whether the island would join the union as a free or slave state prevented Polk from moving forward. Debate about the possible annexation of Hawaii ran into the same obstacle. Hawaii was below the 36°30′ parallel and therefore would have been admitted as a slave state, an outcome unacceptable to both Hawaiians and northerners. Southern states were, however, unwilling to back down and opposed territorial expansion that risked threatening slavery rather than consolidating it. As Matthew Karp observes, "The preservation of slave institutions took priority over the acquisition of new land."[92]

The sectional divide over slavery not only worked against territorial expansion into the Caribbean, Latin America, and Pacific, but it also encouraged a hands-off approach when it came to the spread of republican values. Monroe in 1823 warned Europeans against "any attempt on their part to extend their system to any portion of this hemisphere."[93] Adams followed up in 1826 with his affirmation that governance in Latin America was "congenial with our own."[94] But when it came to concrete steps to advance the fortunes of democracy among its southern neighbors, the United States did virtually nothing. Slaveholders were fearful that the North's progressive agenda, if embraced for Latin America, would eventually come their way.[95] The same went for policy toward Europe. The South generally opposed direct U.S. support to liberal movements in Europe, concerned that doing so would eventually threaten slaveholding at home. If the United States interfered in the affairs of other nations, warned the *New Orleans Bulletin*, "we will be the first who will be interfered with. . . . Of all the people upon the earth's surface, the Southern people are the last to think of, much less attempt to enforce, doctrines of this character."[96]

Southern opposition played a role in blocking material support to the liberal revolutions that swept Europe in 1848. The upheaval elicited intense interest in the United States and provoked heated debate about whether Americans should take action to buttress the fortunes of European democracy. But paralleling the reaction to the Greek Revolution in the 1820s, the U.S. government ended up providing only its best wishes. Lazlo Kossuth, a leader of the Hungarian Revolution who fled the country in the face of Austrian repression, was greeted as a hero when he visited the United States in 1851–1852. During Kossuth's visit, Henry Clay acknowledged that republican government in Europe was under siege and affirmed that "you require material aid." But he went on to argue that "far better it is for ourselves, for Hungary, and for the cause of liberty, that, adhering to our wise, pacific system, and avoiding the distant wars of Europe, we should keep our lamp burning brightly on this Western shore as a light to all nations, than to hazard its utter extinction amid the ruins of fallen or falling republics in Europe."[97] President Millard Fillmore (1850–1853) agreed, affirming that the nation's "true mission is not to propagate our opinions, or impose upon other countries our form of government, by artifice or force." Instead, the United States should "teach by example and show by our success, moderation and justice, the blessings of self-government and the advantages of free institutions."[98]

* * *

Between the end of the War of 1812 and the outbreak of the Civil War, the United States took advantage of its rapid growth in population and wealth to push its way to the Pacific coast while adding to the union a sizable portion of Mexico's territory. Determined U.S. diplomacy with European powers helped reduce their imperial footprint in the Americas. The United States also relied on its growing naval strength to expand significantly overseas trade.

Nonetheless, when it came to geopolitical engagement beyond North America, U.S. grand strategy remained fundamentally isolationist. Despite the country's growing ability to project its power and the political temptation to do so, the United States continued to steer clear of foreign commitments. Fear of the strategic dangers that would likely accompany foreign entanglement, a tenacious ideological attachment to unilateralism, populist resistance to the centralization of power that would necessarily accompany foreign ambition, and racism and the sectional divide over slavery all combined to prevent any significant departure from the doctrine of geopolitical detachment handed down by the Founders.

The Civil War, Reconstruction, and the Rise of American Power: Restraint Amid Ascent

The Civil War had the potential to be a strategic turning point for the United States. The defeat of the Confederacy and the abolition of slavery seemingly removed a political cleavage that had long blocked expansion into the Caribbean and Latin America. The exertions of the war bequeathed to the United States a strengthened central government, including a large military establishment, new powers of taxation, and a more unified currency system. The second half of the nineteenth century was also an era of unprecedented economic growth for the United States; the nation emerged as one of the world's leading industrial powers, giving it the wherewithal to acquire commensurate geopolitical influence.

Despite its increasing ability to extend its strategic reach well beyond its own territory, the United States continued to pursue a grand strategy of geopolitical isolation. To be sure, territorial expansion had strong advocates. William Seward, secretary of state under President Lincoln and President Andrew Johnson (1865–1869), was an avowed expansionist, keen to annex Canada and Alaska as well as territories in Latin America and the Caribbean. Johnson's successor, President Ulysses Grant (1869–1877), was a strong supporter of southward expansion. President Benjamin Harrison (1889–1993) fashioned an effective protectorate over Samoa alongside Britain and Germany, attempted to annex Hawaii, and ordered the construction of the nation's first battleships, a move that laid the foundation for a navy capable of projecting the nation's geopolitical strength to distant theaters, not just protecting the nation's coasts and commerce.

But despite the country's impressive economic growth, the rapid expansion of foreign trade, and the increase in the size and range of the U.S. Navy, the opponents of foreign entanglement staunchly stood their ground—and

generally prevailed. Seward, with the Senate's consent, did succeed in purchasing Alaska from Russia in 1867. Americans laid claim to additional guano
islands. The United States also secured access to three maritime footholds in the
Pacific—Midway Atoll in 1867, Pago Pago in Samoa in 1878, and Pearl Harbor
in Hawaii in 1887. Nonetheless, these ports were to serve as forward coaling stations to support seaborne commerce, not strategic outposts for projecting the
nation's geopolitical ambition. In the meantime, Congress refused to go further,
consistently rejecting proposals to annex Santo Domingo, Cuba, the Danish
West Indies, Hawaii, and other territories to the south and west. The United
States had the material capability to acquire sizable territory beyond North
America—but not yet the political inclination.

The main strategic and political arguments that sustained the isolationist consensus from the founding era until the Civil War continued to guide U.S. grand
strategy during the second half of the 1800s. The temptation to assert control
over weaker neighbors could not overcome fear of entanglement in foreign
conflicts and aversion to interference in the affairs of other nations. The defeat
of the Confederacy ended the formal discord over the extension of slavery that
stymied southward expansion prior to the Civil War. But racism continued to
shape foreign policy, with most Americans opposed to incorporating into the
union or ruling over nonwhite populations. In addition, the nation's expanding
commercial engagement in East Asia meant that anti-immigrant sentiment focused not just on blacks and Latin Americans. Congress in 1882 passed legislation banning arrivals of laborers from China, for the first time—but not the
last—imposing restrictions on immigration based on country of origin.

Isolationism continued its hold on U.S. grand strategy through the balance
of the 1800s—but it did not quite last the century. President William McKinley
(1897–1901) in 1898 launched a war against Spain that led to not only its expulsion from Cuba but also America's imperial expansion into the Caribbean
and Pacific—the subject of the next chapter. But the harbingers of a change
of course became apparent even before McKinley took office. A succession
of post–Civil War presidents made a run at annexing territory outside North
America. Harrison embarked on the construction of battleships and was an
avowed expansionist. Had Grover Cleveland (1885–1889, 1893–1897) not
won a second term in 1892 and denied Harrison reelection, territorial expansion
into the Caribbean and Pacific may well have occurred under Harrison's watch.
And Cleveland himself, although opposed to the annexation of new territories,
did continue the construction of battleships and flexed the United States' diplomatic muscle in Latin America.

These stirrings of geopolitical ambition had multiple sources. Domestic
developments, discussed in the next chapter, were paramount, but events abroad
also played a role. The closing decades of the 1800s were an era of national

consolidation in Europe. Germany and Italy became unified countries in the early 1870s, both a product and a cause of rising nationalist sentiment in Europe. German unification and industrialization would soon upset Europe's balance of power and contribute to intensified competition and expansion in the imperial periphery. Americans responded by taking steps, including securing access to Pago Pago and Pearl Harbor, to maintain and expand trade across the Pacific. Technological change—internal-combustion engines, telephones, radios, electric lights—hastened the pace of shifts in the balance of power and increased commercial and political interaction across national boundaries. Americans took full advantage of these and other innovations, contributing to a rapid rise in American power. In this respect, the forces leading to the Spanish-American War and the burst of U.S. expansion that accompanied it were long in the making. Nonetheless, isolationism continued its virtual lock on U.S. grand strategy from the end of the Civil War in 1865 until the outbreak of war against Spain in 1898.

The Civil War: "One War at a Time"

The outbreak of the Civil War effectively put on hold consideration of potential expansion into the Caribbean, Latin America, and the Pacific. The divided nation focused its resources and attention on the conflict at home. Foreign trade plummeted, primarily due to the North's blockade of southern ports. The South's hope of expanding the union into the Caribbean in order to protect slavery and enhance the power of slaveholding states was extinguished in step with the Confederacy's defeat. As historian Robert May puts it, "the [South's] dream of a Caribbean empire became one of the first casualties of the Civil War."[1]

The demands of the Civil War not only put on hold consideration of territorial expansion, but they also reinforced the North's aversion to European entanglements. The Confederacy sought assistance from both Britain and France, seeking to draw them into the conflict. Although both countries remained nominally neutral during the war, London effectively sided with the Confederacy. The South's successful secession would break the union into two weaker halves, countering the threat that a rising and unitary United States would pose to Britain's geopolitical sway. Despite British discomfort with the South's commitment to slavery, London also preferred its more conservative social order to the North's liberalizing ambition and its challenge to European monarchism.[2] Accordingly, London's declaration of neutrality did not prevent it from aiding the Confederacy. The British recognized the Confederacy as a legal belligerent, British shipyards delivered a number of warships to the South, and British privateers skirted the blockade to deliver munitions. London also sent thousands of troops to Canada and put its fleet on a war footing in response to a diplomatic crisis stemming from the U.S. seizure of two Confederate commissioners from the RMS *Trent*—a British mail packet headed across the Atlantic late in 1861. The envoys were on their way to Britain and France to try to convince both governments to recognize the Confederacy as a sovereign nation and provide support.

Secretary of State Seward was not one to shrink from the prospect of conflict with European powers. In early April 1861, only days before the outbreak of the Civil War, he had broached with Lincoln the need for the United States to stand up to Europe—including through the use of force if necessary—over its interference in American affairs. It was time, Seward wrote to Lincoln, to "send agents into Canada, Mexico, and Central America to rouse a vigorous continental spirit of independence on this continent against European intervention."[3] By the time the war was in full swing, however, Seward had backed off, ultimately agreeing with Lincoln's admonition that the United States could fight only "one war at a time."[4] Guided by this prudence, the Lincoln administration promptly responded to the *Trent* crisis by releasing the two Confederate emissaries it had seized from the British ship, thereby defusing the situation.

The United States practiced similar restraint with respect to Spain and France. Spain in 1861 recolonized Santo Domingo—in direct violation of the Monroe Doctrine. The United States did express its discontent, but took no further steps to counter the reassertion of Spanish rule over the island.[5] In 1862, France established effective control over much of Mexico, and the following year, Napoleon III appointed Maximilian, the Archduke of Austria, as the Emperor of Mexico. The United States, its hands tied by the Civil War and keen to avoid French support to the Confederacy, did little other than protest.[6]

The cautionary restraint exercised by the North during the war diminished after the conflict ended in 1865. Thereafter, the United States had the wherewithal to take a much stronger stand against European interference in its neighborhood. Seward led the charge, guided by his conviction that "nature designed this whole continent—not merely these thirty-six states—but that this whole continent shall be sooner or later within the magic circle of the American Union."[7] He pushed hard for the annexation of Canada as well as British Columbia.[8] Seward maintained that Britain should cede both territories to the United States as compensation for losses imposed on the Union by Confederate vessels constructed in British dockyards. British-built ships provided to the Confederacy sank or captured hundreds of Union vessels, with the *Alabama* alone destroying some seventy Union ships.[9]

Seward's proposal that Britain transfer territory to the United States to compensate for damages incurred during the Civil War enjoyed reasonably strong support in Congress and among the public.[10] Unlike expansion into the Caribbean and Latin America, the annexation of British North America meant bringing into the body politic a primarily white population. As Kagan describes the sentiment of the day, "Canada could be absorbed without injecting a tropical, dark-skinned poison into the nation's bloodstream."[11] That some Confederate soldiers had taken refuge in Canada and sporadically attacked U.S. towns along the border strengthened political support for efforts to wrest control of America's northern neighbor. Irish-Americans were particularly keen to deal Britain a decisive blow in the Western Hemisphere, hoping that the loss of Canada might encourage and advance the cause of Irish independence.[12]

Despite the substantial political backing, the U.S. proposal to wrest control of British territory in North America went nowhere. Although some residents of British Columbia and Canada expressed enthusiasm for annexation, most were opposed to the prospect of joining the United States. Anti-imperialist sentiment in Britain was mounting, but opposition from Canadians and from British investors in Canada helped dissuade the British government from pursuing the transfer.[13] Yet another U.S. attempt to annex Canada—in this instance through diplomacy rather than force—fell short. Nonetheless, the effort to hold Britain accountable for its support to the Confederacy did in the end yield concrete results. At the recommendation of an arbitration commission, the British ultimately compensated the United States for the damage done by British-built ships during the war, agreeing in 1872 to pay the sum of $15.5 million.

The United States had more success in easing European powers out of its southern neighborhood. Spain withdrew from Santo Domingo in 1865. The main causes of the retreat were a violent insurrection against Madrid's rule by many of the island's inhabitants and the toll that disease was taking on Spanish troops. In addition, the Spanish also anticipated possible U.S. intervention, appreciating that the conclusion of the Civil War would free up the United States to enforce the Monroe Doctrine. According to historian Wayne Bowen, "by early 1865, with the American Civil War coming to a close, there was great fear in Madrid that the forbearance of the United States would soon come to an end."[14]

As for France's imperial venture in Mexico, General Ulysses Grant dispatched some 50,000 troops to the Mexican border after the close of the Civil War. In the meantime, Seward stiffened U.S. diplomacy, informing the French late in 1865 that relations between the countries would be in "imminent jeopardy, unless France could deem it consistent with her interest and honor to desist from the prosecution of armed intervention in Mexico."[15] The use of American force ultimately proved unnecessary to prompt a French withdrawal. Already facing significant Mexican resistance to French rule, Napoleon decided to start pulling out French forces in 1866. The Mexican republic was reestablished the following year, after the capture and execution of Maximilian. The end of the Civil War thus led to a more assertive U.S. posture in the Western Hemisphere. But Spain's withdrawal from Santo Domingo and the French retreat from Mexico rendered moot the question of whether the United States was prepared to use force to back up its firmer policy.

The Reconstruction Era: Commerce, Not Colonies

Alongside this strengthened determination to resist Europe's imperial presence in the Western Hemisphere came renewed consideration of territorial acquisitions in Latin America, the Caribbean, and the Pacific. Both refreshed cause and additional capability colored this reopened debate about expansion. Many citizens in the victorious Union perceived the Civil War as a moral crusade. Having defeated the Confederacy and rid the nation of the stain of slavery, the United States had burnished its credentials as a redeemer nation. It could and should return to its messianic calling and endeavor to spread beyond its borders its unique experiment in political and economic liberty.[16] The fervor of the second Great Awakening had died out, but American messianism, in both its religious and secular variants, still had strong appeal. In the public imagination, according to Tuveson, "perhaps, even, Armageddon had been fought."[17] During congressional debate over the potential acquisition of Santo Domingo in 1871, Representative Job Stevenson (R-Ohio) revealed the clear linkage between the nation's redemptive mission and enthusiasm for further territorial expansion:

> We rise from the rebellion conscious of our power, full of hope and confidence, inspired for the first time in our history by the enjoyment of universal liberty. Such a nation cannot shrink from her destiny. She does not shrink. She welcomes it, and goes forth joyously to meet and greet it. Some gentlemen seem to fear the expansion of the Republic . . . yet every acquisition which has been developed has proved a priceless blessing, and the grand result is what the world beholds. Away with such timid misgivings![18]

The United States also had greater ability than before the Civil War to extend political and strategic commitments well beyond its borders. At the close of the war, the Union had more than one million men under arms—compared with a Regular Army that stood at less than 20,000 in 1861. The Union Navy, which started the war with fewer than 100 vessels, had almost 700 ships by the end of the war—including state-of-the-art submarines and ironclad warships. The conflict had strengthened federal institutions. Conscription, a federal bank, a single currency, and new forms of taxation combined to endow the U.S. government with unprecedented political power. The United States emerged from its internal struggle with the tools and institutions necessary to project its geopolitical strength outward. The demands of the Civil War had effectively handed victory to the Hamiltonians in their long-running debate with Jeffersonians over the appropriate reach of the federal government.

So, too, did foreign commerce boom during the second half of the 1800s, with the United States particularly focused on tapping new markets in Asia. In 1868, the United States signed the Burlingame-Seward Treaty with China, facilitating commerce and promoting Chinese immigration to the United States while limiting American interference in China's internal affairs. America's political and commercial ties with Japan deepened after the Meiji Revolution in 1868 set Japan on a new course of economic openness and modernization. Following a belligerent and ultimately futile attempt to open Korea to U.S. trade in 1871— the episode involved the landing of U.S. forces and both American and Korean casualties—efforts to negotiate a commercial treaty continued, finally leading to the conclusion of a Treaty of Peace, Amity, Commerce and Navigation in 1882.

But despite the renewed sense of moral mission, the nation's increased ability to extend its reach beyond its borders, and the growing volume of foreign trade, the United States remained focused on its domestic agenda—the efforts of Reconstruction to repair the union while securing the rights of emancipated slaves, the further construction of infrastructure, and the continued settlement of the West. As before the Civil War, foreign policy was about keeping the outside world at geopolitical bay while fueling economic growth by expanding foreign trade. Aversion to foreign entanglement continued to foil those calling for a more ambitious brand of statecraft. Despite the abolition of slavery, the management of race relations still acted as a brake on territorial expansion. The defeat of the Confederacy and the emphasis on Reconstruction fueled optimism that sectional reconciliation was at hand. Nonetheless, discord over the political and social status of African Americans continued to plague the nation's politics and serve as a block on expansion into the Caribbean and Latin America. Many southerners sought to maintain white supremacy, while frustrated Republicans in the North—most northern Whigs had migrated to the newly formed Republican Party in the mid-1850s—contemplated more intrusive measures to advance the social and political rights of freed slaves. Reconstruction ran out of steam during the 1870s—without delivering on its primary objectives. The political fortunes of Republicans and the search for sectional reconciliation ultimately took precedence over the civil rights of blacks.[19] The timing was hardly ripe for bringing nonwhite territories into the union.

In short, isolationism continued its lock on U.S. grand strategy until the Spanish-American War. In the aftermath of the Civil War, the United States bought Alaska, stiffened its resistance to European interference in the Western

Hemisphere, and continued to invest in the expansion of foreign trade. But it went no further. In the words of Walter LaFeber, "U.S. overseas expansion had two main characteristics after 1870; it was almost entirely interested in markets (not land), and it moved along not one but many routes to all corners of the earth."[20] As for Latin America, according to historian Foster Rhea Dulles, "throughout the 1860s and 1870s, opposition to any European encroachments in the Western Hemisphere, as set forth in unwavering defense of the Monroe Doctrine, constituted the sum and total of popular interest in the countries lying south of the Rio Grande." And in the Pacific, Dulles maintains, "the basic aims of American Far Eastern policy in the latter half of the nineteenth century were cultivation of friendly relations and the promotion of foreign trade. Unlike the European powers, the United States had no territorial ambitions."[21]

Moreover, as Paul Kennedy points out, deepening American engagement abroad—and in the Pacific, in particular—was the result not of deliberate decisions by policy makers but the work of both private citizens and public officials acting on their own initiative. Kennedy puts these developments in historical context:

> For almost the entire duration of the nineteenth century, the United States had so faithfully followed the precepts of Washington and Jefferson in maintaining a reserve and aloofness to the activities and disputes of the other nations of the world that this had become not merely a policy but an integral part of America's national tradition and political philosophy. The exceptions which had occurred to interrupt this general rule were the result of the activities of individual pressure groups, enterprises and statesmen rather than the deliberate choice of the American people themselves or their representatives in Washington.[22]

The pace and scope of demobilization after the close of the war were revealing indicators of this lack of geopolitical ambition. The nation was saddled with enormous debt as a consequence of the costs of the Civil War, putting a political premium on efforts to hold down expenditures. The Army and Navy were subjected to deep budget cuts soon after the war ended. The Army shrank from over one million to roughly 50,000 men. Within five years, the Navy contracted from 700 to roughly 200 vessels, with many of them unfit for service; according to Jay Sexton, "the state-of-the-art ironclad navy that British naval planners had feared in 1865 soon became obsolete."[23] The diplomatic corps remained tiny and, for the most part, poorly trained. Some members of Congress proposed closing all foreign missions other than those in London and Berlin.[24] This downsizing did not take place, but the State Department remained minimally staffed. As of the 1880s, the country had only twenty-five ministers serving abroad (none of which held ambassadorial rank) and roughly sixty officers and clerks working in Washington.[25]

New Acquisitions: Alaska and Midway Atoll

Despite the nation's military demobilization and its focus on domestic repair, Seward, who remained in office until the end of the Johnson administration, did have one notable success in his bid to implement a more expansionist foreign policy: the purchase of Alaska in 1867. After the Russian government concluded that holding on to Alaska was not worth the cost, it indicated to the United States in early 1867 that the territory was available for purchase.[26] Seward seized the opportunity, reaching an agreement with the Russians by the end of March. He then promptly sought Congress's approval of the purchase. Seward rested his case on a number of arguments. If the United States did not acquire Alaska, he maintained, Britain would purchase the territory, further strengthening its imperial presence in North America. In contrast, should the United States take possession of Alaska, British Columbia would be sandwiched between U.S. territories—and likely seek annexation, cutting back Britain's imperial footprint. In addition, the Aleutian Islands, which were stepping stones to East Asia, would clear the way for increased trade across the Pacific. Finally, Seward maintained that Russia, unlike Britain and France, had supported the Union during the Civil War. A positive response to its offer to sell Alaska to the United States would therefore be to reciprocate the goodwill and invest in a strong relationship with a major European power.[27]

The Senate moved quickly to consider the treaty. Senator Charles Sumner (R-Massachusetts), the influential chair of the Foreign Relations Committee, argued strongly in favor of the acquisition, laying out five main supporting arguments. First, he made an economic case for the purchase, affirming that "not only does the Treaty extend the coasting trade of California, Oregon, and Washington Territory northward, but it also extends the base of commerce with China and Japan. To unite the east of Asia with the west of America is the aspiration of commerce." Second, Sumner appealed to patriotism and the spirit of Manifest Destiny: "Our territorial acquisitions are among the landmarks of our history.... With an increased size on the map there is an increased consciousness of strength, and the citizen throbs anew as he traces the extending line." Third, he claimed that the purchase would further the nation's mission of spreading its values and institutions. Buying Alaska, Sumner maintained, would constitute "the extension of republican institutions. . . . By it we dismiss one more monarch from the continent." Fourth, echoing Seward, Sumner argued that London would buy Alaska if Washington failed to do so; accordingly, the United States

needed to go ahead with the deal to prevent Britain from expanding its imperial holdings in North America. Finally, Sumner maintained that ratification of
the purchase "attests and assures the amity of Russia" and an "entente cordiale"
between the two countries. Aware that some of his colleagues were skeptical of
what critics called "Seward's Icebox" and the costs and responsibilities that came
with territorial expansion, he reassured the Senate that "this Treaty must not be
a precedent for indiscriminate and costly annexation."[28] The Senate, after a relatively short debate, approved the treaty by a vote of 37 to 2 in April 1867.

The House, which had to approve the sale price of $7.2 million, was more
reluctant. Securing a positive vote on Alaska took months of lobbying and debate.[29] Supporters reiterated the arguments that carried the day in the Senate,
focusing in particular on the claim that Alaska's commercial potential more than
offset the purchase price, and that the United States needed to counter British
influence in North America. Opponents argued that the country was finan-
cially strapped and should not incur additional debt. As Representative Shelby
Cullom (R-Illinois) put it, "our peoples are already burdened with a public debt
as much as they can bear."[30] Opponents also questioned the need for additional
territory. Representative John Peters (R-Maine) claimed that "the territory is
intrinsically and virtually worthless."[31] Representative Orange Ferriss (R-Iowa)
insisted that "nobody asked for it, and nobody wanted it."[32] In the words of
Representative Hiram Price (R-New York), "I must characterize such legislation
as foolish, inane, and wicked, and I earnestly request gentlemen to use a little
common sense in this matter, and to remember that 'those who buy what they
do not want will soon want what they cannot buy.' "[33]

Others maintained that adding Alaska to the nation's territory risked
overburdening, and therefore dangerously strengthening, the executive branch.
Indeed, members of the House complained that the Johnson administration had
overreached in presenting the purchase of Alaska as a *fait accompli*, with Seward
having already sealed the deal with Russia before approaching Congress.[34] It
did not help matters that President Johnson, a southern Democrat confronted
with a Republican majority in Congress, vetoed legislation aimed at protecting
the political and economic rights of emancipated slaves. The move radicalized
Republicans and helped trigger impeachment proceedings against the president, which passed in the House but failed in the Senate. In the end, partisan animosity toward Johnson and misgivings about buying Alaska proved insufficient
to block the purchase. In July, the House finally approved funding by a vote of
113 to 43 (with 44 abstentions).

Alongside Alaska, the only other notable territorial acquisition of the 1860s
was Midway Atoll (initially called the Middlebrook Islands after their discov-
erer), which ended up in U.S. hands more by accident than by design. Midway,
consisting of two main pieces of land together comprising roughly 2.4 square

miles, was initially reported by a U.S. sealing vessel in 1859. The captain of the ship, N. C. Middlebrooks, obtained the island for the United States under the Guano Islands Act of 1856. The atoll is roughly equidistant from North America and Asia—and thus an opportune site for a replenishing station for vessels crossing the Pacific. In 1867, a U.S. Navy captain, William Reynolds, formally took possession of the island for the United States—without congressional approval.[35] Congress thereafter appropriated $50,000 to dredge the lagoon and develop a deep-water port.[36] But after a failed attempt to construct a harbor in 1870, development of the island's infrastructure would await the early twentieth century.

Failed Attempts at Caribbean and Pacific Expansion

From the close of the Civil War through the end of the Grant administration in 1877, Alaska and Midway were the only noteworthy additions to the nation's territory. The absence of other acquisitions was not for a lack of trying. Indeed, both the Johnson and Grant administrations made concerted attempts to extend the nation's territorial reach into the Caribbean, with Santo Domingo, Haiti, the Danish West Indies (now known as the U.S. Virgin Islands), and Cuba all in the mix.[37] Congress, however, would have none of it, rejecting all such proposals that came its way. So, too, was there considerable opposition to expansion in influential publications. The *Philadelphia Press* argued after the conclusion of the Civil War that "the true interests of the American people will be better served at this important period of our national history by a thorough and complete development of the immense resources of our existing territory than by any rash attempts to increase it."[38] The *Nation* was hardly an outlier when it asserted in 1868 after the annexation of Alaska that "if the national future be in peril at all, it is not for want of territory but from excess of it."[39]

Seward was not deterred by the lack of enthusiasm for further territorial expansion. In 1867, he concluded a deal to purchase the Danish West Indies from Denmark for $7.5 million. When the House first caught wind of Seward's intentions, it raced to block him by advancing a resolution that affirmed "in the present financial condition of the country any further purchases of territory are inexpedient."[40] In the Senate, Republican animosity toward President Johnson played a role in stiffening opposition to the purchase. The Senate ultimately refused to take up Seward's treaty, considering the move, according to DeConde, "extravagant and unnecessary."[41] The Grant administration considered making another run at winning Senate approval, but faced similar domestic opposition and eventually let the treaty lapse in 1870.[42]

Fearful of an invasion from Haiti (which had occupied Santo Domingo from 1822 to 1844), the government of Santo Domingo in 1867 broached with the

United States the possibility of annexation. The Johnson administration was favorably disposed, and asked Congress to consider the annexation of Santo Domingo as well as a separate proposal to establish a protectorate over both Haiti and Santo Domingo. Seward and other expansionists argued that the United States needed a naval base in the Caribbean to support and protect trade and to establish a strategic presence capable of countering a potential resurgence of European ambitions in the region. Both Haiti's harbor at Môle St. Nicholas and Santo Domingo's Samana harbor would serve as appropriate sites. Seward was also interested in the construction of an isthmian canal, a project that would make a U.S. foothold in the Caribbean of even greater geopolitical importance.[43]

Congress considered both proposals. The proposal to annex Santo Domingo was tabled after little debate. The proposal to establish a protectorate over Haiti and Santo Domingo also failed, but only after a heated debate. Deliberations in Congress focused less on the strategic and commercial benefits of expansion touted by Seward and more on southward expansion being part of the nation's destiny and redemptive mission. A good number of members were confident that the islands of the Caribbean would eventually end up as American territory. In the words of Representative Rufus Spalding (R-Ohio), "it was the destiny of the American Government to spread itself not only over the whole continent of America, but over all the islands adjacent thereto. . . . It is merely a question of time."[44] Representative James Mullins (R-Tennessee) agreed: "If there was a destiny of God in the formation of this Government . . . then it is that we shall inhabit this land and all adjacent to it. This Saxon people are a burning meteor rushing on in space, and their empire is land and dominion upon earth." Representative Benjamin Butler (R-Massachusetts) was of a similar mind: "There is no precedent for our position in the history of the world." When it came to the "young republics of South America," he affirmed, the United States could not be a bystander, instead "in every act extending a helping hand."

Even if committed to the spread of republican institutions, other representatives were more cautious than Butler about U.S. interference in the affairs of the country's island neighbors. In the minds of many, the nation should extend its reach only as the countries of the hemisphere became stable republics and willingly came America's way. To force the process would be to compromise America's values and institutions. As for "these little islands," Mullins said, "we do not propose to fight their battles. . . . I would let them alone; they will come to us themselves." Representative Columbus Delano (R-Ohio) agreed, maintaining that "when these islands are ready to come to us let us take them. . . . When we find a people ripe for our institutions and ready for our plan of government let us incorporate them and then protect them afterwards. But to go out as a protector of other nations who are struggling among themselves for self-government is to adopt a policy which will end in the overthrow of our institutions and in ruin to our nation." Representative Norman Judd (R-Illinois) maintained that the implementation of a protectorate could itself constitute "the delegation to the executive department of a power which we cannot control."

Other members opposed further territorial expansion altogether—regardless of the timing and conditions. They voiced traditional concerns about compromising the natural security afforded by geographic isolation and insisted that the United States continue to pursue its messianic mission only by serving as an exemplar, not through more activist means. Representative Samuel Shellabarger (R-Ohio) was firmly in this camp:

> This Government, sir, may be strong in itself, may be irresistible in itself, may, God grant, be perpetual. But, sir, that immortality is to be found in our being to ourselves and for ourselves a Government of ourselves; not involving or embroiling ourselves in or interfering with the affairs of other Governments. . . . In departing from the inculcations of the fathers of the Republic, when they told us to let foreign wars alone, we embark on new seas—seas you and I have not explored. I pause; I fear; I refuse to go. . . . We want republics to be established all over the world. If we take care well of our own Government we become . . . the light-house to the other Governments of the world. In that light . . . will be found the moral power which is to furnish the true, the real and effective protectorate of the struggling or the feeble or the threatened republics of the world.

As before the Civil War, racism and sectional tension continued to serve as a check on expansion. Representative George Washington Woodward (D-Pennsylvania) declared that "it is a marvel to me that . . . [colleagues] should want more negroes brought within our limits in view of the actual condition of things in this country at this time." Woodward recommended that Congress should put off consideration of southward expansion until "after we had settled our own disturbed affairs in the southern States."

Amid these multiple sources of opposition, neither the proposal to annex Santo Domingo nor the idea of establishing protectorates over Haiti and Santo Domingo passed muster in Congress. But the debate was not over. Although the Grant administration did not pursue Seward's designs on either the Danish West Indies or Haiti, it did make another run at annexing Santo Domingo. To the strategic, commercial, and ideological rationales for annexation touted by the previous administration, Grant added a new twist; he saw taking possession of Santo Domingo as a means of fostering racial reconciliation at home.[45]

Faced with Reconstruction's shortcomings, Grant sought alternative means of advancing the economic and political fortunes of freed blacks. Annexation of Santo Domingo provided one option. Southern blacks facing discrimination could move to the island and enjoy rule by their own race—a potential means of sidestepping southern opposition to political equality across racial lines. Grant hoped that the example of blacks embracing democracy and wage labor in Santo Domingo would ultimately convince southerners to overcome their prejudice. However, "if Providence designed that the two races shall not live together," he wrote in a memo making the case for annexation, then black Americans "would find a home in the Antillas."[46] Grant elaborated in his memoir that "colored people would go there in great numbers so as to have independent states governed by their own race. They would still be States of the Union, and under the protection of the General Government; but the citizens would be almost wholly colored."[47]

Prior to the Civil War, many southerners saw southward expansion as a way of increasing the political power of slaveholding states and protecting slavery. Northerners objected—one of the reasons that expansion into the Caribbean did not take place. After the conflict and in the wake of emancipation, Grant looked to territorial expansion as a means of forging a consensus between North and South on race relations. Annexing Santo Domingo and exporting freed slaves there to govern themselves held promise of addressing what was arguably the primary challenge of the Reconstruction era—dealing with the political implications of emancipation and fostering sectional reconciliation. Expansion abroad was a vehicle for tackling political challenges at home.

The Grant administration's push to annex Santo Domingo ran into staunch opposition in Congress, making the issue "one of the biggest foreign policy controversies of the Reconstruction era."[48] The Senate was determined to assert its authority over matters of foreign policy.[49] Opponents deployed traditional strategic arguments against the annexation, maintaining that extending the nation's reach into the Caribbean risked drawing it into unwanted conflicts. By taking islands at a distance from the mainland and therefore difficult to defend against potential aggressors, the United States would be needlessly abandoning the natural advantages of its insular geography. Senator Carl Schurz (R-Missouri) insisted that taking possession of one island would inevitably lead to other acquisitions; first Santo Domingo, then Cuba, then Puerto Rico. "But there you will not stop," he asserted. "The Anglo-Saxon race is somewhat notorious for its land hunger, and such appetites are always morbidly stimulated by eating." In addition, whatever strategic advantages might accrue to the United States would not be worth the financial costs of annexation.[50]

The debate in the Senate focused on issues of race as much as strategy, making clear that many senators did not share Grant's view that annexation would advance race relations. With controversy already raging over whether and how to integrate blacks into American society, there was strong opposition to adding more to the population. Some northerners feared that the South might attempt to use territorial expansion to preserve slavery in Latin America, if not to resuscitate it at home. In addition, members contended that the population of Santo Domingo was unfit to practice democracy and become citizens of the United States. According to Senator Sumner, "the island of San Domingo, situated in tropical waters and occupied by another race, never can become a permanent possession of the United States."[51] Senator Schurz held a similar view, noting that the nation should be looking north, not south, if it wanted to pursue expansion. "If we annex them [Canadians] today they would be good Americans and republicans tomorrow," he asserted. "On the other hand, if the people of the West India islands even desired at this moment annexation it does not have the least effect upon their capability of being assimilated with us, of being absorbed by our population, of being fitted for our institutions." In tropical latitudes, he emphasized, workers "exhibit a strong tendency to run into shiftlessness," and republican institutions are destined to fail.[52] Representative John Franklin Farnsworth (R-Illinois), amid a separate debate in the House about the status of Santo Domingo, agreed that the United States should keep its distance from "a motley mixture of French, Spanish, and other Europeans, with Indians, savages, and negroes from every part of Western Africa."[53]

The opponents of annexation prevailed. As with Seward's effort to assert control over Santo Domingo during the Johnson administration, Grant's bid to do so also failed. Unconvinced of the strategic and commercial case for annexation and averse to integrating Santo Domingo's population into the union, the Senate voted down the treaty, 28 to 28, with 16 abstentions, on June 30, 1870.

Like Seward, Grant was also interested in laying the groundwork for an isthmian canal, but he lacked Congress's support on that issue as well. In addition, the possible annexation of Cuba was in play. Successive administrations had been eyeing Cuba for decades, and the Johnson and Grant administrations were no different. Seward visited Havana in 1866 on a trip that also took him to the Danish West Indies, Santo Domingo, and Haiti. Although he recognized that Spain would likely keep hold of Cuba for the time being, he ventured that the island would "by means of constant gravitation . . . fall into the United States."[54] In late 1868, Cubans revolted against Spain and declared independence. The Grant administration, which took office the following March, faced a measure of political pressure to recognize the rebels as belligerents, provide them assistance, and even intervene with armed force.

Congress was divided on the issue. Representative Morton Smith Wilkinson (R-Minnesota) argued that "for nearly two years there has been a struggle going on in Cuba . . . an island which of right belongs to the Government of the United States. . . . I believe it is the duty of the United States . . . to take hold of and control all the islands of the West Indies and to command the commerce of these islands. . . . I would rather have war with Spain a hundred times over, war with Spain and France combined, rather than that it should be understood that we are afraid to express our just sympathy for the oppressed Cubans."[55] Representative John Coburn (R-Indiana) disagreed: "Our own national attitude . . . is not that of an aggressive, grasping, arrogant people, but rather that of a peacemaker, a mediator, an exemplar of national good behavior. . . . We are not buccaneers, not filibusters, not knights errant. . . . We want no wars for glory or conquest. We want no annexation, purchase, or seizure of territory. We have room enough. . . . Populations of diverse languages, nationalities, tastes, sympathies, and races, are an element of weakness in a great republic."[56]

The Grant administration demurred, guided by Secretary of State Hamilton Fish, who was a strong advocate of avoiding actions that could provoke conflict with Spain. He was also concerned that recognizing the Cuban rebels as belligerents and supporting them could alienate Britain and thereby undercut his efforts to extract Civil War reparations from London.[57] The administration's decision not to support the revolt did not stop private individuals in the United States, including Cuban exiles, from sending aid to the rebels. Moreover, the smuggling of arms to Cuba almost ensnared the United States in the conflict. The Grant administration put the U.S. Navy on alert after a Spanish gunboat in 1873 seized a U.S. ship, the *Virginius*, which was running arms to the rebels. Spain charged as pirates and executed fifty-three of the crew and passengers on board. The Spanish eventually agreed to pay compensation to the families of those it put to death, deescalating the situation. The Cuban uprising then ended in 1878, and a decade of turmoil on the island came to an end without any formal U.S. intervention.

With the exception of Midway, American expansion into the Pacific similarly consisted of false starts. Seward was keen to establish footholds for the U.S. Navy in the Pacific as well as the Caribbean. He negotiated a trade reciprocity treaty with Hawaii, which he envisaged as a first step toward establishing a naval base there. The Senate repeatedly turned down the treaty between 1867 and 1870. In 1875, the Grant administration concluded a treaty granting Hawaiian sugar and other products duty-free access to the American market, which the Senate approved. The treaty did obligate Hawaii to refrain from granting other countries privileged access to its ports or territory, but it did not entail any strategic ties between the United States and Hawaii. Samoa was also in play. In 1872, a U.S. naval commander, acting under his own authority, negotiated a treaty with Samoa for exclusive control over the harbor at Pago Pago. The Senate refused even to consider the treaty. Thereafter, the Samoan chiefs requested that the United States annex their islands, a proposal that Secretary of State Fish promptly rejected.[58]

Despite their repeated attempts to expand the nation's reach into the Caribbean and Pacific, the Johnson and Grant administrations thus came to a close with little to show for their efforts. They were foiled more often than not by a recalcitrant Congress. Indeed, Congress's repeated defeat of attempts at territorial aggrandizement—in particular, the bruising rejection of Grant's bid to annex Santo Domingo—cautioned Johnson's and Grant's successors against undertaking expansionist policies.[59] Seward openly lamented his failure to extend the nation's southern reach, protesting that "we have already come to value dollars more, and dominion less."[60] He also complained that "the public mind refuses to dismiss these [domestic] questions even so far as to entertain the higher but more remote questions of national extension and aggrandizement."[61] On another occasion, he observed "how sadly domestic disturbances demoralize the national ambition."[62] Grant, too, bemoaned the lack of enthusiasm for expansion. "It is with extreme regret that I inform you of the failure of the treaty for the annexation of San Domingo to the United States," he wrote to the president of Santo Domingo on July 7, 1870. In defending his efforts, Grant placed more blame than did Seward on Congress instead of the public, noting, "I had hoped a different result. I believe now that if the subject was submitted to a popular vote of the people it would carry by an overwhelming majority."[63]

From Reconstruction to the Spanish-American War: Ascent without Expansion

America's reluctance to expand beyond North America continued for the next several decades—until the Spanish-American War. The ongoing adherence to isolationism was particularly striking given the nation's rapid economic growth. Between 1865 and 1898, coal production rose by 800 percent and railway track mileage by 567 percent, while petroleum production increased from approximately three million barrels to over fifty-five million barrels per year. By the middle of the 1880s, the United States had surpassed Britain as the world's leading producer of manufactured goods and steel. Agricultural output also rose dramatically—wheat and corn production both grew by more than 200 percent and refined sugar by more than 450 percent. The country's impressive economic performance attracted and was fueled by throngs of immigrants. Between 1865 and 1900, the American population more than doubled.[64]

New enthusiasm for expanding overseas commerce accompanied these economic gains.[65] Developing transpacific trade and tapping into growing markets in East Asia was a particular priority. Hawaii became home to a large and prosperous community of American citizens. American traders and missionaries flocked to Japan, China, and Korea during the second half of the 1800s. Europe's markets were crowded and its politics ossified, while Asia offered alluring opportunities for extending commerce and American values.[66] In the meantime, geopolitical competition was heating up across both the Pacific and the Atlantic. Japan after the Meiji Restoration of 1868 embarked on an ambitious program of modernization and industrialization accompanied by the buildup of its army and navy. Growing rivalry between Britain, France, and Germany triggered a scramble for colonies in Africa as well as imperial forays into East Asia.

Despite unprecedented economic growth at home, the rapid increase in overseas commerce, and the more competitive global environment, Americans nonetheless remained determined to avoid geopolitical commitments abroad. The expansion of foreign fleets did help build political support for a substantial strengthening of the U.S. Navy. But America's growing strength and its increasing commercial and cultural engagement with the rest of the world did not readily translate into a willingness to extend its geopolitical reach beyond the homeland. Instead, there were more false starts. Prompted in part by French plans to build a canal across Panama, the Chester Arthur administration (1881–1885) concluded the Frelinghuysen-Zavala Treaty in an effort to build a U.S.-controlled canal across Nicaragua. But the Senate balked—U.S. construction of a canal would violate the Clayton-Bulwer Treaty that the United States had concluded with Britain in 1850—and President Grover Cleveland withdrew the treaty after taking office.[67] In the Pacific, the United States did establish two naval stations—at Pago Pago in 1878 and Pearl Harbor in 1887. However, the purpose of securing access to these ports of call was to support transoceanic trade, not acquire overseas possessions or project the nation's geopolitical ambition.

America's deepening commercial engagement with Asia also prompted a domestic backlash that took the form of restrictions against immigration. Following the influx of laborers from China after the friendship treaty of 1868, Congress in 1882 passed the Chinese Exclusion Act, which prohibited the entry of workers from China for ten years—a provision that was repeatedly extended—and made it more difficult for Chinese immigrants to become naturalized citizens. Concern about protecting labor markets combined with racism to build support for the new restriction, which was preceded by regular acts of violence against Chinese immigrants—particularly in California.[68] The following decade, the American Federation of Labor lobbied to restrict immigration from European countries as well, but the effort fell short largely due to pressure from the business community to sustain a healthy supply of cheap labor.[69]

The United States thus adhered to an isolationist grand strategy through the balance of the nineteenth century—but there were clear signs that a tectonic shift was in the making. The nation's wealth was rapidly rising, as was its overseas trade. The influx of immigrants and outflow of Americans contributed to the emergence of a more cosmopolitan and outward-looking society. As the historian Frank Ninkovich has argued, the cultural foundations of a new internationalism were evolving.[70] The harbors at Pago Pago and Pearl Harbor may have been only replenishing stations to support transoceanic trade, but they did constitute a new willingness to establish outposts far from the nation's borders. That the nation could be approaching a turning point in grand strategy looked all the more likely after 1890, when the United States started to build battleships, an indication that it was departing from the traditional focus of its navy on coastal defense and commerce protection. As the next section makes clear, the stirrings of a new and more ambitious brand of statecraft were apparent well before the outbreak of the Spanish-American War in 1898.

New Instruments of Geopolitical Ambition: Battleships

In his seventh Annual Message to Congress on December 7, 1875, President Grant was forthright in acknowledging that the U.S. Navy fell far short of the maritime capability possessed by European powers. Nonetheless, he asserted that existing force levels were more than adequate to meet the nation's requirements:

> The condition of our Navy at this time is a subject of satisfaction. It does not contain, it is true, any of the powerful cruising ironclads which make so much of the maritime strength of some other nations, but neither our continental situation nor our foreign policy requires that we should have a large number of ships of this character, while this situation and the nature of our ports combine to make those of other nations little dangerous to us under any circumstances.
>
> Our Navy does contain, however, a considerable number of ironclads of the monitor class, which, though not properly cruisers, are powerful and effective for harbor defense and for operations near our own shores. Of these all the single-turreted ones, fifteen in number, have been substantially rebuilt, their rotten wooden beams replaced with iron, their hulls strengthened, and their engines and machinery thoroughly repaired, so that they are now in the most efficient condition and ready for sea as soon as they can be manned and put in commission.[71]

Such satisfaction about the state of the navy was to wane during the final two decades of the 1800s. The United States emerged as a world-class industrial power during the decades after the Civil War, with exports quadrupling by the end of the century. The booming economy and growth in foreign trade provided the resources as well as the rationale for increasing the capability of the nation's navy. During the 1880s, the United States consequently embarked on a naval building program for the first time since the Civil War. The increase in fleet strength was modest and the new vessels were primarily cruisers, along with a few "sea-going double-bottomed armored vessels," which came to be called "second-class" battleships.[72] Nonetheless, the decision to invest in new ships did mark the beginning of efforts to reverse the deterioration of the fleet that began in the mid-1860s. In addition, the Naval War College was founded in 1884, and the Navy began to post intelligence attachés abroad in 1889.[73]

The 1890s marked an even more consequential turning point; the United States completed the construction of second-class battleships and began to build larger and more powerful warships in the service of acquiring a blue-water navy. The decision to begin building a battleship fleet was itself a strategic breakpoint; the United States was at least contemplating the abandonment of isolationism by acquiring the ability to project its power over significant distances and to engage in the game of great-power competition that it had sworn off since the founding era. Nonetheless, the possession of the ability to project the nation's power abroad did not necessarily translate into the political will to do so. During his second term (1893–1897), President Cleveland continued the battleship program initiated by his predecessor, Benjamin Harrison. But Cleveland was also a committed isolationist who sought to *withdraw* the United States from the strategic commitments in Samoa and Hawaii undertaken by Harrison.

During the 1890s, the nation was passing through a strategic inflection point; until 1898, it was intent on acquiring the ability to project its growing power well beyond its territory, but not yet convinced of the merits of following through. Americans were tempted by the allure of translating their new economic strength into geopolitical heft, but the nation's statecraft was still guided by its isolationist instincts and traditions. To be sure, once it was armed with new naval strength, it would not take long for the United States to embrace exactly the kind of geopolitical ambition that it had long shunned. In 1898, President McKinley, pressed by Congress, went to war against Spain and put the United States in control of Cuba, Puerto Rico, the Philippines, Guam, and Hawaii. The following year, the United States took possession of Wake Island and established sovereignty over Samoa's eastern islands (including Pago Pago). But prior to the nationalist fervor that helped drive America's outward push in 1898, the public mind had been up for grabs. During the 1890s, two incompatible conceptions of the nation's role in the world were competing head-to-head, producing marked inconstancy in U.S. statecraft.

The initial turn toward building up naval strength began under President James Garfield, who took office in 1881 and installed a strong advocate of naval construction, William Hunt of Louisiana, as secretary of the navy. Garfield served only a matter of months before he was fatally shot. His vice president, Chester Arthur, replaced him. Both Garfield and Arthur were Republicans keen to pursue a more outward-looking foreign policy that would favor the North's industrialists and financiers and strengthen the federal government. Jeffersonian and Jacksonian traditions still had sway in the South, making Democrats—on both principled and partisan grounds—skeptical of a larger navy and more powerful executive. Under Garfield, a newly established naval planning board recommended the procurement of sixty-eight vessels—including state-of-the-art ships that would be steel-hulled and steam-powered.[74] Once he took office, Arthur strongly supported the board's call for the construction of a steel-hulled navy. Even though the nation's financial situation had dramatically improved by the 1880s—indeed, the Treasury was running a surplus—Congress balked at the size of the naval board's recommendation. Legislators instead approved construction of a handful of new, modern cruisers.[75]

President Cleveland took office in 1885, putting Democrats in control of the White House for the first time in sixteen years. In his inaugural address, he made clear that he intended to adhere to the isolationist admonitions of the Founders:

> The genius of our institutions, the needs of our people in their home life, and the attention which is demanded for the settlement and development of the resources of our vast territory dictate the scrupulous avoidance of any departure from that foreign policy commended by the history, the traditions, and the prosperity of our Republic. It is the policy of independence, favored by our position and defended by our known love of justice and by our power. It is the policy of peace suitable to our interests. It is the policy of neutrality, rejecting any share in foreign broils and ambitions upon other continents and repelling their intrusion here. It is the policy of Monroe and of Washington and Jefferson—"Peace, commerce, and honest friendship with all nations; entangling alliance with none."[76]

In keeping with his party's opposition to a more expansive foreign policy, Cleveland withdrew from Senate consideration the Frelinghuysen-Zavala Treaty, which had been submitted by the Arthur administration to clear the way for the construction of a canal across Nicaragua. Cleveland thereby avoided a break with Britain over the Clayton-Bulwer Treaty. In general, his administration was committed to steering clear of entanglement in Europe's great-power ambitions. Cleveland's secretary of state, Thomas Bayard, affirmed in 1885 that "so long as I am head of this Department, I shall not give myself the slightest trouble to thwart the small politics or staircase intrigues in Europe, in which we have not the slightest share or interest, and upon which I look with impatience and contempt."[77]

Although Cleveland's leanings were distinctly isolationist, he nonetheless continued the naval building program that began under Garfield and Arthur—a sign that even some Democrats were embracing the need for a more muscular navy. Congress approved some thirty new vessels, including heavier cruisers and two second-class battleships intended primarily to keep pace with acquisition programs in Latin America.[78] Importantly, however, the naval upgrade that proceeded over the course of the 1880s did not lead to a redefinition of the fleet's core missions—commerce protection and coastal defense. According to Harold and Margaret Sprout, "all we needed for offensive purposes, according to the controlling opinion of that day, was a fleet of fast unarmored cruisers to raid hostile merchant shipping, to engage an enemy's light cruisers, and to harry the battleships of an attacking fleet."[79]

That "controlling opinion" began to lose its hold on Congress and the executive branch after President Benjamin Harrison took office in 1889. Early in the new administration, Harrison's secretary of the navy, Benjamin Tracy, issued a report calling for twelve armored battleships for service in the Atlantic and eight for the Pacific. The naval policy board was even more ambitious, calling for the construction of some 200 new ships, including both short-range and long-range battleships. The policy board asserted that a nation's naval strength should be "commensurate with the wealth of the country and the interests at stake," and went on to conclude that "when we consider the wealth of our country, or our ability to maintain a navy, and the interests at stake in case of war, we are forced to admit that our navy is insignificant and totally disproportionate to the greatness of the country."[80] Tracy, backed by the board, maintained that coastal defense and commerce protection were no longer sufficient to safeguard the nation; the United States needed a battleship fleet capable of taking offensive actions against enemies in distant theaters. Admiral Alfred Thayer Mahan was a key voice shaping the evolution of U.S. naval strategy at this inflection point.[81] He advocated for not just a blue-water navy, but also permanent naval bases in the Caribbean and the Pacific. Mahan argued that the United States needed to build and control an isthmian canal to connect the Atlantic and Pacific oceans, which in turn would require naval bases in Hawaii and the Caribbean to secure the canal's western and eastern approaches.

The advocates of this new naval strategy ultimately carried the day—although Congress's appetite for battleships was much more limited than that of the naval board. The Naval Act of 1890 approved America's first three "sea-going, coast-line battleships."[82] One more was approved in 1892, two more in 1895, and an additional three in 1896. The Naval Act of 1890 referred to the new vessels as "coast-line" ships and specifically limited the ships' proposed cruising range, in part to sidestep opposition from those opposed to acquisition of a blue-water fleet.[83] But the new vessels were much larger and heavier than the second-class battleships approved earlier—and ended up being used for offensive operations during the Spanish-American War.

The battleship program might have proceeded far more modestly than its strongest advocates had wanted, but its commencement nonetheless marked a turning point in U.S. statecraft. For the first time in its history, the United States was investing in a blue-water navy, indicating that it was ready to begin extending its geopolitical reach—not just its trade—beyond its immediate neighborhood. Although naval programs in Latin America were a main impetus behind this naval buildup, the new battleships would enable the nation to engage in offensive action in distant waters—potentially against great-power rivals. Unlike the lighter vessels that the U.S. Navy had long used for coastal defense and deployed abroad to defend U.S. trade and citizens, battleships implicated the United States in geopolitical entanglement. Not surprisingly, this turn in U.S. strategy did not come without heated debate. The report of the naval board, according to Sprout and Sprout, "raised a storm of protest," and in both the House and Senate, the proposed building program "evoked great opposition which ranged over a broad field."[84]

The bill's opponents objected to the costs of the program, its departure from the navy's traditional focus on coastal defense and trade protection, and the risk that a battleship fleet would draw the nation into great-power rivalry. Senator John McPherson (D-New Jersey) argued that the battleship was "a class of ships which this country has no use for whatever," and called the proposed building program "the greatest scheme of mad extravagance that I ever witnessed." He contended that the United States, as it had done throughout its history, should invest in only armored vessels capable of coastal protection and long-range cruisers "to show the people of the world that there is an American nation, and in case of war to prey upon the enemy's commerce."[85] Senator Joseph Dolph (R-Oregon) claimed that "a great navy is more likely to lead us into war with foreign nations than it is to preserve the peace." He asserted that "we want no navy for aggressive warfare. We seek no colonization and our conquests are conquests of peace. We have no occasion to compare navies or armies with European countries. Our policy with Europe is non-intervention."[86]

Members of Congress in favor of the battleship program embraced many of the arguments made by the navy and other advocates within the Harrison administration. For Representative Jonathan Dolliver (R-Iowa), building the new fleet was about patriotism: "With us it is a matter of national pride; . . . I am in favor of such a policy as will give us a navy built by our own labor, out of our own material; a navy which will restore the dignity and strength of our country upon every sea."[87] Representative Charles Boutelle (R-Maine) maintained that coastal defense was no longer sufficient to meet the country's strategic needs. Instead, he argued, the nation needed battleships "that can meet assault outside of the headlands of our coast and decide the safety of our territory before the fleet or army of a foe has invaded our harbors or gained foothold upon the soil of our country."[88] From the perspective of Representative Hilary Herbert (D-Alabama), who later became Cleveland's secretary of the navy, the building program was required to counter the rapid expansion of the fleets of other major powers: "There is a remarkable consensus of opinion all over the world, among all nations, or at least among those who control the naval policies of all nations, that battle-ships heavily armored are essential to a modern navy. England, France, Germany, Spain, China, Russia, all are providing for and building new battle-ships. . . . There is not a naval power in the world but that has been building and greatly improving battle-ships from year to year."[89]

So, too, did some members of Congress believe that the nation's messianic calling needed to be backed up with greater material strength. According to Senator William Stewart (R-Nevada), the cost of a battleship fleet "is a very small sum for this great nation. It is a very small sum compared with the benefits of having some influence and protecting the independence of the various Governments upon this hemisphere." Stewart recognized that "the moral effect of a Republican power ought to have its effect in preserving Republican institutions for man on this hemisphere." But he then went on to claim that "the nations of the earth respect physical power. . . . Moral power with physical power behind it is very persuasive."[90]

Congress ultimately approved the building program by a vote of 33 to 18 in the Senate and 131 to 105 in the House. The passage of the naval bill was facilitated by the fact that Republicans were in simultaneous control of the White House, Senate, and House for the first time since 1875, providing Harrison ready congressional support. The vote did not, however, run strictly along partisan lines, making clear that enthusiasm for a more ambitious brand of statecraft was building on both sides of the aisle. Inasmuch as the building program engaged trade and manufacturing interests, it garnered more support in industrializing and coastal states reliant on foreign commerce than it did in the agrarian interior. Accordingly, sectional interests at times trumped partisan affiliation. Of the twenty-six Democrats voting for the battleship bill in the House, twenty-four were from constituencies in seaboard states. Of the twenty-three Republicans opposed to the bill, twenty-two represented communities in the country's interior.[91]

Pacific Temptations: The Debates over Samoa and Hawaii

The decision to embark on the construction of a battle fleet was not the only sign that the country was contemplating a break with the strict version of isolationism it inherited from the Founders. The establishment of naval stations at Pago Pago in 1878 and Pearl Harbor in 1887 was a clear indication that the United States was intent on increasing its maritime and commercial engagement in the Pacific. The Harrison administration was then prepared to go a significant step further by turning these naval footholds into more durable strategic and political commitments.

In 1878, the United States concluded and ratified a treaty "of friendship and commerce" permitting the United States to establish at Pago Pago a coaling station for naval and commercial vessels.[92] According to the treaty, "naval vessels of the United States shall have the privilege of entering and using the port of Pago Pago and establishing therein and on the shores thereof a station for coal and other naval supplies."[93] The harbor provided the Pacific Squadron as well as merchant ships a strategic port serving both the western and southern Pacific—although it was little used during its first decade.[94] The United States was not alone in seeking access to the islands. Amid mounting rivalry among Europe's imperial powers in both Africa and East Asia, Germany and Britain stepped up their efforts to secure footholds in the South Pacific. By the end of the 1870s, Berlin and London had also signed treaties of friendship and commerce with Samoan leaders.

The United States, Germany, and Britain sought to manage cooperatively Samoan affairs, but over the course of the 1880s, the three countries ended up jockeying for the upper hand amid infighting among Samoa's political factions.[95] The Cleveland administration, despite its aversion to overseas territorial commitments, feared mounting rivalry with Germany and Britain might lead to the loss of access to Pago Pago. Congress agreed, in early 1889 appropriating $600,000 to develop and ensure U.S. control of the harbor. The commercial value of Pago Pago, coupled with its potential strategic worth should great-power tensions intensify, loomed large in the congressional debate, as the remarks of Representative William McAdoo (D-New Jersey) made clear:

> The islands are located . . . in the Pacific Ocean, on the ocean route between San Francisco and Australia. They are in the course of commercial travel. They are of infinite advantage for a coaling station on the very long voyage . . . . The United States has secured in an honorable way the right of making the harbor of Pago Pago a coaling depot, which would be of great use to us in case of war, because the modern war vessel is propelled by steam, the steam is made by coal, and when the coal gives out the vessel is like a dead whale. . . . Therefore all the greatest nations of the world are trying to secure for themselves places where they can get supplies of coal in emergencies so as to steam from point to point with facility.[96]

President Harrison, who took office in March, would soon deepen American involvement in Samoa. With the United States tightening its hold on Pago Pago and Germany and Britain seeking to strengthen their own influence, civil strife among Samoans almost brought the three powers to blows during the spring of 1889.[97] To deescalate the situation and clarify American, German, and British rights and responsibilities, delegates from the three countries convened in Berlin. The result—the General Act of Berlin signed in June—effectively established a tripartite protectorate over the islands. Although the agreement nominally acknowledged "the independence and the neutrality of the Islands of Samoa," it effectively turned the territory into a colony collectively run by the three powers, which on occasion did not even bother to translate the results of their policy conferences into Samoan.[98]

The Harrison administration's primary motivation for entering the pact was to maintain unfettered access to Pago Pago. In the words of Harrison's secretary of state, James Blaine, "the interests of the United States require the possession of a naval station in those remote parts of the Pacific, and by a treaty with the lawful authorities of Samoa they have been put in control of the harbor of Pago Pago for these purposes. We cannot consent to the institution of any form of government in Samoa . . . [that] might check or control the use or the development of this American right."[99] Notably, Blaine was careful to qualify the aims behind this new readiness to assume a strategic commitment some 5,000 miles from the nation's west coast. In a speech in August 1890 on the subject of reciprocal trade, he said, "our great demand is expansion. I mean expansion of trade with countries where we can find profitable exchanges. We are not seeking annexation of territory."[100] Harrison himself was of a similar mind, writing to Blaine that "you know I am not much of an annexationist, though I do feel that in some directions, as to naval stations and points of influence, we must look forward to a departure from the too conservative opinions which have been held heretofore."[101]

Meeting in executive session, the Senate ratified the Berlin Act the following February by a vote of 38 to 12, with only Democrats casting negative votes. According to the *Chicago Tribune*, Senator James Eustis (D-Louisiana) was a vociferous opponent, charging that if the treaty "involved the United States in an entangling alliance with foreign powers, that it committed this country to a policy from which it has heretofore kept clear."[102] Senator Wilkinson Call (D-Florida) also spoke against the treaty, contending that it did not sufficiently protect U.S. access to Pago Pago—a claim that was refuted both on the floor of the Senate and in the press.[103] Media coverage of the issue was relatively limited, and there was no groundswell of opposition to the treaty in newspapers.

The Senate's acquiescence to the treaty as well as the lack of public attention to the issue may well have been a function of Samoa's low political salience in the United States. Far from the American mainland, Samoa was home to only a handful of American citizens and maintaining access to a coaling station at Pago

Pago was the primary, if not the only, U.S. interest. The status of the Samoan Islands thus had none of the political resonance that accompanied debates over, say, Santo Domingo, Cuba, or Hawaii.

At the same time, the lack of more pronounced opposition to the treaty was an early sign that the nation's political establishment was warming up to a more ambitious brand of statecraft. Even if on only a small scale, the tripartite protectorate effectively breached key tenets of the founding era. The Berlin agreement violated the isolationist playbook by establishing a legally binding strategic commitment quite far from the nation's shores. It violated unilateralism by making that strategic commitment a joint one; in the service of governing Samoa, the United States was suddenly "entangled" with both Britain and Germany. And it violated the traditional American aversion to imperialism. The United States and its European partners were effectively ruling over the people of Samoa. As the *New York Times* commented following the treaty's ratification, "the United States are for the first time involved in a combination with foreign powers to maintain a Government in a foreign country."[104] In Samoa in 1889, the United States was, as it were, sticking its toe in the water, testing its own readiness to move from strict isolationism to a statecraft that countenanced overseas commitments and foreign entanglement. And, surprisingly, it was doing so with little fanfare or opposition.

Harrison also tested the nation's appetite for a new level of foreign ambition when it came to Hawaii. In 1887, the United States and Hawaii both ratified an extension of the trade reciprocity treaty of 1875. The Senate had since 1884 refrained from ratification, awaiting an amended version of the treaty that would grant the United States exclusive access to Pearl Harbor and clear the way for a U.S. lease for the port.[105] As had happened in 1889 with Pago Pago and the Samoan Islands, Harrison would soon seek to build on U.S. access to Pearl Harbor to assert broader control over the Hawaiian Islands. In January 1893, the increasingly sizable and influential expatriate community in Hawaii—many of whom were American owners of sugar plantations—orchestrated a successful coup against the Hawaiian monarch. The rebellion was the culmination of a long-running power struggle between wealthy settlers and the monarchy and its native Hawaiian supporters. The rebellion enjoyed the support of the U.S. minister, John Stevens, who called in U.S. marines and sailors to backstop the overthrow of Queen Liliuokalani. Although Stevens acted without explicit authorization from Washington, the Harrison administration supported the provisional government, responded favorably to its request for rapid annexation of Hawaii by the United States, and the month following the coup submitted the annexation treaty for Senate approval. Times had certainly changed since 1857, when the United States intervened in Nicaragua to *reverse* a coup carried out by an American citizen.

Unlike the treaty establishing a tripartite protectorate over Samoa, which stirred up relatively little debate, the proposed annexation of Hawaii proved quite controversial.[106] For the most part, Republicans supported the treaty and Democrats opposed it. Senator William Washburn (R-Minnesota) spoke for many in his party in arguing that "there is only one way to act in the matter . . . and that is to take the islands into the fold. Hawaii is our meat, and the more speedily we act in the matter the better it will be for all concerned, and especially for the United States. . . . The fact of the matter is that Hawaii is a rich prize, and to permit the present opportunity to get it to go by would be a political crime."[107] There were, however, exceptions to the partisan divide. Senator Richard Pettigrew (R-South Dakota) opposed annexation, noting that "from a strategic point there is nothing to gain. Already we have exclusive rights in Pearl Harbor."[108] Senator John Morgan (D-Alabama) meanwhile supported annexation, agreeing with Washburn that "it would be a political crime not to gather in such desirable territory as the Hawaiian group."[109]

Critics of annexation reprised many of the same objections that had blocked previous attempts to extend the nation's strategic reach. As he did during earlier debates over annexing Santo Domingo and other Caribbean islands, the former senator Carl Schurz continued to stress the strategic benefits of geographic isolation:

> In our present condition, we have over all the nations of the world one advantage of incalculable value. We are the only one that is not in any of its parts threatened by powerful neighbors; the only one not under any necessity of keeping up a large armament either on land or water for the security of its possessions; the only one that can turn all the energies of its population to productive employment; the only one that has an entirely free hand. This is a blessing for which the American people can never be too thankful. . . . We occupy a compact part of the American Continent, bounded by great oceans on the east and west, and on the north and south by neighbors neither hostile in spirit nor by themselves formidable in strength. . . . In other words, in our compact continental stronghold we are substantially unassailable. . . . In fact, we can hardly get into a war unless it be of our own seeking.[110]

A good number of newspapers joined Schurz in opposing annexation. The *Boston Herald* asserted that "Hawaii would be our one weak point, liable to assault in a foreign war." The *Pittsburg Dispatch* was of a similar mind: "The talk of defending our Pacific coast by a naval station 2,000 miles away is worse than absurd. The United States has attained its greatness simply by staying at home and minding its own business. . . . Do we wish to throw to the winds the policy which has made this country powerful and prosperous?" The *St. Paul Globe* expressed similar concern, fearing that annexation would "launch the country on a crusade of territorial extension without limit, and divert it from what is its real 'manifest destiny,' the working out on this continent of the evolution of the latest and highest type of humanity."[111]

Paralleling previous debates over potential expansion into territory populated by many nonwhites, racism also provoked opposition to the annexation of Hawaii. According to the *Chicago Herald*, "any sort of a popular government . . . would be impracticable, owing to the character of the masses of the people. The most that could be made of it would be a sort of satrapy, and its political management probably would be profligate and corrupt beyond anything possible, except the negro governments in the South after the war." *The Nation* was concerned that making the republic more racially diverse would only stoke racism, noting "the power of race hatred to convert Anglo-Saxons, at least, into devils incarnate. Do we want more material to feed this apparently inextinguishable passion?"[112] The editor of *The Nation*, E. L. Godkin, expressed his opposition to integrating into the national population "scanty, ignorant, superstitious, and foreign-tongued" voters.[113]

In light of such opposition, it is by no means clear that the Senate would have ratified the annexation treaty if it had had the chance to do so. But it ran out of time. Grover Cleveland began his second term in March 1893—only a few weeks after Harrison submitted the annexation treaty to the Senate—and promptly withdrew it from consideration.[114] Indeed, Cleveland staunchly opposed Harrison's expansionist agenda, making clear that the nation's turn toward a more ambitious brand of statecraft was still tentative and lacked strong bipartisan support.

Cleveland's Pullback

During Cleveland's first term, the expansionism advocated by some of his predecessors was effectively off the table. During his second term, Cleveland's isolationist instincts were only reinforced by the views of his cautious secretary of state, Walter Gresham. Gresham opposed, on both pragmatic and moral grounds, the overseas extension of U.S. commitments and was convinced that "the only safeguard against all the evils of interference in affairs that do not specially concern us is to abstain from such interference altogether."[115] He believed that the ongoing naval buildup was at odds with the restraint counseled by the Founders and maintained that Americans "should stay home and attend to their own business." Otherwise, "they would go to hell as fast as possible." Accordingly, Gresham was dead set against the annexation of Hawaii, fearing that the demands of protecting even a small number of modest commitments in the Pacific would inevitably lead to additional and more onerous burdens that would leave the United States strategically exposed. He opposed U.S. rule over other peoples, asserting that "a free government cannot pursue an imperial policy." Should it engage in colonialism, a "popular government will not long survive," because it would lose its moral compass and its legitimacy. Harkening back to the founding years, Gresham was also concerned that the military buildup needed to maintain an imperial policy would undermine republican practices and institutions at home.[116]

These concerns resonated with public discomfort over the prospect of creeping foreign entanglement. In addition, Gresham combined his warnings against foreign ambition with a sharp critique of growing greed and corruption within American society. In so doing, he strengthened his political credibility amid mounting public anxiety about the increasing power of corporations and banks and the social ills and inequality that had come with industrialization and urbanization. Gresham's call for the restoration of public virtue went hand-in-hand with his desire to immunize the nation against the political and geopolitical dangers that accompanied foreign ambition—foreshadowing a strain of anti-imperialism that was to grow much stronger after 1898.[117]

Cleveland and Gresham were of a single mind on the importance of withdrawing the Hawaiian annexation treaty from Senate consideration. Gresham maintained that annexation of the islands would be tantamount to "stealing territory" and a violation of "international morality." In his view, the United States would end up governing Hawaii as "Rome governed her provinces, by despotic rule."[118] Cleveland concurred that Americans had taken control of Hawaii by illegitimate means. In a message to Congress on December 18, 1893, he explained that "it appears that Hawaii was taken possession of by the United States forces without the consent or wish of the government of the islands. . . Therefore the military occupation of Honolulu by the United States . . . was wholly without justification, either as an occupation by consent or as an occupation necessitated by dangers threatening American life and property." Cleveland viewed this forcible brand of regime change as inconsistent with U.S. practice and principle. "While naturally sympathizing with every effort to establish a republican form of government," he continued, "it has been the settled policy of the United States to concede to people of foreign countries the same freedom and independence in the management of their domestic affairs that we have always claimed for ourselves." He also complained about the haste with which the Harrison administration had acted, especially because annexation would have constituted "a departure from unbroken American tradition in providing for the addition to our territory of islands of the sea more than 2,000 miles removed from our nearest coast."[119] "Upon the facts developed," Cleveland asserted in his Annual Message to Congress on December 4, "it seemed to me the only honorable course for our Government to pursue was to undo the wrong that had been done by those representing us and to restore as far as practicable the status existing at the time of our forcible intervention."[120]

Supporters of Hawaii's annexation were outraged. Senator Henry Cabot Lodge (R- Massachusetts), who had embraced Mahan's ambitions for the nation's navy and saw Hawaii as "the vantage ground of the control of the naval 'Key of the Pacific,'" called the administration's policy "grotesque and miserable."[121] Cleveland and Gresham were unfazed by such criticism. Indeed, they followed the withdrawal of the Hawaiian treaty by seeking to undo the nation's commitments in Samoa. Gresham saw the tripartite protectorate as colonialism by another name, arguing that it was "inaccurately styled an 'autonomous government,'" but was in reality "a tripartite foreign government, imposed upon the natives and supported and administered jointly by the three treaty powers."[122] Cleveland was concerned that U.S. commitments in Samoa could draw the country into unwanted and unnecessary conflicts. In his Annual Message on December 4, he asserted that the commitments stemming from the tripartite protectorate, especially in light of continuing unrest among Samoan factions, "signally illustrate the impolicy of entangling alliances with foreign powers."[123] Factional infighting among Samoans made Cleveland and Gresham particularly uneasy inasmuch as it increased the likelihood of U.S. involvement in hostilities—including, potentially, against Germany and Britain.

Over the course of the next two years, the Cleveland administration made several attempts to convince the Senate to abrogate the nation's participation in the tripartite protectorate. Cleveland began the effort in May of 1894 by sending to the Senate a report on Samoa drafted by Gresham. Although Gresham did not formally request withdrawal from the Berlin treaty, he made clear that the administration had serious misgivings about the arrangements:

> [In Samoa] we have made the first departure from our traditional and well established policy of avoiding entangling alliances with foreign powers in relation to objects remote from this hemisphere.... Every nation, and especially every strong nation, must sometimes be conscious of an impulse to rush into difficulties that do not concern it, except in a highly imaginary way. To restrain the indulgence of such a propensity is not only the part of wisdom, but a duty we owe to the world as an example of the strength, the moderation, and the beneficence of popular government.

Tripartite control, Gresham continued, was "fraught with so much peril to our 'safety and prosperity,' we look in vain for any compensating advantage." Trade with the islands was negligible and, in any case, "we have never found it to be necessary to interfere in the affairs of a foreign country in order to trade with it."[124]

President Cleveland himself took up the issue a few months later. Increasingly concerned about unrest on the islands, Cleveland in August 1894 sent a confidential letter to the Senate urging withdrawal from the Berlin Act. He requested that the Senate "concur in the termination of the general act of Berlin, if such termination could be brought about on acceptable terms."[125] The Senate did not take up the issue. Cleveland tried again in December, this time in public. He maintained that the joint protectorate was failing to bring stability to Samoa and that the arrangement constituted "plain defiance of the conservative teachings and warnings of the wise and patriotic men who laid the foundations of our free institutions."[126] The Senate Foreign Relations Committee on this occasion did debate the issue. Swayed mainly by a commitment to maintaining the naval station at Pago Pago, a bipartisan majority emerged in favor of declining Cleveland's entreaty to withdraw from the Samoan protectorate. Maintaining the nation's naval presence in the Pacific had come to enjoy support on both sides of the aisle.[127]

Cleveland, the Monroe Doctrine, and the Venezuelan Crisis

Cleveland was not uniformly opposed to pursuing a more muscular foreign policy. Even though he canceled the bid to annex Hawaii and sought to withdraw the nation from the tripartite protectorate over Samoa, on other issues he demonstrated a more internationalist orientation. As during his first term, he supported and added to the naval program launched by his Republican predecessor. His administration ordered five additional battleships—two in 1895 and three in 1896—and accelerated the construction of a new fleet of torpedo boats.[128] That a Democrat launched this building program made clear that bipartisan support for a blue-water navy was mounting.

As he looked to expand the nation's naval strength, Cleveland was more focused on flexing the nation's muscles in Latin America than in the Pacific. Indeed, his readiness to embrace an expansive interpretation of the Monroe Doctrine provoked a diplomatic crisis with Britain in 1895–1896. The issue in play was a dispute between Britain and Venezuela over the border of British Guiana. In late 1895, Cleveland received overwhelming support from both houses of Congress to insert the United States into the dispute and to fund a commission that would resolve the issue through neutral arbitration. Senator Lodge warned that Britain's handling of its confrontation with Venezuela without regard to U.S. interests was an affront to Americans, and that "the United States must either maintain the Monroe doctrine and treat its infringement as an act of hostility or abandon it."[129] Representative Charles Grosvenor (R-Ohio) similarly asserted that Cleveland should either take a strong stand or "cease to discuss the subject and abandon the Monroe doctrine permanently. . . . To temporize is cowardice, to equivocate dishonor."[130]

Amid the charged atmosphere, Richard Olney, Cleveland's new secretary of state (Gresham died in May 1895), promptly dispatched a letter to the British urging them to agree to address the dispute through arbitration. Olney's interpretation of the Monroe Doctrine was fulsome: "Today the United States is practically sovereign on this continent, and its fiat is law upon the subjects to which it confines its interposition. . . . Its infinite resources combined with its isolated position render it master of the situation and practically invulnerable as against any or all other powers."[131]

The British government initially rejected the U.S. request to resolve the dispute through arbitration as well as the claim that the Monroe Doctrine provided the United States a say in the matter. Indeed, the British effectively dismissed the Monroe Doctrine in their reply, noting that no country, regardless of its power, is "competent to insert into the code of international law a novel principle which was never recognized before, and which has not since been accepted by the government of any other country."[132] Blustery talk of war ensued in Washington, and the administration ordered the U.S. Navy to maintain readiness.[133] In February 1896, the Senate debated the status of the Monroe Doctrine, reinforcing the chamber's commitment to stand firm on the Venezuela border dispute. Senator Newton Blanchard (D-Louisiana) proclaimed that any British effort to seize territory from Venezuela "would be held by us to be tantamount to a declaration of war against both the United States and Venezuela, and would be resisted accordingly. That is the inevitable logic of the position we have assumed. We do not shrink from it, because it is right: it is the bold assertion of a great national policy that we are prepared to enforce and feel ourselves able to enforce against the British Empire and all comers."[134]

The heated atmosphere in Washington helped convince the British prime minister, Lord Salisbury, to back down and agree to submit the border dispute to neutral arbitration. Weighing heavily on his mind were the Royal Navy's anxieties about going to war with the United States while also facing rising threats to British interests in Europe, Asia, and South Africa.[135] The British were particularly concerned about the increasingly aggressive tone of congressional and public debate. Indeed, the British government seemed at least as concerned about rampant war-fever among the American public as it was about the strategic intentions of the Cleveland administration. The General Staff openly expressed its worries that public passions could press Washington to take hostile action, and Lord Salisbury, according to historian Stuart Anderson, "distrusted the emotionalism that often found its way into American foreign policy."[136] The British also went out of their way to acknowledge U.S. sway in the Western Hemisphere,

perhaps to the end of moderating public attitudes in the United States. Arthur
Balfour, leader of the House of Commons and First Lord of the Treasury, told
Parliament that in the dispute with Venezuela, "there has never been, and there
is not now, the slightest intention on the part of this country to violate what is
the substance and the essence of the Monroe Doctrine . . . a principle of policy
which both they [the United States] and we cherish."[137]

Cleveland's decision to confront Britain over the border dispute between
Venezuela and British Guiana, while out of character given his isolationist
leanings, was in keeping with the more assertive stance toward the hemisphere
that took shape during the 1890s. Indeed, U.S. forces were becoming increasingly active in the region. Interventions continued to be limited in scope and
duration, focused narrowly on protecting U.S commercial interests and citizens.
Nonetheless, between 1890 and the outbreak of the Spanish-American War in
1898, the United States intervened in Latin America eight times—in Argentina
(1890), Haiti (1891), Chile (1891), Brazil (1894), Nicaragua (1894, 1896,
1898), and Colombia (1895). By means of comparison, during the previous
decade, U.S. forces intervened in the region only twice—in Panama (1885) and
Haiti (1888).[138]

The United States' growing military activism in Latin America notwithstanding, Cleveland's blustery response to the Venezuela crisis still stands out
as a clear step forward in the nation's readiness to embrace and enforce a more
activist conception of the Monroe Doctrine. The nation's citizens and their commercial interests were not at stake in the dispute, but Washington was nonetheless
prepared to take a firm stand and risk a breach—and potential hostilities—
with Britain. To explain this escalation in U.S. engagement in the region, many
historians interpret Cleveland's move as a political gambit aimed at bolstering
the administration's flagging popular support.[139] In 1893, the country experienced a financial panic that produced a severe economic downturn lasting much
of the decade. Hundreds of banks failed, thousands of businesses collapsed, and
unemployment spiked. The Cleveland administration took much of the blame
for the economic duress. In the 1894 midterms, the Democrats suffered a huge
reversal, losing more than 120 seats in the House and four in the Senate.

These setbacks compelled Cleveland to look for ways to reclaim popular support. Rallying the public around the flag by precipitating a diplomatic crisis with
Britain over the Monroe Doctrine was his option of choice. Indeed, Democrats
more generally responded to their declining political fortunes by becoming
more nationalistic and moving away from the hostility toward foreign engagement that had long been a hallmark of the party.[140] The fact that Cleveland and
his party turned to foreign ambition and potential great-power entanglement
as a means of building public support was a clear indicator of the turn that
was taking place in popular attitudes. Since the founding era, politicians had

demonstrated their mettle and bolstered their popularity largely by shunning foreign commitments. But by the 1890s, Congress and the public were coming to embrace foreign ambition, especially when it came to a more robust interpretation and enforcement of the Monroe Doctrine. Republican supporters of expansion clearly helped drive this transformation by standing at the ready to criticize Democrats for their lack of spine whenever they opposed a more muscular foreign policy. Indeed, Lodge and Roosevelt, who had been vociferous critics of Cleveland over his cancellation of Hawaii's annexation, also charged that he was too accommodating of Britain during the dispute over Venezuela.[141]

* * *

By Cleveland's second term, the United States was in a strategic no-man's-land of sorts. A fundamental transition in American statecraft was clearly under way, but it was inchoate and incomplete. On one hand, the United States had passed through an inflection point. It was in the midst of building a battle fleet, a clear sign of its readiness to project its geopolitical influence well beyond its own neighborhood. Congress was ready to support and fund distant coaling stations at Pearl Harbor and Pago Pago. Moreover, even Cleveland, a president with impressive isolationist *bona fides*, in 1895 found it politically expedient to provoke a diplomatic crisis with Britain over the Monroe Doctrine. The fact that Britain backed down in the face of U.S. pressure only strengthened public confidence in a more ambitious brand of statecraft.

On the other hand, the nation's appetite for assuming wide-ranging strategic commitments was limited. The United States was building battleships, but many in Congress, especially southern Democrats, were still skeptical of the merits of doing so, and feared that projecting power into distant theaters would undermine, not enhance, American security. Harrison was enthusiastic about annexing Hawaii and exercising joint control over Samoa, but Cleveland wanted nothing to do with either island chain. Even in the Western Hemisphere, Cleveland was skittish about taking on new strategic commitments. He stood firm during the Venezuela crisis, but, as in his first term, he continued to oppose U.S. construction of an isthmian canal. When another bloody revolt against Spanish rule in Cuba broke out in 1895, Cleveland rejected U.S. involvement—despite interventionist pressure from Congress. Cleveland similarly rebuffed congressional pressure to intervene on behalf of Armenians facing persecution and massacre in the Ottoman Empire.[142] And even if Secretary of State Olney was adept at sending blustery messages to the British during the Venezuela crisis, he nonetheless appreciated the merits of a foreign policy of caution and restraint: "Thus far in our history, we have been spared the burdens and evils of immense standing armies and all the other accessories of huge warlike establishments, and the exemption has largely contributed to our national greatness and wealth as well as to the happiness of every citizen."[143]

In short, the internationalist turn had begun—but only in a tentative and halting way. It would not be until 1898 that the United States would break with its isolationist roots. Moreover, the embrace of foreign ambition exhibited in 1898 would prove to be only fleeting. Soon after the bout of imperialism that accompanied the Spanish-American War, many Americans would have buyer's remorse, questioning the merits of great-power entanglement and longing for the natural security that had come with isolation.

PART II

THE DEFEAT OF REALIST AND IDEALIST INTERNATIONALISM, 1898–1941

Part II of this book covers the second era of U.S. grand strategy, which runs from the Spanish-American War of 1898 until the nation's entry into World War II in 1941. The Spanish-American War marked a watershed in U.S. foreign policy. The United States embarked on a war of choice with Spain to expel it from Cuba, and ended up seizing control of and ruling over not only that island, but a host of other territories in the Caribbean and the Pacific. The era of isolationism came to an abrupt halt. Four decades of experimentation with both realist and idealist brands of internationalism were under way.

The imperial turn of 1898 was bound up with America's growing power as well as a change in the exceptionalist narrative driven in significant part by the closing of the nation's western frontier. With westward expansion at its geographic limits, the supporters of extra-continental expansion argued that it was time for Americans to capitalize on their growing economic and naval strength to take Manifest Destiny abroad. They argued not only that the nation's political and economic dynamism required continued expansion, but also that the country had an enduring obligation to bring republicanism and liberty to the rest of the world now that the task was complete at home. Preserving the American experiment no longer required isolating the union from the outside world. On the contrary, America's exceptionalist calling mandated that the United States venture out to share its ideals and fulfill its messianic mission.

President William McKinley's decision to expel Spain from Cuba—ostensibly to liberate the island from imperialism and oppression—was the opening salvo as Americans began to pursue this more activist brand of exceptionalism. This initial gambit was a success; the war went well, with the U.S. Navy handily defeating the Spanish fleets in the Caribbean and the Pacific. But popular enthusiasm for the nation's new geopolitical ambition quickly began to dissipate. Far from serving, as promised, as a liberator and guardian of freedom, the United States emerged from the war with a host of colonial appendages; rather than defeating imperialism, the country had embraced it. A public reaction against republican imperialism soon set in, fueling calls for a return to Washington's "great rule." A strategic pullback followed. A realist brand of internationalism failed to sustain popular support.

President Woodrow Wilson, who took office in 1913, then tried a different tack. Well aware of the political backlash against the imperial turn of 1898, he initially adhered to a traditional strategy of nonentanglement when World War I broke out in 1914. The arguments against U.S. involvement drew on the isolationist logics that had dominated grand strategy prior to 1898. The war was too distant from America's shores to affect U.S. security. The United States could not compromise its exceptionalist calling by inserting itself into yet another pointless power struggle among Europe's great powers. Instead, the nation needed to stand apart as a repository of democracy, a mediator, and an architect of a more peaceful postwar world. So, too, did Wilson fear that entanglement in the war would compromise liberty at home and serve as an obstacle to progressive economic reform.

Prompted by Germany's attacks on U.S. shipping in early 1917, Wilson changed his mind and decided to enter the war. He justified U.S. intervention on purely idealist grounds. With the United States itself under attack, Wilson maintained, the lofty goals of defending democracy and building a cooperative postwar order could be fulfilled only through resort to force. But just as the realist internationalism of 1898 failed to endure, Wilson's idealist alternative proved equally vulnerable. Americans were prepared to stand by their exceptionalist calling, but dying on the Western front required justification that went beyond altruism and ideological ambition. A brand of internationalism devoid of realist concerns about concrete strategic interests failed to sustain political support. So, too, did Wilson overreach ideologically when it came to the League of

Nations—his vehicle of choice for preserving postwar peace. The Senate rejected U.S. participation in the League, clearing the way for the stubborn isolationism of the interwar era.

The United States won the Spanish-American War and World War I. But neither military victory led to a durable internationalist consensus. The internationalism that accompanied war with Spain was too realist, while Wilson's was too idealist. America's break with isolationism was in one significant respect irreversible: the nation maintained the activist dominance of the Western Hemisphere that began in 1898; there was no pullback to the continentalism of the nineteenth century.

From more distant strategic theaters, however, the United States did beat a decisive retreat during the interwar era. During the 1920s, the United States pulled back militarily but stayed engaged economically, seeking to use its commercial and financial strength to advance geopolitical stability in both the European and Asian theaters. After the Great Depression, the United States began to go it alone even on economic issues, withdrawing into hemispheric isolation as geopolitical tension and conflict swept Europe and Asia. At the end of the 1930s, President Roosevelt finally took on the isolationists and began to provide economic and military support to nations fighting fascism. But he did so in the service of helping others fight for themselves so that the United States could stay out of the war. Only after Japan brought the war to Americans did Roosevelt reverse course and finally abandon the nation's isolationist perch.

The Spanish-American War and the Onset of Imperial Ambition

The American colonies went to war against Great Britain in 1775 as a matter of necessity; their political independence was at stake. The United States also had first-order interests on the line in the War of 1812; its ability to conduct foreign trade without interference was at stake. In contrast, the Spanish-American War was clearly a war of choice. Spain was indeed committing atrocities as it put down the ongoing rebellion in Cuba, but the Spanish posed no meaningful threat to the United States and did not impair its maritime commerce. That the United States took advantage of the war not just to expel Spain from Cuba but also to wrest control of territories in the Caribbean and the Pacific made clear that the United States had arrived at a strategic turning point. After more than a century of forswearing the imperial ambitions of Europe's great powers, the United States was playing their game.

A second era in U.S. grand strategy was opening. The nation's aversion to foreign entanglement prevailed from 1789 until the spring of 1898, but thereafter Americans were ready to expand beyond the homeland.[1] Such an about-face in U.S. grand strategy warrants a pause in this book's historical narrative to consider why the imperial turn came about. Clarifying the causes of this inflection point will lay a foundation for exploration of the trajectory of the nation's foreign policy after 1898.

It was inevitable that the United States would eventually seek to extend its geopolitical reach beyond the homeland. The history of the rise and fall of great powers demonstrates that as countries ascend economically, they eventually seek to acquire geopolitical influence commensurate with their economic strength.[2] Even while Americans were struggling for their independence with limited resources at their disposal, the Founders envisaged that their emerging nation would eventually come to dominate the Western Hemisphere. Given America's endowments of land and resources and the growth in population and economy that took place over the course of the nineteenth century, it was only a matter of time before the nation would seek to translate its material strength into geopolitical influence.

Even if this inflection point was inevitable, why the imperial turn happened when it did and why it took the form it did are nonetheless compelling puzzles. The Monroe Doctrine had been on the books since the 1820s, but the United States did little to stand behind it for another eighty years. Even after the Civil War, despite numerous opportunities for territorial expansion into the Caribbean, Latin America, and the Pacific, the United States shunned major strategic commitments beyond its own territory. What changed in 1898? How did isolationism, which had heretofore wielded controlling influence over U.S. foreign policy, lose its political grip? What ideological and political forces prompted the executive branch, Congress, and the public to abandon the commitment to isolationism that had long served the nation well and enabled it to rise in largely unmolested fashion? Why did the United States not only kick Spain out of Cuba—a move consistent with America's long-standing desire to rid its hemisphere of European powers—but also go on to assert control over Cuba, Puerto Rico, Hawaii, Guam, the Philippines, Wake Island, and Samoa—a move entirely inconsistent with the nation's founding principles and prior history? Americans had aggressively expanded across their continent, subjugating peoples who stood in the way of securing the envisaged homeland. But, in both principle and practice, they rejected the colonial ambitions of European powers. How could a polity whose creed was about rejecting and defeating imperialism suddenly embrace it?

This stark turn in strategy had multiple causes—the most important of which was the reinterpretation of American exceptionalism that took place during the late nineteenth century. Since the founding era, the United States' role as redeemer nation had meant advancing the American experiment by shielding the nation from the outside world and spreading that experiment only by example. But by the end of the nineteenth century, many Americans viewed this passive approach to realizing the country's exceptionalist calling as no longer sufficient; to save the world, the United States needed to venture out beyond its shores in the service of exporting the American experiment. In the words of Robert Tucker, the United States was beginning to transition from "exemplar" to "crusader."[3]

The origins of this transition in the nation's creed were twofold. One source of this new narrative was the nation's success. Americans had completed their messianic mission at home; the fulfillment of Manifest Destiny meant that productive settlement, democracy, and Christian civilization spanned from coast to coast. With the closing of the frontier, it was now time for Americans to take their mission abroad. The other source of the changing conception of exceptionalism emerged from the nation's shortcomings. Industrialization and the maturing economy had increased urbanization, inequality, and social immobility. Too-powerful corporations and trusts were becoming the new enemy within. In the public mind, the American dream was at risk as the faceless worker toiling in the urban factory replaced the yeoman farmer tilling land on the western frontier. Expansion abroad and the renewed prosperity that would accompany it was the needed redress.

These two sources of change in the American narrative, although they had different starting points, actually reinforced each other. For those focused on exporting the American experiment beyond the nation's borders, the intensi-fication of social ills at home was a clear sign of the adverse domestic impact of the closing of the frontier. For those more concerned about alleviating do-mestic poverty and inequality, restoring the American dream required expan-sion abroad and access to new markets now that free land was no longer available at home.

The New Frontier of American Exceptionalism

The reconceptualization of exceptionalism that took place in the 1890s emerged in part from confidence: Americans believed that they had successfully completed the North American chapter of their messianic mission. Over the course of the nineteenth century, they had not just made it to the Pacific coast, but had also succeeded in consolidating a secure, democratic, and prosperous republic. And they had done so while maintaining their liberty and proving un-founded the fears of the Founders that the American republic, like those before it, would eventually veer toward tyranny. But with their primary task behind them and the American frontier closed, Americans needed to look abroad to continue their messianic mission, retain their social dynamism, and sustain the American experiment. The foot soldiers of Manifest Destiny needed their next calling. The advancing frontier had given purpose, opportunity, and energy to American society, and expansion abroad would do the same moving forward. According to LaFeber, "there can be no doubt that one important part of the ra-tionale for an expansive foreign policy in the 1890s was a fervent . . . belief held by many Americans that their unique and beneficent internal frontier no longer existed."[4] For McDougall, the new brand of secular expansionism was also the product of a decline in religious messianism; the United States needed to be ex-ceptional for what it did, rather than what it was.[5]

The historian Frederick Jackson Turner popularized the notion of the closing of the frontier in an essay he prepared for delivery at a meeting of the American Historical Association in 1893.[6] Turner began his essay by quoting from the of-ficial census of 1890, which noted that heretofore, "the country had a frontier of settlement, but at present the unsettled area has been so broken into by isolated bodies of settlement that there can hardly be said to be a frontier line." Turner understood this development to have profound implications:

> This brief official statement marks the closing of a great historic move-
> ment. Up to our own day American history has been in a large degree
> the history of the colonization of the Great West. The existence of an
> area of free land, its continuous recession, and the advance of American
> settlement westward, explain American development. . . . And now,
> four centuries from the discovery of America, at the end of a hundred
> years of life under the Constitution, the frontier has gone, and with its
> going has closed the first period of American history.

The closing of the frontier was of momentous import for Turner because he attributed to westward expansion core features of the American experiment and its exceptional trajectory. For starters, he understood the advancing frontier to have shaped "the evolution of American political institutions" and consolidated its democratic character. According to Turner, "complex society is precipitated by the wilderness into a kind of primitive organization based on the family. The tendency is anti-social. It produces antipathy to control, and particularly to any direct control. . . . The frontier individualism has from the beginning promoted democracy." Turner referenced an 1830 statement from a western Virginian politician to underscore his point. The Virginian noted that when politicians from the Old Dominion return home, "they have negroes to fan themselves asleep." In contrast, when a politician from the frontier returns home, "he takes off his coat and takes hold of the plow. This gives him bone and muscle, sir, and preserves his republican principles pure and uncontaminated."

Turner also took the expanding frontier to be a source of common identity and national solidarity: "the frontier promoted the formation of a composite nationality for the American people." The eastern seaboard had been populated primarily by English settlers, while Scotch-Irish, Germans, Dutch, and other immigrants headed west. "In the crucible of the frontier," according to Turner, "the immigrants were Americanized, liberated, and fused into a mixed race." So, too, in his view, did western migration and settlement ameliorate sectionalism and moderate cultural and political differences among the nation's regions. Turner maintained that "particularism was strongest in colonies with no Indian frontier." In contrast, in areas of western expansion, "North and South met and mingled into a nation. Interstate migration went steadily on—a process of cross-fertilization of ideas and institutions." Turner concluded that "nothing works for nationalism like intercourse within the nation. Mobility of population is death to localism, and the western frontier worked irresistibly in unsettling population."

Finally, Turner attributed to frontier life the ongoing renewal of the nation's exceptionalist calling: "American social development has been continually beginning over again on the frontier. This perennial rebirth, this fluidity of American life, this expansion westward with its new opportunities, its continuous touch with the simplicity of primitive society, furnish the forces dominating the American character." He maintained that "to the frontier the American intellect owes its striking characteristics. That coarseness and strength combined with acuteness and inquisitiveness; that practical, inventive turn of mind, quick to find expedients; that masterful grasp of material things, lacking in the artistic but powerful to effect great ends; that restless, nervous energy; that dominant individualism, working for good and for evil, and withal that buoyancy and exuberance which comes with freedom—these are traits of the frontier."

Although Turner focused his attention on the contributions of the frontier to American life, he was not silent on the implications of the frontier's closing for the nation's next steps. "He would be a rash prophet who should assert that the expansive character of American life has now entirely ceased. Movement has been its dominant fact, and, unless this training has no effect upon a people," Turner maintained, "the American energy will continually demand a wider field for its exercise."

Turner articulated a set of arguments that would go on to provide an intellectual and political foundation for overseas expansion. Over the course of the 1890s, a growing number of Americans came to believe that preserving the nation's exceptional character and furthering its messianic mission mandated expansion abroad now that the western frontier had closed. Up until the 1890s, Americans tended to deem foreign entanglement to be at odds with their unique political experiment; being true to the American creed meant shielding the nation from the rest of the world while playing the role of global exemplar. By the end of the century, the American narrative was beginning to embrace the opposite claim: sustaining the vitality of the nation's unique character and pursuing its role as redeemer nation required expansion abroad. American ideals and aspirations—spreading republican government, protecting individual liberty, expanding economic opportunity—had not changed, but isolationism had to give way to foreign ambition to ensure their attainment. Playing the role of exemplar was no longer enough.

This logic began to figure prominently in a recast version of American exceptionalism. Brooke Adams, an influential writer of the time, maintained that "the continent which, when Washington lived, gave a boundless field for the expansion of Americans has been filled." The nation, in his view, now needed to look farther afield, and "the risk of isolation promises to be more serious than the risk of an alliance."[7] Others saw both an opportunity and an obligation to extend to other nations the Anglo-Saxon values that had successfully spread from coast to coast.

The Protestant pastor Josiah Strong worried about the effects on American society of both rapid industrialization and the dwindling supply of arable land. "We have seen that our manufacturing interests must inevitably become relatively greater," Strong wrote, "so that our national welfare will be increasingly dependent on foreign markets; and it has been further shown that we are dependent on such markets not simply for industrial prosperity, but also for political and social health."[8] Strong concluded, in the words of LaFeber, that sustaining the nation's vitality and prosperity required "ever increasing involvement in world politics."[9]

The claim that the nation's chosen status justified and mandated expansion abroad helped build public support for leaving behind the nation's isolationist past. If the United States was acting out of altruism and moral obligation rather than the quest for wealth and glory that fueled European imperialism, then its behavior still conformed to the nation's founding mission. The country was venturing abroad to spread American ideals; its conquests had noble intent. In the public mind, ejecting Spain from Cuba was a humanitarian cause, as was the occupation of the Philippines. Strong saw overseas expansion as a religious duty; with North America having been Christianized, it was time to bring the gospel to other nations. As LaFeber summarizes Strong's views, "salvation lay in the fulfillment of the Anglo-Saxon mission to reshape the world in the mold of western civilization."[10] For Frederick Wells Williams, a historian based at Yale during the 1890s, "American imperialism represented freedom."[11] He encouraged Americans to abandon "vain fears of imperialism," and instead venture abroad to expand commerce and spread Anglo-Saxon liberty and Christian values.[12]

Americans were thus coming to see overseas expansion as central to their exceptionalist calling—a calling with exclusively benign intentions. By expanding abroad they could both revitalize the American experiment at home and finally fulfill their redemptive mission abroad by bringing their experiment to others. According to Bernard Fensterwald, "most Americans of the day believed that our motives were anti-imperialist."[13] Those seeking to spread Christianity and Anglo-Saxon values, according to Jonathan Monten, believed that "because the United States was an agent of progressive historical change, it was a benign custodian of power."[14] Kagan agrees: "The Spanish-American War was . . . an expression of who the American people were and what they had made of the nation."[15]

The New Vulnerability of American Exceptionalism

The reconfiguration of American exceptionalism during the 1890s was also driven by an alternative line of argumentation—one that was rooted in the *vulnerability* rather than the success of the American experiment. Industrialization had wrought social transformation. By the late 1800s, the United States had a significant number of urban poor, greater ethnic

heterogeneity as a result of immigration, and more pronounced social stratification due to the increasing affluence of the most wealthy and the growth of
corporations, trusts, and banks. The financial panic and economic downturn
of 1893 only exacerbated the societal anxiety emerging from these changes,
threatening the American narrative of opportunity, mobility, and social
egalitarianism. In the words of Louis Hartz, "one of the earliest sources of
American nationalism was a sense of equality that came from knowing that
the social conflicts of Europe were not established here."[16] But by the 1890s,
those conflicts had arrived on America's shores, undermining a key plank of
the nation's creed. Corporate power and class stratification cast doubt on the
ability of ordinary citizens to realize the American dream.

These adverse economic and social developments prompted progressive
voices to begin embracing overseas expansion as the antidote; venturing abroad
was needed to help resolve challenges at home now that the American frontier
had closed. For much of American history, westward expansion had fueled economic growth and the vitality and equality of American society. But with the
closing of the frontier, progressive reformers argued that expansion overseas
was now needed to serve the same function.[17] James Phelan, the mayor of San
Francisco, laid out the case in 1898:

> We are confronted with the world-fact, that commerce enriches a na-
> tion, gives lucrative employment to the people, and thus contributes to
> their prosperity and happiness; and furthermore, that in these modern
> days, commerce cannot be secured and the balance of trade maintained
> unless a country is bold and enterprising, and stands behind its
> merchants wherever they may assert themselves, even in the remotest
> corners of the globe. We live in the world, and we of the United States
> are not so insular—that is, continental—as to say that the world is not
> a legitimate field for our activities.[18]

Progressive reformers were not alone in coming to see expansion as a valuable instrument for advancing economic growth. Indeed, they ended up in an
unlikely political alliance with both the business community and politicians
and strategists driven principally by realist considerations. Progressives wanted
to redress economic hardship and social stratification, while business leaders
envisaged increased profits. But both saw overseas expansion as furthering their
interests.[19] The realists were happy to play along. Admiral Mahan, although
motivated more by geopolitical than domestic considerations, aided and abetted
the cause by claiming that expanding overseas markets was key to the nation's
prosperity and that building a battleship fleet was necessary to make the oceans
safe for American commerce. Economists and other academic professionals
often lent their support to such arguments.[20] These shifts in elite opinion helped

transition the American narrative from one focused on isolation to one focused on expansion.

That progressives connected domestic prosperity and equality to foreign ambition helped convince the public that the nation's expansive impulse emerged from benign intentions; the United States was venturing forth to promote equality and liberty at home and abroad, not to replicate a European brand of imperialism that was about usurpation and oppression. Moreover, average American workers—not just shipbuilders, industrialists, and financiers—would be the beneficiaries of expansion. Opportunity and mobility would return to American society. Foreign peoples would benefit from the arrival of republican institutions and growing prosperity. The success of the American experiment and the fulfillment of its redemptive mission were both coming to require the projection of American power. Isolationism was giving way to a brand of internationalism ostensibly consistent with America's exceptionalist calling at home and abroad.

The New Global and Domestic Landscape

Three additional developments contributed to this shift in the American narrative—and amplified its consequence. First, the rapid pace of Europe's imperial expansion during the late nineteenth century helped convince American decision makers that they needed to act before it was too late. Importantly, the United States did not abandon isolationism because its security was directly threatened. The naval building program that began in the 1880s was in part intended to protect the country against the growing fleets of other powers. But the United States by the end of the 1800s was remarkably secure. It had emerged as a major industrial economy, come to dominate the Western Hemisphere, and was in the midst of orchestrating rapprochement with its most threatening adversary—Great Britain.

The situation in other strategic theaters, however, looked far less auspicious. During the 1880s and 1890s, Europe's great powers were busy carving up Africa and extending their colonial holdings in Asia. At the Berlin Conference (1884–1885) European diplomats formalized and mapped out their colonial claims to much of Africa. Germany, Japan, and Russia also entered the game, intensifying the race for territorial acquisitions. Japan's defeat of China in the Sino-Japanese War (1894–1895) made clear that a new power was emerging in the western Pacific. And unlike the laissez-faire British, the Germans, French, Japanese, and Russians were not committed free traders. If tapping into new international markets was essential to revitalizing the American experiment, then the nation had better get going.

From this perspective, it was not only America's western frontier that was closing, but also the opportunity to expand elsewhere. The last chapter made clear that this sentiment was shaping U.S. policy well before 1898. The decisions to gain access to Pago Pago and Pearl Harbor were largely about getting naval footholds in the Pacific while the United States still could. As Secretary of State Thomas Bayard put it in 1888 while seeking to justify the U.S. outpost in Samoa, European advances in the region meant that "of the vast aggregate of territory in the Pacific Ocean, but a few island groups, containing a few thousand square miles, remain today as independent and autonomous."[21] In the middle of the 1890s, Senator Lodge put forth a similar argument when making the case that the United States needed to extend its reach abroad on an urgent basis: "The great nations are rapidly absorbing for their future expansion and their present defense all the waste places of the earth. It is a movement which makes for civilization and the advancement of the race. As one of the great nations of the world, the United States must not fall out of the line of march."[22] A further sign that the United States was trying to keep pace with the international competition was its decision to supplement the imperial push of 1898 with its 1899 Open Door policy toward China—an effort to ensure that Americans enjoyed access to the Chinese market. As historian Julius Pratt concludes, "the thought of entering the scramble for colonies ere it was too late was not wholly a stranger to the minds of some American statesmen in 1898."[23]

A second important development took place at home. Political power in the United States had become more centralized and its governing institutions more capable, better equipping the government to pursue an ambitious foreign policy.[24] The republic had survived more than a century without falling prey to tyranny; by the 1890s most Americans no longer feared that building a battleship fleet or projecting the nation's power abroad would spell the end of domestic liberty. Southern Democrats, long supportive of isolationism and a weak central government, had warmed up to overseas expansion—in part because they feared appearing weak in the face of Republican calls for a more ambitious foreign policy. Democrats in the end played an influential role in pressing President McKinley—a Republican—to intervene militarily in Cuba. So, too, did progressives, who had feared that a strong executive would end up doing the bidding of corporate interests, come to believe that a more capable federal government was needed to address inequality and the social ills that had accompanied industrialization and urbanization.

Finally, the American economy had matured in ways that strengthened the voice and political power of domestic groups with vested interests in overseas expansion.[25] The U.S. Navy, the steel and shipbuilding sectors, shipping lines, finance, exporters of both agricultural and manufactured goods, and progressives looking to boost employment all joined forces to back a new American internationalism. Expansionism also began to enjoy greater cross-sectional support—including among Democrats—as these vested interests opened for business in the South as well as the North and in the interior of the country as well as the coastal states.[26] The transcontinental railroad and the steamship helped bring heartland farmers and ranchers into the global marketplace. Emerging technologies, such as wireless telegraphy, promised to facilitate links between American merchants and foreign markets. Not surprisingly, growing enthusiasm for expansion began to show up among academic specialists and in the media. Public opinion followed the same trajectory. Indeed, Congress's and the public's clamor for U.S. intervention in Cuba helped push the McKinley administration to war in 1898.

* * *

Material and ideological change worked hand in hand to lure the United States away from its isolationist creed. The nation's extraordinary economic ascent during the closing decades of the nineteenth century provided Americans the option of building a world-class navy and seeking to extend their geopolitical reach well beyond their own shores. Ideological change then induced them to exercise that option. Confronted with the closing of the western frontier and a new set of domestic ills stemming from industrialization and urbanization, Americans became convinced that it was time to take their exceptionalist calling abroad. Moreover, in light of the growing ambition and reach of other major powers, the nation had to act sooner rather than later if it was to gain the naval footholds and tap the foreign markets needed to realize the new and more activist version of exceptionalism that was taking hold.

8

Republican Imperialism and the Isolationist Backlash

In the 1896 election, Republicans took back the White House and retained control of both houses of Congress. The Republican sweep cleared the way for pursuit of a more ambitious brand of statecraft. Nonetheless, a consensus in favor of overseas expansion took time to materialize. The official and public minds were still in a strategic limbo of sorts; the nation was ready to translate its economic strength into geopolitical ambition, but still reluctant to countenance the commitments that would accompany expansion. Soon after taking office, President William McKinley tried to annex Hawaii, but the Senate was not on board. On Cuba, the tables were turned; McKinley initially resisted Congress's enthusiasm for the forcible expulsion of Spain from the island. Despite growing pressure from the legislature, the press, and the public, McKinley steered clear of intervention in Cuba during his first year in office, wary of conflict with Spain and deterred by the prospect of either ruling over or incorporating into the union the island's large and largely nonwhite population.

McKinley's political room for maneuver on Cuba shrank considerably as the result of escalating violence between Spanish forces and the rebels. More than 100,000 Cubans died from fighting and starvation, and Spain herded hundreds of thousands more into concentration camps, prompting many Americans to call for intervention. On February 15, 1898, an explosion in Havana's harbor sank the USS *Maine* and killed more than 250 American servicemen; McKinley had dispatched the vessel to Cuba to protect U.S. citizens and interests. Although the cause of the explosion was uncertain, a Navy investigation concluded that the ship hit a mine. Prowar newspapers helped stoke widespread outrage in the United States. Prodded by Congress and public pressure, McKinley in April took the nation to war in the service of Cuban independence.

The Spanish-American War served as a tipping point in American grand strategy. The isolationist dam, as it were, broke, unleashing pent-up political enthusiasm for exerting the nation's geopolitical influence and marking its arrival as a major power. The United States wrested from Spain control over not only Cuba, but also Puerto Rico, Guam, and the Philippines. The McKinley administration did not stop with former Spanish possessions. It proceeded to annex Hawaii and the western portion of the Samoan islands, and took possession of Wake Island, which lies between Guam and Hawaii. Successive administrations embraced a new level of diplomatic activism and military interventionism in Latin America. Soon after the turn of the century, the United States at last started construction of an isthmian canal across Panama—first sending warships to help Panama achieve independence from Colombia. This more activist brand of statecraft also reached across the Pacific. In 1889, the Asiatic Squadron was composed of five obsolescent ships. By 1902, the U.S. Navy had forty-eight vessels on station in the squadron.[1]

The same strategic and economic objectives that triggered the launch of the battleship fleet were behind this new activism. Less than two weeks before the outbreak of the Spanish-American War, the German Reichstag passed the first of a series of naval laws aimed at the acquisition of a world-class battleship fleet. With most of the world's major powers enlarging their navies and imperial holdings, the main shapers of American strategy—McKinley, Lodge, and Mahan among them—were convinced that safeguarding the nation's security and prosperity required overseas expansion. In their minds, this reality provided a compelling response to Washington's cautionary question in his Farewell Address: "Why quit our own to stand upon foreign ground?"

But even if realist logic and material considerations figured prominently in the acquisition of a high-seas fleet and the embrace of expansive designs, the political will to act on these designs came primarily from ideological conviction. Congress, the media, and the public clamored for war against Spain to fulfill a perceived humanitarian obligation that was part and parcel of advancing America's mission as redeemer nation. The war represented an opportunity— indeed, an obligation—to take Manifest Destiny abroad and to share the American experiment with the rest of the world through action rather than just example. Expelling Spain from Cuba and bringing independence and democracy to the island—this was the obvious place to start.

It was no accident that in his message to Congress requesting a declaration of war, McKinley justified U.S. intervention on primarily ideological grounds. He led his case for war by insisting that the United States needed to act "in the cause of humanity. . . . It is no answer to say this is all in another country, belonging to another nation, and is therefore none of our business. It is specially our duty, for it is right at our door."[2] As Nichols describes the address, McKinley was portraying the United States as a "hemispheric force for democracy and a defender of a universal vision of justice."[3] This ideological justification for taking on geopolitical commitments beyond the nation's shores helped rally support on both sides of the aisle. On April 19, a joint resolution authorizing the use of force passed the House by a vote of 311 to 6 and the Senate by 42 to 35, and Congress on April 25 approved, by unanimous consent, the formal declaration of war.

Resting the case for geopolitical ambition on primarily idealist grounds helped anchor popular support for abandoning the nation's isolationist strictures. However, it also set the stage for the isolationist recoil that would soon follow. Americans projected their power abroad to defeat imperialism and spread their exceptional values. But in doing so, the United States itself became an imperial overseer, embracing the very values and practices it had set out to defeat. American exceptionalism may have mandated military intervention in Cuba and the expulsion of Spain from the Caribbean and Pacific. But America's experimentation with republican imperialism came back to haunt the nation by compromising its exceptional character. The result was an anti-imperialist backlash that eroded the nation's new internationalism. "We [Americans] had acquired an empire," according to Fensterwald, "and we spent the next forty years either trying to get rid of it or trying to ignore it."[4]

A second contradiction emerging from the ideological origins of the Spanish-American War would prove even more problematic—indeed, it continues to plague American grand strategy to this day. Americans ventured out to redeem the world, to extend Manifest Destiny abroad now that the mission at home had been completed, to do for others what Americans had done for themselves. To shed a national narrative that had long taken isolationism to be part of the American creed required redefining exceptionalism in expansive terms. The war fever of 1898 was predicated on the proposition that henceforth Americans could remain true to their exceptional character only by exporting their political experiment in the service of transforming the world.

This shift in the national narrative and redefinition of exceptionalism, however, set Americans up for frustration, disappointment, and retreat. Pacifying and democratizing Cuba and the Philippines were far more difficult and elusive than expected. And although Americans were keen to share their values with other peoples, they were unconvinced that expending blood and treasure to do so was worth the effort. The transition from exemplar to crusader proved more attractive in theory than in practice, leaving Americans with a core dilemma. They needed to believe that they were bringing their experiment to the rest of the world if they were to venture abroad. But the high hurdles and costs standing in the way of realizing that objective left the nation's new internationalism on vulnerable political ground. Hence the temptation to return to an isolationist brand of exceptionalism.

These contradictions born of the imperialism that accompanied the Spanish-American War left the country in an awkward middle ground. The United States emerged from the war with an empire. But the acquisition of empire and the bloody war in the Philippines soured the public on the nation's outward turn. McKinley remained popular enough to win reelection in 1900 against his anti-imperialist competitor, William Jennings Bryan. McKinley was then assassinated, only six months into his second term, and the presidency passed to Theodore Roosevelt (1901–1909), whose imperialist leanings were at least as strong as those of his predecessor. Indeed, Roosevelt intensified the nation's new activism in Latin America; it was during his watch that the United States started construction of the Panama Canal and stepped up its heavy-handed diplomacy and regular military interventions throughout the Caribbean and Latin America. Spain's exit from the region along with rapprochement between Washington and London after the Venezuela crisis left the United States as the uncontested regional hegemon; mission accomplished when it came to the Monroe Doctrine.

But beyond the hemisphere, Roosevelt too had buyer's remorse and scaled back the nation's ambition. According to McDougall, "from the point of view of hard national interest almost everyone, including Teddy Roosevelt, soon concluded that annexing the Philippines had been a mistake. The islands were a military Achilles' heel and an economic drain, and he hoped to set them free as soon as possible."[5] Roosevelt did keep hold of all the Pacific territories taken during the Spanish-American War. But he also returned to a foreign policy in Asia focused on maintaining market access and preserving a regional balance of power rather than extending strategic commitments. Roosevelt's successor, William Howard Taft (1909–1913), went a step further, making commercial expansion the focal point of U.S. grand strategy—a move that came to be known as dollar diplomacy. The United States had a growing battleship fleet and a new set of far-flung strategic commitments, neither of which the nation was prepared to give up. But many Americans, the president included, were tempted to return to the more familiar and tested approach of the Founders. Jefferson, after all, had given dollar diplomacy a solid pedigree: "Commerce with all nations, alliance with none, should be our motto."[6]

The Taft era set the stage for Woodrow Wilson, who was acutely aware that the Spanish-American War, although it produced a stunning victory for the United States, ended up pitting the nation's new foreign ambition against its historic mission as a redeemer nation. Wilson would pivot toward a brand of internationalism that was more genuinely idealist than that of McKinley; Wilson sought to eradicate rather than embrace empire. But the allure of isolationism and unilateralism as well as ongoing doubts about the feasibility and merits of taking Manifest Destiny abroad would mean that Wilson's effort to reconcile internationalism with the nation's ideals would ultimately fail.

The Imperial Moment

The 1896 Republican platform called for an expansionist policy that included the annexation of Hawaii, the purchase of the Danish West Indies, the construction of an isthmian canal, and a sizable enlargement of the navy.[7] Backed by the business community in the Northeast, the party was keen to increase international commerce as well as orders for shipyards. Concern about Japan's potential designs on Hawaii put the islands at the top of the Republican agenda.[8] McKinley acted quickly; only three months after taking office, he made a new run at annexing Hawaii. On June 16, 1897, his administration signed a treaty with the Republic of Hawaii—which was governed by white settlers who had taken power in 1893—and soon thereafter dispatched it to the Senate for approval.

Despite the fact that a Republican president was requesting consent from a Republican-controlled Senate, the treaty garnered nowhere near the necessary two-thirds majority. The outcome was heavily influenced by a lobbying campaign launched by native Hawaiians. Over the course of September and October, activists garnered some 20,000 signatures on a petition opposing annexation—representing roughly half of the native Hawaiian and mixed-race population. A delegation led by the Hawaiian queen then took the petition to Washington, where the chair of the Senate Foreign Relations Committee, Senator George Hoar (R-Massachusetts), presented it to the chamber. The Hawaiian delegation also met with many individual senators as well as the secretary of state. Only forty-six of ninety senators ended up supporting annexation, leaving McKinley well short of the numbers required for ratification.[9]

When it came to an island much closer to home—Cuba—Congress was considerably more forward leaning. Amid Spain's violent crackdown against the renewed rebellion that began in 1895, Congress in early 1896 passed resolutions calling for the United States to support the rebels, provide financial aid to victims of the civil war, and play a direct role in negotiating a resolution to the crisis. Later in the year—after McKinley's election and the Republican retention of Congress—the Senate Foreign Relations Committee passed a resolution in favor of recognizing Cuba as an independent republic. The so-called yellow press added to the pressure for U.S. action by regularly running sensationalist stories about the bloodshed and repression occurring in Cuba.

Like Cleveland, McKinley was averse to military intervention, especially when expelling Spain from Cuba entailed the sobering prospect of armed conflict with a European power. McKinley's top priority was economic recovery from the sharp downturn that began in 1893, an objective that the business community advised would be hindered by war.[10] McKinley was also concerned about the aftermath of conflict and the likelihood that the United States would find itself in effective control of Cuba after Spain's departure. In line with virtually all of his predecessors, McKinley was opposed to annexation given Cuba's primarily nonwhite population. The main alternative—establishing some form of colonial rule—was equally unappealing as it would be inconsistent with American values and its anti-imperialist calling. Accordingly, it was best to steer clear.[11]

Such restraint became politically unsustainable following the sinking of the *Maine* in February 1898. Indignation over the loss of American lives and the escalating violence and suffering in Cuba produced mounting war fever among elites and the public alike. Senator Lodge was among those calling for a forceful response: "The men who were hurled from the sleep of life into the sleep of death call upon us from their graves to root out forever the causes which made their slaughter possible."[12] In late March, the United States offered to serve as a mediator and put a number of demands to the Spanish— including an armistice and the end of concentration camps—which generally went unmet. McKinley on April 11 requested authorization from Congress "to secure a full and final termination of hostilities between the Government of Spain and the people of Cuba . . . and to use the military and naval forces of the United States as may be necessary."[13] Two weeks later, Madrid severed diplomatic relations with Washington and Congress declared war against Spain.[14]

From the outset, the McKinley administration had more than Cuba in its sights.[15] Within days of the declaration of war, McKinley authorized the U.S. Asiatic Squadron to attack the Spanish fleet in the Philippines. The Navy had been planning for months to expand the conflict to the Pacific in the event of war with Spain over Cuba.[16] In the Battle of Manila Bay on May 1, the U.S. fleet destroyed Spain's Pacific Squadron, and soon thereafter McKinley ordered a military expedition of some 15,000 U.S. soldiers to occupy and secure the Philippines.[17] On May 10, the secretary of the navy instructed a U.S. cruiser headed for Manila to seize Guam as it made its way across the Pacific.[18] Spanish authorities surrendered Guam on June 20.[19] The United States also went on to win handily in the Caribbean, on July 3 destroying Spain's fleet in the Battle of Santiago de Cuba.[20]

An armistice was signed in August. In December, through the Treaty of Paris, Spain ceded to the United States control over Cuba, Puerto Rico, Guam, and the Philippines. The United States agreed to pay Spain $20 million for the Philippines.[21] The following month Filipinos, led by General Emilio Aguinaldo, declared the founding of the Philippine Republic. Aguinaldo's republican aspirations were, however, quite premature; the Philippines was by the beginning of 1899 governed by the U.S. military, as were Cuba, Puerto Rico, and Guam. The Philippines would not gain independence from the United States until 1946.

Amid U.S. successes against the Spanish fleets in the Pacific and Caribbean, McKinley took advantage of the jubilant atmosphere in Washington to try again to annex Hawaii. Not only had triumphs against Spain whetted the national appetite for expansion, but the war also gave the proponents of Hawaii's annexation another rationale for moving forward. Now that the United States had new commitments in the western Pacific—pacifying the Philippines most prominent among them—Pearl Harbor became of greater strategic importance. As during earlier debates over annexation, proponents touted Hawaii as a way station for transpacific trade and a strategic outpost needed to protect the western approaches to the United States. In the words of Representative Robert Hitt (R-Illinois), the United States needed Hawaii "because of the supreme importance and value of the islands on account of their position. . . . Coal has become an essential of maritime war . . . and across that wide ocean any vessel of war coming to attack the United States must stop for coal and supplies at the Hawaiian Islands before it can attack us." Pearl Harbor was a prized asset not just for defensive purposes; it was also deemed essential to resupplying the war effort in the Philippines. According to Hitt, "a great and successful blow was struck in Manila by gallant Admiral Dewey and his fleet . . . yet it is not possible to send support to Dewey to-day without taking on coal and supplies at Honolulu in the Hawaiian islands."[22] In its report on Hawaii's proposed annexation, the House Foreign Affairs Committee concluded that "annexation, and that alone, will securely maintain American control in Hawaii" and access to Pearl Harbor.[23]

Chastened by his earlier defeat in the Senate, McKinley requested approval of Hawaiian annexation through a joint resolution of Congress rather than Senate ratification. A joint resolution would require only a simple majority in both chambers. The move did provoke some opposition; Representative Hugh Dinsmore (D-Arkansas) asserted that "I do not believe that we have any constitutional authority by the method proposed to us now to take" Hawaii. He also contended that annexation "is strictly in conflict with every tradition of our Government," and that Hawaii's strategic value is "greatly exaggerated."[24] Representative James "Champ" Clark (D-Missouri) agreed, noting that Admiral Dewey did not require U.S. ownership of Hawaii to defeat the Spanish fleet, and that "if his great victory proves anything at all about these islands it is that we have no earthly use for them."[25] Despite such constitutional and strategic objections from Dinsmore, Clark, and other opponents, Congress complied with McKinley's request for approval of annexation. The resolution passed easily in both chambers (290 to 91 in the House, 42 to 21 in the Senate), and Hawaii finally became a U.S. territory in August 1898.

The United States also raised its flag over Wake Island during the summer of 1898 when a U.S. officer on his way to the Philippines claimed the territory. The following January, McKinley ordered a U.S. naval commander to land on the island and formally establish it as a U.S. possession. Congress was not involved. McKinley followed the same game plan for Samoa. In 1899, he split the islands with Germany following Britain's withdrawal from the tripartite protectorate, and in 1900 proceeded to annex the U.S. portion while dispensing with all forms of congressional authorization or approval. To be sure, the acquisitions of Wake Island and Samoa were relatively uncontroversial; Wake was uninhabited and Samoa's chiefs welcomed rather than resisted U.S. annexation. Nonetheless, times had clearly changed; after decades of congressional vetoes over territorial expansion, Congress was finally ready to approve a succession of acquisitions— and in some cases content to be merely a passive bystander as the executive branch extended the nation's geopolitical reach.

The Expansionists: Realists, Redeemers, and Reformers

From the founding era through Grover Cleveland's second term, isolationism maintained its hold on U.S. grand strategy because it enjoyed support, often for disparate reasons, across the political spectrum. In similar fashion, the imperial turn of 1898 was made possible by an ideological consensus behind expansionism that united Americans of disparate political persuasions. Three main ideological camps came together to pull the nation away from its isolationist roots. The realists maintained that U.S. security and prosperity mandated that the nation extend its geopolitical reach beyond its borders. The redeemers contended that Americans had an obligation to take Manifest Destiny on the road now that the mission at home was complete. The reformers saw overseas expansion and the spread of republican government as a pathway to stimulating economic growth and political rejuvenation at home. These three lines of argumentation intermingled and overlapped, leading to a solid bipartisan consensus in favor of the nation's outward turn.

The Realists

For the realists—the likes of Alfred Thayer Mahan, Henry Cabot Lodge, and Theodore Roosevelt (who served as McKinley's assistant secretary of the navy from 1897 to 1898)—the Spanish-American War was an opportunity to break away from an isolationist grand strategy that was obsolete in favor of an expansionist policy consistent with the nation's newly acquired economic and geopolitical strength. The expulsion of Spain from Cuba was less of a paramount strategic objective than it was a handy justification for launching what Lodge liked to call a "large policy."[26] In the words of Pratt, the realists "aimed at no less than making the United States the indisputably dominant power in the western hemisphere, possessed of a great navy, owning and controlling an Isthmian canal, holding naval bases in the Caribbean and the Pacific, and contesting, on at least even terms with the greatest powers, the naval and commercial supremacy of the Pacific Ocean and the Far East."[27] The relevance and influence of the realist camp are evident in the results of the war. The United States did not just drive Spain from the Caribbean; it used the war as an excuse to push outward and establish imperial control over a host of noncontiguous territories.

In both political and ideological terms, Lodge was a pivotal figure in orchestrating the seismic change in U.S. foreign policy that took place in 1898. The core of his position was that geopolitical detachment had long served the country well, but that the United States had outgrown it. In Lodge's words, "isolation in the United States has been a habit, not a policy. It has been bred by circumstances and by them justified. When the circumstances change, the habit perforce changes too, and new policies are born to suit new conditions."[28] The nation's circumstances had indeed changed in two important respects: the United States had grown far more powerful, and the increasing strength and colonial reach of other great powers necessitated that the nation project power abroad to safeguard its security and prosperity. "We have come indeed to the parting of the ways," Lodge insisted, "and I believe we can no longer remain isolated. A nation of seventy millions, with an extending commerce must be a world power."[29]

Others echoed Lodge's evolutionary justification for abandoning isolationism. In the words of Senator Orville Platt (R-Connecticut), "a policy of isolation did well enough when we were an embryo nation, but today things are different. . . . We are 65,000,000 of people, the most advanced and powerful on earth, and regard to our future welfare demands an abandonment of the doctrines of isolation."[30] James Bridge, the editor of the *Overland Monthly*, wholeheartedly agreed: "The subjugation of a continent was sufficient to keep the American people busy at home for a century. . . . But now that the continent is subdued, we are looking for fresh worlds to conquer."[31]

In Lodge's mind, the first objective of the nation's new ambition was to finally rid the hemisphere of European interlopers. "My desire is to get Europe out of America," he declared.[32] But for Lodge and his fellow realists, pushing Spain and Great Britain out of America's neighborhood was not enough. With European and Asian powers expanding their battle fleets and their imperial holdings, the United States needed to keep pace to ensure its security. As Roosevelt wrote to Mahan months before the outbreak of the Spanish-American War, "if I had my way, we would annex those islands [Hawaii] tomorrow. If that is impossible I would establish a protectorate over them. I believe we should build the Nicaragua Canal at once, and in the meantime that we should build a dozen new battleships, half of them on the Pacific Coast."[33] According to McDougall, "U.S. naval officers and their supporters in Congress knew that sooner or later the United States would have to expand its purview, if only to secure North America from the fleets of the imperial powers."[34] The need for territorial expansion followed logically from the need for a naval buildup. If the United States had to build a world-class navy to defend its security, then it would have to acquire overseas outposts to sustain the fleet. In Mahan's own words, "I am frankly an imperialist, in the sense that I believe that no nation, certainly no great nation, should henceforth maintain the policy of isolation which fitted our early history."[35]

Lodge, Mahan, and their ideological kin also argued that enlarging the nation's geopolitical ambition would expand its wealth. Lodge and Mahan both maintained that access to new overseas markets would lead to economic growth at home. A battle fleet, supported by overseas naval stations, would help ensure such access. Influential scholars joined the chorus. Historian Gary Marotta maintains that academic associations—such as the American Historical Association, the American Economic Association, and the American Academy of Political and Social Science—were "intellectually predisposed toward an imperial policy." Many economists, for example, "approvingly saw a profound connection between the development of economics at home and the deliberate pushing into foreign markets."[36] Important voices within the scholarly community thus lent their support to the realist case for expansion.

Notably, realists like Lodge may have been keen to abandon isolationism, but they nonetheless adhered steadfastly to another tradition handed down to them by the Founders—unilateralism. The nation needed to expand, but it needed to act alone, not in partnership with other powers. The United States was expelling Spain from its neighborhood, not embroiling itself in European affairs. As the nation emerged as a world power, in Lodge's view, "this involves no entangling alliances but it does involve leaving our isolation . . . and the only question is whether we shall do it intelligently or clumsily."[37] The same went for the nation's diplomatic engagements. If and when the United States supported international institutions, it had to do so in a way that would not impair the nation's freedom of action. For example, the United States in 1899 backed the establishment of the Permanent Court of Arbitration in the Hague. But the U.S. delegation was careful to stipulate that "nothing contained in this convention shall be so construed as to require the United States of America to depart from its traditional policy of not intruding upon, interfering with, or entangling itself in the political questions or policy or internal administration of any foreign State; nor shall anything contained in the said Convention be construed to imply a relinquishment by the United States of America of its traditional attitude toward purely American questions."[38]

The marriage between internationalism and unilateralism that emerged in 1898 would prove to have remarkable staying power. As discussed in the next chapter, Lodge would ultimately take the lead in defeating Woodrow Wilson's bid to join the League of Nations on unilateralist, not isolationist, grounds. And to this day, a strong strain of unilateralism and hostility to pacts perceived to compromise the nation's freedom of action continue to shape U.S. internationalism—especially on the political right.

The Redeemers

The realists may have been the plotters behind the imperial turn, but it was the redeemers who successfully justified the nation's new expansionism among the broader public. Although ending European imperialism in the Western Hemisphere was entirely consistent with America's exceptionalist narrative and its encapsulation in the Monroe Doctrine, wresting control of and ruling over territorial possessions in the Caribbean and Pacific were not. Indeed, military occupation and colonial rule were in direct contradiction to the long-standing equation of America's exceptional character with its role as anti-imperialist beacon of republican government. In this regard, portraying the Spanish-American War as the next step in the country's exceptional mission—rather than a departure from it—was key to providing ideological justification for the conflict.

Building on the societal anxiety that emerged from the 1893 economic crisis and concern about the closing of the frontier, the redeemers successfully cast the war and the bout of expansionism that accompanied it as the logical follow-on to the completion of Manifest Destiny at home. Advancing the American experiment had since the founding era meant shunning foreign ambition due to the threat that entanglement would pose to the nation's natural security, the liberty of its citizens, and the deeply held conviction that all peoples should be free to govern themselves. But now that the United States was a major power and its experiment secure, it had an obligation to pursue its redemptive mission through more activist means. It was time for Americans to move beyond their role as exemplar and literally bring their Anglo-Saxon way of life to the rest of the world. The ends justified the new means. In the service of exporting the American experiment, Americans were destined to project their power abroad even if doing so transgressed the isolationist admonitions of the Founders.[39]

McKinley headed the effort to justify America's new foreign policy in terms of the nation's redemptive mission. As he prepared to take the nation to war to expel Spain from Cuba he insisted that he was acting in "the cause of humanity."[40] McKinley justified the U.S. occupation of the Philippines on similar grounds: "There was nothing left for us to do but to take them all, and to educate the Filipinos, and uplift and civilize and Christianize them, and by God's grace do the very best we could for them, as our fellow-men for whom Christ also died."[41] "Territory sometimes comes to us when we go to war in a holy cause, and whenever it does the banner of liberty will float over it and bring, I trust, blessings and benefits to all people," he explained during a speaking tour in the fall of 1898.[42] During another stop on the tour, he insisted that "we cannot escape the obligations of victory. . . . Accepting war for humanity's sake, we must accept all obligations which the war in duty and honor imposed upon us. . . . There must be a constant movement toward a higher and nobler civilization."[43] In reacting to the insurgency that sought to expel U.S. troops from the Philippines, McKinley pointedly asked: "Do we need their consent to perform a great act of humanity?"[44] He similarly reached for ideological justification in making the case for annexing Hawaii, claiming that "we need Hawaii just as much as and a good deal more than we did California. It is manifest destiny."[45]

McKinley was hardly alone in justifying U.S. expansion in terms of the nation's messianic mission. Amid heated debate over the merits of taking possession of the Philippines, Senator Knute Nelson (R-Minnesota) insisted that "we come as ministering angels, not as despots."[46] Wresting control of the islands, Senator John Spooner (R-Wisconsin) maintained, will not compromise the nation's democratic principles because the United States "will religiously maintain the best ideals of the Republic, and will be in harmony with justice, generosity, and the highest civilization."[47] Senator Albert Beveridge (R-Indiana) went to the Philippines amid the insurgency, and returned to instruct his colleagues that the nation had to stay the course "with gratitude for a task worthy of our strength, and thanksgiving to Almighty God that He has marked us as his chosen people, henceforth to lead in the regeneration of the world."[48] Religious leaders and missionaries joined the expansionist chorus, with Reverend R. L. Bachman reminding his congregation in Utica, New York, that Christ's command "did not pertain to one people, or to some favored section of the globe. In its reach and scope it took in the whole earth." On the eve of the outbreak of war, the *California Christian Advocate* declared, "this war is the *Kingdom of God coming!*"[49]

This shift in the country's global role from exemplar to crusader, which represented a striking change in the national narrative, was not just about exporting the American experiment. An activist conception of the redemptive mission was also aimed at making the world safe for American engagement. Isolation enabled Americans to cordon themselves off from peoples perceived as inferior. Expansion meant that Americans would now be in their midst. The United States may have been compelled to become a global power for reasons of security, prosperity, and national mission. But, if so, Americans would have to raise up the outside world to make it a more hospitable and inviting place for Anglo-Saxons to venture.

In this regard, a strong sense of racial superiority still shaped U.S. grand strategy. Instead of retreating from the nonwhite, non-Christian world, however, Americans would bring to that world Anglo-Saxon values and practices. As McKinley put it, Americans had "to educate the Filipinos, and uplift and civilize and Christianize them." In the words of Pastor Josiah Strong, "it is chiefly to the English and American peoples that we must look for the evangelization of the world. . . . It seems to me that God, with infinite wisdom and skill, is training the Anglo-Saxon race for an hour sure to come in the world's future. . . . Then this race of unequaled energy . . . of the largest liberty, the purest Christianity, the highest civilization . . . will spread itself over the earth."[50] If the United States could not separate itself from lesser peoples, then it would have to civilize them.

Taking on this more activist approach to spreading republican government required one other change in strategic logic: Americans had to have at least a measure of confidence that their efforts would bear fruit. Such optimism about the ability of the United States to effect political change abroad was new. Over the course of the nineteenth century, Americans had systematically held back from foreign intervention in support of republicanism in part because they were skeptical that doing so would yield positive results; most of the world simply was not ready to embrace democratic rule. By 1898, Americans were ready to try their hand at exporting democracy.

McKinley may have sincerely believed that "the banner of liberty will float over" the territories taken by the United States in the Spanish-American War. But, if so, his optimism was not the product of changed circumstances abroad or a reasoned reassessment of the likelihood of success. Rather, the U.S. government was keen to begin flexing its geopolitical muscle and justified its outward push as central to the nation's exceptionalist calling; Americans needed to believe the forcible spread of republicanism would work. As discussed below, this "rigged" optimism about the likely consequences of taking Manifest Destiny abroad would backfire on the redeemers. Exporting republicanism proved to be as difficult as Americans had previously presumed, ultimately prompting the United States to engage in the imperialist practices that it was ostensibly going to war to end. This sobering reality would make relatively short-lived the country's imperial turn. However, this more activist approach to the promotion of democracy would continue into the twenty-first century—often with results that were as frustrating and elusive as those that emerged from the efforts of 1898.

The Reformers

The progressive movement aimed at reforming the nation's political economy in order to address the social ills that were a by-product of modernization and mounting prosperity. The closing decades of the nineteenth century came to be

called the Gilded Age due to the growing affluence and conspicuous consump-
tion of wealthier Americans. With that wealth came increasing concern about
rising inequality, the plight of the working poor, the excessive political power of
corporations and trusts, and the social dislocations associated with industrialization and urbanization. The downturn of 1893 exacerbated anxiety about the
health of the American experiment. Businesses collapsed and the ranks of the
unemployed and poor swelled. The Pullman strike of 1894 brought train traffic
through the Chicago hub to ten percent of its usual volume.[51] Protests and work
stoppages led to unprecedented levels of violence between labor and management. The *New York Times* commented that "we cannot too soon face the unwelcome fact that we have dangerous social elements to contend with."[52]

In the eyes of many Americans, these developments threatened core elements
of the nation's exceptional character. Yeoman farming had cultivated a uniquely
American ruggedness and individualism that the drudgery and uniformity of
factory life were coming to compromise. The United States still had no aris-
tocracy, but the increasing concentration of wealth and political power in the
hands of corporate and financial elites was threatening ideals of upward mobility and equality of opportunity. As Edward Bellamy, a prominent novelist and
progressive, explained, "we are today confronted by portentous indications in
the conditions of American industry, society and politics, that this great experiment, on which the last hopes of the race depends, is to prove, like all former
experiments, a disastrous failure. Let us bear in mind that, if it be a failure, it will
be the final failure. There are no more new worlds to be discovered, no fresh
continents to offer virgin fields for new ventures."[53]

The progressive movement was a response to these concerns. Reformers
saw trusts, inequality, and poverty as the new enemy within. Tackling these
challenges was primarily the provenance of domestic policy—stronger federal
control of the economy, more regulatory and administrative oversight, and court
supervision and intervention to check the power of trusts and monopolies. But
reformers also viewed overseas expansion as an effective means of stimulating
economic growth at home and defending progressive values abroad.

Senator Beveridge, a reformist Republican who would later join Roosevelt in
founding the Progressive Party, tied his strong advocacy of overseas expansion
to its beneficial economic effects: "American factories are making more than the
American people can use; American soil is producing more than they can consume. Fate has written our policy for us; the trade of the world must and shall
be ours."[54] William Jennings Bryan, a progressive Democrat who lost the 1896
election to McKinley, saw the war against Spain as a noble and principled effort to bring liberty to the Cuban people. In Bryan's words, "until the right has
triumphed in every land and love reigns in every heart, Governments must, as a

last resort, appeal to force. As long as the oppressor is deaf to the voice of reason, so long must the citizen accustom his shoulder to the musket and his hand to the saber. Our Nation exhausted diplomacy in its efforts to secure a peaceful solution of the Cuban question. . . . History will vindicate the position taken by the United States in the war with Spain." In backing the war, Bryan presumed that the United States would serve as a liberator and not an occupier. He did, however, have early reservations, caveating his support for the war in a manner that would prove prophetic: "In saying this I assume that the principles which were invoked in the inauguration of the war will be observed in its prosecution and conclusion."[55] Bryan would soon turn against the conflict precisely because the principles invoked to justify its launch would not be upheld in its prosecution. Indeed, he would again run against McKinley in 1900, this time on a staunchly anti-imperialist platform. Nonetheless, Bryan's initial backing for the war helped build strong support on both sides of the aisle.

As historian William Leuchtenburg has noted, "at the outbreak of the Spanish-American War few men saw any conflict between social reform and democratic striving at home and the new imperialist mission; indeed, the war seemed nothing so much as an extension of democracy to new parts of the world, and few political figures exceeded the enthusiasm of William Jennings Bryan for the Spanish-American War."[56] Fellow historian Gerald Markovitz agrees that "the great majority of progressives saw reform at home and an imperial policy abroad as complementary," asserting that they "joined others in defining commercial expansion overseas as essential to the normal functioning of the economy." Reformers, Markovitz maintains, believed that "new markets (especially in what we now call the Third World) *had* to be secured and maintained if economic depression, social strife and class warfare were to be averted. . . . Reformers acted upon the assumption that America's growth and development could only proceed hand-in-hand with the regeneration of the world along the lines of America's 'democratic capitalism.' "[57]

For progressives, expansion was about not just spreading liberal values abroad and stimulating growth through foreign trade and new orders for steel mills and shipyards; it was also about restoring vigor to American society. Life on the expanding frontier encouraged vitality, stamina, and a spirit of adventure; the closing of that frontier risked societal stagnation. Expansion abroad was the needed corrective. As Roosevelt proclaimed in 1899, the projection of American power abroad was part of "the strenuous life" needed to toughen up the American people. "Above all," Roosevelt declared, "let us shrink from no strife, moral or physical, within or without the nation, provided that we are certain that the strife is justified, for it is only through strife, through hard and dangerous endeavor, that we shall ultimately win the goal of true national greatness."[58]

Other influential voices made similar arguments, contending that the country's new zeal for overseas expansion was not only consistent with its chosen status, but would also advance its unique republican character. Washington Gladden, the Congregationalist pastor and leading progressive, insisted that "in saving others we may save ourselves."[59] Henry Demarest Lloyd, a progressive political activist and journalist, maintained that reform at home required activism abroad and that the United States could not "progress from perfection to perfection while Chinese ossified, and the Cubans and Philippine people were disembowelled [*sic*], and the Africans continued to eat each other."[60] Americans may have deemed it their duty to share their exceptional values and institutions with others—through force if necessary. But doing so was not just an act of altruism; it would also help reinvigorate American society.

This enthusiasm for territorial expansion among progressives helped clear the way for an unusual alliance between left and right in support of the Spanish-American War. The American Federation of Labor and labor activists like Samuel Gompers teamed up with realists like Lodge and Mahan to build bipartisan support for expelling Spain from Cuba.[61] Many progressives may not have shared Mahan's desire to guide the nation into the realm of great-power competition and naval rivalry, but they nonetheless supported shipbuilding for their own reasons. According to historian Robert Beisner, "those who supported naval reconstruction were not all dedicated Mahanites; many were merely aware that such a building program would produce a healthy din in their districts' shipyards, fire the hearths in underemployed steel mills, or consume enough government revenue to justify the continuation of current protectionist tariff rates."[62] And Mahan may not have been a progressive, but he was more than happy to make the case that expansion would reinvigorate American society. In one of Mahan's many essays encouraging the nation to "look outward," he summoned the spirit of Manifest Destiny, claiming that "nowhere does a vigorous foreign policy find more favor than among the people west of the Rocky Mountains," thanks to "men who have all the aggressive spirit of the advanced line of national progress."[63]

By 1898, realists, redeemers, and reformers had come together to overturn the aversion to foreign entanglement that had shaped U.S. grand strategy for over a century. At least temporarily, internationalism triumphed over isolationism. However, the Spanish-American War soon confronted the American people with an inescapable contradiction. The United States ventured abroad to spread republican values but ended up establishing imperial rule over other peoples. This reality would quite quickly cause a political backlash against the nation's outward push.

Navigating Republican Imperialism

The realists drove the imperial turn of 1898. In their minds, the United States extended its geopolitical reach into the Caribbean and Pacific because it could and because it had to. The country enjoyed an era of unprecedented economic growth, making possible the sizable expansion of the U.S. Navy that began in the 1880s. Other major powers were enlarging their fleets and imperial holdings, compelling the United States to respond in kind in order to advance its security and prosperity. Lodge, Mahan, and kindred spirits argued that America's time had come. Conditions at home allowed and conditions abroad necessitated a "large policy."

The realists may have been behind the imperial turn, but it was the redeemers and reformers who succeeded in selling it to the public. Convincing Americans to forsake their isolationist roots required an ideological justification that was consistent with the nation's redemptive mission. A realist rationale would not have resonated; indeed, it would have contradicted the exceptionalist narrative. Expansion had to be about furthering the nation's republican calling, not abandoning it. It had to be about taming corporate power, not submitting to it. Taking Manifest Destiny abroad was the next step in the nation's unique political experiment.

Accordingly, American officials from President McKinley on down studiously avoided any reference to empire or colonies as they unfurled the nation's new foreign policy.[64] On the contrary, they went out of their way to distinguish U.S. policy from the imperialist practices of other great powers and to attribute altruistic rather than self-interested motives for acquiring overseas territories. In his war message, McKinley insisted that the United States would undertake "forcible intervention . . . as a neutral to stop the war, according to the large dictates of humanity and following many historical precedents where neighboring states have interfered to check the hopeless sacrifices of life by internecine conflicts beyond their borders." After winning the war and taking possession of Spanish territories in the Caribbean and the Pacific, he reassured Americans that "no imperial designs lurk in the American mind. They are alien to American sentiment, thought, and purpose. Our priceless principles undergo no change under a tropic sun. They go with the flag."[65]

As it debated the merits of going to war to expel Spain from Cuba, Congress took explicit steps to reassure itself as well as the public that the conflict would not serve as a pretext for annexing or ruling over Cuba. The Teller Amendment to the joint war resolution, which was proposed by Senator Henry Teller (R-Colorado) and embraced by both chambers, forswore imperial intent. The amendment stated that the United States "hereby disclaims any disposition or intention to exercise sovereignty, jurisdiction, or control over said Island except for the pacification thereof, and asserts its determination, when that is accomplished, to leave the government and control of the Island to its people."[66] In backing the resolution, Senator Hoar proclaimed that it would "lead to the most honorable single war in all history. . . . It is a war in which there does not enter the slightest thought or desire of foreign conquest or of national gain or advantage. I have not heard throughout this whole discussion in the Senate or House an expression of a desire to subjugate and occupy Cuba for the purposes of our own country. There is nothing of that kind suggested. It is disclaimed by the President, disclaimed by the committee, disclaimed by everybody, so far as I am aware."[67]

Especially among redeemers and reformers, the Teller Amendment eased misgivings about the potential for the war to contravene the United States' anti-imperialist pedigree. Moreover, the McKinley administration adhered to Congress's instructions; at no point did it attempt to annex Cuba. Indeed, McKinley instructed Leonard Wood, the U.S. Army officer who served as Cuba's military governor after Spain's departure, to "prepare Cuba, as rapidly as possible, for the establishment of an independent government, republican in form; to arrange for an efficient administration of justice; and a good school system."[68]

The problem was that the McKinley administration, despite the president's instructions to Woods, abided by its commitment to Cuba's independence only in name. The U.S. military occupied and governed Cuba from the end of the war until 1902, after which the Platt Amendment superseded the Teller Amendment. The Platt Amendment, which was effectively forced on Cuba's government, provided the United States the right to lease or buy land (the naval base at Guantanamo Bay resulted) and stipulated that "the government of Cuba consents that the United States may exercise the right to intervene for the preservation of Cuban independence . . . [and] the maintenance of a government adequate for the protection of life, property, and individual liberty."[69] Under these provisions, the U.S. military returned to Cuba in 1906 and occupied the island for another three years. The American military came back to Cuba in 1912 and intervened again from 1917 through 1922. The Platt Amendment was not repealed until 1934. At least in nominal terms, the United States stood by its anti-imperialist credentials. But the reality on the ground was a different matter altogether. As critics of the war were quick to point out, Cuba had effectively become a military protectorate of the United States.

Navigating imperialism was even more politically perilous when it came to the other territories that passed to U.S. control in 1898 and 1899. Hawaii was the least controversial. It was an "incorporated territory" and thus part of the U.S. body politic—the same status enjoyed by other territories annexed by the United States and destined for statehood. Hawaii was viewed as already part of the American system; its politics and economy were dominated by its white settlers and English was used in government, the courts, schools, and commerce. Hawaii's population was much smaller than that of Cuba, so there were far fewer nonwhites to incorporate into the nation's population. White residents and native Hawaiians were eligible for U.S. citizenship, while Japanese and Chinese immigrants were not.[70] Many in Congress viewed the annexation of Hawaii as an unexceptional development. According to Representative Hitt, chair of the Committee on Foreign Affairs, the matter "is not a case of greed for territory and overweening influence brought to bear by a great and powerful Government upon one of the smallest in the world. . . . There is no oppression on our side, there is no unwillingness on the other side. . . . It is the pursuance of a policy long discussed and well known there and to our people here and to all the world."[71]

The status of the Philippines, Puerto Rico, and Guam were, from a political standpoint, much more problematic inasmuch as they effectively became American colonies. They were "unincorporated territories"—they belonged to, but were not part of, the United States. They were governed, at least initially, by U.S. military authorities. The U.S. Army governed the Philippines and Puerto Rico (Puerto Rico transitioned to a U.S.-led civilian government in 1900). The U.S. Navy ran Guam, and trained the local inhabitants to work on the U.S. naval base. Samoa received similar treatment. The populations of these territories had not consented to acquisition by the United States, they had no say in Congress, and they were not eligible for U.S. citizenship. This was uncharted territory for the United States. Congress and the courts struggled to clarify the status and rights of these new appendages, uneasily encountering the reality that the United States had launched a war to defeat imperialism and then itself become an empire.[72]

Acquisition of the Philippines ended up provoking the broadest and most passionate opposition, in no small part because American soldiers were soon killing and being killed by Filipino insurgents. But even before the insurgency broke out in early 1899, Americans were forced to confront the contradictions between the consequences of their "large policy" and their founding principles. McKinley himself tried to square the circle by conceiving of the U.S. objective in the Philippines as one of "benevolent assimilation." On December 21, 1898— prior to Senate ratification of the Treaty of Paris—he issued his "Benevolent Assimilation Proclamation," which he dispatched to the U.S. military governor of the Philippines. McKinley wrote that "it will be the duty of the commander of the forces of occupation to announce and proclaim in the most public manner that we come, not as invaders or conquerors, but as friends, to protect the natives in their homes, in their employments, and in their personal and religious rights. . . . The mission of the United States is one of benevolent assimilation, substituting the mild sway of justice and right for arbitrary rule." At the same time, he also announced "the actual occupation and administration of the entire group of the Philippine islands" and went on to call for "the strong arm of authority to repress disturbance and to overcome all obstacles to the bestowal of the blessings of good and stable government."[73]

Members of Congress confronted head-on the inescapable contradiction between "benevolent assimilation" and "the strong arm of authority." As the terms of the Treaty of Paris became clear and the Senate began contemplating ratification, intense debate ensued about the legality and desirability of taking possession of and ruling over Spain's former territories. Senator George Vest (D-Missouri) proposed a joint resolution opposing on constitutional grounds the prospect of establishing American colonies:

> That under the Constitution of the United States no power is given to the Federal Government to acquire territory to be held and governed permanently as colonies. The colonial system of European nations cannot be established under our present Constitution, but all territory acquired by the Government, except such small amount as may be necessary for coaling stations, correction of boundaries, and similar governmental purposes, must be acquired and governed with the purpose of ultimately organizing such territory into States suitable for admission into the Union.[74]

Senator Platt sharply disagreed, noting that "I believe that our power to govern any province, country, or land which we have the right to acquire is full and plenary, and is given by that clause in the Constitution, which says: 'The Congress shall have power to dispose of and make all needful rules and regulations respecting the territory or other property belonging to the United States.'"[75]

Senator Hoar took exception to Platt's view: "When the Senator from Connecticut undertakes to declare that we may do such things not for . . . the general welfare of the people of the United States . . . but for any fancied or real obligation to take care of distant peoples beyond our boundaries, . . . then I deny his proposition and tell him he can find nothing either in the text of the Constitution or the exposition of the fathers . . . to warrant or support his doctrine." Hoar asserted that "the power to conquer alien peoples and hold them in subjugation is nowhere expressly granted" and "nowhere implied as necessary . . . by the Constitution." He concluded by hoisting McKinley himself on his own petard: "A year ago last December the President of the United States sent a message to Congress. In that message he said: 'I speak not of forcible annexation, because that is not to be thought of, and under our code of morality that would be criminal aggression.' . . . Who shall haul him down? Who shall haul down the code? Who shall haul down the President?"[76] Senator William Mason

(R-Illinois) pursued a similar line of argument: "Those of us who pointed out in the early summer this present situation . . . knew that it meant war for expansion, war for conquest, war in the denial of our very proposition made in this Chamber when we declared war for the liberation of Cuba."[77]

Such strong and principled objections to the effective establishment of U.S. colonies did take a toll on congressional and public support for the Treaty of Paris. In the end, however, opponents of the treaty fell short; the Senate by a vote of 57 to 27—just clearing the required two-thirds majority—ratified the treaty on February 6, 1899. The public patriotism that accompanied military victory appears to have helped McKinley's case. As measured by the position taken by newspapers, public support for U.S. control over Spain's former territories built over the course of 1898. In August, some forty percent of a sample of newspapers supported permanent retention of the Philippines, while over sixty percent favored that position by the end of the year.[78] The patriotic atmosphere also raised the political risks of opposing ratification. The novelist Henry Adams, after returning from nearly a year in Europe, summarized the national mood as follows: "I find America so cheerful, and so full of swagger and self-satisfaction, that I hardly know it."[79]

Amid the patriotic fervor, supporters of expansion did not hesitate to tar their opponents as traitors to the national cause. As Representative Hitt remarked during the debate over Hawaii's annexation in the summer of 1898, "there is no one in our country so recreant to his duty as an American that he would refuse to support the President in succoring Dewey after his magnificent victory."[80] Representative Joseph Walker (R-Massachusetts) agreed: "The time of our swaddling clothes has gone. . . . We can not shut our eyes to the fact we have attained to-day . . . to a stature such as none of us dreamed we should ever reach in our day or even in that of our immediate children. We can not shirk its responsibilities. We can not return again to the place of a physical pygmy or a moral dwarf."[81]

Even though military victory spawned a blustery patriotism, the Senate ratified the Treaty of Paris by the smallest of margins. The anti-imperialist movement may have failed in its effort to block the treaty, but its message clearly contributed to a building backlash against republican imperialism.

The Anti-Imperialist Backlash

Support for the use of force to expel Spain from Cuba was broad and deep, cutting across political, ideological, and sectional lines. Realists, redeemers, and reformers could all agree on the need to liberate Cuba and banish Spain from the Caribbean. The political consensus readily eroded, however, as it became clear that a war launched in the name of humanitarianism, liberation from oppression, and the Monroe Doctrine was turning the nation into an imperialist republic. Indeed, in effectively establishing new colonies in the Western Hemisphere, the United States was turning the Monroe Doctrine on its head, not standing by it.

The Anti-Imperialist League was founded in June 1898, only a matter of weeks after Dewey's victory in Manila Bay. Its ranks grew in the lead-up to Senate ratification of the Treaty of Paris, which confirmed that the United States would emerge from military victory owning and ruling over Spain's former colonies in the Caribbean and the Pacific. Clearly, the nation was not abiding by Bryan's stipulation that "the principles which were invoked in the inauguration of the war will be observed in its prosecution and conclusion." The League's appeal widened after the Senate's approval of the treaty and the spread of the insurgency in the Philippines. Chapters existed in a dozen cities by the end of 1899. The membership was diverse; it included, among others, leading politicians, intellectuals, corporate heads, clergy, labor activists, and farmers.[82]

The movement's critique of the imperial turn rested on several core arguments. For starters, it maintained that ruling over other peoples violated the nation's founding principles. A just war to liberate Cuba from Spanish oppression had turned into an episode of territorial aggrandizement entirely inconsistent with the American creed. Prominent supporters of the war became some of the most vocal critics of the nation's new expansionism. Samuel Gompers, who became vice president of the New England Anti-Imperialist League, lamented that "the first moment we have the opportunity of laying our hands upon territory . . . we are at once asked to violate every declaration we have made, or promise that we have given and insist that these islands, with their subjugated people, shall come under our domination."[83]

William Jennings Bryan, who served in the Nebraska militia during the conflict, stood by his initial support for going to war against Spain, but denounced what followed: "Shall we contemplate a scheme for the colonization of the Orient merely because our fleet won a remarkable victory in the harbor of Manila?" Military success has seduced many fellow citizens, he observed with regret, to "turn to thoughts of aggrandizement and yield allegiance to those who clothe covetousness in the attractive garb of 'National destiny.' "[84] Bryan at times resorted to sarcasm to make his point: "When the desire to steal becomes uncontrollable in an individual he is declared to be a kleptomaniac and is sent to an asylum; when the desire to grab land becomes uncontrollable in a nation we are told that the 'currents of destiny are flowing through the hearts of men' and that the American people are entering upon 'a manifest mission.' "[85] The United States, he insisted on another occasion, could not "endure half republic and half colony—half free and half vassal."[86] To charges from the McKinley administration that the anti-imperialists dishonored the sacrifices of U.S. soldiers in the

Philippines, Bryan responded, "a thousand times better to haul down the stars and stripes and substitute the flag of an independent republic than to surrender the doctrines that gave glory to 'Old Glory.' . . . The mission of that flag is to float—not over a conglomeration of commonwealths and colonies—but over 'the land of the free and the home of the brave'; and to that mission it must remain forever true—forever true."[87]

William Sumner, an influential Yale professor, offered a similar critique:

> We have beaten Spain in a military conflict, but we are submitting to be conquered by her on the field of ideas and policies. Expansionism and imperialism . . . appeal to national vanity and national cupidity. They are seductive . . . they are delusions, and they will lead us to ruin unless we are hard-headed enough to resist them. . . . Patriotism is being prostituted into a nervous preoccupation which is fatal to an apprehension of truth. . . . If we Americans believe in self-government, why do we let it slip away from us? Why do we barter it away for military glory as Spain did? . . . If we believe in liberty, as an American principle, why do we not stand by it?

In the same address, Sumner also raised an objection to imperial expansion pointed to by many Americans before him—that compromising the liberty of other peoples would ultimately imperil liberty at home: "The question of imperialism, then, is the question whether we are going to give the lie to the origin of our own national existence, by . . . sacrific[ing] our existing civil and political system . . . by throwing the Constitution into the gutter here at home." He concluded that "it was fundamentally antagonistic to our domestic system to hold dependencies which are unfit to enter the Union. Our system cannot be extended to take them in, or adjusted to them to keep them out without sacrificing its integrity."[88] Former president Grover Cleveland was of a similar mind: "If the suggestion is made that the time has come for our nation to abandon its old landmarks, and to follow the lights of monarchical hazards, and that we should attempt to force the simple machinery of our popular and domestic government to serve the schemes of imperialism, your challenge of the proposition is entirely in order."[89]

Racism also figured prominently in the debate between expansionists and their anti-imperialist critics. Both camps, for example, agreed that the people of the Philippines were ill suited for democratic governance. But that shared assessment led them to diametrically opposed prescriptions. For the expansionists, that Filipinos were not ready for republican rule was a justification for military occupation; the only way to make "inferior peoples" into good democrats was to rule over them and inculcate in them Anglo-Saxon values and practices. Herein was the next chapter of Manifest Destiny. To critics who charged that occupation ran counter to the nation's own Declaration of Independence, Senator Beveridge retorted that "the Declaration applies only to people capable of self-government. How dare any man prostitute this expression of the very elect of self-governing peoples to a race of Malay children of barbarism, schooled in Spanish methods and ideas."[90]

The anti-imperialists, who opposed on principled grounds ruling over other peoples, maintained that the United States was obligated to integrate into the union any newly acquired territory—just as it had done during the era of westward expansion. That option, however, was as unacceptable as colonial rule in light of the fact that the peoples in question were not fit for inclusion in the American body politic. Senator John Daniel (D-Virginia) called the population of the Philippines a "mess of Asiatic pottage," while Representative Clark remarked that "no matter whether they are fit to govern themselves or not, they are not fit to govern us, and that is precisely what they will do if we let them in as States."[91] Recognizing the undesirability of either ruling over other peoples or bringing them into the union, William Sumner captured the core dilemma confronting republican imperialism:

> We must either rule over them as inferior possessions, to be ruled and exploited by us after the fashion of the old colonial system, or we must take them in on an equality with ourselves, where they will help to govern us and to corrupt a political system which they do not understand, and in which they cannot participate. From that dilemma there is no escape except to give them independence and to let them work out their own salvation or go without it. . . . It was an enormous blunder in statecraft to engage in a war which was sure to bring us into this predicament.[92]

Finally, many progressive reformers, even those who had initially backed intervention in Cuba and viewed overseas expansion as a means of improving economic conditions at home, opposed the territorial acquisitions that came with military victory. Confronted with the reality that the war, although successful, had effectively turned the United States into an imperial power, they gravitated back to the more traditional reformist agenda of tackling domestic problems through domestic solutions. In addition, the events of 1898 prompted many in the progressive movement to embrace a pacifist and anti-militarist agenda. This growing pacifism on the left would play an influential role in shaping foreign policy moving forward—especially during the presidency of Woodrow Wilson.[93]

William James, a philosopher and psychologist, and Jane Addams, a social worker and author, were among the leaders of progressive opposition to the new expansionism. James rejected the notion that the acquisition of overseas territories furthered domestic reform, arguing that it compromised and corrupted core American principles. He called instead for domestic measures aimed at expanding prosperity and social mobility and at scaling back the power of trusts and corporations. He also took exception to the notion that military struggle and territorial expansion were needed to restore vitality to American society, a task that he thought could be better fulfilled through domestic projects such as building infrastructure, taming the nation's wilderness, and caring for the country's less advantaged citizens. "The passion of military conquest," he maintained, "should have been kept chained by a native wisdom nourished assiduously for a century on opposite ideals."[94]

In similar fashion, Jane Addams marshaled a pacifist critique of expansionism while calling for an ambitious domestic agenda focused on social work, public education, and public health. In Addams's mind, promoting social welfare and pluralism in America's crowded and diverse cities would produce a cosmopolitan patriotism that would lay "the simple and inevitable foundations for an international order." "There arises the hope," she wrote, "that when this newer patriotism becomes large enough, it will overcome arbitrary boundaries and soak up the notion of nationalism. We may then give up war, because we shall find it as difficult to make war upon a nation at the other side of the globe as upon our next-door neighbor."[95] Gompers and other labor leaders joined this reformist, anti-imperialist chorus, adding to the critique of expansion their charge that immigrants from new U.S. territories would take away jobs and depress wages on the mainland.

The failure of the anti-imperialists to block ratification of the Paris Treaty was a clear setback for the movement. However, the building insurgency in the Philippines would soon give the movement new momentum. Some 125,000 U.S. soldiers would serve in the Philippines to pacify the islands.[96] Between its outbreak in 1899 and the end of the insurrection in 1902, over 4,000 American soldiers lost their lives and around 20,000 Filipino fighters and hundreds of thousands of civilians died from violence, disease, and starvation. Reports of American atrocities circulated in the U.S. press, some of the stories coming from letters sent home by U.S. soldiers. The anti-imperialists now had a second target; they could oppose not just the acquisition and occupation of overseas territories, but also America's new war against the Philippine insurrection. Mark Twain chronicled how this conflict had turned him from a "red-hot imperialist" into a dedicated opponent of expansion:

I wanted the American eagle to go screaming into the Pacific. It seemed tiresome and tame for it to content itself with the Rockies. Why not spread its wings over the Philippines, I asked myself, and I thought it would be a real good thing to do. I said to myself here are our people who have suffered for three centuries. We can make them as free as ourselves, give them a government and a country of their own, put a miniature of the American Constitution afloat in the Pacific, start a brand new republic to take its place among the free nations of the world. It seemed to me a great task to which we had addressed ourselves. But I have thought some more since then and I have read carefully the treaty of Paris and I have seen that we do not intend to free, but to subject the people of the Philippines. We have gone there to conquer, not to redem [sic]. . . . And so I am an anti-imperialist. I am opposed to having the eagle put its talons on any other land.[97]

The war in the Philippines, even as it brought new activists like Twain to the ranks of the anti-imperialists, at the same time served to undercut the movement. As during earlier debates over the annexation of Hawaii and ratification of the Treaty of Paris, anti-imperialism ran up against patriotism. With Americans fighting and dying in the Philippines, many Americans—elected officials and the public alike—rallied behind the troops, charging opponents of the war with sedition and disloyalty. "Who shall haul down the flag that floats over our dead in the Philippines?" McKinley accusingly asked.[98] In a letter to Leonard Wood, the U.S. military governor of Cuba, Roosevelt wrote that anti-imperialist journalists are "simply unhung traitors, and are liars, slanderers and scandalmongers to boot."[99] According to one study of the anti-imperialist movement in Chicago, public reaction to the bloodshed in the Philippines tended to fall along party lines, fostering a greater partisan divide over the nation's outward push. Republicans congregated behind McKinley, while Democrats trended against the war and therefore came to constitute a much larger percentage of anti-imperialist activists than they did before the insurgency began.[100]

Building polarization over foreign policy would captivate the presidential contest of 1900 in which Bryan again ran against McKinley, effectively making the election a referendum on the nation's new "large policy." A main plank of McKinley's campaign was a stout defense of his ambitious brand of statecraft. Notably, he continued to justify overseas expansion as part of the nation's redemptive mission. In his speech accepting the Republican nomination, McKinley claimed that "a just war has been waged for humanity" and that the people living in newly acquired U.S. territories "recognize American sovereignty as the symbol and pledge of peace, justice, law, religious freedom, education, the security of life and property." He reaffirmed that "our steps have been guided by honor and duty. There will be no turning aside, no wavering, no retreat. No blow has been struck except for liberty and humanity, and none will be."[101] Republicans charged that Bryan simply failed to understand the nation's geopolitical ascent and the opportunities and obligations that came with it.[102]

The Democratic comeback aimed directly at McKinley's principled defense of territorial expansion. The party's platform, the first three pages of which focused exclusively on foreign policy, asserted that "any government not based upon the consent of the governed is a tyranny; and that to impose upon any people a government of force is to substitute the methods of imperialism for those of a republic." The party stated that it was "unalterably opposed to the seizing or purchasing of distant islands to be governed outside the constitution and whose people can never become citizens." The platform went on to assert that the nation's imperial turn was fundamentally at odds with its core values and thereby imperiled the republic:

> We assert that no nation can long endure half republic and half empire, and we warn the American people that imperialism abroad will lead quickly and inevitably to despotism at home.... Militarism ... will impose upon our peace-loving people a large standing army, an unnecessary burden of taxation, and would be a constant menace to their liberties. . . . For the first time in our history and coeval with the Philippine conquest has there been a wholesale departure from our time-honored and approved system of volunteer organization. We denounce it as un-American, undemocratic and unrepublican and as a subversion of the ancient and fixed principles of a free people.[103]

In his speech accepting the Democratic nomination, Bryan pursued a similar line of attack: "Those who would have this nation enter upon a career of empire must consider not only the effect of imperialism on the Filipinos, but they must also calculate its effect upon our own nation. We cannot repudiate the principles of self-government in the Philippines without weakening that principle here." Bryan went further, claiming that the Republicans were forsaking the nation's founding principles: "The Republican party has accepted the European idea and planted itself upon ground taken by George III and by every ruler who distrusts the capacity of the people for self-government or denies them a voice in their own affairs." Bryan declared: "Let them censure Jefferson; of all the statesmen of history, none has used words so offensive to those who would hold their fellows in political bondage. Let them censure Washington, who declared that the colonies must choose between liberty and slavery."[104]

Bryan's passionate appeals fell short; against the backdrop of the sacrifices of American soldiers in the Philippines and continuing public enthusiasm for the nation's new status as a major power, his message had only limited appeal. McKinley's running mate, Theodore Roosevelt, had led the "Rough Riders"— a cavalry regiment that contributed to the U.S. victory in Cuba—and thus campaigned as a national hero of sorts. The economy was on the upswing, favoring the incumbent Republicans. In addition, the anti-imperialist movement was poorly organized and weakened by personal rivalries. As scholar Allen Merriam concludes, "the anti-imperialists failed to persuade the nation because they never became a united political force, often argued among themselves, and were forced into a negative position in a nation optimistic about America's role in the new century."[105]

McKinley handily won a second term, dealing the anti-imperialists another serious setback. The outcome revealed the sea change that had taken place in American attitudes toward foreign entanglement; geopolitical ambition and territorial expansion beyond the nation's shores had become more of a political asset than a liability. A majority of the public clearly continued to greet with approval the nation's arrival as a great power and its military victory over Spain. At the same time, the anti-imperialist movement and the backlash against the war in the Philippines did leave an indelible imprint on the nation's politics. At a minimum, Bryan and other anti-imperialists ensured that Americans confronted the inescapable dilemmas that accompanied the nation's imperial turn. Was territorial expansion furthering or compromising the country's role as redeemer nation? Was taking Manifest Destiny abroad succeeding in spreading American values? Was it worth the effort? Was expansion on balance contributing to or detracting from American security and prosperity?

The absence of consensus on these issues would mean that America's embrace of republican imperialism peaked quickly. McKinley by no means gave up any of the territories that the United States took between 1898 and 1900, but the backlash against expansion did dampen enthusiasm for new targets of conquest—particularly in Asia. With his hands full in the Philippines and the anti-imperialists pushing back, McKinley returned to a more traditional policy of expanding commerce rather than strategic commitments in the Pacific. In 1899, Secretary of State John Hay issued the Open Door notes to ensure U.S. access to the Chinese market amid the European push for exclusive concessions. In 1900, McKinley dispatched more than 5,000 U.S. troops to China during the Boxer Rebellion.[106] The Boxers were protesting foreign influence in China as well as economic deprivation. American forces worked with those of a number of other countries to defend foreign legations and citizens and to put down the rebellion. However, their mission was limited in scope and Hay wrote to the U.S. minister in China that "there must be no alliances."[107] The international coalition ended up exacting from the Chinese government punitive damages. The operation thus represented a temporary exigency in line with many other short-term U.S. interventions during the previous century. At least for the time being, the United States had acquired quite enough territory in the Pacific. McKinley's pivot back to a foreign policy focused more on commerce than territorial expansion set the stage for his immediate successors.

Theodore Roosevelt and the End of the Imperial Turn

Following the assassination of McKinley on September 6, 1901, Theodore Roosevelt entered the presidency with impressive expansionist credentials. He had long been an avid advocate of a world-class battle fleet, had fought in Cuba, and had been a staunch defender of the Treaty of Paris and the strategic and economic value of the nation's territorial prizes in the Caribbean and the Pacific. In his second Annual Message, delivered on December 2, 1902, Roosevelt encouraged the nation to enlarge further its international aspirations: "As a people we have played a large part in the world, and we are bent upon making our future even larger than the past. In particular, the events of the last four years have definitely decided that, for woe or for weal, our place must be great among the nations."[108] Five months later, he made clear that he took America's growing role in the world to be a matter of destiny, not preference: "We have no choice, we people of the United States, as to whether or not we shall play a great part in the world. That has been determined for us by fate, by the march of events. We have to play that part."[109] Roosevelt was dismissive of the anti-imperialists, insisting that overseas expansion was a logical and necessary extension of the westward march of Americans across their own continent. "The simple truth," he contended, "is that there is nothing even remotely resembling 'imperialism' or 'militarism' involved in the present development of that policy of expansion which has been part of the history of America from the day when she became a nation."[110]

Roosevelt oversaw the steady expansion of the battle fleet; during his presidency, Congress authorized an average of two new battleships per year as well as many smaller vessels. By the time he left office, the United States had the second-largest navy in the world.[111] He ordered the Great White Fleet, which consisted of sixteen battleships and numerous supporting vessels, to broadcast America's new naval strength by circumnavigating the globe between 1907 and 1909. In the Caribbean and Central America, the United States did much more than show the flag; it effectively became the region's overseer, militarily intervening in Colombia, Cuba, Santo Domingo, Honduras, and Panama under Roosevelt's watch. After a succession of false starts by his predecessors, Roosevelt finally began construction of the Panama Canal in 1904, enhancing the United States'

strategic and commercial interests in Central America and its neighboring waters. Soon after he took office, the United States and Britain concluded the Hay-
Pauncefote Treaty, which superseded the Clayton-Bulwer Treaty and cleared the
way for the United States to construct, fortify, and operate an isthmian canal.

Paternalism and the Roosevelt Corollary

Roosevelt's readiness to insert the United States more regularly and forcefully
into the affairs of its southern neighbors stemmed in part from his conviction that the nation could and should deploy its resources to promote good
governance in other countries. Prior to 1898, his predecessors tended to believe that such efforts were both inappropriate and futile. They were inappropriate because Americans should not dictate to others how they should govern
themselves. They were futile because "inferior peoples" were not well suited
to republican government. The McKinley administration was the first to take
a different approach and intrude abroad in the service of effecting political
change.

Roosevelt embraced the views of his predecessor; indeed, he adopted an
even more paternalistic stance. He believed that domestic conditions in other
countries—particularly those in America's neighborhood—had a direct bearing
on the strategic and economic interests of the United States; disorder inside
other polities meant disorder outside them. Accordingly, governments that were
incapable of upholding a basic social contract with their citizens were legitimate
targets of U.S. intervention. As Roosevelt put it in his first Annual Message to
Congress in 1901, "wars with barbarous or semi-barbarous peoples . . . [are]
a most regrettable but necessary international police duty which must be
performed for the sake of the welfare of mankind."[112] This outlook informed his
approach to managing the nation's new appendages—Cuba and the Philippines,
in particular—as well as his broader strategy in the Caribbean and Central
America, where Roosevelt set out, in the words of historian Cyrus Veeser, to
"remake tropical societies."[113]

In addition to his serial military interventions, another prominent manifestation of Roosevelt's paternalism was his insistence in 1904 that the United
States take over Santo Domingo's custom houses—against the will of the island's
government. Santo Domingo had become delinquent on its debt payments to
American and European companies. In part to head off the prospect of European
intervention—Germany and Britain had blockaded Venezuela's coast in 1902
when it failed to pay its debts—Roosevelt turned to U.S. authorities to take
over duty collection and directly pay back creditors. In his Annual Message to
Congress in December 1904, he laid out the logic behind this policy. Roosevelt
disavowed any territorial ambitions in the Western Hemisphere, but also made

clear that the United States would view domestic disorder as a justification for intervention:

> It is not true that the United States feels any land hunger or entertains any projects as regards the other nations of the Western Hemisphere save such as are for their welfare. All that this country desires is to see the neighboring countries stable, orderly, and prosperous. Any country whose people conduct themselves well can count upon our hearty friendship. If a nation shows that it knows how to act with reasonable efficiency and decency in social and political matters, if it keeps order and pays its obligations, it need fear no interference from the United States. Chronic wrongdoing, or an impotence which results in a general loosening of the ties of civilized society, may in America, as elsewhere, ultimately require intervention by some civilized nation, and in the Western Hemisphere the adherence of the United States to the Monroe Doctrine may force the United States, however reluctantly, in flagrant cases of such wrongdoing or impotence, to the exercise of an international police power. . . . We would interfere with them only in the last resort, and then only if it became evident that their inability or unwillingness to do justice at home and abroad had violated the rights of the United States or had invited foreign aggression to the detriment of the entire body of American nations.[114]

In asserting "international police power," Roosevelt was establishing the United States as the custodian of the Western Hemisphere—a policy that came to be known as the Roosevelt Corollary to the Monroe Doctrine. He was effectively granting the United States the right to intervene in the region when and as it saw fit.

In theory, the Roosevelt Corollary could have served as license for the continuation of republican imperialism. After all, a doctrine maintaining that the United States could and should intervene abroad to maintain order and good governance in other countries had considerable potential to draw Americans into one colonial adventure after another. Indeed, during Roosevelt's presidency and continuing for the next three decades, the United States regularly dispatched expeditionary forces to Latin America and embarked on a number of lengthy military occupations. But Roosevelt—as well as his successors—stepped back from imperial ambition and no longer sought to add to the nation's portfolio of territorial acquisitions. He focused more on expanding the nation's commerce and influence than on extending its strategic commitments. It was not an ideological shift that drove this change; Roosevelt remained committed to increasing the nation's geopolitical heft—as made clear by the rapid expansion of the U.S. Navy during his presidency—and to the nation's redemptive mission abroad. Rather, he became acutely aware that the domestic appetite for the further enlargement of America's territorial commitments had since 1898 dramatically diminished.

Domestic Constraints on Imperial Ambition

It is not accidental that Roosevelt went out of his way to reassure Congress and the electorate that U.S. expansion entailed "nothing even remotely resembling 'imperialism' or 'militarism.'" The prolonged campaign against the Philippine insurgency and lingering discomfort about the nation's embrace of imperial rule took a significant toll on public enthusiasm for a "large policy." Simon Rofe and John Thompson note that throughout his presidency Roosevelt "always accepted the fact that his freedom for maneuver would be limited by the American public." Stephen Wertheim and other historians of the era maintain that Roosevelt, pressed by public and congressional opinion as well as fear of strategic overstretch, backed away from his earlier support for imperial expansion and limited the ambition of his foreign policy in order to maintain popular support.[115]

Congress discernibly distanced itself from the brand of internationalism that it had initially supported during McKinley's tenure. In early 1905, the Senate took up consideration of the protocol negotiated with Santo Domingo to set up U.S. control of its customs collection. Opponents of the deal were reluctant to see the United States take on additional commitments in the Caribbean and were resentful that Roosevelt had kept Congress in the dark by presenting the arrangements to the Senate as a *fait accompli*.[116] Indeed, when news of the deal leaked in the press before Roosevelt sent the protocol to Congress, Senator Augustus Bacon (D-Georgia) expressed dismay that the president appeared to have concluded a treaty "which shall virtually take over the affairs of another government and seek to administer them by this Government, without submitting that question to the consideration and judgment of the Senate."[117] The Senate refused to act on the issue before it adjourned its regular session on March 4, forcing Roosevelt to call the Senate into a special session devoted almost exclusively to the issue. After the Senate's further deliberations remained inconclusive, Roosevelt resorted to an executive agreement to finalize the deal, which took effect on April 1.[118]

Congress similarly balked when it came to authorizing funds for naval expansion. Roosevelt's request in 1907 for four additional battleships provoked, in the words of Sprout and Sprout, "one of the bitterest legislative struggles in American naval history."[119] Unable to garner sufficient support in either the House or Senate, Roosevelt was forced to settle for only two new battleships. Congress also blocked efforts to build up U.S. naval bases in Guam and the

Philippines. Roosevelt was particularly frustrated that Congress rejected or substantially reduced his administration's repeated requests for the money needed to construct a major naval base at Subic Bay in the Philippines. Naval officers overseeing the Asiatic fleet consistently warned about the neglect of base.[120] In 1907, the naval station's commandant complained that its facilities as well as its stores of coal were woefully inadequate. According to William Braisted, a historian of the U.S. naval presence in the Pacific, "the great Far Eastern naval base of the United States was indeed mostly make-believe." Roosevelt recognized as much, confiding to William Howard Taft, who served as the first civilian governor of the Philippines and then as secretary of war from 1904 to 1908, that the administration should consider granting independence to the islands as quickly as possible because Americans were unwilling to allocate the resources necessary to defend them. Roosevelt eventually abandoned his efforts to construct a major base at Subic Bay, instead relying on Pearl Harbor as the main U.S. naval facility in the Pacific. Taft would endorse this decision after he succeeded Roosevelt in 1909.[121]

Faced with such domestic constraints, Roosevelt ended up pursuing a far more modest and restrained grand strategy than would have been suggested by his reputation as an ardent expansionist. He was intent on increasing foreign commerce and looked out for the business interests of U.S. companies, but the nation's territorial expansion ground to a halt during his watch; he kept what the United States had taken during McKinley's presidency but went no further. And although he did not let go of the Philippines, Roosevelt, according to Wertheim, "ended up preparing the islands for independence. . . . He left office favoring the relinquishment of the islands within a single generation."[122] In 1907, Roosevelt acknowledged that "personally I should be glad to see the islands made independent."[123] To this end, he wound down the war, replaced U.S. military rule with a civilian governor general, and oversaw the establishment of a bicameral legislature, an independent judiciary, and local autonomy.[124]

Roosevelt made clear that public constraints weighed heavily on his mind as he loosened the U.S. grip on the Philippines: "Statesmen have to take into account both the ideals, and the lack of knowledge of the peculiar difficulties in the Philippines, among our people. Our people do not desire to hold foreign dependencies, and do believe in self-government for them."[125] Wertheim contends that Roosevelt soured on retaining the Philippines largely because of domestic opposition to imperialism. "What made Roosevelt regard the islands as the heel rather than the arm of Achilles," he concludes, "was the public's lack of imperial commitment, transmitted through the Congress."[126]

Beyond maintaining the U.S. presence in the Philippines and the nation's other newly acquired Pacific possessions, Roosevelt kept interventionism in the region to a minimum. America's naval presence in the western Pacific increased markedly during Roosevelt's presidency, but U.S. troops generally steered clear of China, Japan, and Korea, intervening only once—in 1905 to protect the U.S. legation in Seoul during the Russo-Japanese War (1904–1905). Roosevelt relied heavily on diplomacy and the symbols of American power—rather than the exercise of force—to pursue U.S. interests. He was eager to expand U.S. trade and influence in the region, and involved himself in mediating an end to the Russo-Japanese War, for which he received the Nobel Peace Prize. His principal objective was to maintain a stable balance of power that would further U.S. market access and the continuation of the Open Door.[127] According to Michael Green, a historian of U.S. strategy toward Asia, "Roosevelt engaged in eight years of strenuous diplomacy aimed at creating a stable regional order."[128]

Green underscores Roosevelt's keen awareness of the constraints facing U.S. engagement in the region, arguing that he "discovered the confounding downsides of geography: the vulnerability of forward defense lines across a huge ocean; the temptations and risks of entrapment on the continent of Asia; and the difficulty of aligning democratic values abroad with growing anti-immigration and anti-imperialist sentiments at home." Roosevelt, Green continues, understood that "American expansion beyond Spain's possessions would have exacerbated great-power rivalry and put the new American island outposts at risk. . . . [He] acted like Bismarck after the Franco-Prussian War, using *self-restraint* to great strategic advantage."[129]

When it came to U.S. guardianship over its southern neighbors, Roosevelt was more of an interventionist than he was in the Pacific, but he still harbored no territorial designs. In his message to the Senate requesting approval of the protocol negotiated with Santo Domingo, he made clear the limits of his ambition:

> It can not be too often and too emphatically asserted that the United States has not the slightest desire for territorial aggrandizement at the expense of any of its southern neighbors, and will not treat the Monroe doctrine as an excuse for such aggrandizement on its part. We do not propose to take any part of Santo Domingo, or exercise any other control over the island save what is necessary to its financial rehabilitation in connection with the collection of revenue. . . . We can point with just pride to what we have done in Cuba as a guaranty of our good faith. We stayed in Cuba only so long as to start her aright on the road to self-government. . . . Our purpose in Santo Domingo is as beneficent.[130]

Privately, Roosevelt communicated the same sentiment in more colorful terms: "I want to do nothing but what a policeman has to do in Santo Domingo. As for annexing the island, I have about the same desire to annex it as a gorged boa constrictor might have to swallow a porcupine wrong-end-to."[131]

Despite his conviction that the United States had the responsibility and right to enforce order and capable governance in the Western Hemisphere—through force if necessary—Roosevelt confined his military interventions largely to the Caribbean and Central America. Toward the rest of Latin America, he focused principally on expanding U.S. trade and market access. Roosevelt on occasion dispatched U.S. troops to the Middle East, but the missions were small, short, and focused principally on protecting American diplomats. In these parts of the world, Roosevelt exhibited the cautionary restraint that had been the hallmark of U.S. strategy prior to the imperial turn.

The developments of 1898 marked a decisive departure from the grand strategy of isolationism that had come before. The United States had arrived as one of the world's leading powers. It had a world-class economy, was in the midst of building one of the world's most capable navies, and had acquired the overseas territories that were significant markers of great-power status. At the same time, the bout of imperial expansionism overseen by McKinley reawakened the nation's isolationist impulses, leaving Roosevelt little choice but to scale back his internationalist ambitions. Territorial expansion ground to a halt, statecraft once again focused at least as much on commercial as strategic objectives, and the war in the Philippines encouraged self-restraint and cautioned against entanglement in major conflicts. As Wertheim points out, "except in the Philippines, Roosevelt sent not a single American into armed combat during seven and a half years as president."[132] His successor's foreign policy would further reveal the strength of isolationism's comeback and the political appeal of an inward turn.

William Howard Taft and Dollar Diplomacy

Theodore Roosevelt was an imperialist whose geopolitical ambitions were tamed by political realities. William Howard Taft made a different transition; he was an isolationist forced by facts on the ground to oversee the grand strategy of a nation that had, whether he liked it or not, become deeply entangled in the geopolitics of the Western Hemisphere and East Asia. "I am not and never have been an expansionist," Taft affirmed in a speech he delivered in 1900 as he prepared to resign his judgeship on the Sixth Circuit Court of Appeals to govern the Philippines. "I have always hoped that the jurisdiction of our nation would not extend beyond territory between the two oceans. We have not solved all the problems of popular government so perfectly as to justify our voluntarily seeking more difficult ones abroad."[133] Nonetheless, by the time he entered office in 1909, Taft had already served as the first civilian governor of the Philippines and as Roosevelt's secretary of war, giving him considerable experience in managing the wide array of strategic commitments that the nation had acquired a decade earlier.

Taft's exposure to shaping and implementing defense policy during the Roosevelt administration did not whet his appetite for further expansion. On the contrary, he was determined to conduct a foreign policy focused on expanding the nation's commercial rather than its geopolitical reach. The term "dollar diplomacy" became popularized during his tenure—primarily as a pejorative description of his foreign policy. Despite the denigration, Taft stuck to his conviction that the nation's commercial interests should guide its grand strategy. His final Annual Message to Congress in 1912 contained Taft's own concise summary of his approach: "The diplomacy of the present administration has sought to respond to modern ideas of commercial intercourse. This policy has been characterized as substituting dollars for bullets. It is one that appeals alike to idealistic humanitarian sentiments, to the dictates of sound policy and strategy, and to legitimate commercial aims. It is an effort frankly directed to the increase of American trade upon the axiomatic principle that the Government of the United States shall extend all proper support to every legitimate and beneficial American enterprise abroad."[134] Henry Pringle, a biographer of Taft, comments that " 'every diplomat a salesman' might, to a degree, have been a slogan of the Taft years."[135]

Taft not only veered away from the geopolitical aspirations of McKinley and Roosevelt, but he also tempered their reliance on realist instruments of statecraft with a more idealist bent. A former lawyer and judge, he believed that the United States should rely on negotiation and compromise to tame rivalry and conflict. His secretary of state, Philander Knox (a former lawyer, bank director, and senator), along with a number of Knox's key deputies, were known for their informal, straight-talking style and can-do attitudes—what was referred to as shirtsleeve diplomacy. His preference for a foreign policy that emphasized dollars rather than bullets reflected his desire not only to expand commerce, but also to move the nation toward a brand of statecraft that relied on compromise instead of coercion.

To this end, the Taft administration sought to conclude arbitration treaties with Britain and France, revealing a new willingness to abandon unilateralism in favor of legalizing and institutionalizing relations with European powers—a move upon which his successors would soon build. Taft was thus not a traditional isolationist, but instead a harbinger of a new brand of internationalism that entailed limiting the nation's strategic commitments while wielding influence abroad through commerce and diplomacy. This "isolationist internationalism" would come into its heyday in the 1920s.

Taft was, however, before his time. Neither arbitration treaty survived close inspection by the Senate. As usual, senators objected to the prospect of both perceived encroachment on U.S. sovereignty and entanglement with foreign powers. Senator Isidor Rayner (D-Maryland) remarked, "the Monroe doctrine is to be left to arbitration. Just think of it!" According to Senator Gilbert Hitchcock (D-Nebraska), the proposed treaty with Britain "certainly is not American. . . . Instead of having an American plan, a democratic plan, to control our international relations by representatives of the people, we will have a monarchical plan." Hitchcock went on to claim that the arbitration treaty "will involve us in an entangling alliance with Great Britain. I have a great admiration . . . for the British people, but I am not in favor of departing from the old American idea of isolation. I do not believe in an entangling alliance with any country."[136]

The Senate ended up dooming the treaties by watering them down through amendments that Taft found unacceptable. In his own words, "they have amended the treaty in the Senate and have put in so many exceptions that really it is very doubtful whether the adoption of such a treaty will be a step forward." Taft lamented setting aside his work, but nonetheless saw the effort as of symbolic importance and a significant legacy. As he noted in his farewell message to Congress, "in the field of work toward the ideals of peace this Government negotiated, but to my regret was unable to consummate, two arbitration treaties which set the highest mark of the aspiration of nations toward the substitution of arbitration and reason for war in the settlement of international disputes."[137]

Domestic pressure as well as ideological inclination prompted Taft to gravitate to a grand strategy that relied primarily on diplomacy and commercial engagement. According to historian Robert Smith, Taft sought to popularize a brand of statecraft focused on commercial diplomacy "because of domestic opposition to colonialism and military rule." Smith observes that dollar diplomacy "was cheaper than military operations" and "it provided an alternative to military and colonial policies, which were being attacked by various groups as inconsistent with traditional ideals."[138] Following Bryan's electoral defeat in 1900, a chastened anti-imperialist movement became more sophisticated and politically astute. The anti-imperialists accepted that the nation had acquired unprecedented power and influence, but they argued that the United States should use its new clout to mediate disputes and tame interstate conflict through diplomacy and international law. In the meantime, the country should address the societal ills that had contributed to the nation's misguided imperial adventurism. In the words of Nichols, the anti-imperialists "presented a much more limited and internally oriented vision for the nation: act in the world primarily as an exemplar, perhaps as mediator, certainly as a commercial and cultural presence, but not as a conqueror or colonizer."[139] The anti-imperialist movement aided and abetted Taft's idealist turn and his emphasis on commercial rather than territorial expansion.

Congress also played a role in restricting intervention abroad. When Taft negotiated agreements for U.S. authorities to take over customs collection in Nicaragua and Honduras—effectively replicating Roosevelt's approach to Santo Domingo—Congress rejected the deals. "Many members," according to historian Emily Rosenberg, "had become uneasy about further expansion of quasicolonial responsibilities."[140] Moreover, Democrats and Republicans alike complained that the proposed arrangements served the interests of only Wall Street. "I do not know how other senators feel about this matter," said Senator William Smith (R-Michigan), "but for myself I wish to say that never shall I give my approval to a treaty that first must be ratified by J. Pierpont Morgan or by any other individual before it is submitted to the United States senate."[141] In 1911, Taft mobilized thousands of troops along the Mexican border amid revolutionary chaos in Mexico that threatened U.S. citizens and interests. Congress was unenthusiastic about U.S. intervention in Mexico and U.S. troops ultimately stayed put on their side of the border.[142]

One of the main impacts of dollar diplomacy was diminished emphasis on the projection of U.S. naval power. Taft did seek to maintain a naval building program on par with Roosevelt's, but Congress repeatedly pared down his requests.[143] Not only did naval construction slow, but as historian Andrew Dunar observes, Taft "did not rely as much on the threat or application of military force as had TR. . . . Taft's belief in the importance of economics in foreign policy . . . meant that the navy would have a diminished role in his administration."[144]

This strategic shift had its most significant impact in East Asia. Taft dispatched U.S. forces to China on a number of occasions to protect U.S. citizens and property. But he effectively replaced Roosevelt's maritime strategy of preserving a balance of power in the region with one focused on intensified commercial engagement. In particular, he looked to U.S. investment in Manchuria and North China to counter Japanese and Russian ambitions, defend Chinese sovereignty, and preserve U.S. access to the Chinese market. In late 1910, Roosevelt wrote to Taft to protest the dismantlement of a maritime-based Asia strategy, arguing that a commercially oriented approach was falling short.[145] Roosevelt had good reason to complain. American businesses were less enthusiastic about investing on the Asian mainland than Taft had expected. Moreover, dollar diplomacy failed to check the ambitions of Moscow and Tokyo; over the course of 1910, Russia and Japan established effective spheres of influence in Manchuria and Japan proceeded to annex Korea.[146]

In the Caribbean and Central America, Taft's foreign policy more closely tracked that of his predecessor. He continued work on the Panama Canal, which would open the year after he left office. Taft retained Roosevelt's interventionist paternalism, intervening militarily in Nicaragua, Honduras, Panama (only to supervise elections), Santo Domingo, and Cuba.[147] Indeed, Secretary of State

Knox outlined to Taft an approach to the region that essentially mimicked the Roosevelt Corollary: "There should be some conventional right to intervene in Central American affairs promptly, without waiting for outbreaks and with a view to averting rather than quelling internal disturbances. The United States and Mexico jointly or the United States alone should be in a position to apply an effective remedy at any time."[148] In keeping with dollar diplomacy, the Taft administration was quite explicit about its commercial objectives in the region. According to a State Department memo from 1909, "If we want foreign trade, a share in foreign investments, a chance to exploit the riches of other lands, our share in the wealth of other nations, we must buy their bonds, help float their loans, build their railroads, establish banks in their chief cities. In South America the giving of advice and the Monroe Doctrine should be made to yield a financial harvest."[149]

* * *

Taft confronted the unenviable task of reconciling America's isolationist past with its imperialist present. His inclination was to reclaim the nation's traditional focus on expanding its commercial rather than its geopolitical reach. Congress generally embraced the same view. And although the anti-imperialist movement and its candidate fell short in the election of 1900, many Americans remained uneasy with a foreign policy that, even if it demonstrated the nation's new power and status, was at odds with its founding principles.

Taft ended up politically stranded between the nation's internationalist and isolationist impulses. On one hand, Americans had built a world-class navy, acquired a host of territorial commitments in the Caribbean and Pacific that they were not prepared to give up, and assumed the role of heavy-handed guardian in Central America. So, too, had many Americans embraced the notion that the completion of Manifest Destiny at home mandated that they take their national mission abroad. On the other hand, Taft's ideological inclinations as well as domestic pressures prompted him to embrace a foreign policy that prioritized commerce and diplomacy rather than territorial expansion and coercion. Congress was looking to limit foreign commitments and slow the buildup of the navy. The anti-imperialist movement had evolved, backing an enlarged American role in the world, but one that would be consistent with the nation's republican values. Along with his background in law, these domestic trends encouraged Taft to veer away from the realist orientation of McKinley and Roosevelt toward an idealist brand of engagement that would rationalize and legalize the nation's foreign relations—as manifest in commercial engagement, shirtsleeve diplomacy, and the arbitration treaties with France and Britain.

Taft's search for a middle ground between the nation's isolationist traditions and the imperial ambition that emerged in 1898 exposed him to critiques by both contemporaries and historians that his foreign policy was at once naïve and ineffective. He needed to manage the wide range of external commitments left behind by his predecessors, but was disinclined to back up those commitments with sufficient power and resolve. Put differently, American purpose lacked the necessary support of American power. According to one of his biographers, Lewis Gould, Taft's foreign policy was "lackluster and pedestrian. No wars, no major crises, no enduring doctrines, only the deriding label of 'dollar diplomacy' remains of what he . . . tried to do."[150] Taft understood that the isolationists had become more internationalist and the internationalists more reluctant. But he ended up pleasing neither camp. His ineffectual image hurt his reelection bid in 1913, which was not helped by the fact that Roosevelt split the Republican vote by running as the candidate of the Progressive Party, clearing the way for Wilson's victory.

Taft set the stage for Wilson's effort to reconnect American power to American purpose. Wilson picked up on Taft's search for a brand of internationalism that would resonate with the American electorate's republican values. In this regard, he embraced Taft's aversion to territorial expansion abroad and his effort to tame international competition through legalized cooperation. At the same time, Wilson was more willing than Taft to back up his idealist ambitions by relying on the nation's geopolitical strength, not just its commercial reach. Indeed, Wilson embarked on an effort to deploy American power in the service of eradicating imperialism and spreading republican government, convinced that he could sustain public support by pursuing a brand of internationalism that would finally align the nation's newfound power with its founding ideals.

Wilsonian Idealism and
the Isolationist Backlash

Woodrow Wilson's ideological disposition prepared him well to address the core contradiction that had confronted the conduct of U.S. grand strategy since the nation's break with isolationism in 1898. Americans had enthusiastically taken advantage of their newly acquired geopolitical heft to expel Spain from the Western Hemisphere and the Pacific. But the main rationale for doing so—fulfilling the nation's redemptive mission—was inescapably at odds with the reality of imperial conquest. In this sense, territorial expansion did more to undermine than to further America's exceptionalist calling—precisely why it reawakened the nation's isolationist impulse.

Wilson sought to resolve this contradiction by pursuing a brand of internationalism that would align rather than clash with American ideals. To do so, he drew on all three of the ideological foundations of the nation's internationalist turn. Wilson was a realist inasmuch as he accepted that the United States should play a role in the world commensurate with its economic might. Although he started off as an isolationist when it came to U.S. involvement in World War I, he later became convinced that the United States had to be more than an exemplar and a commercial heavyweight; wielding influence would require the projection of U.S. military power. Indeed, Wilson in early 1917 decided to do what had been virtually unthinkable since the nation's founding. He entangled the United States in Europe's geopolitics and dispatched millions of American soldiers across the Atlantic to fight in World War I.

Unlike McKinley and Roosevelt, however, who foresaw the nation's ascent through mastery of the game of great-power politics, Wilson wanted to use U.S. power and diplomacy to eradicate that game. He guided the nation into World War I to vanquish the balance-of-power system that had caused that war—and the many that had come before it. Wilson was thus a committed redeemer whose overriding foreign policy objective was to remake the world in America's image. The United States had brought democracy, peace, and prosperity to its own territory, and it now had an obligation to do the same for the rest of the world. The League of Nations—an international body that would resolve disputes and organize collective action against any aggressors that might emerge—was Wilson's brainchild for achieving this goal. At the close of World War I and the conclusion of the Versailles Treaty that contained the League Covenant, Wilson was optimistic that his mission had been accomplished. "The miasma of distrust, of intrigue, is cleared away," Wilson told the participants at the Paris Peace Conference.[1]

Wilson was also a committed reformer. His priorities at home included regulating commerce and banking, strengthening workers' rights, lowering tariffs, and limiting the political power of corporations and party machines. His progressive domestic agenda and his progressive foreign policy went hand in hand. In Wilson's mind, countries that embraced democracy and practiced good governance at home would be best suited to contribute to an international order based on justice, equality, and cooperation. Wilson's progressive priorities helped him build bipartisan support for his ambitious brand of internationalism. Left-leaning politicians and activists who might have otherwise objected to the nation's entry into World War I rallied behind Wilson due to his strong support of a reformist agenda at home and abroad. His insistence on entering World War I to make the world safe for democracy and reform a war-prone international system resonated with the public, garnering strong bipartisan support for U.S. participation in exactly the kind of great-power bloodletting that the Founders admonished the nation to shun forever. Both the Senate and the House backed by overwhelming margins Wilson's request for a declaration of war in April 1917.

Ironically, with military victory came political defeat. In the end, Wilson ideologically overcorrected and politically overreached. His idealist objectives proved elusive and lost their popular appeal as the war proceeded. Especially after the costs of the conflict mounted, many Americans second-guessed the merits of abandoning nonentanglement to make the world safe for democracy. Justifying entry into World War I on principled grounds rather than on concrete strategic interests left Wilson vulnerable when that war took the lives of over 100,000 Americans. Repression of antiwar dissent, the wartime centralization of power, and the sacrifice of progressive reform to the demands of the wartime economy undercut the administration's support among establishment liberals and labor.

So, too, did Wilson's moralistic case for U.S. participation in the League run up against the nation's unilateralist traditions. After all, when the likes of Senator Henry Cabot Lodge backed a "large policy" in the years before Wilson's presidency, they hardly did so in the service of guiding the nation into a host of international pacts and alliances. Accordingly, Lodge and many other senators saw the League as a vehicle that would infringe on the nation's sovereignty, saddle it with unwanted international obligations, and drag it into unwanted conflicts. Especially amid the partisan wrangling over foreign policy that was a legacy of the Spanish-American War and the anti-imperialist movement, Wilson proved unwilling to make the political compromises that could have secured Lodge's support and salvaged U.S. participation in the League.

The nation's entry into World War I ultimately provoked an isolationist backlash that cleared the way for America's interwar retreat. The Senate voted three times on ratification of the Versailles Treaty, on each occasion rejecting U.S. participation in the League and effectively rebuffing Wilson's rationale for entering the war to begin with. Wilson's idealist aspirations may have lined up with the nation's exceptionalist calling, but they ran up against cold political and geopolitical realities—as well as Wilson's refusal to make pragmatic compromises with his political opponents.

The Wilsonian era thus demonstrates the degree to which a stable brand of American internationalism must rest on solid realist as well as idealist foundations. Americans backed away from the imperial turn of 1898 because it was too realist; indeed, it contravened the nation's exceptionalist narrative. But they backed away from World War I and the League because they were too idealist; Wilson's vision violated the realities of power politics and the prerogatives of national sovereignty. The strength of the exceptionalist narrative means that Americans, if they are to venture out into the world, need to believe that they are fulfilling their redemptive mission. But to sustain the burdens associated with that mission they also need to be convinced that their material interests are directly at stake.

Finding a grand strategy that relied on equal parts of realism and idealism would prove to be a key challenge as Wilson's successors confronted the challenges of the interwar era. It would not be until World War II and the Cold War that a sustainable brand of internationalism would emerge—one that was in many respects built on Wilson's idealist foundations, but also grounded on political and strategic realities.

Wilson's Ideology

Wilson grew up in a deeply religious family. His father was a Presbyterian minister who reared his son in notions of divine justice and order.[2] This moral compass informed his reform agenda at home and his idealist aspirations abroad. He entered public life at an opportune moment for a figure pledging a more virtuous brand of governance. Amid discontent with the nation's missteps abroad, mounting social tensions at home, and Taft's lackluster presidency, Americans

welcomed an individual offering moral ambition and lofty rhetoric—and especially concrete steps to improve the lives of ordinary workers. First as governor
of New Jersey and then as president, Wilson took noteworthy steps to fight poverty, reform labor laws, and regulate commerce, banking, and trusts.

In Wilson's mind, improving domestic governance at home as well as in other
countries was a necessary first step on the path to forging a more peaceful international system. Like Roosevelt, he maintained that the United States needed
to alter the internal makeup of foreign nations if it was to change their external
behavior. Accordingly, the pacification of global affairs would require that the
United States work assiduously to change the way that states govern themselves,
not just the way they interact with each other. For Wilson, doing so was a matter
of changing character and habits more than institutions. "It is the aid of our character they need," he wrote in 1901, "and not the premature aid of our institutions.
Our institutions must come after the ground of character and habit has been
made ready for them; as effect, not cause, in the order of political growth." Such
evolution was a matter of destiny, not choice: "Every man now knows that the
world is to be changed—changed according to an ordering of Providence."[3]

Wilson firmly believed that the United States was destined to be the driving
force in effecting change abroad. Indeed, the nation's exceptionalism—its success as a republic of liberty, its prosperity, its redemptive calling—made it
uniquely suited to the task: "No other modern nation has been schooled as we
have been in big undertakings and the mastery of novel difficulties. We have become confirmed in energy, in resourcefulness, in practical proficiency, in self-
confidence." The United States therefore had to play a "leading part" in ensuring
that "nations and peoples which have stood still the centuries through are to
be quickened, and made part of the universal world of commerce and of ideas."
Wilson deemed it "our peculiar duty to impart to the peoples thus driven out
upon the road of change, so far as we have opportunity or can make it, our own
principles of self-help; teach them order and self-control in the midst of change;
impart to them, if it be possible by contact and sympathy and example, the drill
and habit of law and obedience."[4]

In line with the arguments of progressive expansionists during the 1890s,
Wilson maintained that the nation's exertions abroad would strengthen its
institutions of governance at home. He shared the view that the closing of the
continental frontier meant that Americans needed to look abroad to sustain
their social vitality and further their redemptive mission. "Until 1890," he wrote,
"the United States had always a frontier; looked always to a region beyond, un-
occupied, unappropriated, an outlet for its energy, a new place of settlement and
of achievement for its people." Westward expansion, Wilson argued, provided "a
certain singular unity in our national task." Moving forward, Americans had to
spread their ideals beyond their shores and "these new duties now thrust upon

us will not break that unity. They will perpetuate it, rather, and make it complete, if we keep but our integrity and our old-time purpose true. . . . The reactions which such experiments in the universal validity of principle and method are likely to bring about in respect of our own domestic institutions cannot be calculated or forecast."[5] Moreover, Wilson was confident that the nation's democratic institutions were sufficiently mature and stable to withstand the ambitious program of national armament that he eventually pursued to equip the country for its international obligations. In his mind, a sizable military establishment would not pose a threat to domestic liberty.[6]

Spreading the American experiment was in part a moral obligation arising from the nation's redemptive mission. But the United States was motivated by self-interest as much as selflessness; Wilson readily admitted that Americans have a "habit of acting under an odd mixture of selfish and altruistic motives."[7] Exporting America's values and its republican institutions might be a noble task, but it would also enhance the nation's security and prosperity by laying the foundation for a more peaceful world. Wilson envisaged an international system in which democracies would band together and turn to disarmament, diplomacy, and cooperation to preserve a stable and just global order.

Even when he took the nation to war in 1917, asking for unprecedented American sacrifice at a great distance from the homeland, his aim was not military victory and the defeat of Germany, but instead the elimination of Old World geopolitics and the establishment of an international order based on law, reason, and negotiation. In his war message to Congress, Wilson declared that "the world must be made safe for democracy. Its peace must be planted upon the tested foundations of political liberty."[8] In the words of political theorist John Kane, Wilson "would commit the nation to participation in a cruel war in Europe, justifying it as a war to end all wars, the prelude to building world peace through general disarmament, arbitration, and a system of international law expressed in and safeguarded by a League of Nations."[9]

Especially when compared with other American leaders of his era, Wilson fully merits his reputation as a high-minded and idealistic leader of strong moral conviction. That he chose as his secretary of state William Jennings Bryan, the anti-imperialist progressive who had lost presidential bids against McKinley in 1896 and 1900 and against Taft in 1908, spoke clearly to his ideological preferences as well as his desire to garner the support of pacifist and left-leaning Democrats. Nonetheless, Wilson did exhibit contradictory impulses, at times pursuing policies that betrayed his own ideological convictions. His speeches were often paeans to democracy and liberty, but he was as interventionist and heavy-handed in the Caribbean and Central America as any of his contemporaries. He regularly deployed lofty rhetoric in favor of national self-determination, but strongly privileged existing multi-ethnic states. He in theory defended the political equality of all peoples, but practiced racism at home and played a prominent role in excluding from the League Covenant collective commitments to racial equality and the protection of minorities. And Wilson proved too bellicose for his own secretary of state, prompting Bryan to resign in protest in 1915 over the president's stern response to Germany's sinking of a British passenger ship, the RMS *Lusitania*.[10]

Despite these and other areas of tension between his ideology and his policies, Wilson does deserve credit for formulating a new version of American internationalism that would ultimately prove to have remarkable staying power. Like McKinley and Roosevelt, Wilson believed that neither the nation's role as exemplar nor dollar diplomacy would be adequate to safeguard American interests; the United States needed to extend its strategic reach and uphold, with military force if necessary, a global range of geopolitical commitments. But Wilson broke with his predecessors on the purposes of American power. Whereas McKinley and Roosevelt wanted the United States to master the practice of great-power politics, Wilson wanted to displace it in favor of an international order grounded on democracy, justice, and multilateral cooperation. Wilson was thus the first American leader to harness American power to the task of globalizing American ideals. In the end, he fell short; the country whose material strength and ideals most shaped the post–World War I order itself refused to join that order, leaving it badly wounded. But Wilson did lay the ideological foundation for the brand of liberal internationalism that would take hold in the 1940s, a formula that proved able to durably overturn the isolationist consensus that returned with a vengeance during the interwar period.

The Western Hemisphere and East Asia

Wilson inherited from his predecessors deep American involvement in the affairs of the nation's southern neighbors—and faced strong incentives to continue the interventionism that began in 1898. The opening of the Panama Canal in 1914 heightened the region's commercial and strategic importance to the United States. By Wilson's presidency, roughly half of U.S. foreign investment flowed to Latin America, which had also become a major market for U.S. manufactured goods.[11] The United States had already inserted itself into the domestic politics of numerous countries in the region—and Wilson's commitment to spreading republican habits and institutions abroad predisposed him to continue such efforts.

At least in rhetorical terms, Wilson sought to align his policies toward Latin America with his idealist convictions. He initially pledged to pursue a more hands-off approach to the Western Hemisphere than did his predecessors, denouncing imperialism and coercion and pledging to help defend the political rights of the region's peoples. In a speech in Mobile, Alabama, on October 27, 1913, he laid out the key elements of his thinking:

> The future, ladies and gentlemen, is going to be very different for this hemisphere from the past. These States lying to the south of us, which have always been our neighbors, will now be drawn closer to us by innumerable ties, and, I hope, chief of all, by the tie of a common understanding of each other. . . . Comprehension must be the soil in which shall grow all the fruits of friendship, and there is a reason and a compulsion lying behind all this which is dearer than anything else to the thoughtful men of America. I mean the development of constitutional liberty in the world. Human rights, national integrity, and opportunity as against material interests—that, ladies and gentlemen, is the issue which we now have to face. I want to take this occasion to say that the United States will never again seek one additional foot of territory by conquest.[12]

Wilson did attempt to fashion policies that at least to some extent reflected his idealist leanings. For example, he explored the potential conclusion of a Pan-American Pact aimed at consolidating republican government, safeguarding sovereignty and territorial integrity, and expanding trade throughout the hemisphere. Negotiations ensued, with a particular focus on engaging Argentina, Brazil, and Chile.[13] But the proposal never bore fruit. Instead, U.S. policy toward the region contrasted sharply with Wilson's public statements and his pledge to honor "national integrity."

During his presidency, Wilson regularly inserted the United States into Mexico's unstable politics, on occasion using the U.S. military to do so. American forces occupied the port of Veracruz for much of 1914. In 1916, Wilson sent several thousand U.S. troops into Mexico in pursuit of Francisco "Pancho" Villa, a Mexican revolutionary who had killed several Americans in a cross-border raid. Wilson also intervened in Haiti (where the United States in 1915 established a protectorate that lasted for the next two decades), Santo Domingo, Cuba, and Panama. American troops remained in Nicaragua throughout Wilson's presidency. In 1916, Wilson bought the Virgin Islands from Denmark, completing the effort initially launched by William Seward in 1867.

Wilson tried to finalize the Weitzel-Chamorro Treaty—essentially a Platt Amendment for Nicaragua—which would have made the country an effective protectorate of the United States and given U.S. forces the right to intervene at will. Notably, the Senate blocked the treaty, just as it did Taft's attempts to take over customs houses in Nicaragua and Honduras. Still chastened by the backlash against colonial rule that followed the Spanish-American War, senators were not looking to take on additional commitments in Latin America.[14] Senator William Borah (R-Idaho), who would emerge as one of Wilson's fiercest critics in Congress, called the treaty "outrageous" and observed that "Uncle Sam gets some queer twists in his mind when he goes to deal with small powers."[15] He charged that the proposed arrangement was the "beginning of that policy whose irrefutable logic is complete dominance and control."[16]

Wilson's interventionism, like that of his predecessors, stemmed in part from awareness of the nation's economic interests abroad—particularly in Latin America. During the 1912 presidential campaign, he explicitly linked domestic prosperity to the penetration of foreign markets, asserting that "if prosperity is not to be checked in this country we must broaden our borders and make conquest of the markets of the world."[17] But Wilson also harbored a progressive skepticism toward banks and corporations and shared none of Taft's optimism that commercial engagement alone would secure U.S. interests. Rather, he sincerely believed that the United States could inculcate among Latin Americans the habits of republican government and the rule of law. As Wilson put it condescendingly in 1913, "I am going to teach the South American republics to elect good men!"[18] According to Arthur Link, one of his leading biographers, Wilson "assumed that it was his responsibility as well as his privilege to teach his unenlightened neighbors how to write good constitutions and elect wise leaders, even though the effort might require a partial or total denial of the sovereignty of the recipients of such assistance." Link also points out the self-evident tension between Wilson's coercive means and his idealist ends: "A certain strain of irony runs through this story. An idealistic President who talked movingly of Pan-American brotherhood and of the equality of nations great and small, and who worked hard in many ways to give reality to these ideals, became in fact the most extraordinary interventionist in Latin America in the history of the United States."[19]

Wilson's disinterest in East Asia stands in stark contrast to his interventionism in Central America. The one exception was the Philippines, where Wilson, in keeping with his progressive, anti-imperialist agenda, orchestrated an overhaul of U.S. policy that led to a considerable degree of self-rule. The Philippine Autonomy Act of 1916 devolved significant powers to an elected Filipino legislature and local administrators. The American governor general retained the right to veto policy decisions, and the islands remained in U.S. hands for another three decades. Nonetheless, the legislation did clear the way for Filipinos to take effective control of the islands' internal affairs.

With respect to Asia's major powers, however, Wilson's approach was one of neglect and disengagement more than purposeful strategy. As for China and the Open Door, Wilson effectively ended dollar diplomacy, rejecting Taft's confidence in the ability of U.S. investment to provide sufficient leverage to preserve market access. He also backed away from Roosevelt's policy of maritime balancing, looking to contain rather than enlarge America's strategic presence in the region. Wilson wanted the United States to rely on its diplomatic and moral authority to check Japanese ambition and support China's political independence and territorial integrity. But since he was unwilling to back up that commitment with American muscle, he could offer only a mild protest when Japan, an ally of Britain, entered World War I and wrested control of a number of German possessions in China and the southern Pacific. When it came to Japanese expansion, Wilson's policy, according to Michael Green, was one of "non-action." "Wilson was not willing to use American power . . . to formulate a new strategic equilibrium to preserve the Open Door," Green writes, noting that he "had no clear plan for shaping the regional order."[20]

Wilson also adopted a hands-off approach when it came to recognizing the anticolonial and nationalist aspirations of Asian nations; once again, his policies were at odds with his rhetoric. Wilson's talk of self-determination raised high hopes that the Versailles Treaty would roll back European imperialism and recognize the equality of all peoples. But Indian nationalists were not even invited to the peace conference, Japan's request for a clause recognizing racial equality was turned down, and Europe's imperial presence in East Asia remained intact. "Wilson barely put up a fight when it came to the rights of non-European peoples," observes Pankaj Mishra. High expectations yielded to frustration and disillusionment, ultimately energizing sharp-edged nationalist and anticolonialist movements throughout Asia. "The Wilsonian moment did alter the relationship between colonizer and colonized," writes Erez Manela, "but it did not do so in the consensual, evolutionary manner that Wilson had envisioned."[21]

In sum, Wilson pursued a policy of strategic retrenchment in East Asia, in general shying away from the expansive commitments that emerged from the Spanish-American War and the Open Door policies. He was far more focused on Latin America and Europe, the latter becoming a preoccupation after the outbreak of World War I.

World War I

After Germany embarked on the construction of a battleship fleet in 1898, the United States kept its distance from Anglo-German naval rivalry and, soon thereafter, building tensions between the Triple Entente (Britain, France, and Russia) and the Triple Alliance (Germany, Austria-Hungary, and Italy). Wilson continued that policy after the outbreak of World War I in 1914, adhering closely to the admonitions of the Founders. He declared neutrality and insisted that the

United States remain aloof from what he saw as yet another round of futile geo-political competition among European rivals. Wilson refused to choose sides, in-stead echoing Washington and Jefferson when he informed Congress on August 19, 1914, that "every man who really loves America will act and speak in the true spirit of neutrality, which is the spirit of impartiality and fairness and friendliness to all concerned."[22] In theory, Wilson was exercising America's right to trade with all belligerents, but in practice his policy was not exactly one of "impartiality and fairness." The British blockade of Germany meant that U.S. trade flowed prima-rily to Britain and its allies. Some historians have therefore concluded that, de-spite his declaratory policy of neutrality, Wilson privately favored Britain and its partners from the outset.[23]

Wilson backed off his effort to maintain an even-handed neutrality after a German submarine torpedoed and sank the RMS *Lusitania* in May 1915. Some 1,200 passengers lost their lives, including 128 Americans. Wilson sent a series of warnings to the Germans and began to support building up the U.S. Army and Navy, a move aimed primarily at strengthening the U.S. role as a neutral mediator and deterring further German attacks on passenger vessels.[24] His more assertive diplomacy helped convince Berlin to cease unrestricted attacks on bel-ligerent passenger ships.

Wilson's more resolute stance toward Germany and his interest in military preparation proved politically controversial. Secretary of State Bryan stepped down on June 9, noting in his resignation letter that he could not support Wilson's more confrontational approach toward Germany "without violating what I deem to be an obligation to my country, and the issue involved is of such moment that to remain a member of the cabinet would be as unfair to you as it would be to the cause which is nearest my heart, namely, the prevention of war."[25] A good number of Democrats and progressive Republicans were less than enthusiastic about the preparedness program, especially after Germany agreed to end unrestricted submarine warfare. Congress did pass defense bills in 1916 that expanded the size of the Army, the National Guard, and the Navy. Naval outlays were quite substantial, but particularly when it came to active-duty ground forces, the increases were modest and fell far short of what Army Chief of Staff Leonard Wood and other supporters of the preparedness movement were recommending. The legislation provoked a firestorm of criticism that it left the United States woefully underprepared in light of international conditions.[26]

To the degree that the war figured in the 1916 presidential election, nonentanglement was Wilson's policy of choice. "He kept us out of war" was one of his main campaign slogans.[27] The former governor of New York, Martin Glynn, noted in his keynote address at the Democratic Convention that "in all the history of the world there is no other national policy that has justified itself so completely and entirely as the American policy of neutrality and isolation from the quarrels of European powers. . . . It has freed us from the paralyzing touch of Europe's balance of power, leaving to Europe the things that are Europe's and preserving to America the independence, the peace, and the happiness that now are hers."[28] In his speech accepting the Democratic nomination, Wilson justified his strict adherence to neutrality on isolationist logic as well as idealist aspiration:

> We have been neutral not only because it was the fixed and traditional policy of the United States to stand aloof from the politics of Europe and because we had had no part either of action or of policy in the influences which brought on the present war, but also because it was manifestly our duty to prevent, if it were possible, the indefinite extension of the fires of hate and desolation kindled by that terrible conflict and seek to serve mankind by reserving our strength and our resources for the anxious and difficult days of restoration and healing which must follow, when peace will have to build its house anew.[29]

Wilson thereafter ran on a peace agenda, emphasizing his success in keeping the United States out of the war. He went on to warn the electorate that a Republican victory would imperil neutrality; should he lose the election, he foresaw a "certain prospect" of the country being pulled "into the embroilments of the European war."[30] Democratic spokespeople made similar arguments across the country. The Republicans took up the bait. Roosevelt, who endorsed the Republican candidate, Charles Evans Hughes, called Wilson's "He kept us out of war" slogan "the phrase of a coward" and reminded voters of "the shadows of the helpless whom Mr. Wilson did not dare protect lest he might have to face danger."[31] Nonetheless, the appeal of Wilson's progressive legislation and his pledge to keep the United States out of the war helped earn him, even if by a relatively narrow margin, a second term.

Even before his reelection, however, Wilson did lay down a clear marker, pledging that the United States would no longer stand aloof should its neutral rights be breached. In his speech accepting the Democratic nomination, he stipulated that should a belligerent violate "the rights of our own citizens" and engage in "direct violations of a nation's sovereignty," the aggressor "must expect to be checked and called to account by direct challenge and resistance. It at once makes the quarrel in part our own."[32] Wilson's warning would prove prophetic when Germany returned to unrestricted submarine warfare in early 1917.

On February 3, 1917, three days after Germany made clear that it would abandon restraints on submarine warfare, Wilson broke relations with Berlin. In a speech to Congress justifying this move, he held out hope that Germany would refrain from following through on its declaration: "I cannot bring myself to believe that they will indeed . . . destroy American ships and take the lives of

American citizens in the willful prosecution of the ruthless naval program they have announced their intention to adopt. Only actual overt acts on their part can make me believe it even now." Wilson went on to specify that "if American ships and American lives should in fact be sacrificed by their naval commanders in heedless contravention of the just and reasonable understandings of international law and the obvious dictates of humanity, I shall take the liberty of coming again before the Congress, to ask that authority be given me to use any means that may be necessary for the protection of our seamen and our people in the prosecution of their peaceful and legitimate errands on the high seas."[33]

Soon thereafter, American citizens lost their lives on belligerent ships sunk by German submarines, which also began to attack U.S. vessels. In late February, the British provided to Wilson an intercepted German telegram to the Mexican government, proposing that Mexico ally with Berlin. In return, Germany would provide generous financial support and help Mexico recover Texas, New Mexico, and Arizona. These developments convinced Wilson that the United States could no longer remain neutral. On April 2, he delivered his war message to Congress: "American ships have been sunk, American lives taken.... I advise that the Congress declare the recent course of the Imperial German Government to be in fact nothing less than war against the government and people of the United States.... Our object ... is to vindicate the principles of peace and justice in the life of the world."[34] Four days later, both the Senate and House approved the declaration of war by overwhelming margins. The first American troops arrived in Europe in June, and units of the American Expeditionary Forces (AEF) were fully engaged on the front lines by October.

The remainder of this chapter charts the evolution of U.S. strategy from isolationist neutrality, to full engagement in World War I, to Wilson's unsuccessful effort to guide the United States into the postwar league for peace that he took the lead in constructing. It was Wilson's idealism that shaped both his isolationism as well as his eventual readiness to entangle the United States in the war. It was also this idealism—untempered by political and geopolitical realities—that was Wilson's undoing.

Isolationism and the Case for Neutrality

Between the outbreak of World War I in August 1914 and the German actions in early 1917 that would convince Wilson to abandon neutrality, isolationism maintained its tight hold on U.S. grand strategy toward Europe. The United States had fully entangled itself in the affairs of the Americas and had major footholds in the Pacific, but when it came to the Old World, bipartisan support for geopolitical separation remained intact. According to historian John Cooper, "the initial impact of the World War on the United States had reinforced the traditional consensus behind isolation."[35] This consensus rested on five main assumptions, all of which drew on the core isolationist logics that had dominated the nation's strategic discourse since its founding.

First, geographic separation meant that the United States could and should cordon itself off from Europe's geopolitical rivalries. Soon after the war started, Wilson argued in his Annual Message to Congress that Europeans had entered into a conflict "with which we have nothing to do, whose causes can not touch us, whose very existence affords us opportunities of friendship and disinterested service which should make us ashamed of any thought of hostility or fearful preparation for trouble."[36] More than a year into the conflict, in his Annual Message for 1915, he held fast to this view: "We have stood apart, studiously neutral. It was our manifest duty to do so. Not only did we have no part or interest in the policies which seem to have brought the conflict on; it was necessary, if a universal catastrophe was to be avoided, that a limit should be set to the sweep of destructive war."[37] Remaining neutral would not just keep the United States out of others' troubles but also enable it to sustain commerce with all parties—just as the Founders had advised. According to Link, Wilson's primary objective in foreign policy "was to win the largest possible freedom of trade with all belligerents for American citizens, within the bounds of neutrality."[38] The strategy paid off handsomely. Despite the British blockade of Germany, American exports to Europe, especially of food and ammunition, rose significantly, and loans to the belligerents helped establish the United States as a major international creditor.[39]

Second, Wilson's belief in America's role as redeemer nation helped convince him that all of Europe's warring parties were unworthy of American sacrifice. A few months before the war began, he invoked George Washington to justify his assessment that none of the belligerents was deserving of American help: "It was not merely because of passing and transient circumstances that Washington said that we must keep free from entangling alliances. It was because he saw that no country had yet set its face in the same direction in which America had set her face. We can not form alliances with those who are not going our way; and in our might and majesty and in the confidence and definiteness of our own purpose we need not and we should not form alliances with any nation in the world."[40]

Privately, Wilson did express concern that Germany's illiberal government was a cause of the country's militarism and he worried that a German victory would mean a more militarized world.[41] But, especially in public, he attributed moral equivalence to the belligerents; the war was not a struggle between democracy and autocracy, but instead a product of the rivalries and jealousies that continued to infect European affairs. According to historian William Langer, "Wilson, like most of his countrymen, regarded this newest and most terrible conflict merely as the latest manifestation of the crass materialism, the ruthless

ambition, the political immorality and the baleful power politics which had always sullied the history of the Old World."[42] Historian Ross Kennedy agrees that
in Wilson's mind "it was the lawless character of the system, the lack of any international security regime for states, that encouraged ambitious, militaristic power
politics, not the nature of the states within the system."[43]

Wilson's public stance on the war changed little as the fighting progressed.
In December 1915, he maintained that the United States needed to remain a
repository of decency and reason, arguing that "some part of the great family of
nations should keep the processes of peace alive."[44] More than two years into the
war, Wilson indicated that he still viewed the parties to the conflict as morally
equivalent, affirming that "the objects which the statesmen of the belligerents
on both sides have in mind in this war are virtually the same."[45] In a speech in
October 1916, Wilson directly addressed the causes of the war: "Have you ever
heard what started the present war? If you have, I wish you would publish it, because nobody else has. So far as I can gather, nothing in particular started it, but
everything in general. There has been growing up in Europe a mutual suspicion,
an interchange of conjectures about what this government and that government was going to do, an interlacing of alliances and understandings, a complex
web of intrigue and spying, that presently was sure to entangle the whole of the
family of mankind on that side of the water in its meshes."[46] Consistent with this
view, Wilson hoped that the conflict would end in a draw; peace without victory
would impress on the belligerents the dangers of Old World geopolitics and the
futility of war, thereby setting the stage for a more pacific postwar order.[47]

Third, Wilson's belief in American exceptionalism and the nation's redemptive mission, buttressed by the idealism and pacifism that informed the progressive movement, led him to envisage the United States as not just a neutral
power but also an impartial mediator that would help end the conflict and construct a new international order. In his declaration of neutrality on August 19,
1914, he called on Americans to fulfill "the proper performance of our duty as
the one great nation at peace, the one people holding itself ready to play a part
of impartial mediation and speak the counsels of peace and accommodation,
not as a partisan, but as a friend."[48] William Jennings Bryan, the progressive intellectual Randolph Bourne, and other influential voices, many associated with
Christian pacifist movements, encouraged Wilson to establish the United States
as both an arbitrator and the architect of the peaceful order that would follow
the conflict's end.[49]

Drawing on the anti-imperialist arguments deployed by progressives after
1898, Wilson and many other reformers contended that remaining true to the
nation's exceptional character entailed resisting rather than falling prey to the
temptations of geopolitical rivalry. Wilson encouraged his fellow citizens to
emulate the "self-mastered man" who exhibits "a much more fundamental and

terrible courage than the irritable, fighting man."[50] He called on the United States to "show herself in this time of peculiar trial a Nation fit beyond others to exhibit the fine poise of undisturbed judgement, the dignity of self-control, the efficiency of dispassionate action."[51]

Wilson's embrace of American exceptionalism, not just his fear of unneeded and unwanted embroilment in Europe's bloodshed, shaped his aversion to taking sides in the war. Insisting that "we need not and we should not form alliances with any nation in the world," he went on to explain that alliances are only for nations that are weak and unjust: "Those who are right, those who study their consciences in determining their policies, those who hold their honor higher than their advantage, do not need alliances. You need alliances when you are not strong, and you are weak only when you are not true to yourself. You are weak only when you are in the wrong."[52] Simply put, geopolitical entanglement with Europe was beneath the nation. Instead, the United States would stand by its exceptional principles and its role as a redeemer nation, taking the lead in forging a postwar order that would do away with alliances and other Old World anachronisms.

Fourth, prominent voices maintained that armament and U.S. entry into the war were inimical to domestic liberty and would compromise the nation's political institutions. Eugene Debs in 1915 laid out the dangers he saw in Wilson's call for national preparedness: "A large standing army, a powerful navy, and stupendous military armament such as President Wilson proposes . . . means [sic] a military autocracy and it can mean nothing else."[53] The American Union Against Militarism (AUAM), an organization that began life in January 1915 as the Anti-Militarism Committee, organized a nationwide campaign against armament and involvement in the war. One full-page AUAM advertisement that ran nationally in 1917 in the *New Republic* was quite explicit about the domestic dangers of entering the European conflict: "We cannot bring democracy to Europe by going to war. We can preserve democracy in the western hemisphere by staying out."[54]

Wilson was also concerned about militarism eventually infecting American politics and encroaching on civil liberties, but for him the chief worry was not armament and the potential onset of military autocracy; American democracy was durable enough to weather wartime sacrifice and the requisite increase in the powers of the federal government. Instead, Wilson feared that involvement in the war would ensnare the nation in Europe's balance-of-power geopolitics and force the United States to play by the rules of the Old World. Unwilling to countenance compromising America's role as redeemer nation, he insisted that "some part of the great family of nations should keep the processes of peace alive."[55] That concern helped convince Wilson to stay out of the war until he felt that German attacks on U.S. ships left him no choice. As discussed below, his belief in the nation's exceptionalist calling also helped persuade him to enter the conflict not as just another acquisitive combatant, but as a peacemaker bent on delivering Europe—and the rest of the world—from war and its causes.[56]

Fifth, picking up on the critique of corporate power that won many adherents during the 1890s, influential progressives—including Wilson—feared that armament and war would come at the expense of domestic reform. "Every reform we have won," Secretary of the Navy Josephus Daniels recalled Wilson saying in 1914, "will be lost if we go into this war."[57] Figures farther to the left claimed that commercial and banking interests were behind the scenes pushing the country toward armament and needless involvement in the war. Debs was one of the most prominent figures charging that the "Northeastern plutocracy," supported by its capitalist allies in other parts of the country, was scheming to ensnare the nation in Europe's bloodletting. In opposing Wilson's call for preparedness and increases in defense spending, Debs warned that "if the American people acquiesce in such an obviously plutocratic program they must not be surprised . . . if they themselves are conscripted and fight and die to maintain plutocratic supremacy in the United States."[58] Although urban workers constituted his political base, Debs's message resonated among southern libertarians, midwestern farmers, and others worried about big government, excessive corporate influence, and inequality. Although he had served as an officer in the Union Army, Representative Isaac Sherwood (D-Ohio) denounced in the House—to rousing applause—"that powerful group of war exploiters in Gotham who value blood-coined dollars as more vital than orderly self-government."[59] Well aware of such public skepticism, Bryan wanted to enhance the ability of the electorate to block potential involvement in the war, following his resignation in 1915 calling for a constitutional amendment requiring that a declaration of war be approved through a popular referendum (except in case of invasion).[60]

Partisan alignments reinforced the political strength of the isolationist camp. Democrats enjoyed majorities in both houses of Congress. Realist Republicans from the Northeast were the most reliable supporters of armament and a more resolute stand against Germany, but they had little influence over Wilson and were mindful of the popular backlash against foreign ambition that resulted from McKinley's imperial forays. Southern Democrats—Wilson's political base—still harbored a traditional libertarian suspicion of large military establishments and, although they generally accepted the nation's new strategic commitments in Latin America, opposed moving beyond hemispheric isolation. Socialists, who were strongest in urban areas but influential in building antiwar sentiment in the agrarian heartland, added to the pressure on Wilson to steer clear of Europe's conflict.

Despite the misgivings within Wilson's own camp, he was able to secure a modest increase in military preparedness in 1916. Partisan loyalty played an important role. Representative Dan Stephens (D-Nebraska) indicated as much, stating that "the truth is I am very distressed over the Administration program. . . . I am equally distressed with the proposition of making a fight against the Administration for to do so would weaken our chances of re-election all along the line." Indeed, Wilson's readiness to back away from his preference for a more substantial expansion of the nation's armed forces stemmed in large part from opposition within his own party.[61]

Leagues for Peace

Even as the isolationist consensus against U.S. involvement in the war held firm, debate proceeded over proposals for a leading U.S. role in building a postwar order that would preserve peace. Not long after the war broke out, influential figures began to call for the creation of an international organization whose members would agree to settle disputes through arbitration and to amass collective military force against any aggressors that might emerge in the future. Interested parties began to coordinate their efforts in June 1915, gathering at Independence Hall in Philadelphia to launch the League to Enforce Peace. At its founding meeting, the League's members elected William Howard Taft as its president. They adopted a resolution affirming that "the time has come to devise and to create a working union of sovereign nations to establish peace among themselves and to guarantee it by all known and available sanctions at their command." The resolution also called for the settlement of all disputes through negotiation and arbitration and a commitment of the signatory powers to "jointly use forthwith both their economic and their military forces against any one of their number that goes to war, or commits acts of hostility, against another of the signatories."[62]

Wilson soon picked up on these ideas, and over the course of 1916 began to articulate his own vision of what would become the League of Nations. He delivered a major speech on the topic in May before a meeting of the League to Enforce Peace. Wilson began by defending neutrality, reiterating that "we are in no sense or degree parties to the present quarrel." But, he observed, "we are not mere disconnected lookers-on." When the conflict comes to a close, he maintained, "we shall be as much concerned as the nations at war to see peace assume an aspect of permanence." Wilson proposed that "the nations of the world must in some way band themselves together to see that that right prevails as against any sort of selfish aggression; that henceforth alliance must not be set up against alliance, understanding against understanding, but that there must be a common agreement for a common object, and that at the heart of that common object must lie the inviolable rights of peoples and of mankind." He concluded that "I am sure that I speak the mind and wish of the people of America when I say that the United States is willing to become a partner in any feasible association of nations formed in order to realize these objects and make them secure against violation."[63]

After this initial statement in May, Wilson further developed—and regularly shared with the public—his ideas for a postwar concert of nations. In October he insisted that "it is our duty to lend the full force of this nation, moral and physical, to a league of nations which shall see to it that nobody disturbs the peace of the world without submitting his case first to the opinion of mankind."[64] In a speech before the Senate on January 22, 1917, Wilson insisted that any meaningful pact for peace would require a means of enforcement, which he specified as a commitment among member states to amass an overwhelming military coalition against aggressors. "Mere agreements may not make peace secure," he warned. "It will be absolutely necessary that a force be created as a guarantor of the permanency of the settlement so much greater than the force of any nation now engaged or any alliance hitherto formed or projected, that no nation, no probable combination of nations, could face or withstand it. If the peace presently to be made is to endure, it must be a peace made secure by the organized major force of mankind." Only this approach, in Wilson's mind, would succeed in doing away with the war-prone geopolitics of the Old World: "The question upon which the whole future peace and policy of the world depends is this: Is the present war a struggle for a just and secure peace, or only for a new balance of power? If it be only a struggle for a new balance of power, who will guarantee, who can guarantee, the stable equilibrium of the new arrangement? Only a tranquil Europe can be a stable Europe. There must be, not a balance of power, but a community of power; not organized rivalries, but an organized common peace."[65]

Wilson's effort to construct a new international order stemmed not just from his idealist conviction that "a community of power" must replace "a balance of power," but also his belief that the United States had, as of 1898, become irreversibly enmeshed in global affairs. Wilson viewed the Spanish-American War as a turning point for the nation: "No war ever transformed us quite as the war with Spain transformed us. . . . The nation that was one hundred and twenty-five years in the making has now stepped forth into the open arena of the world."[66] Pointing out that the 1890 census had acknowledged the closing of the U.S. frontier and thereby strengthened the case for overseas expansion, he observed in 1916 that "it is not by accident . . . that only eight years elapsed before we got into the politics of the world." Ever since, he asserted, "we have been caught inevitably in the net of the politics of the world."[67] In his 1916 address to the League to Enforce Peace, Wilson elaborated: "We are participants, whether we would or not, in the life of the world. The interests of all nations are our own also. We are partners with the rest. What affects mankind is inevitably our affair as well as the affair of the nations of Europe and of Asia."[68]

It followed that if the United States could no longer shield itself from the world, it would have to remake the world to render it safe for American engagement. To be sure, the nation's messianic calling was part of the impetus; as historian N. Gordon Levin notes, Wilson strongly believed that "an exceptionalist America had a mission to lead mankind toward the orderly international society of the future."[69] But American self-preservation also drove Wilson's effort to establish a league of nations. Exporting American ideals to the rest of the world would ensure that the United States could engage in that world without sacrificing its exceptional character. And since such engagement was in the end unavoidable, protecting the American experiment entailed changing Europe and eradicating Old World geopolitics.

Wilson understood that his vision of America's new role in the world would likely provoke intense political controversy; inasmuch as it entailed deep entanglement in global affairs, it was out of step with the nation's isolationist and unilateralist traditions. He sought to counter the most obvious objections by arguing that his plan, far from imposing entanglement and alliance on the nation, would liberate the country from both by fundamentally overhauling the international system. In May 1916, only a matter of days after his speech to the League to Enforce Peace, Wilson pledged that "I shall never, myself, consent to an entangling alliance. But I would gladly assent to a disentangling alliance—an alliance which would disentangle the peoples of the world from those combinations in which they seek their own separate and private interests and unite the people of the world to preserve the peace of the world upon a basis of common right and justice. There is liberty there, not limitation. There is freedom, not entanglement."[70] He pursued a similar line of argument before the Senate the following January: "I am proposing that all nations henceforth avoid entangling alliances which would draw them into competitions of power, catch them in a net of intrigue and selfish rivalry, and disturb their own affairs with influences intruded from without. There is no entangling alliance in a concert of power. When all unite to act in the same sense and with the same purpose all act in the common interest and are free to live their own lives under a common protection."[71]

Wilson was prescient in anticipating objections to his plans for a concert of nations; his views indeed elicited fierce opposition from both the left and right. On the left, Bryan and other pacifists strongly objected to Wilson's proposed activism, insisting that the United States return to its pre-1898 strategy of sharing its values only through example. Bryan maintained that any scheme that would potentially involve the country in war "would be a descent and would impair our influence and jeopardize our moral prestige."[72] Entering into a pact to enforce peace would be, he contended, to accept that Americans "are tired of being good and hunger for the excitement of the camp and the man hunt."[73] Randolph

Bourne argued that a league would drag the United States into unwanted conflicts and force it to play by the rules of power politics. He preferred instead a league of neutrals to serve as a redoubt of democracy, peace, and justice.[74]

Republican critics, meanwhile, focused their ire on what they saw as the potentially limitless commitments and loss of national autonomy that would accompany the realization of a league to enforce peace. After Wilson began laying out his ideas in the spring of 1916, Roosevelt remarked that "if his words meant anything they would mean that hereafter we intended to embark on a policy of violent meddling in every European quarrel, and in return to invite Old World nations violently to meddle in everything American."[75] Senator Albert Cummins (R-Iowa) reacted to Wilson's proposal by complaining that "we will be involved either in almost continuous war waged all over the world or we will be engaged in almost continuous rebellion against the authority which he proposes to set over us."[76] Lodge was similarly opposed to any scheme that would compromise U.S. sovereignty by granting an international league authority over matters of war and peace.[77]

These Democratic and Republican critiques of Wilson's plan for a new postwar order foreshadowed the objections that would ultimately sink U.S. participation in the League of Nations when the Senate took three votes on the matter in 1919 and 1920. But prior to Wilson's losing battle to win ratification of the Versailles Treaty, he first needed to secure Congress's approval of entry into World War I—a battle that he handily won.

Idealism and the Case for War

After Germany in early 1917 returned to unrestricted submarine warfare and began sinking U.S. ships, Wilson began making preparations to enter the war. He asked for a declaration of war on April 2. Congress readily complied on April 6; the vote in the Senate was 82 to 6, and in the House, 373 to 50.

Wilson's case for entering World War I was strikingly idealist in content and tone. Indeed, in his address to a joint session of Congress on April 2 he justified his decision to go to war by appropriating the same ambitious objectives that he had used to defend neutrality. Wilson insisted that "our motives and our objects" had not changed and that "my own thought has not been driven from its habitual and normal course by the unhappy events of the last two months." He still envisaged the role of the United States to be that of peacemaker and architect of a cooperative postwar order. But now that Americans were under direct attack, Wilson maintained, the United States could attain those objectives only by inserting itself into the conflict. He believed that the nation had no choice but to resort to force if it was to have the leverage and moral authority to forge a world in which acts of aggression would be met with a collective response. "We will not choose the path of submission and suffer the most sacred rights of our Nation and our people to be ignored or violated," Wilson insisted. "The wrongs against which we now array ourselves are no common wrongs; they cut to the very roots of human life."[78] As Link describes Wilson's thinking, the United States "could not submit to Germany's flagrant . . . assault on American sovereignty without yielding its honor and destroying its influence for constructive work in the world. . . . American belligerency now offered the surest hope for early peace and the reconstruction of the international community."[79]

In his war message to Congress, Wilson asserted that U.S. involvement in the war was a matter of principle and was not driven by realpolitik concerns about security or prosperity. Indeed, he explicitly disavowed the notion that material interests were at stake: "We have no selfish ends to serve. We desire no conquest, no dominion. We seek no indemnities for ourselves, no material compensation for the sacrifices we shall freely make." The United States needed to take up arms not to protect its citizens and vessels, but to defend its core ideals and the interests of mankind: "The present German submarine warfare against commerce is a warfare against mankind. It is a war against all nations. . . . Our motive will not be revenge or the victorious assertion of the physical might of the nation, but only the vindication of right, of human right."

Wilson went on to argue that the United States would not just help bring the war to an end and secure political liberty, but also help craft a new postwar order that would defend the principles for which the United States was fighting. The goal, as he put it, would be "to set up amongst the really free and self-governed peoples of the world such a concert of purpose and of action as will henceforth insure the observance of those principles." He went on to insist that only democracies would be capable of upholding a league for peace: "A steadfast concert for peace can never be maintained except by a partnership of democratic nations. No autocratic government could be trusted to keep faith within it or observe its covenants." This "concert of free peoples," he explained, would seek to "bring peace and safety to all nations and make the world itself at last free." Wilson was clearly picking up on the notion of a "community of power" that he had shared with the Senate on January 22. But on April 2, he was going a significant step further, arguing that "neutrality is no longer feasible or desirable" and that the United States would have to enter the war if a concert of democratic nations was to be realized.

As he laid out his case for war, Wilson was thus elevating, not just maintaining, his ideological ambition. When he had been defending neutrality, he had effectively portrayed the belligerents as morally equivalent; the main cause of the war was Europe's balance-of-power system, not the governing structures or proclivities of its individual nations. The democratization of Germany was not one of his aims, as reflected in his call for "peace without victory." By the spring of 1917, however, Wilson was ready to blame the war on the nature of Germany's government, claiming that "Prussian autocracy was not and could never be our friend." He insisted that "we have no quarrel with the German people," instead viewing the conflict as "provoked and waged in the interest of dynasties or of little groups of ambitious men who were accustomed to use their fellow men as pawns and tools." Wilson also offered a more generic critique of nondemocratic governments, stating that "the menace to . . . peace and freedom lies in the existence of autocratic governments backed by organized force which is wholly controlled by their will, not by the will of their people."[80]

This shift in perspective and rhetoric clearly marked an evolution in Wilson's mindset.[81] The change could have reflected the new strategic reality that emerged after U.S. vessels had been sunk; now that Germany was attacking U.S. property and citizens, he attributed to its government a more malign character.[82] Alternatively, Wilson may have had new license to launch broadsides against autocracy as the result of the Russian revolution; the Tsar abdicated in March, ending absolutist government in one of America's prospective war partners. Wilson's shift may have also been a tactical maneuver aimed at garnering popular support for the war by tapping into the nation's exceptionalist narrative. Indeed, as the war progressed, Wilson regularly reminded the electorate that the nation was fighting in Europe to fulfill its messianic mission. In July 1918, he told Americans that they had an obligation to ensure that the Founders, in "character and purpose and of the influences they were setting afoot . . . spoke and acted, not for a single people only, but for all mankind."[83] Whatever the motivation behind Wilson's change of mind, he was openly identifying democratization and regime change as one of his top war aims—overturning the cautionary restraint of most of his predecessors and helping lay a foundation for the liberal internationalism that the nation would embrace after it entered World War II.

Wilson's insistence that the United States enter the war as an "associated power" rather than a formal "ally" sheds further light on the scope of his ideological ambition. To be sure, American forces would be joining the fight against Germany alongside British and French soldiers, but they were to operate independently and remain under U.S. command.[84] Several considerations shaped this decision. By designating the United States as an associated power, Wilson was able, at least in nominal terms, to abide by the Founders' injunction against "entangling alliances." This stance helped him win support for entering the war from committed unilateralists. Wilson was also conscious of the potential need to distance U.S. forces from the war aims of Britain and France should they end up pursuing expansive and punitive objectives. The United States needed to indemnify itself against such objectives in order to preserve its moral authority and its role as a peacemaker. In Wilson's mind, the nation was entering the war not as just another belligerent, but as Europe's deliverer and redeemer.[85]

Antiwar Voices

A combination of Wilson's persuasive powers, the call of patriotism, and partisan loyalty among Democrats produced overwhelming support for the declaration of war in both chambers. Many members had misgivings about entering the war but felt the nation should stay unified as it faced the prospect of armed conflict. Allegiance to Wilson among Democrats meant reduced opposition from southern libertarians and from progressive pacifists. Wilson's redemptive justification for the war also earned him strong support from religious institutions and communities.[86] The members who remained unpersuaded by Wilson—six in the Senate and fifty in the House—were an ideologically diverse group.

Among the Democratic opponents was the House Majority Leader, Representative Claude Kitchin (D-North Carolina), a progressive antimilitarist who had joined Bryan to oppose preparedness.[87] After the sinking of the *Lusitania*, he argued against a diplomatic confrontation with Germany and instead supported legislation to prohibit Americans from sailing on belligerent vessels. Amid the debate over the war declaration, he resurrected one of the main arguments that Wilson had deployed to defend neutrality: "Half the civilized world is now a slaughterhouse for human beings. This Nation is the last hope of peace on earth, good will toward men. I am unwilling for my country by statutory command to pull up the last anchor of peace in the world and extinguish during the long night of a worldwide war the only remaining star of hope for Christendom."[88]

Senator James Vardaman (D-Mississippi) took a different tack, contemptuously dismissing Wilson's idealist objectives: "If our joining in this war in Europe would relieve the world of this burning, devouring, devastating social cancer that is destroying the world body politic, there might be some justification for the adoption of this resolution. I do not believe that we will relieve the situation by becoming a party to the horrors and brutalities of the conflict." Vardaman mocked Wilson's ambitious war aims, observing that the "President hopes that by sacrificing millions of Americans, spending a few billion dollars, taken from the products of the toiling masses of this country, we may be able to 'organize the parliament of man,' and bring about 'the federation of the world.' . . . It is a fine, big idea the President has for the salvation of the world.[89]

Republican opponents, who represented more than two-thirds of the fifty negative votes in the House, deployed a wide range of arguments against entering the war. Representative Henry Cooper (R-Wisconsin) based his opposition on traditional grounds of geographic isolation: "There is no reason in it, since a brave man might well defend his own home, his wife and children from marauders and yet not be willing to go 100 miles away to engage in a brawl." Representative Frederick Britten (R-Illinois) shared Vardaman's dismissive attitude toward Wilson's idealist justification for entering the war: "Let us not deceive ourselves that we are going into this war in the interest of humanity. The man who deceives himself is a fool."[90] Representative Jeannette Rankin (R-Montana), the first woman elected to Congress, opposed the war declaration as a committed pacifist.

Republican progressives saw U.S. entry into the war as a setback for domestic reform and a product of pressure from war-profiteering banks and corporations. Senator George Norris (R-Nebraska) claimed that "this war madness has taken possession of the financial and political powers of our country." With the country preparing to enter the conflict, he asserted that "we are committing a sin against humanity and against our countrymen. I would like to say to this war god, You shall not coin into gold the lifeblood of my brethren. . . . I feel that we are about to put the dollar sign upon the American flag." Norris concluded "that we would not be on the verge of war now if it were not for the influence of money."[91]

The appeal of sustaining national unity as the country prepared to join the fight in Europe did reduce the numbers of those opposing the war declaration, helping produce the lopsided votes in both chambers. Senator Borah, whose iso-lationist leanings would soon prompt him to lead the fight against the League of Nations, voted in favor of the declaration of war, making clear his reluctance, but also his sense of duty to the country: "I join no crusade; I seek or accept no alliances; I obligate this Government to no other power. I make war alone for my countrymen and their rights, for my country and its honor."[92] Moreover, members of Congress who expressed their opposition to the war did end up being labeled as unpatriotic. After her vote against the war declaration, the *Helena Independent* called Representative Rankin "a dagger in the hands of the German propagandists, a dupe of the Kaiser, a member of the Hun army in the United States, and a crying schoolgirl."[93] Senator Norris sought to preempt con-demnation of his negative vote by promising to stand with the majority once the decision for war was final: "I am bitterly opposed to my country entering the war, but if, notwithstanding my opposition, we do enter it, all of my energy and all of my power will be behind our flag in carrying it on to victory." His qualifica-tion failed to avert harsh reproach. Senator James Reed (D-Missouri) critiqued Norris's stance by remarking, "if that be not treason it takes on a character and guise that is so near to treason that the enemies of America will gain from it much consolation."[94]

Pacifists, socialists, and other antiwar activists continued their vocal oppo-sition even after Congress's declaration of war and the dispatch of U.S. forces to Europe. But their ranks did thin as they faced harsh criticism and charges of disloyalty to the nation from the Wilson administration, the media, and other pro-war organs. The administration set up both official and unofficial vehicles to spread wartime propaganda, build patriotic fervor, and isolate dissenters.

According to Nichols, "by positing America as a force for global democracy and mobilizing patriotism toward that cause, the administration further marginalized would-be dissenters, casting free-speech advocates, progressive reformers, suffragists, socialists, and others as unpatriotic if they did not support the war." The pressure induced numerous left-wing activists and pacifists to break with the antiwar movement and throw their support behind Wilson. Some justified their shift by arguing that American participation in the conflict gave the nation greater leverage in negotiating a peaceful postwar order.[95]

Nonetheless, prominent voices of dissent refused to yield to patriotic pressure. Randolph Bourne held his ground, warning that the nation was being seduced by the game of power politics and that joining the fight would compromise the nation's exceptional character. "The promise of American life is not yet achieved, perhaps not even seen," he insisted, "and that, until it is, there is nothing for us but stern and intensive cultivation of our garden." Bourne counseled a "turning within in order that we may have something to give without," and told Americans that they had before them a stark choice: "The war—or American promise: one must choose. One cannot be interested in both."[96]

Since soon after the war began, Eugene Debs had been arguing that plutocrats were responsible for the conflict. "No war," he insisted in the fall of 1914, "was ever caused by the working class but always and everywhere by the exploiting class. But the exploiting class never fights."[97] As calls for national unity mounted, he responded, "socialists are not required to demonstrate their patriotism for the benefit of the capitalist class."[98] Especially after the nation's entry into the war, Debs expanded his target audience, taking his antiwar message beyond urban workers to rural areas, particularly in the South. His message attracted considerable support in farming communities. Hugh Alexander, president of the North Carolina Farmers Union, captured the flavor of the antiwar sentiment building among his constituents: "We are driven to war by the munitions mongers, the bankers, speculators, the jingo press and the devil, and all for their profit, while all that is expected of the farmers is that they furnish the men to do the fighting and then bear the great bulk of war taxes."[99]

Antiwar organizing in rural areas and among urban workers took a toll on public support for the war. Some 330,000 Americans failed to report for conscription. A sizable number—estimates range up to 3.6 million—failed to register for conscription or otherwise avoided the draft. Most of those who refused to serve were poor farmers and laborers. Conscription proved to be a step too far even for some who had voted in favor of war. Senator Borah, for example, opposed the draft, asserting that "I am unwilling to Prussianize this country in order to de-Prussianize Germany. I do not think it necessary."[100]

Concern about the political effects of antiwar sentiment led to far-reaching efforts to repress dissent. The Espionage Act of 1917 and the Sedition Act of

1918 gave the U.S. government broad powers to clamp down on antiwar voices, including through incarceration, censorship, and the confiscation by the Post Office of antiwar and anticonscription material. Debs himself was convicted of obstruction of the war effort and sentenced to a ten-year term. He ended up running for president in the 1920 election from jail. A series of Supreme Court cases in 1919 upheld the crackdown, decisions that, in the words of historian David Kennedy, would "weave into the legal fabric of the nation restrictions on freedom of speech that had been unknown before 1917."[101] Indeed, the American Civil Liberties Union was founded in 1920, in large part as a response to war-time repression of free speech. Alongside these constraints on democratic debate came the harassment and persecution of German-Americans and a surge in anti-immigrant sentiment, clearing the way for the numerical limits and quota system that Congress would adopt in 1921. As Americans from George Washington to Randolph Bourne had feared, war had come at the expense of domestic liberties.

Ideological Overreach

Although Wilson went to war with overwhelming support and used coercive measures to repress dissent, his critics did help lay a groundwork for the isolationist backlash that lay ahead. As the war dragged on, its costs climbed, and domestic opposition to Wilson's peace plans mounted, his exclusive reliance on idealist justifications for U.S. participation became increasingly vulnerable. Completely missing from his case for war was a realist assessment of the geopolitical and economic stakes for the nation. War is inescapably about power balances, geopolitical threats, and national interests, but the language of realpolitik was nowhere to be found in Wilson's lexicon. In the words of historians Norman Graebner and Edward Bennett, "Wilson made himself the prophet of a world free of power politics, one in which the old balance of power would recede before a new community of power." Bernard Fensterwald also faults Wilson for "his attempts to place our war effort upon an altruistic basis. . . . It is one of the pities of history that the war slogans were not less altruistic and more self-interested. The main effect of these high-minded sentiments was to build up American hopes and expectations to a height from which the descent was dizzying."[102]

Americans believed that their troops were heading to Europe to serve as redeemers, not belligerents. The narrative of redemption only deepened as the war progressed, with Wilson in January 1918 delivering a speech to Congress articulating the Fourteen Points—the principles on which a new international order would rest. Counseling Americans that "unless justice be done to others it will not be done to us," he called for open diplomacy, freedom of navigation, equality of trade, disarmament, a raft of territorial adjustments in the service of national self-determination, and a "general association of nations" that would provide mutual guarantees of political independence and territorial integrity.[103] Soon after the conclusion of an armistice in November 1918, Wilson crossed the Atlantic to bring his ideas to life in a negotiated peace treaty. Apart from a brief return to the United States in February, Wilson was abroad from early December through early July, tirelessly working to turn his idealist aspirations into reality.

The problem was that Wilson's lofty ambition was fundamentally at odds with the brutal reality of war. Americans, nearly five million of whom served in the military during the war, were witnessing bloodshed and cruelty, not peace and magnanimity under U.S. tutelage. At home, the war did benefit some Americans by boosting orders for many goods, but it also put on hold progressive reforms and coincided with widespread worker discontent; strikes in 1917 numbered 4,450, the highest in the nation's history. In 1919, one in five industrial laborers engaged in a work stoppage. The prospect of creeping Bolshevism and class warfare loomed, spawning the Red Scare of 1918–1920 and a crackdown on left-wing activism.[104]

Entanglement in European geopolitics brought to the home front not only social disorder but also repression; it appeared, as the Founders had warned, that the United States was unable to engage in Europe's rivalries without falling prey to its retrograde politics. Domestic repression took a serious toll on support for the war, especially among progressives. Many of them had supported Wilson's decision to join the conflict because he promised that U.S. entry would further liberal ends—but it had done just the opposite. Liberals also grew disillusioned with the results of Wilson's peacemaking efforts, arguing that he was ultimately ceding too much ground to the realist ambitions of his European partners and settling for a more punitive peace than he had promised.

Randolph Bourne may have been motivated by a desire to vindicate his unyielding opposition to the war, but he accurately captured the backlash that occurred within the ranks of Wilson's supporters in insisting that "American liberals who urged the nation to war are . . . suffering the humiliation of seeing their liberal strategy for peace transformed into a strategy for a prolonged war."[105] For many Americans, especially those on the left, Wilson had taken the nation to war under false pretenses. He pledged that the United States would change the world, but instead the world changed the United States. John Kane eloquently describes this realization as follows:

> Wilson had mobilized American military power and risked American innocence in the hope of establishing the universal reign of peace and Christian virtue on earth. Nonentanglement had been compromised and domestic freedoms endangered for this transcendent cause, but as in the case of imperialist adventure, the results had been profoundly

disillusioning. Instead of a new international rule of law and virtue, the postwar settlement produced only a resurgence of bad old European power politics.[106]

Realist Republicans hardly came to Wilson's rescue. If the left felt that Wilson had forsaken his idealist agenda, the right felt that he had taken his idealism too far. Republicans found Wilson's peace plans naïve and called for the decisive defeat of Germany. They also resented the accumulation of the federal government's wartime powers—in particular, its steps to establish more control over the economy, which included a takeover of the nation's railroads. Senator Lodge contended that the public was turning against Wilson in part due to "the dread deep down in the people's hearts of the establishment of a dictatorship."[107]

In the absence of reliable public opinion surveys, it is difficult to judge the degree to which the reality of war undermined public confidence in Wilson and his idealist agenda. But it speaks volumes that in the midterm elections of 1918—just as the United States and its "associates" were achieving military victory—the Democrats lost both houses of Congress. Wilson importuned the public on the eve of the election to deliver a vote of confidence in his stewardship and his handling of the war by returning Democratic majorities to both houses. He got just the opposite. That setback for Wilson, particularly because Republicans explicitly ran against Wilson's Fourteen Points and his peace plans, did not augur well for the coming battle over ratification of the Versailles Treaty. The bipartisanship that accompanied the nation's entry into the war had entirely disappeared by its end.

The Treaty Fight

Marking the first trip to Europe by a sitting U.S. president, Wilson left New York Harbor on December 4, 1918, on his way to France for the Versailles peace conference. He also visited the United Kingdom, Italy, Belgium, and the Holy See during his sojourn. Although rejected at home in the November midterms, he was warmly welcomed in Europe and often greeted by cheering throngs. Wilson was more than prepared to take advantage of his popularity. He was mindful that securing his vision of a new postwar order could well entail rallying mass support to put pressure on European leaders. He needed to woo Europe's left away from its socialist and Bolshevik leanings, while simultaneously convincing conservatives to refrain from imposing a punitive settlement on Germany.

Wilson ended up agreeing to a more realist peace settlement than he would have preferred; he accepted onerous war reparations on Germany, strict limits on

German military strength, and the occupation of the Rhineland by the victors. Despite his rhetorical support for self-determination, the treaty sanctioned the continuation of colonialism and the subjugation of national populations—in part by granting Japan the right to control some of Germany's former possessions in Asia. But Wilson did secure some of his chief idealist objectives. He successfully resisted calls at home and in Europe for invading Germany and pressing for an unconditional surrender. He convinced European leaders to include the Covenant of the League of Nations in the peace treaty rather than making it a stand-alone agreement. And he talked the French out of stripping away from Germany the Saar and the Rhineland. Wilson deeply believed that "moderation . . . is necessary to show toward Germany. We neither wish to destroy Germany, nor could we do so; our greatest error would be to give her powerful reasons for one day wishing to take revenge. Excessive demands would most certainly sow the seeds of war."[108]

Wilson returned to the United States in February for consultations on the draft covenant that he had negotiated. He went back to France in early March and succeeded in attaining additional concessions to respond to the feedback he had heard at home. To circumvent criticism that the League would invite European meddling in America's own hemisphere, for example, the final version of the covenant included language ensuring that the pact would not "affect the validity of international engagements, such as treaties of arbitration or regional understandings like the Monroe Doctrine."[109] He arrived back in New York Harbor on July 8, and two days later—in person—submitted the Versailles Treaty to the Senate.[110]

Wilson was ebullient about his accomplishments, effectively claiming that the United States had finally realized its messianic obligation to secure a world of democracy and peace. Through open diplomacy, dispute settlement, collective security, and disarmament (in the language of the covenant, "the reduction of national armaments to the lowest point consistent with national safety"), he saw the League as doing away with an international system infected by balance-of-power thinking. In Wilson's mind, the results of his labor represented the consummation of the nation's efforts to export its founding principles to the rest of the world. When presenting the treaty to the Senate in July, he explicitly reached back to the founding era and called forth the image of America as the chosen nation, pointing to divine inspiration, not just his own handiwork and that of predecessors, as the source of his achievements. "It has come about," he concluded his address, "by no plan of our conceiving, but by the hand of God who led us into this way. We cannot turn back. We can only go forward, with lifted eyes and freshened spirit, to follow the vision. It was of this that we dreamed at our birth. America shall in truth show the way. The light streams upon the path ahead, and nowhere else."[111]

While crisscrossing the country to build public support for the treaty, Wilson focused on the same themes. He shared the following reflection with an audience in Portland, Oregon:

> I am glad for one to have lived to see this day. I have lived to see a day in which, after saturating myself most of my life in the history and traditions of America, I seem suddenly to see the culmination of American hope and history—all the orators seeing their dreams realized, if their spirits are looking on; all the men who spoke the noblest sentiments of America heartened with the sight of a great Nation responding to and acting on those dreams, and saying, "At last, the world knows America as the savior of the world!"

During a stop in Cheyenne, Wyoming, Wilson reaffirmed that "America had the infinite privilege of fulfilling her destiny and saving the world."[112]

Wilson may have been convinced that the nation was at the brink of fulfilling its messianic calling, but many of his fellow citizens thought otherwise. Indeed, Wilson faced formidable opposition in the Senate—precisely why he embarked on a speaking tour to rally the public. But his best efforts to secure domestic support for his vision of a new postwar order fell short. Three camps of widely disparate ideological complexion staunchly opposed U.S. participation in the League and ultimately blocked ratification of the Versailles Treaty in the Senate.

Die-hard isolationists—a group known as "irreconcilables"—were part of the blocking coalition. They wanted nothing to do with Wilson's vision of an America that would remain in and of a global community of like-minded nations, preferring to return to the era of geopolitical detachment. The irreconcilables were, however, too few in number to defeat the treaty on their own. Realist Republicans, although inclined toward sustained international engagement, joined the irreconcilables in opposing the treaty. For them, Wilson's idealist aspirations went too far. By committing the United States to join the fight against aggression wherever and whenever it might occur, the president had, in their minds, violated the constitutional authority of Congress to declare war and compromised the ability of the U.S. government to act as it saw fit. And even though most Democrats, at least initially, lined up behind Wilson out of party loyalty, he also faced sharp resistance from the left on the grounds that Wilson had given away too much to the realists, acceding to a postwar order still beholden to balance-of-power logic. Internationalist Democrats and internationalist Republicans thus had little common ground. A small but tenacious isolationist bloc, coupled with disagreement among Democratic and Republican internationalists about the form that U.S. engagement abroad should take, set the stage for the defeat of Wilson's effort to make America "the savior of the world."

The irreconcilables—a group of some fifteen senators dead set against ratification of the treaty in any form—consisted mostly of Republicans.[113] Their ringleader was Senator Borah, who not only railed against the League in Congress, but also, like Wilson, undertook a national speaking tour to sway the public. Borah had come to regret his reluctant vote in favor of the nation's entry into World War I.[114] Against the backdrop of what he saw as the nation's ill-advised war in Europe, he recoiled at the prospect of U.S. participation in the League. During the Senate's debate over ratification in November 1919, Borah delivered a lengthy broadside against the proposed body, linking his discontent with the war to his antipathy toward the League:

> We are in the midst of all the affairs of Europe. We have entangled ourselves with all European concerns. We have joined in alliance with all the European nations. . . . We are sitting there dabbling in their affairs and intermeddling in their concerns. . . . We have forfeited and surrendered, once and for all, the great policy of "no entangling alliances" upon which the strength of this Republic has been founded for 150 years. . . . We are a part of the European turmoils and conflicts from the time we enter this league.

Under no circumstances, Borah insisted, would he "consent to exchange the doctrine of George Washington for the doctrine of Frederick the Great translated into the mendacious phrases of peace."[115]

As for Wilson's success in including in the treaty recognition of the Monroe Doctrine, Borah dismissed the revision as worthless. "Do you think that you can intermeddle in European affairs and keep Europe from meddling in your affairs?" he asked. "If we intermeddle in her affairs," he continued, "if we help to adjust her conditions, inevitably and remorselessly Europe then will be carried into our affairs, in spite of anything you can write upon paper." Borah went on to claim that ratification of the treaty would defile American values and jeopardize its exceptional political character; the United States could not at once join the League and preserve domestic liberty. The "distinguishing virtues of a real republic you cannot commingle with the discordant and destructive forces of the Old World and still preserve them. . . . When you shall have committed this Republic to a scheme of world control based upon force . . . you will have soon destroyed the atmosphere of freedom, of confidence in the self-governing capacity of the masses, in which alone a democracy may thrive." At stake was not just the nation's institutions but the ideals at the heart of America's identity and sense of nationhood:

> This treaty . . . imperils what I conceive to be the underlying, the very
> first principles of this Republic. It is in conflict with the right of our
> people to govern themselves free from all restraint, legal or moral, of
> foreign powers. It challenges every tenet of my political faith. . . . I claim
> no merit save fidelity to American principles and devotion to American
> ideals. . . . I will not, I cannot, give up my belief that America must, not
> alone for the happiness of her own people, but for the moral guidance
> and greater contentment of the world, be permitted to live her own life.

"Americanism," Borah concluded, "shall not, cannot, die."[116] After the Senate vote, Borah reportedly called the defeat of the treaty "the second winning of the independence of America" and "the greatest victory since Appomattox."[117]

Other irreconcilables rallied behind Borah's attack on the treaty. Some echoed his call to defend U.S. sovereignty and "Americanism." In a January 1919 letter to one of his sons, Senator Hiram Johnson (R-California) wrote that "our difficulty has been the past two years that we were Pro-Belgian, Pro-English, Pro-French—anything but Pro-American, and that it is time to be Pro-American now."[118] Other irreconcilables justified their opposition to the League on racial and religious grounds. Senator Reed, one of the few Democrats to join the irreconcilable clan, argued that the United States could not join an organization in which blacks might outnumber whites. (Reed argued in favor of immigration restrictions that would have barred nonwhites from permanent settlement in the United States.) He also complained that the United States would end up having to submit to the will of autocrats: "A victor in the war, shall she nevertheless emerge a mere constituent state of a league dominated by European monarchs and Asiatic despots?"[119]

Voicing an objection shared by many, Senator Lawrence Sherman (R-Illinois) maintained that membership in the League would weaken, not strengthen, American influence because the United States would be outnumbered and outvoted in the international body. Sherman worried in particular about the potential predominance of Catholic member states "spiritually dominated by the Vatican"—an imbalance that could yield to the papacy unwelcome sway over global affairs.[120] He also foresaw unlimited demands on U.S. "lives and treasures" and urged the nation to resist becoming "the knight-errant of the world."[121] As his Republican colleagues were proposing potential amendments to the League Covenant, Sherman quipped, "I will vote for any pertinent amendment that comes along. I hope every one of them will be adopted. . . . So vote them in; and then, after every one of the amendments is voted into the treaty and the league, I will vote to reject it all."[122]

Realist Republicans were led by Senator Lodge, who had become the chair of the Foreign Relations Committee after the 1918 midterms. Unlike the irreconcilables, they were at least open to working with Wilson. Nonetheless, a combination of partisan animosity and principled disagreement blocked the emergence of a compromise. Democrats and Republicans had been sparring over Wilson's peace plans ever since he had begun laying them out in 1916—and the acrimony only intensified in the run-up to the 1918 midterms. Thereafter, it did not help matters that Wilson included not a single senator and only one low-ranking Republican in the commission that he brought with him to Europe for the peace negotiations. By the time of the treaty debate, personal relations between Wilson and Lodge were deeply strained; indeed, Lodge had already confided to Roosevelt in 1915 that "I never expected to hate anyone in politics with the hatred I feel towards Wilson." The *Piedmont*, a newspaper in South Carolina, concluded that "the Senate's chief objection to the League idea is that Wilson is a Democrat."[123]

Partisanship aside, substantive disagreements also pitted realist Republicans against the League. Lodge offered fourteen "reservations"—essentially revisions to the treaty—the most important of which aimed at diluting Article X, the provision obligating signatories of the covenant "to respect and preserve as against external aggression the territorial integrity and existing political independence of all Members of the League."[124] Lodge wanted to qualify this provision to ensure that the United States would not be forced to go to war at the behest of an international body. His reservation stipulated that "the United States assumes no obligation to preserve the territorial integrity or political independence of any other country or to interfere in controversies between nations . . . unless in any particular case the Congress, which, under the Constitution, has the sole power to declare war or authorize the employment of the military or naval forces of the United States, shall by act or joint resolution so provide."[125]

The League Covenant actually did *not* automatically obligate members to take up arms in response to aggression. Article X specified that the League Council—the great-power directorate that would oversee the body—"shall advise upon the means by which this obligation [to defend against aggression and preserve territorial integrity] shall be fulfilled." Moreover, "except where otherwise expressly provided," the Council would take decisions only by "the agreement of all the Members of the League represented at the meeting," giving the United States an effective veto.[126] Even though the covenant itself provided prospective members latitude in deciding how they would respond to acts of aggression, Wilson refused to accede to Lodge's proposed revision. He insisted that all signatories would have a moral obligation to act should a League member be attacked. Explicitly weakening Article X would break the moral backbone of the covenant and undermine the core commitment of members to provide for collective security. To accept Lodge's proposed amendment would, in Wilson's own words, "not provide for ratification but, rather, for the nullification of the treaty."[127] Wilson insisted that it would be "better a thousand times to go down fighting than to dip your colors to dishonorable compromise."[128]

The standoff between Wilson and Lodge provided mainstream Republicans a wide opening, enabling them to charge that the League trampled on the Constitution as well as the nation's sovereignty and autonomy. While most of the irreconcilables were calling for a return to geopolitical detachment and avoidance of foreign entanglement of any sort, realist Republicans were more concerned about preserving the nation's freedom of action. As described by historian William Appleman Williams, "association with other nations they accepted, but not equality of membership or mutuality of decision."[129] After Wilson first presented the draft treaty to the Senate in February 1919, Lodge invoked the Founders to make his case:

> We abandon entirely by the proposed constitution the policy laid down by Washington in his Farewell Address. . . . The principles of the Farewell Address in regard to our foreign relations have been sustained and acted upon by the American people down to the present moment. Washington declared against permanent alliances. . . . Now, in the twinkling of an eye, while passion and emotion reign, the Washington policy is to be entirely laid aside and we are to enter upon a permanent and indissoluble alliance. . . . Let us not overlook the profound gravity of this step.

Lodge acknowledged that the League Council "is to have the power of advice, which I do not suppose is binding at all." But he went on to argue that the League's guarantee of the political independence and territorial integrity of its member states would be binding, effectively meaning that the United States would lose control over decisions of war and peace should it commit to uphold it. The "people of America," he insisted, need to decide "whether they are willing to have the United States forced into war by other nations against her own will." Lodge charged that Wilson was asking Americans "to substitute internationalism for nationalism and an international state for pure Americanism."[130] As debate over ratification ensued during the fall of 1919, Senator Andrieus Jones (D-New Mexico), although a supporter of the treaty, succinctly captured the main Republican objection: "The chief reasons advanced for opposition to the covenant are founded upon the assumption that this covenant creates a super-state, superpower, or some superentity to which the sovereignty of the United States is to be surrendered."[131]

As Republicans rallied to either block or revise the treaty, most Democratic senators stood behind Wilson. Nonetheless, the defection of influential liberals— many of whom had been staunch backers of Wilson—weighed on public debate and helped build insurmountable opposition to the treaty. As discussed above, repression of dissent, the administration's wartime propaganda and its accumulation of executive powers, and the accommodation of European calls for punitive measures against Germany alienated a critical group of Wilson's potential supporters. Indeed, the administration was marginalizing, if not silencing, the very constituency that it needed to help build public enthusiasm for the League.

George Creel, who led the Committee on Public Information—the administration's propaganda organ during the war—confided to Wilson his misgivings on this front following the Republican victory in the 1918 midterms:

> All the radical or liberal friends of your anti-imperialist war policy were either silenced or intimidated. The Department of Justice and the Post-office were allowed to silence or intimidate them. There was no voice left to argue for your sort of peace. When we came to this election the reactionary Republicans had a clear record of anti-Hun imperialistic patriotism. Their opponents, your friends, were either besmirched or obscured.[132]

Oswald Garrison Villard, a liberal journalist and a founder of the Anti-Imperialist League, agreed, noting that Wilson had suppressed "adequate discussion of the peace aims. . . . At the very moment of his extremist trial our liberal forces are by his own act scattered, silenced, disorganized, some in prison." At the time of the armistice, Walter Weyl, one of the founding editors of the *New Republic*, long an ardently pro-Wilson publication, confided in his diary that "liberalism is crumbling about our ears, & we are doing little or nothing."[133]

In the end, the *New Republic* broke with Wilson and opposed ratification of the treaty, denying the president a key source of support. The magazine's critique was stinging, revealing the scope of the ideological estrangement that had emerged between Wilson and establishment liberals. The *New Republic*'s editorial, titled "Peace at Any Price," charged that Wilson and his colleagues at Versailles had effectively abandoned liberal principles:

> They crave at any cost the emotional triumph of imposing on the German nation the ultimate humiliation of solemnly consenting to its own abdication as a self-governing and self-respecting community. . . . It is the most shameless and, we hope, the last of those treaties which, while they pretend to bring peace to a mortified world, merely write the specifications for future revolution and war. . . . If a war which was supposed to put an end to war culminates . . . in a treaty of peace which renders peace impossible, the liberalism which preached this meaning for the war will have committed suicide.

The *New Republic* in principle expressed strong support for the establishment of a League of Nations, but insisted that the treaty as drafted would kill the League, not bring it to life: "The League is not powerful enough to redeem the treaty. But the treaty is vicious enough to incriminate the League. It would convert the League into the instrument of competitive imperialist nationalism."[134]

Confronted with opposition from across the political spectrum, Wilson fought valiantly against the odds, tirelessly traveling across the country to rally support for ratification—and suffering a debilitating stroke while doing so. But to no avail. On November 19, Democrats joined irreconcilables to vote down the treaty with Lodge's reservations; the margin was 39 to 55—not even a simple majority. Realist Republicans then joined irreconcilables and seven Democrats to vote down the treaty as submitted by Wilson by a margin of 38 to 53. On March 19, 1920, the Senate again voted on the treaty with Lodge's reservations. A good number of Democrats defied Wilson to support the treaty, but the vote was 49 to 35, seven votes short of the two-thirds majority needed for ratification.[135]

Wilson refused to give up, envisaging the presidential election of 1920 as a national referendum on the League and the new brand of internationalism that he had put on offer. Ohio governor James Cox ran against Senator Warren Harding (R-Ohio), who embraced a platform staunchly opposed to U.S. participation in the international body. In his speech accepting the Republican nomination on July 22, Harding did not mince his words:

> It is better to be the free and disinterested agents of international justice and advancing civilization with the covenant of conscience, than to be shackled by a written compact which surrenders our freedom of action and gives the military alliance the right to proclaim America's duty to the world. No surrender of rights to a world council or its military alliance, no assumed mandatory, however appealing, ever shall summon the sons of this republic to war.

"We stand," Harding said in summation, "for the policies of Washington and the doctrine of Monroe and against the internationalism and the permanent alliance with foreign nations proposed by the President."[136]

Helped by a recession and public skepticism toward the reform agenda of the progressive era, Harding won in a landslide, carrying some sixty percent of the popular vote. In his inaugural speech on March 4, 1921, he effectively closed the door on the Wilsonian era of idealist internationalism:

> We seek no part in directing the destinies of the Old World. We do not mean to be entangled. . . . We crave friendship and harbor no hate. But

America, our America, the America builded on the foundation laid by
the inspired fathers, can be a party to no permanent military alliance. . . .
A world super government is contrary to everything we cherish and can
have no sanction by our Republic. This is not selfishness, it is sanctity. It
is not aloofness, it is security. It is not suspicion of others, it is patriotic
adherence to the things which made us what we are.[137]

* * *

The Wilsonian era—at least in terms of the aspirations of its primary architect—
constitutes the high-water mark of an idealist brand of American internationalism. Woodrow Wilson was determined to deliver on the pledge of the Founders
to make the world anew. In his own words, the United States should serve as
the "chief interpreter to the world of those democratic principles which we believe to constitute the only force which can rid the world of injustice and bring
peace and happiness to mankind."[138] It was this conviction that initially guided
him to neutrality; amid Europe's descent, the nation needed to remain above the
fray as the world's repository of democracy and reason. It was also this conviction that convinced Wilson to take the nation to war after German submarines
started attacking U.S. vessels. If the United States could not cordon itself off from
Europe's ills, then it would have to remake the Old World in the American image.
If the United States had to be in the world, then it would have to make that world
safe for American democracy. As Adam Tooze describes the mindset of Wilson
and other American statesmen engaged in crafting the postwar order, "it was
their sense of America's god-given, exemplary role that they sought to impose
on the world."[139]

In the end, Wilson dramatically overreached, ultimately provoking a political
backlash that produced the opposite of what he had intended. In the words of
Louis Hartz, rather than convincing Americans "to define and reconstruct alien
things in terms of an American image," Wilson prompted "a withdrawal from
alien things . . . the polar counterpart of the crusading impulse."[140] He shunned
talk of power and interests and was ready to issue global guarantees of territorial
integrity that were morally, if not legally, binding. Many Americans, however, saw
such guarantees as a violation of U.S. sovereignty, while others were simply not
ready to part ways with the nation's protective isolationism, viewing participation
in the League as entirely incompatible with "Americanism." Having given ground
to European leaders who similarly judged his idealism to be excessive, Wilson
even lost the confidence of many establishment liberals. His faltering health did
not help matters. And Wilson's partisan and uncompromising attitude certainly
contributed to political stalemate over the League, the Republican victory in the
1918 midterms, and the rout of Democrats in the 1920 presidential election.

The defeat of Wilsonian idealism was hugely consequential. After 1898, Americans decisively soured on the realist brand of internationalism on offer, readily seeing through the charade of republican imperialism. Wilson accordingly offered a brand of internationalism that would be in keeping with American exceptionalism and the nation's democratic ideals. But that approach also proved unable to sustain domestic support. The Senate's rejection of the Versailles Treaty not only left the League profoundly wounded, but also set the stage for a sharp American retreat. During the 1920s, the United States returned to focusing on commercial and diplomatic engagement abroad while limiting strategic commitment. A decisive isolationist turn followed in the 1930s despite—and, indeed, because of—rising fascism and militarism in Europe and East Asia. Wilsonian ideas were not finished for good. They would make a comeback during and after World War II—although tempered with a strong dose of realism. But before the resuscitation of U.S. internationalism, the nation would pass through a most illusory and destructive bout of isolationism.

10

The 1920s:
Influence without Responsibility

The internationalism that Woodrow Wilson sought to instill among Americans took a pummeling at the close of World War I. The United States may have been on the winning side of the war, but the experience of entanglement and the results it produced bore no resemblance to the idealist vision laid out by Wilson. As after 1898, Americans felt they had paid a high price for a false bill of goods. Not only did Wilson lose the fight for the League, but President Warren Harding (1921–1923), who ran "against the internationalism" of his predecessor and "for the policies of [George] Washington," won the 1920 presidential contest in one of the most lopsided elections in American history.[1]

Harding entered office by insisting that "we seek no part in directing the destinies of the Old World. We do not mean to be entangled."[2] He immediately delivered on his promise. According to historian John Gaddis, "the most significant geopolitical development of the early postwar years was surely the fact that the United States . . . made no significant attempts after 1920 to shape political-military developments on the [European] Continent."[3] The same went for East Asia; America sought geopolitical detachment. Even in Latin America, where the United States had been continuously interventionist since 1898, the 1920s was a decade of relative restraint and retrenchment.

Nonetheless, the United States did not return to the mix of isolationism and stiff-necked unilateralism that came before 1898. Instead, the country sought to secure geopolitical detachment through commercial and diplomatic engagement. The U.S. government relied heavily on Wall Street to wield influence in Europe and East Asia. Bankers and diplomats, not U.S. forces, would keep the peace. Republicans, who controlled the White House and Congress throughout the decade, were picking up on Taft's dollar diplomacy and his efforts to tame geopolitical rivalry through economic leverage.

So, too, did Republicans return to Taft's efforts to promote international stability through the legalization of interstate relations. The Senate had three times rejected Wilson's bid for U.S. membership in the League of Nations, but it was thereafter ready for international pacts—provided that the agreements codified nonentanglement instead of commitments to collective action. The Harding administration agreed to negotiated limits on the nation's naval strength—the Washington Naval Treaties of 1922 placed caps on the U.S., British, French, Italian, and Japanese fleets—as a means of dampening geopolitical competition and defending the Open Door policy toward China. In 1928, the administration of President Calvin Coolidge (1923–1929) took the lead in concluding the Kellogg-Briand Pact, an international agreement outlawing war that was eventually signed by more than sixty countries. The United States acquired a new appetite for multilateral agreements—as long as they enabled the nation to avoid, not make, strategic commitments. As aptly put by Nichols, Americans embraced an "isolationist internationalism."[4] They were seeking geopolitical clout without strategic liability.

This pronounced strategic retreat grew out of the experience of World War I, which intensified the political resonance of the multiple logics of isolationism that had shaped the nation's statecraft since its founding. In the words of William Leuchtenburg, World War I was viewed as "a dirty, unheroic war which few remembered with any emotion save distaste."[5] Contrary to Wilson's promises, entanglement in Europe had compromised, not advanced, the nation's exceptional character at home and its messianic mission abroad. For most Americans, entry into the war had been a grave mistake—an unnecessary conflict pushed on the country by arms merchants and greedy banks. As the next chapter will chronicle, America's determination to shun strategic entanglement would deepen considerably after the Great Depression. But the story of the 1930s begins in the 1920s as the United States searched for a grand strategy that would provide it influence without responsibility.

Isolationist Internationalism

As he ran for the presidency in 1920, Warren Harding promised to bring back "normalcy." "America's present need is not heroics," he insisted, "but healing; not nostrums, but normalcy; not revolution, but restoration; . . . not submergence in internationality but sustainment in triumphant nationality." He charged Wilson with trying "to revise human nature and suspend the fundamental laws of life and all of life's requirements." Instead, the United States needed peace "so we may set our own house in order." Refurbishing the economy and restoring the regular functions of republican government would again enable the nation to be "the commanding example of world leadership today." By putting its own house in order, Harding insisted, "we shall do more to make democracy safe for the world than all armed conflict ever recorded."[6]

After accepting the Republican nomination, Harding continued to argue that domestic renewal required geopolitical detachment. Americans, he observed in August 1920, had come to "a new realization of the menace to our America in European entanglements which emphasizes the prudence of [George] Washington.... It would be a sorry day for this republic if we allowed our activities in seeking for peace in the old world to blind us to the essentials of peace at home." Harding asserted that "we want a free America again. We want America free at home, and free in the world.... I had rather have industrial and social peace at home, than command the international peace of all the world."[7]

Harding was rejecting not just the idealist internationalism of Wilson, but also the realist expansionism embraced by his own party at the turn of the century. He did not want to retreat from the world, but as he made clear in his first Annual Message to Congress in 1921, he understood the rationale for engagement to rest exclusively on "our inescapable relationship to world affairs in finance and trade."[8] He was, Bear Braumoeller observes, unambiguously calling for reliance on "banks rather than tanks" to pursue U.S. interests abroad.[9] Harding acknowledged that geopolitical stability was an important ingredient of robust international commerce, but insisted that tranquility "must be worked out by the nations more directly concerned. They must themselves turn to the heroic remedies for the menacing conditions under which they are struggling." The United States would then be willing to lend a hand "because the commerce and international exchanges in trade, which marked our high tide of fortunate advancement, are possible only when the nations of all continents are restored to stable order and normal relationship."[10]

Harding's reclamation of a foreign policy focused on pursuing the nation's commercial interests represented a reaction against World War I and Wilson's idealist overreach. It also reflected the ascendance among Republicans of a conservative, pro-business agenda aimed at reducing government spending, scaling back taxes, and undoing progressive-era and wartime regulation of the private sector. In order to cut spending and reduce the risks of militarism and foreign entanglement, they took direct aim at the navy that the Republican Party had so enthusiastically supported during the days of McKinley and Roosevelt. Confronted with an economic downturn and social unrest at home, Harding's top priority was improving the performance of the nation's economy. The Emergency Tariff of 1921 and the Fordney-McCumber Act of 1922 raised tariffs, in part to provide relief to farmers suffering from depressed prices for agricultural goods.

Harding put up barriers to the inflow of immigrants as well as imports. World War I had brought to a head the fears of ethnic dilution that had been building since the late nineteenth century.[11] Congress in 1917 passed, over Wilson's veto, the nation's first widely restrictive legislation, imposing a literacy test, an arrival tax, and a ban on entry from an "Asiatic Barred Zone."[12] Wilson resisted more draconian legislation that would have imposed quotas on the basis of national origin.[13] Soon after taking office, Harding proceeded with the approach that Wilson had rejected, and the United States for the first time in its history imposed national quotas on immigration.

Although Harding's death in August 1923 cut short his tenure, his vice president, Calvin Coolidge, embraced much of his agenda after taking over the presidency. Coolidge signed into law the Immigration Act of 1924, which further tightened the restrictions put in place under Harding by reducing quotas and establishing the makeup of the nation's population in the census of 1890 as the baseline for the allocation of national slots.[14] As President Coolidge had proclaimed in his first Annual Message to Congress in December 1923, "America must be kept American."[15] The 1924 act reflected a rising nativism that had ethnic, racial, and religious dimensions. In the words of historian John Higham, "a nationalism so committed to isolation, so distrustful of entanglement with Europe, should find expression in a general revulsion against all foreigners. Indeed, indiscriminate anti-foreignism did extend far and wide in the early twenties."[16] As intended, the legislation succeeded in substantially raising the proportion of immigrants from the British Isles and northern Europe while reducing the inflow of Jews from eastern Europe and Catholics from southern Europe. At the beginning of the decade, roughly two-thirds of annual arrivals came from eastern and southern Europe. After the legislation passed in 1924, immigration from these areas shrunk to about ten percent of the total. Japanese, who had been exempted from the Asian ban imposed in 1917, were also barred from entry. Immigrants from these areas already in the United States moved elsewhere in growing numbers as they found the country an increasingly inhospitable place for resettlement.[17]

Coolidge also followed in Harding's footsteps when it came to reviving dollar diplomacy. Soon after winning reelection in 1924, Coolidge famously stated that "the chief business of the American people is business. They are profoundly concerned with producing, buying, selling, investing and prospering in the world. I am strongly of the opinion that the great majority of people will always find these are moving impulses of our life."[18] He presided over the downsizing of the federal government, slashed taxes, reduced the deficit, scaled back regulations, and imposed draconian cuts on the naval budget, which by 1926 reached the lowest level of the interwar period.[19] The U.S. Army also shrank in dramatic fashion. Over two million men were on active duty during World War I, compared with around 140,000 during the 1920s.[20] Cutbacks to the tools of statecraft reflected Coolidge's priorites. According to historian George Herring, Coolidge "showed little interest in and much ignorance of the world," happily leaving the conduct of foreign policy to Charles Evans Hughes, his secretary of state.[21]

Like Harding, Coolidge thus pursued a foreign policy that shunned geopolitical entanglement in favor of commercial and financial engagement. America's
diplomats were not sidelined; indeed, the 1924 Rogers Act consolidated the
State Department's diplomatic and consular services by establishing the Foreign
Service.[22] But in both Europe and East Asia, the United States was focused
on using the nation's economic power—rather than its military strength—to
wield influence and promote geopolitical stability. Through the Dawes Plan,
Washington in 1924 arranged for partial relief of Germany's onerous war
reparations and provided for major loans from U.S. investment banks to German
industry. The United States pressed Europeans to stabilize their currencies on
the basis of the gold standard.[23] It offered famine aid to Russia and earthquake
assistance to Japan.[24] In East Asia, major U.S. investments and loans were to enforce the Open Door and bind both China and Japan to the U.S. economy. As
Michael Green notes, U.S. strategy toward the region rested on the "assumption that America's enormous financial and industrial power at the end of the
First World War would increase both Chinese and Japanese dependence on
American capitalism."[25]

The U.S. government worked hand-in-hand with the private sector as it sought
to use the nation's economic strength as its main instrument of foreign engagement. Federal authorities regularly devolved to private firms responsibility for
both designing and carrying out policy. J. P. Morgan, for example, played a prominent role in fashioning U.S. relations with Germany, Japan, and China. As the
scholar Peter Trubowitz observes, this strategy entailed "private initiative rather
than government action." He notes that American businessmen were encouraged
to assume a leading role in stabilizing the war-ravaged European economies
through bank loans and private investment and to create the conditions in
which American influence could spread." Green concurs, concluding that "the
Republican administrations of the 1920s were uniquely willing to outsource
major diplomatic tasks to leading industrialists and bankers."[26]

The revival of an updated, more ambitious, and more effective version of
dollar diplomacy had its biggest impact on strategy toward Europe and East Asia;
the United States sought strategic detachment from both theaters. Nonetheless,
these trends also affected policy toward Latin America. The United States had
since 1898 regularly intervened in the region. But, as George Herring notes, "the
excess of Wilsonian interventionism had produced a backlash at home, raising
demands for the liquidation of military occupations and abstentions from future
interventions."[27] A bipartisan coalition came together to press for a U.S. pullback
from the region. The left objected to the militarism of U.S. engagement; progressives charged that self-interested banks and corporations were behind the
quasi-imperial character of policy. Meanwhile, the right opposed the entanglement of military occupation. Senator Borah based his own critique of U.S. policy

on a mix of these objections, stating in 1922 that "the people of Nicaragua are today being exploited in shameless fashion by American corporations protected by United States Marines."[28]

The political appeal of pulling back from Latin America became clear even before Wilson left office. Harding's campaign platform called for an end to the U.S. occupations of Haiti and Santo Domingo. In an address to Congress during the campaign, he revealed a disdainful attitude toward the nation's repeated interventions in the region:

> If I should be, as I fully expect to be, elected President of this just and honorable Republic, I will not empower an assistant secretary of the navy [a reference to Theodore Roosevelt] to draft a constitution for helpless neighbors in the West Indies and jam it down their throats at the point of bayonets borne by the United States marines. We have a higher service for our gallant marines than that. Nor will I misuse the power of the Executive to cover with a veil of secrecy repeated acts of unwarranted interference in domestic affairs of the little republics of the western hemisphere, such as in the past few years have not only made enemies of those who should be our friends, but have rightfully discredited our country as their trusted neighbor.[29]

In August of 1923, Secretary of State Hughes delivered a speech before the American Bar Association in which he dwelled on the same theme: "I utterly disclaim, as unwarranted . . . a claim on our part to superintend the affairs of our sister republics, to assert an overlordship, to consider the spread of our authority beyond our own domain as the aim of policy, and to make our power the test of right in this hemisphere."[30]

President Coolidge and President Herbert Hoover (1929–1933) embraced similarly skeptical attitudes toward U.S. interference in Latin America. During the presidential campaign of 1928, Republicans and Democrats alike advocated for ending the long era of U.S. interventions and occupations in the region. The Republican Party platform affirmed that "our policy absolutely repudiates any idea of conquest or exploitation." The Democratic platform asserted that "interference in the purely internal affairs of Latin-American countries must cease."[31] Coolidge, and Hoover after him, enjoyed bipartisan support for pulling back from the region. As Herring summarizes the strategic trend of the time, "the Republicans significantly altered the means, if not the ends, of U.S. Latin American policies in the 1920s, shifting away from the gunboat diplomacy and military interventionism that had marked the previous twenty years."[32]

Turning the commitment to retrenchment into actual shifts in policy occurred in fits and starts. The economic interests of influential U.S. corporations were at stake, outbreaks of political instability continued to invite U.S. interventions, and the Republican administrations of the 1920s still exhibited a paternalistic approach toward the region. The Harding administration withdrew U.S. troops from Cuba in 1922, and the Coolidge administration withdrew forces from the Dominican Republic in the middle of the decade, while also briefly removing them from Nicaragua in 1925. At the same time, the United States repeatedly intervened in the Caribbean Basin over the course of the 1920s, including in Guatemala (1920), Costa Rica (1921), Panama (1920, 1921, 1925), and Honduras (1924, 1925). American forces also returned to Nicaragua from 1926 to 1933, and the occupation of Haiti continued from 1915 until 1934.[33]

It was not until Hoover's "Good Neighbor" policy that the United States in earnest began to embrace a stance of noninterference.[34] He put in place plans to end the U.S. occupation of Haiti in order to, in his own words, "extricate ourselves from the mess into which we had been plunged."[35] He also withdrew U.S. troops from Nicaragua and resisted pressure to intervene elsewhere in the region.[36] By the time Hoover left office, he had weaned U.S. policy of its heavy reliance on military intervention, clearing the way for President Franklin Roosevelt (1933–1945) to take further steps, including completion of the withdrawal from Haiti and ratification of a new treaty with Cuba abrogating the 1903 treaty that had given the United States the right to intervene in Cuba at will.[37] Roosevelt's version of the Good Neighbor policy aimed at more broadly normalizing relations with Latin America and making good on the principle of recognizing the rights of all nations in the hemisphere to sovereignty and self-determination.

In sum, the United States during the 1920s embraced what Nichols calls "isolationist internationalism"—in Trubowitz's words, "semi-internationalism" or "independent internationalism."[38] As Wilson had acknowledged, Americans understood that since 1898 they had become "participants, whether we would or not, in the life of the world."[39] But in the aftermath of World War I, they rejected the global obligations that Wilson had insisted need accompany such participation and were keen to scale back spending on defense—in part to forestall the temptations of foreign entanglement. Accordingly, Americans were searching for a form of engagement that came without strategic responsibility; they wanted influence, but also limited liability, if not strategic immunity. As Herring puts it, "Republican leaders involved the United States to an unprecedented extent in reconstructing postwar Europe and promoting stability in East Asia, even assuming the sort of leadership the United States had not previously considered. The key, of course, was to do this without political entanglements."[40]

In political terms, this "isolationist internationalism" represented an ideological meeting ground between left and right—a new "sweet spot" in American politics. The left emerged from the Wilsonian era internationalist but staunchly antimilitarist. Mainstream Republicans had lost much of their appetite for flexing the nation's military muscle, but they valued the country's new economic power (and prosperity) and were more than happy to work with the private sector to wield U.S. influence abroad. The unilateralists and strident nationalists were content as long as the nation returned to a posture of strategic detachment outside the Western Hemisphere. As Nichols observes, "the vision for how America might lead other nations was cooperative enough to satisfy many internationalists, while it was nonentangled enough to placate many among the unilateralist-oriented isolationists."[41]

There were also signs in society at large that internationalism—even if in a limited, commercialized form—was going mainstream. In 1919, Georgetown University founded the School of Foreign Service, and other graduate schools of international affairs would soon open. Notably, the initial mission of the School of Foreign Service was to educate students in the practice of international commerce. The Council on Foreign Relations (CFR), founded in 1921 and headquartered in New York, became a principal venue for private-sector representatives, politicians, diplomats, military leaders, journalists, and academics to debate U.S. foreign policy. That the CFR was located in New York made clear the central role that the private sector played in the formulation and conduct of U.S. statecraft. According to its incorporating charter, the CFR's role was "to afford a continuous conference on international questions affecting the United States."[42] The organization also sought to help stimulate public debate on foreign policy, in 1922 launching a quarterly journal, *Foreign Affairs*.

Pacts of Inaction:
Naval Arms Control and Outlawing War

Another marker of the nation's new "isolationist internationalism" was its unprecedented readiness for participation in multilateral pacts. In concluding the Washington Naval Treaties and the Kellogg-Briand Pact, the executive branch demonstrated its willingness to negotiate, and the legislative branch its readiness to ratify, agreements that subjected the conduct of U.S. foreign policy to an international accord. Coming so soon after the resounding rejection of U.S. participation in the League, this embrace of multilateralism constituted a quite remarkable about-face. At the same time, the naval treaties and Kellogg-Briand Pact were multilateral agreements that effectively limited rather than augmented the strategic commitments of its signatories. The United States was entering international pacts that constrained its ability to act as it saw fit, but to the end of avoiding strategic obligations abroad. Accordingly, the treaties were exemplary signs of the "isolationist internationalism" that had taken root.

With the strategic situation in Europe appearing stable after the close of World War I, the United States looked to naval arms control to limit geopolitical competition in East Asia. In 1921–1922, the Harding administration gathered in Washington, Britain, France, Italy, and Japan to discuss naval disarmament. Belgium, China, the Netherlands, and Portugal participated in a broader negotiation focused on enforcing the Open Door.[43] The resulting Five-Power Treaty capped the aggregate capital ship tonnage of the United States, Britain, France, Italy, and Japan for a ten-year period.[44] Article 19 of the agreement also prohibited the United States, the British Empire, and Japan from further fortification of existing bases in East Asia.[45] The treaty not only reduced the likelihood of naval rivalry, but also enabled Harding to cancel ambitious plans for the construction of battleships and substantially reduce the naval budget, a top Republican priority. The Four-Power Treaty committed the United States, Great Britain, France, and Japan to the territorial status quo in East Asia and to consultations in the event of disputes or crises. The Nine-Power Treaty committed all of the nations taking part in the Washington Conference to honor the Open Door policy and China's territorial sovereignty.

The strategic stability promoted by naval arms control and multilateral agreement to preserve the territorial status quo would enable the United States to pursue a strategy toward East Asia focused almost exclusively on economic engagement. Secretary of State Hughes and his colleagues believed that the nation's economic strength would enable it to maintain preeminence in the region as long as geopolitical rivalry could be averted. This approach, at least in theory, attained a chief strategic aim of the Harding and Coolidge administrations; it provided the United States geopolitical influence while limiting strategic liability. According to Michael Green, U.S. officials operated under the assumption that "the strategic environment had been totally changed by the treaties, that international norms were now more effective instruments of deterrence than military power, alliance, or economic sanctions." Green contends that policy makers presumed that the "balance of power no longer mattered," encouraging them to believe "America could now maintain the peace without greater commitments." Adam Tooze arrives at the same conclusion, assessing that American policy makers deemed that "through naval disarmament and a China settlement, the Washington Conference would reanimate the vision of the Open Door, creating an international space swept clean of militarism in which the free flow of American capital would unify and pacify."[46]

Unlike the Versailles Treaty, which imposed international obligations on the United States, the Washington agreements absolved the United States of such strategic commitments. When President Harding presented the treaties to the Senate in February 1922, he noted that the "proposed commitments are . . . fraught with vastly less danger, than our undertakings in the past." He also went out of his way to distinguish the conclusions of the naval conference from the results of Versailles: "There is no commitment to armed force, no alliance, no written or moral obligation to join in defence, no expressed or implied commitment to arrive at any agreement except in accordance with our constitutional methods." Moreover, the Washington treaties provided for no means of enforcement or oversight; the United States would not be submitting its will to some "superentity." Adherence to the terms of the agreements depended solely on the will of the individual signatories.[47]

The Five-Power Treaty limiting naval strength enjoyed strong bipartisan and public support; it was approved by the Senate by a vote of 74 to 1. The Nine-Power Treaty defending the Open Door to China also had strong backing, passing by a vote of 66 to 0. In contrast, the Four-Power Treaty ensuring the territorial status quo in East Asia provoked considerable opposition—precisely because it was the one component of the treaty package that could be interpreted as extending a U.S. commitment to intervene abroad. Indeed, the Senate insisted on adding a reservation stipulating that "the United States understands that under the statement in the preamble or under the terms of this Treaty there is no commitment to armed force, no alliance, no obligation to join in any defense." Even with this reservation, the Four-Power Treaty passed by the narrow margin of 67 to 27.

Opponents of the Four-Power Treaty included Democrats who staunchly backed the League of Nations and saw the results of the Washington Conference as woefully inadequate. Others took the opposite position, charging that the treaty too closely resembled the League. Senator Borah again led the irreconcilable camp in opposing ratification. Borah argued that "whether it is an alliance or not," the treaty "has the effect of constituting in the Pacific Ocean a political group, or diplomatic group, for certain purposes and certain objects to be attained." Consequently, he asserted, "there is no departure from old and long-discredited practices. The system of political grouping of nations is as old as recorded history. . . . Its evils, its deplorable result, fill the pages of history since recorded time. . . . There has never been organized, so far as my knowledge goes, a political group of this kind that did not give rise to a counter political group."[48] Borah repeatedly pointed to the political jockeying in the run-up to World War I to demonstrate the dangers associated with the formation of competing blocs. "I want policies, not promises," he concluded. "I want disarmament, not political alliances the members of which continue to arm, continue to practice imperialism."[49] Despite such pointed objections, Republican loyalty to Harding and Hughes, combined with the prospect of averting geopolitical rivalry through economic engagement and self-restraint, produced more than the two-thirds majority needed for ratification.[50]

Like the Washington Naval Treaties, the Kellogg-Briand Pact was the result of American initiative—in this case, the product of teamwork between Coolidge's secretary of state, Frank Kellogg, and his French counterpart, Aristide Briand. In the spring of 1927, Briand had proposed to Kellogg a bilateral security treaty—in effect, a mutual nonaggression pact. Uncomfortable with the prospect of fashioning a special relationship with France that could end up again entangling the United States in Europe's rivalries, Kellogg, pushed along by a vocal peace movement, counterproposed a much broader agreement. The resulting accord was in essence a multilateral agreement to outlaw war that ideally would be signed and adhered to by all countries. The operative clause in the accord affirmed that "the High Contracting Parties solemnly declare in the names of their respective peoples that they condemn recourse to war for the solution of international controversies, and renounce it, as an instrument of national policy in their relations with one another."[51] The agreement contained no enforcement mechanisms and relied solely on the will of the signatories to abide by their commitment to repudiate the use of force as an instrument of policy. Fifteen nations initially signed the pact in August 1928. Some sixty nations had signed the accord by the end of the 1930s.

Kellogg-Briand was yet another manifestation of America's new "isolationist internationalism." The United States was ready to play an ongoing role in shaping the international system as long as it enjoyed strategic immunity while doing so. The peace pact offered an attractive way for the nation to wield geopolitical influence without taking on geopolitical obligations. The Senate approved the Kellogg-Briand Pact by a vote of 85 to 1. As with the Washington Naval Treaties, the accord enjoyed the Senate's support largely because it entailed a commitment to collective inaction, not to collective responsibility.

A good number of senators viewed the pact as a way of compensating for the nation's rejection of participation in the League of Nations. Senator Carter Glass (D-Virginia) indicated as much during the debate over ratification, calling Kellogg-Briand "one of the many devices that have been contrived to solace the awakened conscience of some people who kept the United States out of the League of Nations."[52] The Senate's rejection of the commitment to collective action spelled out in the League Covenant was hardly out of character for the United States; nonentanglement and unilateralism had long guided the nation's strategy. But walking away from the League was at odds with America's exceptionalist calling. In effect, the United States was defecting from an ambitious international effort, orchestrated by its own president, to realize a national mission dating to the Founders: to ban geopolitical rivalry and fashion a more peaceful world. Kellogg-Briand offered a means of returning to this mission and refurbishing the nation's exceptionalist calling—while avoiding geopolitical entanglement.

For the pacifist movement, Kellogg-Briand was even better than what the Versailles Treaty had put on offer. The pact relied solely on law and moral

suasion to prevent war, avoiding the distasteful threat of collective coercion that
was at the heart of the League. Emily Balch and other leaders of the peace movement lobbied hard both at home and abroad for the agreement.[53] The liberal
establishment also threw its weight behind the pact. The *New Republic*, which
had opposed the League as a sell-out to the logic of realpolitik, backed Kellogg-
Briand—despite concerns that the pact was merely "a gesture of good will." "If
put to the test of a real war," the editors wrote, "the treaty would probably go to
pieces. Nevertheless, the New Republic believes it should be signed. . . . This is a
necessary first step which must be taken, however awkwardly, before we can go
on to a real struggle with the curse of militarism." The scholar and public intellectual John Dewey, a regular contributor to the magazine, was more enthusiastic,
arguing that "there appears to be but one course for American lovers of peace,
namely, to get firmly and unanimously behind Kellogg's proposal for a general
treaty of renunciation of war."[54]

Paradoxically, pacifists and liberals found in Senator Borah, who led the
irreconcilables' effort to defeat the League and the Four-Power Treaty, a passionate partner when it came to Kellogg-Briand. Borah viewed the League as
a vehicle for the permanent entanglement of the United States in the geopolitics of the Old World and an affront to "Americanism." In contrast, he saw
Kellogg-Briand not as a constraint on the nation's autonomy but as a vehicle
for freeing the United States from international obligations and an expression
of American values. In an opinion piece supporting the accord published in the
New York Times Magazine, Borah insisted that "the United States will never become identified or cooperate with a system of peace based upon 'pledges to wage
war.' But the United States now stands ready to cooperate and identify itself with
a system based upon pledges *not* to wage war." Kellogg-Briand, in Borah's mind,
"would put an end to any questions of war commitments under the League
Covenant or other alliances. . . . This gives us international laws based upon
peace and not upon war."[55] If each nation minded its own business and exercised
geopolitical restraint, international peace would prevail and all nations would
enjoy full sovereignty and autonomy.

The Republican mainstream was less convinced of the merits of Kellogg-
Briand than either Balch or Borah, but had few reservations about the agreement, which enjoyed strong public support. Republican senators, harkening
back to the debate over the League, were particularly keen on attaining
assurances that the pact would entail neither a legal nor moral obligation to respond to aggression. Secretary Kellogg repeatedly provided such assurances, on
one occasion asking rhetorically, "where is there a statement in the treaty, or
anywhere else, of any moral obligation to punish an aggressor?"[56] Moreover, the
pact, by deemphasizing traditional geopolitics, was entirely consistent with a
Republican foreign policy aimed at relying on the nation's economic strength to

wield U.S. influence abroad. So, too, would Kellogg-Briand, like the Washington Naval Treaty, help the United States avoid the expenses and dangers associated with arms races. Herbert Hoover, Coolidge's secretary of commerce, called the pact "a magnificent step toward world peace" as he campaigned for the presidency in 1928.[57]

Many senators, Republicans and Democrats alike, although not wildly enthusiastic about the pact, nonetheless voted in favor of ratification because they deemed the agreement innocuous. During the Senate debate, Senator Hiram Johnson, another irreconcilable, stated that "I will vote for this pact with a hope, only a hope. I am willing to indulge in any hope that peace may come on earth."[58] He wrote to his son that "I could not find myself getting excited over the Treaty. I think it just a piece of bunk utilized by so-called statesmen the world over to fool their people."[59] Some Democrats shared the sentiment. Senator Reed labeled the pact a "sort of international kiss." Senator Kenneth McKellar (D-Tennessee) remarked, "at least it can do no great harm."[60] Senator Glass felt compelled to instruct his constituents not to presume that "I am simple enough to suppose that it is worth a postage stamp in the direction of accomplishing permanent international peace."[61] Senator David Walsh (D-Massachusetts) did not put great stock in the treaty, but argued that rejecting it, especially since the United States had taken the lead in negotiating it, would undercut the country's diplomatic clout and send a signal that Americans opposed efforts to pursue international peace.[62]

As it had done when it attached a reservation to the Four-Power Treaty, the Senate did end up passing a measure (the Reed-Moses Resolution) stipulating that participation in Kellogg-Briand would in no way limit the nation's right to self-defense, require it to act against any party that violated the agreement, or impair the exercise of the Monroe Doctrine.[63] It is quite revealing that the Senate felt compelled to offer such caveats to an agreement that was essentially a collective commitment to inaction and nonentanglement. Even as the United States seemingly took the lead in a multilateral effort to pacify global affairs, it insisted on doing so in a way that came without geopolitical responsibility and reinforced the country's detachment from strategic commitments outside its own hemisphere. Kellogg-Briand was in important respects the pinnacle of an American effort to shape world affairs while cordoning itself off from that world.

* * *

The United States after World War I sought to return to a grand strategy of geopolitical detachment, limiting its strategic exposure in Europe and East Asia and even beginning a pullback from Latin America. The most restrictive immigration legislation in the nation's history was part of this effort to distance the United States from the outside world. At the same time, U.S. grand strategy reflected a new reality: the nation had become a leading world power. Largely as a result of the war, the United States had also emerged as a major creditor. Reconciling its global influence with its aversion to foreign entanglement produced a grand strategy that sought to parlay economic and diplomatic leverage into geopolitical heft. As part of this new grand strategy, the United States, for the first time in its history, turned to multilateral agreements—the Washington Naval Treaties and Kellogg-Briand Pact—to preserve geopolitical quiescence and magnify the sway of its economic strength.

This "isolationist internationalism" was a good fit for a nation that was seeking to maximize its influence and its prosperity while limiting its strategic obligations. The core weakness of this approach was that it depended entirely on fleeting circumstances. America's economic and diplomatic leverage would soon dwindle as a result of the Great Depression. The Washington Naval Treaties and the Kellogg-Briand Pact depended upon the goodwill and like-mindedness of other major powers; they worked as long as the signatories were willing to adhere to the agreements.[64] Both accords lacked enforcement mechanisms—precisely why they appealed to U.S. leaders and could pass muster in the Senate.

These shortcomings became readily apparent during the 1930s as Germany, Japan, and Italy rendered these accords virtually meaningless. As the strategic architecture of the 1920s fell apart, the United States doubled down on its search for geopolitical immunity. The isolationist consensus grew so strong that the country did not enter World War II until it was attacked by Japan—eight years after Hitler had come to power in Germany and begun to dismantle the Versailles peace settlement and ten years after Imperial Japan had invaded Manchuria and begun its effort to carve up China.

From the Great Depression to Pearl Harbor: Delusions of Strategic Immunity

The Great Depression recast U.S. grand strategy in fundamental ways. President Herbert Hoover and President Franklin Roosevelt both orchestrated an inward geopolitical turn as they focused on the challenge of economic recovery. Amid unprecedented economic duress at home, the United States had fewer resources at its disposal for tasks abroad; it was no longer willing to provide assistance, make loans, ease debt burdens, and oversee financial stability. As credit and investment from the private sector dried up, so too did the leverage that had come with Wall Street's role as an instrument of U.S. diplomacy. The United States effectively abandoned the activist dollar diplomacy of the 1920s in favor of financial detachment. The nation's efforts to use its economic strength to shape geopolitical outcomes in Europe and East Asia came to an end.

Economic leadership gave way to not just financial disengagement, but also protectionism and unilateralism. During Hoover's watch, the United States resorted to the infamous Smoot-Hawley Tariff to promote domestic employment, prompting other countries to do the same and producing a plunge in international commerce. Roosevelt's top priority was his program for promoting economic growth at home, the New Deal; in his inaugural address, he devoted only one sentence to traditional matters of diplomacy—and the subject was Latin America. He would soon veto efforts to create an international vehicle for stabilizing exchange rates, preferring to go it alone. The "isolationist internationalism" of the 1920s had quickly dissipated.

A decisive strategic pullback accompanied this economic retreat. As Germany, Japan, and Italy rearmed and engaged in overt acts of aggression—moves that flouted their commitments under the Versailles Treaty, the Washington Naval Treaties, and the Kellogg-Briand Pact—Roosevelt's main response was to shepherd through Congress a series of neutrality acts that aimed to cordon off the United States from trouble abroad. In the opinion of many Americans, U.S. entry into World War I had been a costly mistake imposed on the nation by corporate interests—the primary conclusion of congressional hearings on the subject that began in 1934. Determined to avoid a repeat of the events that drew the nation into World War I, Congress passed tightening versions of neutrality that banned arms exports to belligerents and then prohibited all trade on U.S. vessels with countries at war—regardless of whether the recipient was aggressor or victim.

The nation was breaking with a guidepost dating to the founding era—"commerce with all nations, alliance with none."[1] Indeed, the United States had twice gone to war—in 1812 and again in 1917—to defend the commercial rights of neutrality. But in the 1930s, the United States was more than ready to abandon that principle in order to build a moat around the nation. Isolationism had since the eighteenth century meant coupling geopolitical detachment with commercial engagement. By the 1930s, it meant severing both commercial and geopolitical ties in the service of cordoning the country off from the prospect of war.[2] The United States did little more than watch as expansive ambition and atrocities began to engulf both Europe and East Asia.

After the Nazi invasion of Poland in September 1939, which prompted Britain and France to declare war against Germany, Roosevelt finally reversed course and convinced Congress to allow the victims of fascism to purchase arms from the United States. But the steps were halting—the items had to be transported on ships provided by the purchaser—even though Germany was already in control of most of Central Europe and Japan had conquered Manchuria and major portions of China. Over the course of 1941, Roosevelt substantially increased the scope of U.S. military assistance to those fighting the Axis powers. But to do so he had to battle a determined isolationist camp, which was by then operating under the banner of the America First Committee. And even after munitions, ships, and aircraft were flowing to countries resisting the Axis powers, Roosevelt kept the United States out of the war—until Japan bombed Pearl Harbor and forced him to join the fight.

Paradoxically, but not surprisingly, isolationism exercised remarkable sway over the conduct of U.S. grand strategy at a time when the world was desperately in need of American power and purpose. The United States abdicated leadership on matters of trade and finance even though Britain in the aftermath of World War I was not up to the task. Americans then ran for cover as militarism and virulent nationalism began to engulf Europe and East Asia. And even after the outbreak of World War II made amply clear the dangerous ambitions of the Axis powers, America was willing to contribute only armaments and financial assistance until the United States itself was attacked by Japan. That the United States was a passive bystander during one of history's darkest decades helps illuminate why isolationism was finally discredited and defeated after the nation entered World War II.

The Economic Pullback

During the 1920s, the United States sought to compensate for its geopolitical re-trenchment by turning to its economic strength to wield influence abroad. In the wake of the Great Depression, this revised version of dollar diplomacy gave way to economic disengagement. That the world's leading power was pulling back economically as well as geopolitically hastened the fragmentation of the inter-national system.[3] The vulnerabilities of the agreements struck during America's era of leadership without responsibility became readily apparent; Germany, Italy, and Japan met little resistance as they made short shrift of the international obligations they had assumed after World War I.

The collapse of financial markets in the United States meant that J. P. Morgan and other investment banks would no longer serve as the levers of U.S. diplomatic influence abroad. Between 1924 and 1931, loans from U.S. entities accounted for roughly sixty percent of international lending. Thereafter, U.S. lending abroad virtually ceased and did not recover for the rest of the decade.[4] As the U.S. government turned most of its attention to the domestic economy, it scaled back efforts to help manage European war debts and other economic travails. Similarly, enforcing the Open Door in China took a backseat to addressing plunging wages and rising unemployment at home.

A retreat on trade accompanied the pullback on investment. In 1930, Hoover signed the Smoot-Hawley Tariff Act, which raised tariffs on more than 20,000 imported goods. America's trading partners responded in kind. Between 1929 and 1934, international trade fell by sixty-six percent, exacerbating the global economic downturn. Smoot-Hawley also projected to the rest of the world a unmistakable message that the United States would take a go-it-alone approach to managing the Depression, undermining the new spirit of multilateralism that the nation had embraced during the 1920s.[5]

Roosevelt took office in March 1933 and made clear from the outset that the urgent need to improve the nation's economy required a near-exclusive focus on domestic policy—even if concentrating on the home front came at the expense of the nation's engagement abroad. In his inaugural address, he stated that "our greatest primary task is to put people to work" and identified as his top priority "putting our own national house in order and making income balance outgo." He maintained that "our international trade relations, though vastly important, are in point of time and necessity secondary to the establishment of a sound national economy. I favor as a practical policy the putting of first things first. I shall spare no effort to restore world trade by international economic readjust-ment, but the emergency at home cannot wait on that accomplishment." In the only sentence in the speech that he devoted to the diplomatic as opposed to economic dimensions of foreign policy, Roosevelt called for a "good neighbor" approach toward Latin America.[6]

A few months later, Roosevelt demonstrated that he was fully prepared to act on his stated priorities, sacrificing multilateral efforts to stabilize the international monetary system in order to maintain maximum flexibility on domestic economic policy. In the summer of 1933, national delegations gathered in London for a World Economic Conference aimed at forging a collective mechanism for preserving the stability of exchange rates. Roosevelt undermined his own team by instructing them that it would be "particularly unwise from political and psychological standpoints to permit limitation of our own action to be imposed by any nation other than our own." He then telegraphed to London a public statement that came to be called the "bombshell" message because it effectively blew up the conference and ended hope of arriving at a collective approach to managing exchange rates.[7]

Roosevelt informed the delegates that "I would regard it as a catastrophe amounting to a world tragedy if the great Conference of Nations . . . should . . . allow itself to be diverted by the proposal of a purely artificial and temporary experiment affecting the monetary exchange of a few Nations only." Instead, each country needs to get its own house in order, beginning with "concerted policies in the majority of Nations to produce balanced budgets and living within their means." Roosevelt asserted that "the sound internal economic system of a Nation is a greater factor in its well-being than the price of its currency." The communique, according to economist Rodney Morrison, "sounded the Conference's death knell." Historians Justus Doenecke and John Wilz soberly summarize the impact of this turn of events: "The United States had announced in no uncertain terms that it would find its own exit from the Great Depression."[8]

The Johnson Debt Default Act of 1934 was a further indicator of America's economic pullback. During the 1920s, the United States sought to restore the economic health of postwar Europe by renegotiating the terms of German reparations and providing loans and assistance to nations in need. The Johnson Act put the U.S. economy first, prohibiting loans to any country that was in default on its debts to the United States.[9] Preoccupation with economic duress at home meant the end of U.S. efforts to mitigate economic dislocation—and its geopolitical consequences—abroad.

The Geopolitical Pullback

Harding and Coolidge orchestrated a major strategic retrenchment after World War I, imposing huge cuts on the naval budget, downsizing the U.S. Army, relying on economic leverage rather than military strength to wield geopolitical influence, and turning to multilateral agreements—the Washington Naval Treaties and the Kellogg-Briand Pact—to dampen rivalry. Hoover followed suit. Indeed, the Great Depression reinforced Washington's aversion to foreign entanglement. According to Green, "the world economic crises only compounded Hoover's resistance to overseas adventures."[10]

Hoover did not build a single battleship during his presidency, and Roosevelt maintained defense spending at relatively modest levels (around two percent of GDP) throughout the 1930s.[11] As the decade progressed, both presidents kept their distance from Japanese, German, and Italian aggression, and pulled back farther from Latin America. Fueled by the financial crisis and by congressional hearings on the causes of World War I, elites and the public alike embraced an unprecedented animosity toward corporations and banks. Senator Gerald Nye (R-North Dakota) oversaw the hearings, which ran from 1934 to 1936, under the auspices of the Special Committee on Investigation of the Munitions Industry. The committee effectively indicted the munitions industry as "merchants of death" responsible for dragging the country into World War I.[12] This conclusion would strengthen the nation's determination to cordon itself off from building geopolitical tensions in Europe and East Asia. Stoked in part by soaring unemployment, the anti-immigrant sentiment that had led to restrictive legislation in the 1920s mounted alongside the growing opposition to foreign entanglement. Over the course of the 1930s, roughly one million persons of Mexican heritage—many of whom were U.S. citizens—were effectively deported to Mexico.[13]

As it had prior to the 1890s, a strict version of isolationism again dominated the nation's politics, cutting across party, region, and ideological orientation. The imperial turn of 1898, World War I, and the bruising fight over the League had already turned mainstream Republicans against geopolitical entanglement. By the 1930s, the Depression compelled them to shy away even from dollar diplomacy and the "isolationist internationalism" that they had embraced in the 1920s. So, too, did many Republicans fear that ambition abroad would come at the expense of political and economic liberty at home—as had happened during World War I. And right-wing Republicans like Senator Borah, even though many of them had backed the Kellogg-Briand Pact in 1928, over the course of the following decade backed away from any hint of political obligation to keep the peace abroad.

Progressives on both sides of the aisle, who had once seen overseas expansion as a source of employment and reform at home, had become staunch isolationists, suspicious that geopolitical ambition emerged from the self-seeking manipulation of foreign policy by banks and industry. Democrats who had believed in the redemptive potential of American power and purpose remained disillusioned by Wilson's failed idealism; they were focused on defending liberal causes at home, not on confronting the rising tide of fascism and militarism abroad. Pacifists were the beneficiaries of these political trends, with the peace movement enjoying unprecedented prominence. The central message of the pacifists—that the nation should cordon itself off from brewing trouble abroad and remain true to its commitment to disavow war as a tool of statecraft—resonated among a public determined to avoid a repeat of the missteps that had drawn the nation into World War I. According to Doenecke and Wilz, "by the mid-1930s, the peace movement had reached its peak of influence. Its solution for keeping America out of war: total isolation."[14]

This isolationist consensus ensured that the United States would be no more than a concerned bystander as the relative quiescence of the 1920s gave way to renewed geopolitical rivalry in Europe and East Asia. Japan invaded Manchuria in 1931, abrogating its commitments under the Washington Naval Treaties and the Kellogg-Briand Pact. The main response of Hoover's secretary of state, Henry Stimson, was to declare that the United States would refuse to recognize the legality of any Japanese actions that violated the Open Door or Kellogg-Briand—what Green calls "the famous and ineffective 'nonrecognition doctrine.'"[15] Hoover himself was determined to avoid U.S. participation in any collective response, especially if it involved the use of force. He made this position quite clear in a policy memorandum: "Neither our obligations to China, nor our own interest, nor our dignity require us to go to war over these questions. These acts do not imperil the freedom of the American people, the economic or moral fiber of our people. I do not propose to sacrifice American life for anything short of this." Stimson informally summarized the administration's priority as not allowing "under any circumstances anybody to deposit that baby on our lap." At the end of 1934, Japan gave official notice of its withdrawal from the Washington Naval Treaty and the updated naval limitations that it had agreed to at the London Naval Conference of 1930—again meeting no significant response from the United States. As Doenecke and Wilz conclude, "the Great Depression had pushed diplomacy to the background of American life."[16]

Hoover, and Roosevelt after him, were similarly intent on keeping away from trouble in Europe. Nazi Germany withdrew from the League of Nations in the fall of 1933 and then announced in 1935 that it would rearm and no longer abide by the military limitations imposed on it by the Versailles Treaty. The following year Hitler remilitarized the Rhineland and in 1938 invaded and annexed Austria and the borderlands of Czechoslovakia. By that time, Nazi anti-Semitism had already taken a violent turn, with synagogues being burned, Jewish shops ransacked, and thousands of Jews headed to concentration camps. Italy, which Benito Mussolini had turned into an effective dictatorship in 1925, had also embarked on an aggressive path by the middle of the decade, invading Ethiopia in 1935 and abandoning its commitments to naval arms control and the

Kellogg-Briand Pact. Italy and Germany signed a treaty of cooperation in 1936, with Mussolini declaring the formation of a Rome-Berlin Axis.

Throughout these developments, the United States steered clear of involvement. Roosevelt may have been somewhat of a reluctant isolationist, but he needed the support of isolationist progressives to advance his domestic agenda and pass New Deal legislation—and was not about to take them on over foreign policy.[17] Indeed, as discussed below, the main U.S. policy response to Europe's strategic descent during the second half of the 1930s was to embargo trade with belligerents to avoid a replay of the chain of events that brought the country into World War I. It would not be until 1939, prompted by the Nazi invasions of Czechoslovakia and Poland, that Roosevelt finally began to reverse course and provide limited assistance to countries resisting fascism. And despite the outflow from Europe of Jews escaping persecution, U.S. immigration quotas remained intact, with authorities in May 1939 infamously sending back to Europe a passenger liner carrying almost 1,000 Jewish refugees from Germany. Roughly half of the refugees returned to Europe perished in the Holocaust.[18]

The stringent isolationism that emerged in the 1930s was primarily directed toward Europe and East Asia, but it also shaped policy closer to home. Picking up on Hoover's Good Neighbor doctrine, Roosevelt sought to retract U.S. forces from the Caribbean and Latin America and bring to an end the long era of U.S. interventionism in the region. In his first inaugural address, he asserted that "in the field of world policy I would dedicate this Nation to the policy of the good neighbor—the neighbor who resolutely respects himself and, because he does so, respects the rights of others—the neighbor who respects his obligations and respects the sanctity of his agreements in and with a world of neighbors."[19]

Roosevelt completed the withdrawal of U.S. forces from Nicaragua in 1933 and from Haiti in 1934, and negotiated agreements with Cuba in 1934, Panama in 1936, and Mexico in 1937 to annul the U.S. right to intervene militarily in their affairs. He made landmark visits to Haiti, Panama, and Colombia in 1934. In 1936, he played a prominent role in organizing the Inter-American Conference for the Maintenance of Peace, which took place in Buenos Aires.[20] One of the goals of the meeting was to transform the unilateralist and paternalistic character of the Monroe Doctrine into a multilateral framework for ensuring hemispheric security. Against the backdrop of the militarism building in both Europe and East Asia, Roosevelt was effectively reinstating the notion of hemispheric detachment that guided U.S. statecraft during the nineteenth century. "The madness of a great war in other parts of the world would affect us and threaten our good in a hundred ways," he told the delegates in Buenos Aires. He went on to reassure participants that Americans "stand shoulder to shoulder in our final determination that others who, driven by war madness or land hunger, might seek to commit acts of aggression against us will find a Hemisphere wholly prepared to consult together for our mutual safety and our mutual good."[21]

According to scholar Peter Smith, "the decade of the 1930s stands out as a golden era of U.S. relations with Latin America. . . . Washington withdrew military troops, refrained from intervention, and initiated a process of consultation and cooperation. The United States began treating Latin American nations as sovereign entities, rather than subordinates, as equal partners engaged in the collective promotion of hemispheric interests."[22] Isolationist sentiment played a role in fostering this transition, as did Hoover's and Roosevelt's growing support for principles of anti-imperialism, nonintervention, and self-determination.[23] At the same time, the switch in policy also reflected frustration that persistent U.S. efforts to help stability and democracy take root in the region had yielded little success. Democratic setbacks in Nicaragua and Cuba were particularly sobering given U.S. exertions in both countries. As a consequence, Roosevelt adopted a pragmatic willingness to work with the leaders of the region—even if they governed in autocratic and repressive ways.[24]

The debate over the Ludlow Amendment during the second half of the 1930s made clear just how fully elites and the public alike had embraced isolationist attitudes. Harkening back to a proposal that William Jennings Bryan had made in 1915, Representative Louis Ludlow (D-Indiana) in 1935 proposed a constitutional amendment that would have required that any declaration of war be approved by popular referendum.[25] Ludlow argued to his colleagues that his amendment would do more "to keep American boys out of slaughter pens in foreign countries than any other measure that could be passed. . . . It is based on the philosophy that those who have to suffer and, if need be, to die and to bear the awful burdens and griefs of war should have something to say as to whether war shall be declared."[26] He also contended that it would protect the nation against manipulation by the arms industry, arguing that "as a Christian nation we should arise above the sordid profits of war trade and we should not be a party, even indirectly, to the slaughter of human beings which we are when we furnish munitions and loads to warring nations."[27]

The House took up Ludlow's bill early in 1938, and a fierce debate ensued over whether to bring the proposal from committee to full consideration on the floor. Opinion surveys, which were a new development of the 1930s, revealed that roughly three-quarters of the public supported the Ludlow Amendment.[28] Representative Hamilton Fish III (R-New York) noted as much in supporting the proposal: "Every public poll taken shows that approximately 80 percent of the people favor a referendum before being involved in a foreign war." Fish affirmed that "I have an abiding faith and profound confidence in the American people, and I believe in their right to make this awful decision as to whether they want to go into any foreign war." Representative Robert Crosser (D-Ohio) stated that "either we are for or against democracy. That is the issue. . . . I say let the people rule and that is all that would be made possible by our providing for a referendum vote. To deny that is to deny the principle of popular government."[29] Representative Gerald Boileau (Progressive Party-Wisconsin) offered one of the more pointed interventions in favor of the amendment:

> A referendum was provided for in connection with the administration's farm program. This administration has supported referendums in connection with farm legislation. I submit to the Members of the House that if it is fair and if it is right to submit to a small group of the people, the farmers, the right to determine whether or not they should lead little pigs to slaughter, it is fair and it is right that all of the people should be permitted by a referendum vote to determine whether or not the sons and the daughters of these same farmers, among other citizens, should be led to slaughter upon the battlefields of foreign countries.[30]

Opponents of the bill were no less passionate. President Roosevelt himself fought hard against the proposal, arguing that it would "cripple" the president's ability to conduct statecraft.[31] Although a staunch isolationist, Senator Arthur Vandenberg took a strong stand against the idea of requiring a popular referendum to declare war, remarking that "it would be as sensible to require a town meeting before permitting the fire department to put out a blaze."[32] During the House debate, Representative Sam Rayburn (D-Texas) stated that "if the Congress of the United States in this hour of trouble in this unhappy world should vote to . . . submit this proposed constitutional amendment—and I measure my words when I make this statement—it would make the most tremendous blunder it has ever made since the formation of our Government under the Constitution." Representative Edith Rogers (R-Massachusetts) warned that "every subversive influence in this country, as well as every potentially hostile nation abroad, would be extremely glad to see the Ludlow resolution passed."[33]

In the end, the House voted not to advance the bill. But the opponents won by a relatively small margin, 209 to 188. Overwhelming public support for the Ludlow Amendment and this close call in Congress made clear just how determined Americans were to stay out of the geopolitical troubles building in both Europe and Asia. Roosevelt's secretary of state, Cordell Hull, called the episode "a striking indication of the strength of isolationist sentiment in the United States."[34]

Redefining Neutrality:
Banning Trade with Belligerents

Staying out of trouble abroad was hardly a novel objective of U.S. grand strategy; the nation had been doing just that from its founding era until the imperial turn of the late nineteenth century. What was new, however, was the tightened version of neutrality that the United States adopted during the second half of the 1930s. In effect, the United States abandoned its traditional insistence on maintaining trade with all belligerents in favor of a policy that prohibited U.S. vessels from conducting trade with any nation at war. This more restrictive version of neutrality was meant to inoculate U.S. ships against attack, thereby avoiding the circumstances that drew it into World War I. President Washington's "great rule" of conduct had been to pursue political connections with none but trade with all. During the 1930s, President Roosevelt went a significant step further, coupling geopolitical with commercial isolation to further distance the nation from the risk of entanglement abroad.[35]

The political push to tighten neutrality grew out of the deliberations of the Nye Committee and the beginning of German rearmament. The conclusion that the arms industry had been responsible for U.S. involvement in World War I, in combination with what appeared to be the stirrings of a new round of great-power rivalry in Europe, produced mounting political pressure to introduce an arms embargo against belligerents. Numerous versions of neutrality legislation circulated in Congress during 1935. The issues under discussion included: whether to grant the president a measure of discretion in defining and implementing neutrality; whether to impose blanket restrictions against all belligerents or distinguish between aggressors and victims; and whether to ban only arms exports to belligerents or cut off all trade.[36]

Prominent isolationists were divided among themselves as to which version of neutrality was preferable. Senator Borah and Representative Fish favored adherence to traditional neutrality; the United States should freely exercise its right to trade with any and all. Senator Johnson supported an embargo on arms exports, but opposed broader restrictions. Senator Nye and Senator Vandenberg advocated for a total ban on trade with belligerents, fearful that all of the alternatives risked a repeat of the sequence of events that led to war in 1917.[37]

Congress passed the first neutrality act of the interwar era in 1935, with successive versions becoming more restrictive in step with mounting turmoil abroad.[38] The 1935 law prohibited arms trade with all belligerents, granting the president no discretion in implementing the ban and making no distinction between aggressor and victim. With memories of the sinking of the *Lusitania* in mind, the bill also stipulated that U.S. citizens traveling on ships passing through war zones did so at their own risk.[39] The United States implemented the ban on arms trade against both Italy and Ethiopia after the outbreak of war between them in 1935—despite the fact that the League determined that Italy was the aggressor. In sharing with the Italian ambassador the rationale for the embargo, Secretary of State Hull explained that "the people of this country are in no state of mind to engage in any activities or steps except those primarily looking towards keeping out of war and in a secondary or subordinate sense manifesting proper interest in peace and the shortening of the duration of the war in the light of our obligations under the Kellogg Pact."[40]

The neutrality legislation of 1936 renewed the embargo on arms trade and added a prohibition against loans to belligerents.[41] In a measure aimed at keeping belligerents away from America's neighborhood, it also exempted from the embargo any American republic at war with a country from outside the hemisphere. The act of 1937 further tightened the restrictions and made them permanent.[42] It gave the president the authority to ban *all* trade with belligerents, not just arms. It barred the sale of munitions to neutral countries that intended to transship the goods to belligerents, prohibited U.S. citizens from traveling on belligerent vessels, prohibited U.S. vessels from transporting passengers or goods to belligerents, and banned the arming of U.S. merchantmen. The 1937 act also applied to civil wars, thereby covering the conflict that had broken out between Spain's Republican government and the rebel militia led by General Francisco Franco. The United States imposed the embargo on both parties even though Franco's forces were backed by Germany and Italy, meaning that their victory would advance the fascist cause. The Roosevelt administration was not only refusing to come to the assistance of a like-minded democracy, but also pursuing a policy that knowingly increased the likelihood of a setback for republicanism.

Even as it tightened the terms of trade with belligerents, Congress did establish a vehicle for permitting trade in non-embargoed goods, in part to ease the costs imposed on American exporters by the new restrictions.[43] The bill granted the president the right to authorize "cash and carry" for nonmilitary items. At the president's discretion, belligerents would be able to purchase non-embargoed goods from the United States as long as they paid cash and transported the purchased items on ships of their own or foreign registry. Taken together, these measures were meant to permit some trade with belligerents, but in a way that effectively closed off the possibility that belligerent attacks on American ships could again draw the nation into an armed conflict beyond the Western Hemisphere.[44]

Roosevelt generally went along with these efforts to backstop geopolitical isolation with commercial detachment, at times playing a leading role in shaping and advancing the legislative process.[45] He was focused on domestic economic priorities, and his views on foreign policy were in line with the isolationist mainstream. Taking consequential diplomatic or military steps to counter Germany, Japan, Italy, or Franco-led rebels in Spain was not under active consideration. A more resolute posture that would have run the risk of American entanglement was simply outside the boundaries of political debate. According to Doenecke, "for most of his first two terms, FDR was singularly indifferent to much of the world. He concentrated almost exclusively on his domestic agenda while major powers in Europe and Asia were turning increasingly predatory."[46]

A 1937 survey revealed strong support for neutrality among elites.[47] As discussed earlier, much of the public backed a proposed a constitutional amendment that would have required approval of a declaration of war by popular referendum. Suspicion of "merchants of death" continued to run strong, producing sustained support for the embargo on arms exports even if the ban disadvantaged victims of aggression and republican regimes. Liberals were as adamant as conservatives that rigid isolationism remained the only course. Pacifists, who had so enthusiastically backed the Kellogg-Briand Pact, responded to the progressive dismantlement of the architecture of peace with a disappointment that only strengthened their support for strategic detachment. For the peace movement, according to Doenecke and Wilz, "ignoring the troubles of the rest of the world was not enough. The United States should complete its insulation by cutting economic ties with warring nations as well."[48]

Mainstream Republicans, who had during the 1920s crafted a foreign policy relying heavily on commercial and financial engagement, arrived at the same conclusion. The circumstances drawing the nation into World War I demonstrated that commercial engagement with belligerents was simply too dangerous. Doenecke and Wilz describe this evolution as follows: "The darkening state of world politics led to demands for rigid neutrality legislation. Americans who sought to avoid 'foreign war' wanted laws designed to prevent a collision with any belligerent. Above all, they feared a repetition of the years 1915–1917 when ships carrying supplies to Britain and France became targets of German submarines. The prescription was alluringly simple: at the onset of war anywhere in the world, the United States should simply terminate trade with all contestants."[49]

The Tide Turns:
Roosevelt Opts for Aid-Short-of-War

From 1935 until early 1939, Roosevelt and Congress worked hand in hand to distance the United States from mounting geopolitical tensions abroad. Thereafter, Roosevelt began to change his stance. As described by Herring, "only toward the end of that tumultuous decade, when the reality of war seemed about to touch the United States directly, did a reluctant nation, led by Roosevelt himself, shift course."[50] By the beginning of 1939, he had concluded that even-handed neutrality, by leaving Germany unchecked, could ultimately mean the fall of Britain, an outcome that would imperil U.S. security. If the Axis conquered Europe, Roosevelt saw Africa and Latin America as the next targets. The result, he maintained, would be "the gradual encirclement of the United States by the removal of first lines of defense."[51] Roosevelt began to make the case to Congress and the public that the United States needed to start providing aid to the victims of Nazi aggression, increasingly setting him at odds with the staunch isolationists. Notably, as he sought to outmaneuver the isolationists, he made the case that providing military assistance to Britain, far from drawing the United States into the war, offered the best hope of checking German expansionism and keeping America disentangled from Europe's broadening conflict.[52]

Several developments convinced Roosevelt to begin looking for ways to counter German expansionism by providing military assistance to its opponents. Franco's forces completed their defeat of Spain's republican government early in 1939, prompting Roosevelt to conclude that imposing a blanket arms embargo on aggressor and victim alike had been a mistake.[53] In his Annual Message to Congress on January 4, Roosevelt not only admitted as much, but also hinted that the United States itself might suffer should it continue to stand so apart from growing threats to peace:

> The world has grown so small and weapons of attack so swift that no na-
> tion can be safe in its will to peace so long as any other powerful nation
> refuses to settle its grievances at the council table. . . . We have learned
> that God-fearing democracies of the world which observe the sanctity
> of treaties and good faith in their dealings with other nations cannot
> safely be indifferent to international lawlessness anywhere. . . . At the
> very least, we can and should avoid any action, or any lack of action,
> which will encourage, assist or build up an aggressor. We have learned
> that when we deliberately try to legislate neutrality, our neutrality
> laws may operate unevenly and unfairly—may actually give aid to an
> aggressor and deny it to the victim. The instinct of self-preservation
> should warn us that we ought not to let that happen anymore.[54]

The German invasion of Czechoslovakia in March consolidated Roosevelt's determination to switch from strict neutrality to a policy that would permit military aid to countries fighting fascism. Over the course of 1939, he tried several times to make cash-and-carry less restrictive by enabling the sale of arms to belligerents on a selective basis.[55] Congress resisted, still unwilling to run the risk that allowing U.S. arms to cross the Atlantic could ensnare the country in the war. Members objected to the very notion of taking sides in the conflict. Senator Robert Reynolds (D-North Carolina) asserted that "the real purpose of lifting the arms embargo is definitely to help one of the belligerents and therefore a complete violation of international law and unneutral." Reynolds also challenged Roosevelt's assertion that Nazi Germany, even if it overran Europe, would pose a threat to the United States. In light of America's geographic separation from Europe, it was unnecessary to lift the arms embargo in order to avert a German victory in Europe:

> Even assuming that Germany should be victorious in Europe and could without too much difficulty hold down her victims, the possibility of her coming across 3,000 miles of ocean to meet a fresh nation, especially one with huge resources, a first-class navy, and the means of raising a huge army, is something which I defy any competent military expert to explain in a convincing fashion. Of course theoretically it is possible, as Orson Welles' famous Invasion From Mars was also a theoretical possibility. Intelligent governments, however, do not embark on costly programs on such remote possibilities."[56]

Congress finally relented after the German invasion of Poland on September 1 and the consequent declaration of war by Britain and France two days later. On November 4, Roosevelt signed a revised neutrality law that repealed the arms embargo, effectively permitting Britain and France to purchase armaments on a cash-and-carry basis. The new policy did, however, continue to buffer the United States from direct involvement in the war; U.S. ships were still prohibited from transporting goods of any kind to belligerents. As David Reynolds puts it, "the new neutrality legislation minimized the dangers of America being entangled unwillingly in another European war. Within that framework, however, it opened up the vast material resources of the United States to Britain and France. It was now up to the Allies to make use of the American arsenal."[57]

The neutrality bill of 1939 was the first in a succession of legislative defeats that Roosevelt would deal the still-strong isolationist bloc in Congress as he incrementally stepped up U.S. assistance to countries resisting Germany and Italy. Following the fall of France in June 1940 and the beginning of German air attacks against Britain, Roosevelt implemented further measures. In August, he sidestepped the neutrality law by transferring to Britain fifty older U.S. destroyers in return for U.S. basing rights on British possessions along the Atlantic seaboard and in the Caribbean.[58] In order to avoid a bruising public debate, he proceeded without congressional approval.[59] In September 1940, the administration introduced selective service, the first peacetime draft in the nation's history.[60] While taking these steps, Roosevelt repeatedly reassured the public that he had no intention whatsoever of entering the war. As he told an audience in Boston during an October campaign stop prior to the 1940 election, "while I am talking to you mothers and fathers, I give you one more assurance. I have said this before, but I will say it again, and again and again: Your boys are not going to be sent into any foreign wars."[61]

Over the course of 1941, Roosevelt substantially increased the American contribution to the war effort. He began the year by seeking to rally congressional and public support for more assistance to the allied powers. To his realist arguments about the strategic necessity of preventing the fall of Britain he added broader idealist objectives related to the nation's exceptionalist calling. In his Annual Message on January 6, Roosevelt explicitly deployed Wilsonian themes:

> In the future days, which we seek to make secure, we look forward to a world founded upon four essential human freedoms. The first is freedom of speech and expression. . . . The second is freedom of every person to worship God in his way. . . . The third is freedom from want. . . . The fourth is freedom from fear. . . . That is no vision of a distant millennium. It is a definite basis for a kind of world attainable in our own time and generation. That kind of world is the very antithesis of the so-called new order of tyranny which the dictators seek to create with the crash of a bomb.[62]

Despite staunch resistance from the isolationist camp, Roosevelt in March succeeded in securing congressional approval for Lend-Lease, a program that authorized the president to "sell, transfer title to, exchange, lease, lend or otherwise dispose of" defense articles to any country "whose defense the President deems vital to the defense of the United States." Items approved for transfer included "any weapon, munition, aircraft, vessel, or boat."[63] The United States itself needed to shoulder the costs of many of the items it would transfer, Roosevelt informed Congress, because "the time is near when they will not be able to pay for them all in ready cash. We cannot, and we will not, tell them that they must surrender, merely because of present inability to pay for the weapons which we know they must have."[64]

As with his earlier justifications for providing support to countries fighting the Axis powers, Roosevelt maintained that Lend-Lease would help the nation steer clear of the war. As historian Warren Kimball notes, "publicly and privately as far as can be determined, Roosevelt stoutly maintained that the purpose of Lend-Lease was to keep America out of war."[65] Even so, as discussed below, the isolationist camp mounted a determined effort to block Lend-Lease. Roosevelt again carried the day, with the legislation passing by comfortable margins—60 to 31 in the Senate, and 260 to 165 in the House.[66] Roosevelt also succeeded in ramping up defense spending in 1941—roughly a fourfold increase over 1940—to strengthen defenses at home and to produce the ships, aircraft, and other military items that would be transferred to the belligerents. After Germany invaded the Soviet Union in June, the administration extended the Lend-Lease program to the Soviets.

Although his intent was to restrict overt U.S. involvement to trade embargoes against aggressors and aid-short-of-war to their victims, Roosevelt also edged the United States toward deeper involvement in the conflict. He ran an informal ring of spies to report on developments in both the European and Asian theaters. Members of the group engaged in illegal activities, including gaining unauthorized access to confidential cables.[67] In August, Roosevelt met with British prime minister Winston Churchill on a ship anchored off the coast of Newfoundland. Although Roosevelt rebuffed Churchill's pleas for the United States to enter the war, the two leaders jointly issued the Atlantic Charter, a document laying out their shared vision of a new postwar international order.

During the spring and summer of 1941, Roosevelt dispatched U.S. troops to Greenland and Iceland to ensure that they did not fall into German hands and to facilitate the transport of defense items across the Atlantic. He extended the range of U.S. patrols and authorized the U.S. Navy to report the positions of German vessels in the western Atlantic, enabling U.S. merchantmen to avoid them and the Royal Navy to attack them. Roosevelt soon thereafter quietly approved of U.S. Navy escorts of Atlantic convoys as far east as Iceland, a mission that ultimately led to the exchange of fire between U.S. ships and German submarines.[68]

In May, a German submarine sank a U.S. merchantman crossing the Atlantic. Roosevelt chose not to escalate. In early September, the USS *Greer* and a German U-boat fired upon each other. Thereafter, Roosevelt ordered U.S. ships and aircraft to attack any German or Italian warship operating "in the waters which we deem necessary for our defense." On September 11, he explained to the public that "we have sought no shooting war with Hitler. We do not seek it now. But neither do we want peace so much, that we are willing to pay for it by permitting him to attack our naval and merchant ships while they are on legitimate business. . . . When you see a rattlesnake poised to strike, you do not wait until he has struck before you crush him. These Nazi submarines and raiders are the rattlesnakes of the Atlantic."[69] On October 17, a torpedo attack on the USS *Kearny* took the lives of eleven U.S. sailors, and another attack later that month sank the USS *Reuben James*, killing 100 personnel. During these same months, German submarines also sank a number of U.S. merchantmen.

After the sinking of the *Kearny*, Roosevelt affirmed that the United States would not flinch in its determination to help defend the sea-lanes across the Atlantic. He convinced Congress to approve the arming of U.S. merchantmen and their entry into combat zones; American ships could finally transport American goods to the victims of aggression. But, unlike Wilson in 1917, he did not see Germany's attacks on U.S. ships as a provocation warranting full-scale war. Indeed, even after the sinking of U.S. vessels and the loss of American lives, Roosevelt made clear that he intended to continue restricting the nation's role in the war to the resupply of the Allies:

> The purpose of Hitler's attack was to frighten the American people off the high seas—to force us to make a trembling retreat. . . . None of us wants to burrow under the ground and live in total darkness like a comfortable mole. The forward march of Hitler and of Hitlerism can be stopped – and it will be stopped. Very simply and very bluntly – we are pledged to pull our own oar in the destruction of Hitlerism. . . . Every day that passes we are producing and providing more and more arms for the men who are fighting on actual battlefronts. That is our primary task. And it is the Nation's will that these vital arms and supplies of all kinds shall neither be locked up in American harbors nor sent to the bottom of the sea. It is the Nation's will that America shall deliver the goods.[70]

The Roosevelt administration's response to Japanese aggression in East Asia, like its approach to the European theater, was cautious and incremental. As mentioned above, Roosevelt during the second half of the 1930s chose not to invoke neutrality laws with regard to the fighting taking place on the Asian mainland. Even after Japan's full-scale invasion of China began in 1937, the administration shied away from imposing economic sanctions. Elites and the public alike saw the war as having little or no strategic consequence for the United States.[71]

In the spring of 1940, Roosevelt decided to keep a significant number of warships in Hawaii instead of at their normal home ports on the West Coast.[72] Prompted in part by the increasing prospect of alliance among Tokyo, Berlin, and Rome—which was formalized in September 1940—he in July began to embargo the export to Japan of aviation fuel and high-grade scrap iron. In September, the administration broadened the embargo to include all scrap metal, and in December extended it again to iron ore, pig iron, and steel. Roosevelt also began offering loans and military assistance to China in 1940 and included it in the Lend-Lease program the following year—even though he did rebuff China's request for a formal military alliance.[73] In effect, Roosevelt followed the same strategy in Asia that he did in Europe. He sought to block further expansion by coupling sanctions against aggressors with aid to victims. At the same time, he was intent on limiting the nation's strategic exposure by stopping short of American entry into the war in either theater.

Over the course of 1941, negotiations between Washington and Tokyo went nowhere. Japan refused to abandon its expansive aims, while the United States refused to back off its trade embargo. As tensions with Japan mounted, Roosevelt strengthened the U.S. military presence in the western Pacific, sending additional forces to the Philippines. After the Japanese invaded southern French Indochina in July, the United States cut off oil exports to Japan. With the conflict in China rapidly consuming Japan's already scarce resources and the trade embargo imposed on the country only tightening, Tokyo was determined to expand deeper into Southeast Asia to secure new sources of oil and other war-making materials.

As far as the Navy General Board was concerned, Japan's continuing expansion warranted an American retreat. The board in October advised the secretary of the navy to abandon the Philippines and the Open Door policy, observing that "it appears sound that the strategic military frontiers are at present approximately determined by the line from the Aleutian Islands through the outlying islands of the Hawaiian Group to Samoa."[74] Tokyo, however, had other ideas. Deeming war to be virtually inevitable, Japan launched a surprise attack against Pearl Harbor on December 7. It hoped to deal a blow to the U.S. fleet sufficient to clear the way for Japan to realize its territorial ambitions and establish a zone of hegemonic control that it called the Greater East Asia Co-Prosperity Sphere. The attack immediately extinguished Roosevelt's hopes of keeping the United States out of World War II.

Roosevelt versus America First

Historians continue to debate Roosevelt's true intent. Was his ultimate objective to avoid the nation's involvement in World War II or to guide the United States into the war?[75] On the basis of his actions, his public statements, and his private papers, there is no compelling evidence to confirm the claim that Roosevelt's aid-short-of-war policy masked an intentional effort to orchestrate the nation's entry into the war. As Warren Kimball writes, "no evidence has surfaced to demonstrate that he lied actively and consistently to the American people about his ultimate intentions." In both the European and Asian theaters, Roosevelt's aim was to defeat the Axis powers by offering the nation's financial resources and its war-making capacity—but not its soldiers. According to Kimball, Roosevelt "did not want to join the war against Hitler in the full, participatory sense—with American ground forces used to the fullest. Nor did he want to fight the Japanese. What he wanted was to gain victory and global political influence without paying the price."[76] This interpretation is bolstered by the fact that Roosevelt did not put the economy on a war footing until after Pearl Harbor.

Even though Roosevelt appeared determined to keep the United States out of World War II—and argued vehemently and consistently that aid-short-of-war offered the best means of doing so—he nonetheless was engaged in a pitched political battle with the isolationist camp during 1940 and 1941. Roosevelt's main argument in favor of running the risk of providing military assistance to Britain was the one he had been making since early 1939—that the fall of the British Isles to Nazi Germany would ultimately imperil U.S. security. In one of his signature fireside chats, broadcast on December 29, 1940, Roosevelt confronted the isolationists head-on:

> If Great Britain goes down, the Axis powers will control the continents of Europe, Asia, Africa, Australasia, and the high seas—and they will be in a position to bring enormous military and naval resources against this hemisphere. It is no exaggeration to say that all of us, in all the Americas, would be living at the point of a gun—a gun loaded with explosive bullets, economic as well as military. We should enter upon a new and terrible era in which the whole world, our hemisphere included, would be run by threats of brute force. To survive in such a world, we would have to convert ourselves permanently into a militaristic power on the basis of war economy. Some of us like to believe that even if Great Britain falls, we are still safe, because of the broad expanse of the Atlantic and of the Pacific. But the width of those oceans is not what it was in the days of clipper ships. . . . Even today we have planes that could fly from the British Isles to New England and back again without refueling. . . . Frankly and definitely there is danger ahead—danger against which we must prepare. But we well know that we cannot escape danger, or the fear of danger, by crawling into bed and pulling the covers over our heads.

After laying out why the nation would be imperiled by a victory of the Axis powers, Roosevelt then sought to co-opt the isolationists by insisting that the provision of military assistance to the victims of aggression offered the best hope of keeping the United States out of the war:

> Thinking in terms of today and tomorrow, I make the direct statement to the American people that there is far less chance of the United States getting into war, if we do all we can now to support the nations defending themselves against attack by the Axis than if we acquiesce in their defeat, submit tamely to an Axis victory, and wait our turn to be the object of attack in another war later on. . . . The people of Europe who are defending themselves do not ask us to do their fighting. They

ask us for the implements of war, the planes, the tanks, the guns, the freighters which will enable them to fight for their liberty and for our security. Emphatically we must get these weapons to them in sufficient volume and quickly enough, so that we and our children will be saved the agony and suffering of war which others have had to endure.

"There is no demand for sending an American Expeditionary Force outside our own borders," Roosevelt reassured Americans. "There is no intention by any member of your Government to send such a force. You can, therefore, nail any talk about sending armies to Europe as deliberate untruth." Roosevelt concluded by expropriating the exceptionalist narrative long deployed by isolationists to defend geopolitical detachment: "We must be the great arsenal of democracy. "[77]

Despite these and other reassurances that his policies would keep the country out of harm's way, the isolationist camp mounted stiff resistance to Roosevelt's aid-short-of-war policy. The America First Committee (AFC) was founded in September 1940 to coordinate the activities and messaging of disparate isolationist voices and bodies. Headquartered in Chicago, AFC opened some 450 chapters and subchapters around the country and attracted roughly 800,000 members. The organization released a statement of principles in March 1941 stating that "our first duty is to keep America out of foreign wars. Our entry would only destroy democracy, not save it." The statement advocated "humanitarian aid" to "the suffering and needy people of England and the occupied countries," but stipulated that "not by acts of war abroad but by preserving and extending democracy at home can we aid democracy and freedom in other lands."[78]

AFC attracted prominent politicians, public figures, and corporate leaders—among them Senator Nye, Senator Burton Wheeler (D-Montana), Frank Lloyd Wright, Charles Lindbergh, and Henry Ford. John F. Kennedy, who graduated from college the year AFC was founded, made a donation to the organization, and Gerald Ford, who was studying at Yale Law School, joined the chapter that opened at Yale. Various pro-Axis groups with anti-Semitic leanings, such as the German-American Bund, quietly and indirectly supported the organization. At one of the Bund's rallies in New York City in 1939, speakers denounced "international Jewry" against a backdrop of swastikas, and one banner read: "Stop Jewish Domination of Christian Americans."[79]

AFC itself earned an anti-Semitic reputation, in part due to the prominent role played by Lindbergh, who became one of the organization's most prominent spokespersons. In an antiwar speech Lindbergh delivered in Des Moines in September 1941, he provocatively warned Jewish Americans against supporting U.S. intervention: "Instead of agitating for war, the Jewish groups in this country should be opposing it in every possible way for they will be among the first to feel its consequences. Tolerance is a virtue that depends upon peace and strength. History shows that it cannot survive war and devastations. A few far-sighted Jewish people realize this and stand opposed to intervention. But the majority still do not. Their greatest danger to this country lies in their large ownership and influence in our motion pictures, our press, our radio and our government."[80] According to historian Sarah Churchwell, "Lindbergh had not a word of condemnation for Hitler's violence, insisting that there was aggression on both sides, and both sides were simply bent on preserving their own power. Indeed, he all but said in so many words that as long as some 'white race' was left in undisputed dominion over Europe, he didn't much care which 'white race' it was."[81] Henry Ford was also a well-known member of AFC who openly espoused anti-Semitism and voiced concern about an international Jewish conspiracy.[82] Father Charles Coughlin, who hosted a popular radio program, was another prominent figure who intertwined isolationism and anti-Semitism.

AFC and its sympathizers in Congress waged a fierce campaign to block Lend-Lease, viewing it as a decisive step closer to war. Robert Wood, the chair of AFC and a top executive at Sears Roebuck, announced that the organization would fight Lend-Lease legislation "with all the vigor it can exert." Roosevelt, Wood charged, was "not asking for a blank check, he wants a blank check book with the power to write away your man power, our laws and our liberties."[83] Prompted by AFC, thousands of Americans wrote the White House and members of Congress opposing the legislation.

In testimony before Congress, opponents of Lend-Lease argued that the policy not only risked drawing the United States into the war, but also represented a usurpation of authority by Roosevelt. Lindbergh charged that passing the legislation and giving the president the authority to transfer armaments would be "a step away from the system of government in which most of us in this country believe," while Senator Nye claimed that the bill would grant the president the power of a "dictator." "What I object to most strenuously in the pending bill is the surrender of constitutional powers by the Congress to the President," Nye said. "I am now more alarmed by the encroachments upon our constitutional status, and the impairment of the regular processes of our Government by forces within the government itself, than about possible aggressions against us by potential, but not necessarily probable, foreign foes."[84] Senator Burton Wheeler expressed similar reservations: "If the American people want a dictatorship— if they want a totalitarian form of Government and if they want war—this bill should be steamrollered through Congress, as is the wont of President Roosevelt. Approval of this legislation means war, open and complete warfare. I, therefore, ask the American people before they supinely accept it: Was the last World War worthwhile?"[85]

Such fervent objections from isolationists failed to convince Congress to reject Lend-Lease. The fighting in Europe had taken a turn for the worse. Germany conquered the Low Countries and France in the late spring of 1940, with Italy invading France in June. The Nazis began bombing raids against British cities in September. Along with Roosevelt's impassioned appeals, these developments helped convince many Americans and a solid majority of their elected representatives that the country urgently needed to contribute its resources—even though not its manpower—to the fight. Prior to Pearl Harbor, most Americans still opposed U.S. entry into the war.[86] However, the public was coming to appreciate Roosevelt's insistence that the United States had to help others stand up to aggression, with a poll in February 1941 revealing that only twenty-two percent of the public was opposed to Congress passing Lend-Lease.[87]

The outbreak of hostilities between U.S. naval vessels and German submarines triggered another round of heated debate between the Roosevelt administration and the isolationist camp. As Roosevelt made the case for the continued U.S. escort of convoys and authorized the Navy to attack enemy vessels in defensive maritime zones, AFC spokespersons blamed the U.S. government for the escalation. Senator Nye insisted that "these incidents involving the Greer and the Kearny are incidents very largely of our own making and our own inviting. We cannot order our ships to shoot to destroy the vessels of certain belligerent nations and hope at the same time that the ships of those nations are not going to seek to destroy our ships."[88] John Flynn, chair of the New York chapter of AFC, accused the Roosevelt administration of "asking for these attacks" in order to precipitate war; he warned Americans to wake up to the fact they were "the victims of a conspiracy to hurry them into this war."[89] Two hundred AFC chapters passed resolutions calling on the administration to withdraw U.S. troops from Iceland and order U.S. naval vessels out of combat zones.[90]

Even though direct U.S. entry into the war was not under active consideration, these debates over the appropriate scope of the country's exposure to the conflicts raging in Europe and East Asia were uniquely divisive. According to historian Arthur Schlesinger, "the debate between interventionists and isolationists in 1940–41 had an inner fury that tore apart families, friends, churches, universities, and political parties."[91] As the Wilson administration had done to its opponents during World War I, the Roosevelt administration launched an effort to discredit and marginalize isolationists, including by launching FBI investigations into their background and activities. As the tide of public opinion began to turn, newspapers dropped columnists opposed to Roosevelt's aid-short-of-war approach.[92] The isolationist label began to take on the pejorative connotation so frequently associated with it during the post–World War II era.[93] Indeed, in September 1941 Lindbergh openly complained about the administration's largely successful efforts to malign and marginalize the isolationist camp:

These plans [for war] were of course, to be covered and assisted by the full power of their propaganda. Our theaters soon became filled with plays portraying the glory of war. Newsreels lost all semblance of objectivity. Newspapers and magazines began to lose advertising if they carried anti-war articles. A smear campaign was instituted against individuals who opposed intervention. The terms "fifth columnist," "traitor," "Nazi," "anti-Semitic" were thrown ceaselessly at any one who dared to suggest that it was not to the best interests of the United States to enter the war. Men lost their jobs if they were frankly anti-war. Many others dared no longer speak.[94]

The Japanese strike on Pearl Harbor on December 7, 1941, brought to an abrupt halt the ongoing debate over engagement versus detachment. With the country having been attacked and many Americans killed, the nation resolutely rallied behind Roosevelt's request for a declaration of war on December 8. "Yesterday," Roosevelt began his address to a joint session of Congress the day after the attack, "December 7, 1941—a date which will live in infamy—the United States of America was suddenly and deliberately attacked by naval and air forces of the Empire of Japan. . . . I believe that I interpret the will of the Congress and of the people when I assert that we will not only defend ourselves to the uttermost but will make it very certain that this form of treachery shall never again endanger us."[95] Within an hour of the president's speech, the Senate, by a vote of 82 to 0, and the House, by a vote of 388 to 1, complied with Roosevelt's request to declare war against Japan. The single dissenter in the House was Jeannette Rankin, the Montana pacifist who had also voted against entry into World War I. Three days later, after Berlin and Rome declared war against the United States, Congress approved declarations of war against Germany and Italy in unanimous votes in both houses (Rankin abstained).

America's entry into World War II effectively silenced the isolationist camp. AFC formally disbanded on December 11—but felt compelled to issue a self-serving statement seeking to vindicate its claim that Roosevelt's aid-short-of-war policy would inevitably draw the country into the war: "Our principles were right. Had they been followed, war could have been avoided." Having put down this marker, the organization proceeded to throw its weight behind the war effort, affirming that "no good purpose can now be served by considering what might have been, had our objectives been attained. . . . We are at war. Today, tho [*sic*] there may be many important subsidiary considerations, the primary objective is not difficult to state. It can be completely defined in one word—victory."[96] Isolationist stalwarts individually arrived at the same conclusion. "We have been stepping closer to war for many months," Lindbergh asserted in a statement issued on December 8. "Now it has come and we must meet it as united

Americans regardless of our attitude in the past toward the policy our government has followed. Whether or not that policy has been wise, our country has
been attacked by force of arms and by force of arms we must retaliate."[97]

The Tragic Staying Power of Interwar Isolationism

Against the backdrop of the march of fascism and aggression that afflicted both
Europe and East Asia, the scope and longevity of America's interwar retreat are
quite striking. From the Great Depression until the outbreak of World War II,
isolationism had a virtual lock on the conduct of U.S. strategy. And even after
the war was under way, Roosevelt provided only financial and military assistance
to the victims of aggression, keeping the nation out of war until the Japanese
brought war to the nation. The public shared the president's reluctance to enter
the war. Before the attack on Pearl Harbor, opinion surveys indicate that only
about twenty percent of Americans were in favor of going to war against the Axis
powers.[98]

All the variants of isolationist logic that had informed the nation's identity
and statecraft since its founding were in full swing, contributing to its political
appeal. Yes, the Midwest's farmers and urban progressives may have made the
region a particularly tenacious advocate of steering clear of geopolitical entanglement.[99] And, yes, Republicans were far more likely than Democrats to oppose
Roosevelt's efforts to lift the arms embargo in 1939. But staying out of World War
II was not an issue that pitted one region or party against another; isolationism's
allure was neither sectional nor partisan, but instead enjoyed support across the
political spectrum and across the country. With so many versions of isolationist
logic in play, virtually all Americans could find much to like in steadfast adherence to a policy of neutrality and strategic detachment.

Despite advances in military technology, North America's geographic distance from Europe and Asia was still a prominent plank of the case for isolationism. Roosevelt did recognize that the nation's flanking oceans no longer
provided the natural security that they once did. As he stated in his Annual
Message to Congress in 1939, "the world has grown so small and weapons of attack so swift that no nation can be safe in its will to peace."[100] But Roosevelt used
this new strategic reality to make the case only for aid-short-of-war. Precisely
because a hostile power could in fact reach across the ocean and do the United
States great harm, that hostile power needed to be stopped on its own side of the
ocean. The United States *had* to help others resist the expansive ambitions of
the Axis powers because otherwise war would eventually come America's way.
Cordoning the nation off from trouble abroad had become more difficult, but

the increased capacity of distant nations to harm the U.S. homeland made geo-political detachment even more of a strategic imperative.[101]

This strategic logic, buttressed by Roosevelt's Good Neighbor policy, strengthened the case for hemispheric isolation. "Fortunate it is," Roosevelt affirmed in his 1939 Annual Message, "that in this Western Hemisphere we have, under a common ideal of democratic government, a rich diversity of re-sources and of peoples functioning together in mutual respect and peace. That Hemisphere, that peace, and that ideal we propose to do our share in protecting against storms from any quarter. Our people and our resources are pledged to secure that protection. From that determination no American flinches."[102] Major George Fielding Eliot, a retired army officer who became a prominent commen-tator on foreign policy during the 1930s, agreed: "We cannot bring peace to a warring world; but we can keep the peace of our own part of the world. We cannot settle the troubles of distant continents; but we can prevent the peoples of those continents from transporting their wars to the Western Hemisphere."[103] Hanson Baldwin, a well-known journalist and editor, added his voice to the chorus: "By frittering away our great strength in foreign theatres, we may well de-stroy that impregnability which today means certain security for the American castle."[104] Roosevelt, Fielding, and Baldwin were three of many voices arguing that the United States and its neighbors in the hemisphere should take advan-tage of protective oceans to shield themselves from the dangers of war.

Geopolitical isolation would protect not just the nation's physical security but also its autonomy and sovereignty. The newly discovered multilateralism of the 1920s turned back into the headstrong unilateralism that had come be-fore. Senator Borah, who served as the chair of the Senate Foreign Relations Committee from 1924 to 1933, might have been an ardent supporter of the Kellogg-Briand Pact in the late 1920s. But by the following decade, he, along with other right-wing Republicans, was of a different mind. In an address be-fore the Council on Foreign Relations in 1934, Borah accepted that the United States was engaged in the world in commercial and financial terms. "But in all matters political, in all commitments of any nature or kind, which encroach in the slightest upon the free and unembarrassed action of our people, or which circumscribe their discretion and judgment, we have been free, we have been in-dependent, we have been isolationist."[105] Especially during 1939 to 1941, when the nation was grappling with the prospect of greater involvement in the conflict, the America First Committee stressed that it was defending the nation's inde-pendence in making its case for strict detachment. As Lindbergh put it in his Des Moines speech in September 1941, AFC stood for "neutrality and indepen-dence" and was determined "to maintain the independent American destiny that our forefathers established in this new world." As domestic debate intensified, according to Doenecke, the isolationists increasingly rested their case on the need for "unimpaired freedom of action."[106]

America's redemptive mission provided a further rationale for remaining detached from World War II. As war spread in Europe and Asia, both the political mainstream and the pacifist left argued ever more passionately that the United States needed to remain the last major repository of law, reason, and peace. Roosevelt himself defended the provision of armaments to Britain as the best way to keep the United States out of the war and ensure that it remain "the great arsenal of democracy." Although he and many others were clearheaded in viewing the Axis powers as dangerous aggressors, supporters of AFC often attributed moral equivalence to the belligerents in World War II—just as the isolationists (including Wilson) had initially done during World War I. In their minds, the United States had no cause, moral or otherwise, to intervene in yet another war resulting from the expansionist urges of the Old World. Opponents of aiding Britain and France noted that both were imperial powers not worthy of American support. "We are not being invited into a campaign to defend powers which can properly be called democratic powers," Senator Nye insisted in 1938. "The defense of the British and French Empires, were we to aid in it, would involve the continued subjugation of hundreds of millions of black and brown peoples."[107] In his 1935 book *Road to War*, Walter Millis argued that World War I had been the result of "the ceaseless, intricate, and insane game of European diplomacy."[108] Even though Millis eventually became a proponent of U.S. involvement in the fight against the Axis powers, *Road to War* was a bible of sorts for isolationists seeking to keep the country out of World War II.[109]

Entry into the war was not only unnecessary, it would also compromise America's unique experiment in political and economic liberty. On the left, the *New Republic* opined that "you cannot end war by waging war. On the contrary, nothing is more likely than that the United States would go fascist through the very process of organizing to defeat fascist nations."[110] Similar worries came from the right, with former president Hoover telling the Council on Foreign Relations in 1938 that war and economic centralization would mean that "step by step more force and coercion must be applied until all liberty—economic and personal and political—is lost."[111] Senator Nye, participating in a radio debate in 1938, agreed: "The one sure way to kill off democracy in the United States is to enter another war." Lindbergh shared the same sentiment, arguing that the administration was using the prospect of war "to justify the restriction of congressional power, and the assumption of dictatorial procedures on the part of the president and his appointees."[112] "If we enter the fighting for democracy abroad, we may end by losing it at home," he warned. "This is the test before America now. This is the challenge—to carry on Western civilization."[113]

Isolationists on the left and right differed on the nature of the economic threat that would accompany entry into the war, but they were equally adamant that staying out of the conflict would advance the nation's economic interests. Liberal isolationists and progressives feared that war would drain resources away from the New Deal, magnify the political power of big business, increase the risk of monopoly capitalism, and stand in the way of domestic reform and social advancement. Senator Robert La Follette, Jr. (R/Progressive Party-Wisconsin), called for directing resources to works programs rather than warships, predicting that "if the United States gears its productive machinery to an expanding armament program, and if that expansion stops, there will be a depression such as the world has never experienced."[114] He spoke bluntly about his concerns on the floor of the Senate: "I should like to say to my liberal and progressive friends in America who saw in defense and war a means of achieving their social and economic aspirations for this Nation that they are being proved tragically wrong. The New Deal is very sick, and the latest bulletin from its bedside is that the patient is sinking fast."[115]

In contrast, conservatives feared excessive political interference in the economy, if not an overweening federal authority that would jeopardize fundamental economic and civic freedoms. War, conservative isolationists claimed, would risk that capitalism give way to creeping socialism.[116] Senator Robert Taft (R-Ohio) warned in 1939 that should the country be entangled in a major conflict, "the additional powers sought by the President . . . would create a socialist dictatorship which it would be impossible to dissolve when the war ended."[117] In June 1941, Malcolm Muir, the publisher of *Newsweek*, noted the "serious apprehension in many quarters that while dictatorship is being fought abroad, the price of war may be state socialism at home."[118]

The isolationists exploited anti-immigrant sentiment, ethnic tensions, and concern about the enemy within—Americans with dual loyalties—to make their case for staying out of the war. AFC members charged that proponents of U.S. intervention were British sympathizers, many of them misled by British propaganda to support an imperial power that was oppressing the Irish and many other peoples. As Lindbergh warned, "we know that England is spending great sums of money for propaganda in America during the present war. . . . But our interest is first in America; and as Americans, it is essential for us to realize the effort that British interests are making to draw us into their war."[119] American Jews, some isolationists charged, were more concerned about their brethren in Europe than the welfare of their own country; they should not be allowed to push the country into an ill-advised war. After Germany attacked the Soviet Union in June 1941, proponents of entry into the war were labeled communist sympathizers.[120] The isolationists were exploiting ethnic and political tensions at home to keep the nation from entanglement abroad.

Finally, pacifism, including Christian pacifism, played its own role in keeping the United States out of World War II. Pacifists were not strict isolationists; most wanted the United States, in the words of Andrew Preston, "to lead the world to a better, warless world." In this respect, they continued the tradition of "isolationist internationalism" that emerged in the 1920s. But pacifists opposed U.S. entry into the war and thus strengthened the isolationist consensus. As Preston notes, "the failure of Wilsonianism, followed by suspicions that the war had been fought to ensure profits for bankers and weapons manufacturers and not to make the world safe for democracy, reinvigorated the faith-based peace movement. For the next twenty years, Christian pacifism was in the ascendance. No longer could one support a war to end all wars. After World War I, this was no longer an acceptable, even glorious paradox but an impossible, hateful contradiction."[121]

* * *

The Japanese attack on Pearl Harbor readily undermined and discredited these multiple variants of isolationist logic and the hold they exercised on American politics. Literally overnight, the country unified behind entry into World War II. The declaration of war against Japan on December 8 drew only one dissenting vote, and AFC disbanded within days and threw its weight behind the war. An opinion poll revealed that ninety-seven percent of the public supported the declaration of war against Japan.[122]

Despite the nation's about-face, Roosevelt remained wary of an isolationist comeback, especially after Republicans did well in the 1942 midterm elections. "Anybody who thinks that isolationism is dead in this country is crazy," he quipped. "As soon as this war is over, it may well be stronger than ever."[123] The nation's isolationist turn after the close of World War I may have given Roosevelt good reason to fear another retreat, but his concerns proved to be misplaced. After the close of World War II, voices calling for full-scale demobilization and the return home of all U.S. troops did emerge. The onset of the Cold War, however, quickly extinguished the urge to return to hemispheric isolation. Indeed, the United States by the second half of the 1940s had become the chief architect and defender of a wide range of multilateral institutions and it maintained troops in both Europe and Asia to help keep the peace and contain the Soviet Union and the spread of communism. Pearl Harbor endured as the historical inflection point at which a durable brand of U.S. internationalism effectively ended isolationism's long run.

Roosevelt's concerns about another inward turn are, however, readily understandable—and not just because of the backlash against World War I. He presided over the country at a time when the isolationist consensus was virtually unbreakable. The greater the expansive ambition of the Axis powers, the firmer the conviction that the United States needed to cordon itself off from trouble abroad. Even after Imperial Japan in 1937 and Nazi Germany in 1939 revealed the scope of their aggressive intent, the United States kept its distance. Roosevelt did end the arms embargo in 1939, shepherd Lend-Lease through Congress early in 1941, and soon thereafter authorize the U.S. Navy to help protect Atlantic convoys. Nonetheless, that the United States, prior to the attack on Pearl Harbor, was able to muster only these limited responses to the simultaneous emergence of great-power aggressors in Europe and Asia was a sure sign of the staying power of the isolationist consensus.

Isolationism's ideological and political strength stemmed in significant part from its historical pedigree and its role as an anchor of the nation's identity. Indeed, several developments magnified the political resonance of isolationism's multiple logics. Between 1898 and 1919, Americans had tried both realist and idealist brands of internationalism—and rebuffed both. The hemispheric hegemony acquired in 1898 remained; after all, that had been a strategic objective of the Founders. But following the Senate's rejection of the Versailles Treaty, the United States shunned geopolitical commitments outside the Western Hemisphere and returned to a foreign policy focused on overseas commerce. From the close of World War I until the Great Depression, successive administrations chose to wield U.S. influence through economic engagement and pacts of restraint dependent upon the goodwill of their signatories.

The Great Depression decisively ended this new era of dollar diplomacy as Hoover and Roosevelt focused near-exclusive attention on the domestic economy. The vilification of the financial community and the arms industry that grew out of the Nye Committee also created new political obstacles to substituting commercial engagement for geopolitical entanglement. So, too, was the multilateralist idealism of the 1920s snuffed out as Japan, Germany, and Italy all abandoned voluntary restraint—and paid virtually no price for doing so. The U.S. reaction to repeated acts of aggression was to sever commercial links to belligerents to avoid any strategic exposure. Geopolitical entanglement was off the table. It followed that commercial engagement had to be cut off lest it draw the country into war. The United States cornered itself into being a passive bystander in the face of momentous danger.

Isolationism served the United States well for much of its history, contributing to its speedy and unmolested ascent. But this past misled the country during the 1930s, prompting a geopolitical retreat at a time when U.S. engagement was desperately needed to check fascism and the genocidal ambition of Nazi Germany. Prior to World War I, Britain had been the global guardian of last resort; Pax Britannica was a key source of financial and geopolitical stability. That task fell to the United States after World War I, but the country refused to assume the responsibilities that came with its newly acquired power.

That abdication—until it was very late—left unchecked not just successive bouts of aggression, but also direct threats to the survival of liberal democracy throughout large swaths of Europe and Asia. Americans may have convinced themselves that the preservation of their exceptional mission required detachment from the dangerous march of fascism. But this assumption represented a delusional search for strategic immunity. If the Axis powers had succeeded in taking control of Eurasia, which they may well have done had the United States not entered the war, America's own security and way of life would have been imperiled. Roosevelt recognized as much—precisely why he ran the political and strategic risks of sending military aid to the Allies. But it took the bombing of Pearl Harbor to finally overwhelm America's isolationist instincts and bring the United States into the war. Japan's attack was responsible for the ultimate demise of American isolationism—and the defeat of Nazism and fascism along with it.

PART III

THE RISE AND FALL OF LIBERAL INTERNATIONALISM, 1941–2020

Part III of this book covers the era of liberal internationalism. Americans had soundly rejected the realist brand of internationalism that had been put on offer in 1898. They did the same to the idealist internationalism of the Wilsonian era. By merging these two alternatives to isolationism— marrying U.S. power to international partnership and justifying foreign entanglement in terms of American interests as well as ideals—liberal internationalism proved far more durable. Indeed, it succeeded in providing a solid political foundation for the nation's global engagement during World War II, the Cold War, and into the twenty-first century. The result was *Pax Americana*—a rules-based international order designed and defended by the United States. If the era of isolationism was about running away from the world and transforming it only by example, the era of liberal internationalism was about running the world and transforming it through American power and purpose.

Liberal internationalism rested on a bipartisan coalition that backed the formula of marrying power to partnership. As a consequence, it enjoyed presidential and congressional support regardless of which party was in control of the White House and Capitol Hill. Developments both abroad and at home encouraged Republicans and Democrats alike to fashion a centrist compact supportive of liberal internationalism. The attack on Pearl Harbor had burst the myth of strategic immunity. Meeting the urgent threat posed by the Axis powers and then the Soviet Union required the projection of U.S. power to distant theaters as well as the entangling alliances needed to ensure forward defense and to amass countervailing force. The protection and spread of democracy and capitalism would advance the nation's interests as well as its redemptive mission. At home, economic growth promoted ideological moderation, and both realists and idealists could find much to like in a brand of international engagement that was about the pursuit of both interests and ideals. The population mobility demanded by industrialization also eased sectional divides, contributing to the emergence of a stable political center. Liberal internationalism enjoyed both bipartisan and cross-sectional support, enabling it to push isolationism and unilateralism to the margins of American politics.

The exertions of the early Cold War—the founding of NATO, U.S. participation in the Korean War, the deployment of additional U.S. troops to Europe—awakened isolationist voices that tested the bipartisan compact behind liberal internationalism. So, too, did the Vietnam War provoke intense domestic opposition and calls for the United States to step back from an excess of foreign entanglements. Nonetheless, liberal internationalism ultimately proved sufficiently durable to outlast the Cold War, sustained in significant part by the Soviet threat.

The collapse of the Soviet Union thereafter cleared the way for liberal internationalism's demise. Absent the disciplining effects of a transcendent external threat, Democrats and Republicans began to go their separate ways. Democrats, long drawn toward idealism, became the party of partnership; Republicans, long the guardians of realism, became the party of power and unilateralism. After decades of a relatively consistent brand of American statecraft, U.S. grand strategy began to experience dramatic swings as political control changed hands in Washington. Growing inequality and the economic stagnation of the working class contributed to deepening polarization, the return of sharp sectional divides, and the erosion of the moderate center. The attacks of September 11 restored bipartisanship in only a fleeting way, with the nation's resulting wars in Afghanistan and Iraq soon exacerbating the partisan divide over matters of statecraft.

American grand strategy began to suffer not just from inconstancy but also overreach. Unchecked by either a peer competitor or the moderation that accompanied bipartisanship, the United States tried to do too much. With the Cold War over and the nation still guided by the activist and expansive version of exceptionalism that took root in the 1940s, Americans understood the completion of their messianic mission to be in reach. Autocracy and communism had been defeated; political freedom and economic liberty were on the march. Democrats invested in too much partnership and Republicans in too much power, saddling the nation with a surfeit of international obligations for which there has been scant public support. The result has been a growing mismatch between America's international commitments and the political will to uphold those commitments.

Amid the far-reaching changes taking place abroad and at home, Presidents Bill Clinton (1993–2001), George W. Bush (2001–2009), and Barack Obama (2009–2017) all tried, through different approaches and with varying degrees of success, to sustain *Pax Americana* and uphold the international order built during the era of liberal internationalism. President Donald Trump then changed course. Supported by many Americans who deemed themselves to be on the losing end of globalization and liberal internationalism, Trump was determined to bring down rather than salvage the order erected during America's watch. Indeed, the isolationism, unilateralism, protectionism, and racism accompanying his America First approach to statecraft were far more reminiscent of U.S. grand strategy before Pearl Harbor than after.

The collapse of liberal internationalism and Trump's return to America First raise profound questions about what brand of U.S. statecraft comes next. The task ahead entails melding America's isolationist and internationalist traditions to craft a grand strategy that both enjoys domestic support and advances the nation's security and prosperity.

World War II and the Cold War: The Era of Liberal Internationalism

The Onset of Liberal Internationalism

The third era of U.S. grand strategy began at the end of 1941. The heyday of iso-lationism ran from 1789 to 1898. Between 1898 and 1941, the nation made a run at both realist and idealist brands of internationalism, but neither garnered sufficient political support to endure. The attack on Pearl Harbor then opened the era of liberal internationalism, leading to the durable melding of the realist and idealist alternatives that had been in play since the turn of the century. Entry into World War II set the stage for a sea change in U.S. grand strategy: Americans were ready to embrace both power and partnership in the service of defeating fascism, defending democracy, and shaping a peaceful postwar order.

On the power front, the United States during World War II projected its ge-opolitical might across the Atlantic and the Pacific, contributing awesome re-sources to the allied cause. The war effort entailed a massive mobilization of manpower and industrial capacity. Some sixteen million Americans served in the armed forces. In 1939, American factories produced around 2,000 warplanes. By the end of the war, U.S. production lines had turned out some 300,000 military aircraft.[1] On the partnership front, the country joined the fight as a full-fledged ally, not an "associated power." American troops were integrated into allied command structures. Even before entering the war, Roosevelt met with British prime minister Winston Churchill and committed the United States to a leading role in building a cooperative postwar order based open trade, the peaceful reso-lution of disputes, and the right of all peoples to choose their own government. The Atlantic Charter they together drafted would go on to inform the aims of the United Nations which was founded at the war's end.

Americans liked what they got from this marriage of interests and ideals, responding to military victory with celebration and a surge in national confidence—a far cry from the regretful and partisan postmortem that followed

World War I. Against the backdrop of an emerging threat from the Soviet Union, the nation's commitment to liberal internationalism endured.

Americans stood by their new willingness to project power and assume strategic responsibilities well beyond their own shores. Far from bringing home all U.S. troops, Roosevelt's successors maintained a global network of overseas bases that sustained a global range of commitments, often backed up by the forward presence of U.S. forces. By one count, the United States had some 2,000 base sites around the world at the close of World War II.[2] The fighting may have ended, but U.S. forces had important peacetime responsibilities in Germany, Japan, and a host of other countries. As of July 1947, the U.S. Army stood at 684,000 personnel, 373,000 of whom were serving abroad.[3]

Despite the continued overseas presence of U.S. forces, the end of World War II initially led to a major military demobilization. Between 1945 and 1947, defense spending fell from $81 billion to $13 billion and the number of military personnel declined from 12.1 to 1.6 million.[4] But the sharp downward trend in defense outlays did not last long. The heating up of the Cold War prompted the remilitarization of U.S. statecraft. The Soviet Union blockaded Berlin in June 1948 and tested an atomic weapon in August 1949. Mao Zedong's forces won China's civil war, leading to the establishment of the People's Republic of China in October 1949 and heightening U.S. concern about the potential for communism's further spread.

These developments strengthened the hand of hardliners like Paul Nitze, the State Department strategist who helped orchestrate the preparation of NSC-68, the blueprint for U.S. grand strategy adopted in 1950. NSC-68 consolidated support for a more confrontational stance toward the Soviet Union than had been advocated by George Kennan, one of the State Department's experts in Russia and the "father" of containment. In Kennan's "Long Telegram," which he dispatched from the embassy in Moscow early in 1946, Kennan had laid out a version of containment that aimed primarily at assisting the political and economic recovery of Western Europe and Japan and exploiting splits within the communist bloc.[5] He opposed confronting the Soviet Union with a major military buildup, presuming that it would only fuel the Kremlin's fears of encirclement and intensify U.S.-Soviet rivalry.

In contrast, Nitze strongly supported the militarization of containment; NSC-68 cleared the way for a major conventional and nuclear buildup. Kennan had wanted the United States to focus on defending key centers of power and warned against military involvement on the Asian mainland. Nitze's new blueprint took a much more expansive view of U.S. interests, contending that "a defeat of free institutions anywhere is a defeat everywhere."[6] Prompted by this strategic logic and North Korea's invasion of South Korea in 1950, the United States soon found itself fighting on the Asian mainland. President Harry

Truman (1945–1953) dispatched U.S. troops to the Korean peninsula without asking Congress for a declaration of war, justifying his action by claiming that he was acting under UN auspices to respond to an act of aggression. "In these circumstances I have ordered United States air and sea forces to give the Korean Government troops cover and support," Truman announced on June 27, 1950.[7]

Some members of Congress vehemently objected, with Senator Taft claiming that the president was overstepping his constitutional authority.[8] Others gave Truman a green light. Senator Tom Connally (D-Texas) reportedly told him that "if a burglar breaks into your house you can shoot him without going down to the police station and getting permission. You might run into a long debate in Congress which would tie your hands completely. You have the right to do it as Commander-in-Chief and under the UN Charter."[9] Truman proceeded as he saw fit.[10] Between 1950 and the end of the Korean War in 1953, some 1.8 million U.S. military personnel fought to preserve the independence of South Korea. Prosecuting the Cold War would entail not only deploying U.S. forces abroad in peacetime, but also sending U.S. troops into battle.

Americans maintained their new enthusiasm for not just projecting power but also sustaining international partnership. The United States upheld many of its foreign commitments through international agreements, not by going it alone. Washington erected a grid of treaty-based military pacts, overcoming the aversion to peacetime alliance that had persisted since George Washington reneged on the alliance with France in 1793. Among these new pacts were the Inter-American Treaty of Reciprocal Assistance (Rio Pact), which took effect in 1948, the North Atlantic Treaty Organization, founded in 1949, and the Southeast Asia Treaty Organization, established in 1954. Washington also concluded a host of other defense pacts—including with Japan, Australia, New Zealand, and the Philippines in 1951.

The enthusiasm for international partnership applied not just to the formation of military alliances. The United States took the lead in designing and rallying international support for the establishment of the United Nations. The Senate had rejected the League of Nations each of the three times it voted on the Versailles Treaty. The United Nations, which confronted the United States with responsibilities similar to those associated with membership in the League, won approval in the Senate by a vote of 89 to 2. The United States similarly led the effort to construct the Bretton Woods system for managing international monetary affairs—a stark contrast with Roosevelt's "bombshell" message that undermined the World Economic Conference in 1933. Washington abandoned the stinginess and protectionism of the 1930s, instead launching the Marshall Plan in 1948 to help rebuild Europe. In addition, it sought to stabilize and liberalize international trade through the General Agreement on Tariffs and Trade, which also took effect in 1948.

This new marriage of power and partnership aimed at three broad objectives. First, the chief geopolitical goal of American grand strategy was to prevent the domination of Eurasia by a hostile power. In the words of historian Melvyn Leffler, "never again could the United States permit an adversary or coalition of adversaries to gain control of the preponderant resources of Europe and Asia." That goal emerged during World War II and remained central to the nation's Cold War strategy of containing the Soviet Union. Second, the United States sought to promote an open trading order. American officials tended to see economic nationalism and mercantilist trade policies as having contributed to the onset of World War II—hence the need for an open trading system that would benefit all democracies and counter the logic of zero-sum competition. An open economic order would also promote growth and prosperity in the United States and other capitalist democracies. Again quoting Leffler, "never again could the United States allow the world economy to be constricted and distorted by artificial restraints and discriminatory practices."[11] Third, liberal internationalism sought to preserve and extend the democratic way of life. To be sure, in the service of checking communism amid the Cold War, the United States partnered with numerous autocratic and repressive regimes. Nonetheless, liberal internationalism was about not only advancing the security and prosperity of the United States and its main allies, but also protecting and spreading democratic institutions and values. It provided a pathway for the country to pursue its exceptionalist calling and fulfill its messianic mission.

These three objectives served as guideposts for U.S. grand strategy from the 1940s into the twenty-first century. The United States maintained a global network of military bases, with hundreds of thousands of forces on station to contain communism, uphold alliances, and defend *Pax Americana*. Between 1948 and 1991, U.S. forces engaged in forty-six military interventions.[12] America's enthusiasm for institutionalized multilateralism continued, as did its passion for free trade. During the second half of the twentieth century, the United States proceeded to conclude a raft of bilateral trade agreements and regional pacts, and threw its weight behind successive rounds of global trade negotiations. Washington also sought to expand the footprint of democracy, regularly using its geopolitical and economic leverage to encourage liberal change. Over the course of the Cold War, the United States attempted on over seventy occasions to topple other nations' governments—most often through covert means.[13] The primacy of geopolitical objectives meant that these attempts at regime change were not always in the service of installing democratic governments. Nonetheless, one of the nation's chief objectives throughout the Cold War was to export political and economic liberty to unfree portions of the world. America's embrace of a more activist conception of its redemptive mission was at the core of the formulation and implementation of liberal internationalism.

Bipartisanship and the New Exceptionalism

As he laid a political foundation for a new brand of American engagement in the world, Roosevelt was mindful of the partisan animosity that had foiled Woodrow Wilson's bid to forge a durable internationalism. He self-consciously reached out to Republicans as he sought to wean the country away from isolationism. In 1940, he appointed two prominent Republicans to his cabinet: Henry Stimson, who had served as Hoover's secretary of state, became the secretary of war; and Frank Knox, who was the Republican nominee for vice president in 1936, became the secretary of the navy. Roosevelt enlisted Wendell Willkie, the Republican he defeated in the 1940 election, to help build internationalism among Republicans. He also ensured that Republicans were included in the Senate advisory committee formed to provide guidance on the creation of the United Nations and in the delegation that went to San Francisco in 1945 to finalize the UN Charter. Roosevelt had help from church communities in building bipartisan support for the UN. Christian pacifists were hardly enthusiastic about the nation's entry into World War II, but they were firmly behind the effort to establish a world body that, under U.S. leadership, would advance peace and justice.[14]

Socio-economic change further facilitated the emergence of a bipartisan compact behind liberal internationalism that outlasted Roosevelt's deliberate efforts to reach across the aisle. The war and the postwar boom fueled rising prosperity for many Americans, easing class tensions and contributing to growing support for economic openness and the liberalization of trade. The advance of industrialization led to an unprecedented mixing of the American population as workers flocked to new production lines, ports, and other nodes of growing economic activity. Such mobility decreased the political salience of sectionalism as the nation's regions became more politically heterogeneous and began sending to Congress balanced bipartisan delegations. Economic growth, mobility, and political heterogeneity helped advance ideological moderation.[15] These socio-economic and political trends contributed to what Arthur Schlesinger dubbed the "vital center."[16]

Roosevelt's political tact and the emergence of the "vital center" set the stage for the chief source of liberal internationalism's staying power: the successful recasting of the nation's exceptionalist mission and the crafting of a grand strategy that balanced realist and idealist objectives. Direct threats to the nation's security necessitated global engagement, which in turn would afford the United States the opportunity to advance its messianic mission. By resting the case for entanglement on strategic imperative while also tapping into a core element of America's identity and narrative dating to the founding era, Roosevelt and his Cold War successors endowed liberal internationalism with immediate appeal to realists and idealists alike. A grand strategy that rested on equal parts power and partnership was especially important given that Republicans and Democrats had followed divergent ideological paths since the late nineteenth century. Beginning with McKinley, Republicans had tilted toward realpolitik and unilateralism. The era of Bryan and Wilson set Democrats on a more idealist trajectory that favored diplomacy and multilateralism. Liberal internationalism, by marrying power and partnership and aligning the nation's interests with its ideals provided a foundation for a durable bipartisan compact on issues of statecraft.

A more activist notion of America's exceptionalist calling had been on offer since the end of the nineteenth century. As the realists had argued in 1898 and the idealists in 1917, the United States could no longer fulfill its mission of reforming the world by remaining aloof from it. Technology had compromised the strategic immunity afforded by protective oceans, and the United States had become too engaged in global affairs to turn its back on the world. Leading only by example was no longer enough. Accordingly, Americans would have to spread their experiment in political and economic liberty through activism and intervention, at once changing the world and making it safe for American engagement now that the nation could no longer afford to shun foreign entanglement. Since the world could not be redeemed by American example, it would have to be redeemed by American action.

This new version of the exceptionalist narrative failed to congeal prior to 1941; McKinley's statecraft was too much about asserting U.S. power and Wilson's too much about asserting U.S. ideals, denying them both a sustainable brand of internationalism. But after Pearl Harbor, the United States successfully and durably transitioned from exemplar to crusader state. Roosevelt and his successors succeeded where McKinley and Wilson fell short because they understood the need to merge realist and idealist strains of statecraft and forge a new version of American exceptionalism around this melding of power and partnership.

The rhetorical linkage between the nation's interests and ideals began immediately after the bombing of Pearl Harbor. When Roosevelt asked Congress for a declaration of war the day after the attack, he warned that "the very life and safety of our Nation" were at stake. The United States was entering World War II to defeat urgent threats to its security and prosperity. But Roosevelt also went on to call upon the "righteous might" of the American people and pledged that "we will not only defend ourselves to the uttermost but will make it very certain that this form of treachery shall never again endanger us."[17] America's war aims were at once narrowly realist and expansively messianic. On one hand, the Axis powers had to be defeated to prevent a global balance of power that would favor fascism and imperil the United States and its way of life. On the other hand, the fascist powers had to be occupied and reborn as democratic stakeholders to ensure "they never again endanger us."

A similar balance between realist and idealist impulses shaped Roosevelt's approach to crafting a postwar order. He initially wanted to avoid the codified formality and commitments associated with institutions like the League of Nations, preferring an informal grouping of great powers known as the Four Policemen. The United States, Britain, the Soviet Union, and China would collectively manage the international system, each taking special responsibility for its own sphere of influence. Under pressure from U.S. colleagues as well as foreign leaders, Roosevelt eventually acquiesced to the establishment of the United Nations. Nonetheless, he made sure that the great powers exercised outsized influence in the world organization and rebuffed calls for a joint UN force—in no small part to safeguard U.S. sovereignty and ensure that U.S. participation could pass muster in the Senate. Roosevelt was committed to building a new international architecture that held out hope of realizing the more just, peaceful, and democratic world envisaged by the Founders. But he was always mindful of geopolitical and political realities. "He is after workable minimums, not impossible maximums," a journalist wrote of his plans for the postwar order after interviewing the president in 1943.[18]

The same amalgam of interests and ideals shaped U.S. strategy throughout the Cold War. The United States had a paramount geopolitical interest in preventing Soviet expansion, but was also dedicated to ensuring that democratic capitalism triumphed over autocratic socialism. When President Truman in 1947 asked Congress to help prevent the spread of communism by approving financial assistance to Greece and Turkey, he began by stressing "the gravity of the situation" and the threat posed to the "national security" of the country. But he also drew a clear link between the nation's security and the fulfillment of its founding mission. The United States, he affirmed, had an obligation to create "conditions in which we and other nations will be able to work out a way of life free from coercion. . . . The free peoples of the world look to us for support in maintaining their freedoms. If we falter in our leadership, we may endanger the peace of the world—and we shall surely endanger the welfare of this Nation."[19]

The linkage between interests and ideals continued once the Cold War was in full swing. According to NSC-68, the chief threat to the United States stemmed from inescapable power realities: "Any substantial further extension of the area under the domination of the Kremlin would raise the possibility that no coalition adequate to confront the Kremlin with greater strength could be assembled. It is in this context that this Republic and its citizens in the ascendancy of their strength stand in their deepest peril." The document then asserted that at stake was the "destruction not only of this Republic but of civilization itself. . . . The assault on free institutions is world-wide now." NSC-68 went on to make the case for not just resisting Soviet expansion, but also redoubling efforts to complete the nation's redemptive mission: "In a shrinking world, which now faces the threat of atomic warfare, it is not an adequate objective merely to seek to check the Kremlin design, for the absence of order among nations is becoming less and less tolerable. This fact imposes on us, in our own interests, the responsibility of world leadership. It demands that we make the attempt, and accept the risks inherent in it, to bring about order and justice by means consistent with the principles of freedom and democracy."[20]

The intermingling of realism and idealism, of power and partnership, of interests and ideals—this formula provided the ideological and political underpinnings of liberal internationalism and ensured its durability. Constructing and defending Pax Americana was a strategic imperative, a moral obligation, and a fulfillment of America's historic destiny.

As scholars of American foreign policy have argued, a proclivity to overreach was a logical consequence of a grand strategy that rested on an expansive notion of the nation's exceptionalist mission.[21] Considering the defeat of free institutions anywhere to be a defeat everywhere was a recipe for trying to do too much. Secondary and tertiary priorities were mistaken for vital ones, and reputational concerns at times blurred the identification of core interests. In the service of fighting communism wherever and whenever it showed signs of spreading, the United States on occasion partnered with regimes that were far from democratic. The scope and longevity of the Vietnam War, the nation's overkill nuclear arsenal, America's support for governments in the Western Hemisphere and beyond that grossly violated the human rights of their citizens—these were clear examples of the strategic excess fueled in part by the nation's messianic objectives.

Nonetheless, the liberal internationalism of the Cold War era, precisely because its idealist aspirations were moderated by realist restraint, ultimately produced a grand strategy that was balanced and effective enough to sustain popular support and achieve the paramount U.S. objectives of containing and eventually facilitating the demise of Soviet power and ideology. Throughout the Cold War, American ambition was held in check by the presence of a formidable geopolitical and ideological counterweight. In addition, nuclear weapons encouraged caution. The United States was keen to spread its republican values, but in the end exercised pragmatism, patience, and restraint as it awaited the internal collapse of its peer competitor.

Isolationist Temptations

The bipartisan support for liberal internationalism that congealed during Roosevelt's presidency, although it ebbed and flowed, continued through the end of the Cold War. The durability of the compact behind liberal internationalism was strengthened by the Soviet threat, which helped to engender political discipline of the sort that emerged during World War II. Senator Vandenberg, who served as chair of the Committee on Foreign Relations from 1947 to 1949, famously and repeatedly warned that politics must stop "at the water's edge," exhorting his colleagues to set partisanship aside when it came to the conduct of statecraft.[22] Congress generally rose to the occasion, with bipartisan voting on foreign policy becoming the norm during the Cold War era.[23] As then-senator Hillary Clinton put it in 2003, "for more than a half a century, we know that we prospered because of a bipartisan consensus on defense and foreign policy."[24] Pearl Harbor brought to a definitive end the bipartisan consensus that had long sustained isolationism. It also cleared the way for the bipartisan compact that then sustained liberal internationalism during the long decades of the Cold War.[25]

Despite its durability and longevity, the Cold War internationalist consensus was tested by isolationist impulses. The scholar Eric Nordlinger is generally correct that after the outbreak of the Korean War, "isolationist ideas went into near-total eclipse."[26] Nonetheless, amid the heating up of the Cold War in the late 1940s and early 1950s, the Truman administration did meet resistance as it sought to commit additional economic and military resources to the containment of communism. The Vietnam War similarly provoked an isolationist resurgence. In the end, however, liberal internationalism ultimately weathered these tests, demonstrating the staying power of the internationalist consensus that had emerged in the early 1940s.

The Early Cold War

After the close of World War II, Americans were ready for a respite and major reduction in the burdens of foreign entanglement.[27] When Truman in 1947 sought to provide economic assistance to Greece and Turkey to help them resist communism, he faced public skepticism as well as staunch opposition from members of Congress opposed to foreign aid and deeper U.S. involvement abroad. He felt compelled to unfurl the Truman Doctrine, delivering a speech that deliberately overstated the threat posed by the Soviet Union in order to rally Congress and the public. Truman confided to his advisers that winning support for his policy would entail the "greatest selling job ever facing a President."[28] The administration succeeded in securing the economic assistance package it was seeking, but it also set the stage for the errant and excessive anti-communist purges orchestrated by Senator Joseph McCarthy (R-Wisconsin) during the early 1950s.

The establishment of NATO in 1949 constituted another major hurdle for the Truman administration. The Senate's consideration of the North Atlantic Treaty, which bound the United States to the defense of Western Europe, provoked intense opposition from a small, but vocal, group of isolationist senators. Senator

Taft led the charge against ratification, emphasizing the dangers entailed in extending a binding and blanket U.S. commitment to the defense of allies: "The present treaty obligates us to go to war if certain facts occur. . . . All kinds of circumstances may arise which will make our obligation most inconvenient." Taft additionally worried that arming the nations of Western Europe "will promote war in the world rather than peace."[29] Critics of NATO also voiced their opposition in the press. Writing in the *New York Times*, Gilbert Macbeth, a professor at Villanova, claimed that the treaty was "out of harmony" with the Constitution. The commitment to collective defense, he wrote, "puts the Senate in the position of trying to bind in advance the President and Congress to an arbitrary definition of what would be an attack upon the United States." Macbeth concluded that "the Senate does not have the power under the Constitution to do this." Andre Visson, a syndicated columnist, lamented in the *Washington Post* that "the North Atlantic Pact is the official burial of American neutrality."[30]

Despite such pointed objections, the Senate backed U.S. participation in NATO, ratifying the treaty by a vote of 82 to 13 on July 21, 1949. Notably, opinion surveys revealed overwhelming public support for an ongoing U.S. role in the defense of Western Europe.[31] Nonetheless, observers worried that the debate over NATO revealed an isolationist reawakening. In November 1949, Adlai Stevenson, the Democratic governor of Illinois, wrote that "old-fashioned isolationism is moribund." He was concerned, however, that although there is little sign "of a resurrection of the body of isolation there is plenty of evidence of a reincarnation of its spirit. There is a conspicuous and growing tendency to be internationally minded in principle, but not in practice, to favor international cooperation in the abstract while opposing concrete steps to make it effective." As an example, Stevenson pointed to the thirteen senators who had voted against the NATO treaty.[32]

Debate over NATO did not end with the Senate's blessing. In what came to be called the Great Debate, President Truman in 1950 and 1951 crossed swords with congressional opponents over his intention to deploy—without congressional approval—four additional U.S. Army divisions to Europe to back up NATO's commitment to collective defense. The administration worried that communist adventurism on the Korean peninsula could be replicated in Western Europe. Truman argued that he did not need to involve Congress in the dispatch of troops to Europe, claiming in January 1951 that "under the President's constitutional powers as Commander in Chief of the Armed Forces he has the authority to send troops anywhere in the world."[33]

Against the backdrop of a series of setbacks for U.S. troops fighting in Korea, prominent critics attacked Truman's plan. Robert Kennedy, U.S. ambassador to Great Britain from 1938 to 1940, vehemently opposed any U.S. participation in a war on the Eurasian landmass in either Europe or Asia, and publicly called for a return to hemispheric isolation. Herbert Hoover, the former president, claimed that "any attempt to make war on the communist mass by land invasion, through the quicksands of China, India or Western Europe is sheer folly." Doing so, he maintained, would "end in the exhaustion of this Gibraltar of Western Civilization."[34] Debate in Congress focused less on the merits of deploying more U.S. troops in Europe than on Truman's intention to act without congressional authorization. Senator Taft insisted on much more congressional input into the administration's plans, called for reliance on nuclear deterrence and strategic airpower rather than land forces, and wanted to preserve the nation's freedom of action by limiting the scope of partnership with allies. Senator John Bricker (R-Ohio) proclaimed that he was far less concerned about losing Europe to communism than about "losing our fundamental freedoms and about destroying the Constitution of the United States."[35]

After extensive and heated deliberation, the Senate in April passed a compromise resolution that approved the dispatch of four divisions to Europe, but also stipulated that any further deployments would require congressional approval. The Truman administration opposed the ostensible constraint imposed on executive authority, but also claimed victory in its effort to bolster Europe's defenses. The deployment of more U.S. troops in Europe, coming on the heels of the Senate's ratification of the North Atlantic Treaty and the nation's participation in the Korean War, reflected the further consolidation of the nation's new internationalism.

At the same time, these developments also heightened concern about a building isolationist backlash. In response to Hoover's criticism of the proposed troop deployment to Europe, the *Nation* charged that the former president had issued a "rallying cry for all the discredited forces of isolationism, to all men who since Pearl Harbor have covertly nursed their infantile illusions of a hemispheric 'Gibraltar' without having the courage to give them voice." Public enthusiasm for Hoover's speech, the magazine claimed, indicated "a widespread revival of blind isolationism."[36]

Arthur Schlesinger sounded a similar alarm in 1952. "The events of 1939–45," Schlesinger wrote, "destroyed the doctrine and the program of the Old Isolationism, but they did not destroy the emotions which underlay and sustained it. . . . Today we face a New Isolationism, bent upon what promises to be a fundamental attack on the foreign policy to which the United States and the free world are presently committed. The internationalist euphoria of the past decade should not lead us to overlook the deep roots which isolationism has in the national consciousness." Schlesinger singled out Senator Robert Taft for particular criticism, disparaging Taft's calls for major reductions in defense spending as well as his aversion to military alliances and his preference for unilateral instead of collective action. Schlesinger was far more concerned about the return of go-it-alone attitudes than he was about an isolationist retreat: "The New Isolationism boggles at the word 'collective' and it recoils from the whole theory of building 'situations of strength.' Its supreme emotional link with the Old Isolationism . . . is its dislike of allies and its desire for unilateral action by the United States."[37]

Adding to this worry about the return of isolationism and unilateralism was an effort during the first half of the 1950s to dilute the power of the executive branch to conclude international agreements. Prompted in part by negotiations under UN auspices over the Human Rights Covenant and an international criminal court, Senator Bricker proposed multiple versions of a constitutional amendment that would have required congressional approval of executive agreements and stipulated that a treaty could become effective as domestic law only through Congress's passage of relevant legislation. The proposal was intended to enhance congressional influence over diplomacy and limit U.S. entanglement abroad.[38] The Bricker Amendment attracted considerable support among Republicans and Democrats alike. Indeed, President Dwight Eisenhower (1953–1961) personally intervened to block Bricker's initiative, helping ensure that it ultimately failed to pass muster in the Senate—albeit by a single vote. The defeat of the Bricker Amendment did not extinguish fears of a return of isolationism. In 1957, Senator Paul Douglas (D-Illinois) warned that "the foreign policy of this country may . . . grow increasingly in the direction of isolation."[39]

The concerns expressed by Stevenson, Schlesinger, Douglas, and other internationalists proved to be a false alarm. The urgency and gravity of the communist threat effectively made isolationism politically untenable, including among most right-wing Republicans. Conservative Republicans continued to prefer reliance on unilateralism and the use of force to the multilateralism and foreign assistance packages favored by liberal internationalists. Yet the communist challenge, along with the anti-communist fervor stoked by McCarthyism, prompted most of them to abandon the resolute anti-interventionism of the America First era.

William Henry Chamberlin, a journalist and historian who had been a staunch opponent of U.S. intervention in World War II, was quite explicit about his own intellectual transition in an essay he published in 1956: "Certainly isolationism, with its flat rejection of foreign alliances and overseas commitments, is not a safe or even a practicable policy for the United States now, when the Communist empire has weighed down the scales of world power so heavily that only United States power can maintain a precarious balance. To advocate isolationism today is, therefore, to aid, albeit unconsciously, the Communist grand design of world domination." Although Chamberlin had jettisoned the isolationism of the interwar conservatives, he had not abandoned their commitment to unilateralism. He went on to warn against "a vague and woozy internationalism. All schemes of world government are unreal fantasies. There is no warrant for submitting American vital interests to chance ballots in that Tower of Babel, the United Nations."[40] The John Birch Society, which was established in 1958, would help crystallize and propagate this brand of conservative internationalism, which combined staunch anti-communism with libertarianism and unilateralism.[41] Its founder, businessman David Welch, went out of his way to disassociate the group from nativism, racism, and anti-Semitism. But as with conservative nationalists during the interwar era, the society did attract a good number of members who harbored racial and religious prejudice.[42]

Not all libertarians made the transition to anti-communist internationalism. In the late 1950s, the economist and historian Murray Rothbard attempted to rally libertarian conservatives behind a return to isolationism. In 1959, Rothbard submitted an essay titled "For a New Isolationism" to the *National Review*, a magazine founded in 1955 by the conservative intellectual William F. Buckley. Rothbard's opening paragraph revealed just how isolated the isolationists had become:

> It is with a heavy heart that I enter the lists against the overwhelming majority of my friends and compatriots on the Right; also with a sense of futility in trying to combat that tough anti-Soviet foreign policy to which the Right is perhaps even more dedicated than it is to anti-Socialism. But I must try, if only for the reason that no one else has done so (if, indeed, there are any outright isolationists left anymore).

Rothbard maintained that the Cold War and the nuclear and conventional arms race it had spawned unnecessarily threatened American security and prosperity. He called for "a genuine policy of peace" focused on world disarmament and "a return to the ancient and traditional American policy of isolationism and neutrality."[43] The *National Review* rejected the essay.

In a book that he wrote in the early 1970s, Rothbard labeled the conservative defection from isolationism a "betrayal" of the right. He complained that "young libertarians coming into the ranks were increasingly infected with the Cold War mentality and had never even heard of the isolationist alternative." For Rothbard, the conservative movement had by the mid-1950s effectively arrived at a new consensus behind anti-communist internationalism. In his mind, "the last great political gasp of the isolationist Right came in the fight for the Bricker Amendment."[44] Other scholars also date the definitive demise of conservative isolationism to the mid-1950s.[45]

Over the course of the 1950s and into the 1960s, liberal internationalism held its ground as isolationism gravitated to the fringes of American politics. The wide range of alliances and other strategic commitments undertaken to contain the Soviet Union enjoyed continuing support. When looking back on the period from the 1990s, Schlesinger himself noted that his concerns in the early 1950s about the emergence of a new isolationism had been misplaced. Joining many others, he attributed the staying power of internationalism to the Soviet threat: "It is now surely clear that the upsurge in American internationalism during the Cold War was a reaction to what was seen as the direct and urgent Soviet threat to the security of the United States."[46]

The Vietnam War

The isolationist impulse made another significant comeback in response to the Vietnam War, which severely strained the liberal internationalist consensus. Beginning in the late 1960s and continuing into the 1970s, a rising chorus of politicians, opinion makers, and public activists called for a U.S. withdrawal from Vietnam, claiming that the intensity of the nation's Cold War internationalism had led to strategic overreach. The term "new isolationism" reemerged as part of regular political dialogue, occasionally used in positive terms by those counseling withdrawal from Vietnam, but more often deployed as a political pejorative against opponents of the war.[47]

During the campaign for the 1972 presidential election, Senator George McGovern (D-South Dakota), the Democratic nominee seeking to block the reelection bid of President Richard Nixon (1969–1974), ran on an antiwar platform. McGovern called for withdrawing all U.S. troops from Korea and Indochina, cutting defense spending by one-third, and reducing by fifty percent the U.S. military presence in Europe. The theme of his acceptance speech at the Democratic convention was "Come Home, America," a phrase for which he would long be remembered. Other prominent politicians who strongly opposed U.S. involvement in the Vietnam War included Senator Michael Mansfield (D-Montana), the majority leader, and Senator William Fulbright (D-Arkansas), the chair of the Committee on Foreign Relations. In 1968, Mansfield called for "a discerning internationalism which will permit us to limit our undertakings abroad to those which promise a reasonable contribution to security and progress."[48] In 1971, he introduced legislation mandating a fifty percent cut in the number of U.S. troops in Europe—which stood at roughly 300,000. Strong bipartisan support for significant cuts to foreign aid accompanied antiwar sentiment in Congress.

Opinion makers added their voices to the call for withdrawal from Vietnam. Most focused on extracting the United States from the conflict, but a few went much further and advocated for a return to a strategy of nonentanglement. Foreign policy analyst Earl Ravenal called for "strategic disengagement," which he took to mean "the dissolution of alliances" and the "rehabilitation of the civilized concept of neutrality." Ravenal argued that the nation's nuclear deterrent provided a protective umbrella that facilitated disengagement and "a gradual and inexorable movement toward unalignment." In Asia, he advocated for a U.S. withdrawal to a "mid-Pacific position." In Europe, "America would witness the continuing devolution of military power. . . . We would initiate the thinning out of our troops and continue a measured and irreversible redeployment to the continental United States." Ravenal recommended that "commitments would be gradually dissolved" and that "in political-military arrangements, we would insulate. Security frontiers would be retracted to defensible lines that corresponded generally to national boundaries and related ocean areas." He stipulated that, as during the heyday of American isolationism, "disengagement should not affect commercial relations, humanitarian expressions or cultural contacts."[49]

Robert Tucker joined Ravenal in calling for a comprehensive pullback. In the *New York Times*, he advocated for the restoration of a grand strategy that advanced commercial engagement while shunning alliances and military intervention. Tucker maintained that "a new isolationism" would not threaten "America's core security." However, he acknowledged that the United States would have to abandon its exceptionalist aspirations: "The world of an isolationist America . . . would clearly not be the order we have dreamed of and sought to establish . . . an order holding out the promise of a world moving progressively, under American leadership, toward the ultimate triumph of liberal-capitalist values."[50]

Ravenal and Tucker were outliers; most strategists and commentators favored retrenchment rather than disengagement. Although he encouraged the United States to avoid formal military alliances, historian Ronald Steel asserted that "obviously we cannot return to isolationism." Anti-interventionists like himself, he argued "in no sense advocate American isolation. . . . They call for retrenchment from commitments that have become exorbitant, unnecessary, and dangerous. They object to a geopolitical strategy that puts the United States in the role of world policeman." Steel concluded that "it is not isolationism that America needs, but an internationalism based on cooperation rather than coercion, one which recognizes our place as a member of the world community and not its jail warden. Beyond the nostalgia of isolationism and the arrogance of interventionism lies a measured disinvolvement that has become imperative."[51]

Journalist Arlen Large took a similar line in the *Wall Street Journal*, calling for "prudent isolationism," by which he meant scaling back the nation's global ambitions, not retreating to the Western Hemisphere. "The Vietnam War is exactly the kind of debilitating conflict the nation's founders tried to prevent," he wrote. Large also complained that "the global responsibilities assumed by Presidents since World War II would require, for complete fulfillment, the power wielded by absolute monarchs."[52] Steel and Large were representative of mainstream antiwar voices inasmuch as they called for reining in the nation's external ambition, not returning to a strategy of nonentanglement.

A considerable segment of the electorate shared such views, fueling sustained public protests against U.S. involvement in the Vietnam War. Opinion surveys revealed diminishing enthusiasm for an activist brand of internationalism. In 1964, only eighteen percent of the public agreed with the statement that "the United States should mind its own business internationally and let other countries get along as best they can on their own." By 1974, 41 percent of respondents agreed with this statement.[53] The centrist political compact behind liberal internationalism also began to fray, with bipartisan voting on foreign policy declining steadily during the 1970s.[54] Nonetheless, public attitudes generally tracked elite attitudes, with the electorate backing retrenchment, but not isolationism. A New York Times summary of a Gallup poll from 1975 noted that "the American public's views on the extent of United States military commitment abroad offer little evidence of a trend toward isolationism since 1971."[55]

In sum, only a handful of voices advocated for a return to traditional isolationism—a pullback to North America or the Western Hemisphere. The backlash against the Vietnam War did reawaken political dialogue about the costs and benefits of nonentanglement, but the debate focused primarily on whether to get out of Vietnam and scale back the nation's global responsibilities, not on whether to end those responsibilities. It was, after all, war hawks, not critics of the Vietnam conflict, who were most keen to revive the isolationist label—primarily in an effort to land political blows against those advocating for retrenchment.

Many observers at the time realized as much, pointing out the regular use of the isolationist moniker as a political cudgel. The political scientist Michael Roskin asked in 1972, "will the real 'isolationism' please stand up?" Roskin concluded that "the meaning of 'isolationism' or 'new isolationism' ... [is] whatever the user happens to oppose in foreign policy."[56] Senator Fulbright remarked that so-called neo-isolationists "are no such thing; the word is an invention of people who confuse internationalism with an intrusive American unilateralism, with a quasi-imperialism."[57] Columnist Joseph Kraft wrote that "the last desperate shift of the Vietnam Warriors is to call those who question their policy neoisolationists. For neoisolationism is a myth born of fear long since outdated by reality and now manipulated for strictly polemical purposes." He maintained that the United States was "bound into the international community by interests, institutions and habits too powerful to assess and too numerous to count." Alarm about the return of isolationism, he concluded, "has about as much relevance as a warning of fire on the eve of Noah's flood."[58] Columnist Stephen Rosenfeld offered a similar assessment: "It seems by now that we Americans are confirmed internationalists, if not by necessity then by choice. For various reasons, good and ill, Americans wish to exercise influence at various points remote from home. Vietnam has sobered us but not queered us on this tendency."[59]

Political outcomes confirmed the accuracy of this confidence in the staying power of American internationalism. Despite McGovern's "Come Home, America" campaign theme, Nixon soundly defeated his Democratic challenger in 1972, carrying forty-nine of fifty states. So, too, did the Senate handily reject Mansfield's effort to cut in half the U.S. force presence in Europe. Rosenfeld was correct that Americans were chastened by the Vietnam War but hardly in full retreat. Congress in 1973 did pass the War Powers Resolution—overriding Nixon's veto—in an effort to wrest back warmaking authority from the executive branch by requiring congressional consent to the entry of U.S. forces into armed conflict. The legislation, however, did not significantly reverse the systematic strengthening of presidential control over national security policy that had taken place both before and during the Cold War.

As during the 1950s, fear of an isolationist comeback during the 1970s proved to be a false alarm. Nonetheless, the political backlash against the Vietnam War did have a significant impact on U.S. strategy. Nixon pursued a broader strategic retrenchment under the rubric of the Nixon Doctrine. In late 1969, he announced that the United States would stand by "all of its treaty commitments," but that in the case of aggression against a partner nation, "we shall look to the nation directly threatened to assume the primary responsibility of providing the manpower for its defense."[60] In East Asia, this approach meant transferring to South Vietnamese forces main responsibility for combat—the "Vietnamization" of the war. Nixon's defense secretary, Melvin Laird, explained to Congress that "Vietnamization provides the American people with a practical middle course between isolationism and the role of world policeman."[61] In the Persian Gulf, the Nixon Doctrine led to the Twin Pillars policy. Moving forward, the United States would look to the twin pillars of Iran and Saudi Arabia to provide security in the Gulf.[62] American arms sales to both countries increased dramatically during the early 1970s. After his reelection, Nixon moved to end the nation's direct military involvement in the Vietnam War, withdrawing U.S. forces early in 1973. To ratchet down the intensity of the Cold War, he pursued détente with the Soviet Union and reached out to China, visiting the country in 1972 and meeting with Chairman Mao Zedong.

Nixon thus made substantial changes to U.S. foreign policy, but he did not shatter the mold; the shifts he orchestrated constituted adjustments to, not the abandonment of, the broad formula of power plus partnership that emerged in the 1940s. America's core military alliances remained intact, as did its commitment to multilateralism. The most significant change was that Nixon deemphasized power in favor of partnership, pulling out of Vietnam, investing in diplomacy with Russia and China, and encouraging allies to do more to defend themselves. Following Nixon's resignation, President Gerald Ford (1974–1977) continued to pursue the path set by his predecessor, relying heavily on diplomacy to reduce Cold War tensions. President Jimmy Carter (1977–1981) went further in the same direction, advancing détente and arms control with the Soviet Union, establishing formal diplomatic relations with China, proposing the withdrawal of U.S. troops from South Korea, and putting a new emphasis on promoting human rights.

The ratcheting down of Cold-War rivalry did not last; the era of détente was relatively short-lived. The Iranian Revolution of 1979, the U.S. hostage crisis in Tehran, and the Soviet invasion of Afghanistan the same year brought it to a close. President Ronald Reagan (1981–1989) labeled the Soviet Union an "evil empire," boosted U.S. defense spending, and provided assistance to anti-communist movements in many quarters of the globe in an effort to "roll back" Soviet influence. Although Reagan's hardline policies and his emphasis on U.S. power provoked considerable criticism, mounting rivalry between Washington and Moscow largely marginalized the voices of retrenchment that had emerged in response to the Vietnam War. At the same time, Reagan's second-term diplomacy with the Soviet leader Mikhail Gorbachev paved the way for a dramatic deescalation of U.S.-Soviet rivalry. Reagan ultimately turned to the liberal internationalist playbook, relying on a combination of power and partnership to finally set the stage for the end of the Cold War.

* * *

The backlash against the Vietnam War strained, but did not break, the Cold War internationalist consensus. Moreover, even though that consensus weakened as a consequence of the war, the bipartisan compact behind liberal internationalism began to firm up again at the end of the 1970s—largely as a result of the Iranian Revolution and the Soviet invasion of Afghanistan. Bipartisan voting on foreign policy rose in step with the intensification of U.S.-Soviet rivalry, although it did not return to the levels of the 1950s and 1960s. The political scars left behind by the Vietnam War, Reagan's polarizing tenure, and tensions over domestic issues—in particular, the Civil Rights movement—all took a toll on bipartisanship.[63] Nonetheless, bipartisan support for liberal internationalism remained intact through the end of the Cold War. Prominent isolationists, like Representative Ron Paul (R-Texas), held their ground. But they were in the political wilderness. When Paul ran in the 1988 presidential election as the candidate of the Libertarian Party, he received less than 0.5 percent of the vote.

After 1941, the United States durably transitioned from following a grand strategy of hemispheric isolation and unilateralism to one of global engagement and multilateralism. To be sure, U.S. foreign policy during the Cold War was not monochromatic. Some scholars see the retrenchment that followed the Vietnam

War as part of a broader pattern of oscillation. Stephen Sestanovich, for example, argues that U.S. strategy has tended to swing between periods of maximalism (characterized by confrontation and the extension of commitments) and minimalism (characterized by accommodation and retrenchment).[64] He labels Harry Truman and Ronald Reagan as maximalists, and Richard Nixon and Jimmy Carter as minimalists. Nonetheless, Republicans and Democrats alike adhered to liberal internationalism throughout the Cold War, making for considerable continuity across administrations even as individual administrations made minor strategic adjustments. The era of U.S. grand strategy that began with the bombing of Pearl Harbor continued through the fall of the Berlin Wall.

13

The End of the Cold War, Overreach, and the Isolationist Comeback

The bipartisan compact behind liberal internationalism, although it weakened during the 1970s as a consequence of the Vietnam War, did not fully unravel until after the end of the Cold War.[1] The turning point was the Republican takeover of Congress in the 1994 midterm election; thereafter, bipartisan cooperation on foreign policy dropped off sharply. With the disappearance of the threat posed by the Soviet Union, Democrats and Republicans no longer felt compelled to adhere to the formula of power plus partnership pioneered by Roosevelt and sustained by his successors. In the absence of the political discipline engendered by the Cold War, politicians ceased their efforts to insulate the conduct of statecraft from partisan jockeying. The erosion of the ideological center, brought on in part by growing economic insecurity, hastened the collapse of bipartisanship. The moderating effects of the economic growth and mobility that followed World War II gave way to the polarizing effects of stagnating wages, mounting inequality, and the return of sharper sectional divides.

The dissolution of the bipartisan compact behind liberal internationalism has left U.S. grand strategy adrift. American statecraft since the 1990s has exhibited marked inconstancy, experiencing wide swings as political power shifts between Democrats and Republicans. The collapse of the nation's only peer competitor prompted Democrats to return to their traditional preference for partnership rather than power. Democrats hardly abandoned the use of force as a tool of statecraft, but they favored policies that emphasized multilateralism and diplomacy. As described by Derek Chollet, a scholar and former policy maker, those on the liberal side of the aisle "believe in the power generated by legitimacy, and maintain that treaties, alliances and agreements are vital ingredients of influence." Republicans meanwhile became the party of power, preferring the unilateral use of force to the multilateralism that the party had embraced in the 1940s. According to Chollet, Republicans returned to unilateralism because "conservatives prioritize freedom of action, which helps explain their . . . suspicions of international institutions and law."[2] The tug-of-war between partnership and power has produced pronounced oscillations in strategy as control of the White House has changed hands.

Amid this inconstancy, two contradictory trends in U.S. grand strategy have emerged since the end of the Cold War. On one hand, the United States has engaged in sustained strategic overstretch. It has been struggling to attain an ambitious array of international objectives that, simply put, are out of reach. On the other hand, Americans are aware of this overstretch and are responding accordingly; they are looking to off-load foreign commitments. These contradictory impulses are producing a grand strategy that risks political insolvency and an isolationist overcorrection—exactly what happened during the interwar period. Indeed, with the COVID-19 pandemic having produced an economic shock not unlike that of the Great Depression, the history of the 1930s offers a stark warning of the potential for a dangerous American retreat.

The United States has been overreaching since soon after the end of the Cold War. Absent a realist check on the nation's idealist aspirations, the pursuit of America's messianic mission has saddled the United States with a surfeit of entanglements. Through an excess of both partnership and power, the United States has simply tried to do too much. In the view of scholar Andrew Bacevich, the nation's inability to discern when and where to stop "captures the essence of the fate that has befallen Americans during the quarter century following the Cold War."[3]

Between 1992 and 2017, the United States carried out 188 military interventions, a fourfold increase over the Cold War era.[4] The enlargement of NATO has unwisely and unnecessarily contributed to a new era of confrontation with Russia and imposed on the United States an expanding range of strategic commitments of questionable merit. Triggered by the terrorist attacks of September 11, Americans have been fighting unwinnable wars in the Middle East for the better part of two decades. The U.S. intervention in Afghanistan was a war of necessity, while the invasion of Iraq was a major strategic mistake. But in both countries the United States proceeded to make a cardinal error. Trying to turn Afghanistan and Iraq into Ohio may have been a laudable goal, but the United States has exhausted itself by seeking to attain the unattainable. With the collapse of the Soviet Union, the United States deluded itself into thinking that it could finally fulfill its founding mission; Fukuyama's "end of history" was in sight.[5] But this hubris paradoxically produced the opposite effect, hastening the demise of *Pax Americana* by encouraging the United States to chronically overreach.

The electorate is acutely aware that endless wars in the Middle East have produced instability and bloodshed, not democratic regimes crafted in the American image. The Middle East is not alone in disappointing expectations of the "end of history." The broad surge in illiberalism around the globe suggests that the world is not breaking America's way. Harkening back to U.S. statecraft during the nineteenth century, Americans have been tempted to cordon themselves off from a dangerous world instead of seeking to remake it. Also contributing to the inward turn are economic dissatisfaction and discomfort with the growing ethnic heterogeneity of American society. As during previous periods in American history, economic and social insecurity are prompting calls for the nation to focus on the home front and to shun expensive international burdens, use tariffs to protect American jobs, and restrict immigration. In short, both international and domestic developments are making the American public increasingly skeptical of liberal internationalism and the sacrifices entailed in upholding *Pax Americana*.

The nation's expansive ambition is thus increasingly at odds with an electorate that is keenly interested in downsizing the nation's foreign entanglements. America's purposes have of late been running well ahead of its political means. A critical gap has opened up between the United States' global commitments and the nation's political appetite for sustaining them. Bringing America's purposes and its means back into equilibrium is critical to restoring the political foundations of U.S. statecraft and preventing an isolationist retreat.

A grand strategy of inconstancy and insolvency has unfolded across the four presidencies of the post–Cold War era. The Clinton presidency was the era of partnership. Amid America's "unipolar moment"—after the collapse of the Soviet Union, the United States was the sole superpower—the expansion and maturation of the international institutions erected during the Cold War were to spread the nation's influence and ideals. The Bush presidency was the era of power. In the aftermath of the terrorist attacks of September 11, 2001, Washington strongly favored power over partnership and set about fighting extremism and enforcing *Pax Americana* primarily through the use of force. The Obama presidency was the era of liberal internationalism lite. Obama sought to respond to the Bush administration's overreach by restoring a balance between partnership and power, but with less of both. If Clinton, Bush, and Obama all sought to preserve the liberal international order, albeit through different means, Trump sought to bring it down by pulling back from both partnership and power. The Trump presidency was the era of America First redux.

The Clinton Presidency: The Era of Partnership

Signs of the breakdown of the bipartisan compact behind liberal internationalism were evident even while President George H. W. Bush (1989–1993) was in office. Following the collapse of the Soviet bloc, public enthusiasm for foreign entanglement fell off. In one opinion poll from 1991, sixty percent of respondents favored withdrawing U.S. troops from Western Europe, and seventy-four percent supported withdrawal from South Korea. Mainstream voices from the foreign policy establishment began to call for a selective disengagement from foreign commitments.[6] So, too, did bipartisan support for the projection of U.S. power start to wane on Capitol Hill. After Iraq's invasion of Kuwait in 1991—a blatant act of aggression in the oil-rich Persian Gulf—the Senate voted by only a slim margin (52 to 47) to authorize the use of force to expel Iraq from Kuwait. The vote fell mainly along party lines—forty-five of fifty-six Democrats voted against the resolution, joined by two of forty-four Republicans.

Democrats made clear their diminishing enthusiasm for sending U.S. forces into harm's way. Senate Majority Leader George Mitchell (D-Maine) cast his vote against the authorization of force, tellingly asking, "how many young Americans will die? . . . Just this morning I heard it said that there may be 'only' a few thousand casualties. But for the families of those few thousand—the fathers and mothers, husbands and wives, daughters and sons—the word 'only' will have no meaning. And the truly haunting question, which no one will ever be able to answer, will be: Did they die unnecessarily?"[7] Even after the American-led coalition handily won the war, Bush was unable to turn a resounding victory on the battlefield into political success, in 1992 losing his bid for reelection to Bill Clinton.

The swift erosion of bipartisan voting on foreign policy after the 1994 midterms underscored the divergent ideological trajectories of Democrats and Republicans. Democrats increasingly favored partnership, while Republicans preferred power. Each party tended to support one half of the liberal internationalist compact, but not the two together. The political landscape was set for oscillation between partnership and power as control changed hands, exposing the conduct of statecraft to a widening partisan divide. As then–Senate minority leader Tom Daschle noted in 1996, "the Cold War exerted a powerful hold on America, and it forced the parties to work together to advance American interests through bipartisan internationalism. . . . The tragedy is that such cooperation increasingly seems an artifact of the past."[8]

The Democrats' preference for partnership rather than power was on display throughout the Clinton presidency. Amid the self-confidence, if not triumphalism, bred by the West's victory in the Cold War and America's status as the world's only superpower, the Clinton team set about consolidating and expanding *Pax Americana* by extending the reach of the liberal order and building out its architecture. As described by Anthony Lake, Clinton's first national security adviser, "the successor to a doctrine of containment must be a strategy of enlargement—enlargement of the world's free community of market democracies." The nation's exceptionalist calling beckoned. Through anchoring the nations of the world in open markets and multilateral institutions, the United States would move closer to fulfilling its messianic mission. As Clinton's second secretary of state, Madeleine Albright, put it in 1998 in justifying a strategy of global engagement and enlargement, "we are America; we are the indispensable nation. We stand tall and we see further than other countries into the future."[9]

During Clinton's first term and at Washington's insistence, NATO decided to open its doors to Europe's new democracies. The goal, in Clinton's words, was "to help consolidate freedom's new gains into a larger and a more lasting peace."[10] The zealous promotion of multilateralism was not restricted to Europe's new democracies. Russia joined the G-7 in 1997, turning it into the G-8. The G-20 was born in 1999 in an effort to widen the circle and make global governance more inclusive. Washington pushed hard for China's admission to the World Trade Organization (WTO), which took effect in 2001. The Clinton administration favored signing the nation up to a host of new pacts, including the Kyoto Protocol to the United Nations Framework on Climate Change, the International Criminal Court, and the Comprehensive Nuclear Test Ban Treaty. And it was an avid proponent of the liberalization of international trade, concluding both the Uruguay Round of multilateral trade negotiations—which led to the founding of the WTO—and the North American Free Trade Agreement (NAFTA). At the signing of NAFTA in the Rose Garden, President Clinton emphasized the pact's strategic and economic value: "Once again, we are leading. And in so doing, we are rediscovering a fundamental truth about ourselves: When we lead, we build security, we build prosperity for our own people."[11]

When it came to the other half of the liberal internationalist compact—the use of force—the Clinton administration demonstrated far less enthusiasm. Clinton downsized the military and, after eight years in office, handed off to his successor a smaller defense budget than he inherited. He used force sparingly. Clinton inherited from the Bush administration a humanitarian mission in Somalia. After eighteen U.S. personnel were killed in the shoot-down of two Black Hawk helicopters in Mogadishu in 1993, he proceeded to end combat operations and withdraw U.S. troops from Somalia. Soon thereafter Clinton told his advisers that, "Americans are basically isolationist. They understand at a basic gut level Henry Kissinger's vital-interest argument. Right now the average American doesn't see our interest threatened to the point where we should sacrifice one American life."[12] He refused to intervene in the Rwandan genocide in 1994, and his administration dragged its feet amid the war in Bosnia, standing on the sidelines during three years of bloodshed before finally organizing NATO's intervention in 1995. Washington did lead NATO's effort to end ethnic conflict in Kosovo in 1999, but Clinton restricted U.S. involvement to a high-altitude air campaign in order to prevent U.S. and allied casualties.

Clinton exercised similar restraint when it came to the military containment of the Iraqi regime; he limited the use of force to several rounds of stand-off cruise missile strikes, air strikes, and the preventive deployment of ground troops in the region. Strikes against Al-Qaeda targets in Afghanistan and Sudan similarly occurred only from the air. The administration expanded NATO, but without taking any significant military steps to back up the credibility of its new commitments. It also disregarded Russian objections to the alliance's enlargement, dismissing legitimate concerns in Moscow about the approach of NATO's eastern frontier.[13] Indeed, Secretary Albright maintained that the enlargement of NATO into eastern Europe would actually advance relations with Moscow, testifying before Congress that "confidence within the region will grow, allowing political and economic ties with Russia to improve, too."[14]

In keeping with his idealist inclinations, Clinton was more enthusiastic when it came to the deployment of U.S. troops for purposes other than full-scale combat. Thousands of American troops participated in NATO's postwar peacekeeping missions in the Balkans and in a peacekeeping and nation-building operation in Haiti that began in 1994.[15] Over the course of his presidency, Clinton also dispatched U.S. troops to a good number of other countries, including the Central African Republic, Sierra Leone, Liberia, and East Timor. But these missions were limited in scope and did not entail the use of significant numbers of troops in a combat setting. Indeed, Clinton's fondness for humanitarian missions prompted the scholar Michael Mandelbaum to criticize his administration for attempting "to turn American foreign policy into a branch of social work." In 2000, Condoleezza Rice, who would soon serve as national security adviser and then secretary of state to President George W. Bush, chided Clinton that "the president must remember that the military is a special instrument. It is lethal, and it is meant to be. It is not a civilian police force. It is not a political referee. And it is most certainly not designed to build a civilian society."[16]

Republicans meanwhile showed little interest in the Clinton administration's expansive idealism. Most supported NATO enlargement, but as an exercise in containing Russia, not enlarging the footprint of liberal multilateralism. Republicans opposed moving forward with U.S. participation in the International Criminal Court and the Kyoto Protocol. In 1999, the Senate rejected the Comprehensive Test Ban Treaty; fifty out of fifty-four Republicans voted against the treaty, joined by not a single Democrat. Many Republicans echoed the views of Senator Borah during the interwar era, claiming that such pacts were intrusions on American sovereignty, not useful tools of American statecraft. According to John Bolton, who would later become President George W. Bush's UN ambassador and President Trump's national security adviser, the "globalists" in the Clinton administration were imposing "harm and costs to the United States . . . [by] belittling our popular sovereignty and constitutionalism, and restricting both our domestic and our international policy flexibility and power."[17] Democrats and Republicans alike remained broadly internationalist, but they were clearly parting company when it came to the form American internationalism should take.

Clinton thus presided over a country that was still predisposed toward international activism—even though he did need to navigate the widening partisan divide over foreign policy. Nonetheless, signs were emerging that Americans were losing interest in matters of statecraft and paying far less attention to developments abroad. The print and broadcast media were dramatically cutting back coverage of foreign affairs.[18] During the Cold War, the foreign policy issue of the day ranked near the top of the public's concerns. By the end of the 1990s, roughly three percent of Americans viewed foreign policy as a primary concern and a solid majority indicated that events in other parts of the world have "very little" impact on the United States.[19] Candidates with isolationist leanings—such as the political commentator Patrick Buchanan and the businessman Ross Perot—ran in the 1992 and 1996 presidential elections. Buchanan ran again in 2000. Neither came close to winning, but Perot received close to twenty percent of the vote in 1992. In *A Republic, Not an Empire*, a book that Buchanan published in 1999, he argued that the United States should have stayed out of World War II. He also wrote that "the savagery of today's attacks on 'isolationism' is a measure of the depth of establishment fear that the destiny of the Republic will be torn away from it and restored to people who carry in their hearts the great tradition of America First."[20]

As during previous eras, politicians with isolationist inclinations at times exhibited racist and anti-Semitic leanings. Buchanan regularly complained about the excessive political influence of American Jews and the Israeli lobby—in 1990, he stated that "Capitol Hill is Israeli-occupied territory"—and charged that immigration was diluting the Christian character of the nation.[21] Ron Paul, who from 1985 to 1997 took a break from representing Texas in the House, also laced his libertarian opposition to U.S. intervention abroad with bigotry. During the 1990s, his company, Ron Paul & Associates, published a series of newsletters that featured racist, anti-Semitic, and homophobic content. One newsletter noted that the 1992 Los Angeles riots came to an end only "when it came time for the blacks to pick up their welfare checks."[22]

These political trends prompted prominent voices to caution against an isolationist comeback. In 1994, former President George H. W. Bush spoke out against the rising influence of "quasi-isolationists" like Perot, cautioning against "that faulted siren's call."[23] In 1995, Arthur Schlesinger published an essay in *Foreign Affairs* warning that the disappearance of the Soviet threat could stoke isolationist sentiment and a "return to the womb in American foreign policy."[24]

As he ran for the presidency in 1999, George W. Bush issued a similar concern: "America's first temptation is withdrawal—to build a proud tower of protectionism and isolation. In a world that depends on America to reconcile old rivals and balance ancient ambitions, this is the shortcut to chaos. . . . Let us reject the blinders of isolationism, just as we refuse the crown of empire."[25] The same year, the *New York Times* published an editorial lamenting that "isolationism—the notion that American interests are best served by minimal involvement in foreign affairs and alliances—has . . . now resurfaced with surprising passion."[26] Clinton himself voiced such concerns at the end of his presidency. In December 2000, he offered the following reflection: "People say I'm a pretty good talker . . . but I still don't think I've persuaded the American people by big majorities that you really ought to care a lot about foreign policy, about our relationship to the rest of the world, about what we're doing."[27] Such warnings were premature—but also prophetic.

The Bush Presidency: The Era of Power

While running for the presidency, George W. Bush may have warned against the temptations of isolationism, but during both his campaign and his initial months in office, he was determined to scale back the nation's foreign commitments. In a campaign speech in September 1999, he complained that U.S. forces were "overstretched" and pledged to "replace diffuse commitments with focused ones" and to "be selective in the use of our military." During one of the presidential debates, he asserted that "I don't think our troops ought to be used for what's called nation-building. . . . I'm worried about overcommitting our military around the world. I want to be judicious in its use."[28] He also wanted to focus greater economic and diplomatic attention on America's own hemisphere; his first two foreign trips were to Mexico and Canada. Bush's initial approach to grand strategy was an early reflection of the inward turn that would later strengthen within the Republican Party.

Bush's efforts to rein in U.S. commitments did not last long. The terror attacks of September 11 abruptly extinguished his preference for strategic restraint. In the aftermath of those attacks, the Bush administration invaded Afghanistan. It then dismissed the warnings and objections of allies and invaded Iraq. After removing the Taliban from power in Afghanistan and bringing about regime change in Iraq, American troops stayed put to battle insurgent resistance. The nation's endless wars were in progress. The U.S. defense budget spiked, roughly doubling in nominal terms over the course of the Bush presidency. If the Clinton presidency had been the era of multilateral diplomacy and partnership, the Bush presidency was the era of unilateralism and power.

The immediate goals of the assertive use of U.S. force were to pursue the perpetrators and supporters of terrorism and to neutralize Iraq's alleged stockpile of weapons of mass destruction. But the Bush team also had more expansive aims. In justifying the invasion of Iraq and the toppling of Saddam Hussein, the Bush administration made clear that it was pursuing the nation's messianic calling. In the words of Vice President Richard Cheney, "regime change in Iraq would bring about a number of benefits to the region. When the gravest threats are eliminated, the freedom-loving peoples of the region will have a chance to promote the values that can bring lasting peace." Bush agreed that a "liberated Iraq can show the power of freedom to transform that vital region, by bringing hope and progress into the lives of millions." On the day that he launched the war, he pledged to the American people that "we will bring freedom to others." Like most of his predecessors, Bush deployed the exceptionalist narrative to justify his actions, stating in 2004 that "like generations before us, we have a calling from beyond the stars to stand for freedom. This is the everlasting dream of America."[29]

Bush's goals were similar to Clinton's—to pursue the nation's redemptive mission of spreading democracy and peace. But Bush opted to do so through power rather than partnership. His 2002 National Security Strategy explicitly stated that "the great strength of this nation must be used to promote a balance of power that favors freedom."[30] He and his team were openly hostile to multilateralism, preferring the autonomy that came with unilateral action. The Bush administration initially turned down NATO's offer of help in Afghanistan and dismissed out of hand staunch European opposition to the invasion of Iraq. Bush supported the continued expansion of NATO to help democracies "stand firm against the enemies of freedom," but he also strong-armed allies in 2008 to commit to eventual membership for Georgia and Ukraine—a move that provoked ire in Russia and contributed to Moscow's later invasions of both countries.[31] He withdrew from the Anti-Ballistic Missile Treaty and turned his back on the Kyoto Protocol and the International Criminal Court. He appointed as his ambassador to the UN John Bolton, an unabashed unilateralist who once quipped that "the [UN] Secretariat building in New York has 38 stories. If it lost 10 stories today, it wouldn't make a bit of difference."[32]

Bush did reverse course somewhat in his second term, rediscovering the merits of partnership as he looked to allies to help out in Afghanistan and Iraq. But this shift was more a product of necessity than of choice given that the United States was in desperate need of assistance in light of the instability and insurgent violence afflicting both countries. The Bush administration also adhered to the liberal internationalist agenda when it came to trade, negotiating a host of bilateral free-trade agreements and trying—unsuccessfully—to complete the Doha Round of multilateral liberalization.

Nonetheless, the damage had been done—both to America's relationships with its traditional allies and to relations between Republicans and Democrats. Even before the launch of the controversial wars in Afghanistan and Iraq, allies were complaining about Bush's abandonment of multilateralism. After he had been in office for only a few months, one of Britain's leading journalists summed up the prevailing view in London as follows: "From here, the main voices in Washington seem to be working their way toward a host of fresh assessments: abrasive toward old enemies, mistrustful of internationalist compromise, America First when it comes to global threats, admonitory toward allies." Amid Bush's dismissive attitude toward European objections to the invasion of Iraq, the *Berliner Zeitung* lamented, "never has a president of the United States been so foreign to us, and never have German citizens been so skeptical about the policies of their most powerful allies."[33] By the time Bush's second term had come to an end, America's image abroad had been seriously tarnished. Before Bush entered office, close to eighty percent of the German and British publics held favorable views of the United States. By the time he left office, those numbers had plunged to roughly thirty percent in Germany and fifty percent in Britain.[34]

As for relations between Republicans and Democrats, Bush presided over a further deterioration in bipartisanship. Despite a temporary uptick after the September 11 attacks, bipartisan voting on foreign policy quickly returned to pre–September 11 levels—and fell further during Bush's second term. Indeed, polarization in Congress reached historically high levels.[35] The Bush administration exacerbated matters by deliberately using foreign policy as a tool of partisan warfare. In the 2004 presidential election, Bush focused his campaign on the threat of terrorism, charging that the country would "invite disaster" if the Democrats were to win.[36] The rhetoric continued in the 2006 midterm elections, with Bush insinuating that a Democratic victory would mean "the terrorists win and America loses."[37] Clearly, partisan politics no longer stopped at the water's edge.

The Obama Era: Liberal Internationalism Lite

Bush handed off to Barack Obama intractable wars in Afghanistan and Iraq, a profoundly polarized political landscape, and an acute financial crisis stemming from the bursting of the U.S. housing bubble. Obama responded to these challenges by seeking to return to the liberal internationalist formula—but on a scaled-backed and less costly basis. Clinton strongly favored partnership, while Bush relied heavily on power. Obama wanted to again marry partnership and power, yet with reduced quantities of both: liberal internationalism lite.

Liberal internationalism lite was to preserve the basic international operating system inherited from the Cold War era, but that system was to be less reliant on American power and therefore less burdensome to a U.S. electorate suffering through an economic downturn.

Obama understood that there was no going back to the formalized multilateralism of the Cold War era given the unilateralist turn among Republicans; most treaties were unlikely to pass muster in the Senate. Accordingly, Obama wanted to reinstate the country's role as a leader of more informal international coalitions. His renewed focus on partnership did not mean that Obama was shy about the use of force. On the contrary, he approved a sizable increase in U.S. force levels in Afghanistan in 2009, picked up the pace of drone strikes and special operations against extremist targets, and oversaw a major military campaign against the Islamic State beginning in 2014. At the same time, he clearly wanted to rein in the nation's foreign commitments—particularly those in the Middle East. He was determined to reduce defense spending, pull back from Bush's strategic excesses, and allocate more resources and attention to the home front. Partnership combined with power, but less of both.

Obama saw liberal internationalism lite as good politics as well as good policy. Returning to the formula of partnership plus power could help reconstitute the liberal internationalist compact among Democrats and Republicans. Repairing the partisan divide was one of Obama's early priorities. As he put it in his 2008 victory speech, "we have never been just a collection of individuals or a collection of red states and blue states. We are, and always will be, the United States of America."[38] Obama similarly saw reducing the nation's strategic footprint abroad as a political winner. When he announced in 2011 his intention to withdraw over 30,000 U.S. troops from Afghanistan, he proclaimed, "America, it is time to focus on nation-building here at home"—a refrain he frequently used as he ran for reelection in 2012.[39]

Obama and Partnership

As for the partnership plank of liberal internationalism lite, Obama was outspoken in his defense of multilateralism. As he asserted in 2014, "after World War II, America had the wisdom to shape institutions to keep the peace and support human progress, from NATO and the United Nations, to the World Bank and IMF. These institutions are not perfect, but they have been a force multiplier. They reduce the need for unilateral American action and increase restraint among other nations." America's way of doing business, he continued, entails "standing with our allies on behalf of international order. Working with international institutions."[40]

Obama wanted to reinstate the nation's embrace of multilateralism in order to help win back the international support that eroded during Bush's watch and fashion more effective institutions and partnerships. Amid ongoing shifts in the global distribution of power, such partnerships would also clear the way for a more equitable distribution of global burdens; allies and emerging powers alike needed to step up. Since the Senate's enthusiasm for treaty-based partnership had diminished since the Cold War era, Obama of necessity relied more on executive agreements and informal pacts that would not require Senate ratification.[41] Liberal internationalism lite thus entailed a less institutionalized and more pragmatic approach to multilateralism—as well as behind-the-scenes teamwork with key partners. As Obama adviser Ben Rhodes observed, Angela Merkel, the German chancellor, would "work closely with Obama. . . . I'd seen them sit together, sometimes for hours, with notepads in front of them, designing strategies that could keep the global economy crawling forward, or hold Afghanistan together."[42]

Obama's reinstatement of the Democrats' traditional preference for multilateralism yielded prompt benefits. His tenure reversed the plunge in global attitudes toward the United States that had occurred during the Bush presidency.[43] International help was easier to come by. The Bush administration struggled to find a handful of partners willing to join the invasion of Iraq in 2003. In contrast, over sixty countries joined the counter-ISIL coalition put together by the Obama administration.[44] The Paris Agreement on climate change and the Iran nuclear deal were signature accomplishments of a president committed to diplomacy and international cooperation. As Obama explained in defense of his eagerness to negotiate with Tehran, "it has been our willingness to work through multilateral channels that kept the world on our side."[45] The administration demonstrated a similar enthusiasm for the liberalization of trade through multilateral deals, working hard to complete both the Trans-Pacific Partnership (TPP) and the Trans-Atlantic Trade and Investment Partnership (TTIP). With China continuing its economic ascent and East Asia poised to be the globe's most dynamic region, TPP was the centerpiece of Obama's effort to orchestrate a "pivot to Asia."

Due to political polarization and the defection of Republicans from the partnership plank of liberal internationalism, Obama turned to executive agreements to conclude both the Paris Agreement and the Iran deal; neither would have been able to garner two-thirds support in the Senate. Both agreements were therefore vulnerable to a change in control of the White House. Indeed, Trump pulled the United States out of both pacts after taking office. Thus, even though liberal internationalism lite offered a pragmatic approach to multilateral cooperation, the agreements it yielded remained vulnerable to domestic politics. The same applied to the trade agreements that Obama pursued. Trump promptly withdrew the United States from TPP, and trade negotiations with Europe languished during his presidency. Liberal internationalism lite did not enjoy the bipartisan support that Obama had hoped for, meaning that U.S. statecraft again changed dramatically as control of the White House shifted hands.

Obama and Power

As for the power plank of the liberal internationalist compact, Obama wanted to sustain the United States' role as "the hub of alliances unrivaled in the history of nations," as he put it in 2014, while nonetheless orchestrating a strategic retrenchment—particularly from the Middle East.[46] According to Rhodes, "Obama did not want to disengage from the world; he wanted to engage more. By limiting our military involvement in the Middle East, we'd be in a better position to husband our resources and assert ourselves in more places, on more issues."[47] His scaled-back version of liberal internationalism aimed at reducing the nation's footprint abroad, but without compromising the nation's unique role in preserving international stability and spreading republican values. "The United States has been, and will always be, the one indispensable nation in world affairs," he insisted at the Air Force Academy in 2012. "It's one of the many examples of why America is exceptional. It's why I firmly believe that if we rise to this moment in history, if we meet our responsibilities, then—just like the 20th century—the 21st century will be another great American century." He stressed the same theme to West Point cadets two years later: "America must always lead on the world stage. If we don't, no one else will."[48]

But even as Obama embraced American exceptionalism as an ideological foundation for U.S. leadership and engagement abroad, he also recognized that the exceptionalist narrative had played a role in inducing overreach. For Obama, the nation had to resist the temptation to interpret its messianic mission as an obligation to solve every international problem or to view even peripheral interests as vital ones. In addition, other countries had become too dependent on U.S. power and needed to shoulder more international responsibilities. The United States was still the world's predominant power, but the unipolar moment was over. The United States may have been the indispensable nation, but it could not do everything and needed more help from international partners.

Well aware of the public's impatience with the nation's overreach in the Middle East, Obama understood the task before him to entail navigating between isolationism and strategic excess. In his own words, "some would have America retreat from our responsibility as an anchor of global security, and embrace an isolation that ignores the very real threats that we face. Others would have America overextended, confronting every evil that can be found abroad.

We must chart a more centered course."[49] "It is absolutely true that in the 21st century American isolationism is not an option," Obama said on a different occasion. "We don't have a choice to ignore what happens beyond our borders." But he also went on to insist that "not . . . every problem has a military solution."[50]

Liberal internationalism lite was Obama's formula for finding that "more centered course."[51] He was looking to sustain the nation's idealist aspirations while also checking them with realist sobriety. Liberal internationalism lite meant that the country had to choose its fights more selectively, be tough-minded about strategic priorities, and be mindful of the limits of American power.

Implementing Pullback

Obama's efforts to scale back the country's strategic commitments took multiple forms. His top priority was to bring to a close the wars in Afghanistan and Iraq. He ended the U.S. military presence in Iraq in 2011. He pledged to do the same in Afghanistan, where he initially surged U.S. force levels from 30,000 to 100,000—but in the service of defeating the Taliban and completing a U.S. withdrawal by the end of his presidency. The fight against extremists was hardly over, but Obama wanted to transition from Bush's land wars and military occupations to much greater reliance on special operations and drone warfare. As he put it in 2013, "our systematic effort to dismantle terrorist organizations must continue. But this war, like all wars, must end. That's what history advises. It's what our democracy demands."[52]

Strategic retrenchment also meant avoiding new conflicts—especially those with escalatory potential. In one of the most controversial decisions of his presidency, Obama in August 2013 chose not enforce his own red line, backing away from using force against the Syrian government in response to its use of chemical weapons against the opposition. Obama was worried about the lack of congressional support as well as the risk of getting drawn into Syria's civil war.[53] The latter concern also steered him away from implementing a no-fly zone, safe haven, or other measures advocated by proponents of U.S. intervention in Syria. Prior to ISIL's arrival in the country, Obama limited U.S. involvement to the training and arming of opposition groups.[54] Obama was also careful to avoid potential escalation with Russia after Moscow introduced its forces into Syria in 2015. He demonstrated similar restraint following Russia's illegal annexation of Crimea and intervention in eastern Ukraine in 2014. Obama refused to provide lethal weapons to Ukraine, preferring to confront Russia primarily with diplomatic isolation and economic sanctions.[55]

A third element of Obama's pullback was the pursuit of rapprochement with adversaries. During his first term, pursuit of a "reset" with Moscow made significant, if temporary, progress in improving relations between the United States and Russia. The two countries reached an agreement to reduce their nuclear arsenals. Obama also reached out to Myanmar and Cuba. In 2012, the administration began easing sanctions against Myanmar and sent a U.S. ambassador to the country for the first time in more than two decades. Obama visited Myanmar in 2014. Engagement with Cuba cleared the way for the resumption of diplomatic relations between the two countries in 2015 and Obama's historic visit to Havana the following year. Engagement with Tehran similarly yielded fruit. Although the nuclear deal concluded in 2015 did not markedly improve relations between Washington and Tehran, it did achieve Obama's chief goal: putting tight controls on Iran's nuclear program and thereby significantly reducing the likelihood of war between Iran and the United States.

Finally, Obama sought to lighten America's load abroad by encouraging other countries to assume greater international burdens—to "pull their weight," as he put it in 2014.[56] According to the president's introduction to his administration's 2010 National Security Strategy, "the burdens of a young century cannot fall on American shoulders alone—indeed, our adversaries would like to see America sap our strength by overextending our power."[57] The United States would in the first instance look to its traditional allies to do more—hence Obama's encouragement of Japan to assume greater defense responsibilities and his insistence at NATO's 2014 summit that allies commit to spending two percent of GDP on defense. As Secretary of Defense Chuck Hagel told a think tank forum in 2014, "going forward, the Department of Defense will not only seek, but increasingly rely on closer integration and collaboration with our allies."[58] So, too, were emerging powers, such as China and India, on the hook. As Obama's introduction to the 2010 National Security Strategy put it, "as influence extends to more countries and capitals, we will build new and deeper partnerships in every region."[59]

His insistence that allies carry their fair share factored into Obama's decisions about the use of force. He agreed to the intervention in Libya only after Britain, France, and other NATO allies were prepared to play major roles in the military operation. Rhodes notes that the intervention in Libya "was what Obama wanted: multilateral, no ground forces, limited objectives."[60] An unnamed Obama adviser was ridiculed for insisting that the United States was "leading from behind."[61] But the phrase accurately connoted Obama's readiness to catalyze collective action only if other countries were prepared to step up. A similar logic governed his approach to strengthening NATO's eastern flank in 2016. Obama was prepared to authorize the deployment of additional U.S. troops— but only after European allies had committed to do the same. The logic also worked in reverse. Obama's reluctance to intervene in Syria stemmed in part from the fact that neither Arab nor NATO partners were demonstrating a readiness to make major contributions to a military mission.

While Obama's multipronged retrenchment strategy produced at least some of the desired results, it proved to be more difficult to arrive at "a more centered course" than it was to articulate it in theory. On one hand, Obama succeeded in reining in the defense budget, bringing it down from roughly $700 billion when he entered office to around $600 billion when he left. He dramatically reduced the size of the U.S. force presence in war zones in the Middle East, shrinking it from roughly 150,000 to 14,000. His reliance on special operations and drone warfare and his regular use of local rather than U.S. forces for combat operations brought U.S. casualties way down. Allies agreed to increase their defense budgets, and countries from around the world shouldered heavy burdens alongside U.S. forces in Afghanistan, Libya, and the counter-ISIL campaign.

On the other hand, developments around the world, and especially in the Middle East, foiled Obama's best efforts to substantially reduce the nation's strategic entanglements. Pressed by allies, he reluctantly agreed to involve U.S. forces in NATO's intervention in Libya in 2011—only to see the country fall apart after the toppling of the Qaddafi regime. American forces quit Iraq at the end of 2011, but Obama had to send them back in 2014 to help the Iraqi government fight ISIL, which had taken control of a sizable swath of land in Iraq and Syria. He initially restricted the U.S. role in Syria's civil war to the provision of financial and military assistance to opponents of the Syrian regime, but later sent in U.S. troops to help local fighters dislodge and defeat ISIL.[62] In Afghanistan, Obama approved a surge in U.S. force levels to defeat the Taliban, clearing the way for him to assert in his 2014 State of the Union address that, "together with our allies, we will complete our mission there by the end of this year, and America's longest war will finally be over."[63] The Taliban did not play along, forcing Obama to extend the U.S. mission beyond his presidency. The expansion of the fight against terrorism also prompted him to increase the U.S. force presence in Africa. Obama left office with roughly 8,000 troops in Afghanistan, 5,000 in Iraq, 500 in Syria, and well over 1,000 in Africa.[64]

Russia played its own role in frustrating Obama's efforts to scale back the nation's strategic burdens. After Vladimir Putin returned to the Kremlin in 2012, he pursued a policy of confrontation with the United States, undermining the earlier progress achieved in advancing rapprochement between Washington and Moscow. Russia's invasion of Ukraine in 2014 was a turning point, with the Obama administration thereafter leading NATO's efforts to bolster its eastern frontier and its ability to respond to potential Russian aggression. American spending on European defense rose, and additional U.S. troops rotated through forward positions on the continent.[65] Europe's new draw on U.S. capabilities coincided with an assertive turn in Beijing's foreign policy. Beijing's growing economic and military ambition beckoned the "pivot to Asia" and more U.S. engagement in the region—even as commitments in the Middle East and Europe made it difficult for Washington to focus its attention and resources on China's rise.

Obama struggled to reconcile his preferences for and pledges of retrenchment with a world that would not let go of American power. At times, that struggle left him in an awkward middle ground. In Afghanistan, he kept acceding to pressure from allies and the Pentagon to extend the U.S. presence, but the prolonged mission made little headway in defeating the Taliban or bringing stability to the country. The conflict dragged on. As for Syria's civil war, Obama insisted that President Assad's slaughter of his own people meant that he had to go, but he was unwilling to use U.S. forces to take down the Assad regime. At the same time, Obama was uncomfortable doing nothing in the face of a humanitarian crisis and a refugee outflow that was destabilizing Syria's neighbors as well as the European Union. Nonetheless, his solution—providing modest assistance to the Syrian opposition—was insufficient to turn the military tide against Assad, especially after Russia intervened on his behalf. The Syrian regime endured. In Libya, Obama approved a NATO mission that morphed from humanitarian protection to regime change, but then joined Europeans in backing away from the follow-up mission that might have prevented Libya's dissolution into a failed state.

Perhaps Obama's own version of exceptionalism was still too expansive to permit the pullback that he sought. He hinted as much in the West Point speech in which he articulated the need for finding a "more centered course" between isolation and overreach. In making the case against isolationism, Obama argued that the United States had to face down traditional threats to the nation's security stemming from nuclear proliferation, terrorism, and potential Russian or Chinese aggression. But he also went further: "And beyond these narrow rationales, I believe we have a real stake, abiding self-interest, in making sure our children and our grandchildren grow up in a world where schoolgirls are not kidnapped and where individuals are not slaughtered because of tribe or faith or political belief. I believe that a world of greater freedom and tolerance is not only a moral imperative, it also helps to keep us safe."[66]

Ensuring that girls in Afghanistan or Nigeria can freely and safely attend school is a laudable goal. But it is also exactly the kind of expansive objective that can lead to chronic overreach. Obama seemingly realized as much, immediately following his call for defending "greater freedom and tolerance" with an important caveat: "But to say that we have an interest in pursuing peace and freedom beyond our borders is not to say that every problem has a military solution. Since World War II, some of our most costly mistakes came not from our restraint, but from our willingness to rush into military adventures without thinking through the consequences."[67] Ambiguity in Obama's own mind about where to draw the strategic line helps explain why he left office struggling to deliver more fully on his pledge to extract the nation from an excess of foreign entanglements. It also explains why Donald Trump hewed to a neo-isolationist platform as he campaigned to succeed him.

The Trump Era: America First Redux

"From this day forward, it's going to be only America first," President Trump proclaimed in his inaugural address on January 20, 2017. By deliberately reprising the isolationist mantra of the interwar era, Trump made clear that he intended a clean break with the era of liberal internationalism. *Pax Americana* and globalization, he insisted, had ultimately worked to the disadvantage of too many Americans:

> For many decades, we've enriched foreign industry at the expense of American industry, subsidized the armies of other countries while allowing for the very sad depletion of our military. We've defended other nations' borders while refusing to defend our own and spent trillions and trillions of dollars overseas while America's infrastructure has fallen into disrepair and decay. We've made other countries rich while the wealth, strength, and confidence of our country has disappeared over the horizon. One by one, the factories shuttered and left our shores, with not even a thought about the millions upon millions of American workers that were left behind. The wealth of our middle class has been ripped from their homes and then redistributed all across the entire world.

Trump pledged that "this American carnage stops right here and stops right now. . . . We assembled here today are issuing a new decree to be heard in every city, in every foreign capital, and in every hall of power. From this day forward, a new vision will govern our land. From this day forward, it's going to be only America first. America first."[68]

Trump's electoral success stemmed in part from his rejection of liberal internationalism.[69] Public anger was brewing over the nation's strategic overreach, deindustrialization and economic dislocation, and an inadequate immigration system. Many aspects of Trump's agenda had considerable popular allure: his call for pulling back on the nation's strategic commitments; his skepticism toward democracy promotion and nation-building; his determination to break free of constricting partnerships and put America first; his promise to protect

American jobs; his pledge to defend the nation's borders and tighten immigration policy; and his not-so-subtle pandering to white nationalism. In the eyes of
many Trump supporters, the liberal internationalist agenda had run its course
and needed to be discarded. So, too, did Trump get political traction through
his irreverent political incorrectness, appealing to voters turned off by liberal
positions on a host of social issues. By taking on the political establishment and
arguing that "nationalists" rather than "globalists" should be responsible for
the conduct of grand strategy, Trump was able to convince many disaffected
Americans that he deserved their vote.

Critics charged that Trump's brand of statecraft was fundamentally at
odds with the nation's history and ideals and represented a sharp break
with its exceptionalist calling. Indeed, Trump did equivocate on American
exceptionalism, on one occasion calling the United States "the most exceptional
republic ever to exist in all of human history," but on another saying that "I don't
like the term. . . . I don't think it's a very nice term. We're exceptional; you're
not."[70] But Trump's inconsistent views on American exceptionalism notwithstanding, a foreign policy of America First is hardly out of step with U.S. history.
The isolationist yearning, the hostility to U.S. participation in international pacts,
the aversion to an activist brand of democracy promotion, the economic protectionism, the racially tinged nationalism—these aspects of Trump's America First
approach to grand strategy were in striking alignment with the foreign policy
pursued by the United States for much of its history prior to the Japanese attack
on Pearl Harbor.

Trump's Nineteenth-Century Grand Strategy

Trump's America First approach to statecraft did not reject the nation's
exceptionalist mission. Instead, it tapped into an earlier incarnation of it.[71]
Since World War II, the country's exceptionalist narrative has admittedly
centered on the idea of defending a liberal international order through
an enduring compact between power and partnership. But before that,
American exceptionalism meant insulating the American experiment from
foreign threats, shunning international entanglements, spreading democracy through example rather than intrusion and coercion, embracing protectionism and fair (not free) trade, and preserving a relatively homogeneous
citizenry through racist and anti-immigrant policies. In short, it was about
America First. Trump's statecraft was no bolt from the blue. It had deep roots
in the nation's identity and resonated with much of its history. And as Walter
Russell Mead has argued, Trump's brand of foreign policy always retained
its allure among "Jacksonian populists"—many of whom reside in states that
constituted Trump's electoral base.[72]

Since his early days as a candidate, Trump cloaked himself in isolationist garb, touting the merits of both nonentanglement and nonintervention. In a campaign speech in which he laid out his America First foreign policy, he questioned the value of the nation's core alliances in Europe and Asia, asserting that unless America's partners spend more on their own defense, the United States "must be prepared to let these countries defend themselves." He pledged to end the era in which "our politicians seem more interested in defending the borders of foreign countries than their own." He also promised that the United States will be "getting out of the nation-building business."[73] After taking office, Trump proceeded to regularly insult allies and harangue them about their inadequate spending on defense.[74] He publicly questioned whether the United States would stand by its commitments to collective defense, announced a reduction in the U.S. military presence in Germany, and privately expressed to his aides his desire to pull the United States out of NATO.[75] He also contemplated withdrawal from the U.S. defense pact with Japan.[76] Trump's attitude toward "entangling alliances" certainly resonated with that of the Founders.

Trump's isolationist inclinations also led him to avoid new conflicts in the Middle East. Despite numerous provocations from Iran, including an attack on Saudi oil installations in September 2019 and ballistic missile strikes against Iraqi bases hosting U.S. forces in January 2020, Trump held back from going to war. He did order the killing of Iran's high-profile commander, Qassem Soleimani—the move that triggered Iran's missile strikes against U.S. forces in Iraq. But Trump thereafter took decisive steps to avoid further escalation. He also sought to extract the United States from ongoing conflicts in the region. Trump announced during the summer of 2019 that he was cutting in half the U.S. military presence in Afghanistan, and he pursued a peace deal with the Taliban aimed at clearing the way for the full withdrawal of U.S. troops. He told his staff that he wanted all U.S. forces out of the country by the 2020 election and that he wanted to close the U.S. embassy in Kabul due to its size and expense.[77] Trump finally got his deal with the Taliban in February 2020, a pact that envisaged a complete U.S. withdrawal by 2021. Ongoing Taliban attacks following the conclusion of the deal, along with pervasive distrust between the Afghan government and the Taliban, left uncertain if and when U.S. troops would actually quit Afghanistan.

The retreat from Syria was considerably more chaotic. In late 2018, Trump announced that he was ordering U.S. troops to pull out of Syria—without consulting his advisers or first setting in place a diplomatic strategy to pave the way for the departure of American forces. James Mattis, the secretary of defense, and Brett McGurk, the special presidential envoy overseeing the counter-ISIL campaign, both resigned over the issue. The following October, frustrated that U.S. forces were still in Syria, Trump again caught his own foreign policy team off guard by ordering U.S. troops to pull back from the Turkish border and vacate northern Syria. Turkey promptly attacked the Syrian Democratic Forces (SDF), the largely Kurdish militia with which the United States had teamed up to fight ISIL. Washington not only abandoned the SDF, which had lost some 11,000 personnel in the fight against ISIL, but also paved the way for territorial gains by Russia and the Syrian regime. Trump's move also undercut U.S. efforts to offset Iranian influence in Syria and led to the escape of significant numbers of Islamic State detainees from detention camps. In justifying his decision, Trump explained that "it's not our border. We shouldn't be losing lives over it. . . . I campaigned on bringing our soldiers back home, and that's what I am doing."[78]

Trump also set about dismantling the multilateralism of the liberal internationalist era in favor of the unilateralism that came before. His broadsides against institutionalized cooperation rivaled those of Senator Borah and other irreconcilables of the interwar era. As a candidate, Trump vowed that "we will no longer surrender this country or its people to the false song of globalism. The nation-state remains the true foundation for happiness and harmony. I am skeptical of international unions that tie us up and bring America down. . . . We will never enter America into any agreement that reduces our ability to control our own affairs."[79] After taking office, he was even more blunt: "We will never surrender America's sovereignty to an unelected, unaccountable global bureaucracy," he proclaimed before the UN General Assembly in 2018. "Sovereign and independent nations are the only vehicle where freedom has ever survived, democracy has ever endured, or peace has ever prospered. And so we must protect our sovereignty and our cherished independence above all." He told the same body the previous year that countries all around the world should follow the United States in putting their own interests first, thereby contributing to "a great reawakening of nations."[80]

Trump backed up this rhetoric with action. He pulled out of one pact after another, including the Paris Agreement on climate change, the Iran nuclear deal, the Intermediate-Range Nuclear Forces Treaty, the Arms Trade Treaty, the UN Human Rights Council, and the UN Educational, Scientific, and Cultural Organization. He halted U.S. contributions to the UN agency that provides medical and educational assistance to Palestinian refugees. With the COVID-19 pandemic in full swing in the spring of 2020, he announced his intention to withdraw the United States from the World Health Organization. He appointed as his third national security adviser John Bolton, well-known for his hostility to compacts that he believes infringe on U.S. sovereignty. Trump was hostile even to institutions of which the United States is not a member. He supported the United Kingdom's withdrawal from the European Union and aligned himself with populist governments in Italy, Poland, and Hungary that were openly skeptical of the project of European integration.

Trump also turned back the clock when it came to the spread of democracy, exhibiting contempt for the activist brand of democracy promotion embraced during the era of liberal internationalism. His disdainful attitude toward the promotion of democracy in the Middle East was reminiscent of John Quincy Adams's views of the prospects for republican rule in Latin America. As Adams put it in 1821, "so far as they are contending for independence, I wish well their cause; but I had seen and yet see no prospect that [Latins] would establish free and liberal institutions of government."[81] In Trump's America First campaign speech, he blamed instability in the Middle East on the "dangerous idea that we could make western democracies out of countries that had no experience or interests in becoming a western democracy." On Inauguration Day, Trump asserted that "we do not seek to impose our way of life on anyone, but rather to let it shine—we will shine—as an example for everyone to follow." In his 2018 speech before the UN General Assembly, he asserted that "I honor the right of every nation in this room to pursue its own customs, beliefs, and traditions. The United States will not tell you how to live or work or worship. We only ask that you honor our sovereignty in return."[82]

At least on the surface, Trump was returning to the original version of the nation's redemptive mission: the United States should spread democracy only by example. But in practice, Trump went much further, exhibiting an unabashed affection for autocracy, preferring strongmen like Vladimir Putin, Viktor Orban, Kim Jong-un, and Abdel Fattah el-Sisi to democratic allies like Angela Merkel and Justin Trudeau. And at home, Trump exhibited ingrained disregard for traditional republican ideals, instead trafficking in untruths, disparaging the media, and resisting congressional and judicial oversight of his decisions and actions. The Founders may have shared Trump's skepticism toward interference in the domestic affairs of other nations. But they had a profound sense of their obligation to build a country that would serve as a beacon of democracy—even if as an exemplar rather than a crusader.

Trump's fondness for autocracy was not a return to an earlier version of exceptionalism. Instead, it was a bald denigration of American ideals. Early Americans were obsessed with the prospect of creeping tyranny and an unchecked government that would trample on the liberties of ordinary citizens. That fear motivated the Founders to build a compound republic that distributed power across multiple authorities and instituted a network of checks and balances. That fear also compelled the Founders to pursue geopolitical isolation lest external ambition lead to the excessive concentration of power in the hands of the federal government. Their concern that ambition abroad would lead to tyranny at home proved to be overblown. But Donald Trump indeed fulfilled some of the worst fears of the Founders through his callous disregard of republican norms and practices and his readiness to use U.S. military units against demonstators protesting racism after the police killing of George Floyd.

On trade, Trump preferred the nation's earlier protectionism to the liberalizing zeal of the last seven decades. Indeed, his calls for fair and reciprocal trade harkened back to the Model Treaty of 1776 and the decades of protectionism that followed. As he put it in his inaugural speech, "protection will lead to great prosperity and strength. . . . We will bring back our jobs. We will bring back our borders. We will bring back our wealth. And we will bring back our dreams." Trump wasted no time in acting on his rhetoric, withdrawing the United States from the Trans-Pacific Partnership on his fourth day in office. Trump then proceeded to slap tariffs on imports from America's main trading partners, os-tensibly to convince the targeted countries to provide greater market access to U.S. goods. In Trump's words, international trade "must be fair and reciprocal. The United States will not be taken advantage of any longer."[83] The strategy, how-ever, yielded limited payoffs. Trump did succeed in replacing NAFTA with the United States Mexico Canada Agreement. Expected gains from the new pact in-clude a small but positive impact on economic output and the return of some manufacturing jobs from Mexico to the United States.[84] When it came to the main prize—U.S. commerce with China—the primary result of Trump's ap-proach was a trade war that hurt many American producers and consumers and contributed to a global economic slowdown.

Finally, Trump was determined to take the nation back to the more homog-enous America of the past. In referring to Haiti and African nations as "shithole countries" and claiming that Nigerians in the United States would never go back to their "huts," Trump sounded very much like nineteenth-century American leaders discussing the need to cordon off the United States from "inferior peo-ples."[85] Not since the interwar era has the U.S. government taken steps as draco-nian as those of the Trump administration to restrict the arrival of newcomers. Trump's hostility to immigration, cuts to refugee admissions, insults toward Hispanic Americans, equivocations on neo-Nazis marching in Charlottesville, Virginia—all these moves were not-so-subtle paeans to the days when Christians of northern European extraction dominated the United States. Making America Great Again meant making it white again.

Implementing America First

Overall, Trump was reasonably successful in turning his rhetoric into action and attaining some of the main objectives of his America First agenda. He dismantled central elements of liberal internationalism in favor of a more isolationist, uni-lateralist, protectionist, and racist approach to statecraft. Like Obama, however, Trump was frustrated by the obstacles he confronted as he struggled to rein in the nation's strategic commitments abroad. Trump's harangues helped convince most NATO allies to spend more on defense, but Europe's strategic dependence on the United States persisted. In the face of ongoing concern about Russian intentions, Trump ended up approving an incremental increase in the U.S. presence in Poland and in U.S. spending on European defense—even though his administration announced in June 2020 that it intended to reduce U.S. troop levels in Germany by roughly twenty-five percent. Tensions with North Korea and China meanwhile made impractical any reduction in the U.S. presence in Asia. America's main strategic obligations in Europe and East Asia thus remained intact and about as onerous as they were before Trump took office. Indeed, the defense budget rose significantly during his watch.[86] Trump himself was of the mind that "getting along with Russia, China, and everyone is a good thing, not a bad thing." But his own National Security Strategy maintained that "China and Russia want to shape a world antithetical to U.S. values and interests," and called for a renewed U.S. focus on great-power competition.[87]

Trump repeatedly tried to quit Syria and Afghanistan, but his advisers kept finding ways to postpone withdrawal. Indeed, his frustration over his foiled efforts to withdraw from Syria played a role in prompting his precipitous order in October 2019 to remove U.S. forces from the country's north. And even though he justified his decision by asserting that he was "bringing our soldiers back home," many of the troops who left Syria stayed in the region and additional U.S. forces arrived in eastern Syria to protect oilfields. In the end, Trump abandoned the Kurds, but overall U.S. force levels in Syria declined only modestly.[88]

Trump's hawkish approach to Iran was at odds with his desire to off-load entanglements in the Middle East inasmuch as it necessitated keeping a sizable U.S. military presence in the Persian Gulf region, including in Iraq, and sending additional forces to Saudi Arabia. Trump imposed sanctions and tried saber-rattling, threatening "the official end of Iran," but he also made clear he would be happy to meet with the country's leaders. Neither coercion nor outreach worked; instead of yielding to Trump's "maximum pressure" or taking him up on his offer of talks, Tehran in 2019 began to breach the limits imposed on its nuclear program under the 2015 deal. A similar dynamic unfolded with North Korea. After threatening to "totally destroy North Korea," he tried face-to-face negotiations with Kim Jong-un to denuclearize and pacify relations with the country, at one point declaring that he and the North Korean leader "fell in love."[89] Nonetheless, Trump could not convince Kim to give up his nuclear arsenal and their dialogue fizzled. Trump tried both bluster and sycophancy to convince the likes of Iran and North Korea to acquiesce to America's demands—but to little effect.

In short, Trump delivered on much of his America First agenda, but his isolationist instincts ran up against a world still heavily dependent on U.S. power to preserve order. The international system continues to pull the United States outward, while the country's domestic politics pull it inward. Resolving this tug-of-war will be a critical challenge for American statecraft moving forward. In the meantime, U.S. allies and adversaries alike will have to continue to adjust their national strategies to an America that seems increasingly discontented with the scope of its entanglement with the world.

The American Public's Inward Turn

Trump's America First grand strategy produced a political firestorm at home and abroad. The U.S. foreign policy establishment generally saw Trump as a heretic who undermined the sacred tenets of a foreign policy that had kept the nation safe since World War II. America's traditional partners in upholding the liberal international order—principally democratic allies in Europe and East Asia—were alienated and unsettled. Forced to contemplate the prospect of life after *Pax Americana*, Europeans began debating how to achieve "strategic autonomy." "We Europeans must really take our destiny into our own hands," Angela Merkel said in 2017, adding that "the times in which we can fully count on others are somewhat over."[90] Japan as well began taking steps to assume more responsibility for its own defense.[91] Countries around the world sought greater self-reliance in reaction to Trump's unpredictability and isolationist leanings. Trump's critics at home and abroad were also waiting him out, assuming that the United States and the world would go back to normal after his departure.

It would be a dangerous mistake, however, to see Trump's brand of statecraft as no more than an aberrant detour from which the nation will readily self-correct. The bipartisan compact behind liberal internationalism has collapsed; at least for the foreseeable future, there is no going back. Americans are not ready for a full retreat from the world or prepared to abandon their exceptionalist calling. But they disagree as to whether the nation should engage through power or partnership. And many Americans found considerable merit in Trump's resurrection of an earlier version of grand strategy that represents a definitive break with the statecraft that the United States has pursued since World War II.

The fact that Democratic and Republican leaders alike have been backing away from liberal internationalism strengthens the case that changes in policy reflect underlying changes in the views of the American electorate. Obama and Trump, although political and ideological opposites, were both determined to scale back the nation's footprint abroad. When Trump and Hillary Clinton were campaigning in advance of the 2016 election, both questioned free trade and pledged not to conclude the pending Trans-Pacific Partnership. Democrats running in the 2020 presidential contest generally supported Trump's readiness to stand up to China on trade. After Trump in late 2018 announced his intention

to start pulling U.S. troops out of Syria and Afghanistan, the Senate passed a resolution opposing the withdrawal. Most of the Democratic senators at that time
running in the 2020 race voted against the resolution, including Cory Booker
(New Jersey), Kirsten Gillibrand (New York), Kamala Harris (California), Amy
Klobuchar (Minnesota), Bernie Sanders (Vermont), and Elizabeth Warren
(Massachusetts). Clearly, these presidential hopefuls viewed supporting the
withdrawals from Syria and Afghanistan to be in their political interests.

Surveys of public opinion confirm that liberal internationalism is in trouble.
Opinion polls are notoriously sensitive to how questions are posed and what
answers are available to respondents, but several trend lines are clear. First, most
Americans want the nation to reduce its strategic commitments abroad and feel
that partners around the world need to shoulder a greater share of international
burdens. The American public wants to off-load at least some of the nation's foreign entanglements. Second, most Americans want their leaders to focus much
more attention on the home front—in particular, to invest in infrastructure, protect American jobs, and effectively control immigration. Third, a wide partisan
gap has opened on the contours of U.S. engagement abroad, tracking the divide
that persists among foreign policy elites. Democratic voters strongly prefer reliance on multilateralism and partnership, while Republican voters strongly
prefer unilateralism and power. This third trend reinforces the tendency for
U.S. strategy to swing widely when control of the White House changes hands.

The Chicago Council on Global Affairs 2018 survey titled "America Engaged,"
seemingly contradicts these assertions. It concludes that Americans largely oppose the Trump administration's efforts "to pull the United States back from
global engagement," reporting that seventy percent of the public "favor the United
States taking an active part in world affairs."[92] According to the Chicago Council,
"solid majorities of the American public have rejected the 'America First' platform."[93] The 2019 survey, titled "Rejecting Retreat," confirmed the trends found
in the 2018 report. According to the findings, sixty-nine percent of Americans
support "taking an active part in world affairs." Drawing on these findings, the
Chicago Council concludes that "retreating from the world, abdicating international leadership, and abandoning alliances and global institutions is not what
the American public has in mind."[94]

However, it is important to ask what *kind* of engagement in world affairs
Americans prefer before concluding that they have rebuffed an America First
approach to statecraft. After all, the United States has been deeply involved in the
international economy since the founding era, but was for much of its history
intent on limiting its strategic engagement outside the Western Hemisphere.
The United States was long a trading nation even while it insisted on geopolitical isolation. The isolationist consensus no longer holds, but Americans today
are far more enthusiastic about international commerce than they are about

strategic entanglements.[95] The 2019 Chicago Council survey found that while eighty-seven percent of respondents saw taking an active part in world affairs to include "engaging in trade with other countries," only fifty-one percent included "intervening militarily in other countries to solve conflicts," and only thirty-six percent included "selling weapons to other countries."[96]

The Center for American Progress (CAP), which provides a more fine-grained analysis of public attitudes in its 2019 survey, titled "America Adrift," offers further evidence that Americans are indeed questioning the scope of the nation's strategic commitments.[97] The CAP report arrives at a quite different conclusion than the Chicago Council report. The CAP survey finds broad public receptiveness "to core elements of 'America First' nationalism, primarily notions that the United States should stop being the world's policeman and that it should focus more on its own problems rather than worrying about what is happening in other countries." The report concluded that "American voters are not isolationist," but that they do favor a pullback from foreign commitments and support "'restrained engagement'—a strategy that favors diplomatic, political, and economic actions over military action." According to the survey, "American voters want their political leaders to make more public investments in the American people in order to compete in the world and to strike the right balance abroad after more than a decade of what they see as military overextension."[98]

Polling from the Pew Research Center confirms that a significant portion of the electorate favors a pullback from the current scope of U.S. engagement in world affairs. Pew surveys reveal that in recent years a historically high share of Americans—around fifty percent—believe that the country "should mind its own business internationally and let other countries get along the best they can on their own."[99] This finding is in line with other surveys. The CAP study found a slight majority of Americans in favor of U.S. global leadership. Fifty-one percent maintain that "America is stronger when we take a leading role in the world," while forty-four percent believe that "America is stronger when we focus on our own problems instead of inserting ourselves in other countries' problems."[100] According to a separate survey carried out by Gallup, the Council on Foreign Relations, and National Geographic, forty-five percent of Americans want the country's role in the world to increase or stay at current levels, while forty-six percent want it to shrink or end altogether.[101]

On the question of what kinds of international engagement Americans favor, the CAP survey reveals a clear preference for economic and diplomatic rather than military engagement, with fifty-six percent favoring the former, and thirty-nine percent the latter. Moreover, a wide partisan divide has opened on the issue: seventy-two percent of Democrats prioritize economic and diplomatic engagement compared with only thirty-seven percent of Republicans.[102] A 2017 survey from the Pew Research Center finds an even starker gap on this issue, with eighty-three percent of Democrats, and only thirty-three percent of Republicans, supporting the view that good diplomacy is the best way to preserve peace.[103] The elite divide over power versus partnership clearly extends to the public.

As for the public's priorities, the CAP study found that the electorates' top foreign policy concerns are "protecting against terrorist threats," "protecting jobs for American workers," and "reducing illegal immigration." Near the bottom of the list of priorities are "promoting democratic values and institutions around the world" and "maintaining an active military presence in other countries."[104] These findings are consistent with the Gallup/Council on Foreign Relations/National Geographic survey, which reports that the electorates' top concerns are trade and immigration.[105] These priorities are in line with core elements of Trump's America First agenda. So is the CAP report's finding that most Americans want U.S. allies to "pay their fair share for security."[106] The public's increasing preoccupation with the domestic economy only intensified as a result of the painful economic impact of the COVID-19 pandemic.

The CAP report concludes its survey by breaking the electorate into four segments—traditional internationalists who support engagement through power and partnership; global activists focused on fighting challenges like climate change and poverty through international cooperation; Trump nationalists who support America First; and voters who are largely disengaged on matters of foreign policy and prefer a strong focus on domestic issues. Traditional internationalists represent only eighteen percent of the electorate—not good news for liberal internationalism—with global activists representing twenty-eight percent of the electorate. Thirty-three percent of the electorate are Trump nationalists, while twenty-one percent favor disengagement. The nation's political landscape is certainly fragmented, but a majority of the public favors either America First or disengagement.[107] It is this political reality that is driving American leaders—Republicans and Democrats alike—to call for a renewed focus on the home front and to cut back on the nation's entanglements abroad. As the CAP report stresses, the American electorate has not become isolationist, but it is clearly turning inward and keen on shedding at least some of the nation's burdens abroad.

Generational change could deepen these trends over time. According to the CAP report, "younger voters are much less committed to traditional international and military engagement than are elder cohorts." They are less interested than older Americans in more conventional foreign policy goals such as preserving alliances and exercising U.S. leadership, instead prioritizing international issues like fighting climate change and defending human rights. While younger voters are less likely than older ones to back an America First approach to statecraft, they are more likely than their elders to favor a strong focus on domestic priorities. Generational change could thus strengthen popular pressure for strategic retrenchment, as well as fill the ranks of Congress with individuals for whom geopolitics is not a priority.[108]

At the same time that opinion surveys reveal the nation's inward turn, they also make clear that the public still strongly supports important elements of an internationalist agenda. Both the Chicago Council and CAP surveys reveal ample public support for the nation's alliances—NATO, in particular—even as Americans want allies to assume greater defense burdens.[109] The 2017 Pew survey indicates that almost three-fifths of the public want the U.S. government to take the views of allies into consideration—even if doing so entails compromise.[110] According to the 2018 Chicago Council report, over ninety percent of the public believes that the United States can more effectively achieve its foreign policy goals by working with other countries.[111] The American public, according to both the Chicago Council and Pew surveys, remains strongly supportive of international trade—even as it prioritizes steps to protect American jobs.[112]

* * *

The American electorate is not clamoring to cordon itself off from the world either geopolitically or economically, but it is demanding an adjustment—a middle course between the nation's original isolationism and its more recent overstretch. Accordingly, rebuilding a bipartisan consensus around an internationalist grand strategy is not out of reach. But it will have to be a new grand strategy—one built for the twenty-first century, not the nineteenth or the twentieth.

Where Isolationism and Liberal Internationalism Meet: The Search for a Middle Ground

The United States is in the midst of a heated and polarizing debate about the nature and scope of its engagement with the world. Such controversy over foreign policy is not new. Alexander Hamilton feuded with Thomas Jefferson over matters of U.S. statecraft during the nation's earliest days; similar bouts have broken out ever since. After the bitter arguments between Franklin Roosevelt and intransigent isolationists over the role that the nation should play in World War II, Walter Lippmann worried about the prospect of an America that was so divided that it would be unable to arrive at "a settled and generally accepted foreign policy." Lippmann warned: "This is a danger to the Republic. For when a people is divided within itself about the conduct of its foreign relations, it is unable to agree on the determination of its true interest. It is unable to prepare adequately for war or to safeguard successfully its peace. . . . The spectacle of this great nation which does not know its own mind is as humiliating as it is dangerous."[1]

Lippmann's worries would prove premature; a consensus behind liberal internationalism would form during the 1940s, consolidate in the early 1950s, and last through the balance of the twentieth century. Today, however, that consensus is gone; Lippmann's apprehensions could not be more apt. Across the Clinton, Bush, Obama, and Trump administrations, American statecraft has been inconsistent and incoherent precisely because the nation is very much "divided within itself about the conduct of its foreign relations." The result is the absence of "a settled and generally accepted foreign policy."

This book puts in historical relief the import of this moment in American history. Not for the first time, the United States is at an inflection point in the nature of its engagement with the world. The Revolutionary War and War of 1812, the Spanish-American War, World War I, the Senate's rejection of U.S. participation in the League of Nations, the Great Depression, World War II—these were all watershed events that profoundly altered the trajectory of U.S. statecraft. By the end of the War of 1812, geopolitical isolation had become doctrine and burgeoning reality, with the United States well on its way to enjoying the natural security afforded by its geography and setting its sights on westward expansion. In 1898, the United States transitioned from North American isolation to republican imperialism. The reaction against empire, the experience of World War I, and the nation's bitter debate over the League of Nations combined to induce Americans to swing back toward "isolationist internationalism" and seek influence without responsibility. The Great Depression then triggered a deluded search for geopolitical immunity from great-power competition. In 1941, the country, after two decades of shunning strategic commitments outside the Western Hemisphere, embraced an ambitious brand of internationalism that would outlast the Cold War. These were transformative moments for both the United States and the world.

As the last chapter made clear, U.S. grand strategy is again at a turning point. The domestic consensus behind liberal internationalism has collapsed, giving way to an inward turn among elites and the public alike as well as wide oscillations in policy as power changes hands in Washington. The ongoing rise of China will soon bring about the end of U.S. primacy, and illiberal forces appear to have reversed democracy's spread, potentially dissuading Americans from continuing to assume the burdens of global leadership that they took on in 1941. The COVID-19 pandemic encouraged Americans as well as other peoples around the world to tighten borders and enforce "social distancing" among nations.

Today, however, the United States should guard against a strategic adjustment on par with previous inflection points. It would be a grave mistake for the country to return to a grand strategy of North American or hemispheric isolation reminiscent of the nineteenth century. America and the world have changed too much. Globalization has fostered economic, social, technological, and strategic interdependence on an unprecedented scope. The economic impact of the spread of pandemic diseases, the shared interests that come with commercial and financial integration, the threats posed by climate change, the opportunities and vulnerabilities of cyberspace, the perils of nuclear proliferation—these are only a few examples of why the United States, even if it wanted to, cannot shield itself from the outside world. Washington's "great rule," wise in its time, is not fit for America in the world of the twenty-first century. As outlined in this chapter, the United States needs to trim its sails and step back from overreach through a strategy of judicious retrenchment. But it cannot afford to beat a precipitous retreat.

Nonetheless, an isolationist overcorrection is possible, if not likely. The strategic, political, and socio-economic forces that long made Americans ambivalent, if not hostile, toward foreign ambition are by no means gone for good. These forces have been largely dormant since the early 1950s, but they are making a comeback. The global balance of power is shifting away from the United States and its latest military ventures have not gone well, potentially prompting Americans to pull away from a world they are less able to control. After all, the United States spent much of its history shielding itself from a recalcitrant world, not trying to transform it. A resurgent unilateralist impulse is undermining international institutions and partnerships built over decades. Economic discontent is fueling protectionism, anti-immigrant sentiment, and political pressure to focus resources on the home front. In Lippmann's words, the country "does not know its own mind" when it comes to the conduct of statecraft, making it very hard to arrive at a purposeful and sustainable brand of internationalism.

The Logics of Isolationism: Then and Now

Amid these conditions, the logics that long sustained isolationism are gaining more traction and again entering mainstream discourse. As laid out in this book's second chapter, these six interlocking logics are: capitalizing on natural security; serving as redeemer nation; advancing liberty and prosperity at home; preserving freedom of action abroad; protecting social homogeneity; and promoting pacifism. These different strains of the isolationist impulse are reemerging in updated form, but, taken together, they strongly resonate with the strategic narrative that long convinced Americans to steer clear of foreign entanglement.

Capitalizing on Natural Security

For geographic reasons alone, banking on the nation's natural security has always had intrinsic appeal. Even amid the internationalist fervor of the Cold War era, a few lonely voices continued to tout the advantages of hemispheric isolation. To be sure, protective oceans are no longer as protective as they used to be. But the Founders' injunction against entanglement abroad arose from an enduring logic based on immutable geographic realities. The Founders were drawn to a grand strategy of isolationism because it would enable the country to capitalize on its enviable location. They envisaged a republic with territorial girth and watery expanse to its east and west, one that was destined to become a continental behemoth that would dominate its own hemisphere; this was the nation's "natural" course. Geography mattered.

According to George Washington, the nation's "detached and distant situation" meant that "Europe has a set of primary interests which to us have none; or a very remote relation." Geopolitical entanglement in Europe would therefore be "artificial."[2] In analyzing the relations between the United States and England, Thomas Paine asserted that "it is evident they belong to different systems; England to Europe, America to itself."[3] Alexander Hamilton similarly saw a world that consisted of discrete and separate regions: "The world may politically, as well as geographically, be divided into four parts [Africa, Asia, America, and Europe], each having a distinct set of interests." "Our situation invites and our interests prompt us to aim at an ascendant in the system of American affairs," Hamilton concluded.[4] The Monroe Doctrine emerged from a similar logic, warning foreign powers against colonial ambition in the Western Hemisphere, where the United States is "of necessity more immediately connected, and by causes which must be obvious to all enlightened and impartial observers." The same logic applied to Europe, where Monroe stipulated that U.S. policy should be "not to interfere."[5] In short, the Founders envisaged a world of regions, with great powers holding sway in their respective spheres of influence.

Two developments could tempt the United States to once again gravitate toward a world of regions. First, the economic and military preponderance that, beginning in 1898, fueled foreign ambition has been slipping away. China will likely become the world's leading economic power over the course of the next decade, and its military capability will eventually catch up with its wealth.[6] Even though the United States is today determined to contain China's rise, this ongoing shift in the material distribution of power could gradually diminish America's enthusiasm for projecting its power to Asia. Most of China's neighbors still look to the United States to hedge against China's ascent—and may continue to do so for quite some time. Nonetheless, as China's economic and military might continues to grow and the United States finds it difficult to keep pace, the countries of the Asia Pacific may over time align themselves with Beijing rather than Washington. It may be a sign of things to come that President Rodrigo Duterte has been wooing China and contemplating whether to terminate the agreement that governs the U.S. military presence in the Philippines.

That "changing of the guard" is exactly what transpired in the Western Hemisphere. The United States began life effectively surrounded by extra-regional powers—France, Great Britain, Russia, and Spain. But one by one, these powers exited or were ejected from America's neighborhood. American hegemony took on a taken-for-granted character as the countries of the region submitted to American power because they had little choice. Today Beijing is following this original American playbook. China is focusing on the growth of its domestic economy; it is looking to tap into new markets abroad and to use trade and investment to enhance its geopolitical leverage; it is avoiding entangling alliances; and it is aspiring to hold sway over its own neighborhood—just as the United States did during its successful ascent. As China eventually reemerges as its region's "natural" hegemon, the United States may well be inclined to pull back from the western Pacific. After all, the United States long steered clear of entanglement in Europe while it ventured into East Asia in part because Europe was home to powers of superior strength.

Second, Americans are acutely aware of the nation's overreach in the Middle East. The wars in Afghanistan, Iraq, Libya, and Syria have been extremely costly. Tens of thousands of U.S. personnel have been wounded or killed, and one study puts the cost of the post–September 11 wars at roughly $6 trillion.[7] Moreover, these conflicts have left behind considerable instability and suffering. A good number of Americans have concluded that the most effective way of dealing with violent extremists in Afghanistan and Iraq may be getting U.S. soldiers out of harm's way, not sending them into Kandahar and Fallujah.

Against this backdrop, U.S. history suggests that a pullback is inevitably coming. The Spanish-American War and the territorial acquisitions that followed marked a clear change of course for the United States. However, many Americans recoiled from the imperial conquests of 1898—in particular, the bloody occupation of the Philippines—and gravitated toward dollar diplomacy and hemispheric isolation. Woodrow Wilson in 1917 departed even further from the Founders' warnings and dispatched millions of U.S. soldiers to fight in Europe. Even though the United States was victorious in World War I, it again pulled back, relying primarily on its economic strength to exercise diplomatic influence beyond the Western Hemisphere as it sought strategic immunity from Europe and Asia. After the Great Depression, Americans pulled back even further, going it alone on economic recovery and using neutrality legislation to cordon the nation off from the risk of entanglement in great-power war. The travails of the Vietnam War prompted another round of retrenchment. With the Cold War still on, very few Americans called for a return to hemispheric isolation. Nonetheless, Nixon, Ford, and Carter all looked to diplomacy to lighten America's load abroad.

While the rise of China, America's overextension in the Middle East, and the nation's record of retrenchment in response to overreach point to the advisability and inevitability of a strategic pullback, they do not warrant or make inevitable a full retreat to hemispheric isolation. The Founders may have based their vision of a world of regions on immutable geographic realities, but their vision was of their time. Nonetheless, geography still matters, the United States is still far from Europe, Asia, the Middle East, and Africa, and the prospect of immunity from the dangers of foreign entanglement still has its intrinsic, even if illusory, appeal. The nation's enviable location will always sustain the isolationist temptation. Indeed, as discussed below, prominent scholars are already calling for the United States not just to pull back from the Middle East, but also to de-camp from Europe and East Asia.

Serving as Redeemer Nation

America's exceptionalist calling—its role as redeemer nation—was central to the nation's long embrace of a grand strategy of isolationism. The United States needed to remain aloof from the outside world to protect its unique experiment in liberty; in the meantime, it would change the world by example. Its messi-anic aspirations were then equally important in sustaining the long run of liberal internationalism. Beginning in 1941, the United States set about changing the world through more activist means. The collapse of the Soviet Union and the end of the Cold War confirmed the value of these efforts.

Today, however, many Americans are questioning whether their exceptionalist calling has led them astray. When they have done so before, isolationist impulses awakened. It was time to take Manifest Destiny abroad and liberate the hem-isphere from oppression, McKinley told Americans as he made the case for expelling Spain from Cuba by force. Instead, Americans acquired an empire that tarnished their exceptionalist credentials, contributing to the political backlash against internationalism that soon followed. Wilson entered World War I to make the world safe for democracy and bring into being the peaceful, rules-based order envisaged by the Founders. But Americans recoiled from the results of their exertions, deciding that their exceptionalist ambitions would be best served by steering clear of foreign entanglement.

Once again, Americans are finding that the results of their exceptionalist exertions are falling well short of expectations. A succession of wars in the Middle East is not leading to the replication of the American experiment. Despite decades of robust global engagement and pronouncements that the end of the Cold War meant the "end of history," the world has of late become more illib-eral, rejecting rather than replicating the American experiment. Obama explic-itly recognized that the nation's ideological ambitions had led it down an errant path. Driven by "interest in pursuing peace and freedom beyond our borders," he maintained, "some of our most costly mistakes came not from our restraint, but from our willingness to rush into military adventures without thinking through the consequences. . . . U.S. military action cannot be the only—or even primary—component of our leadership in every instance. Just because we have the best hammer does not mean that every problem is a nail." Trump arrived at a similar conclusion, although he preferred to echo America's nineteenth- century leaders in asserting that some peoples simply are not cut out for democracy. The nation's wars in the Middle East were futile, he concluded, because the countries there "had no experience or interests in becoming a western democracy. We tore up what institutions they had and then were surprised at what we unleashed." Trump counseled that Americans "not seek to impose our way of life on anyone" but instead offer their model "as an example for everyone to follow."[8]

If history is any guide, Americans may well return to a brand of exceptionalism in which they play the role of exemplar, not crusader. Recent political trends point to the same conclusion. Bipartisanship is a rare commodity in contemporary America. But Democrats and Republicans alike appear to be converging around the need to step back from the activist version of the exceptionalist narrative that both parties embraced in 1941.

Advancing Liberty and Prosperity at Home

The Founders held firmly to the conviction that ambition abroad would come at the expense of liberty and prosperity at home. Indeed, they feared domestic threats to democracy more than they did foreign enemies. They embraced isolationism in part because they foresaw a future of tyranny rather than republican freedom should the United States acquire the powerful federal institutions and large military establishment that would accompany entanglement in great-power competition. So, too, would the expense of foreign ambition require high taxation and other disruptions to the U.S. economy. During the first half of the twentieth century, Americans looked to isolationism to help counter other internal threats to the nation's economic welfare, including corporations with vested interests in expansion, growing inequality and job loss due to foreign trade, and an influx of foreign workers that would further increase unemployment.

These concerns are again front and center. The Founders' fears that foreign ambition would mean tyranny at home proved to be unfounded. Nonetheless, presidential control over foreign policy, which began to mount in the late nineteenth century, has increased substantially over time. The Founders would recoil at the prospect of Truman taking the nation to war in Korea without congressional authorization. The United States since the attacks of September 11 has relied on the Authorization for Use of Military Force (AUMF) that Congress passed in 2001 and in 2002 to launch one war after another in the broader Middle East. The 2001 legislation enabled the president to take action against those who "planned, authorized, committed or aided" the September 11 attacks, while the 2002 legislation authorized the U.S. invasion of Iraq that began in 2003. These two acts hardly provide a compelling and convincing legislative foundation for the wide range of military operations that the United States has carried out over the past twenty years.[9] Steps to increase domestic surveillance have also encroached upon the privacy and civil liberties of American citizens.[10] The fight against both foreign and domestic terrorism led to a network of surveillance— wiretapping, financial monitoring, electronic data collection—that both

Congress and the courts deemed to be excessive.[11] Entanglement abroad has in fact compromised liberty at home.[12]

In the minds of many Americans, the economic costs of foreign entanglement far exceed its negative impact on domestic liberties. Not for the first time in American history, economic duress has been fueling pressure for the United States to distance itself from the global economy. Indeed, Trump's political success stemmed in no small part from the explicit linkage he drew between globalization and America's domestic ills. According to his account, the globalization of trade and finance has impoverished American workers and led to unprecedented inequality.Unchecked immigration is only worsening the plight of the working class. In the meantime, the nation's allies are free riding on America's strategic reach, failing to shoulder their fair share of defense burdens. The health crisis and economic downturn spawned by COVID-19, a disease that rapidly spread across national boundaries, added further pressure for the United States to distance itself from the outside world. In response to economic dislocation at home—what Trump called "this American carnage"—Republicans abandoned their long-running commitment to free trade and supported draconian cuts to immigration.

Many Democrats have joined Republicans in pulling back from free trade— especially when it comes to China. Progressive Democrats have also revived arguments frequently made by early- twentieth-century reformers, charging that corporations are ensuring the enrichment of the few at the expense of the many. Left-leaning voices have been calling for higher taxes on the rich, the breakup of large corporations like Amazon, Apple, Facebook, and Google, and significant reductions to the defense budget. Progressives charge that corporations are manipulating foreign policy to further their self-interest. In the words of Elizabeth Warren, "the coziness between defense lobbyists, Congress, and the Pentagon . . . tilts countless decisions, big and small . . . toward the desires of giant corporations that thrive off taxpayer dollars." Bernie Sanders offered a similar critique: "It is time to invest in the working families of this country and not a bloated military budget."[13] Many Americans have concluded, as the Founders warned, that foreign ambition has come at the expense of liberty and prosperity at home.

Preserving Freedom of Action Abroad

Isolationism also emerged from the Founders' determination to preserve the nation's freedom of action abroad. Indeed, isolationism and unilateralism have been intertwined since the founding era. President Washington's failure to honor the alliance with France in 1793 may have been a bald act of infidelity, but it enabled the United States to act as it saw fit amid war between Britain and France. In his Farewell Address three years later, Washington's doctrinal admonition against alliance allowed the nation not only to enjoy its geographic good fortune, but also to avoid the encumbrances that would accompany obligations to others. The prospect of U.S. participation in the 1826 Panama Congress provoked a political firestorm in Congress due to the nation's aversion not only to potential strategic commitments beyond its borders, but also to entanglement in the politics and diplomacy of Latin America. The Senate's rejection of U.S. participation in the League of Nations may have been a harbinger of the isolationism of the interwar era. But it was unilateralism, not isolationism, that sank the League. Senator Lodge and his Republican cohort were internationalist in outlook. They voted against ratification because they believed the treaty, without revision, would subjugate U.S. policy to the collective will of the League.

Today, American unilateralism, which has been regaining potency for the past three decades, again runs stronger than isolationism. To be sure, political pressure has been mounting to off-load foreign commitments and reduce the nation's strategic footprint abroad. But at least for now, it is America's go-it-alone attitudes, more than its strategic pullback, that is causing global consternation. America's traditional allies may still enjoy the protection of U.S. troops, but they share profound discontent over the unilateralist turn in U.S. diplomacy. In their view, the United States is undermining the very institutions and habits of strategic and economic cooperation that it worked so hard to build and sustain from the 1940s into the twenty-first century. Especially within the Republican Party, this unilateralist impulse is likely to endure for the foreseeable future. Not for the first time in American history, allies and adversaries alike are questioning America's reliability and the credibility of its international agreements. When the United States last defected from making common cause with like-minded nations—the 1930s—the consequences were ruinous.

Protecting Social Homogeneity

America's quest for social homogeneity and the racial, ethnic, and religious tensions it fueled were long a source of the isolationist impulse. Prior to the Civil War, the North and South could not agree whether targets of acquisition would be free or slave-holding, blocking expansion beyond North America. After the Civil War and the end of slavery, the troubled politics of race relations still compelled the United States to steer clear of expansion into the Caribbean and Latin America; the prospect of bringing more nonwhites into the body politic was too controversial. Concern about preserving the Anglo-Saxon character of the nation, combined with efforts to protect labor markets, produced successive waves of anti-immigrant legislation—targeting Chinese in the 1880s, the "Asiatic Barred Zone" in 1917, and southern and eastern Europeans in the 1920s. During the 1930s, around a million individuals of Mexican descent, many of them U.S. citizens, were deported to Mexico. Prominent members of the America First Committee, as well as libertarian nationalists during the Cold War era, on occasion trafficked in racism and anti-Semitism.

Anti-immigrant sentiment and fear of social dilution have again been having outsized influence on American politics. Trump's efforts to build a wall along the border with Mexico and to scale back dramatically both legal and illegal immigration raised the salience and emotional intensity of identity politics. Indeed, Trump made immigration a wedge issue by integrating it into his America First agenda. There was no direct linkage between Trump's determination to withdraw from Syria and Afghanistan and his efforts to cut back on immigration. But as during previous periods in American history, concern about the social dilution of American society was entangled with the impulse to cordon the nation off from the outside world. It is hardly accidental that Trump's America First agenda melded anti-immigrant measures with economic protectionism and strategic pullback. These logics have regularly intersected and reinforced each other across the nation's isolationist past.

Promoting Pacifism

Pacifism helped sustain isolationism from the founding years through the interwar era. Although the pacifist strain of isolationism has arguably been weaker than the others, pacifist sentiment has played a role in dampening foreign ambition. The passionate opposition of pacifists to the War of 1812 and the Mexican-American War failed to prevent those conflicts. Indeed, northern opposition to the War of 1812 helped bring about the collapse of the Federalist Party after the war's end. But the pacifist movement, which was initially concentrated in New England but then evolved into a national network, did reinforce the isolationist consensus that prevailed through the balance of the nineteenth century. The influence of pacifists increased substantially after the Spanish-American War. They helped fuel the anti-imperialist movement, which, although it fell short of blocking the Treaty of Paris that formalized republican imperialism, shaped both Taft's strategic pullback and Wilson's idealist turn. So, too, did the pacifists play a role in blocking ratification of the League of Nations, which the left found too wedded to the rules of realpolitik. Pacifists also bolstered the isolationist coalition that formed during the 1930s, joining a political bloc that succeeded in keeping the United States out of World War II until the attack on Pearl Harbor.

The United States today is absent a strong pacifist movement. However, the progressive wing of the Democratic Party has embraced elements of a traditional pacifist agenda. Unlike Trump, the left generally backs international teamwork and close cooperation with U.S. allies. But as they campaigned for the presidency, both Bernie Sanders and Elizabeth Warren supported substantial decreases in defense spending, blamed corporate America for promoting militarism, and called for a reduction in the nation's foreign entanglements. Sanders was quite blunt on this front: "The time is long overdue for us to take a hard look at military spending, including the 'war on terror,' and whether it makes sense to spend trillions more on endless wars, wars that often cause more problems than they solve. Call me a radical, but maybe before funding a new space force, we should make sure no American goes bankrupt because of a medical bill or dies because they can't afford to go to a doctor on time."[14]

Warren was equally adamant, outlining a set of foreign policy priorities that echoed those of Emily Balch, Jane Addams, Randolph Bourne, and other pacifists of their era:

> We must not accept yet another unnecessary, costly, and counterproductive war. Instead, we should refocus our attention and resources on the challenges that will define our national security for the next generation: promoting prosperity and lessening inequality; addressing the climate crisis; answering resurgent right-wing demagogues who are undermining the strength of our democratic alliances; and countering globalized corruption and authoritarianism led from Moscow and Beijing. America should end its military involvement in conflicts in the Middle East and bring our troops home from these endless wars in smart, responsible ways.[15]

Another Democratic candidate, Representative Tulsi Gabbard (D-Hawaii), offered a similar perspective: "Stupid regime change wars suck badly needed funds from our domestic needs such as healthcare, infrastructure, protecting the environment, and more. This will end when I'm president."[16]

Pacifism is not a dominant political force in American politics. Nonetheless, years of wars in the Middle East have pushed progressives in a pacifist direction. Progressives and conservatives share scant common ground ideologically. But left and right increasingly agree, albeit for different reasons, that the nation needs to pull back from a surfeit of foreign entanglements. As made clear at the close of World War I and during the interwar era, progressive pacifists and conservative nationalists can together serve as a formidable coalition behind isolationism.

Managing Overreach: The Risk of Overcorrection

America's isolationist past should not be its future. Global interdependence makes it both unfeasible and unwise for the United States to return to being a North American or hemispheric redoubt. Nonetheless, the strategic, political, and socio-economic forces that gave rise to isolationism, and the interlocking logics that long sustained it, are making a comeback. The result is a growing gap between the nation's global commitments and the readiness of the American electorate to uphold those commitments. This gap is contributing to the inability of the United States to arrive at a steady grand strategy that enjoys public support. As Lippmann warned, "the nation must maintain its objectives and its power in equilibrium, its purposes within its means and its means equal to its purposes." If not attended to, the growing gap between means and ends could well trigger an isolationist retreat that would be both disruptive and dangerous.

Across the nation's history, and especially prior to 1941, the United States has often turned to isolationist recourse to keep its means and purposes in equilibrium—to both good and ill effect. Moreover, the isolationist impulse can come from multiple quarters. At times, it has been the executive branch that shuns foreign ambition. George Washington was unequivocal as he laid down his "great rule" in 1796. As both secretary of state and president, John Quincy Adams counseled against foreign entanglement, famously proclaiming in 1821 that the United States "goes not abroad, in search of monsters to destroy." Secretary of State Hamilton Fish refused to involve the United States in a Cuban revolt against Spain that broke out in 1868 and rebuffed Samoan chiefs when they requested that the United States annex their islands. Cleveland during his first term canceled plans to build a canal across Nicaragua, and during his second term he withdrew the Hawaiian annexation treaty and tried—unsuccessfully—to convince Congress to allow him to pull out of the Samoan protectorate, both of which were left behind by his predecessor. Taft reverted from republican imperialism to dollar diplomacy, while Wilson shunned U.S. involvement in World War I until Germany began sinking U.S. ships in early 1917. During the 1920s, Harding and Coolidge both backtracked from Wilsonian idealism to "isolationist internationalism." From the Great Depression through the outbreak of World War II, Hoover and Roosevelt pulled back from economic and strategic engagement outside the Western Hemisphere.

Congress has played its own important role in enforcing the isolationist impulse. Over the course of the nineteenth century, Congress repeatedly blocked the efforts of the executive branch to expand into the Caribbean and Pacific. Among the territories rejected were Santo Domingo, Cuba, the Danish West Indies, and Hawaii. Until the early 1900s, Congress turned away successive attempts to construct an isthmian canal. The effort to build a blue-water navy that began in the 1880s provoked a firestorm of opposition among legislators. It was the Senate that sank the League of Nations. Congress in the 1930s led the effort to tighten neutrality legislation, even refusing during much of 1939 to allow Franklin Roosevelt to provide arms to the victims of aggression through the "cash and carry" program. As the Cold War heated up, Truman had to strong-arm Congress to win support for foreign assistance to fight the spread of communism and to acquiesce to his decision to deploy additional U.S. forces to Europe.

So, too, has the public itself at times imposed significant constraints on foreign ambition. The anti-imperialist movement had a telling impact on U.S. grand strategy during the early 1900s. Even an avowed expansionist like Theodore Roosevelt had to rein in his enthusiasm for international ambition due to concern about losing public support. The America First Committee wielded considerable influence over the electorate, contributing to strong public support for staying out of World War II. The public's skepticism toward foreign entanglement also contributed to several near misses on constitutional reform. The Ludlow Amendment, which would have subjected declarations of war to popular referendum, did not pass, but it enjoyed quite strong support in the public and in Congress. The Bricker Amendment, which would have imposed significant constraints on the ability of the executive branch to conclude and implement international agreements, similarly had quite strong public backing. It took Eisenhower's direct intervention to block its passage. Given this track record, it is hardly surprising that Arthur Schlesinger and many others worried about a potential resurgence of isolationism during both the Cold War and its aftermath.

Signs abound that Americans once more deem their means and their purposes to be out of kilter. As in the past, the demand signal for retrenchment is again coming from multiple quarters. The previous chapter revealed that the electorate favors "restrained engagement" and a pullback from the current scope of U.S. commitments. The American people twice elected Barack Obama, a Democrat who called for "nation-building at home." They then elected Donald Trump, a Republican who unabashedly pursued a grand strategy of America First. Trump bullied allies into shouldering greater defense burdens and openly mused about withdrawing from NATO and U.S. defense commitments in Asia. Indeed, Trump's America First approach to foreign policy and his isolationist overtones uncannily resonated with U.S. grand strategy during the nineteenth century.[17] Democrats complained bitterly. But most of the Democratic senators seeking to succeed Trump supported his decision late in 2018 to begin the withdrawal from Syria and Afghanistan. Congress and the American electorate may be deeply polarized, but there is an emerging consensus that the nation should pull back from the role of global guardian that it has played since the 1940s.

Debate among foreign policy experts tracks with these political trends. An expanding chorus of mainstream international relations scholars and public intellectuals is clamoring for the nation to pursue strategic retrenchment.[18] Indeed, prominent academics from the nation's premier universities are filling the pages of *Foreign Affairs* with calls for the United States to dismantle the primary strategic commitments it has upheld since World War II.[19] John Mearsheimer and Stephen Walt are among the growing cadre of influential scholars calling for a grand strategy of offshore balancing. Mearsheimer and Walt want the United States to quit Europe, leaving stability on the continent to Europeans themselves. They hedge when it comes to East Asia, acknowledging that at least some U.S. forces should remain in the region to balance China. But others go further. Barry Posen, even though he does not explicitly recommend a complete withdrawal from the region, calls for Japan and other maritime Asian countries "even without the United States as a backstop . . . [to] make common cause against China." Stephen Wertheim similarly calls for the United States to "significantly reduce its forward-deployed military presence in Asia and Europe alike."[20]

The libertarian Cato Institute used to be the sole prominent home in the nation's capital for strategists advocating that the United States return to policies of nonentanglement. But in 2019, George Soros, a generous benefactor of liberal causes, and Charles Koch, a conservative philanthropist, teamed up to provide funding for a new Washington think tank—the Quincy Institute for Responsible Statecraft—which "promotes ideas that move U.S. foreign policy away from endless war and toward vigorous diplomacy in the pursuit of international peace."[21] The Quincy Institute, named after John Quincy Adams, institutionalizes the same unusual alliance between anti-war progressives on the left and libertarian nationalists on the right that existed during the interwar era.

These developments indicate that a strategic pullback is coming—a product of changes in America's political landscape, the nation's chronic strategic overreach since the Cold War's end, the economic discontent of many Americans, and the public's awareness that a shift in the global distribution of power necessitates a more equitable sharing of global responsibilities. The COVID-19 crisis renders this pullback all the more inevitable. The pandemic made clear that the country had dramatically underspent on preparedness for healthcare emergencies. Its dire economic consequences reinforced the electorate's insistence on investments at home rather than abroad. And the rapid transmission of the virus around the globe prompted the United States to close its borders and stoked anti-foreign sentiment.

The central question is not whether the United States retrenches, but whether it does so by design or by default. By design is far preferable. A planned, paced, and measured retrenchment has the potential to preserve a stable, rules-based order even as the United States sheds strategic commitments and shares global responsibilities with other players. Indeed, Obama tried to do as much. Liberal international lite—in Obama's own words, a "more centered course" between "isolation" and "confronting every evil that can be found abroad"—was an explicit effort to orchestrate retrenchment by design.

The more likely outcome, however, is retrenchment by default—an unplanned and perilous American retreat from global affairs. American grand strategy risks becoming politically insolvent as the gap grows between the scope of the nation's commitments abroad and the willingness of the body politic to uphold those commitments. The result could be strategic overcompensation; dangerous overreach could turn into even more dangerous underreach. The interwar era puts into sobering relief the disastrous consequences that can potentially ensue when the United States takes excessive and irresponsible steps to cordon itself off from trouble abroad. This book's historical narrative makes clear that a disruptive inward turn is a real possibility. The ambitious internationalism of the last eight decades is the exception, not the rule, in U.S. history; it should *not* be interpreted as a sign that the nation's zealous engagement in shaping the globe's geopolitical affairs is here to stay. Charting the future on the basis of the nation's post-Pearl Harbor grand strategy would be a mistake. It is important to take into consideration the full sweep of the nation's history.

Isolationism has from the outset been part of the American creed; it is part and parcel of the American experience. A strategy of nonentanglement has had powerful political allure during much of the nation's history—and has considerable potential to do so again. The isolationist temptation reemerges even when the internationalists deem it to be extinguished for good. When the likes of McKinley, Mahan, Roosevelt, and Lodge orchestrated the "large policy" of 1898, little did they know that their actions would trigger a potent anti-imperialist movement and a quick retreat to dollar diplomacy. When Wilson entered World War I to erect a U.S.-led and rules-based international order, he had overwhelming support in both houses of Congress. Little did he know that the Senate would soon walk away from the League of Nations or that U.S. participation in the Great War would set the stage for the stubborn isolationism of the interwar era. The retrenchment that followed the Vietnam War was more modest and incremental in scope. But that pullback occurred during the Cold War, when the liberal internationalist compact was still intact. With the Cold War over and America's political center in remission, a pullback today could well go much farther—indeed, too far—as it has done multiple times in the past.

Today, the potential for a disruptive retreat is magnified by the fact that the last two American presidents, although they tried to step back from overreach, fell short. Trump, and Obama before him, actively sought to respond to the electorate's demand for retrenchment. But both ran into multiple obstacles. Obama faced considerable pressure at home and abroad to turn to the

U.S. military to respond to instability in the broader Middle East and the spread of violent extremism. He reluctantly kept U.S. troops in Afghanistan, embarked with allies on a war in Libya, responded to ISIL's conquests by sending U.S. forces to Iraq and Syria, and deployed a sizable number of troops across Africa primarily to fight extremists. Trump sensed the public's impatience, which was exactly why he campaigned on a retrenchment platform.

Yet Trump, too, struggled to make good on his pledges to bring the troops home, leading to frustration and impetuous missteps. As for Afghanistan, Trump in early 2020 cut a deal with the Taliban that was to reduce the fighting and ostensibly clear the way for U.S. troops to be out of the country by 2021. But the Taliban was back on the warpath within days of signing the agreement and Trump's own team was confused about its apparently vague terms.[22] As for Syria, Trump in 2019 recklessly decided to pull U.S. forces out of the country's north—without first putting in place an accompanying military or diplomatic strategy for doing so. Turkey promptly invaded Syria, America's Kurdish partners were on their own, and Russia markedly strengthened its sway over Syria. A few months later, the Syrian regime and its Russian backers intensified their assault on Idlib Province, drawing Turkey more deeply into the conflict and triggering yet another surge in humanitarian suffering and the flow of displaced persons. Turkey then pressured Europe to get more deeply involved by encouraging migrants in Turkey to head to Greece, threatening the European Union with a new wave of refugees. An impetuous withdrawal had quite adverse knock-on effects. It is precisely this kind of rash and unplanned retreat that the nation must avoid.

Trump regularly protested that he was hemmed in by the "deep state"—a complaint that was not without justification. One of the obstacles standing in the way of a more measured and considered retrenchment is America's own foreign policy establishment. As Stephen Walt and others have chronicled, this establishment still tends to support a brand of U.S. statecraft that entails global activism and the regular projection of U.S. power.[23] Indeed, many of its members continue to charge that advocates of retrenchment are deluded isolationists—a term that still carries the pejorative connotation that it earned in the 1930s. According to James Carafano, a scholar at the Heritage Foundation, supporters of retrenchment are the "'new' isolationists [who] would prefer America step off the playing field and wave from the sidelines."[24] The conservative intellectual William Kristol responded to the founding of the Quincy Institute with the following tweet: "75 years of a US-led liberal international order . . . has enabled remarkable peace and prosperity. But let's go back to the 1920s and 30s."[25] Such cheap shots, however, only raise the chances of a perilous retreat by standing in the way of the open and honest conversation that Americans need to have about the nation's role in the world. If retrenchment is coming—and it is—the nation needs to embark on a searching debate about how to arrive at the middle ground between doing too much and doing too little.

A Strategy of Judicious Retrenchment

The history of isolationism presented in this book speaks for itself. It illuminates the long-running debate among Americans over the scope and nature of their nation's entanglement in the world, underscores the contingent nature of U.S. engagement in global affairs, and clarifies the costs and benefits of isolationist and internationalist alternatives. Given the outsized role that the United States continues to play in global affairs, Americans as well as the many other peoples affected by U.S. policy need to be aware of this history as debate over the future of U.S. grand strategy advances. The historical record does not dictate specific policy recommendations. On the contrary, readers should and will take away different lessons from this exploration of the *longue durée* of U.S. statecraft.

As they debate the future of U.S. grand strategy, Americans should keep in mind that isolationism and internationalism both have strategic upsides and strategic downsides. Isolationism succeeded in enhancing America's security and prosperity during the nineteenth century and helped the nation resist the imperial temptation after 1898, but misled the nation into dangerous delusion during the interwar era. Liberal internationalism was an effective and sustainable grand strategy during the Cold War, but a successful brand of internationalism has been the exception in U.S. history. Americans rejected the realist internationalism of 1898 as well as Wilson's idealist ambition that came soon thereafter. Since the Cold War's end, the nation's internationalist calling has again gone awry, producing pronounced strategic excess.

A principal challenge moving forward will be to draw on both isolationist and internationalist traditions to find a sustainable brand of statecraft that constitutes the middle road between overreach and underreach. Good policy requires good politics. If Democrats and Republicans are again to unite behind "a settled and generally accepted foreign policy," it will need to be one that brings purposes and means back into equilibrium. It will need to be a grand strategy that aims to do less while still doing enough. Tension between isolationism and internationalism has shaped strategic debate since the founding era; politicians and strategists need to tap into that tension to forge a new and stable equilibrium between the excesses of isolation and overstretch.

This book concludes by offering three broad guidelines that Americans should consider as they debate the contours of a strategy of retrenchment.[26] First, judicious retrenchment should focus on shedding U.S. entanglements in the periphery, not in the strategic heartland of Eurasia. America's main strategic error since the end of the Cold War has been unnecessary embroilment in wars of choice in the Middle East. The terror attacks of September 11 fully justified the invasion of Afghanistan to take down Al-Qaeda and neutralize the Taliban. But the subsequent effort to politically and socially reengineer the country, the toppling of regimes in Iraq and Libya, the attempt to bring down the Syrian government—these have been bouts of misguided excess. Most Americans have realized as much. That realization, alongside economic distress and faltering infrastructure inside the United States, has understandably prompted much of the electorate to call for a renewed focus on the home front.

The United States should end its endless wars in the Middle East. It would, however, be a grave error for legitimate frustration over an excess of foreign entanglements in the periphery to also prompt withdrawal from essential commitments in the strategically core areas of Europe and East Asia. Trump and his predecessors are right that America's allies need to shoulder a fairer share of the burdens of common defense. But pulling back from Europe and East Asia constitutes precisely the kind of rash overcorrection that the United States must avoid. Americans still have an overriding interest in dampening and preventing great-power competition in Europe and Asia. The expansionist threats that both Russia and China pose to their neighbors mean that the same objective that guided U.S. entry into World War II and the Cold War—to prevent the domination of Eurasia by a hostile power—still applies today and for the foreseeable future.

An American withdrawal from Europe and Asia would only unsettle allies and embolden adversaries, inviting arms racing and intensifying rivalry. It would be far riskier and far more costly for the United States to decamp from these core strategic theaters—only to have to rush back after war has broken out. Moreover, the history of the interwar era reveals how politically difficult it may be for Washington, once it has pulled out of Eurasia, to return in a timely fashion. The United States militarily disengaged from Europe and East Asia after World War I, seeking instead to use its diplomatic and economic leverage to preserve stability in both regions. The strategy initially worked. However, when geopolitical rivalries began to heat up in both theaters, America was desperately slow to reengage militarily, preferring to bank on the illusion of strategic immunity. This mistake the United States cannot afford to repeat.

If and when Europe and East Asia are able to build stable, self-sustaining regional orders, then, perhaps, the world of regions envisaged by the Founders would draw closer.[27] But those days are far off. For now, America needs to stop spinning its wheels in wars of choice in the strategic periphery, but should remain the principal pacifier of great-power politics in Eurasia.

Second, even as they pursue retrenchment Americans must sustain the enthusiasm for international partnership that they embraced during the second half of the twentieth century. The United States cannot afford to return to the stubborn unilateralism that guided the nation's grand strategy for much of its history prior to entry into World War II. Too many of today's global challenges require broad international cooperation if they are to be effectively addressed. Managing the globalization of trade and finance, combating climate change, preventing nuclear proliferation, addressing global pandemics—these and other challenges make going it alone a nonstarter. Moreover, as the United States pulls back from its role as global policeman, it will want like-minded partners to help fill the gap. These necessary partnerships become stronger through diplomacy and teamwork, not through unilateral action.

Determined diplomacy will be particularly important in a world that, for the first time in history, will be globalized and interdependent—but without a captain at the helm to provide oversight. Globalization took off during *Pax Britannica* and deepened during *Pax Americana*, with Britain and then America supplying stewardship. But no country or region will similarly dominate the twenty-first century. It will be neither an American century nor a Chinese century; it will be "No One's World."[28] As economic and military might diffuses across the international system, the challenges of coordinating policy across numerous zones of power will only grow. Multipolarity may make multilateralism more difficult, but the dispersion of power also makes teamwork more important.

To be sure, America's divided political landscape is making teamwork harder to come by. The country has been gravitating back toward its earlier preference for unilateralism and strategic autonomy. These political realities mean that multilateral cooperation will often have to take the form of pragmatic partnerships rather than the formalized treaties and institutions of the Cold War era. The United States should view itself as the leader of an international posse, defending rules-based institutions when possible, and putting together "coalitions of the willing" when necessary. The increasing polarization of the United States and the diffusion of power around the globe mean that pragmatic teamwork, flexible concerts, and task-specific coalitions must become the staples of a new brand of U.S. multilateralism.

Third, even as it scales back the scope of its international ambition, the United States should stand by its exceptionalist calling. Illusions of completing America's messianic mission have admittedly lured the nation toward overreach; a realist course correction is overdue, and judicious retrenchment is just that. But the United States cannot afford to abandon its role as a beacon of republican values and institutions. Today's world desperately needs an anchor of republican ideals—a role that only the United States has the power and credentials to fulfill. Illiberalism is on the rise within the West and beyond, fueled in part by the efforts of Russia and China to legitimate and replicate alternatives to liberal democracy. The progressive flow of history may end if the United States is no longer seeking to tip the scales toward freedom and human dignity. Indeed, it is precisely because the world is potentially at a historical inflection point that the United States must reclaim its exceptionalist mantle and continue to advance the cause of liberty.

As they chart the next phase of their exceptionalist mission, Americans must realize that they must start by putting their own house in order. The United States cannot serve as a model for the world when its political landscape is so deeply polarized and its republican institutions so dysfunctional. The first priority is to tackle the root causes of the political ills afflicting the nation, including inequality and the profound sense of economic insecurity that pervades much of the electorate. The country also needs a credible and effective immigration policy to help ensure that the exceptionalist narrative embraces a racially and ethnically pluralistic notion of nationhood instead of the nativist version that has been in the ascendant. As sectarian passions cleave the Middle East, Hindu nationalism unsettles India, the Chinese "reeducate" Uighurs, and discord over the future of immigration and multiculturalism test European solidarity, the United States must demonstrate unity amid diversity. Congress also needs to claw back from the executive branch its constitutional responsibility to exercise more sway over matters of war and peace.[29] The Founders quite deliberately granted Congress— and Congress alone—the power to declare war and the power of the purse. The full exercise of those rights can both guide judicious retrenchment and help restore public confidence in the nation's republican institutions.

Finally, to reclaim its exceptionalist mantle and mission while pursuing judicious retrenchment, the United States should return to its original plan for sharing the American experiment, which was to serve as an exemplar rather than a crusader. Working to spread democracy through advocacy and example rather than more intrusive means will help the United States find the middle ground between isolation and overreach. This middle course will require that Americans become comfortable engaging in the world as it is, not as they would like it to be. For much of its history, the United States cordoned itself off from a world that it feared would spoil the American experiment. Beginning with World War II, the United States swung to the opposite extreme, seeking to recast the world in America's image. Moving forward, the United States will need to engage in a messy and imperfect world while resisting the temptation either to recoil from it or to remake it.

This new brand of statecraft would require that Americans accept a more pluralistic global order. The United States would need to operate in a world of political diversity and respectfully work with democratic and nondemocratic regimes alike. Liberal democracy would compete in the marketplace of ideas with other approaches to governance, demonstrating an abiding American confidence in the ability of liberal forms of government to ultimately prevail against authoritarian alternatives. This approach, after all, is hardly out of step with America's longer diplomatic traditions. President Monroe in 1823 warned European powers against any new imperial adventures in the Western Hemisphere, articulating the doctrine that came to bear his name. But he also acknowledged Europe's monarchical preferences and committed the United States "not to interfere in the internal concerns of any of its powers; to consider the government de facto as the legitimate government for us; to cultivate friendly relations with it."[30] Such pragmatism and prudence are again in order.

* * *

Isolationism served the United States well during its long ascent. After the nation's arrival as a great power, Americans experimented with both realist and idealist brands of internationalism, neither of which proved capable of durably displacing isolationism. By merging realism and idealism and marrying power to partnership, liberal internationalism finally guided the United States away from its isolationist roots and anchored U.S. statecraft from World War II into this new century. The result was the long run of *Pax Americana*.

But those days are over. America needs a grand strategy that is still idealist in vision and voice—even if more realist in practice. Building an inclusive order of democracies and nondemocracies—while still working over the long haul to advance the exceptionalist mission of universal republicanism—will offer the right blend of idealism and realism needed if the United States is to find a middle course between doing too much and doing too little. Isolationism ruled for much of American history. An unstinting internationalism followed. It is now time to find the stable middle ground.

NOTES

Chapter 1

1. Donald Trump, "Inaugural Address," January 20, 2017, *The American Presidency Project* (*TAPP*), https://www.presidency.ucsb.edu/node/320188.
2. Barack Obama, "Remarks and an Exchange With Reporters Following a Press Briefing by White House Press Secretary James F. 'Jay' Carney," August 20, 2012, *TAPP*, https://www.presidency.ucsb.edu/node/302263.
3. Barack Obama, "Address to the Nation on the Situation in Syria," September 10, 2013, *TAPP*, https://www.presidency.ucsb.edu/node/304920.
4. John Kerry, "Statement of Hon. John Kerry, Secretary of State," September 10, 2013, in *Proposed Authorization to Use Military Force in Syria: Committee on Armed Services, House of Representatives*, 113th Cong., 1st Sess., p. 8, https://www.hsdl.org/?view&did=794380.
5. Obama, "Address to the Nation on the Situation in Syria." John Kerry during Q&A portion of *Proposed Authorization to Use Military Force in Syria: Committee on Armed Services, House of Representatives*, pp. 20–21.
6. "Public Opinion Runs Against Syrian Airstrikes," Pew Research Center, September 3, 2013, http://www.people-press.org/2013/09/03/public-opinion-runs-against-syrian-airstrikes/.
7. Barack Obama quoted in Jeffrey Goldberg, "The Obama Doctrine," *Atlantic*, vol. 317, no. 3 (April 2016), https://www.theatlantic.com/magazine/archive/2016/04/the-obama-doctrine/471525/.
8. "Obama Campaign Ad: Foreign Policy," *Wall Street Journal*, October 22, 2012, https://www.youtube.com/watch?v=Cc3nES1esyU; Barack Obama, "Presidential Debate in Boca Raton, Florida," October 22, 2012, *TAPP*, https://www.presidency.ucsb.edu/node/303198.
9. On "deep engagement," see Stephen Brooks, G. John Ikenberry, and William Wohlforth, "Don't Come Home America: The Case against Retrenchment," *International Security*, vol. 37, no. 3 (Winter 2012/13), pp. 7–51. See also Thomas Wright, "The Folly of Retrenchment: Why America Can't Withdraw from the World," *Foreign Affairs*, vol. 99, no. 2 (March/April 2020), pp. 10–18.
10. George Washington, "Washington's Farewell Address," *Yale Law School Avalon Project* (*YLSAP*), http://avalon.law.yale.edu/18th_century/washing.asp.
11. In World War I and World War II, U.S. troops fought alongside the forces of partner nations in a collective effort to defeat their adversaries. In neither war, however, did the United States extend binding security guarantees to its partners.
12. Scholars of isolationism do not agree on a single, precise definition of the term. Selig Adler views isolationism as resting on "our twin policies of neutrality and non-intervention." "American isolationism," he writes, "coupled a determination to stay out of foreign wars with an unwavering refusal to enter into alliances" (pp. 27–28). Christopher Nichols defines isolationism as a grand strategy of avoiding "entangling alliances as well as conflicts abroad" (p. 6).

For Manfred Jonas, isolationism is the "basic conviction that political commitments tying American policy to the policies of other nations were unnecessary and dangerous" (p. 6). Eric Nordlinger sees isolationism as resting on the assumption that the United States is "strategically immune in being insulated, invulnerable, impermeable, and impervious and thus has few security reasons to become engaged politically and militarily" (p. 6). I add to the injunctions against alliance, intervention, and foreign war the avoidance of strategic commitments outside North America. This more exacting definition captures the continentalism that guided U.S. statecraft during the nineteenth century. It also puts into starker relief the serial defeat of the efforts to acquire territorial possessions in the Caribbean and Pacific that took place prior to 1898. The annexation of Santo Domingo, for example, would not have violated the injunctions against alliance, intervention, and foreign war. It would, however, have meant the assumption of a strategic commitment beyond the continental homeland—one of the main reasons that repeated efforts to acquire the island all failed. See note 16 below for full citations.

13. See Barbara Salazar Torreon and Sofia Plagakis, "Instances of Use of United States Armed Forces Abroad, 1798–2020," Congressional Research Service, R42738, January 13, 2020, https://fas.org/sgp/crs/natsec/R42738.pdf.

14. As Albert Weinberg notes, Americans understood westward expansion to be an important element in realizing strategic isolation because it would push European powers out of America's neighborhood and provide the nation "natural boundaries." See Albert Weinberg, *Manifest Destiny: A Study of Nationalist Expansionism in American History* (Baltimore: Johns Hopkins Press, 1935), chap. 2, pp. 43–71.

15. Walter Russell Mead, *Special Providence: American Foreign Policy and How It Changed the World* (New York: Knopf, 2001), pp. 6–7.

16. Seminal works on isolationism during specific historical periods include the following: Felix Gilbert, *To the Farewell Address: Ideas of Early American Foreign Policy* (Princeton: Princeton University Press, 1961); Christopher McKnight Nichols, *Promise and Peril: America at the Dawn of a Global Age* (Cambridge: Harvard University Press, 2011); John Milton Cooper, *The Vanity of Power: American Isolationism and the First World War, 1914–1917* (Westport: Greenwood, 1969); John Milton Cooper, *Breaking the Heart of the World: Woodrow Wilson and the Fight for the League of Nations* (New York: Cambridge University Press, 2001); Manfred Jonas, *Isolationism in America, 1935–1941* (Ithaca: Cornell University Press, 1966); Selig Adler, *The Isolationist Impulse: Its Twentieth-Century Reaction* (New York: Abelard-Schuman, 1957); Wayne Cole, *Roosevelt and the Isolationists, 1932–45* (Lincoln: University of Nebraska Press, 1983); Eric Nordlinger, *Isolationism Reconfigured: American Foreign Policy for a New Century* (Princeton: Princeton University Press, 1996).

17. Franklin Roosevelt, "Message to the National Convention of Young Democrats," August 21, 1941, *TAPP*, https://www.presidency.ucsb.edu/node/209883; Harry Truman, "Address on Foreign Economic Policy, Delivered at Baylor University," March 6, 1947, *TAPP*, https://www.presidency.ucsb.edu/node/232807; Harry Truman, "Address at the Dedication of the Credit Union National Association's Filene House, Madison, Wisconsin," May 14, 1950, *TAPP*, https://www.presidency.ucsb.edu/node/230597; and Harry Truman, "Address in Miami at the Golden Jubilee Convention of the Veterans of Foreign Wars," August 22, 1949, *TAPP*, https://www.presidency.ucsb.edu/node/229860.

18. Acheson quoted in Robert Beisner, *Dean Acheson: A Life in the Cold War* (New York: Oxford University Press, 2009), p. 156.

19. Robert W. Tucker, *A New Isolationism: Threat or Promise?* (New York: Universe Books, 1972).

20. John Kerry, "Statement of Hon. John F. Kerry, Secretary of State, U.S. Department of State, Washington, DC," September 3, 2013, in *The Authorization of Use of Force in Syria: Hearing before the Committee on Foreign Relations, United States Senate*, 113th Cong., 1st Sess., p. 11, https://www.foreign.senate.gov/download/transcript-the-authorization-of-the-use-of-force-in-syria-090313.

21. Bret Stephens, "The Robert Taft Republicans Return," *Wall Street Journal*, September 3, 2013, p. A13; Niels Lesniewski, "McCain Still Fighting 'Wacko Birds,'" *Roll Call*, March 25, 2013, http://www.rollcall.com/news/mccain_still_fighting_wacko_birds-223417-1.html.

22. See, for example, "Open Letter on Donald Trump from GOP National Security Leaders," *War on the Rocks*, March 2, 2016, https://warontherocks.com/2016/03/open-letter-on-donald-trump-from-gop-national-security-leaders/.

23. Andrew Bacevich, "70 Years of 'New Isolationism,' " *American Conservative*, October 24, 2013, http://www.theamericanconservative.com/articles/70-years-of-new-isolationism/.

24. Thomas Jefferson, "Thomas Jefferson to Alexander von Humboldt," December 6, 1813, *Founders Online*, https://founders.archives.gov/documents/Jefferson/03-07-02-0011.

25. Bernard Fensterwald, Jr., "The Anatomy of American 'Isolationism' and Expansionism. Part I," *Journal of Conflict Resolution*, vol. 2, no. 2 (June 1958), p. 112.

26. See Nordlinger, *Isolationism Reconfigured*, p. 60.

27. Nichols, *Promise and Peril*, p. 341.

28. See Arthur Schlesinger, *The Imperial Presidency* (Boston: Houghton Mifflin, 1973).

29. Walter Lippmann, *U.S. Foreign Policy: Shield of the Republic* (Boston: Little Brown, 1943), p. 7.

30. Andrew Kohut, "American International Engagement on the Rocks," Pew Research Center, July 11, 2013, http://www.pewglobal.org/2013/07/11/american-international-engagement-on-the-rocks/.

31. Michael Dimock et al., "America's Place in the World 2013," Pew Research Center, December 3, 2013, http://www.pewresearch.org/wp-content/uploads/sites/4/2013/12/12-3-13-APW-VI-release1.pdf.

32. On the case for a comprehensive pullback, see Barry Posen, *Restraint: A New Foundation for U.S. Grand Strategy* (Ithaca: Cornell University Press, 2014).

33. Barack Obama, "Commencement Address at the United States Air Force Academy in Colorado Springs, Colorado," May 23, 2012, *TAPP*, https://www.presidency.ucsb.edu/node/301082.

34. Donald Trump, "Address Before a Joint Session of the Congress on the State of the Union," February 4, 2020, *TAPP*, https://www.presidency.ucsb.edu/node/335440.

35. On the impact of exceptionalism on U.S. foreign policy, see Louis Hartz, *The Liberal Tradition in America: An Interpretation of American Political Thought since the Revolution* (New York: Harcourt Brace, 1955); Walter McDougall, *Promised Land, Crusader State: The American Encounter with the World since 1776* (Boston: Houghton Mifflin, 1997); and Samuel Huntington, *American Politics: The Promise of Disharmony* (Cambridge: Harvard University Press, 1983).

36. Herman Melville, *White-Jacket; or, The World in a Man-of-War* (New York: Harper and Brothers, 1956), p. 151.

37. Washington, "Washington's Farewell Address."

38. Thomas Paine, *Common Sense* (New York: Penguin, 2012), p. 85. On the wide readership and significant impact of *Common Sense*, see Walter LaFeber, *The American Age: United States Foreign Policy at Home and Abroad since 1750* (New York: Norton, 1994), pp. 18–19.

39. John Quincy Adams, *An Address Delivered at the Request of the Committee of the Citizens of Washington; on the Occasion of Reading the Declaration of Independence on the Fourth of July, 1821* (Washington: Davis and Force, 1821), p. 29.

40. Albert Weinberg, "The Historical Meaning of the American Doctrine of Isolation," *American Political Science Review*, vol. 34, no. 3 (June 1940), p. 542.

41. See Daniel Rodgers, *As a City on a Hill: The Story of America's Most Famous Lay Sermon* (Princeton: Princeton University Press, 2018).

42. See, for example, Gilbert, *To the Farewell Address*. For further discussion of the protective nature of oceans and "the stopping power of water," see John Mearsheimer, *The Tragedy of Great Power Politics* (New York: Norton, 2001).

43. See, for example, Robert Kagan, *Dangerous Nation: America's Place in the World from Its Earliest Days to the Dawn of the Twentieth Century* (New York: Knopf, 2006).

44. See, for example, Peter Trubowitz, *Defining the National Interest: Conflict and Change in American Foreign Policy* (Chicago: University of Chicago Press, 1998); Alexander DeConde, "The South and Isolationism," *Journal of Southern History*, vol. 24, no. 3 (August 1958), pp. 332–46; William Carleton, "Isolationism and the Middle West," *Mississippi Valley Historical Review*, vol. 33, no. 3 (December 1946), pp. 377–90; Ralph Smuckler, "The Region of Isolationism," *American Political Science Review*, vol. 47, no. 2 (June 1953), pp. 386–401.

45. See Trubowitz, *Defining the National Interest.*

46. On the weak correlation between sectionalism and isolationist voting in Congress, see Peter Boyle, "The Roots of Isolationism: A Case Study," *Journal of American Studies,* vol. 6, no. 1 (April 1972), pp. 41–50.

47. Adler, *The Isolationist Impulse,* p. 9.

48. Jonas, *Isolationism in America,* p. 23.

49. Thomas Jefferson, "Inaugural Address," March 4, 1801, *TAPP,* https://www.presidency.ucsb.edu/node/201948.

50. Nichols, *Promise and Peril,* p. 2.

51. Robert Tucker, "Exemplar or Crusader? Reflections on America's Role," *National Interest,* no. 5 (Fall 1986), pp. 64–75. See also McDougall, *Promised Land, Crusader State;* and Colin Dueck, *Reluctant Crusaders: Power, Culture, and Change in American Grand Strategy* (Princeton: Princeton University Press, 2006).

52. Richard Olney, *International Isolation of the United States* (New York: Houghton Mifflin, 1898), p. 7.

53. Mead, *Special Providence,* pp. 58–59.

54. Hartz, *The Liberal Tradition in America,* p. 286.

55. See Francis Fukuyama, *The End of History and the Last Man* (New York: Free Press, 1992).

56. Charles Krauthammer, "The Unipolar Moment," *Foreign Affairs,* vol. 70, no. 1 (Winter 1990/1991), pp. 23–33.

57. George W. Bush, "National Security Policy of the United States: Foreword by President George W. Bush", September 17, 2002, https://2001-2009.state.gov/r/pa/ei/wh/15434.htm.

58. Hartz, *The Liberal Tradition in America,* p. 286.

59. "Era of Good Feelings," *Columbian Centinel* (Boston), no. 3471, July 12, 1817, p. 2. Accessed via Readex: America's Historical Newspapers, https://www.readex.com/content/americas-historical-newspapers.

60. Woodrow Wilson, "Address to a Joint Session of Congress Requesting a Declaration of War Against Germany," April 2, 1917, *TAPP,* https://www.presidency.ucsb.edu/node/207620.

61. The term "isolationist internationalism" is from Nichols, *Promise and Peril,* pp. 276–77. See chapter 10 for further discussion.

Chapter 2

1. Alfred Thayer Mahan, "The United States Looking Outward," *Atlantic,* vol. 66, no. 398 (December 1890), https://www.theatlantic.com/magazine/archive/1890/12/the-united-states-looking-outward/306348/. See also McDougall, *Promised Land, Crusader State,* pp. 39–40.

2. Arthur H. Vandenberg, Jr., ed., *The Private Papers of Senator Vandenberg* (Boston: Houghton Mifflin, 1952), p. 1.

3. Washington, "Washington's Farewell Address."

4. Alexander Hamilton, *Federalist No. 11,* "The Utility of the Union in Respect to Commercial Relations and a Navy," November 23, 1787, *YLSAP,* https://avalon.law.yale.edu/18th_century/fed11.asp; See also, Gilbert, *To the Farewell Address,* p. 114.

5. Kagan, *Dangerous Nation,* pp. 3, 10.

6. Bear Braumoeller, "The Myth of American Isolationism," *Foreign Policy Analysis,* vol. 6, no. 4 (October 2010), p. 350.

7. Warren Cohen, *Empire without Tears: America's Foreign Relations, 1921–1933* (New York: Knopf, 1987); Melvyn Leffler, *Safeguarding Democratic Capitalism: U.S. Foreign Policy and National Security, 1920–2015* (Princeton: Princeton University Press, 2017), chap. 3, pp. 76–116. See also William Appleman Williams, "The Legend of Isolationism in the 1920s," *Science and Society,* vol. 18, no. 1 (Winter 1954), pp. 1–20. For discussion of the conceptual limitations of the isolationism versus internationalism dichotomy, see Andrew Johnstone, "Isolationism and Internationalism in American Foreign Relations," *Journal of Transatlantic Studies,* vol. 9, no. 1 (2011), pp. 7–20.

8. Alexander Hamilton, *Federalist No. 24*, "The Powers Necessary to the Common Defense Further Considered," December 19, 1787, *YLSAP*, https://avalon.law.yale.edu/18th_century/fed24.asp.

9. Adler, *The Isolationist Impulse*, p. 30.

10. Edward Herbert of Cherbury, *The life and reign of King Henry the Eighth* (London: Printed by Mary Clark for Ann Mearn, 1683), p. 18, https://catalog.hathitrust.org/Record/009019355. See also Paul Kennedy, *The Rise and Fall of British Naval Mastery* (London: Macmillan, 1983), chap. 1, pp. 13–36.

11. See Gilbert, *To the Farewell Address*, pp. 21–23.

12. "Of Alliances," in *A Political Grammar, Adapted to the Meridian of Great Britain* (London: [No publisher], 1742), p. 18, https://books.google.com/books?id=5VAsAQAAMAAJ.

13. See Gilbert, *To the Farewell Address*, pp. 35–36; McDougall, *Promised Land, Crusader State*, p. 41.

14. On the contrast between the economic orientation of the Anglo-American tradition and the geopolitical orientation of Continental realism, see Mead, *Special Providence*, pp. 36–40.

15. Washington, "Washington's Farewell Address."

16. Alexander Hamilton, *Federalist No. 8*, "The Consequences of Hostilities Between the States," November 20, 1787, *YLSAP*, https://avalon.law.yale.edu/18th_century/fed08.asp.

17. Paine, *Common Sense*, p. 38.

18. Hamilton, *Federalist No. 8*.

19. Washington, "Washington's Farewell Address."

20. Gilbert, *To the Farewell Address*, p. 133.

21. Paine, *Common Sense*, p. 44.

22. Paine, *Common Sense*, p. 38.

23. Washington, "Washington's Farewell Address."

24. Paine, *Common Sense*, p. 38.

25. Paine, *Common Sense*, p. 43.

26. LaFeber, *The American Age*, p. 12; Jerald Combs, *The History of American Foreign Policy: Volume 1, To 1920*, 3rd ed. (Armonk: Sharpe, 2008), p. 5.

27. Abraham Lincoln, "Address Before the Young Men's Lyceum of Springfield, Illinois, January 27, 1838," in John G. Nicolay and John Hay, eds., *Complete Works of Abraham Lincoln*, vol. 1 (New York: Francis D. Tandy, 1894), pp. 35–36.

28. Paine, *Common Sense*, p. 38; Washington, "Washington's Farewell Address"; Thomas Jefferson, "From Thomas Jefferson to Thomas Lomax," March 12, 1799, *Founders Online*, https://founders.archives.gov/documents/Jefferson/01-31-02-0056; John Quincy Adams, "To Richard Anderson," May 27, 1823, in Worthington Chauncey Ford, ed., *Writings of John Quincy Adams, Volume 7, 1820–1823* (New York: Macmillan, 1917), p. 468.

29. Paine, *Common Sense*, p. 37.

30. Lawrence Kaplan, *Entangling Alliances with None: American Foreign Policy in the Age of Jefferson* (Kent: Kent State University Press, 1987), p. 12. For an alternative view of the Founders' thinking on free trade, see James Hutson, "Intellectual Foundations of Early American Diplomacy," *Diplomatic History*, vol. 1, no. 1 (Winter 1977), pp. 1–19.

31. Thomas Jefferson, "From Thomas Jefferson to John Adams," July 31, 1785, *Founders Online*, https://founders.archives.gov/documents/Jefferson/01-08-02-0265. See also Thomas Jefferson, "Report on the Privileges and Restrictions on the Commerce of the United States in Foreign Countries," December 16, 1793, *YLSAP*, https://avalon.law.yale.edu/18th_century/jeffrep2.asp.

32. Alexander Hamilton, *Federalist No. 6*, "Concerning Dangers from Dissensions Between the States," November 14, 1787, YLSAP, http://avalon.law.yale.edu/18th_century/fed06.asp.

33. Washington, "Washington's Farewell Address"; Gilbert, *To the Farewell Address*, pp. 130–31, 145.

34. Kaplan, *Entangling Alliance with None*, p. 79.

35. McDougall, *Promised Land, Crusader State*, pp. 55–56.

36. Ernest Lee Tuveson, *Redeemer Nation: The Idea of America's Millennial Role* (Chicago: University of Chicago Press, 1968), pp. 1–52; Jonathan Monten, "The Roots

of the Bush Doctrine: Power, Nationalism, and Democracy Promotion in U.S. Strategy," *International Security*, vol. 29, no. 4 (Spring 2005), pp. 126–28.

37. See Roger Finke and Rodney Starke, *The Churching of America, 1776–2005: Winners and Losers in Our Religious Economy* (New Brunswick: Rutgers University Press, 2005).

38. Gilbert, *To the Farewell Address*, pp. 4–5; LaFeber, *The American Age*, pp. 8–10.

39. On the Great Awakenings, see Walter Hixson, *The Myth of American Diplomacy: National Identity and U.S. Foreign Policy* (New Haven: Yale University Press, 2008); Donald Matthews, "The Second Great Awakening as an Organizing Process, 1780–1830: An Hypothesis," *American Quarterly*, vol. 21, no. 1 (Spring 1969), pp. 23–43; Andrew Preston, "Bridging the Gap between the Sacred and the Secular in the History of American Foreign Relations," *Diplomatic History*, vol. 30, no. 5 (November 2006), pp. 783–812; Sean Wilentz, *The Rise of American Democracy: Jefferson to Lincoln* (New York: Norton, 2006), pp. 267–72, 347–52.

40. Andrew Preston, *Sword of the Spirit, Shield of Faith: Religion in American War and Diplomacy* (New York: Anchor Books, 2012), p. 92.

41. Timothy Dwight, "America: or, A poem on the settlement of the British colonies; addressed to the friends of freedom, and their country," Evans Early American Imprint Collection, http://name.umdl.umich.edu/N13258.0001.001.

42. Paine, *Common Sense*, pp. 4, 85.

43. Susan Matarese, *American Foreign Policy and the Utopian Imagination* (Amherst: University of Massachusetts Press, 2001), p. 66.

44. John Jay, *Federalist No. 2*, "Concerning Dangers from Foreign Force and Influence," October 31, 1787, *YLSAP*, http://avalon.law.yale.edu/18th_century/fed02.asp.

45. LaFeber, *The American Age*, p. 45.

46. Andrew Jackson, "Farewell Address," March 4, 1837, *TAPP*, https://www.presidency.ucsb.edu/node/201770.

47. Richard Price, *Political Writings* (New York: Cambridge University Press, 1991), pp. 119–20.

48. Horace Bushnell, *Work and Play; or Literary Varieties* (New York: Charles Scribner, 1864), p. 45.

49. J. Sullivan Cox, "Imaginary Commonwealths," *United States Magazine, and Democratic Review*, vol. 19, no. 99 (September 1846), p. 184.

50. Melville, *White-Jacket*, chap. 37.

51. Washington Gladden, "Migrations and Their Lessons," *Publications of the Ohio Archeological and Historical Society*, vol. 3 (1891), p. 195.

52. Roderick Frazier Nash, *Wilderness and the American Mind* (New Haven: Yale University Press, 2001), p. 69. See also pp. 34–35.

53. Henry David Thoreau, *The Writings of Henry David Thoreau*, Journal, vol. 2, *1850–September 15, 1851* (New York: Houghton Mifflin, 1906), pp. 152–53.

54. Matarese, *American Foreign Policy*, p. 22.

55. Matarese, *American Foreign Policy*, pp. 67–68.

56. Henry Clay, "On Sending a Minister to South America," May 10, 1820, in Calvin Colton, ed., *The Speeches of Henry Clay*, vol. 1 (New York: A. S. Barnes, 1857), p. 243.

57. Timothy Dwight, "A Valedictory to the Young Gentlemen who commenced bachelors of arts at Yale College, July 25, 1776," Evans Early American Imprint Collection, p. 13, http://name.umdl.umich.edu/N11665.0001.001.

58. James Monroe, "Seventh Annual Message," December 2, 1823, *TAPP*, https://www.presidency.ucsb.edu/node/205755.

59. Alexis de Tocqueville, *Democracy in America*, vol. 2 (Cambridge: Sever and Francis, 1862), p. 122.

60. Thomas Jefferson, "Jefferson's Observations on DéMeunier's Manuscript," June 22, 1786, *Founders Online*, https://founders.archives.gov/documents/Jefferson/01-10-02-0001-0005.

61. Hartz, *The Liberal Tradition in America*, pp. 206, 37.

62. Kaplan, *Entangling Alliances with None*, pp. 79–80.

63. Bushnell, *Work and Play*, p. 45.

64. Gladden, "Migrations and Their Lessons," p. 180.

65. Josiah Strong, *The New Era, or the Coming Kingdom* (New York: Baker and Taylor, 1893), p. 81.

66. Hartz, *The Liberal Tradition in America*, p. 17.

67. Hartz, *The Liberal Tradition in America*, pp. 68–76.

68. Nash, *Wilderness and the American Mind*, pp. 84–88.

69. On the tension between passive exemplarism and activist messianism, see H. W. Brands, *What America Owes the World: The Struggle for the Soul of Foreign Policy* (New York: Cambridge University Press, 1998); McDougall, *Promised Land, Crusader State*; Jonathan Monten, "The Roots of the Bush Doctrine," esp. pp. 112–17.

70. James Monroe, "Letter of James Monroe, Secretary of State, to Joel Robert Poinsett, United States Consul General at Buenos Aires," April 30, 1811, in William Manning, ed., *Diplomatic Correspondence of the United States Concerning the Independence of the Latin-American Nations*, vol. 1 (New York: Oxford University Press, 1925), p. 11.

71. See Monten, "The Roots of the Bush Doctrine," pp. 124–35.

72. See Gilbert, *To the Farewell Address*, pp. 54–75. Some Christian communities, the Mennonites and the Quakers in particular, promoted a religious rather than rationalist brand of pacifism. On the religious roots of pacifism, see Peter Brock, *Pacifism in the United States: From the Colonial Era to the First World War* (Princeton: Princeton University Press, 1968).

73. Quincy Adams, *An Address Delivered at the Request of the Committee of the Citizens of Washington*, p. 29.

74. John Quincy Adams quoted in Charles Francis Adams, ed., *Memoirs of John Quincy Adams, Comprising Portions of His Diary from 1795 to 1848*, vol. 5 (Philadelphia: J. B. Lippincott, 1874–1875), p. 325.

75. Drawing on arguments borrowed from the European Enlightenment, John Adams, Thomas Paine, and other influential voices did argue that the end of monarchy and the spread of free trade would promote a more peaceful world. But these positions hardly enjoyed the status of conventional wisdom. See Gilbert, *To the Farewell Address*, pp. 63–75.

76. Hamilton, *Federalist No. 6*.

77. Charles Kupchan, *How Enemies Become Friends: The Sources of Stable Peace* (Princeton: Princeton University Press, 2010), pp. 94–102.

78. On these ideological differences between the North and South, see Mead, *Special Providence*, chaps. 4–7.

79. John Jay, *Federalist No. 5*, "The Same Subject Continued: Concerning Dangers From Foreign Force and Influence," November 10, 1787, *YLSAP*, https://avalon.law.yale.edu/18th_century/fed05.asp.

80. Combs, *The History of American Foreign Policy*, p. 4.

81. Alexander Hamilton, *Federalist No. 22*, "The Same Subject Continued: Other Defects of the Present Confederation," December 14, 1787, *YLSAP*, http://avalon.law.yale.edu/18th_century/fed22.asp.

82. Alexander Hamilton, *Federalist No. 7*, "The Same Subject Continued: Concerning Dangers from Dissensions Between the States," November 15, 1787, *YLSAP*, http://avalon.law.yale.edu/18th_century/fed07.asp.

83. Washington, "Washington's Farewell Address."

84. Alexander Hamilton, *Federalist No. 23*, "The Necessity of a Government as Energetic as the One Proposed to the Preservation of the Union," December 18, 1787, *YLSAP*, http://avalon.law.yale.edu/18th_century/fed23.asp.

85. Hamilton, *Federalist No. 7*, "The Same Subject Continued."

86. Nordlinger, *Isolationism Reconfigured*, p. 241.

87. Thomas Jefferson, "From Thomas Jefferson to David Humphreys," March 18, 1789, *Founders Online*, https://founders.archives.gov/documents/Jefferson/01-14-02-0422.

88. Washington, "Washington's Farewell Address."

89. Washington, "Washington's Farewell Address"; Thomas Jefferson, "From Thomas Jefferson to Joseph Jones," August 14, 1787, *Founders Online*, https://founders.archives.gov/documents/Jefferson/01-12-02-0038.

90. See LaFeber, *The American Age*, p. 33.

91. James Madison, *Federalist No. 51*, "The Structure of the Government Must Furnish the Proper Checks and Balances Between the Different Departments," February 8, 1788, *YLSAP*, http://avalon.law.yale.edu/18th_century/fed51.asp.

92. James Madison, "From James Madison to Thomas Jefferson," May 13, 1798, *Founders Online*, https://founders.archives.gov/documents/Madison/01-17-02-0088.

93. LaFeber, *The American Age*, pp. 34, 39.

94. Alexander Hamilton, "Constitutional Convention. Remarks on Equality of Representation of the States in the Congress," June 29, 1787, *Founders Online*, https://founders.archives. gov/documents/Hamilton/01-04-02-0109. See also Robert Yates, *Secret Proceedings and Debates of the Convention Assembled at Philadelphia, in the Year 1787, for the Purpose of Forming the Constitution of the United States of America* (Albany: Websters and Skinners, 1821), pp. 185–187.

95. See, for example, Mead, *Special Providence*.

96. See Gilbert, *To the Farewell Address*, pp. 129–45.

97. Washington, "Washington's Farewell Address."

98. Thomas Jefferson, "From Thomas Jefferson to Elbridge Gerry," January 26, 1799, *Founders Online*, https://founders.archives.gov/documents/Jefferson/01-30-02-0451.

99. John Adams, "From John Adams to the President of Congress," February 5, 1783, *Founders Online*, https://founders.archives.gov/documents/Adams/06-14-02-0152.

100. See Mead, *Special Providence*, pp. 185–88.

101. Thomas Jefferson, "From Thomas Jefferson to Albert Gallatin," December 13, 1803, *Founders Online*, https://founders.archives.gov/documents/Jefferson/01-42-02-0100.

102. Preston, *Sword of the Spirit, Shield of Faith*, pp. 11–12.

103. George Washington, "From George Washington to Alexander Hamilton," May 8, 1796, *Founders Online*, https://founders.archives.gov/documents/Washington/99-01-02-00497.

104. John Jay, *Federalist No. 4*, "The Same Subject Continued: Concerning Dangers From Foreign Force and Influence," November 7, 1787, *YLSAP*, https://avalon.law.yale.edu/18th_century/fed04.asp.

105. Jefferson, "From Thomas Jefferson to Elbridge Gerry."

106. Washington, "Washington's Farewell Address." Italics added.

107. LaFeber, *The American Age*, pp. 54–56.

108. Thomas Jefferson, "From Thomas Jefferson to James Monroe," November 24, 1801, *Founders Online*, https://founders.archives.gov/documents/Jefferson/01-35-02-0550.

109. Nichols, *Promise and Peril*, pp. 14, 56–57.

110. LaFeber, *The American Age*, p. 80.

111. See Nichols, *Promise and Peril*, pp. 96–97; Combs, *The History of American Foreign Policy*, pp. 163–64.

112. Society of *Friends, The testimony of the people called Quakers, given forth by a meeting . . . held at Philadelphia the twenty-fourth day of the first month, 1775 and subsequent documents, 1776 to 1777* (Philadelphia: Printed by John Dunlap, 1777), https://www.loc.gov/item/2006566657/.

113. George Washington, "Authority to Collect Clothing," November 1, 1777, *Founders Online*, https://founders.archives.gov/documents/Washington/03-12-02-0070; George Washington, "From George Washington to the Pennsylvania Council of Safety," January 19, 1777, *Founders Online*, https://founders.archives.gov/documents/Washington/03-08-02-0114.

114. Jonathan Whipple, *Autobiography*, Duane I. Schultz, ed. (Quakertown Online, 2009), http://quakertownonline.net/The_Autobiography_of_Jonathan_Whipple_introduction.htm. See also Brock, *Pacifism in the United States*.

115. Henry David Thoreau, "Resistance to Civil Government," in Elizabeth Peabody, ed., *Æsthetic Papers* (New York: G. P. Putnam, 1849), pp. 189, 200.

Chapter 3

1. Washington, "Washington's Farewell Address."

2. Samuel Flagg Bemis, *The Diplomacy of the American Revolution* (Bloomington: Indiana University Press, 1957), pp. 14–15.

3. John Hutson, *John Adams and the Diplomacy of the American Revolution* (Lexington: University Press of Kentucky, 1980), p. 4.

4. John Adams quoted in Charles Francis Adams, ed., *The Works of John Adams, Second President of the United States: with a Life of the Author, Notes and Illustrations*, vol. 2 (Boston: Little Brown, 1856), p. 505.

5. Paine, *Common Sense*, pp. 21–22.

6. Hamilton, *Federalist No. 11*.

7. Jefferson, "From Thomas Jefferson to James Monroe," November 24, 1801.

8. See Mark Anderson, *The Battle for the Fourteenth Colony: America's War of Liberation in Canada, 1774–1776* (Hanover: University Press of New England, 2013).

9. Robert Coakley and Stetson Conn, *The War of the American Revolution: Narrative, Chronology, and Bibliography* (Washington: Center of Military History, 2010), pp. 34–35.

10. John Sullivan, "Autograph Letter to General Schuyler," June 19, 1776, quoted in Benson John Lossing, *The Life and Times of Philip Schuyler*, vol. 2 (New York: Sheldon, 1873), p. 87.

11. John Adams quoted in L. H. Butterfield, ed., *Diary and Autobiography of John Adams, Volume 4, Autobiography Parts Two and Three, 1777–1780* (Cambridge: Belknap Press, 1962), p. 182, http://www.masshist.org/publications/adams-papers/index.php/view/ADMS-01-04-02-0002-0001#DJA04d112n16.

12. Bemis, *The Diplomacy of the American Revolution*, pp. 198, 207–208.

13. Gilbert, *To the Farewell Address*, p. 139.

14. Douglas Irwin estimates that exports accounted for twelve percent of the nation's GDP around 1790. See Douglas Irwin, "Revenue or Reciprocity? Founding Feuds over Early U.S. Trade Policy," in Douglas Irwin and Richard Sylla, eds., *Founding Choices: American Economic Policy in the 1790s* (Chicago: University of Chicago Press, 2010), p. 93.

15. *Journals of the Continental Congress*, vol. 26, 1784, January 1–May 10, pp. 180–85, 317–22. The complete *Journals of the Continental Congress* are available online from the Library of Congress here: https://memory.loc.gov/ammem/amlaw/lwjc.html.

16. John Adams, "From John Adams to James Warren," March 20, 1783, *Founders Online*, https://founders.archives.gov/documents/Adams/06-14-02-0227.

17. Thomas Jefferson, "American Commissioners to De Thulemeier," March 14, 1785, *Founders Online*, https://founders.archives.gov/documents/Jefferson/01-08-02-0015.

18. Gilbert, *To the Farewell Address*, pp. 71–72.

19. Hamilton, *Federalist No. 6*.

20. John Adams, "From John Adams to the Comte de Vergennes," July 18, 1781, *Founders Online*, https://founders.archives.gov/documents/Adams/06-11-02-0317.

21. *Journals of the Continental Congress*, vol. 5, 1776, June 5–October 8, pp. 768–79.

22. Continental Congress, "The Continental Congress: Instructions to Franklin, Silas Deane, and Arthur Lee as Commissioners to France," September 24–October 22, 1776, *Founders Online*, https://founders.archives.gov/documents/Franklin/01-22-02-0371. See also Bemis, *The Diplomacy of the American Revolution*, p. 48.

23. *Journals of the Continental Congress*, vol. 5, pp. 813–17; Gilbert, *To the Farewell Address*, pp. 53–54.

24. *Journals of the Continental Congress*, vol. 6, 1776, October 9–December 31, p. 1104.

25. Kaplan, *Entangling Alliances with None*, pp. xiii, 81–83.

26. John Adams, "From John Adams to John Jackson," December 30, 1817, *Founders Online*, https://founders.archives.gov/documents/Adams/99-02-02-6833.

27. "Treaty of Amity and Commerce Between The United States and France," February 6, 1778, *YLSAP*, https://avalon.law.yale.edu/18th_century/fr1788-1.asp.

28. "Treaty of Alliance Between The United States and France," February 6, 1778, *YLSAP*, http://avalon.law.yale.edu/18th_century/fr1788-2.asp.

29. "Treaty of Alliance Between The United States and France."

30. Jonathan Dull, *A Diplomatic History of the American Revolution* (New Haven: Yale University Press, 1985), pp. 119, 151.

31. Bemis, *The Diplomacy of the American Revolution*, pp. 84–86.

32. Bemis, *The Diplomacy of the American Revolution*, p. 255.

33. For more on the League of Armed Neutrality, see Isabel de Madariaga, *Britain, Russia, and the Armed Neutrality of 1780: Sir James Harris's Mission to St. Petersburg during the American Revolution* (London: Hollis and Carter, 1962).

34. *Journals of the Continental Congress*, vol. 24, *1783, January 1–August 29*, p. 349.

35. William Carpenter, "The United States and the League of Neutrals of 1780," *American Journal of International Law*, vol. 15, no. 4 (July 1921), pp. 521–22. See also "Continental Congress Report on American Participation in a European Neutral Confederacy," June 12, 1783, *Founders Online*, https://founders.archives.gov/documents/Hamilton/01-03-02-0251.

Chapter 4

1. Paul Smith, "The American Loyalists: Notes on Their Organization and Numerical Strength," *William and Mary Quarterly*, vol. 25, no. 2 (April 1968), pp. 259–77.

2. Thomas Jefferson, "To George Washington from Thomas Jefferson," May 23, 1792, *Founders Online*, https://founders.archives.gov/documents/Washington/05-10-02-0268.

3. See, for example, Alexander Hamilton, "Alexander Hamilton's Final Version of the Report on the Subject of Manufactures," December 5, 1791, *Founders Online*, https://founders.archives.gov/documents/Hamilton/01-10-02-0001-0007.

4. Thomas Jefferson, "To George Washington from Thomas Jefferson," July 31, 1793, *Founders Online*, https://founders.archives.gov/documents/Washington/05-13-02-0212.

5. Thomas Jefferson, "To James Madison from Thomas Jefferson," February 8, 1786, *Founders Online*, https://founders.archives.gov/documents/Madison/01-08-02-0254.

6. Hamilton, *Federalist No. 7*.

7. "Constitution of the United States," initially signed September 17, 1787, *YLSAP*, https://avalon.law.yale.edu/18th_century/usconst.asp.

8. James Madison, *Federalist No. 41*, "General View of the Powers Conferred by the Constitution," January 19, 1788, *YLSAP*, http://avalon.law.yale.edu/18th_century/fed41.asp.

9. Hamilton, *Federalist No. 8*.

10. See Philippe Girard, *The Slaves Who Defeated Napoleon: Toussaint Louverture and the Haitian War of Independence, 1801–1804* (Tuscaloosa: University of Alabama Press, 2011), pp. 277–78.

11. See Tim Matthewson, "Jefferson and the Nonrecognition of Haiti," *Proceedings of the American Philosophical Society*, vol. 140, no. 1 (March 1996), pp. 22–48.

12. Kagan, *Dangerous Nation*, p. 130.

13. Kagan, *Dangerous Nation*, pp. 102, 56, 64.

14. Kagan, *Dangerous Nation*, pp. 52, 118.

15. See, for example, Alexander Hamilton, "The Stand No. III," April 7, 1798, *Founders Online*, https://founders.archives.gov/documents/Hamilton/01-21-02-0233; Alexander Hamilton, "Views on the French Revolution," 1794, *Founders Online*, https://founders.archives.gov/documents/Hamilton/01-26-02-0002-0442.

16. Washington, "Washington's Farewell Address."

17. John Adams, "From John Adams to the President of Congress, No. 85," June 17, 1780, *Founders Online*, https://founders.archives.gov/documents/Adams/06-09-02-0270.

18. Adams quoted by Benjamin Rush, "To John Adams from Benjamin Rush," August 14, 1805, *Founders Online*, https://founders.archives.gov/documents/Adams/99-02-02-5095. See also Hutson, *John Adams and the Diplomacy of the American Revolution*, pp. 11, 30.

19. Hamilton, *Federalist No. 6*.

20. Kaplan, *Entangling Alliances with None*, p. 89.

21. Thomas Jefferson, "Response to the Address of Welcome," March 11, 1790, *Founders Online*, https://founders.archives.gov/documents/Jefferson/01-16-02-0130.

22. "The Paris Peace Treaty of September 30, 1783," *YLSAP*, http://avalon.law.yale.edu/18th_century/paris.asp.

23. The treaty was signed late in 1814, but it was not until early 1815 that word spread and brought the fighting to an end.

24. Kaplan, *Entangling Alliances with None*, pp. 89–94; and Combs, *The History of American Foreign Policy*, pp. 30–31.

25. Alexander Hamilton and Thomas Jefferson, "Cabinet Meeting. Opinion on a Proclamation of Neutrality and on Receiving the French Minister," April 19, 1793, *Founders Online*, https://founders.archives.gov/documents/Hamilton/01-14-02-0226.

26. Alexander Hamilton, "Enclosure: Answer to Question the 3d. Proposed by the President of the UStates," May 2, 1793, *Founders Online*, https://founders.archives.gov/documents/Hamilton/01-14-02-0262-0002.

27. Kaplan, *Entangling Alliances with None*, p. 90. See also Alexander Hamilton and Thomas Jefferson, "Cabinet Opinion on Washington's Questions on Neutrality and the Alliance with France," April 19, 1793, *Founders Online*, https://founders.archives.gov/documents/Jefferson/01-25-02-0530.

28. Combs, *The History of American Foreign Policy*, p. 30. See also Mlada Bukovansky, "American Identity and Neutral Rights From Independence to the War of 1812," *International Organization*, vol. 51, no. 2 (Spring 1997), pp. 209–43; "Editorial Note: Jefferson's Opinion on the Treaties with France," *Founders Online*, https://founders.archives.gov/documents/Jefferson/01-25-02-0562-0001.

29. George Washington, "The Proclamation of Neutrality 1793," April 22, 1793, *YLSAP*, http://avalon.law.yale.edu/18th_century/neutra93.asp.

30. Edmond Charles Genêt, "To George Washington from Edmond Charles Genêt," August 13, 1793, *Founders Online*, https://founders.archives.gov/documents/Washington/05-13-02-0288.

31. Alexander Hamilton, "Pacificus No. 5," July 13–17, 1793, *Founders Online*, https://founders.archives.gov/documents/Hamilton/01-15-02-0072. Complete text of the debate between Hamilton and Madison can be found in Morton Frisch, ed., *The Pacificus-Helvidius Debates of 1793–1794: Toward the Completion of the American Founding* (Indianapolis: Liberty Fund, 2007), https://oll.libertyfund.org/titles/hamilton-the-pacificus-helvidius-debates-of-1793-1794.

32. James Madison, "Helvidius No. 3," September 7, 1793, *Founders Online*, https://founders.archives.gov/documents/Madison/01-15-02-0066; James Madison, "Helvidius No. 1," August 24, 1793, *Founders Online*, https://founders.archives.gov/documents/Madison/01-15-02-0056. See also Hamilton and Madison, *The Pacificus-Helvidius Debates of 1793–1794*.

33. Jefferson, "To George Washington from Thomas Jefferson," July 31, 1793.

34. George Washington, "From George Washington to the United States Senate," April 16, 1794, *Founders Online*, https://founders.archives.gov/documents/Washington/05-15-02-0473.

35. "The Jay Treaty," November 19, 1794, *YLSAP*, http://avalon.law.yale.edu/18th_century/jay.asp.

36. Alexander Hamilton, "Conversation with George Hammond," July 1–10, 1794, *Founders Online*, https://founders.archives.gov/documents/Hamilton/01-16-02-0529.

37. Kagan, *Dangerous Nation*, pp. 93–94; James Field, Jr., "All Economists, All Diplomats," in William Becker and Samuel Wells, Jr., *Economics and World Power: An Assessment of American Diplomacy Since 1789* (New York: Columbia University Press, 1984), pp. 20–21.

38. Benjamin Russell of the *Columbian Centinel* (Boston), April 24 and May 8, 1799, cited in Charles Warren, *Jacobin and Junto, or Early American Politics as viewed in the Diary of Dr. Nathaniel Ames, 1758–1822* (Cambridge: Harvard University Press, 1931), pp. 71–96, quotes on p. 92; McDougall, *Promised Land, Crusader State*, pp. 29–30.

39. Combs, *The History of American Foreign Policy*, pp. 33–34.

40. For details of French intervention in the campaign, see Alexander DeConde, "Washington's Farewell, the French Alliance, and the Election of 1796," *Mississippi Valley Historical Review*, vol. 43, no. 4 (March 1957), pp. 641–58; Alexander DeConde, *Entangling Alliance: Politics & Diplomacy under George Washington* (Durham: Duke University Press, 1958).

41. DeConde, *Entangling Alliance*, pp. 65, 462–65.

42. DeConde, "Washington's Farewell, the French Alliance, and the Election of 1796," pp. 648–50; Gilbert, *To the Farewell Address*, pp. 125–47.

43. All quotations are from Washington, "Washington's Farewell Address."

44. On the geographic logic informing Washington's remarks, see Gilbert, *To the Farewell Address*, pp. 114, 126–47. Hamilton played a particularly influential role in shaping Washington's thinking on geopolitical issues (p. 130). For Hamilton, "states situated in the *same geographical area* were tied together in a continuous power struggle arising from clashing interests."

(emphasis added) The "natural" strategic theater for the United States was therefore the Americas; in contrast, geopolitical connections to Europe would be "artificial." As America's power increased, Hamilton envisaged the United States becoming dominant in its neighborhood, but not beyond: "Our situation invites and our interests prompt us to aim at an ascendant in the system of American affairs" (p. 114). See also Hamilton, *Federalist No. 11*.

45. Jasper Dwight [pseudonym], *A Letter to George Washington, President of the United States: Containing Strictures on His Address of the Seventeenth of September, 1796, Notifying His Relinquishment of the Presidential Office* (Philadelphia: [No publisher], 1796), p. 41. See also DeConde, "Washington's Farewell, the French Alliance, and the Election of 1796," p. 651. Historians have also attributed the letter to Duane's bookkeeper, Treziulney.

46. James Madison, "From James Madison to James Monroe," September 29, 1796, *Founders Online*, https://founders.archives.gov/documents/Madison/01-16-02-0262.

47. See "Washington's Farewell Address," United States Senate, https://www.senate.gov/artandhistory/history/minute/Washingtons_Farewell_Address.htm.

48. Until the Twelfth Amendment was ratified in 1804, the candidate receiving the most electoral votes (as long as the total represented a majority of electors) won the presidency, and the candidate receiving the second-highest number of votes became vice president. The Twelfth Amendment altered the voting procedure by stipulating that electors cast separate votes for president and vice president.

49. Timothy Pickering, "No. 119. France," February 28, 1798, in *American State Papers: Foreign Relations*, vol. 1, 4th Cong., 2nd Sess., pp. 748–49. The complete *American State Papers* are available here: https://memory.loc.gov/ammem/amlaw/lwsplink.html.

50. Timothy Pickering, "Report of the Secretary of State respecting the depredations inflicted on the commerce of the United States, since the 1st of October, 1796," in *American State Papers: Foreign Relations*, vol. 2, 5th Cong., 1st Sess., pp. 28–63. See also LaFeber, *The American Age*, p. 49.

51. Congress's vote left the alliance and the commercial treaty in an ambiguous status. The French claimed that the unilateral act of Congress had no effect on the treaties; they could be abrogated only by mutual consent. Moreover, as the debate following Washington's declaration of neutrality had made clear, Americans themselves were divided over the respective authorities of the president and Congress with respect to annulling treaties. As DeConde notes, it was "an open question as to whether or not Congress had the power, even with the consent of the President, to cancel, unilaterally, a contract with another nation." See Alexander DeConde, *The Quasi-War: The Politics and Diplomacy of the Undeclared War with France, 1797–1801* (New York: Scribner, 1966), p. 235.

52. "An Act in Addition to the Act, Entitled 'An Act for the Punishment of Certain Crimes Against the United States,'" July 14, 1798, *YLSAP*, http://avalon.law.yale.edu/18th_century/sedact.asp.

53. "Chap. 58—An Act concerning Aliens," June 25, 1798, in Statutes at Large, 5th Cong., 2nd Sess., pp. 570–72, https://www.loc.gov/rr/program/bib/ourdocs/alien.html.

54. "An Act in Addition to the Act, Entitled 'An Act for the Punishment of Certain Crimes Against the United States.'"

55. Thomas Jefferson, "To James Madison from Thomas Jefferson," November 3, 1798, *Founders Online*, https://founders.archives.gov/documents/Madison/01-17-02-0119.

56. William Shaw, "From William Smith Shaw to Abigail Smith Adams," May 20, 1798, *Founders Online*, https://founders.archives.gov/documents/Adams/04-13-02-0018.

57. "Virginia Resolution—Alien and Sedition Acts," December 24, 1798, *YLSAP*, http://avalon.law.yale.edu/18th_century/virres.asp.

58. "Kentucky Resolution—Alien and Sedition Acts," December 3, 1799, *YLSAP*, http://avalon.law.yale.edu/18th_century/kenres.asp.

59. Douglas Bradburn, "A Clamor in the Public Mind: Opposition to the Alien and Sedition Acts," *William and Mary Quarterly*, 3rd series, vol. 65, no. 3 (July 2008), pp. 565–600; James M. Smith, *Freedom's Fetters: The Alien and Sedition Laws and American Civil Liberties* (Ithaca: Cornell University Press, 1956); Jeffrey Pasley, *The Tyranny of Printers: Newspaper Politics in the Early American Republic* (Charlottesville: University of Virginia Press, 2001), chaps 5–8.

60. "France—Convention of 1800: Text of the Treaty," *YLSAP*, http://avalon.law.yale.edu/19th_century/fr1800.asp.

61. Combs, *The History of American Foreign Policy*, p. 38.
62. James Madison, "From James Madison to Thomas Jefferson," April 4, 1800, *Founders Online*, https://founders.archives.gov/documents/Madison/01-17-02-0223.
63. Kagan, *Dangerous Nation*, p. 125.
64. Thomas Jefferson, "Inaugural Address," March 4, 1801, *TAPP*, https://www.presidency.ucsb.edu/node/201948.
65. Thomas Jefferson, "From Thomas Jefferson to William Short," October 3, 1801, *Founders Online*, https://founders.archives.gov/documents/Jefferson/01-35-02-0307.
66. Kaplan, *Entangling Alliances with None*, p. 95.
67. Thomas Jefferson, "Inaugural Address."
68. Donald Adams, Jr., "American Neutrality and Prosperity, 1793–1808: A Reconsideration," *Journal of Economic History*, vol. 40, no. 4 (December 1980), pp. 713–37.
69. Kagan, *Dangerous Nation*, p. 99.
70. Mead, *Special Providence*, p. 17.
71. Kagan, *Dangerous Nation*, p. 144.
72. James Madison, "Fourth Annual Message," November 4, 1812, *TAPP*, https://www.presidency.ucsb.edu/node/204504.
73. LaFeber, *The American Age*, pp. 58–61; Kaplan, *Entangling Alliances with None*, p. 119.
74. Madison, "Fourth Annual Message."
75. John C. Calhoun, "Speech on the Petition of the Citizens of Albany to repeal the Embargo," May 6, 1812, in Richard K. Crallé, ed., *The Works of John C. Calhoun, Volume 2, Speeches of John C. Calhoun Delivered in the House of Representatives and in the Senate of the United States* (New York: D. Appleton, 1860), p. 20.
76. Madison, "Fourth Annual Message"; Padraig Riley, *Slavery and the Democratic Conscience: Political Life in Jeffersonian America* (Philadelphia: University of Pennsylvania Press, 2016), pp. 160, 172.
77. *The National Advocate* (New York), March–April 1815 quoted in Harvey Strum, "New York Federalists and Opposition to the War of 1812," *World Affairs*, vol. 142, no. 3 (Winter 1980), p. 183.
78. Strum, "New York Federalists and Opposition to the War of 1812," p. 169; Riley, *Slavery and the Democratic Conscience*, pp. 182–83, 186–91.
79. See Kaplan, *Entangling Alliances with None*, pp. 112–13.
80. Kaplan, *Entangling Alliances with None*, pp. 120–21, 134–35.
81. Kaplan, *Entangling Alliances with None*, pp. 128, 141–42.
82. Thomas Jefferson, "Thomas Jefferson to James Maury," April 25, 1812, *Founders Online*, https://founders.archives.gov/documents/Jefferson/03-04-02-0551.
83. Strum, "New York Federalists and Opposition to the War of 1812," p. 173.
84. Rufus King, "R. King to C. Gore," July 17, 1812, in Charles King, ed., *The Life and Correspondence of Rufus King, Volume 5, 1807–1816* (New York: Knickerbocker Press, 1898), p. 272.
85. LaFeber, *The American Age*, p. 63.
86. Strum, "New York Federalists and Opposition to the War of 1812," pp. 177–79, 183.
87. *Plebian* (Kingston, NY), April 20, 1813, quoted in Strum, "New York Federalists and Opposition to the War of 1812," p. 176.
88. Riley, *Slavery and the Democratic Conscience*, pp. 164–68, 176.
89. Combs, *The History of American Foreign Policy*, pp. 52–53.
90. Kaplan, *Entangling Alliances with None*, pp. 141–42.
91. Thomas Jefferson, "Thomas Jefferson to Thomas Leiper," June 12, 1815, *Founders Online*, https://founders.archives.gov/documents/Jefferson/03-08-02-0431.

Chapter 5

1. James Monroe, "To General Jackson," December 14, 1816, in Stanislaus Hamilton, ed., *The Writings of James Monroe, Volume 5, 1807–1816* (New York: Knickerbocker Press, 1901), p. 342.
2. "Era of Good Feelings."
3. On divisions among Republicans, see Andrew R. L. Cayton, "The Debate over the Panama Congress and the Origins of the Second American Party System," *Historian*, vol. 47, no. 2 (February 1985), pp. 219–38.

4. Bradford Perkins, *The Cambridge History of American Foreign Relations, Volume 1, The Creation of a Republican Empire, 1776–1865* (New York: Cambridge University Press, 1995), p. 47.

5. Combs, *The History of American Foreign Policy*, p. 57.

6. Ruth Schwartz Cowan, *A Social History of American Technology* (New York: Oxford University Press, 1997), p. 104.

7. Lincoln, "Address Before the Young Men's Lyceum of Springfield, Illinois, January 27, 1838."

8. Tuveson, *Redeemer Nation*, p. 125.

9. The Free Soil Party existed from 1848 to 1856 and focused primarily on opposing the expansion of slavery to western territories.

10. California was admitted as a free state as a result of the Compromise of 1850, a package of five pieces of legislation aimed at resolving a number of disputes between slave and free states.

11. In 1859 the United States and Britain confronted each other over the border in the San Juan Islands, but the crisis was resolved diplomatically.

12. Amy S. Greenberg, *A Wicked War: Polk, Clay, Lincoln, and the 1846 U.S. Invasion of Mexico* (New York: Knopf, 2012), p. 8.

13. McDougall, *Promised Land, Crusader State*, p. 90; Dov Levin and Benjamin Miller, "Why Great Powers Expand in Their Own Neighborhood: Explaining the Territorial Expansion of the United States, 1819–1848," *International Interactions*, vol. 37, no. 3 (September 2011), pp. 241–43.

14. "Treaty of Guadalupe Hidalgo," February 2, 1848, *YLSAP*, http://avalon.law.yale.edu/19th_century/guadhida.asp.

15. Reginald Horsman, "Scientific Racism and the American Indian in the Mid–Nineteenth Century," *American Quarterly*, vol. 27, no. 2 (May 1975), pp. 164, 166; Greenberg, *A Wicked War*, p. 131.

16. LaFeber, *The American Age*, p. 125.

17. Greenberg, *A Wicked War*, pp. 268–69.

18. LaFeber, *The American Age*, pp. 136–37.

19. LaFeber, *The American Age*, pp. 138–40; Kagan, *Dangerous Nation*, pp. 228–32.

20. In 1822, the American Colonization Society (ACS), a privately operated and funded organization, established in Liberia a "colony" for the resettlement of emancipated African-Americans. The ACS effectively governed the settlement, which never became a formal U.S. territory. Liberia established itself as an independent country in 1847. See J. H. Mower, "The Republic of Liberia," *The Journal of Negro History*, vol. 32, no. 3 (July 1947), pp. 265–306.

21. McDougall, *Promised Land, Crusader State*, pp. 50, 79.

22. Daniel Immerwahr, *How to Hide an Empire: A History of the Greater United States* (New York: Farrar, Straus, and Giroux, 2019), pp. 46–58. On the legal status of the guano islands, see Christina Duffy Burnett, "The Edges of Empire and the Limits of Sovereignty: American Guano Islands," *American Quarterly*, vol. 57, no. 3 (September 2005), pp. 779–803.

23. John Quincy Adams, "First Annual Message," December 6, 1825, *TAPP*, https://www.presidency.ucsb.edu/node/206789.

24. Earl Swisher, "Commodore Perry's Imperialism in Relation to America's Present-Day Position in the Pacific," *Pacific Historical Review*, vol. 16, no. 1 (February 1947), pp. 30–40.

25. Hamilton, *Federalist No. 11*.

26. Henry Clay, "Speech on South American Independence," May 10, 1820, in James Hopkins, ed., *The Papers of Henry Clay, Volume 2, The Rising Statesman, 1815–1820* (Lexington: University Press of Kentucky, 1961), pp. 857–58.

27. Henry Clay, "Toast and Response at Public Dinner," May 19, 1821, in James Hopkins and Mary W. M. Hargreaves, eds., *The Papers of Henry Clay, Volume 3, Presidential Candidate: 1821–1824* (Lexington: University Press of Kentucky, 1963), p. 80.

28. Monroe, "James Monroe, Secretary of State, to Joel Robert Poinsett, United States Consul General at Buenos Aires."

29. Kaplan, *Entangling Alliances with None*, pp. 181–83; McDougall, *Promised Land, Crusader State*, pp. 65–66; Kagan, *Dangerous Nation*, pp. 161–62.

30. John Quincy Adams, "The Department of State—First Term," September 19, 1820, in Adams, ed., *Memoirs*, vol. 5, p. 176.

31. Clay, "Toast and Response at Public Dinner."
32. Quincy Adams, "Department of State—First Term," March 9, 1821, in Adams, ed., *Memoirs*, vol. 5, pp. 324–25.
33. Quincy Adams, *An Address Delivered at the Request of the Committee of the Citizens of Washington*, p. 29.
34. Quincy Adams, "Department of State—First Term," March 9, 1821.
35. Quincy Adams, *An Address Delivered at the Request of the Committee of the Citizens of Washington*, pp. 28–29.
36. John Quincy Adams, "To Edward Everett," January 31, 1822, in Ford, ed., *Writings*, vol. 7, p. 201.
37. Quincy Adams, "Department of State—First Term," March 9, 1821.
38. Quincy Adams, *An Address Delivered at the Request of the Committee of the Citizens of Washington*, p. 29.
39. See William Spence Robertson, "The Recognition of the Hispanic American Nations by the United States," *Hispanic American Historical Review*, vol. 1, no. 3 (August 1918), pp. 239–69; Kaplan, *Entangling Alliances with None*, pp. 183–84; LaFeber, *The American Age*, pp. 80–81.
40. George Canning, "George Canning, Secretary of State for Foreign Affairs of Great Britain, to Richard Rush, United States Minister to Great Britain," August 20, 1823, in William R. Manning, ed., *Diplomatic Correspondence of the United States Concerning the Independence of Latin-American Nations*, vol. 3 (New York: Oxford University Press, 1926), pp. 1478–479; George Dangerfield, *The Era of Good Feelings* (New York: Harcourt Brace, 1952), p. 286.
41. James Monroe, "To James Madison from James Monroe," October 17, 1823, *Founders Online*, https://founders.archives.gov/documents/Madison/04-03-02-0147.
42. See George Herring, *From Colony to Superpower: U.S. Foreign Relations since 1776* (New York: Oxford University Press, 2011), p. 153; DeConde, *A History of American Foreign Policy*, pp. 121–23.
43. Thomas Jefferson, "From Thomas Jefferson to James Monroe," October 24, 1823, *Founders Online*, https://founders.archives.gov/documents/Jefferson/98-01-02-3827.
44. Jefferson, "From Thomas Jefferson to James Monroe," October 24, 1823.
45. James Madison, "From James Madison to James Monroe," October 30, 1823, *Founders Online*, https://founders.archives.gov/documents/Madison/04-03-02-0159.
46. Worthington Chauncery Ford, "John Quincy Adams and the Monroe Doctrine," *American Historical Review*, vol. 8, no. 1 (October 1902), p. 28.
47. John Quincy Adams, "The Department of State—Second Term," November 7, 1823, in Charles Francis Adams, ed., *Memoirs of John Quincy Adams: Comprising Portions of His Diary From 1795 to 1848*, vol. 6 (Philadelphia: J. B. Lippincott, 1875), pp. 178–79.
48. Kagan, *Dangerous Nation*, p. 173.
49. Quincy Adams, "The Department of State—Second Term," November 22, 1823, pp. 197–98. For an overview of the debate on Greece, see Lawrence Kaplan, "The Monroe Doctrine and the Truman Doctrine: The Case of Greece," *Journal of the Early Republic*, vol. 13, no. 1 (Spring 1993), pp. 1–21.
50. John Randolph, "The Greek Cause," January 20, 1824, in *Annals of Congress*, 18th Cong., 1st Sess., House of Representatives, p. 1111. The complete *Annals of Congress* are available from the Library of Congress here: https://memory.loc.gov/ammem/amlaw/lwac.html.
51. Angelo Repousis, "'The Cause of the Greeks': Philadelphia and the Greek War for Independence, 1821–1828," *Pennsylvania Magazine of History and Biography*, vol. 123, no. 4 (October 1999), pp. 338–40.
52. James Monroe, "Monroe Doctrine," December 2, 1823, *YLSAP*, http://avalon.law.yale.edu/19th_century/monroe.asp.
53. Metternich letter to Nesselrode, January 19, 1824, and French newspaper *Étoile*, January 4, 1824, quoted in Dexter Perkins, *The Monroe Doctrine, 1823–1826* (Cambridge: Harvard University Press, 1927), pp. 167, 30.
54. Tsar Alexander letter to Baron Tuyll, March 5, 1824, quoted in Kori Schake, *Safe Passage: The Transition from British to American Hegemony* (Cambridge: Harvard University Press, 2017), p. 54. See also Perkins, *The Monroe Doctrine*, p. 168.
55. Dangerfield, *The Era of Good Feelings*, p. 304.

56. "Important Proposition," *Niles' Weekly Register*, vol. 28, no. 711, April 30, 1825, in H. Niles, ed., *Niles' Weekly Register from March, 1825, to September, 1825—Vol. XXVIII or, Vol. IV—Third Series* (Baltimore: Franklin Press, 1825), p. 132; Cayton, "The Debate over the Panama Congress," pp. 219–38.

57. Charles Wilson Hackett, "The Development of John Quincy Adams's Policy with Respect to an American Confederation and the Panama Congress, 1822–1825," *Hispanic American Historical Review*, vol. 8, no. 4 (November 1928), p. 526.

58. Jeffrey J. Malanson, "The Congressional Debate over U.S. Participation in the Congress of Panama, 1825–1826: Washington's Farewell Address, Monroe's Doctrine, and the Fundamental Principles of U.S. Foreign Policy," *Diplomatic History*, vol. 30, no. 5 (November 2006), p. 813.

59. Quincy Adams, "First Annual Message."

60. Malanson, "The Congressional Debate," pp. 818–19.

61. *Executive Proceedings of the Senate of the United States on the Subject of the Mission to the Congress of Panama* (Washington: Gales and Seaton, 1826), 19th Cong., 1st Sess., p. 76; Malanson, "The Congressional Debate," p. 821.

62. Malanson, "The Congressional Debate," pp. 824–25.

63. Cayton, "The Debate over the Panama Congress," pp. 235–36.

64. Malanson, "The Congressional Debate," p. 837.

65. John Quincy Adams, "Special Message," December 26, 1825, *TAPP*, https://www.presidency.ucsb.edu/node/200537. Italics added.

66. Robert Hayne, "On the Panama Mission—(in conclave)," March 14, 1826, in *Register of Debates*, 19th Cong., 1st Sess., Senate, p. 171. The complete *Register of Debates* is available from the Library of Congress here: https://memory.loc.gov/ammem/amlaw/lwrd.html.

67. Hugh White, "On the Panama Mission—(in conclave.)," March 14, 1826, in *Register of Debates*, 19th Cong., 1st Sess., Senate, pp. 198, 201. See also Malanson, "The Congressional Debate," pp. 821–22, 824.

68. John Quincy Adams, "Special Message," March 15, 1826, *TAPP*, https://www.presidency.ucsb.edu/node/207536.

69. Washington, "Washington's Farewell Address."

70. Quincy Adams, "Special Message," March 15, 1826.

71. The Federalist Party survived in Delaware into the 1820s.

72. Louis McLane, "Mission to Panama," April 4, 1826, in *Register of Debates*, 19th Cong., 1st Sess., House of Representatives, p. 2011.

73. James Hamilton, "Mission to Panama," April 10, 1826, in *Register of Debates*, 19th Cong., 1st Sess., House of Representatives, p. 2160.

74. James Buchanan, "Mission to Panama," April 11, 1826, in *Register of Debates*, 19th Cong., 1st Sess., House of Representatives, pp. 2172, 2182.

75. Edward Livingston, "Mission to Panama," April 12, 1826, in *Register of Debates*, 19th Cong., 1st Sess., House of Representatives, p. 2212.

76. William Rives, "Mission to Panama," April 5, 1826, in *Register of Debates*, 19th Cong., 1st Sess., House of Representatives, p. 2059.

77. John Berrien, "On the Panama Mission—(in conclave.)," March 14, 1826, in *Register of Debates*, 19th Cong., 1st Sess., Senate, p. 289.

78. John Forsyth, "Mission to Panama," April 17, 1826, in *Register of Debates*, 19th Cong., 1st Sess., House of Representatives, p. 2323.

79. Malanson, "The Congressional Debate," pp. 834–36.

80. Malanson, "The Congressional Debate," p. 833.

81. Quincy Adams, "First Annual Message."

82. Robert Remini, *John Quincy Adams* (New York: Times Books, 2002), p. 81.

83. Martin Van Buren, "On the Panama Mission—(in conclave.)," March 14, 1826, in *Register of Debates*, 19th Cong., 1st Sess., Senate, pp. 236–37.

84. Cayton, "The Debate over the Panama Congress," p. 220.

85. Malanson, "The Congressional Debate," p. 814.

86. Cayton, "The Debate over the Panama Congress," pp. 228, 236–37.

87. Matthew Karp, *This Vast Southern Empire: Slaveholders at the Helm of American Foreign Policy* (Cambridge: Harvard University Press, 2016), p. 13.

88. John Randolph, "Negro Slavery in South America," March 1, 1826, in *Register of Debates*, 19th Cong., 1st Sess., Senate, p. 112.

89. Paul D. Naish, *Slavery and Silence: Latin America and the U.S. Slave Debate* (Philadelphia: University of Pennsylvania Press, 2017), p. 7.

90. John Berrien, "On the Panama Mission—(in conclave.)," March 14, 1826, p. 330.

91. Karp, *This Vast Southern Empire*, pp. 13–14; Cayton, "The Debate over the Panama Congress," pp. 225, 231–32.

92. Karp, *This Vast Southern Empire*, pp. 6–7.

93. Monroe, "Monroe Doctrine."

94. Quincy Adams, "Special Message," March 15, 1826.

95. Kagan, *Dangerous Nation*, pp. 204–207.

96. Kagan, *Dangerous Nation*, pp. 256–57.

97. Henry Clay speech to Kossuth in Calvin Colton, ed., *The Works of Henry Clay*, vol. 3 (New York: Knickerbocker Press, 1904), pp. 222–24.

98. Millard Fillmore, "Second Annual Message," December 2, 1851, *TAPP*, https://www.presidency.ucsb.edu/node/200741.

Chapter 6

1. Robert May, *The Southern Dream of a Caribbean Empire, 1854–1861* (Gainesville: University Press of Florida, 2002), p. 247.

2. Foster Rhea Dulles, *Prelude to World Power: American Diplomatic History, 1860–1900* (New York: Macmillan, 1965), pp. 3–8. For a comprehensive treatment of Britain's role in the American Civil War, see Amanda Foreman, *A World on Fire: Britain's Crucial Role in the American Civil War* (New York: Random House, 2011).

3. William Seward, "Some Thoughts for the President's Consideration," April 1, 1861, Library of Congress, p. 3, https://www.loc.gov/resource/mal.0866000/.

4. See Dean Mahin, *One War at a Time: The International Dimensions of the American Civil War* (Washington: Brassey's, 2000). Walter Stahr in *Seward: Lincoln's Indispensable Man* (New York: Simon & Schuster, 2012), pp. 618–19, note 81, attempts to track down the origins of this famous Lincoln homily. He reports, "the best evidence I can find that Lincoln said 'one war at a time' is the *Norfolk [MA] County Journal*, which reported on December 28, 1861, that 'President Lincoln never spoke a wiser word than when he said "one war at a time."'"

5. See Dulles, *Prelude to World Power*, pp. 25–26; Francis Loomis, "The Position of the United States on the American Continent—Some Phases of the Monroe Doctrine," *Annals of the American Academy of Political and Social Science*, vol. 22 (July 1903), pp. 3–6; James Cortada, "A Case of International Rivalry in Latin America: Spain's Occupation of Santo Domingo, 1853–1865," *Revista de Historia de América*, no. 82 (July-December 1976), pp. 53–82; Wayne Bowen, *Spain and the American Civil War* (Columbia: University of Missouri Press, 2011).

6. See Office of the Historian, "French Intervention in Mexico and the American Civil War, 1862–1867," U.S. Department of State, https://history.state.gov/milestones/1861-1865/french-intervention; Marvin Goldwert, "Matías Romero and Congressional Opposition to Seward's Policy Toward the French Intervention in Mexico," *Americas*, vol. 22, no. 1 (July 1965), p. 22.

7. William Seward, "Remarks Of Mr. Seward," *Boston Herald*, June 24, 1867, p. 2. Accessed via Readex: America's Historical Newspapers.

8. David Shi, "Seward's Attempt to Annex British Columbia, 1865–1869," *Pacific Historical Review*, vol. 47, no. 2 (May 1978), pp. 217–38.

9. Doris W. Dashew, "The Story of an Illusion: The Plan to Trade the *Alabama* Claims for Canada," *Civil War History*, vol. 15, no. 4 (December 1969), p. 334.

10. Dashew, "The Story of an Illusion," pp. 332–33.

11. Kagan, *Dangerous Nation*, p. 280.

12. DeConde, *A History of American Foreign Policy*, pp. 251–52.

13. See Shi, "Seward's Attempt to Annex British Columbia," pp. 217–38. See also Dashew, "The Story of an Illusion," pp. 343–44.

14. Bowen, *Spain and the American Civil War*, p. 104.

15. William Seward, "Mr. Seward to Mr. Bigelow," December 16, 1865, in *Foreign Relations of the United States 1865–'66 (FRUS)*, part 3, p. 429. The University of Wisconsin hosts all *FRUS* volumes between 1861 and 1960 here: http://digicoll.library.wisc.edu/FRUS/Browse.html. See also Frederic Bancroft, "The French in Mexico and the Monroe Doctrine," *Political Science Quarterly*, vol. 11, no. 1 (March 1896), pp. 30–43.

16. See Kagan, *Dangerous Nation*, pp. 263–69, 280–83; Tuveson, *Redeemer Nation*, pp. 187–205.

17. Tuveson, *Redeemer Nation*, p. 192.

18. Job Stevenson, "Republic of Dominica—Again," July 10, 1871, in the *Congressional Globe*, 41st Cong., 3rd Sess., p. 409. A complete copy of the *Congressional Globe* is available from the Library of Congress: http://memory.loc.gov/ammem/amlaw/lwcg.html.

19. See Andrew Slap, *The Doom of Reconstruction: The Liberal Republicans in the Civil War Era* (New York: Fordham University Press, 2006); Michael Green, "Reconstructing the Nation, Reconstructing the Party: Postwar Republicans and the Evolution of a Party," in Paul Cimbala and Randall Miller, eds., *The Great Task Remaining Before Us: Reconstruction as America's Continuing Civil War* (New York: Fordham University Press, 2010), pp. 183–203.

20. LaFeber, *The American Age*, p. 161.

21. Dulles, *Prelude to World Power*, pp. 39, 94.

22. Paul Kennedy, *The Samoan Tangle: A Study in Anglo-German-American Relations, 1878–1900* (Dublin: Irish University Press, 1974), p. 133.

23. Jay Sexton, "The Civil War and U.S. World Power," in Don Doyle, ed., *American Civil Wars: The United States, Latin America, Europe, and the Crisis of the 1860s* (Chapel Hill: University of North Carolina Press, 2017), p. 21.

24. Combs, *The History of American Foreign Policy*, p. 115; Robert Beisner, *From the Old Diplomacy to the New, 1865–1900* (New York: Thomas Y. Crowell, 1975), pp. 12–13; Kagan, *Dangerous Nation*, pp. 341–42.

25. Dulles, *Prelude to World Power*, pp. 120–21.

26. Shi, "Seward's Attempt to Annex British Columbia," p. 223.

27. Dulles, *Prelude to World Power*, pp. 48–57; Shi, "Seward's Attempt to Annex British Columbia," pp. 223–24; Beisner, *From the Old Diplomacy to the New*, pp. 45–47.

28. Charles Sumner, *Speech of Honorable Charles Sumner of Massachusetts, on The Cession of Russian American to the United States* (Washington: Congressional Globe Office, 1867), pp. 12–16, http://name.umdl.umich.edu/aaz9604.0001.001.

29. Debate over the purchase of Alaska was mired in controversy stemming from an outstanding financial claim against the Russian government dating back to the Crimean War (the Perkins claim) as well as reports of bribery and a Russian-financed influence campaign during congressional consideration of the purchase. The House Committee on Public Expenditure led an inconclusive investigation into the controversy. See "Alaska Investigation," February 27, 1869, Report No. 35, 40th Cong., 3rd Sess.; Stahr, *Lincoln's Indispensable Man*, pp. 506–19; Lee A. Farrow, *Seward's Folly: A New Look at the Alaska Purchase* (Fairbanks: University of Alaska Press, 2016), chap. 5; and William A. Dunning, "Paying for Alaska," *Political Science Quarterly*, vol. 27, no. 3 (September 1912), pp. 385–98.

30. Shelby Cullom, "Purchase of Alaska—Mr. Cullom," July 10, 1868, in *Cong. Globe*, Appendix, 40th Cong., 2nd Sess., p. 474.

31. John Peters, "Purchase of Alaska," July 1, 1868 in *Cong. Globe*, 40th Cong., 2nd Sess., p. 3668.

32. Orange Ferriss, "Purchase of Alaska," July 1, 1868 in *Cong. Globe*, 40th Cong., 2nd Sess., p. 3667.

33. Hiram Price, "Purchase of Alaska—Mr. Price," July 1, 1868, in *Cong. Globe*, Appendix, 40th Cong., 2nd Sess., p. 381.

34. David M. Pletcher, *The Diplomacy of Involvement: American Economic Expansion Across the Pacific, 1784–1900* (Columbia: University of Missouri Press, 2001), pp. 35–40. See also "Purchase of Alaska," July 14, 1867, in *Cong. Globe*, 40th Cong., 2nd Sess., pp. 4052–4055; "Treaty with Russia for the Purchase of Alaska," Library of Congress, April 25, 2017, https://www.loc.gov/rr/program/bib/ourdocs/alaska.html.

35. Because the acquisition of Midway took place as an act of executive authority without congressional approval, it has contributed to debate about the legal status of such territories. See David Forman, M. Casey Jarman, and Jon Van Dyke, "Filling in a Jurisdictional Void: The New U.S. Territorial Sea," *Territorial Sea Journal*, vol. 2, no. 1 (1992), pp. 1–66; Duffy Burnett, "The Edges of Empire and the Limits of Sovereignty."

36. "Naval Appropriation Bill," February 22, 1869, in *Cong. Globe*, 40th Cong., 3rd Sess., pp. 1453–457. For details of the harbor dredging, see George Read, *The Last Cruise of the Saginaw* (Boston: Houghton Mifflin, 1912), pp. 3–11.

37. Other territories in the Caribbean under consideration as potential targets of U.S. expansion included Culebra (an island off the coast of Puerto Rico), Martinique, French Guiana, and St. Bartholomew. Seward also pursued the construction of an isthmian canal and sent an emissary to Greenland and Iceland to examine their geographic value and their natural resources. See Fareed Zakaria, *From Wealth to Power: The Unusual Origins of America's World Role* (Princeton: Princeton University Press, 1998), pp. 59–60, 62–63.

38. The *Philadelphia Press* quoted in Donald Marquand Dozer, "Anti-Expansionism during the Johnson Administration," *Pacific Historical Review*, vol. 12, no. 3 (September 1943), p. 256.

39. "The Earth-Hunger," *Nation*, January 2, 1868, p. 5.

40. "Purchase of Territory," November 25, 1867, in *Cong. Globe*, 40th Cong., 1st Sess., p. 792.

41. DeConde, *A History of American Foreign Policy*, p. 269.

42. See Willis Fletcher Johnson, "The Story of the Danish Islands," *North American Review*, vol. 204, no. 730 (September 1916), pp. 381–90.

43. See Glyndon G. Van Deusen, *William Henry Seward* (New York: Oxford University Press, 1967), pp. 526–34; Sumner Welles, *Naboth's Vineyard: The Dominican Republic, 1844–1924* (New York: Payson and Clarke, 1928), pp. 346–408.

44. The quotations from the debate over establishing a protectorate over Haiti and Santo Domingo are from: "Hayti [*sic*] and San Domingo Protectorate," January 13, 1869, in *Cong. Globe*, 40th Cong., 3rd Sess., pp. 333–40.

45. See Nicholas Guyatt, "America's Conservatory: Race, Reconstruction, and the Santo Domingo Debate," *Journal of American History*, vol. 97, no. 4 (March 2011), pp. 974–1000; and Paul Frymer, *Building an American Empire: The Era of Territorial and Political Expansion* (Princeton: Princeton University Press, 2017), pp. 211–18. Some historians argue that Grant's enthusiasm for annexing Santo Domingo also stemmed from the influence of his personal connections with Americans who had economic interests on the island. See LaFeber, *The American Age*, pp. 162–63.

46. Ulysses S. Grant, "Memorandum—Reasons why San Domingo should be annexed to the United States," in John Y. Simon, ed., *The Papers of Ulysses S. Grant, Volume 20, November 1, 1869–October 31, 1870* (Carbondale: Southern Illinois University Press, 1995), pp. 74–76.

47. Ulysses S. Grant, *Personal Memoirs of U. S. Grant*, vol. 2 (New York: Charles L. Webster, 1886), p. 550.

48. Kagan, *Dangerous Nation*, p. 276.

49. Zakaria, *From Wealth to Power*, pp. 67–70.

50. Carl Schurz, "Annexation of San Domingo," January 11, 1871, in *Cong. Globe*, 41st Cong., 3rd Sess., Appendix, p. 26.

51. Charles Sumner, "Annexation of Dominica," December 21, 1870, in *Cong. Globe*, 41st Cong., 3rd Sess., p. 231. See also Kagan, *Dangerous Nation*, pp. 277–79.

52. Schurz, "Annexation of San Domingo," January 11, 1871, in *Cong. Globe*, 41st Cong., 3rd Sess., Appendix, pp. 27, 30.

53. John Farnsworth, "Republic of Dominica," January 10, 1871, in *Cong. Globe*, 41st Cong., 3rd Sess., p. 412.

54. Seward quoted in Stahr, *Lincoln's Indispensable Man*, p. 456.

55. Morton Wilkinson, "Independence of Cuba," June 14, 1870, in *Cong. Globe*, 41st Cong., 2nd Sess., Appendix, pp. 491–92.

56. John Coburn, "Independence of Cuba," June 14, 1870, in *Cong. Globe*, 41st Cong., 2nd Sess., Appendix, pp. 491–92.

57. Zakaria, *From Wealth to Power*, p. 71.

58. See Barry Rigby, "The Origins of American Expansion in Hawaii and Samoa," *International History Review*, vol. 10, no. 2 (May 1988), pp. 221–37.

59. Zakaria, *From Wealth to Power*, p. 74.

60. Seward, "Mr. Seward to Mr. Yeaman," September 23, 1867, U.S. Department of State, in *Compilation of Reports of the Committee on Foreign Relations: Treaties and Legislation Respecting Them*, vol. 8 (Washington: GPO, 1901), p. 188.

61. Seward, "Mr. Seward to Mr. Spalding," July 5, 1868, U.S. Department of State, in *Papers Relating to the Annexation of the Hawaiian Islands to the United States* (Washington: GPO, 1893), p. 140.

62. Seward, "Seward to Bigelow," October 8, 1868, in John Bigelow, *Retrospections of an active life, Volume 4, 1867–1871* (New York: Doubleday, Page, 1913), p. 225.

63. Ulysses S. Grant, "Letter to Buenaventura Báez," July 7, 1870, in Simon, ed., *The Papers of Ulysses S. Grant*, vol. 20, p. 188.

64. David M. Pletcher, "1861–1898: Economic Growth and Diplomatic Adjustment," in Becker and Wells, *Economics and World Power*, p. 120; Zakaria, *From Wealth to Power*, pp. 45–46.

65. For discussion of the tension between protectionist and liberalizing trends during this era of economic growth, see Marc-William Palen, *The "Conspiracy" of Free Trade: The Anglo-American Struggle over Empire and Economic Globalization, 1846–1896* (New York: Cambridge University Press, 2016).

66. See Dulles, *Prelude to World Power*, pp. 94–98, 110.

67. Through the Clayton-Bulwer Treaty, the United States and Great Britain agreed that neither party would build an isthmian canal without the consent and cooperation of the other and that the canal, should it be built, would be open to all shipping.

68. Dulles, *Prelude to World Power*, pp. 81–85.

69. Eric Rauchway, *Blessed Among Nations: How the World Made America* (New York: Hill and Wang, 2006), pp. 69–70.

70. Frank Ninkovich, *Global Dawn: The Cultural Foundation of American Internationalism, 1865–1890* (Cambridge: Harvard University Press, 2009).

71. Ulysses S. Grant, "Seventh Annual Message," December 7, 1875, TAPP, https://www.presidency.ucsb.edu/node/203765.

72. These heavier ships had more armor than previous ships and incorporated advances in firepower, but were nonetheless out of date by international standards by the time they were commissioned.

73. Beisner, *From the Old Diplomacy to the New*, pp. 88–90. See also Mark Shulman, *Navalism and the Emergence of American Sea Power, 1882–1893* (Annapolis: Naval Institute Press, 1995).

74. Nathan Miller, *The U.S. Navy: A History*, 3rd edition (Annapolis: Naval Institute Press, 1997), pp. 148–50.

75. See Harold Sprout and Margaret Sprout, *The Rise of American Naval Power, 1776–1918* (Princeton: Princeton University Press, 1967), pp. 183–201.

76. Grover Cleveland, "Inaugural Address," March 4, 1885, TAPP, https://www.presidency.ucsb.edu/documents/inaugural-address-40.

77. Thomas Bayard quoted in Charles Callan Tansill, *The Foreign Policy of Thomas F. Bayard, 1885–1897* (New York: Fordham University Press, 1940), p. xxviii.

78. "An act to increase the Naval establishment," August 3, 1886, 49th Cong, 1st Sess., Chap. 849, https://www.loc.gov/law/help/statutes-at-large/49th-congress/session-1/c49s1ch849.pdf; Sprout and Sprout, *Rise of American Naval Power*, pp. 184, 189–90.

79. Sprout and Sprout, *Rise of American Naval Power*, p. 195.

80. Navy Department, "Report of Policy Board," January 20, 1890, in *The Proceedings of the United States Naval Institute*, vol. 16, no. 2 (Annapolis: Naval Institute Press, 1890), pp. 201–77, quotes on pp. 202–203.

81. See Alfred Thayer Mahan, *The Influence of Sea Power upon History* (Boston: Little Brown, 1890); Sprout and Sprout, *Rise of American Naval Power*, pp. 202–22.

82. "An act making appropriations for the Naval service for the fiscal year ending June thirtieth, eighteen hundred and ninety-one, and for other purposes," June 30, 1890, 51st Cong., 1st Sess., Chap. 849, https://www.loc.gov/law/help/statutes-at-large/51st-congress/session-1/c51s1ch640.pdf.

83. Sprout and Sprout, *Rise of American Naval Power*, pp. 212–13. For the congressional debates over the 1890 naval authorization, see *Congressional Record: Containing the Proceedings and Debates of the Fifty-First Congress, First Session and Special Session of the Senate*, vol. 21, parts 4 and 6 (Washington: GPO, 1889), pp. 3161–71, 3221–3, 3256–71, 5173–82, 5236–8, 5276–97. Hereafter citations to the *Congressional Record* will be abbreviated as "Volume # *Cong. Rec.*, # Cong., # Sess., part #, page #." In this instance 21 *Cong. Rec.*, 51st Cong., 1st Sess., parts 4 and 6, pp. 3161–71, 3221–3, 3256–71, 5173–82, 5236–8, 5276–97. The entire *Congressional Record* can be found here: https://www.govinfo.gov/app/collection/crecb/160_crecb.

84. Sprout and Sprout, *Rise of American Naval Power*, pp. 211–12. See also Kagan, *Dangerous Nation*, pp. 343–44.

85. John McPherson, "Naval Appropriation Bill," May 22, 1890, in 21 *Cong. Rec.*, part 6, pp. 5138–139.

86. Joseph Dolph, "Naval Appropriation Bill," May 23, 1890, in 21 *Cong. Rec.*, part 6, pp. 5173, 5177.

87. Jonathan Dolliver, "Navy Appropriation Bill," April 8, 1890, in 21 *Cong. Rec.*, part 4, p. 3167.

88. Charles Boutelle, "Naval Appropriation Bill," April 8, 1890, in 21 *Cong. Rec.*, part 4, p. 3171.

89. Hilary Hebert, "Naval Appropriation Bill," April 10, 1890, in 21 *Cong. Rec.*, part 4, p. 3257.

90. William Stewart, Naval Appropriation Bill, May 26, 1890, in 21 *Cong. Rec.*, part 6, p. 5281.

91. Sprout and Sprout, *Rise of American Naval Power*, pp. 206, 212.

92. The Senate unanimously approved the treaty in executive session, leaving behind no official record of its deliberations. The *New York Tribune* reported that "the consideration of the treaty occupied very little time in the Senate, and was confirmed without a division." See "The Treaty with Samoa," *New York Tribune*, January 31, 1878, p. 1. Accessed via the Library of Congress: *Chronicling America: Historic American Newspapers*. As discussed below, Samoa's low political salience, the increasing presence of European powers in the Pacific, and a bipartisan commitment to increasing transpacific commerce may have all contributed to the treaty's easy passage.

93. "Samoa: Friendship and Commerce," January 17, 1878, 20 Stat. 704; Treaty Series 312, https://www.loc.gov/law/help/us-treaties/bevans/b-ws-ust000011-0437.pdf.

94. See Peter Shulman, *Coal and Empire: The Birth of Energy Security in Industrial America* (Baltimore: Johns Hopkins University Press, 2015), pp. 132–33.

95. See Kennedy, *The Samoan Tangle*.

96. William McAdoo, "Naval Appropriation Bill," February 2, 1889 in 20 *Cong. Rec.*, 50th Cong., 2nd Sess., part 2, p. 1439.

97. Holger Droessler, "Colonialism by Deferral: Samoa Under the Tridominium, 1889–1899," in Søren Rud and Søren Ivarsson, eds., *Rethinking the Colonial State* (Bingley: Emerald, 2017), pp. 208–209.

98. "Neutrality and Autonomous Government in Samoa (General Act of Berlin)," June 14, 1889, 26 Stat. 1497; Treaty Series 313, p.116, https://www.loc.gov/law/help/us-treaties/bevans/m-ust000001-0116.pdf; Droessler, "Colonialism by Deferral," p. 210.

99. James Blaine, "Mr. Blaine to Messrs. Kasson, Phelps, and Bates," April 11, 1889, in *FRUS 1890*, p. 201; Henry Ide, "Our Interest in Samoa," *North American Review*, vol. 165, no. 489 (August 1897), pp. 155–73.

100. James Blaine, "Mr. Blaine's Plea for Reciprocal Trade," August 30, 1890, in *American: A National Weekly Journal of Politics, Literature, Science, Art, and Finance*, volumes 20–21 (Philadelphia: The American Company, Ltd., 1890), p. 416.

101. Benjamin Harrison, "230. Harrison to Blaine," in Albert Volwiler, ed., *The Correspondence Between Benjamin Harrison and James G. Blaine, 1882–1893* (Lancaster: Lancaster Press, 1940), p. 202; Beisner, *From the Old Diplomacy to the New*, pp. 96–97.

102. "Ratified the Treaty: In Executive Session the Senate Acts on the Samoan Matter," *Chicago Tribune*, February 5, 1890, p. 2.

103. "Samoan Treaty Ratified: Little Opposition Made by the Democrats," *New York Times*, February 5, 1890, p. 5. The *Times* refers to "Pango-Pango harbor." For the challenge to Senator Call's claim, see "Ratified the Treaty," *Chicago Tribune*; "The Samoan Treaty," *Washington Post*, February 7, 1890, p. 2.

104. "Samoan Treaty Ratified," *New York Times*.

105. Dulles, *Prelude to World Power*, pp. 107–10; Ralph Kuykendall, *The Hawaiian Kingdom, Volume 3: 1874–1893, The Kalakua Dynasty* (Honolulu: University of Hawaii Press, 1967), pp. 373–400.
106. The Senate debate over the annexation of Hawaii in 1893 occurred in executive session and a record of the deliberations is therefore not available. Accordingly, the following summary relies on coverage of the debate in the media and in George W. Baker Jr., "Benjamin Harrison and Hawaiian Annexation: A Reinterpretation," *Pacific Historical Review*, vol. 33, no. 3 (August 1964), pp. 295–309.
107. "Senator Washburn on Money and Hawaii," *New York Tribune*, March 14, 1893, p. 4.
108. "Talk About Hawaii," *New York Tribune*, February 27, 1893, p. 2.
109. "Senator Morgan on Hawaii," *New York Tribune*, February 26, 1893, p. 3.
110. Carl Schurz, "Manifest Destiny," *Harper's*, vol. 87, no. 521 (October 1893), pp. 743-44.
111. Newspaper editorials found in Philip S. Foner and Richard C. Winchester, eds., *The Anti-Imperialist Reader: Volume I, From the Mexican War to the Election of 1900* (New York: Holmes and Meier, 1984), pp. 71–76.
112. Foner and Winchester, eds., *The Anti-Imperialist Reader*, p. 74.
113. E. L. Godkin, "Hawaii," *The Nation*, vol. 56, no. 1441, February 9, 1893, in *The Nation: A Weekly Journal Devoted to Politics, Literature, Science & Art*, vol. 56 (New York: Evening Post Publishing Company, 1893), p. 96.
114. Grover Cleveland, "Special Message," March 9, 1893, *TAPP*, https://www.presidency.ucsb.edu/node/206153.
115. Walter Gresham, "Affairs in the Samoan Islands," May 9, 1894, in *FRUS 1894, Appendix I*, p. 508.
116. Walter Gresham letters to John Overmyer, July 25, 1894, and Noble C. Butler, November 23, 1893, quoted in Charles W. Calhoun, "Rehearsal for Anti-Imperialism: The Second Cleveland Administration's Attempt to Withdraw from Samoa, 1893–1895," *Historian*, vol. 48, no. 2 (February 1986), pp. 210–12; and in Kagan, *Dangerous Nation*, p. 364.
117. Calhoun, "Rehearsal for Anti-Imperialism," pp. 210–11. For a comprehensive biography of Gresham, see Charles W. Calhoun, *Gilded Age Cato: The Life of Walter Q. Gresham* (Lexington: University Press of Kentucky, 1988).
118. Calhoun, "Rehearsal for Anti-Imperialism," p. 212.
119. Grover Cleveland, "Special Message," December 18, 1893, *TAPP*, https://www.presidency.ucsb.edu/node/205550.
120. Grover Cleveland, "First Annual Message (second term)" December 4, 1893, *TAPP*, https://www.presidency.ucsb.edu/node/206263.
121. Lodge quoted in John A. Garraty, *Henry Cabot Lodge: A Biography* (New York: Knopf, 1953), p. 150.
122. Gresham, "Affairs in the Samoan Islands," *FRUS 1894, Appendix I*, p. 511.
123. Cleveland, "First Annual Message (second term)."
124. Gresham, "Affairs in the Samoan Islands," *FRUS 1894, Appendix I*, pp. 504, 509.
125. Grover Cleveland, "Message to the Senate of the United States," August 10, 1894, in *Journal of the Senate, Including the Journal of the Executive Proceedings of the Senate*, vol. 29, part 1 (Washington: GPO, 1909), p. 772.
126. Grover Cleveland, "Second Annual Message (second term)," December 3, 1894, *TAPP*, https://www.presidency.ucsb.edu/node/206266.
127. Calhoun, "Rehearsal for Anti-Imperialism," pp. 220–24.
128. Sprout and Sprout, *Rise of American Naval Power*, pp. 217–22.
129. Henry Cabot Lodge, "England, Venezuela, and the Monroe Doctrine," *North American Review*, vol. 160, no. 463 (June 1895), pp. 657–58.
130. Joseph Wheeler and Charles H. Grosvenor, "Our Duty in the Venezuelan Crisis," *North American Review*, vol. 161, no. 468 (November 1895), p. 632.
131. Richard Olney, "Mr. Olney to Mr. Bayard," July 20, 1895, in *FRUS 1895*, part 1, p. 558; Charles Campbell, *From Revolution to Rapprochement: The United States and Great Britain, 1783–1900* (New York: John Wiley & Sons, 1974).
132. Robert Arthur Talbot Gascoyne-Cecil, "Lord Salisbury to Sir Julian Pauncefote," November 26, 1895, in *FRUS 1895*, part 1, p. 566.

133. Beisner, *From the Old Diplomacy to the New*, pp. 98–103. See also Odeen Ishmael, *The Trail of Diplomacy: The Guyana-Venezuela Border Issue* (Bloomington: Xlibris, 2013), p. 200.

134. Newton Blanchard, "The Monroe Doctrine," February 11, 1896, in 28 *Cong. Rec.*, 54th Cong., 1st Sess., part 2, p. 1579.

135. See Kupchan, *How Enemies Become Friends*, pp. 76–77.

136. Stuart Anderson, *Race and Rapprochement: Anglo-Saxonism and Anglo-American Relations, 1895–1904* (London: Associated University Presses, 1981), p. 87.

137. Arthur Balfour, "Address in Answer to Her Majesty's Most Gracious Speech," February 11, 1896, in *The Parliamentary Debates, Fourth Series, Commencing with the Second Session of the Twenty-Sixth Parliament of the United Kingdom of Great Britain and Ireland, 59 Victoriæ*, vol. 37 (London: Waterlow and Sons, 1896), pp. 109–10; Stephen Rock, *Appeasement in International Politics* (Lexington: University Press of Kentucky, 2000), p. 27.

138. Torreon and Plagakis, "Instances of Use of United States Armed Forces Abroad, 1798–2018."

139. See Combs, *The History of American Foreign Policy*, p. 135; Kagan, *Dangerous Nation*, p. 369; Dulles, *Prelude to World Power*, pp. 137–38; Lars Schoultz, *Beneath the United States: A History of U.S. Policy Toward Latin America* (Cambridge: Harvard University Press, 1998), pp. 107, 113–14; Melvin Small, *Democracy and Diplomacy: The Impact of Domestic Politics on U.S. Foreign Policy, 1789–1994* (Baltimore: Johns Hopkins University Press, 1996), p. 27; and Nelson M. Blake, "Background of Cleveland's Venezuelan Policy," *American Historical Review*, vol. 47, no. 2 (January 1942), pp. 259–77. For a contrary view, see Beisner, *From the Old Diplomacy to the New*, pp. 100–101, and Walter LaFeber, "The Background of Cleveland's Venezuelan Policy: A Reinterpretation," *American Historical Review*, vol. 66, no. 4 (July 1961), pp. 947–67.

140. Kagan, *Dangerous Nation*, pp. 368–69, 382–85; Dulles, *Prelude to World Power*, pp. 138–48.

141. Nichols, *Promise and Peril*, p. 39.

142. See Karine Walther, *Sacred Interests: The United States and the Islamic World, 1821–1921* (Chapel Hill: University of North Carolina Press, 2015), pp. 241–70.

143. Richard Olney, "Mr. Olney to Mr. Bayard," July 20, 1895.

Chapter 7

1. For a history of American expansion beyond North America, see Immerwahr, *How to Hide an Empire*.

2. See Paul Kennedy, *The Rise and Fall of the Great Powers: Economic Change and Military Conflict from 1500 to 2000* (New York: Random House, 1987); Robert Gilpin, *War and Change in World Politics* (New York: Cambridge University Press, 1981).

3. Tucker, "Exemplar or Crusader?" See also McDougall, *Promised Land, Crusader State*.

4. Walter LaFeber, *The New Empire: An Interpretation of American Expansion, 1860–1898* (Ithaca: Cornell University Press, 1998), p. 64.

5. McDougall, *Promised Land, Crusader State*, pp. 101–107.

6. The Turner quotations in this chapter are all from: Frederick Jackson Turner, "The Significance of the Frontier in American History," delivered at the 1893 meeting of the American Historical Association in Chicago, in *Annual Report of the American Historical Association for the Year 1893* (Washington: GPO, 1894), pp. 197–227. A copy of the speech is also available at: https://www.historians.org/about-aha-and-membership/aha-history-and-archives/historical-archives/the-significance-of-the-frontier-in-american-history.

7. Brooke Adams, "The Spanish War and the Equilibrium of the World," *Forum*, vol. 25, no. 6 (August 1898), p. 651.

8. Josiah Strong, *Expansion Under New World-Conditions* (New York: Baker and Taylor, 1900), p. 254.

9. LaFeber, *The New Empire*, p. 76.

10. LaFeber, *The New Empire*, p. 77.

11. Gary Marotta, "The Academic Mind and the Rise of U.S. Imperialism: Historians and Economists as Publicists for Ideas of Colonial Expansion," *American Journal of Economics and Sociology*, vol. 42, no. 2 (April 1983), p. 230.

12. Frederick Wells Williams, "The Real Menace of Russian Aggression," *Annals of the American Academy of Political and Social Science*, vol. 13, supplement (May 1899), p. 197.

13. Fensterwald, "The Anatomy of American 'Isolationism' and Expansionism," p. 118.

14. Monten, "The Roots of the Bush Doctrine," p. 137.

15. Kagan, *Dangerous Nation*, p. 416.

16. Hartz, *The Liberal Tradition in America*, p. 81.

17. See William Leuchtenburg, "Progressivism and Imperialism: The Progressive Movement and American Foreign Policy, 1898–1916," *Mississippi Valley Historical Review*, vol. 39, no. 3 (December 1952), pp. 483–504; Gerald E. Markowitz, "Progressivism and Imperialism: A Return to First Principles," *Historian*, vol. 37, no. 2 (February 1975), pp. 257–75.

18. James Phelan, "Two Opinions of Oriental Expansion," *Overland Monthly*, vol. 32, ser. 2 (July–December 1898), pp. 364–65, https://hdl.handle.net/2027/iau.31858036877029.

19. LaFeber, *The American Age*, pp. 220–25; LaFeber, *The New Empire*, pp. 407–17.

20. See Marotta, "The Academic Mind and the Rise of U.S. Imperialism."

21. Thomas Bayard, "Mr. Bayard to Mr. Pendleton," January 17, 1888, in *FRUS 1888–1890*, part 1, p. 599.

22. Henry Cabot Lodge, "Our Blundering Foreign Policy," *Forum*, vol. 19 (March 1895), p. 17.

23. Julius W. Pratt, "The 'Large Policy' of 1898," *Mississippi Valley Historical Review*, vol. 19, no. 2 (September 1932), p. 220.

24. See Stephen Skowronek, *Building a New American State: The Expansion of National Administrative Capacities, 1877–1920* (New York: Cambridge University Press, 1982); and see Zakaria, *From Wealth to Power*, pp. 90–180.

25. LaFeber, *The New Empire*, p. 7.

26. See Trubowitz, *Defining the National Interest*.

Chapter 8

1. Secretary of the Navy, *Report of the Secretary of the Navy, 1889, Part 1* (Washington: GPO, 1890), p. 34; Secretary of the Navy, *Annual Reports of the Navy Department for the Year 1902* (Washington: GPO, 1902), p. 445.

2. William McKinley, "Message to Congress Requesting a Declaration of War With Spain," April 11, 1898, *TAPP*, https://www.presidency.ucsb.edu/node/304972.

3. Nichols, *Promise and Peril*, p. 49.

4. Fensterwald, "The Anatomy of American 'Isolationism' and Expansionism," pp. 117–18.

5. McDougall, *Promised Land, Crusader State*, p. 114.

6. Jefferson, "Letter from Thomas Jefferson to Thomas Lomax."

7. "Republican Party Platform of 1896," June 18, 1896, *TAPP*, https://www.presidency.ucsb.edu/node/273316.

8. See William Morgan, "The Anti-Japanese Origins of the Hawaiian Annexation Treaty of 1897," *Diplomatic History*, vol. 6, no. 1 (Winter 1982), pp. 23–44.

9. Noenoe K. Silva, *Aloha Betrayed: Native Hawaiian Resistance to American Colonialism* (Durham: Duke University Press, 2004), pp. 145–63. See also "The 1897 Petition Against the Annexation of Hawaii," National Archives, https://www.archives.gov/education/lessons/hawaii-petition.

10. On opposition to the war within the business community and the media, see Piero Gleijeses, "1898: The Opposition to the Spanish-American War," *Journal of Latin American Studies*, vol. 35, no. 4 (November 2003), pp. 681–719.

11. Zakaria, *From Wealth to Power*, p. 155.

12. Henry Cabot Lodge, "Intervention in Cuban Affairs," April 13, 1898, in 31 *Cong. Rec.*, 55th Cong., 2nd Sess., part 4, p. 3784.

13. McKinley, "Declaration of War With Spain," April 11, 1898.

14. On the politics behind McKinley's decision for war, see Peter Trubowitz, *Politics and Strategy: Partisan Ambition and American Statecraft* (Princeton: Princeton University Press, 2011), pp. 90–97.

15. On the considerations informing the decision to take over the Philippines, see Philip Zelikow, "Why Did America Cross the Pacific? Reconstructing the U.S. Decision to Take

the Philippines, 1898–99," *Texas National Security Review*, vol. 1, no. 1 (December 2017), pp. 36–67.

16. Pratt, "The 'Large Policy' of 1898," p. 221.

17. "Report of Quartermaster General," October 31, 1898, in *Annual Reports of the War Department for the Fiscal Year Ended June 30, 1898* (Washington: GPO, 1898), p. 393.

18. John D. Long, "Secretary Of The Navy John D. Long to Captain Henry Glass," May 18, 1898, Navy History and Heritage Command, https://www.history.navy.mil/research/publications/documentary-histories/united-states-navy-s/the-capture-of-guam/secretary-of-the-nav.html.

19. Henry Glass, "Captain Henry Glass To Secretary Of The Navy John D. Long," June 24, 1898, Naval History and Heritage Command, https://www.history.navy.mil/research/publications/documentary-histories/united-states-navy-s/the-capture-of-guam/captain-henry-glass.html.

20. "Report of the Secretary of the Navy," November 15, 1898, in *Annual Report of the Secretary of the Navy for the Year 1898* (Washington: GPO, 1898), pp. 13–14.

21. The payment to Spain was in part to secure U.S. sovereignty over the entire Philippine archipelago and avoid potential partition. See Paolo Coletta, "McKinley, the Peace Negotiations, and the Acquisition of the Philippines," *Pacific Historical Review*, vol. 30, no. 4 (November 1961), pp. 345–48.

22. Robert Hitt, "Hawaii," June 11, 1898, in 31 *Cong. Rec.*, part 6, pp. 5771–72.

23. U.S. Congress, House of Representatives, Committee on Foreign Affairs, "Joint Resolution for the Annexation of Hawaii: Report (to Accompany H. Res. 259)," May 17, 1898, 55th Cong., 2nd Sess., House Report 1355, https://hawaiiankingdom.org/blog/report-of-the-house-committee-on-foreign-affairs-annexation-of-hawaii/.

24. Hugh Dinsmore, "Hawaii," June 11, 1898, in 31 *Cong. Rec.*, part 6, pp. 5776–77.

25. James Clark, "War Revenue Bill," June 11, 1898, in 31 *Cong. Rec.*, part 6, p. 5789.

26. Henry Cabot Lodge, "Lodge to Roosevelt," May 24, 1898, in Henry C. Lodge, ed., *Selections from the Correspondence of Theodore Roosevelt and Henry Cabot Lodge, 1884–1918*, vol. 1 (New York: Charles Scribner's Sons, 1925), pp. 299–300.

27. Pratt, "The 'Large Policy' of 1898," p. 223.

28. Henry Cabot Lodge, *The Story of the Revolution* (New York: Charles Scribner's Sons, 1903), p. 575.

29. Henry Cabot Lodge, "Letter to Elihu Hayes," May 18, 1898, quoted in Nichols, *Promise and Peril*, p. 52.

30. Orville Platt, "Financial Movements," *Railway World*, 37th year, vol. 19, no. 5, February 4, 1893, p. 97.

31. James Bridge, "America's Interest in China," *Overland Monthly*, vol. 31, no. 182 (February 1898), pp. 177–78.

32. Henry Cabot Lodge, "Letter to Thomas Brackett Reed," September 1897, quoted in Garraty, *Henry Cabot Lodge*, p. 184.

33. Theodore Roosevelt, "Letter to Alfred Thayer Mahan," May 3, 1897, in Elting Morison, ed., *The Letters of Theodore Roosevelt: Volume 1, The Years of Preparation, 1868–1898* (Cambridge: Harvard University Press, 1951), p. 607.

34. McDougall, *Promised Land, Crusader State*, p. 108.

35. Alfred Thayer Mahan, *From Sail to Steam: Recollections of Naval Life* (New York: Harper & Brothers, 1907), p. 324.

36. Marotta, "The Academic Mind and the Rise of U.S. Imperialism," p. 217.

37. Henry Cabot Lodge, "Letter to Fred," May 21, 1898, quoted in Nichols, *Promise and Peril*, p. 52. See note 93, p. 364. Nichols believes Fred is "most likely George 'Fred' Williams."

38. "Report of Mr. White, Mr. Low, and Mr. Holls, to the American Commission to the International Conference at the Hague, Regarding the Work of the Third Committee of the Conference," July 31, 1899, *YLSAP*, http://avalon.law.yale.edu/19th_century/hag99-10.asp.

39. McDougall argues that the decline of a religious conception of messianism was in part responsible for the United States' outward turn. Religious messianism gave way to a civil religion that took the form of "progressive imperialism." See McDougall, *Promised Land, Crusader State*,

pp. 104–21; and Walter McDougall, *The Tragedy of U.S. Foreign Policy: How America's Civil Religion Betrayed the National Interest* (New Haven: Yale University Press, 2016).

40. McKinley, "Declaration of War With Spain," April 11, 1898.
41. General James F. Rusling, "Interview with President McKinley," *Christian Advocate*, vol. 78, no. 4, January 22, 1903, p. 17; Nichols, *Promise and Peril*, pp. 49–53.
42. William McKinley, "Speech at Charlton, Iowa," October 13, 1898, in *Speeches and Addresses of William McKinley: From March 1, 1897 to May 30, 1900* (New York: Doubleday and McClure, 1900), p. 114.
43. William McKinley, "Speech at the Citizens' Banquet in the Auditorium, Chicago," October 19, 1898, in *Speeches and Addresses*, pp. 133–35; Robert Saldin, "William McKinley and the Rhetorical Presidency," *Presidential Studies Quarterly*, vol. 41, no. 1 (March 2011), pp. 119–34.
44. William McKinley, "Speech at Dinner of the Home Market Club, Boston," February 16, 1899, in *Speeches and Addresses*, p. 189.
45. William McKinley quoted in Charles Sumner Olcott, *William McKinley*, vol. 1 (New York: Houghton Mifflin, 1916), p. 379. The quote is said to appear in George Cortelyou's diary entry, June 8, 1898.
46. Knute Nelson, "Acquisition of Territory," January 20, 1899, in 32 *Cong. Rec.*, 55th Cong., 3rd Sess., part 1, p. 838.
47. John Spooner, "Acquisition of Territory," February 2, 1899, in 32 *Cong. Rec.*, part 2, p. 1388.
48. Albert Beveridge, "Policy Regarding the Philippines," January 9, 1900 in 33 *Cong. Rec.*, 56th Cong., 1st Sess., part 1, p. 704.
49. Bachman and the *California Christian Advocate*, quoted in Preston, *Sword of the Spirit, Shield of Faith*, pp. 180, 212.
50. Josiah Strong, *Our Country: Its Possible Future and Its Present Crisis* (New York: American Home Missionary Society, 1885), pp. 160–61, 174–5.
51. Richard Welch, *The Presidencies of Grover Cleveland* (Lawrence: University Press of Kansas, 1988), p. 142.
52. "Political Aspects of the Trouble," *New York Times*, July 25, 1877, p. 4; see also Zakaria, *From Wealth to Power*, pp. 116–23.
53. Edward Bellamy, "Letter of Regret to the People's Party," October 22, 1892, in *New Nation*, vol. 2, no. 43, p. 645. Matarese, *American Foreign Policy*, pp. 24–25.
54. Claude G. Bowers, *Beveridge and the Progressive Era* (New York: Literary Guild, 1932), p. 69. See also Emily S. Rosenberg, *Spreading the American Dream: American Economic and Cultural Expansion, 1890–1945* (New York: Hill and Wang, 1982).
55. "Mr. Bryan on the War," *New York Times*, June 15, 1898, p. 3.
56. Leuchtenburg, "Progressivism and Imperialism," p. 485.
57. Markowitz, "Progressivism and Imperialism," pp. 257, 259.
58. Theodore Roosevelt, "The Strenuous Life," April 10, 1899, Voices of Democracy: The U.S. Oral History Project, http://voicesofdemocracy.umd.edu/roosevelt-strenuous-life-1899-speech-text/.
59. Washington Gladden, *Our Nation and Her Neighbors* (Columbus: Quinius and Ridenour, 1898), p. 39.
60. Caro Lloyd, *Henry Demarest Lloyd, 1847–1903: A Biography*, vol. 2 (New York: G. P. Putnam's Sons, 1912), p. 134; see also Markowitz, "Progressivism and Imperialism."
61. See Delber McKee, "Samuel Gompers, the A. F. of L., and Imperialism, 1895–1900," *Historian*, vol. 21, no. 2 (February 1959), p. 193; and Nichols, *Promise and Peril*, pp. 12–13.
62. Beisner, *From the Old Diplomacy to the New*, p. 83.
63. Mahan, "The United States Looking Outward."
64. Nichols, *Promise and Peril*, p. 64.
65. McKinley, "Declaration of War With Spain," April 11, 1898; McKinley, "Speech at Dinner of the Home Market Club, Boston," February 16, 1899.
66. "Appendix A: Joint Resolution For the recognition of the independence of the people of Cuba. . . ," April 20, 1898, 55th Cong., 2nd Sess., https://link.springer.com/content/pdf/bbm%3A978-94-015-0749-3%2F1.pdf.
67. George Hoar, "Intervention in Cuban Affairs," April 14, 1898, in 31 *Cong. Rec.*, part 4, p. 3835.

68. Leonard Wood, "The Military Government of Cuba," *Annals of the American Academy of Political and Social Science*, vol. 21 (March 1903), pp. 156–57. See also J. H. Hitchman, "The American Touch in Imperial Administration: Leonard Wood in Cuba, 1898–1902," *Americas*, vol. 24, no. 4 (April 1968), pp. 394–403.

69. "Relations with Cuba," May 22, 1903, 33 Stat. 2248; Treaty Series 437, p. 1117, https://www.loc.gov/law/help/us-treaties/bevans/b-cu-ust000006-1116.pdf.

70. See Lanny Thompson, "The Imperial Republic: A Comparison of the Insular Territories under U.S. Dominion after 1898," *Pacific Historical Review*, vol. 71, no. 4 (November 2002), pp. 535–74; and Alfred Hartwell, "The Organization of a Territorial Government for Hawaii," *Yale Law Journal*, vol. 9, no. 3 (December 1899), pp. 107–13.

71. Hitt, "Hawaii," June 11, 1898, p. 5771.

72. See Thompson, "The Imperial Republic," for a discussion of the relevant legal cases.

73. William McKinley, "Executive Order," December 21, 1898, *TAPP*, https://www.presidency.ucsb.edu/node/205913.

74. George Vest, "Acquisition of Territory," December 12, 1898, in 32 *Cong. Rec.*, part 1, p. 93.

75. Orville Platt, "Acquisition of Territory," December 12, 1898, in 32 *Cong. Rec.*, part 1, p. 96.

76. George Hoar, "Acquisition of Territory," January 9, 1899, in 32 *Cong. Rec.*, part 1, pp. 495–99.

77. William Mason, "Government of Foreign People," January 10, 1899, in 32 *Cong. Rec.*, part 1, p. 530.

78. John Thompson, *A Sense of Power: The Roots of America's Global Role* (Ithaca: Cornell University Press, 2015), p. 30.

79. Henry Adams, "Henry Adams to Sir Robert Cunliffe," January 25, 1900, in Worthington Chauncey Ford, ed., *Letters of Henry Adams (1892–1918)* (New York: Houghton Mifflin, 1938), pp. 254–55.

80. Hitt, "Hawaii," June 11, 1898, p. 5772.

81. Joseph Walker, "War Revenue Bill," June 11, 1898, in 31 *Cong. Rec.*, part 6, p. 5795.

82. See Fred H. Harrington, "The Anti-Imperialist Movement in the United States, 1898–1900," *Mississippi Valley Historical Review*, vol. 22, no. 2 (September 1935), pp. 211–30; Maria Lanzar-Carpio, *The Anti-Imperialist League* (Ann Arbor: University of Michigan Press, 1928), doctoral dissertation; E. Berkeley Tompkins, *Anti-Imperialism in the United States: The Great Debate, 1890–1920* (Philadelphia: University of Pennsylvania Press, 1970).

83. Samuel Gompers, "Imperialism, Its Dangers Right and Wrong," October 18, 1898, in Stuart Kaufman et al., eds., *The Samuel Gompers Papers, Volume 5, An Expanding Movement at the Turn of the Century, 1898–1902* (Urbana: University of Illinois Press, 1995), p. 23.

84. Bryan quoted in "Mr. Bryan on the War," *New York Times*.

85. William Jennings Bryan, "Jackson Day Speech at Chicago," January 7, 1899, in William Jennings Bryan et al., *The Second Battle or the New Declaration of Independence, 1776–1900: An Account of the Struggle of 1900* (Chicago: W. B. Conkey, 1900), p. 99; see also Paolo Coletta, "Bryan, McKinley, and the Treaty of Paris," *Pacific Historical Review*, vol. 26, no. 2 (May 1957), pp. 131–46.

86. William Jennings Bryan, "The Savannah Interview," December 13, 1898, in Bryan, *The Second Battle*, p. 88.

87. William Jennings Bryan, "The National Emblem," December 23, 1898, in Bryan, *The Second Battle*, p. 90.

88. William Sumner, *The Conquest of the United States by Spain* (Boston: Dana Estes, 1899), pp. 3–19.

89. Grover Cleveland, *American Citizenship: Founder's Day Address* (Princeton: Princeton University Press, 1898), pp. 11–12.

90. Albert Beveridge, "Policy Regarding the Philippines," January 9, 1900, 33 *Cong. Rec.*, part 1, p. 710. See also Allen Merriam, "Racism in the Expansionist Controversy of 1898–1900," *Phylon*, vol. 39, no. 4 (4th Quarter 1978), pp. 369–80.

91. John Daniel, "Acquisition of Territory," February 3, 1899, 32 *Cong. Rec.*, p. 1430; James Clark, "Diplomatic and Consular Appropriation Bill," February 5, 1990, in 33 *Cong. Rec.*, part 2, p. 1520; see also Christopher Lasch, "The Anti-Imperialists, the Philippines, and the Inequality of Man," *Journal of Southern History*, vol. 24, no. 3 (August 1958), pp. 319–31.

92. Sumner, *The Conquest of the United States by Spain*, pp. 14, 19.
93. See Nichols, *Promise and Peril*, chap. 2, pp. 68–112.
94. William James, *Essays, Comments, and Reviews* (Cambridge: Harvard University Press, 1987), pp. 154–55.
95. Jane Addams, *Newer Ideals of Peace* (New York: Macmillan, 1907), pp. 18–19.
96. Allan Millett, Peter Maslowski, and William B. Feis, *For the Common Defense: A Military History of the United States from 1607 to 2012*, 3rd edition (New York: Free Press, 2012), p. 313.
97. Mark Twain, *The New York Herald*, October 15, 1900, reprinted in "Mark Twain Talks Books and Politics," *The Evening Bulletin*, October 27, 1900, p. 6, https://chroniclingamerica.loc.gov/lccn/sn82016413/1900-10-27/ed-1/seq-6/.
98. McKinley quoted in Coletta, "Bryan, McKinley, and the Treaty of Paris," p. 134.
99. Theodore Roosevelt, "Letter to Leonard Wood," April 17, 1901, in Elting Morison, ed., *The Letters of Theodore Roosevelt: Volume 3, The Square Deal, 1901–1903* (Cambridge: Harvard University Press, 1951), p. 60. See also Robert Beisner, "1898 and 1968: The Anti-Imperialists and the Doves," *Political Science Quarterly*, vol. 85, no. 2 (June 1970), pp. 187–216; Coletta, "Peace Negotiations."
100. See James Zimmerman, "Who Were the Anti-Imperialists and the Expansionists of 1898 and 1899? A Chicago Perspective," *Pacific Historical Review*, vol. 46, no. 4 (November 1977), p. 596.
101. William McKinley, "Address Accepting the Republican Presidential Nomination," July 12, 1900, *TAPP*, https://www.presidency.ucsb.edu/node/276593.
102. Nichols, *Promise and Peril*, p. 92.
103. Democratic National Committee, "Platform of the Kansas City Convention," in Democratic National Committee, *National Democratic Campaign Book: Presidential Election, 1900*, (Washington: Globe Printing Company, 1900), pp. 4–6.
104. William Jennings Bryan, "Bryan's Speech of Acceptance," in Democratic National Committee, *National Democratic Campaign Book*, pp. 18–19, 22.
105. Merriam, "Racism in the Expansionist Controversy of 1898–1900," p. 370. See also Tompkins, *Anti-Imperialism in the United States*, chap. 14, pp. 214–35.
106. Sources vary on the size of the U.S. force sent to China. The figure of 5,000 is from: Elihu Root, "Report of the Secretary of War," November 30, 1900, in *Annual Reports of the War Department for the Fiscal Year Ended June 30, 1900*, part 1 (Washington: GPO, 1900), pp. 12–15.
107. John Hay, "Mr. Hay to Mr. Conger," June 10, 1900, in *FRUS 1900*, p. 143; Dulles, *Prelude to World Power*, p. 216.
108. Theodore Roosevelt, "Second Annual Message," December 2, 1902, *TAPP*, https://www.presidency.ucsb.edu/node/206194.
109. Theodore Roosevelt, "Address at Mechanics' Pavilion in San Francisco, California," May 13, 1903, *TAPP*, https://www.presidency.ucsb.edu/node/298063.
110. Theodore Roosevelt, "Accepts the Nomination of the Republican Party to the Office of Vice-President," September 15, 1900, in Republican National Committee, *Republican National Committee* (New York: Republican National Committee, 1900), p. 6; see also Greg Russell, "Theodore Roosevelt's Diplomacy and the Quest for Great Power Equilibrium in Asia," *Presidential Studies Quarterly*, vol. 38, no. 3 (September 2008), pp. 433–55.
111. Lawrence Sondhaus, *Naval Warfare: 1815–1914* (New York: Routledge, 2001), pp. 197–208; Sprout and Sprout, *Rise of American Naval Power*, chap. 15, pp. 250–85; Tom Parker, "The Realistic Roosevelt," *National Interest*, no. 77 (Fall 2004), p. 146.
112. Theodore Roosevelt, "First Annual Message," December 3, 1901, *TAPP*, https://www.presidency.ucsb.edu/node/206187.
113. Cyrus Veeser, "Inventing Dollar Diplomacy: The Gilded-Age Origins of the Roosevelt Corollary to the Monroe Doctrine," *Diplomatic History*, vol. 27, no. 3 (June 2003), p. 301. See also Russell, "Theodore Roosevelt's Diplomacy"; Walter LaFeber, *The Cambridge History of American Foreign Relations, Volume II: The American Search for Opportunity, 1865–1913* (New York: Cambridge University Press, 1993), pp. 195–99; and Jeffrey Engel, "The Democratic Language of American Imperialism: Race, Order, and Theodore Roosevelt's

Personifications of Foreign Policy Evil," *Diplomacy & Statecraft*, vol. 19, no. 4 (December 2008), pp. 671–89.

114. Theodore Roosevelt, "Fourth Annual Message," December 6, 1904, *TAPP*, https://www. presidency.ucsb.edu/node/206208.

115. Simon Rofe and John Thompson, "'Internationalists in Isolationist Times'—Theodore and Franklin Roosevelt and a Rooseveltian Maxim," *Journal of Transatlantic Studies*, vol. 9, no. 1 (March 2011), p. 51; Stephen Wertheim, "Reluctant Liberator: Theodore Roosevelt's Philosophy of Self-Government and Preparation for Philippine Independence," *Presidential Studies Quarterly*, vol. 39, no. 3 (September 2009), pp. 494–518.

116. Veeser, "Inventing Dollar Diplomacy," p. 315; "Affairs in Santo Domingo," January 24, 1905, in 39 *Cong. Rec.*, 58th Cong., 3rd Sess., part 2, pp. 1283–88.

117. Augustus Bacon, "Affairs in Santo Domingo," January 24, 1905, in 39 *Cong. Rec.*, part 2, p. 1281.

118. The Senate did finally approve a revised treaty with the Dominican Republic in 1907. See Jacob Hollander, "The Convention of 1907 Between the United States and the Dominican Republic," *American Journal of International Law*, vol. 1, no. 2 (April 1907), pp. 287–96; W. Stull Holt, *Treaties Defeated by the Senate: A Study of the Struggle Between President and Senate over the Conduct of Foreign Relations* (Baltimore: Johns Hopkins Press, 1933), pp. 212–30; *FRUS 1905*, pp. 298–413.

119. Sprout and Sprout, *Rise of American Naval Power*, p. 264.

120. See, for example, Department of the Navy, "Report of the United States Asiatic Fleet, Flagship Kentucky," July 30, 1903, in *Annual Reports of the Navy Department for the Year 1903* (Washington: GPO, 1903), p. 602.

121. William Braisted, "The Philippine Naval Base Problem, 1898–1909," *Mississippi Valley Historical Review*, vol. 41, no. 1 (June 1954), pp. 21–40. Quote on p. 32.

122. Wertheim, "Reluctant Liberator," p. 496.

123. Theodore Roosevelt, "Letter to William Taft," Washington, August 21, 1907, in Elting Morison, ed., *The Letters of Theodore Roosevelt: Volume 5, The Big Stick, 1905–1909* (Cambridge: Harvard University Press, 1952), p. 762.

124. Paul D. Hutchcroft, "Colonial Masters, National Politicos, and Provincial Lords: Central Authority and Local Autonomy in the American Philippines, 1900–1913," *Journal of Asian Studies*, vol. 59, no. 2 (May 2000), pp. 277–306; William H. Taft and Jacob M. Dickinson, *Special Report on the Philippines to the President* (Washington: GPO, 1919).

125. Theodore Roosevelt, "Letter to Silas McBee," Washington, August 27, 1907, in Morison, ed., *The Big Stick*, pp. 774–75.

126. Wertheim, "Reluctant Liberator," p. 509.

127. See Russell, "Theodore Roosevelt's Diplomacy," and LaFeber, *The Cambridge History of American Foreign Relations*, pp. 201–209.

128. Michael J. Green, *By More Than Providence: Grand Strategy and American Power in the Asia Pacific Since 1783* (New York: Columbia University Press, 2017), p. 96. See also Gregory Russell, *The Statecraft of Theodore Roosevelt: The Duties of Nations and World Order* (Boston: Martinus Nijhoff Publishers, 2009).

129. Green, *By More Than Providence*, pp. 79, 87. Italics in original.

130. Theodore Roosevelt, "Message from the President of the United States, transmitting a protocol of an agreement between the United States and the Dominican Republic, providing for the collection and disbursement by the United States of the customs revenues of the Dominican Republic," February 15, 1905, in *FRUS 1905*, pp. 334–42.

131. Theodore Roosevelt, "Letter to Joseph Bucklin Bishop," Washington, February 3, 1904, in Elting Morison, ed., *The Letters of Theodore Roosevelt: Volume 4, The Square Deal, 1903–1905* (Cambridge: Harvard University Press, 1951), p. 762.

132. Wertheim, "Reluctant Liberator," p. 510.

133. William Taft quoted in "Taft's Position Novel," *Washington Weekly Post*, March 6, 1900, p. 1; see also Adam Burns, "Adapting to Empire: William H. Taft, Theodore Roosevelt, and the Philippines, 1900–08," *Comparative American Studies: An International Journal*, vol. 11, no. 4 (December 2013), pp. 418–33.

134. William Taft, "Fourth Annual Message," December 3, 1912, *TAPP*, https://www.presidency.ucsb.edu/node/207239.

135. Henry Pringle, *The Life and Times of William Howard Taft*, vol. 2 (New York: Farrar & Rinehart, 1939), p. 679.

136. Isidor Rayner, "General Arbitration Treaties," January 16, 1912, in 48 *Cong. Rec.*, 62nd Cong., 2nd Sess., part 1, p. 965; Gilbert Hitchcock, "Arbitration Treaty with Great Britain," January 4, 1916, in 48 *Cong. Rec.*, part 1, pp. 646–47.

137. William Howard Taft, "What I Am Trying to Do," *World's Work*, vol. 24 (June 1912), pp. 174–75; Taft, "Fourth Annual Message."

138. Robert Freeman Smith, "Cuba: Laboratory for Dollar Diplomacy, 1898–1917," *Historian*, vol. 28, no. 4 (August 1966), pp. 587–88.

139. See Nichols, *Promise and Peril*, chaps. 1–2. Quote on p. 110.

140. Emily Rosenberg, "The Invisible Protectorate: The United States, Liberia, and the Evolution of Neocolonialism, 1909–40," *Diplomatic History*, vol. 9, no. 3 (July 1985), p. 195.

141. "U.S. Government Morgan Catspaw?" *Chicago Daily Tribune*, May 25, 1911, p. 1.

142. "20,000 Troops and Two Naval Divisions to Mobilize Near Mexican Border," *New York Times*, March 8, 1911, pp. 1–2; "Unity in Washington on Hands-Off Policy," *New York Times*, May 10, 1911, p. 9; "No Intervention in Mexic [*sic*] Trouble," *Atlanta Constitution*, April 19, 1911, p. 1; Clarence Clendenen, *Blood on the Border: The United States Army and the Mexican Irregulars* (London: Macmillan, 1969), pp. 144–50. For congressional debates, see April 13 and 20 as well as May 9 and 11, 1911, in 47 *Cong. Rec.*, 62nd Cong., 1st Sess., parts 1 and 2, pp. 196–201, 447–52, 1131–135, 1180–182.

143. Sprout and Sprout, *Rise of American Naval Power*, chap. 16, pp. 286–303.

144. Andrew Dunar, *America in the Teens* (Syracuse: Syracuse University Press, 2016), p. 60.

145. Theodore Roosevelt, "Letter to William Taft," December 22, 1919, in Elting Morison, ed., *The Letters of Theodore Roosevelt: Volume 7, The Days of Armageddon, 1909–1914* (Cambridge: Harvard University Press, 1954), pp. 189–90.

146. Green, *By More Than Providence*, pp. 117–22; Raymond Esthus, "The Changing Concept of the Open Door, 1899–1910," *Mississippi Valley Historical Review*, vol. 46, no. 3 (December 1959), pp. 435–54.

147. Torreon and Plagakis, "Instances of Use of United States Armed Forces Abroad, 1798–2018," pp. 7–8; Walter V. Scholes and Marie V. Scholes, *The Foreign Policies of the Taft Administration* (Columbia: University of Missouri Press, 1970).

148. Philander Knox, "Letter to William Howard Taft," September 28, 1909, quoted in Richard Challener, *Admirals, Generals, and American Foreign Policy, 1898–1914* (Princeton: Princeton University Press, 1973), pp. 288–89; Benjamin Harrison, "The United States and the 1909 Nicaragua Revolution," *Caribbean Quarterly*, vol. 41, nos. 3/4 (September–December, 1995), pp. 45–63.

149. "Bureau of Latin American Affairs Memorandum," purportedly written by Philander Knox, October 6, 1909, quoted in Smith, "Cuba: Laboratory for Dollar Diplomacy," p. 587.

150. Lewis L. Gould, *The William Howard Taft Presidency* (Lawrence: University Press of Kansas, 2009), p. 79.

Chapter 9

1. Woodrow Wilson, "Preliminary Peace Conference, Protocol No. 3, Plenary Session of February 14, 1919," in *FRUS, The Paris Peace Conference, 1919*, vol. III, p. 215; see also Ross Kennedy, "Woodrow Wilson, World War I, and an American Conception of National Security," *Diplomatic History*, vol. 25, no. 1 (Winter 2001), pp. 1–31.

2. Arthur S. Link, *Wilson: Volume 2, The New Freedom* (Princeton: Princeton University Press, 1956), pp. 60–70.

3. Woodrow Wilson, "Democracy and Efficiency," *Atlantic*, vol. 87, no. 521 (March 1901), https://www.theatlantic.com/magazine/archive/1901/03/democracy-and-efficiency/520041/.

4. Wilson, "Democracy and Efficiency."

5. Wilson, "Democracy and Efficiency."

6. John Kane, *Between Virtue and Power: The Persistent Moral Dilemma of U.S. Foreign Policy* (New Haven: Yale University Press, 2008), chap. 9, pp. 144–64.

7. Wilson, "Democracy and Efficiency."

8. Wilson, "Address to a Joint Session of Congress Requesting a Declaration of War Against Germany."

9. Kane, *Between Virtue and Power*, p. 144.

10. Bryan was also upset about Wilson's heavy reliance on Edward House—who went by Colonel House even though he did not serve in the military—as his primary foreign policy adviser. When Bryan met with Wilson to tender his resignation, he complained that "Colonel House has been Secretary of State, not I, and I have never had your full confidence." Edward Mandell House, *Diary Entry*, June 24, 1915. From Yale University Library, *Edward Mandell House Papers*, Series II (1912–1926), Diaries, vol. 3, p. 174, http://digital.library.yale.edu/cdm/compoundobject/collection/1004_6/id/3896.

11. David Steigerwald, "The Reclamation of Woodrow Wilson?" *Diplomatic History*, vol. 23, no. 1 (Winter 1999), p. 84. See also Kane, *Between Virtue and Power*, p. 150.

12. Woodrow Wilson, "Address Before the Southern Commercial Congress in Mobile, Alabama," October 27, 1913, *TAPP*, https://www.presidency.ucsb.edu/node/206417.

13. See Mark Gilderhus, "Pan-American Initiatives: The Wilson Presidency and 'Regional Integration,' 1914–17," *Diplomatic History*, vol. 4, no. 4 (Fall 1980), pp. 409–423.

14. See Benjamin T. Harrison, "Woodrow Wilson and Nicaragua," *Caribbean Quarterly*, vol. 51, no. 1 (March 2005), pp. 25–36.

15. Borah quoted in Claudius O. Johnson, *Borah of Idaho* (New York: Longmans, Green, 1936), pp. 191–92; see also George W. Baker, Jr., "The Wilson Administration and Nicaragua, 1913–1921," *Americas*, vol. 22, no. 4 (April 1966), pp. 339–76.

16. Borah quoted in "Unite in Applause of Isthmian Canal," *New York Times*, July 22, 1913, p. 2; see also Link, *The New Freedom*, chap. 10, pp. 319–46.

17. Woodrow Wilson speech in Gloucester, N.J., August 15, 1912, quoted in "Wilson on Tariff," *Washington Post*, August 16, 1912, p. 1.

18. Wilson quoted in Burton Hendrick, *The Life and Letters of Walter H. Page*, vol. 1 (Garden City: Doubleday, Page, 1923), pp. 204–205; see also Robert Freeman Smith, "Latin America, The United States and the European Powers, 1830–1930," in Leslie Bethell, ed., *The Cambridge History of Latin America*, vol. 4 (New York: Cambridge University Press, 1986), pp. 105–11.

19. Arthur S. Link, *Wilson: Volume 3, The Struggle for Neutrality, 1914–1915* (Princeton: Princeton University Press, 1960), pp. 495, 497. See also Tony Smith, *Why Wilson Matters: The Origin of American Liberal Internationalism and Its Crisis Today* (Princeton: Princeton University Press, 2017), pp. 84–92.

20. Green, *By More Than Providence*, pp. 125, 130–31.

21. Pankaj Mishra, *From the Ruins of Empire: The Revolt Against the West and the Remaking of Asia* (New York: Farrar, Straus and Giroux, 2012), pp. 199–200, quote on p. 199; Erez Manela, *The Wilsonian Moment: Self-Determination and the International Origins of Anticolonial Nationalism* (New York: Oxford University Press, 2007), p. 222.

22. Woodrow Wilson, "Message on Neutrality," August 19, 1914, *TAPP*, https://www.presidency.ucsb.edu/node/206513.

23. Steigerwald, "The Reclamation of Woodrow Wilson," p. 82; Combs, *History of American Foreign Policy*, p. 204; Kendrick Clements, "Woodrow Wilson and World War I," *Presidential Studies Quarterly*, vol. 34, no. 1 (March 2004), pp. 62–82.

24. LaFeber, *The American Age*, p. 274; Sprout and Sprout, *Rise of American Naval Power*, pp. 333–34. Sprout and Sprout write that on June 21, the same day that Wilson sent his third *Lusitania* note to the German government, he also "directed his Secretaries of War and the Navy to have the experts in their respective departments draw up plans for strengthening the army and navy."

25. William Jennings Bryan, "From William Jennings Bryan," June 9, 1915, *The Papers of Woodrow Wilson Digital Edition* [hereafter *TPWWDE*], http://rotunda.upress.virginia.edu/founders/WILS-01-33-02-0361.

26. Justus Doenecke, *Nothing Less Than War: A New History of America's Entry into World War I* (Lexington: University Press of Kentucky, 2011), chap. 7, pp. 188–216; Sprout and Sprout, *Rise of American Naval Power*, chaps. 17 and 18, pp. 304–46.

27. Arthur S. Link, *Wilson: Volume 5, Campaigns for Progressivism and Peace, 1916–1917* (Princeton: Princeton University Press, 1965), pp. 48, 109. See also S. D. Lovell, *The Presidential Election of 1916* (Carbondale: Southern Illinois University Press, 1980).

28. Martin Glynn, "Address of Martin H. Glynn, as Temporary Chairman," June 14, 1916, in *Official Report of the Proceedings of the Democratic National Convention, Held at Saint Louis, Missouri, June 14, 15 and 16, 1916* (Chicago: [No listed publisher], 1916), pp. 19–20; Cooper, *The Vanity of Power*.

29. Woodrow Wilson, "Address at Sea Girt, New Jersey Accepting the Democratic Nomination for President," September 2, 1916, *TAPP*, https://www.presidency.ucsb.edu/node/206580.

30. Woodrow Wilson quoted in "Wilson Thrills Crowd; Bitterly Flays Opponents," *New York Times*, October 1, 1916, pp. 1–2.

31. Theodore Roosevelt quoted in "Roosevelt Blames Wilson for Raids," *New York Times*, October 11, 1916, p. 6, and "Roosevelt Bitterly Attacks Wilson," *New York Times*, November 4, 1916, p. 4; Doenecke, *Nothing Less Than War*, p. 212.

32. Wilson, "Address at Sea Girt."

33. Woodrow Wilson, "Address to a Joint Session of Congress on the Severance of Diplomatic Relations with Germany," February 3, 1917, *TAPP*, https://www.presidency.ucsb.edu/node/206606.

34. Wilson, "Address to a Joint Session of Congress Requesting a Declaration of War Against Germany."

35. Cooper, *The Vanity of Power*, p. 32.

36. Woodrow Wilson, "Second Annual Message," December 8, 1914, *TAPP*, https://www.presidency.ucsb.edu/node/207586.

37. Woodrow Wilson, "Third Annual Message," December 7, 1915, *TAPP*, https://www.presidency.ucsb.edu/node/207590.

38. Link, *The Struggle for Neutrality*, p. 105.

39. LaFeber, *The American Age*, pp. 272–73. On the evolution of policy, see Ernest R. May, *The World War and American Isolation, 1914–1917* (Cambridge: Harvard University Press, 1959), chap. 2, pp. 34–53; John M. Cooper, "The Command of Gold Reversed: American Loans to Britain, 1915–1917," *Pacific Historical Review*, vol. 45, no. 2 (May 1976), pp. 209–30; Richard van Alstyne, "Private American Loans to the Allies, 1914–1916," *Pacific Historical Review*, vol. 2, no. 2 (June 1933), pp. 180–93.

40. Woodrow Wilson, "An Address on Commodore John Barry," May 16, 1914, *TPWWDE*, http://rotunda.upress.virginia.edu/founders/WILS-01-30-02-0039.

41. Kennedy, "Woodrow Wilson, World War I, and an American Conception of National Security," pp. 7–8.

42. William Langer, "From Isolation to Mediation," in Arthur Dudden, ed., *Woodrow Wilson and the World of Today* (Philadelphia: University of Pennsylvania Press, 1957), p. 24.

43. Kennedy, "Woodrow Wilson, World War I, and an American Conception of National Security," p. 6.

44. Wilson, "Third Annual Message."

45. Woodrow Wilson, "The President's Suggestion of December 18, 1916, that the Belligerent Governments Communicate Their Terms of Peace," in *FRUS 1916, Supplement, The World War*, p. 98.

46. Woodrow Wilson, "A Luncheon Address to Women in Cincinnati," October 26, 1916, *TPWWDE*, http://rotunda.upress.virginia.edu/founders/WILS-01-38-02-0452.

47. Link, *Campaigns for Progressivism and Peace*, p. 411.

48. Wilson, "Message on Neutrality."

49. See Nichols, *Promise and Peril*, chap. 4, pp. 145–78; Cooper, *The Vanity of Power*, pp. 54–81.

50. Wilson quoted in Cooper, *The Vanity of Power*, p. 36.

51. Wilson, "Message on Neutrality."

52. Wilson, "An Address on Commodore John Barry."

53. Eugene Debs, "EVD to *New York Sun*," November 29, 1915, in J. Robert Constantine, ed., *Gentle Rebel: Letters of Eugene V. Debs* (Urbana: University of Illinois Press, 1995), p. 105.

54. American Union Against Militarism, "The Argument Against War," advertisement, *New Republic*, vol. 10, no. 126, March 31, 1917, p. 275; see also Doenecke, *Nothing Less Than War*, pp. 195–96.

55. Wilson, "Third Annual Message."

56. See Kennedy, "Woodrow Wilson, World War I, and an American Conception of National Security."

57. Josephus Daniels quotes Wilson in Ray Stannard Baker, ed., *Woodrow Wilson: Life and Letters, Volume 5, Neutrality, 1914–1915* (New York: Doubleday, Doran, 1935), p. 77. See also David M. Kennedy, *Over Here: The First World War and American Society* (New York: Oxford University Press, 1980), p. 11.

58. Debs, "EVD to *New York Sun*," in Constantine, ed., *Gentle Rebel*, p. 105; Nichols, *Promise and Peril*, pp. 200–201.

59. Isaac Sherwood, "National Defense," January 4, 1916, in 53 *Cong. Rec.*, 64th Cong., 1st Sess., part 1, p. 462.

60. "Bryan Now Springs a War Referendum," *New York Times*, October 18, 1915, p. 5; William Jennings Bryan, "Wasting Time: Let the Jingoes Die First," *Commoner*, vol. 15, no. 8 (August 1915), p. 5; Cooper, *The Vanity of Power*, p. 123.

61. Cooper, *The Vanity of Power*, pp. 87–98. Stephens quote on pp. 95–96.

62. "League to Enforce Peace Is Launched," *New York Times*, June 18, 1915, p. 4.

63. Woodrow Wilson, "Address delivered at the First Annual Assemblage of the League to Enforce Peace: 'American Principles,'" May 27, 1916, *TAPP*, https://www.presidency.ucsb.edu/node/206570.

64. Woodrow Wilson, "Semi-Centennial Address at Omaha, Nebraska," October 5, 1916, in Edith Phelps, ed., *Selected Articles on a League of Nations* (New York: H.W. Wilson, 1919), p. 6.

65. Woodrow Wilson, "Address to the Senate of the United States: 'A World League for Peace,'" January 22, 1917, *TAPP*, https://www.presidency.ucsb.edu/node/206603; see also Phelps, ed., *Selected Articles on a League of Nations*.

66. Woodrow Wilson, "A Commemorative Address," December 26, 1901, *TPWWDE*, http://rotunda.upress.virginia.edu/founders/WILS-01-12-02-0241.

67. Woodrow Wilson, "An Address in Omaha," October 5, 1916, *TPWWDE*, http://rotunda.upress.virginia.edu/founders/WILS-01-38-02-0329; Lloyd Ambrosius, "The Orthodoxy of Revisionism: Woodrow Wilson and the New Left," *Diplomatic History*, vol. 1, no. 3 (Summer 1977), pp. 199–214.

68. Wilson, "American Principles."

69. N. Gordon Levin, Jr., *Woodrow Wilson and World Politics: America's Response to War and Revolution* (New York: Oxford University Press, 1968), p. 3.

70. Woodrow Wilson, "A Memorial Day Address," May 30, 1916, *TPWWDE*, http://rotunda.upress.virginia.edu/founders/WILS-01-37-02-0134.

71. Wilson, "A World League for Peace."

72. William Jennings Bryan, "Labor's Interest in Peace," extract from speech delivered at Carnegie Hall, June 19, 1915, in *Commoner*, vol. 15, no. 7 (July 1915), p. 9.

73. William Jennings Bryan, "Making the Issue Clear," in *Commoner*, vol. 15, no. 7 (July 1915), p. 2.

74. Cooper, *Vanity of Power*, pp. 55–75.

75. Theodore Roosevelt quoted in "Colonel Attacks Wilson for Note and Alleged Leak," *New York Times*, January 4, 1917, pp. 1, 3.

76. Albert Cummins, "Foreign Policy," January 30, 1917, in 54 *Cong. Rec.*, 64th Cong., 2nd Sess., part 3, p. 2231.

77. Cooper, *Vanity of Power*, pp. 143–55.

78. Wilson, "Address to a Joint Session of Congress Requesting a Declaration of War Against Germany."

79. Link, *Campaigns for Progressivism and Peace*, pp. 411–14.

80. Wilson, "Address to a Joint Session of Congress Requesting a Declaration of War Against Germany."

81. See Kennedy, "Woodrow Wilson, World War I, and an American Conception of National Security," pp. 10–14.

82. See Ido Oren, "The Subjectivity of the 'Democratic' Peace: Changing U.S. Perceptions of Imperial Germany," *International Security*, vol. 20, no. 2 (Fall 1995), pp. 147–84.

83. Woodrow Wilson, "An Address at Mount Vernon," July 4, 1918, *TPWWDE*, http://rotunda. upress.virginia.edu/founders/WILS-01-48-02-0538.

84. Despite these restrictions, two U.S. divisions (the 27th and the 30th) did end up attached to and effectively integrated into British forces. See Mitchell A. Yockelson, *Borrowed Soldiers: Americans under British Command, 1918* (Norman: University of Oklahoma Press, 2008).

85. Kane, *Between Virtue and Power*, p. 162; Nichols, *Promise and Peril*, p. 157.

86. See Preston, *Sword of the Spirit, Shield of Faith*, pp. 233–90.

87. Together they coauthored an antipreparedness pamphlet, *Do You Advocate Peace or War: What the Preparedness Program Means*. See Michael Kazin, *War Against War: The American Fight for Peace, 1914–1918* (New York: Simon & Schuster, 2017), pp. 94–95.

88. Claude Kitchin, "German Intrigues to Involve the United States in War with Mexico and Japan," April 5, 1917, in 55 *Cong. Rec.*, 65th Cong., 1st Sess., part 1, p. 332.

89. James Vardaman, "War with Germany," April 4, 1917, in 55 *Cong. Rec.*, part 1, p. 209.

90. Henry Cooper and Frederick Britten, "War with Germany," April 5, 1917, in 55 *Cong. Rec.*, part 1, pp. 312, 318.

91. George Norris, "War with Germany," April 4, 1917, in 55 *Cong. Rec.*, part 1, pp. 212–14.

92. William Borah, "War with Germany," April 4, 1917, in 55 *Cong. Rec.*, part 1, p. 253.

93. Hannah Josephson, *Jeannette Rankin, First Lady of Congress: A Biography* (Indianapolis: Bobbs-Merrill, 1974), p. 77.

94. George Norris, "War with Germany," April 4, 1917, in 55 *Cong. Rec.*, part 1, p. 212; James Reed, "War with Germany," in 55 *Cong. Rec.*, part 1, April 4, 1917, p. 214.

95. Nichols, *Promise and Peril*, pp. 216–17. Quote on p. 157.

96. Randolph Bourne, "A War Diary," September 1917, in *Seven Arts*, vol. 2 (New York: Arno Press, 1917), p. 546.

97. Eugene Debs quoted in "Debs Greeted by Big Crowd," *Freedom's Banner* of Iola, Kansas, October 24, 1914, citing the *Cincinnati Commercial Tribune*.

98. Eugene Debs, "EVD to Daniel W. Hoan," August 17, 1916, in Constantine, ed., *Gentle Rebel*, p. 111.

99. Hugh Alexander quoted in Nichols, *Promise and Peril*, p. 208. Nichols cites a letter from Alexander to Claude Kitchin, dated April 6, 1917. George Brown Tindall, in *The Emergence of the New South, 1913–1945* (Baton Rouge: Louisiana State University Press, 1967), attributes the quote to an exchange between Alexander and Reuben Dean Bowen, dated April 9, 1917.

100. Nichols, *Promise and Peril*, pp. 213–14. See note 108, p. 400, for an extended discussion of the 330,000 figure. Borah quote on p. 243, citing a letter from Borah to Frank R. Gooding, dated April 16, 1917.

101. Kennedy, *Over Here*, p. 86.

102. Norman Graebner and Edward Bennett, *The Versailles Treaty and Its Legacy: The Failure of the Wilsonian Vision* (New York: Cambridge University Press, 2011), p. 13; Fensterwald, "The Anatomy of American 'Isolationism' and Expansionism," p. 121. See also Ambrosius, "The Orthodoxy of Revisionism."

103. Woodrow Wilson, "Address to a Joint Session of Congress on the Conditions of Peace ['The Fourteen Points']," January 8, 1918, *TAPP*, https://www.presidency.ucsb.edu/node/206651.

104. Kennedy, *Over Here*, pp. 262, 272, 287–92.

105. Randolph Bourne, "The Collapse of American Strategy," August 1917, in *Seven Arts*, vol. 2, p. 423.

106. Kane, *Between Virtue and Power*, p. 163.

107. Henry Cabot Lodge quoted in Kennedy, *Over Here*, pp. 244–45, referencing a letter from Lodge to James Bryce dated December 14, 1918.

108. Woodrow Wilson, "Mantoux's Notes of Two Meetings of the Council of Four," March 27, 1919, *TPWWDE*, http://rotunda.upress.virginia.edu/founders/WILS-01-56-02-0156.

109. "The Covenant of the League of Nations," *YLSAP*, http://avalon.law.yale.edu/20th_century/leagcov.asp.

110. Woodrow Wilson, "Address to the Senate on the Versailles Peace Treaty," July 10, 1919, *TAPP*, https://www.presidency.ucsb.edu/node/310230; "Woodrow Wilson Addresses the Senate," July 10, 1919, United States Senate, https://www.senate.gov/artandhistory/history/minute/Woodrow_Wilson_Addresses_the_Senate.htm.

111. "The Covenant of the League of Nations"; Wilson, "Address to the Senate on the Versailles Peace Treaty."

112. Woodrow Wilson, "Address at Luncheon, Hotel Portland, Portland Oreg.," September 15, 1919, and Wilson, "Address at Cheyenne Wyoming," September 24, 1919, in *Senate Documents*, 66th Cong., 1st Sess., vol. 11, *Addresses Delivered by President Wilson on His Western Tour* (Washington: GPO, 1919), pp. 206, 336. See also J. Michael Hogan, *Woodrow Wilson's Western Tour: Rhetoric, Public Opinion, and the League of Nations* (College Station: Texas A&M University Press, 2006).

113. See Ralph Stone, *The Irreconcilables: The Fight Against the League of Nations* (Lexington: University Press of Kentucky, 1970).

114. Nichols, *Promise and Peril*, p. 231.

115. William Borah, "Treaty of Peace with Germany," November 19, 1919, in 58 *Cong. Rec.*, 66th Cong., 1st Sess., part 9, pp. 8782, 8784.

116. William Borah, "The League of Nations," November 19, 1919, in Wendy Wolff, ed., *The Senate, 1789–1989: Classic Speeches, 1830–1993*, vol. 3, bicentennial edition (Washington: GPO, 1994), pp. 572–74.

117. Borah quoted in "The Rejection of the Treaty," *Literary Digest*, vol. 63, no. 9 (November 29, 1919), p. 11.

118. Hiram Johnson, "Letter to Jack Johnson," January 24, 1919, in Hiram Johnson Papers, *Online Archive of California*, https://oac.cdlib.org/ark:/28722/bk0016t6x6v/?brand=oac4.

119. James Reed, "League of Nations," February 22, 1919, in 57 *Cong. Rec.*, 65th Cong., 3rd Sess., part 4, pp. 4026–4033, quote on page 4026.

120. Lawrence Sherman, "The League of Nations," June 20, 1919, in 58 *Cong. Rec.*, part 2, p. 1437; see also Aaron Chandler, "Senator Lawrence Sherman's Role in the Defeat of the Treaty of Versailles," *Journal of the Illinois State Historical Society*, vol. 94, no. 3 (Autumn 2001), pp. 279–303.

121. Lawrence Sherman, "The League of Nations," March 3, 1919, in 57 *Cong. Rec.*, part 5, p. 4864.

122. Lawrence Sherman, "Treaty of Peace with Germany," October 16, 1919, in 58 *Cong. Rec.*, part 7, p. 7000.

123. Henry Cabot Lodge, "Letter to Theodore Roosevelt," March 1, 1915, image 109 of *Theodore Roosevelt Papers: Series 1: Letters and Related Material, 1759—1919*, https://www.loc.gov/resource/mss38299.mss38299-199_0001_0918/?sp=109. See also Garraty, *Henry Cabot Lodge*, p. 312. Newspaper quote in Thomas Bailey, *Woodrow Wilson and the Great Betrayal* (New York: Macmillan, 1945), p. 42.

124. "The Covenant of the League of Nations."

125. *Reservations to the Treaty of Peace with Germany* (Washington: GPO, 1919), Senate Doc. No. 143, 66th Cong., 1st Sess.

126. "The Covenant of the League of Nations."

127. Woodrow Wilson, "To Gilbert Monell Hitchcock," November 18, 1919, *TPWWDE*, http://rotunda.upress.virginia.edu/founders/WILS-01-64-02-0067.

128. Wilson quoted in Edith Bolling Wilson, *My Memoir* (Indianapolis: Bobbs-Merrill, 1939), p. 297.

129. Williams, "The Legend of Isolationism in the 1920's," p. 10.

130. Henry Cabot Lodge, "Constitution of the League of Nations," February 28, 1919, https://www.senate.gov/artandhistory/history/resources/pdf/LodgeLeagueofNations.pdf.

131. Andrieus Jones, "Treaty of Peace with Germany," September 15, 1919, in 58 *Cong. Rec.*, part 6, p. 5390.

132. George Creel, "From George Creel," November 8, 1918, *TPWWDE*, http://rotunda.upress.virginia.edu/founders/WILS-01-51-02-0651.

133. Oswald Villard, "The German Collapse," *Nation*, vol. 107, no. 2783, November 2, 1918; Weyl's diary quoted in Charles Forcey, *The Crossroads of Liberalism: Croly, Weyl, Lippmann, and the Progressive Era, 1900–1925* (New York: Oxford University Press, 1961), p. 288. For more on liberals and the League of Nations, see Wolfgang J. Helbich, "American Liberals in the League of Nations Controversy," *Public Opinion Quarterly*, vol. 31, no. 4 (Winter 1967–1968), pp. 568–96.

134. "Peace at Any Price," *New Republic*, vol. 19, no. 238, May 24, 1919, pp. 100–102, quotes on pp. 101, 102.

135. In the first November 1919 vote, only four Democrats voted in favor of the treaty with Lodge's reservations, while twenty-one did so in the March 1920 vote. The sizable Democratic defection from Wilson's camp in the March vote reflected growing interest among Democrats in salvaging the treaty by accepting Lodge's reservations as well as growing frustration even among Wilson's supporters with his unwillingness to compromise. See Cooper, *Breaking the Heart of the World*, chaps. 7 and 8, pp. 283–375.

136. Warren Harding, "Statement of Candidate Harding," July 22, 1920, *Advocate of Peace*, vol. 82, no. 8 (August 1920), pp. 281–83.

137. Warren Harding, "Inaugural Address," March 4, 1921, *TAPP*, https://www.presidency.ucsb.edu/node/206688.

138. Woodrow Wilson, "A Message to Teachers," June 28, 1918, *TPWWDE*, http://rotunda.upress.virginia.edu/founders/WILS-01-48-02-0473.

139. Adam Tooze, *The Deluge: The Great War, America and the Remaking of the Global Order, 1916–1931* (New York: Penguin, 2014), p. 27.

140. Hartz, *The Liberal Tradition in America*, p. 297.

Chapter 10

1. Harding, "Statement of Candidate Harding," July 22, 1920, pp. 281–83. Harding's twenty-six-percentage-point victory in the popular vote remains the greatest margin of victory in a contested American presidential election.

2. Warren Harding, "Inaugural Address."

3. John Lewis Gaddis, *We Now Know: Rethinking Cold War History* (New York: Oxford University Press, 1998), p. 7.

4. Nichols, *Promise and Peril*, pp. 276–77.

5. William Leuchtenburg, *The Perils of Prosperity, 1914–1932* (Chicago: University of Chicago Press, 1958), p. 104.

6. Warren Harding, "National Ideals and Policies," May 14, 1920, in *The Protectionist: Devoted to Political Economy* (Boston: Home Market Club, 1920/1921), vol. 32, May 1920 to April 1921, inclusive, pp. 74–75. See also Warren Harding "Back to Normal," May 14, 1920, University of Virginia Miller Center, https://millercenter.org/the-presidency/presidential-speeches/may-14-1920-readjustment.

7. Warren Harding, "A Speech by Senator Warren G. Harding to Delegation from Wayne County, Ohio," August 4, 1920, in Warren Harding, *Speeches of Senator Warren G. Harding of Ohio, Republican Candidate for President, From His Acceptance of the Nomination to October 1, 1920* (New York: Republican National Committee, 1920), pp. 44–46.

8. Warren Harding, "First Annual Message," December 6, 1921, *TAPP*, https://www.presidency.ucsb.edu/node/206691.

9. Braumoeller, "The Myth of American Isolationism."

10. Harding, "First Annual Message."

11. On the evolution of nativist sentiment from the nineteenth century into the 1920s, see John Higham, *Strangers in the Land: Patterns of American Nativism, 1860–1925* (New Brunswick: Rutgers University Press, 1983).

12. "Chap. 29.—An Act To regulate the immigration of aliens to, and the residence of aliens in, the United States," February 5, 1917, H.R. 10384; Public, No. 301, 64th Cong., 2nd Sess., https://www.loc.gov/law/help/statutes-at-large/64th-congress/session-2/c64s2ch29.pdf.; Office of the Historian, "The Immigration Act of 1924 (The Johnson-Reed Act)," in U.S. Foreign Policy Milestones: 1921–1936," U.S. Department of State, https://history.state.gov/milestones/1921-1936/immigration-act.

13. "The National-Origin Immigration Plan," *Editorial Research Reports 1929*, vol. 1 (Washington: CQ Press, 1929), http://library.cqpress.com/cqresearcher/cqresrre1929031200.

14. Immigration visas were restricted to two percent of the number of foreign-born people of that national origin in the United States as of the 1890 census.

15. Calvin Coolidge, "First Annual Message," December 6, 1923, *TAPP*, https://www.presidency.ucsb.edu/node/206712.

16. Higham, *Strangers in the Land*, pp. 270–71.

17. Steven Koven and Frank Götzke, *American Immigration Policy: Confronting the Nation's Challenges* (New York: Springer, 2010), p. 133.

18. Calvin Coolidge, "Address to the American Society of Newspaper Editors, Washington, D.C.," January 17, 1925, *TAPP*, https://www.presidency.ucsb.edu/node/269410.

19. Phillips Payson O'Brien, *British and American Naval Power: Politics and Policy, 1900–1936* (Westport: Praeger, 1998), pp. 180–82.

20. "Military Personnel on Active Duty: 1789 to 1970 (Series Y 904–16)," in U.S. Bureau of the Census, *Historical Statistics of the United States, Colonial Times to 1970*, part 2 (Washington: GPO, 1975), pp. 1141.

21. Herring, *From Colony to Superpower*, p. 442.

22. See Office of the Historian, "The Rogers Act," U.S. Department of State, https://history.state.gov/departmenthistory/short-history/rogers.

23. For an extensive view of global financial decision-making in the interwar period, see Liaquat Ahamed, *Lords of Finance: The Bankers Who Broke the World* (New York: Penguin, 2009).

24. "American Relief Activities in Soviet Russia," *FRUS 1921*, vol. 2, pp. 804–42; "American Assistance to the Japanese Following the Earthquake of September 1, 1923," in *FRUS 1923*, vol. 2, pp. 465–503.

25. Green, *By More Than Providence*, pp. 144–45.

26. Trubowitz, *Defining the National Interest*, p. 99; Green, *By More Than Providence*, p. 145. See also Herbert Feis, *The Diplomacy of the Dollar: First Era, 1919–1932* (Baltimore: Johns Hopkins Press, 1950); Joan Hoff Wilson, *American Business & Foreign Policy, 1920–1933* (Lexington: University Press of Kentucky, 1971); and Leffler, *Safeguarding Democratic Capitalism*, chap. 3.

27. Herring, *From Colony to Superpower*, p. 470.

28. Borah quoted in Johnson, *Borah of Idaho*, p. 343, citing a report from the *New York Call*, December 8, 1922.

29. Warren Harding, "A Speech by Warren G. Harding to Delegation of Indiana Citizens," August 28, 1920, in *Speeches of Senator Warren G. Harding of Ohio*, p. 91.

30. Charles Evan Hughes, "Observations on the Monroe Doctrine," August 30, 1923, in *Advocate of Peace through Justice*, vol. 85, no. 12 (December 1923), pp. 412–20, quote on p. 416.

31. "Republican Party Platform of 1928," June 12, 1928, *TAPP*, https://www.presidency.ucsb.edu/node/273379; "1928 Democratic Party Platform," June 26, 1928, *TAPP*, https://www.presidency.ucsb.edu/node/273212.

32. Herring, *From Colony to Superpower*, p. 470.

33. Torreon and Plagakis, "Instances of Use of United States Armed Forces Abroad, 1798–2018." See also Alan McPherson, ed., *Encyclopedia of U.S. Military Interventions in Latin America*, 2 volumes (Santa Barbara: ABC-CLIO, 2013).

34. See Alexander DeConde, *Herbert Hoover's Latin-American Policy* (Stanford: Stanford University Press, 1951); and Dana G. Munro, *The United States and the Caribbean Republics 1921–1933* (Princeton: Princeton University Press, 1974).

35. Herbert Hoover, *The Memoirs of Herbert Hoover: The Cabinet and the Presidency, 1920–1933* (New York: Macmillan, 1952), p. 333.

36. Alan McPherson, *A Short History of U.S. Intervention in Latin America and the Caribbean* (Malden: Wiley Blackwell, 2016), pp. 120–25.

37. Despite Roosevelt's preference for a less interventionist policy, the days of heavy-handed meddling were hardly over. Roosevelt's ambassador to Cuba, with the backing of U.S. warships, in 1933 orchestrated the overthrow of the Cuban government and installed a more pro-American leader.

38. Trubowitz, *Defining the National Interest*, p. 99; Nichols, *Promise and Peril*, pp. 276–77.

39. Wilson, "American Principles."

40. Herring, *From Colony to Superpower*, p. 450.

41. Nichols, *Promise and Peril*, p. 277.

42. Peter Grose, *Continuing the Inquiry: The Council on Foreign Relations from 1921 to 1996* (New York: Council on Foreign Relations, 2006), p. 9.

43. "Preliminary Arrangements for the Washington Conference on the Limitation of Armament," in *FRUS 1921*, vol. 1, pp. 18–87.

44. The Five Power Treaty established a tonnage limit of 525,000 (for the United States and Britain), 315,000 (for Japan), and 175,000 (for France and Italy) for capital ships, equivalent to a 15:9:5 ratio, with a lower limit (135,000 to 80,000 to 60,000 tons) for aircraft carriers. It did not limit submarines or other vessels, like cruisers, that were under a 10,000-ton limit. See "Conference on the Limitation of Armament, Washington, November 12, 1921–February 6, 1922," in *FRUS 1922*, vol. 1, pp. 1–377. See also "Limitation of Naval Armament (Five-Power or Washington Treaty)," 43 Stat. 1655; Treaty Series 671, Library of Congress, http://www.loc.gov/law/help/us-treaties/bevans/m-ust000002-0351.pdf. The Five Powers also agreed to a treaty banning the use of poison gas and the use of submarines for commerce raiding, but France's refusal to ratify the agreement prevented its entry into force.

45. Some influential military voices opposed the restrictions placed on the fortification of U.S. bases in the western Pacific, viewing this constraint as inconsistent with the long-term goals of expanding U.S. commerce and influence in the region. See Green, *By More Than Providence*, pp. 141–42.

46. Green, *By More Than Providence*, pp. 137, 143–44; Tooze, *The Deluge*, p. 397.

47. Warren Harding, "Message of President Harding to the Senate, February 10, 1922," in *FRUS, 1922*, vol. 1, pp. 298–306, quotes on pp. 303, 302. For the text of the Senate reservation, see "Insular Possessions and Dominions in the Pacific (Four-Power Treaty)," 43 Stat. 1646; Treaty Series 669, Library of Congress, https://www.loc.gov/law/help/us-treaties/bevans/m-ust000002-0332.pdf. See also Charles Evan Hughes, "The Secretary of State to the Ambassador in Great Britain (Harvey)," April 4, 1922, no. 454, in *FRUS, 1922*, vol. 1, p. 379; and Quincy Wright, "The Washington Conference," *American Political Science Review*, vol. 16, no. 2 (May 1922), pp. 285–97.

48. William Borah, "Four-Power Treaty," March 13, 1922, in 62 *Cong. Rec.*, 67th Cong., 2nd Sess., part 4, p. 3787.

49. William Borah, "The Four-Power Treaty," March 23, 1922, in 62 *Cong. Rec.*, part 5, p. 4331.

50. On the politics of ratification, see Thomas H. Buckley, "The Washington Naval Treaties" in Michael Krepon and Dan Caldwell, eds., *The Politics of Arms Control Ratification* (New York: Palgrave Macmillan, 1991), pp. 65–124.

51. "Kellogg-Briand Pact 1928," *YLSAP*, http://avalon.law.yale.edu/20th_century/kbpact.asp. For an account of the negotiation of the pact and an assessment of its impact, see Oona Hathaway and Scott Shapiro, *The Internationalists: How a Radical Plan to Outlaw War Remade the World* (New York: Simon & Schuster, 2017).

52. Carter Glass, "Multilateral Peace Treaty," January 15, 1929, in 70 *Cong. Rec.*, 70th Cong., 2nd Sess., part 2, p. 1728.

53. See Nichols, *Promise and Peril*, pp. 300–12.

54. "The Mental Age of the Senate," *New Republic*, vol. 57, no. 738, January 23, 1929, p. 257; "Should the Kellogg Treaty Be Rejected?" *New Republic*, vol. 56, no. 716, August 22, 1928, p. 8; John Dewey, "As an Example to Other Nations," *New Republic*, vol. 54, no. 692, March 7, 1928, p. 89.

55. William Borah, "One Great Treaty to Outlaw All Wars," *New York Times*, February 5, 1928, p. S127. Emphasis added.

56. "Hearings before the Senate Committee on Foreign Relations, United States Senate, 70th Congress, on The General Pact for the Renunciation of War signed at Paris, August 27, 1928," December 7, 1928, *YLSAP*, http://avalon.law.yale.edu/20th_century/kbhear.asp.

57. Hoover quoted in "Party Peace Record Lauded by Hoover in Reply to Critics," *New York Times*, September 8, 1928, p. 1.

58. Hiram Johnson, "Multilateral Peace Treaty," January 19, 1929 in 70 *Cong. Rec.*, part 2, p. 1728.

59. Hiram Johnson quoted in Nichols, *Promise and Peril*, p. 308, citing a letter dated January 19, 1929, in the Hiram Johnson papers.

60. James Reed, "Multilateral Peace Treaty," January 5, 1929, in 70 *Cong. Rec.*, part 2, p. 1186; Kenneth McKellar, "Multilateral Peace Treaty," January 9, 1929, in 70 *Cong. Rec.*, part 2, p. 1414.

61. Carter Glass, "Multilateral Peace Treaty," January 9, 1929, in 70 *Cong. Rec.*, part 2, p. 1728.

62. George Wickersham, "The Pact of Paris: A Gesture or a Pledge?" *Foreign Affairs*, vol. 7, no. 3 (April 1929), pp. 356–71.

63. Nichols, *Promise and Peril*, pp. 304, 307; Robert Ferrell, *Peace in Their Time: The Origins of the Kellogg-Briand Pact* (New Haven: Yale University Press, 1952), pp. 242–43.

64. Defenders of Kellogg-Briand point out that the pact did provide some of the legal basis for the prosecution of Nazi war crimes. See *Trial of the Major War Criminals Before the International Military Tribunal* (Nuremburg: International Military Tribunal, 1947), p. 218, https://www. loc.gov/rr/frd/Military_Law/pdf/NT_Vol-I.pdf.

Chapter 11

1. Jefferson, "Letter from Thomas Jefferson to Thomas Lomax."

2. Cutting off trade with belligerents was not unprecedented. As discussed in Chapter Four, President Thomas Jefferson in 1807 imposed an embargo on U.S. exports in response to British and French interference with U.S. shipping during the Napoleonic Wars. The goal, however, was not, as during the 1930s, to protect U.S. ships from attack. It was to impose economic pain on Britain and France, thereby encouraging them to cease their harassment of U.S. shipping. Jefferson was, in effect, attempting to use coercive diplomacy to defend the nation's neutral rights. Roosevelt was abandoning those rights to avoid potential confrontation with belligerents. Jefferson's trade embargo ultimately failed; it imposed high costs on the U.S. economy and was abandoned in 1809.

3. David Kennedy, for example, argues that Roosevelt's refusal in 1933 to agree to a multilateral pact to manage exchange rates helped convince Hitler that the United States would not join collective efforts to check German expansionism. See David Kennedy, *Freedom From Fear: The American People in Depression and War, 1929–1945* (New York: Oxford University Press, 1999), pp. 154–55. See also Justus D. Doenecke and John E. Wilz. *From Isolation to War, 1931–1941* (New York: John Wiley & Sons, 2015), p. 52.

4. Nicholas Crafts and Peter Fearon, "Lessons from the 1930s Great Depression," *Oxford Review of Economic Policy*, vol. 26, no. 3 (Autumn 2010), pp. 289, 294.

5. "Protectionism in the Interwar Period" in Office of the Historian, "U.S. Foreign Policy Milestones: 1921–1936," U.S. Department of State, https://history.state.gov/milestones/ 1921-1936/protectionism.

6. Franklin Roosevelt, "Inaugural Address," March 4, 1933, *TAPP*, https://www.presidency. ucsb.edu/node/208712.

7. Franklin Roosevelt, "President Roosevelt to the Acting Secretary of State," July 1, 1933, in *FRUS 1933*, vol. 1, *General*, p. 669; Rodney J. Morrison, "The London Monetary and Economic Conference of 1933: A Public Goods Analysis," *American Journal of Economics and Sociology*, vol. 52, no. 3 (July 1993), pp. 307–21.

8. Franklin Roosevelt, "Wireless to the London Conference," July 3, 1933, *TAPP*, https:// www.presidency.ucsb.edu/node/208290; Morrison, "The London Monetary and Economic Conference of 1933," p. 313; Doenecke and Wilz, *From Isolation to War*, p. 52.

9. See Doenecke and Wilz, *From Isolation to War*, pp. 54–55.

10. Green, *By More Than Providence*, p. 154.

11. M. Slade Kendrick, *A Century and a Half of Federal Expenditures* (New York: National Bureau of Economic Research, 1955), occasional paper 48, pp. 11–12, https://www.nber.org/ books/kend55-1.

12. See David Reynolds, *From Munich to Pearl Harbor: Roosevelt's America and the Origins of the Second World War* (Chicago: Ivan R. Dee, 2001), pp. 29–32; John E. Wilz, "The Nye Committee Revisited," *Historian*, vol. 23, no. 2 (February 1961), pp. 211–33.

13. See Francisco Balderrama and Raymond Rodríguez, *Decade of Betrayal: Mexican Repatriation in the 1930s* (Albuquerque: University of New Mexico Press, 1995); Kevin R. Johnson, "The Forgotten Repatriation of Persons of Mexican Ancestry and Lessons for the War on Terror," *Pace Law Review*, vol. 26, no. 1 (2005), pp. 1–26.

14. Doenecke and Wilz, *From Isolation to War*, p. 15.

15. Green, *By More Than Providence*, pp. 154–55. See also Richard Current, "The Stimson Doctrine and the Hoover Doctrine," *American Historical Review*, vol. 59, no. 3 (April 1954), pp. 513–42.

16. Hoover memo in Ray Wilbur and Arthur Hyde, *The Hoover Policies* (New York: Charles Scribner's Sons, 1937), p. 601; Doenecke and Wilz, *From Isolation to War*, p. 30. Stimson quote on p. 33.

17. Trubowitz, *Politics and Strategy*, p. 68; James MacGregor Burns, *Roosevelt: The Lion and the Fox* (New York: Harcourt, Brace, 1956), p. 263.

18. See Sarah Churchwell, *Behold, America: A History of America First and the American Dream* (London: Bloomsbury, 2018), pp. 253–54. See also Peter Schrag, *Not Fit for Our Society: Nativism and Immigration* (Berkeley: University of California Press, 2010), p. 150.

19. Roosevelt, "Inaugural Address."

20. See Charles G. Fenwick, "The Inter-American Conference for the Maintenance of Peace," *Proceedings of the American Society of International Law*, vol. 31 (Washington: American Society of International Law, 1937), pp. 34–44.

21. Franklin Roosevelt, "Address before the Inter-American Conference for the Maintenance of Peace, Buenos Aires, Argentina," December 1, 1936, TAPP, https://www.presidency.ucsb.edu/node/208508; Cole, *Roosevelt and the Isolationists*, pp. 358–60.

22. Peter Smith, *Talons of the Eagle: Latin America, the United States, and the World* (New York: Oxford University Press, 2008), p. 65.

23. See Alan McPherson, "Herbert Hoover, Occupation Withdrawal, and the Good Neighbor Policy," *Presidential Studies Quarterly*, vol. 44, no. 4 (December 2014), pp. 623–39.

24. Smith, *Talons of the Eagle*, pp. 70–71.

25. Excepted from the referendum requirement were an actual or imminent attack on the United States and an attack in the Western Hemisphere by a non-American state.

26. Louis Ludlow, [Note: There is no subheading for Ludlow's remarks], April 6, 1937, in 81 *Cong. Rec.*, 75th Cong. 1st Sess., part 3, p. 3198.

27. Ludlow quoted in Cole, *Roosevelt and the Isolationists*, p. 256, citing a letter sent to Roosevelt, September 11, 1937. See also Walter Griffin, "Louis Ludlow and the War Referendum Crusade, 1935–1941," *Indiana Magazine of History*, vol. 64, no. 4 (December 1968), pp. 267–88.

28. Hadley Cantril, ed., *Public Opinion, 1935–1946* (Princeton: Princeton University Press, 1951), p. 1025.

29. Hamilton Fish III, "Referendum on War," January 10, 1938, in 83 *Cong. Rec.*, 75th Cong., 3rd Sess., part 1, p. 278; Robert Crosser, "Referendum on War," January 10, 1938, in 83 *Cong. Rec.*, part 1, pp. 278–79.

30. Gerald Boileau, "Referendum on War," January 10, 1938, in 83 *Cong. Rec.*, part 1, p. 282.

31. Franklin Roosevelt, "Letter to the Speaker of the House on a Proposed Referendum to Declare War," January 6, 1938, TAPP, https://www.presidency.ucsb.edu/node/209568.

32. Vandenberg quoted in Willard Edwards, "Vandenberg Rips Roosevelt Ideas on Peace Policy," *Chicago Tribune*, December 23, 1937, p. 8.

33. Samuel Rayburn, "Referendum on War," January 10, 1938, in 83 *Cong. Rec.*, part 1, p. 281; Edith Rogers, "Referendum on War," January 10, 1938, in 83 *Cong. Rec.*, part 1, p. 281.

34. Cordell Hull, *The Memoirs of Cordell Hull*, vol. 1 (New York: Macmillan, 1948), p. 564.

35. On the relationship between neutrality and isolationism, see Brooke Blower, "From Isolationism to Neutrality: A New Framework for Understanding American Political Culture, 1919-1941," *Diplomatic History*, vol. 38, no. 2 (April 2014), pp. 345–76.

36. For discussion of these and other options, see Cole, *Roosevelt and the Isolationists*, esp. chaps. 12, 15, 22.

37. See Nichols, *Promise and Peril*, pp. 332–33; Jonas, *Isolationism in America*, pp. 50–58.

38. Prior neutrality legislation passed in 1934, but the bill was restricted to Bolivia and Paraguay during the Chaco War.

39. "'Neutrality Act' of August 31, 1935," in U.S. Department of State, *Peace and War: United States Foreign Policy, 1931–1941* (Washington: GPO, 1943), pp. 266–71.

40. Cordell Hull, "Memorandum by the Secretary of State," November 22, 1935, in *FRUS 1935*, vol. 1, *General, The Near East and Africa*, p. 828.

41. "'Neutrality Act' of February 29, 1936," in U.S. Department of State, *Peace and War*, pp. 313–14.

42. "'Neutrality Act' of May 1, 1937," in U.S. Department of State, *Peace and War*, pp. 355–65.

43. On pressure from the private sector to permit trade in non-embargoed goods, see Jonas, *Isolationism in America*, pp. 195–98. See also James Garner, "The United States Neutrality Act of 1937," *American Journal of International Law*, vol. 31, no. 3 (July 1937), pp. 385–97.

44. The Roosevelt administration decided not to apply the neutrality restrictions to transpacific trade. Japan began its full-scale invasion of China in 1937, but China and Japan were not legal belligerents since neither declared war. Although criticized by staunch isolationists in Congress for doing so (Representative George Tinkham (R-Massachusetts) and Representative Fish even proposed impeachment over the issue), Roosevelt decided not to invoke the neutrality restrictions in part to maintain the flexibility to provide assistance to China. He ended up sending munitions to China on British vessels. See Ronald Powaski, *Toward an Entangling Alliance: American Isolationism, Internationalism, and Europe, 1901–1950* (New York: Greenwood, 1991), p. 72; C. H. McLaughlin, "Legislative Neutrality in the United States," *Minnesota Law Review*, vol. 22, no. 5 (April 1938), pp. 647–48, https://scholarship.law.umn.edu/mlr/925.

45. Cole, *Roosevelt and the Isolationists*, p. 165.

46. Justus Doenecke, "The Roosevelt Foreign Policy: An Ambiguous Legacy," in Justus Doenecke and Mark Stoler, *Debating Franklin D. Roosevelt's Foreign Policies: 1933–1945* (Lanham: Rowman & Littlefield), p. 6.

47. "American Neutrality," *Living Age*, vol. 351, no. 4445 (February 1937), pp. 555–56; Jonas, *Isolationism in America*, p. 33.

48. Doenecke and Wilz, *From Isolation to War*, p. 15.

49. Doenecke and Wilz, *From Isolation to War*, p. 55.

50. Herring, *From Colony to Superpower*, p. 484.

51. Roosevelt quoted in Cole, *Roosevelt and the Isolationists*, p. 305, referencing "Conference with the Senate Military Affairs Committee," January 31, 1939.

52. See Reynolds, *From Munich to Pearl Harbor*, p. 48. See also Justus Doenecke, *Storm on the Horizon: The Challenge to American Intervention, 1939–1941* (Lanham: Rowman & Littlefield, 2000).

53. Cole, *Roosevelt and the Isolationists*, p. 238.

54. Franklin Roosevelt, "Annual Message to Congress," January 4, 1939, *TAPP*, https://www.presidency.ucsb.edu/node/209128.

55. Robert Divine, *The Illusion of Neutrality* (Chicago: University of Chicago Press, 1962), esp. chaps. 7–9; James Patterson, "Eating Humble Pie: A Note on Roosevelt, Congress, and Neutrality Revision in 1939," *Historian*, vol. 31, no. 3 (May 1969), pp. 407–14.

56. Robert Reynolds, "Neutrality and Peace of the United States," October 21, 1939, in 85 *Cong. Rec.*, 76th Cong., 2nd Sess., part 1, pp. 697–98.

57. Reynolds, *From Munich to Pearl Harbor*, p. 68.

58. "Negotiations for Transfer of American Destroyers to the British Navy and for Establishment of American Naval and Air Bases in British Possessions in the Western Hemisphere," in *FRUS 1940*, vol. 3, *The British Commonwealth, The Soviet Union, The Near East and Africa*, pp. 49–77.

59. William Casto, "Advising Presidents: Robert Jackson and the Destroyers-For-Bases Deal," *American Journal of Legal History*, vol. 52, no. 1 (January 2012), pp. 1–135.

60. J. Garry Clifford and Samuel R. Spencer, Jr, *The First Peacetime Draft* (Lawrence: University Press of Kansas, 1986).

61. Franklin Roosevelt, "Campaign Address at Boston, Massachusetts" October 30, 1940, *TAPP*, https://www.presidency.ucsb.edu/node/209314/.

62. Franklin Roosevelt, "Annual Message to Congress on the State of the Union," January 6, 1941, *TAPP*, https://www.presidency.ucsb.edu/node/209473.

63. "Transcript of Lend-Lease Act," March 11, 1941, https://www.ourdocuments.gov/doc. php? doc=71.

64. Roosevelt, "Annual Message," January 6, 1941.

65. Warren Kimball, *The Most Unsordid Act: Lend-Lease, 1939–1941* (Baltimore: Johns Hopkins Press, 1969), p. 234.

66. See "Promotion of National Defense," March 8, 1941, and March 11, 1941, in 87 *Cong. Rec.*, 77th Cong. 1st Sess., part 2, pp. 2097, 2178. The first House vote took place on February 9, 1941. The House voted again in March after Senate amendments, passing the revised legislation by a margin of 317–71.

67. Joseph E. Persico, *Roosevelt's Secret War: FDR and World War II Espionage* (New York: Random House, 2002).

68. See John Schuessler, "The Deception Dividend: FDR's Undeclared War," *International Security*, vol. 34, no. 4 (Spring 2010), pp. 133–65; Waldo Heinrichs, "President Franklin D. Roosevelt's Intervention in the Battle of the Atlantic, 1941," *Diplomatic History*, vol. 10, no. 4 (Fall 1986), pp. 311–32.

69. Franklin Roosevelt, "Fireside Chat," September 11, 1941, *TAPP*, https://www.presidency. ucsb.edu/node/210065.

70. Franklin Roosevelt, "Address for Navy and Total Defense Day," October 27, 1941, *TAPP*, https://www.presidency.ucsb.edu/node/210207.

71. Doenecke and Wilz, *From Isolation to War*, pp. 132–33, 165–67.

72. Green, *By More Than Providence*, pp. 178–79.

73. See Doenecke and Wilz, *From Isolation to War*, pp. 140–49; *FRUS 1940*, vol. 4, *The Far East*, pp. 688–705.

74. "Memorandum, General Board to the Secretary of the Navy," October 18, 1941, cited in Green, *By More Than Providence*, p. 181.

75. In support of the thesis that Roosevelt was deliberately taking actions that would bring the United States into the war, see Charles Beard, *American Foreign Policy in the Making, 1932–1940: A Study in Responsibilities* (New Haven: Yale University Press, 1946); Charles Beard, *President Roosevelt and the Coming of the War, 1941: A Study of Appearances and Reality* (New Haven: Yale University Press, 1948); Charles Tansill, *Back Door to War: The Roosevelt Foreign Policy, 1933–1941* (Chicago: Regnery, 1952); and Mark Trachtenberg, *The Craft of International History: A Guide to Method* (Princeton: Princeton University Press, 2006), chap 4. Books arguing that Roosevelt aimed to keep the United States out of the war include Robert Dallek, *Franklin D. Roosevelt and American Foreign Policy, 1932–1945* (New York: Oxford University Press, 1995); Waldo Heinrichs, *Threshold of War: Franklin D. Roosevelt and American Entry into World War II* (New York: Oxford University Press, 1988); Mark Stoler, *Allies and Adversaries: The Joint Chiefs of Staff, The Grand Alliance, and U.S. Strategy in World War II* (Chapel Hill: University of North Carolina Press, 2000); David Reynolds, *The Creation of the Anglo-American Alliance, 1937–1941: A Study in Competitive Co-operation* (Chapel Hill: University of North Carolina Press, 1982); and Warren Kimball, *Forged in War: Roosevelt, Churchill, and the Second World War* (New York: William Morrow, 1997). Reviews of this ongoing debate include: John Zimmerman, "Pearl Harbor Revisionism: Robert Stinnett's *Day of Deceit*," *Intelligence and National Security*, vol.17, no. 2 (Summer 2002), pp. 127–46; Justus Doenecke, "Beyond Polemics: An Historiographical Re-Appraisal of American Entry into World War II," *History Teacher*, vol. 12, no. 2 (February 1979), pp. 217–51; and Wayne Cole, "American Entry into World War II: A Historiographical Appraisal," *Mississippi Valley Historical Review*, vol. 43, no. 4 (March 1957), pp. 595–617.

76. Kimball, *Forged in War*, pp. 18, 113.

77. Franklin Roosevelt, "Fireside Chat," December 29, 1940, *TAPP*, https://www.presidency. ucsb.edu/node/209416.

78. Wayne Cole, "The America First Committee," *Journal of the Illinois State Historical Society*, vol. 44, no. 4 (Winter 1951), pp. 308–12. See also Wayne Cole, *America First: The Battle Against Intervention, 1940–1941* (Madison: University of Wisconsin Press, 1953).

79. Churchwell, *Behold, America*, p. 251.

80. Charles Lindbergh, "Des Moines Speech," September 11, 1941, http://www.charleslindbergh.com/americanfirst/speech.asp.

81. Churchwell, *Behold, America*, pp. 259–60.

82. See Schrag, *Not Fit for Our Society*, p. 143; Higham, *Strangers in the Land*, pp. 282–84.

83. Robert Wood quoted in "Wood Urges Protest on Aid to Britain Bill," *New York Times*, January 12, 1941, p. 7.

84. Charles Lindbergh, "Statement of Col. Charles Lindbergh, Lloyd Neck, N.Y.," in *To Promote the Defense of the United States, Hearings before the Committee on Foreign Relations*, United States Senate, 77th Cong., 1st Sess., part 1, January 27–February 3, 1941 (Washington: GPO, 1941), p. 490; Gerald Nye, "Promotion of National Defense," March 4, 1941, in 87 *Cong. Rec.*, part 2, p. 1735. See also Cole, *Roosevelt and the Isolationists*, pp. 414–20.

85. Burton Wheeler, "Address by Senator Burton K. Wheeler," in 87 *Cong. Rec.*, part 10, Appendix, p. A179. Senator Wheeler originally made the remarks on a radio broadcast on the American Forum of the Air, January 12, 1941.

86. "Gallup and Fortune Polls," *Public Opinion Quarterly*, vol. 6, no. 1 (Spring 1942), p. 164. The American Institute of Public Opinion (AIPO) reported a poll on October 4, 1941, in which seventy-nine percent of respondents said the "U.S. should not enter war now."

87. "Gallup and Fortune Polls," *Public Opinion Quarterly*, vol. 5, no. 2 (June 1941), p. 323, reporting an AIPO poll from February 9, 1941. According to Cole, "public opinion polls indicated a comfortable but not overwhelming majority of the American people supported lend-lease and that support grew in the course of the debate." See Cole, *Roosevelt and the Isolationists*, p. 414. See also Adam Berinsky, *In Time of War: Understanding American Public Opinion from World War II to Iraq* (Chicago: University of Chicago Press, 2009), pp. 48–51; Robert Eisinger and Jeremy Brown, "Polling as a Means Toward Presidential Autonomy: Emil Hurja, Hadley Cantril and the Roosevelt Administration," *International Journal of Public Opinion Research*, vol. 10, no. 3 (Fall 1998), pp. 244–45.

88. Nye quoted in Associated Press, "Part of Greer Story Hidden, Nye Charges," *Washington Post*, October 18, 1941, p. 4.

89. Flynn quoted in "Flynn Warns of 'Plot,'" *New York Times*, October 18, 1941, p. 3.

90. See Justus Doenecke, ed., *In Danger Undaunted: The Anti-Interventionist Movement of 1940–1941 as Revealed in the Papers of the America First Committee* (Stanford: Hoover Institution Press, 1990), p. 42, citing an America First Committee press release of November 2, 1941.

91. Arthur Schlesinger, *War and the American Presidency* (New York: Norton, 2004), p. 10.

92. Justus Doenecke, "American Isolationism, 1939–1941," *Journal of Libertarian Studies*, vol. 6, nos. 3–4 (Summer/Fall 1982), p. 212; Richard W. Steele, "Franklin D. Roosevelt and His Foreign Policy Critics," *Political Science Quarterly*, vol. 94, no. 1 (Spring 1979), pp. 15–32.

93. See David Green, *Shaping Political Consciousness: The Language of Politics in America from McKinley to Reagan* (Ithaca: Cornell University Press, 1987), pp. 134–63.

94. Lindbergh, "Des Moines Speech."

95. Franklin Roosevelt, "Address to Congress Requesting a Declaration of War with Japan," December 8, 1941, *TAPP*, https://www.presidency.ucsb.edu/node/210408.

96. "America First Will Dissolve; Urges War Aid," *Chicago Tribune*, December 12, 1941, p. 16.

97. "Isolation Groups Back Roosevelt," *New York Times*, December 9, 1941, p. 44.

98. Doenecke and Wilz, *From Isolation to War*, p. 168.

99. See Smuckler, "The Region of Isolationism," pp. 386–401.

100. Roosevelt, "Annual Message to Congress," January 4, 1939.

101. Jonas, *Isolationism in America*, p. 263.

102. Roosevelt, "Annual Message to Congress," January 4, 1939.

103. George Fielding Eliot, *The Ramparts We Watch: A Study of the Problems of American National Defense* (New York: Reynal & Hitchcock, 1938), p. 355.

104. Hanson Baldwin, "Impregnable America," *American Mercury*, vol. 47, no. 187 (July 1939), p. 267.

105. William Borah, "American Foreign Policy in a Nationalistic World," January 8, 1934, printed in *Foreign Affairs*, vol. 12, no. 2, special supplement (January 1934), p. xi.

106. Lindbergh, "Speech in Des Moines;" Doenecke, "American Isolationism." See also McDougall, *Promised Land, Crusader State*, p. 150.

107. Nye quoted in "What Does the European Situation Mean to Us?—A Debate," March 28, 1938, in A. Craig Baird, ed., *Representative American Speeches, 1937–1938* (New York: H. W. Wilson, 1938), p. 57.

108. Walter Millis, *Road to War: America 1914–1917* (New York: Houghton Mifflin, 1935), p. 21.

109. Walter Millis, "Walter Millis, Author of 'Road to War,' Defends Book Against Heated Criticism," *Harvard Crimson*, January 14, 1941, https://www.thecrimson.com/article/1941/1/14/walter-millis-author-of-road-to/.

110. "Positive Neutrality," *New Republic*, vol. 92, no. 1195, October 27, 1937, p. 327.

111. Herbert Hoover, "The Protection of Democracy," in Baird, ed., *Representative American Speeches*, p. 95.

112. Nye, "What Does the European Situation Mean to Us?" in Baird, ed., *Representative American Speeches*, p. 58; Lindbergh, "Speech in Des Moines."

113. Charles Lindbergh, "Col. Charles A. Lindbergh's Radio Address, September 15, 1939," *World Affairs*, vol. 102, no. 3 (September 1939), pp. 164–66.

114. Robert La Follette Jr., in a speech before the Chicago Committee to Keep America Out of War, April 24, 1938, quoted in "La Follette Warns of Arms Program," *New York Times*, April 25, 1938, p. 7.

115. Robert La Follette Jr., "Promotion of National Defense," February 24, 1941, in 87 *Cong. Rec.*, part 2, p. 1307.

116. Doenecke, "American Isolationism," p. 201; Jonas, *Isolationism in America*, pp. 63–72, 86–99; Trubowitz, *Politics and Strategy*, pp. 67–69; Doenecke, *In Danger Undaunted*, p. 31.

117. Robert Taft, "Let Us Stay Out of War," January 22, 1939, in *Vital Speeches of the Day*, vol. 5, no. 8 (February 1, 1939), p. 255.

118. Malcolm Muir, "Shadows of State Socialism," June 27, 1941, in *Vital Speeches of the Day*, vol. 7, no. 24 (October 1, 1941), p. 760.

119. Lindbergh, "Speech in Des Moines." See also Steven Usdin, *Bureau of Spies: The Secret Connections Between Espionage and Journalism in Washington* (New York: Prometheus, 2018).

120. Jonas, *Isolationism in America*, pp. 232–33. See also Edward Shapiro, "The Approach of War: Congressional Isolationism and Anti-Semitism, 1939–1941," *American Jewish History*, vol. 74, no. 1 (September 1984), pp. 45–65. Such suspicion of dual loyalties contributed to the incarceration of more than 100,000 Japanese Americans once the United States had entered the war.

121. Preston, *Sword of the Spirit, Shield of Faith*, pp. 297–98. Some Christian pacifists, such as the theologian Reinhold Niebuhr, broke with the movement to support U.S. involvement in the war, arguing, in Preston's words, that "it was sometimes necessary to use coercive means to achieve a just end." His views provoked considerable controversy within the religious community. See pp. 297–314; quote on p. 305.

122. Lydia Saad, "Gallup Vault, A Country Unified After Pearl Harbor," Gallup, December 5, 2016, https://news.gallup.com/vault/199049/gallup-vault-country-unified-pearl-harbor.aspx.

123. Roosevelt quoted in Robert Sherwood, *Roosevelt and Hopkins: An Intimate History* (New York: Grosset and Dunlap, 1948), p. 827.

Chapter 12

1. See "Table 2-5: Military Aircraft Production by Month, 1939–1945," in Rudolf Modley, ed., *Aviation Facts and Figures, 1945* (New York: McGraw-Hill, 1945), p. 8. Counting differences between civilian and military aircraft results in different totals in Richard Overy, *The Air War, 1939–1945* (New York: Stein and Day, 1980), pp. 21, 150; and Kennedy, *Rise and Fall of the Great Powers*, pp. 324, 345.

2. See James Blaker, *United States Overseas Basing: An Anatomy of the Dilemma* (New York: Praeger, 1990), p. 9. On the evolution of this network of overseas bases, see Immerwahr, *How to Hide an Empire*, pp. 336–71.

3. Secretary of War, *Annual Report of the Secretary of War, 1948* (Washington: GPO, 1949), p. 6.

4. See "Outlays of the Federal Government, by Major Function: 1940 to 1970 (Series Y 472–87)," and "Military Personnel on Active Duty: 1789 to 1970 (Series Y 904–916)," in *Historical Statistics of the United States, Colonial Times to 1970*, pp. 1115, 1141.

5. "Moscow Embassy Telegram #511: 'The Long Telegram,'" in Thomas Etzold and John Lewis Gaddis, eds., *Containment: Documents on American Policy and Strategy, 1945–1950* (New York: Columbia University Press, 1978), pp. 50–63.

6. "A Report to the National Security Council—NSC 68," April 12, 1950, *President's Secretary's File, Truman Papers*, p. 8, https://www.trumanlibrary.gov/library/research-files/report-national-security-council-nsc-68.

7. Harry Truman, "Statement by the President on the Situation in Korea," June 27, 1950, *TAPP*, https://www.presidency.ucsb.edu/documents/statement-the-president-the-situation-korea.

8. See Nordlinger, *Isolationism Reconfigured*, p. 245.

9. Connally quoted in William Conrad Gibbons, *The U.S. Government and the Vietnam War: Executive and Legislative Roles and Relationships: Part 1: 1945–1960* (Princeton: Princeton University Press, 1986), p. 75.

10. On Truman's increasingly tight grip on policy making and his handling of the Korean War, see Melvyn P. Leffler, *A Preponderance of Power: National Security, the Truman Administration, and the Cold War* (Stanford: Stanford University Press, 1992), chap. 9, pp. 361–97.

11. Melvyn Leffler, "American Grand Strategy from World War to Cold War, 1940–1950," in Paul Kennedy and William I. Hitchcock, eds., *From War to Peace: Altered Strategic Landscapes in the Twentieth Century* (New Haven: Yale University Press, 2000), p. 56. See John Lewis Gaddis, *The United States and the Origins of the Cold War, 1941–1947* (New York: Columbia University Press, 1972), pp. 18–23.

12. Monica Duffy Toft, "Why Is America Addicted to Military Interventions?" *National Interest*, December 10, 2017, https://nationalinterest.org/feature/why-america-addicted-foreign-interventions-23582.

13. Lindsay O'Rourke, "The U.S. tried to change other countries' governments 72 times during the Cold War," *Washington Post*, December 23, 2016, https://www.washingtonpost.com/news/monkey-cage/wp/2016/12/23/the-cia-says-russia-hacked-the-u-s-election-here-are-6-things-to-learn-from-cold-war-attempts-to-change-regimes/.

14. Preston, *Sword of the Spirit, Shield of Faith*, pp. 384–409.

15. See Charles Kupchan and Peter Trubowitz: "Dead Center: The Demise of Liberal Internationalism in the United States," *International Security*, vol. 32, no 2 (Fall 2007), pp. 16–20.

16. Arthur Schlesinger, *The Vital Center: The Politics of Freedom* (Boston: Houghton Mifflin, 1949).

17. Franklin Roosevelt, "Address to Congress Requesting a Declaration of War with Japan."

18. Forrest Davis, "What Really Happened at Tehran," *Saturday Evening Post*, May 20, 1944, p. 44.

19. Harry Truman, "Special Message to the Congress on Greece and Turkey: The Truman Doctrine," March 12, 1947, *TAPP*, https://www.presidency.ucsb.edu/node/232818.

20. "A Report to the National Security Council—NSC 68," pp. 4, 8, 9.

21. See, for example, McDougall, *The Tragedy of U.S. Foreign Policy*.

22. Vandenberg, *Private Papers of Senate Vandenberg*, pp. 112, 334, 473, 552.

23. See, for example, Peter Trubowitz and Nicole Mellow, "'Going Bipartisan': Politics by Other Means," *Political Science Quarterly*, vol. 120, no. 3 (Fall 2005), pp. 433–53; James McCormick and Eugene Wittkopf, "Bipartisanship, Partisanship, and Ideology in Congressional-Executive Foreign Policy Relations, 1947–1988," *Journal of Politics*, vol. 52, no. 4 (November 1990), pp. 1077–100; Joanne Gowa, "Politics at the Water's Edge: Parties, Voters, and the Use of Force Abroad," *International Organization*, vol. 52, no. 2 (Spring 1998), pp. 307–24.

24. Hillary Clinton, "Remarks by Senator Hillary Rodham Clinton," Council on Foreign Relations, December 15, 2003, https://www.cfr.org/event/remarks-senator-hillary-rodham-clinton.

25. See Kupchan and Trubowitz, "Dead Center," pp. 7–20.

26. Nordlinger, *Isolationism Reconfigured*, p. 15.

27. One the evolution of U.S. grand strategy during the early Cold War, see Leffler, *A Preponderance of Power*.

28. Truman quoted in Howard Jones, *"A New Kind of War": America's Global Strategy and the Truman Doctrine in Greece* (New York: Oxford University Press, 1989), p. 43. See also Gaddis, *The United States and the Origins of the Cold War*, pp. 341–46.

29. Robert Taft, "The North Atlantic Treaty," July 11, 1949, in 95 *Cong. Rec.*, 81st Cong., 1st Sess., part 7, pp. 9205–206.

30. Gilbert Macbeth, "Objections to Atlantic Treaty," *New York Times*, July 9, 1949, p. 12; Andre Visson, "Atlantic Pact Paradoxes," *Washington Post*, March 20, 1949, p. B4.

31. Ted Galen Carpenter, "United States' NATO Policy at the Crossroads: The 'Great Debate' of 1950–1951," *International History Review*, vol. 8, no. 3 (August 1986), p. 389.

32. Adlai Stevenson, "The Challenge of a New Isolationism," *New York Times Magazine*, November 6, 1949, p. 9.

33. Harry Truman, "The President's News Conference," January 11, 1951, *TAPP*, https://www.presidency.ucsb.edu/documents/the-presidents-news-conference-538.

34. Hoover quoted by Senator Wayne Morse in "Comments on the Address to the Nation by Herbert Hoover," December 21, 1950, in 96 *Cong. Rec.*, 81st Cong., 2nd Sess., part 12, p. 16913.

35. John Bricker, "Assignment of Ground Forces to Duty in the European Area," March 29, 1951, in 97 *Cong Rec.*, 82nd Cong., 1st Sess., part 3, p. 2972. See also Leffler, *A Preponderance of Power*, pp. 406–7.

36. "Hoover's Folly," *The Nation*, December 30, 1950, p. 688, quoted in Carpenter, "United States' NATO Policy at the Crossroads."

37. Arthur Schlesinger, Jr., "The New Isolationism," *Atlantic*, vol. 189, no. 5 (May 1952), https://www.theatlantic.com/past/docs/politics/foreign/asiso.htm.

38. See Duane Tananbaum, "The Bricker Amendment Controversy: Its Origins and Eisenhower's Role," *Diplomatic History*, vol. 9, no. 1 (Winter 1985), pp. 73–93; Philip Grant, "The Bricker Amendment Controversy," *Presidential Studies Quarterly*, vol. 15, no. 3 (Summer 1985), pp. 572–82; Arthur Dean, "The Bricker Amendment and Authority over Foreign Affairs," *Foreign Affairs*, vol. 32, no 1. (October 1953), pp. 1–19.

39. Paul Douglas, "A New Isolationism—Ripples or Tide?" *New York Times Magazine*, August 18, 1957, p. 56.

40. William Henry Chamberlin, "A New Nationalism," *National Review*, vol. 2, no. 14 (August 25, 1956), pp. 15–16.

41. On the evolution of the John Birch Society and its impact on the American right, see Joyce Mao, *Asia First: China and the Making of Modern American Conservatism* (Chicago: University of Chicago Press, 2015); D.J. Mulloy, *The World of the John Birch Society: Conspiracy, Conservatism, and the Cold War* (Nashville: Vanderbilt University Press, 2014); Lisa McGirr, *Suburban Warriors: The Origins of the New American Right* (Princeton: Princeton University Press, 2001).

42. Donald Critchlow, *The Conservative Ascendancy: How the GOP Right Made Political History* (Cambridge: Harvard University Press, 2007), pp. 65–66; Seymour Martin Lipset and Earl Raab, *The Politics of Unreason: Right-Wing Extremism in America, 1790–1970* (New York: Harper & Row, 1970), pp. 265–69.

43. Murray Rothbard, "For a New Isolationism," April 1959, https://www.lewrockwell.com/1970/01/murray-n-rothbard/for-a-new-isolationism/.

44. Murray Rothbard, *The Betrayal of the American Right* (Auburn: Ludwig von Mises Institute, 2007), pp. 127, 139, https://cdn.mises.org/The%20Betrayal%20of%20the%20American%20Right_2.pdf.

45. Jerome Himmelstein, *To the Right: The Transformation of American Conservatism* (Berkeley: University of California Press, 1990), pp. 31–45; George Nash, *The Conservative Intellectual Movement in America Since 1945*, 30th anniversary edition (Wilmington: Intercollegiate Studies Institute, 2006), p. 186.

46. Arthur Schlesinger, "Back to the Womb? Isolationism's Renewed Threat," *Foreign Affairs*, vol. 74, no. 4 (July/August 1995), p. 5.

47. See, for example, James A. Johnson, "The New Generation of Isolationists," *Foreign Affairs*, vol. 49, no. 1 (October 1970), pp. 136–46.

48. Mansfield quoted in Phil Williams, "Isolationism or Discerning Internationalism: Robert Taft, Mike Mansfield and US Troops in Europe," *Review of International Studies*, vol. 8, no. 1 (January 1982), p. 37.

49. Earl Ravenal, "The Case for Strategic Disengagement," *Foreign Affairs*, vol. 51, no. 3 (April 1973), pp. 505–21.

50. Robert Tucker, "What This Country Needs Is a Touch of New Isolationism," *New York Times*, June 21, 1972, p. 43. See also Tucker, *A New Isolationism*.

51. Ronald Steel, "A Spheres of Influence Policy," *Foreign Policy*, no. 5 (Winter 1971–1972), pp. 107–18.

52. Arlen Large, "A Cheer for Prudent Isolationism," *Wall Street Journal*, April 30, 1971, p. 6.

53. Survey conducted by the Gallup Poll and Potomac Associates, as reported in William Mayer, *The Changing American Mind: How and Why American Public Opinion Changed between 1960 and 1988* (Ann Arbor: University of Michigan Press, 1992), p. 65.

54. Kupchan and Trubowitz, "Dead Center," pp. 22–24.

55. "Gallup Poll Finds Little Evidence of a Trend Toward Isolationism," *New York Times*, May 11, 1975, p. 16.

56. Michael Roskin, "What 'New Isolationism'?" *Foreign Policy*, no. 6 (Spring 1972), p. 119.

57. J. William Fulbright, "Reflections: In Thrall to Fear," *New Yorker*, vol. 47, no. 47, January 8, 1972, p. 58.

58. Joseph Kraft, "The Isolationist Myth," *Washington Post*, March 14, 1971, p. D7.

59. Stephen Rosenfeld, "Word on a Word: Isolationism," *Washington Post*, June 23, 1972, p. A18.

60. See Richard Nixon, "Address to the Nation on the War in Vietnam," November 3, 1969, *TAPP*, https://www.presidency.ucsb.edu/node/240027.

61. Melvin Laird, "Statement of Hon. Melvin R. Laird, Secretary of Defense," in *Hearings Before the Committee on Foreign Relations*, United States Senate, 91st Cong., 1st Sess., November 18 and 19, 1969 (Washington: GPO, 1969), p. 63.

62. On the evolution of U.S. strategy toward the Persian Gulf and Nixon's Twin Pillars policy, see Charles Kupchan, *The Persian Gulf and the West: The Dilemmas of Security* (London: Allen & Unwin, 1987), chap. 2, pp. 10–43.

63. Kupchan and Trubowitz, "Dead Center," pp. 23–24.

64. Stephen Sestanovich, *Maximalist: America in the World From Truman to Obama* (New York: Knopf, 2014). Frank Klingberg similarly argues that the United States has oscillated between periods of "introversion" and "extroversion" throughout its history. See Frank Klingberg, "The Historical Alternation of Moods in American Foreign Policy," *World Politics*, vol. 4, no. 2 (January 1952), pp. 239–73.

Chapter 13

1. See Kupchan and Trubowitz, "Dead Center," pp. 22–23; and Charles Kupchan and Peter Trubowitz, "Grand Strategy for a Divided America," *Foreign Affairs*, vol. 86, no. 4 (July/August 2007), pp. 71–83.

2. Derek Chollet, *The Long Game: How Obama Defied Washington and Redefined America's Role in the World* (New York: Public Affairs, 2016), p. 42. On the evolution of post–Cold War U.S. statecraft, see also Hal Brands, *Making the Unipolar Moment: U.S. Foreign Policy and the Rise of the Post–Cold War Order* (Ithaca: Cornell University Press, 2016).

3. Andrew Bacevich, *The Age of Illusions: How America Squandered Its Cold War Victory* (New York: Metropolitan Books, 2020), p. 202. See also Leffler, *Safeguarding Democratic Capitalism*, chap. 8, pp. 243–80.

4. Toft, "Why Is America Addicted to Foreign Interventions?"

5. Fukuyama, *The End of History and the Last Man*.

6. See Nordlinger, *Isolationism Reconfigured*, pp. 18–20.

7. George Mitchell, "The Persian Gulf," January 10, 1991, in 137 *Cong. Rec.*, 102nd Cong., 1st Sess., part 1, p. 409. See also Adam Clymer, "Congress Acts to Authorize Use of Force in Persian Gulf," *New York Times*, January 13, 1991, pp. 1, 11.

8. Tom Daschle, "The Water's Edge," *Foreign Policy*, no. 103 (Summer 1996), pp. 4–5.

9. Anthony Lake, *From Containment to Enlargement* (Washington: Executive Office of the President, 1993), p. 5, reprinting September 21, 1993, speech delivered at Johns Hopkins School of Advanced International Studies; Madeleine Albright, "Interview on NBC-TV 'The Today Show' with Matt Lauer," February 19, 1998, U.S. Department of State: Archive, https://1997-2001.state.gov/statements/1998/980219a.html.

10. William Clinton, "Remarks to Future Leaders of Europe in Brussels," January 9, 1994, *TAPP*, https://www.presidency.ucsb.edu/node/218369.

11. William Clinton, "Remarks on Signing the North American Free Trade Agreement Implementation Act," December 8, 1993, *TAPP*, https://www.presidency.ucsb.edu/node/219946.

12. Clinton quoted in George Stephanopoulos, *All Too Human: A Political Education* (New York: Little Brown, 1999), p. 214.

13. On the evolution of U.S. policy toward NATO enlargement, see Mary Elise Sarotte, "How to Enlarge NATO: The Debate inside the Clinton Administration, 1993–95," *International Security*, vol. 44, no. 1 (Summer 2019), pp. 7–41.

14. Madeleine Albright, "Prepared statement before the Senate Armed Services Committee, Subject: NATO Enlargement," April 23, 1997, U.S. Department of State: Archive, https://1997-2001.state.gov/statements/970423.html.

15. Torreon and Plagakis, "Instances of Use of United States Armed Forces Abroad, 1798–2018," pp. 14–18.

16. Michael Mandelbaum, "Foreign Policy as Social Work," *Foreign Affairs*, vol. 75, no. 1 (January/February 1996), pp. 18; Condoleezza Rice, "Promoting the National Interest," *Foreign Affairs*, vol. 79, no. 1 (January/February 2000), p. 53.

17. John Bolton, "Should We Take Global Governance Seriously?" *Chicago Journal of International Law*, vol. 1, no. 2 (Fall 2000), p. 206.

18. See, for example, Michael Parks, "Foreign News: What's Next," *Columbia Journalism Review*, vol. 40, no. 5 (January/February 2002), pp. 52–57.

19. See James Lindsay, "The New Apathy: How an Uninterested Public Is Reshaping Foreign Policy," *Foreign Affairs*, vol. 79, no. 5 (September/October 2000), pp. 2–8.

20. Patrick J. Buchanan, *A Republic, Not an Empire: Reclaiming America's Destiny* (Washington: Regnery, 1999)

21. Buchanan on the McLaughlin Group, June 15, 1990, in "Pat Buchanan: In His Own Words," Anti-Defamation League, https://www.adl.org/resources/profiles/pat-buchanan-in-his-own-words.

22. "A Special Issue on Racial Terrorism," *Ron Paul Political Report*, vol. 6, no. 6 (June 15, 1992), p. 6, https://web.archive.org/web/20080216011808/http:/www.tnr.com/downloads/sponraceterrorism.pdf.

23. Bush quoted in "Bush Criticizes Isolationism," *New York Times*, November 24, 1994, p. A29.

24. Schlesinger, "Back to the Womb."

25. George W. Bush, "A Distinctly American Internationalism," November 19, 1999, https://www.mtholyoke.edu/acad/intrel/bush/wspeech.htm.

26. "Isolationism's Return," *New York Times*, October 31, 1999, p. WK14.

27. Clinton quoted in Marc Lacey, "Clinton Gives a Foreign Policy Send-Off," *New York Times*, December 9, 2000, p. 8. For a comprehensive overview of the Clinton administration's foreign policy, see Derek Chollet and James Goldgeier, *America Between the Wars: From 11/9 to 9/11* (New York: Public Affairs, 2008).

28. George W. Bush, "A Period of Consequences," September 23, 1999, http://www3.citadel.edu/pao/addresses/pres_bush.html; George W. Bush, "Second Presidential Debate," October 11, 2000, https://www.debates.org/voter-education/debate-transcripts/october-11-2000-debate-transcript/.

29. Richard Cheney, "Vice President Speaks at VFW 103rd National Convention," August 26, 2002, https://georgewbush-whitehouse.archives.gov/news/releases/2002/08/20020826.html; George W. Bush, "Remarks at the American Enterprise Institute Dinner," February 26, 2003; *TAPP*, https://www.presidency.ucsb.edu/node/211998; George W. Bush, "Address to the Nation on Iraq," March 19, 2003, *TAPP*, https://www.presidency.ucsb.edu/node/213155; George W. Bush, "Remarks Accepting the Presidential Nomination at the Republican

National Convention in New York City," September 2, 2004, *TAPP*, https://www.presidency. ucsb.edu/node/215510.

30. "The National Security Strategy of the United States of America," September 2002, p. 1, https://2009-2017.state.gov/documents/organization/63562.pdf.

31. George W. Bush, "Remarks to the Prague Atlantic Student Summit in Prague," November 20, 2002, *TAPP*, https://www.presidency.ucsb.edu/node/213464.

32. Bolton quoted in Matt Haag, "3 Examples of John Bolton's Longtime Hard-Line Views," *New York Times*, March 22, 2018, https://www.nytimes.com/2018/03/22/us/politics/ john-bolton-national-security-adv.html.

33. Hugo Young, "We've Lost That Allied Feeling," *Washington Post*, April 1, 2001, p. B1; *Berliner Zeitung* quoted in Steven Erlanger, "Protest, and Friends Too, Await Bush in Europe," *New York Times*, May 22, 2002, p. A10.

34. "Global Public Opinion in the Bush Years (2001–2008)," Pew Research Center, December 18, 2008, https://www.pewresearch.org/global/2008/12/18/global-public-opinion-in-the-bush-years-2001-2008/.

35. Kupchan and Trubowitz, "Dead Center," pp. 26–27.

36. George W. Bush, "Remarks in Marlton, New Jersey," October 18, 2004, *TAPP*, https://www. presidency.ucsb.edu/node/212861.

37. George W. Bush, "Remarks at a Georgia Victory 2006 Rally in Statesboro, Georgia," October 30, 2006, *TAPP*, https://www.presidency.ucsb.edu/node/271011.

38. Barack Obama, "Transcript: 'This is your victory,' says Obama," *CNN*, November 4, 2008, http://edition.cnn.com/2008/POLITICS/11/04/obama.transcript/.

39. Barack Obama, "Commencement Address at the United States Military Academy in West Point, New York," May 28, 2014, *TAPP*, https://www.presidency.ucsb.edu/node/305525; Barack Obama, "Address to the Nation on the Drawdown of United States Military Personnel in Afghanistan," June 22, 2011, *TAPP*, https://www.presidency.ucsb.edu/node/290660.

40. Obama, "Commencement Address at the United States Military Academy in West Point."

41. See Sarah Kreps, Elizabeth Saunders, and Kenneth Shultz, "The Ratification Premium: Hawks, Doves, and Arms Control," *World Politics*, vol. 70, no. 4 (October 2018), pp. 479–514.

42. Ben Rhodes, *The World As It Is: A Memoir of the Obama White House* (New York: Random House, 2018), p. 231.

43. See Richard Wike, "Seven charts on the how the world views President Obama," Pew Research Center, June 25, 2015, https://www.pewresearch.org/fact-tank/2015/06/24/7-charts-on-how-the-world-views-president-obama/.

44. Kathleen McInnis, "Coalition Contributions to Countering the Islamic State," Congressional Research Service, R44135, August 24, 2016, p. 1, https://fas.org/sgp/crs/natsec/R44135. pdf.

45. Obama, "Commencement Address at the United States Military Academy in West Point."

46. Obama, "Commencement Address at the United States Military Academy in West Point."

47. Rhodes, *The World As It Is*, p. 275.

48. Barack Obama, "Commencement Address at the United States Air Force Academy in Colorado Springs, Colorado," May 23, 2012, *TAPP*, https://www.presidency.ucsb.edu/ node/301082; Obama, "Commencement Address at the United States Military Academy in West Point."

49. Obama, "Address to the Nation on the Drawdown of United States Military Personnel in Afghanistan."

50. Obama, "Commencement Address at the United States Military Academy in West Point."

51. Obama, "Address to the Nation on the Drawdown of United States Military Personnel in Afghanistan."

52. Barack Obama, "Remarks at National Defense University," May 23, 2013, *TAPP*, https:// www.presidency.ucsb.edu/node/304467.

53. See Samantha Power, *The Education of an Idealist: A Memoir* (New York: Dey Street, 2019), pp. 359–71.

54. Carla Humud et al., "Armed Conflict in Syria: Overview and U.S. Response," Congressional Research Service, RL33487, February 12, 2020, pp. 1, 26, 28, https://fas.org/sgp/crs/mid-east/RL33487.pdf.

55. Barack Obama, "The President's News Conference With Chancellor Angela Merkel of Germany," February 9, 2015, *TAPP*, https://www.presidency.ucsb.edu/node/309454. During the Obama administration the State Department did approve direct commercial sales of light weaponry to Ukraine. See Peter J. Marzalik and Aric Toler, "Lethal Weapons to Ukraine: A Primer," Atlantic Council, January 26, 2018, https://www.atlanticcouncil.org/blogs/ukrainealert/lethal-weapons-to-ukraine-a-primer.

56. Obama, "Commencement Address at the United States Military Academy in West Point."

57. Barack Obama, "Introduction to the National Security Strategy of the United States of America," May 2010, https://nssarchive.us/wp-content/uploads/2020/04/2010.pdf.

58. Chuck Hagel, "Remarks by Secretary Hagel at the Woodrow Wilson International Center Forum on NATO Expansion and European Security," May 2, 2014, U.S. Department of Defense, https://archive.defense.gov/Transcripts/Transcript.aspx?TranscriptID=5423.

59. Obama, "Introduction to the National Security Strategy of the United States of America."

60. Rhodes, *The World As It Is*, p. 120.

61. Ryan Lizza, "The Consequentialist: How the Arab Spring remade Obama's foreign policy," *New Yorker*, vol. 87, no. 11, May 2, 2011, p. 55. For more on the controversy tied to the phrase, see Jason Ukman, "Obama and the ghost of 'leading from behind,'" *Washington Post*, July 11, 2011, https://www.washingtonpost.com/blogs/checkpoint-washington/post/obama-and-the-ghost-of-leading-from-behind/2011/07/10/gIQAgsdf8H_blog.html.

62. Humud et al., "Armed Conflict in Syria," pp. 1, 25, 26, 28.

63. Barack Obama, "Address Before a Joint Session of the Congress on the State of the Union," January 28, 2014, *TAPP*, https://www.presidency.ucsb.edu/node/305034.

64. Sources differ as to the number of troops in these locations at the end of the Obama presidency. See Christi Parsons and W. J. Hennigan, "A military at war for all eight years; Obama had wanted to sow peace, but conflicts became a constant," *Los Angeles Times*, January 13, 2017, pp. A1, A13; "Letter from the President—Supplemental 6-month War Powers Letter," December 5, 2016, https://obamawhitehouse.archives.gov/the-press-office/2016/12/05/letter-president-supplemental-6-month-war-powers-letter; "Counts of Active Duty and Reserve Service Members and APF Civilians," Defense Manpower Data Center, December 31, 2016, https://www.dmdc.osd.mil/appj/dwp/dwp_reports.jsp.

65. Office of the Press Secretary, "Statement by the President on the FY2017 European Reassurance Initiative Budget Request," White House, February 2, 2016, https://obamawhitehouse.archives.gov/the-press-office/2016/02/02/statement-president-fy2017-european-reassurance-initiative-budget; Paul Belkin and Hibbah Kaileh, "The European Deterrence Initiative: A Budgetary Overview," Congressional Research Service, IF10946, June 16, 2020, https://fas.org/sgp/crs/natsec/IF10946.pdf.

66. Obama, "Commencement Address at the United States Military Academy in West Point."

67. Obama, "Commencement Address at the United States Military Academy in West Point."

68. Donald Trump, "Inaugural Address," January 20, 2017, *TAPP*, https://www.presidency.ucsb.edu/node/320188.

69. See Bacevich, *The Age of Illusions*, p. 198.

70. Trump, "Address Before a Joint Session of the Congress on the State of the Union"; Trump quoted in Greg Sargent, "Donald Trump's revealing quote about 'American exceptionalism,'" *Washington Post*, June 7, 2016, https://www.washingtonpost.com/blogs/plum-line/wp/2016/06/07/donald-trumps-revealing-quote-about-american-exceptionalism/.

71. Charles Kupchan, "Trump's Nineteenth-Century Grand Strategy: The Themes of His UN General Assembly Speech Have Deep Roots in U.S. History," *Foreign Affairs*, September 26, 2018, https://www.foreignaffairs.com/articles/2018-09-26/trumps-nineteenth-century-grand-strategy. See also, Hal Brands, *American Grand Strategy in the Age of Trump* (Washington: Brookings, 2018).

72. See Mead, *Special Providence*.

73. Donald Trump, "Remarks on Foreign Policy," April 27, 2016, *TAPP*, https://www.presidency.ucsb.edu/node/317913.

74. Julie Hirschfeld Davis, "U.S. Pushes Allies to Lift Spending for the Military," *New York Times*, July 12, 2018, pp. A1, A8.

75. Eileen Sullivan, "President Questions NATO's Mission of Mutual Defense," *New York Times*, July 19, 2018, p. A8; Julian E. Barnes and Helene Cooper, "As Russia Works to Weaken NATO, Trump Talks of a U.S. Withdrawal," *New York Times*, January 15, 2019, p. A8.

76. Jennifer Jacobs, "Trump Muses Privately About Ending Postwar Japan Defense Pact," *Bloomberg*, June 24, 2019, https://www.bloomberg.com/news/articles/2019-06-25/trump-muses-privately-about-ending-postwar-japan-defense-pact.

77. Courtney Kube and Carol Lee, "Trump wants to pull all U.S. troops out of Afghanistan by 2020 election, officials say," *NBC News*, August 2, 2019, https://www.nbcnews.com/news/military/trump-wants-pull-all-troops-out-afghanistan-2020-election-n1038651.

78. Trump quoted in Lauren Egan, "Trump Dismisses Turkey's invasion of Syria: 'It's not our border,'" *NBC News*, October 16, 2019, https://www.nbcnews.com/politics/donald-trump/trump-says-turkey-s-incursion-syria-not-our-problem-calls-n1067391.

79. Trump, "Remarks on Foreign Policy."

80. Donald Trump, "Remarks to the United Nations General Assembly in New York City," September 25, 2018, *TAPP*, https://www.presidency.ucsb.edu/node/332698; Donald Trump, "Remarks to the United Nations General Assembly in New York City," September 19, 2017, *TAPP*, https://www.presidency.ucsb.edu/node/331184.

81. Quincy Adams, "State—First Term," March 9, 1821.

82. Trump, "Remarks on Foreign Policy"; Trump, "Inaugural Address"; Trump, "Remarks to the United Nations General Assembly in New York City," September 25, 2018.

83. Trump, "Inaugural Address"; Trump, "Remarks to the United Nations General Assembly in New York City," September 25, 2018.

84. Editorial Board, "New NAFTA Is Better Than No NAFTA," *New York Times*, December 13, 2019, p. A30.

85. Julie Hirschfeld Davis et al., "In Vulgar Terms, Trump Disparages Some Immigrants," *New York Times*, January 12, 2018, pp. A1, A15.

86. Total national defense budgetary authority increased from $634 billion in fiscal year 2017 to $740 billion in fiscal year 2021. See Greg Jaffe and Damian Paletta, "Trump administration to seek major increase in defense spending for 2019," *Washington Post*, January 27, 2018, p. A8; Joe Gould, "Divided Senate passes 2-year budget deal with military boost," *Defense News*, August 1, 2019, https://www.defensenews.com/congress/2019/08/01/divided-senate-passes-2-year-budget-deal-with-military-boost/.

87. Donald Trump (@realDonaldTrump), "Had a long and very good conversation with President Putin of Russia. As I have always said, long before the Witch Hunt started, getting along with Russia, China, and everyone is a good thing, not a bad thing," *Twitter*, May 3, 2019, 1:06 p.m., https://twitter.com/realdonaldtrump/status/1124359594418032640; "National Security Strategy of the United States of America," December 2017, p. 25, https://www.whitehouse.gov/wp-content/uploads/2017/12/NSS-Final-12-18-2017-0905-2.pdf.

88. Egan, "Trump Dismisses Turkey's invasion of Syria: 'It's not our border'"; Eric Schmitt and Helene Cooper, "Both Coming and Going, U.S. Troops in Syria May Total Nearly the Same," *New York Times*, October 31, 2019, p. A11.

89. Alex Ward, "Trump Vows to bring about 'the official end of Iran' if it threatens the US again," May 20, 2019, *Vox*, https://www.vox.com/2019/5/20/18632247/trump-iran-end-threat-twitter-north-korea; Trump, "Remarks to the United Nations General Assembly in New York City," September 19, 2017; John Bacon, "President Trump to Kim Jong Un: 'We fell in love' over 'beautiful letters,'" *USA Today*, September 30, 2018, https://www.usatoday.com/story/news/politics/2018/09/30/trump-north-koreas-kim-love-beautiful-letters/1478834002/.

90. Samuel Osborne, "Angela Merkel says Germany can no longer rely on Donald Trump's America: 'We Europeans must take our destiny into our own hands,'" *Independent*, May 28, 2017, https://www.independent.co.uk/news/world/europe/angela-merkel-donald-trump-germany-us-no-longer-rely-european-union-climate-change-g7-a7760486.html.

91. See, for example, Lully Miura, "How Trump forced Japan to take security into its own hands," *South China Morning Post*, January 13, 2019, https://www.scmp.com/week-asia/geopolitics/article/2181764/how-trump-forced-japan-take-security-its-own-hands.

92. Dina Smeltz et al., "America Engaged: American Public Opinion and US Foreign Policy," Chicago Council on Global Affairs, 2018 survey, p. 2, https://www.thechicagocouncil.org/sites/default/files/report_ccs18_america-engaged_181002.pdf.

93. Smeltz et al.,"America Engaged," p. 6.

94. Dina Smeltz et al., "Rejecting Retreat: Americans Support US Engagement in Global Affairs," Chicago Council on Global Affairs, 2019 survey, p. 2, https://www.thechicagocouncil.org/sites/default/files/report_ccs19_rejecting-retreat_20190909.pdf.

95. One of the most striking trends in the 2019 report is a marked increase in support for international trade since the Trump administration took office. The 2016 Chicago Council survey found that fifty-nine percent of respondents believed trade is good for the U.S. economy, consistent with figures in previous years. By the 2017 survey, support for trade had jumped to seventy-two percent, and in the 2019 survey, support reached eighty-seven percent.

96. Smeltz et al., "Rejecting Retreat," p. 13.

97. John Halpin et al., "America Adrift: How the U.S. Foreign Policy Debate Misses What Voters Really Want," Center for American Progress, May 2019, https://cdn.americanprogress.org/content/uploads/2019/05/08120943/ForeignPolicyPoll-report.pdf.

98. Halpin et al., "America Adrift," p. 4.

99. Michael Dimock et al., "Public Sees U.S. Power Declining as Support for Global Engagement Slips," Pew Research Center, December 3, 2013, pp. 4, 107, https://www.pewresearch.org/wp-content/uploads/sites/4/2013/12/12-3-13-APW-VI-release1.pdf; Carroll Doherty et al., "Public Uncertain, Divided Over America's Place in the World," Pew Research Center, May 5, 2016, pp. 11, 97, https://www.pewresearch.org/wp-content/uploads/sites/4/2016/05/05-05-2016-Foreign-policy-APW-release.pdf.

100. Halpin et al., "America Adrift," p. 11.

101. Gallup, "U.S. Adults' Knowledge About the World," survey commissioned by National Geographic and the Council on Foreign Relations, December 2019, p. 33, https://cdn.cfr.org/sites/default/files/report_pdf/NatGeo_CFR_US%20Knoweldge.pdf?ga=2.246905600.507854710.1577376140-403618011.1575644522. Only two percent of respondents want the United States to end its role in the world, confirming the CAP report's finding that few Americans embrace strict isolationism.

102. Halpin et al., "America Adrift," p. 33.

103. Carroll Doherty et al., "The Partisan Divide on Political Values Grows Even Wider," Pew Research Center, October 5, 2017, p. 25, https://www.people-press.org/wp-content/uploads/sites/4/2017/10/10-05-2017-Political-landscape-release-updt..pdf.

104. Halpin et al., "America Adrift," p. 36.

105. Gallup, "U.S. Adults' Knowledge About the World," p. 35.

106. Halpin et al., "America Adrift," pp. 5, 36.

107. Halpin et al., "America Adrift," pp. 47–48.

108. Halpin et al., "America Adrift," p. 6. A 2016 Council on Foreign Relations/National Geographic survey of young Americans between the ages of eighteen and twenty-six showed limited knowledge of global affairs. The study "revealed significant gaps between what young people understand about today's world and what they need to know to successfully navigate and compete in it." See "Global Literacy Survey," https://www.cfr.org/global-literacy-survey.

109. Smeltz et al., "America Engaged," p. 4; Halpin et al., "America Adrift," p. 36.

110. Doherty et al., "The Partisan Divide on Political Values Grows Even Wider," p. 24.

111. Smeltz et al., "America Engaged," pp. 5, 13.

112. Smeltz et al., "America Engaged," p. 21; Doherty et al., "The Partisan Divide on Political Values Grows Even Wider," p. 23.

Chapter 14

1. Lippmann, U.S. Foreign Policy: Shield of the Republic, pp. 3–4.

2. Washington, "Washington's Farewell Address."

3. Paine, Common Sense, p. 44.

4. Hamilton, Federalist No. 11.

5. Monroe, "Monroe Doctrine."

6. Estimates vary as to when China's aggregate GDP will surpass that of the United States, and the coronavirus outbreak and associated economic disruption added additional uncertainty. HSBC estimates that China will have the world's largest economy by 2030. See Janet Henry and James Pomeroy, "The world in 2030," HSBC, September 25, 2018, https://insights. hsbc.co.uk/content/dam/hsbc/gb/wealth/pdf/the-word-in-2030.pdf. China has already surpassed the United States in terms of purchasing power parity. See John Hawskworth et al., "The Long View: How will the global economic order change by 2050?" PwC, February 2017, https://www.pwc.com/gx/en/world-2050/assets/pwc-the-world-in-2050-full-report-feb-2017.pdf. See also Hugh White, *The China Choice: Why America Should Share Power* (Collingwood: Black, 2013), pp. 31–81.

7. Nese DeBruyne, "American War and Military Operations Casualties: Lists and Statistics," Congressional Research Service, September 14, 2019, RL32492, pp. 10–18, https://fas.org/sgp/crs/natsec/RL32492.pdf; Neta Crawford, "United States Budgetary Costs of the Post-9/11 Wars Through FY2019: $5.9 Trillion Spent and Obligated," Brown University Watson Institute for International and Public Affairs, Costs of War, November 14, 2018, https://watson.brown.edu/costsofwar/files/cow/imce/papers/2018/Crawford_Costs%20of%20War%20Estimates%20Through%20FY2019%20.pdf.

8. Obama, "Commencement Address at the United States Military Academy in West Point"; Trump, "Remarks on Foreign Policy"; Trump, "Inaugural Address."

9. "Authorization for Use of Military Force," 115 Stat. 224, September 18, 2001, https://www.congress.gov/107/plaws/publ40/PLAW-107publ40.pdf; "Authorization for Use of Military Force against Iraq Resolution of 2002," 116 Stat. 1498, October 16, 2002, https://www.congress.gov/107/plaws/publ243/PLAW-107publ243.pdf.

10. Kim Lane Scheppele, "The Migration of Anti-Constitutional Ideas: The Post-9/11 Globalization of Public Law and the International State of Emergency," in Sujit Choudhry, ed., *The Migration of Constitutional Ideas* (New York: Cambridge University Press, 2006), pp. 347–373.

11. In 2015, upon expiration of the 2001 PATRIOT Act, Congress passed the USA FREEDOM Act, which reauthorized many elements of the PATRIOT Act, but placed restrictions on some of its more controversial provisions, including the FBI's ability to collect "business records" without a warrant. In 2018, the Supreme Court ruled that cell-site location data is protected under the Fourth Amendment, barring government access to phone location metadata without a warrant. An appeals court ruled in late 2019 that the FBI practice of searching through the National Security Agency's raw data from internet and phone calls for information relating to U.S. citizens, if done without a warrant, could violate the Fourth Amendment. See "USA PATRIOT Act of 2001," 114 Stat. 272, October 26, 2001, https://www.congress.gov/107/plaws/publ56/PLAW-107publ56. pdf; "USA FREEDOM Act of 2015," 129 Stat. 268, June 2, 2015, https://www.congress.gov/114/plaws/publ23/PLAW-114publ23.pdf; "Carpenter v. United States," 138 S. Ct. 2206, June 22, 2018, https://www.supremecourt.gov/opinions/17pdf/16-402_h315.pdf; "United States of America v. Agron Hasbajrami," No. 15-2684 (2d Cir. 2019), December 18, 2019, https://cases.justia.com/federal/appellate-courts/ca2/15-2684/15-2684-2019-12-18.pdf?ts=1576692009.

12. See Bruce Ackerman and Oona Hathaway, "Limited War and the Constitution: Iraq and the Crisis of Presidential Legality," *Michigan Law Review*, vol. 109, no. 4 (February 2011), pp. 447–518; Schlesinger, *The Imperial Presidency*; Nordlinger, *Isolationism Reconfigured*, chap. 10, pp. 240–62.

13. Elizabeth Warren, "It's Time to Reduce Corporate Influence at the Pentagon," *Medium*, May 16, 2019, https://medium.com/@teamwarren/its-time-to-reduce-corporate-influence-at-the-pentagon-98f52ee0fcf1; Bernie Sanders, "Deficit hawks show their hypocrisy on the Pentagon," *Washington Post*, December 17, 2019, p. A19.

14. Sanders, "Deficit hawks show their hypocrisy on the Pentagon."

15. Elizabeth Warren, "We Can End Our Endless Wars," *Atlantic*, January 27, 2020, https://www.theatlantic.com/ideas/archive/2020/01/elizabeth-warren-we-can-end-our-endless-wars/605497/.

16. Tulsi Gabbard (@TulsiGabbard), "Stupid regime change wars suck badly needed funds from our domestic needs such as healthcare, infrastructure, protecting the environment, and more. This will end when I'm president," *Twitter*, June 2, 2019, 6:00 a.m., https://twitter.com/ TulsiGabbard/status/1135123892563922944.

17. Kupchan, "Trump's Nineteenth-Century Grand Strategy."

18. See, for example, Posen, *Restraint*; Bacevich, *The Age of Illusions*; Richard Haass, *Foreign Policy Begins at Home: The Case for Putting America's House in Order* (New York: Basic Books, 2013); Stephen Walt, *The Hell of Good Intentions: America's Foreign Policy Elite and the Decline of U.S. Primacy* (New York: Farrar, Straus and Giroux, 2018); John Mearsheimer, *The Great Delusion: Liberal Dreams and International Realities* (New Haven: Yale University Press, 2018); Colin Dueck, *The Obama Doctrine: American Grand Strategy Today* (New York: Oxford University Press, 2015); Michael Mandelbaum, *Mission Failure: America and the World in the Post–Cold War Era* (New York: Oxford University Press, 2016); Ian Bremmer, *Superpower: Three Choices for America's Role in the World* (New York: Penguin, 2015); Christopher Preble, *Peace, War, and Liberty: Understanding U.S. Foreign Policy* (Washington: Cato Institute, 2019); A. Trevor Thrall and Benjamin Friedman, eds., *US Grand Strategy in the 21st Century: The Case for Restraint* (New York: Routledge, 2018); Tudor Onea, *US Foreign Policy in the Post–Cold War Era: Restraint Versus Assertiveness from George H. W. Bush to Barack Obama* (New York: Palgrave Macmillan, 2013). For scholarship challenging the case for retrenchment, see Ivo Daalder and James Lindsay, *The Empty Throne: America's Abdication of Global Leadership* (New York: PublicAffairs, 2018); Stephen Brooks and William Wohlforth, *America Abroad: Why the Sole Superpower Should Not Pull Back from the World* (New York: Oxford University Press, 2016). For an overview of recent publications on U.S. national security strategy, see Heather Hurlburt, "More Diplomacy, Less Intervention, but for What? Making Sense of the Grand Strategy Debate," *Lawfare*, June 7, 2019, https://www.lawfareblog.com/ more-diplomacy-less-intervention-what-making-sense-grand-strategy-debate.

19. See John Mearsheimer and Stephen Walt, "The Case for Offshore Balancing: A Superior U.S. Grand Strategy," *Foreign Affairs*, vol. 95, no. 4 (July/August 2016), pp. 70–83; Barry Posen, "Pull Back: The Case for a Less Activist Foreign Policy," *Foreign Affairs*, vol. 92, no. 1 (January/February 2013), pp. 116–28; Stephen Wertheim, "The Price of Primacy: Why America Shouldn't Dominate the World," *Foreign Affairs*, vol. 99, no. 2 (March/April 2020), pp. 19–29; Graham Allison, "The New Spheres of Influence: Sharing the Globe With Other Great Powers," *Foreign Affairs*, vol. 99, no. 2 (March/April 2020), pp. 30–40.

20. Mearsheimer and Walt, "The Case for Offshore Balancing"; Posen, "Pull Back," p. 123; Wertheim, "The Price of Primacy," pp. 27–28.

21. See https://www.quincyinst.org. See also Daniel Drezner, "Charles Koch and George Soros teamed up on a new foreign-policy think tank. I have questions," *Washington Post*, July 11, 2019, https://www.washingtonpost.com/outlook/2019/07/11/some-questions-about-quincy-institute/.

22. David Sanger, Eric Schmitt, and Thomas Gibbons-Neff, "U.S. Lawmakers Balk Over Secret Benchmarks Within Taliban Peace Accord," *New York Times*, March 9, 2020, p. A6.

23. Walt, *The Hell of Good Intentions*.

24. James Carafano, "What those decrying America's 'endless wars' are really talking about," *Fox News*, July 2, 2019, https://www.foxnews.com/opinion/james-carafano-what-those-decrying-americas-endless-wars-are-really-talking-about.

25. Bill Kristol (@BillKristol), "75 years of a US-led liberal international order, based on a US forward presence and backed by US might, with regional and bilateral alliances and relatively free trade, has enabled remarkable peace and prosperity. But let's go back to the 1920's and 30's!" *Twitter*, July 1, 2019, 5:16 a.m., https://twitter.com/BillKristol/status/ 1145622150096797697.

26. The analysis in this section draws on Kupchan and Trubowitz, "Grand Strategy for a Divided America"; Charles Kupchan, "The Clash of Exceptionalisms: A New Fight Over an Old Idea," *Foreign Affairs*, vol. 97, no. 2 (March/April 2018), pp. 139-148; and Charles Kupchan and Adam Mount, "The Autonomy Rule," *Democracy: A Journal of Ideas*, no. 12 (Spring 2009), pp. 8–21.

27. For further discussion, see Charles Kupchan, "After Pax Americana: Benign Power, Regional Integration, and the Sources of a Stable Multipolarity," *International Security*, vol. 23, no. 2 (Fall 1998), pp. 40–79.

28. See Charles Kupchan, *No One's World: The West, the Rising Rest, and the Coming Global Turn* (New York: Oxford University Press, 2012).

29. Congress has begun to take steps to curtail the president's war-making authority. The House in January 2020 voted to repeal the 2002 AUMF. Both the House and Senate also passed legislation requiring that the president secure approval from Congress before taking further military action against Iran. Congress in 2019 passed legislation aimed at cutting off U.S. assistance to the Saudi-led military campaign in Yemen, but it was vetoed by President Trump. See Catie Edmondson, "House Votes to Repeal Law Allowing Use of Force in Iraq," *New York Times*, January 31, 2020, p. A21; Catie Edmondson, "House Votes to Claw Back Power to Use Force on Iran," *New York Times*, March 12, 2020, p. A8.

30. Monroe, "Monroe Doctrine."

INDEX

For the benefit of digital users, indexed terms that span two pages (e.g., 52–53) may, on occasion, appear on only one of those pages.